CONTEMPORARY'S

ESSENTIAL
SKILLS
FOR THE
WORKPLACE
LEVEL ONE

Using Forms and Documents

Series Developer
Lori Strumpf
President, Center for Remediation Design

Author
Beth Blanchard-Smith

Project Editor
Sarah Conroy Williams

CONTEMPORARY
BOOKS
CHICAGO

Library of Congress Cataloging-in-Publication Data

Strumpf, Lori.
    Essential skills for the workplace. Using forms and documents /
Lori Strumpf & Beth Blanchard-Smith.
      p. cm.
    ISBN 0-8092-3901-9 (paper)
    1. Office practice—Handbooks, manuals, etc. 2. Business—
Forms—Handbooks, manuals, etc. 3. Business records—
Handbooks, manual, etc. 4. Secretaries—Vocational guidance—
Handbooks, manuals, etc. I. Blanchard-Smith, Beth. II. Title.
HF5547.5.S8172   1993
651.7—dc20   93-22805
                                             CIP

Photographs on page 72 © The Image Bank

Published by Contemporary Books, Inc.
Two Prudential Plaza, Chicago, Illinois 60601-6790
Manufactured in the United States of America
International Standard Book Number: 0-8092-3901-9

10   9   8   7   6   5   4   3

Published simultaneously in Canada by
Fitzhenry & Whiteside
195 Allstate Parkway
Markham, Ontario L3R 4T8
Canada

Editorial Director Caren Van Slyke	*Production Editor* Thomas D. Scharf
Editorial Chris Benton Eunice Hoshizaki Lynn McEwan Scott Gutmann Gerilee Hundt	*Art & Production* Todd Peterson Jan Geist
	Typography Point West, Inc. Carol Stream, Illinois
Editorial Assistant Maggie McCann	Cover design by Georgene Sainati Cover photo © Westlight
Editorial Production Manager Norma Fioretti	Photo manipulation by Kristin Nelson, Provizion

Essential Skills for the Workplace stems from a national demonstration project conducted by the Center for Remediation Design (CRD), a joint project of the U.S. Conference of Mayors, the National Association of Private Industry Councils, the Partnership for Training and Employment Careers, and the National Association of Counties. The CRD's primary goal is to help employers and training providers link basic skills training to the needs of the workplace.

The Project of the States, conducted by the CRD, the Center for Human Resources at Brandeis University, and select JTPA entities since 1987, focuses on the use of reading, writing, computation, problem solving, and communication skills in the workplace. Competencies singled out by this project's labor market studies as being essential to a successful workforce are the foundation for the lessons in this series.

CONTENTS

ACKNOWLEDGMENTS

Time sheet on pages 20, 22, and 24 used by permission of King County Work Training Program.

Application on page 41 reprinted by permission of Group Health Cooperative of Puget Sound, Seattle, Washington.

Enrollment form on page 43 reprinted by permission of the Washington State Department of Retirement Systems.

Application on page 49 and agreement on page 51 reprinted by permission of Texaco Refining and Marketing, Inc.

Credit terms on page 53 and application on page 56 from Sears, Roebuck and Company.

Flier on page 58 and billing statement on page 61 reprinted by permission of Seattle Water Department.

Occupational descriptions on page 73 and chart on page 76 excerpted from *Plan for Tomorrow Today*. Reprinted by permission of Washington State Workforce Training and Education Coordinating Board.

Program descriptions on page 75 reprinted by permission of Renton Technical College, Renton, Washington.

Application on page 83 reprinted courtesy of Oregon State Board of Nursing.

Application on page 85 reprinted courtesy of Washington State Department of Licensing.

Advertisements on pages 97, 99, and 100 and order form on pages 98, 99, and 100 reprinted courtesy of The Reliable Corporation, Chicago, Illinois.

Money order on pages 108 and 109 reprinted courtesy of Travelers Express Company, Inc.

Warranty on page 124 reprinted by permission of Gillette Corporation.

Definition on page 126 reprinted by permission. From *Webster's Ninth New Collegiate Dictionary* ©1991 by Merriam-Webster Inc., publisher of the Merriam-Webster® dictionaries.

Definitions on page 127 copyright ©1989 by Houghton Mifflin Company. Reproduced by permission from the *Houghton Mifflin Student Dictionary*.

Warranty information on page 128 reprinted by permission of Maple Chase Company.

Warranty and service information on page 131 reprinted by permission of Whirlpool Corporation; ®Registered Trademark Whirlpool Corporation, ©1988 Whirlpool Corporation.

Back side of non-negotiable traffic ticket on page 134 used by permission of the Office of the Administrator for the Courts, Olympia, Washington.

Notice of Hearing and summons/subpoena/notice on page 139 reprinted by permission of the Lynnwood Municipal Court, City of Lynnwood, Washington.

Subpoena on pages 141 and 171 reprinted by permission of Aurelia Pucinski, Clerk of the Circuit Court of Cook County, Illinois.

Warranty on page 170 reprinted by permission of Emerson Radio Corporation.

TO THE LEARNER

Contemporary's *Essential Skills for the Workplace* series has four books—two books in Level One, two books in Level Two. Each book **integrates,** or combines, the reading, math, writing, communication, and problem-solving skills you need to complete tasks at the workplace and in everyday life.

Essential Skills for the Workplace will take you out of the classroom and into the world of work. Each task in these books is a task you may encounter at the workplace. In addition, each task is part of the "big picture"—part of the process required to make a business purchase, for example, or to prepare a business delivery.

This book, *Using Forms and Documents,* is part of Level One of the series. In this book, you'll work with forms and documents used in many jobs and in everyday life. You'll practice the skills you need to complete basic tasks in the workplace. When you finish the two workbooks in Level One, you'll be ready for Level Two. At this level, you will actually focus on a specific type of job. You will use the basic skills learned in Level One to help you complete several projects involved with a certain type of job.

In Level One, you will

- be guided through basic workplace tasks
- practice the skills needed to complete these tasks
- apply these skills to a related task

Features in Level One include

- a Skill Preview that tells you what each lesson is about
- a Skill Mastery that lets you demonstrate your skills
- Self-Check suggestions that help you check your work
- Workwise activities that let you think about the world of work
- a Glossary that defines more than 100 workplace-related terms

In the back of the book, you'll find an answer key and blank copies of some important forms and documents.

We hope you enjoy *Essential Skills for the Workplace Level One: Using Forms and Documents.* We wish you the best of luck with your studies.

The Editors

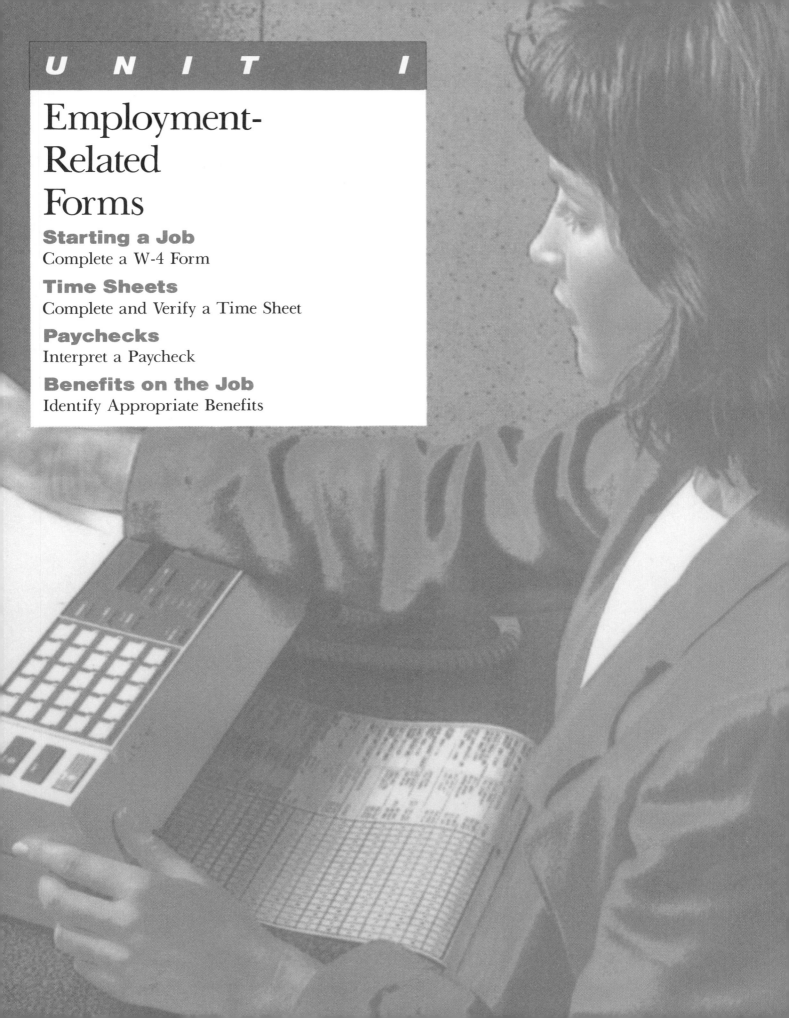

U N I T   I

Employment-Related Forms

Starting a Job
Complete a W-4 Form

Time Sheets
Complete and Verify a Time Sheet

Paychecks
Interpret a Paycheck

Benefits on the Job
Identify Appropriate Benefits

STARTING A JOB

Starting a new job is a challenge. New employees want to do well, get along with their co-workers, and be treated with respect. Hiring a new employee is also a challenge for employers. They want the new employee to do well, fit in, and become productive.

One of the first things an employer and a new employee must do is fill out forms.

SKILL PREVIEW

You may have filled out some **employment forms** in your life. On the lines below, list all of the forms you can think of that a new employee must fill out.

_____

_____

_____

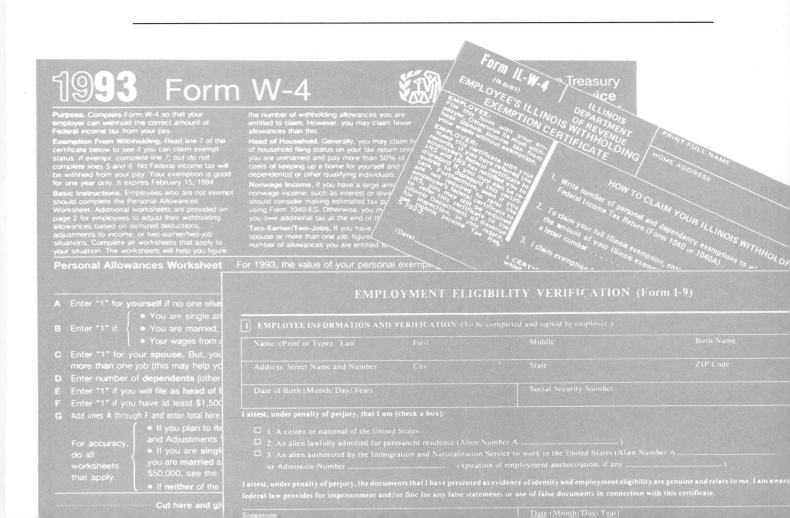

ASKING QUESTIONS

Starting a new job is a time to ask questions. New employees are often nervous about asking questions. They are not always sure whom to talk to or what to ask.

One way to decide what to ask is to think like a newspaper reporter. Reporters want to cover as many facts as possible. To get all the facts, a reporter asks

Who?	*Where?*
What?	*How?*
When?	*Why?*

A new employee could use these six **reporters' questions** to create questions about employment forms. Look at these examples:

Who requires these forms?
What information is needed on the forms?
When do these forms have to be completed?
Where do I turn in the forms?
How can I get help if I need it?
Why are these forms required?

GUIDED PRACTICE

Fill in the correct reporters' word to complete each question below.

Example: __Who__ can help me fill out these forms?

1. _____ is a Form W-4 for?

2. _____ do I know if I've filled it out incorrectly?

3. _____ will I become eligible for company health insurance?

4. _____ do I sign my name?

5. _____ do I need to fill out new tax forms with each new job?

You were correct if you answered 1. *What*; 2. *How*; 3. *When*; 4. *Where*; 5. *Why*.

Form IL-W-4	ILLINOIS DEPARTMENT OF REVENUE	PRINT FULL NAME	SOCIAL SECURITY NO.
(R-8/81) EMPLOYEE'S ILLINOIS WITHHOLDING EXEMPTION CERTIFICATE		HOME ADDRESS	

EMPLOYEE:
File this form with your employer. Otherwise he must withhold Illinois income tax from your wages without exemption.

EMPLOYER:
Keep this certificate with your records. If you have referred the employee's federal certificate to IRS and IRS has notified you to disregard it, you may also be required to disregard this certificate. Furthermore, even if you are not required to refer the employee's federal certificate to IRS, you may still be required to refer this certificate to the Illinois Department of Revenue for inspection. In this regard, see Illinois Income Tax Reg. S 702-2.

HOW TO CLAIM YOUR ILLINOIS WITHHOLDING EXEMPTION

1. Write number of personal and dependency exemptions to which you are ENTITLED on your Federal Income Tax Return (Form 1040 or 1040A) . . . .

2. To claim your full Illinois exemption, enter the amount shown on Line 1. If you elect to reduce the amount of your Illinois exemption for purposes of withholding Illinois income tax, enter a lesser number . . . .

3. I claim exemption from withholding (to be checked only if line 3, Federal Form W-4 is checked)

I CERTIFY that the withholding exemption(s) claimed on this certificate does not exceed the amount to which I am entitled on my federal income tax return.

(Date) _____ , 19 _____   (Signed) _____

APPLIED PRACTICE 1: ASKING QUESTIONS ABOUT A TAX FORM

The form above is the **income tax withholding form** for the State of Illinois. Look at the form. You probably have some questions about it. Use the six reporters' words to write your questions below.

Example: _Who should fill out this form?_ _____

1. _____

2. _____

3. _____

4. _____

5. _____

WORKWISE

Practice your employment form skills by filling out the Form W-4 above. Even if you don't work in Illinois, the extra practice will help prepare you for filling out a Form W-4 in your own state. If you're not sure what some of the words mean, come back to this form after you've completed this lesson.

INTERPRETING A FORM W-4

The federal Form W-4 is a tax form. The Internal Revenue Service (IRS) requires all paid employees in the United States to fill it out. Form W-4 tells employers how much federal income tax to withhold from an employee's paycheck.

GUIDED PRACTICE

To understand this tax form, you need to know the following vocabulary words:

Exempt or **exemption** means that you do not need to have income tax withheld.

Withholding allowances are reasons you can give for having less tax withheld.

Dependents are people you support financially, such as a spouse or children.

Liability means something you're legally responsible for paying.

What does **head of household** mean? Look at the center column at the top of the form. Read the description under Head of Household. In your own words, write the definition here:

_____

You should have written something like this: *You're a head of household if you're single and you pay more than one-half of the costs of a home for you and your dependents.*

APPLIED PRACTICE 2: FINDING ANSWERS ON FORM W-4

Use the Form W-4 on page 9 to answer the following questions.

1. Read item 7 near the bottom of the form. What would make you exempt from income tax withholding?

   _____

   _____

2. Read through lines A through G on the Personal Allowances Worksheet in the center of the form. If you were filling out this worksheet for yourself, how many allowances could you claim?

   _____

   _____

. . . .
Reading: Identifying factual details and specifications within text

1993 Form W-4

Department of the Treasury
Internal Revenue Service

Purpose. Complete Form W-4 so that your employer can withhold the correct amount of Federal income tax from your pay.

Exemption From Withholding. Read line 7 of the certificate below to see if you can claim exempt status. *If exempt, complete line 7; but do not complete lines 5 and 6.* No Federal income tax will be withheld from your pay. Your exemption is good for one year only. It expires February 15, 1994.

Basic Instructions. Employees who are not exempt should complete the Personal Allowances Worksheet. Additional worksheets are provided on page 2 for employees to adjust their withholding allowances based on itemized deductions, adjustments to income, or two-earner/two-job situations. Complete all worksheets that apply to your situation. The worksheets will help you figure the number of withholding allowances you are entitled to claim. However, you may claim fewer allowances than this.

Head of Household. Generally, you may claim head of household filing status on your tax return only if you are unmarried and pay more than 50% of the costs of keeping up a home for yourself and your dependent(s) or other qualifying individuals.

Nonwage Income. If you have a large amount of nonwage income, such as interest or dividends, you should consider making estimated tax payments using Form 1040-ES. Otherwise, you may find that you owe additional tax at the end of the year.

Two-Earner/Two-Jobs. If you have a working spouse or more than one job, figure the total number of allowances you are entitled to claim on all jobs using worksheets from only one Form W-4. This total should be divided among all jobs. Your withholding will usually be most accurate when all allowances are claimed on the W-4 filed for the highest paying job and zero allowances are claimed for the others.

Advance Earned Income Credit. If you are eligible for this credit, you can receive it added to your paycheck throughout the year. For details, get Form W-5 from your employer.

Check Your Withholding. After your W-4 takes effect, you can use Pub. 919, Is My Withholding Correct for 1993?, to see how the dollar amount you are having withheld compares to your estimated total annual tax. Call 1-800-829-3676 to order this publication. Check your local telephone directory for the IRS assistance number if you need further help.

Personal Allowances Worksheet

For 1993, the value of your personal exemption(s) is reduced if your income is over $108,450 ($162,700 if married filing jointly, $135,600 if head of household, or $81,350 if married filing separately). Get Pub. 919 for details.

A Enter "1" for **yourself** if no one else can claim you as a dependent . . . . **A** _____

B Enter "1" if:
  - You are single and have only one job; or
  - You are married, have only one job, and your spouse does not work; or
  - Your wages from a second job or your spouse's wages (or the total of both) are $1,000 or less.
  . . **B** _____

C Enter "1" for your **spouse.** But, you may choose to enter -0- if you are married and have either a working spouse or more than one job (this may help you avoid having too little tax withheld) . . . . **C** _____

D Enter number of **dependents** (other than your spouse or yourself) whom you will claim on your tax return . . . . . **D** _____

E Enter "1" if you will file as **head of household** on your tax return (see conditions under **Head of Household,** above) . **E** _____

F Enter "1" if you have at least $1,500 of **child or dependent care expenses** for which you plan to claim a credit . . **F** _____

G Add lines A through F and enter total here. **Note:** *This amount may be different from the number of exemptions you claim on your return* ▶ **G** _____

For accuracy, do all worksheets that apply.
  - If you plan to **itemize or claim adjustments to income** and want to reduce your withholding, see the Deductions and Adjustments Worksheet on page 2.
  - If you are **single** and have **more than one job** and your combined earnings from all jobs exceed $30,000 OR if you are **married** and have a **working spouse or more than one job,** and the combined earnings from all jobs exceed $50,000, see the Two-Earner/Two-Job Worksheet on page 2 if you want to avoid having too little tax withheld.
  - If **neither** of the above situations applies, **stop here** and enter the number from line G on line 5 of Form W-4 below.

- - - - - - - - - - - - - - - **Cut here and give the certificate to your employer. Keep the top portion for your records.** - - - - - - - - - - - - - - -

---

Form **W-4**
Department of the Treasury
Internal Revenue Service

Employee's Withholding Allowance Certificate

▶ **For Privacy Act and Paperwork Reduction Act Notice, see reverse.**

OMB No. 1545-0010

1993

1 Type or print your first name and middle initial	Last name	2 Your social security number

Home address (number and street or rural route)	3 ☐ Single ☐ Married ☐ Married, but withhold at higher Single rate. **Note:** *If married, but legally separated, or spouse is a nonresident alien, check the Single box.*
City or town, state, and ZIP code	4 If your last name differs from that on your social security card, check here and call 1-800-772-1213 for more information · · · · ▶ ☐

5 Total number of allowances you are claiming (from line G above or from the worksheets on page 2 if they apply) . **5** _____

6 Additional amount, if any, you want withheld from each paycheck . . . . **6** $ _____

7 I claim exemption from withholding for 1993 and I certify that I meet **ALL** of the following conditions for exemption:
  - Last year I had a right to a refund of **ALL** Federal income tax withheld because I had **NO** tax liability; **AND**
  - This year I expect a refund of **ALL** Federal income tax withheld because I expect to have **NO** tax liability; **AND**
  - This year if my income exceeds $600 and includes nonwage income, another person cannot claim me as a dependent.

  If you meet all of the above conditions, enter "EXEMPT" here . . . . ▶ **7**

Under penalties of perjury, I certify that I am entitled to the number of withholding allowances claimed on this certificate or entitled to claim exempt status.

Employee's signature ▶ _____   Date ▶ _____ , 19 ___

8 Employer's name and address (Employer: Complete 8 and 10 only if sending to the IRS)	9 Office code (optional)	10 Employer identification number

Cat. No. 10220Q

INTERPRETING A FORM I-9

The U.S. government requires all paid employees to complete Form I-9. This form proves that it is legal for an employee to work in the United States.

GUIDED PRACTICE

Answer these questions using the Form I-9 on page 11.

1. Which part of the I-9 should the employee fill out? _____

2. What could happen if an employee signed a Form I-9 that has false information? (*Hint:* Read the lines in **bold** type above the first signature line on the form.)

   _____

You are correct if you answered 1. *the top*; 2. *the employee could go to jail or be fined.*

APPLIED PRACTICE 3: FINDING ANSWERS ON FORM I-9

Use the Form I-9 on page 11 to answer these questions.

1. Skim through the top part of the form. In what three ways can a person be legally eligible to work in the United States? (*Hint:* Look at the list of three small boxes.)

   _____

   _____

2. Read through the bottom part of Form I-9. What must employees show to prove they can legally work in the United States?

   _____

   _____

   _____

3. What information from the documents should the employer write on this form?

   _____

. . . .
Reading: Identifying factual details and specifications within text

10 • USING FORMS AND DOCUMENTS

EMPLOYMENT ELIGIBILITY VERIFICATION (Form I-9)

1 **EMPLOYEE INFORMATION AND VERIFICATION:** (To be completed and signed by employee.)

Name: (Print or Type) Last	First	Middle	Birth Name
Address: Street Name and Number	City	State	ZIP Code
Date of Birth (Month/Day/Year)		Social Security Number	

I attest, under penalty of perjury, that I am (check a box):

☐ 1. A citizen or national of the United States.

☐ 2. An alien lawfully admitted for permanent residence (Alien Number A _____)

☐ 3. An alien authorized by the Immigration and Naturalization Service to work in the United States (Alien Number A _____ ,
or Admission Number _____ , expiration of employment authorization, if any _____)

I attest, under penalty of perjury, the documents that I have presented as evidence of identity and employment eligibility are genuine and relate to me. I am aware that federal law provides for imprisonment and/or fine for any false statements or use of false documents in connection with this certificate.

Signature	Date (Month/Day/Year)

PREPARER/TRANSLATOR CERTIFICATION (To be completed if prepared by person other than the employee). I attest, under penalty of perjury, that the above was prepared by me at the request of the named individual and is based on all information of which I have any knowledge.

Signature	Name (Print or Type)
Address (Street Name and Number)	City	State	Zip Code

2 **EMPLOYER REVIEW AND VERIFICATION:** (To be completed and signed by employer.)

Instructions:
Examine one document from List A and check the appropriate box, **OR** examine one document from List B **and** one from List C and check the appropriate boxes.
Provide the **Document Identification Number** and **Expiration Date** for the document checked.

List A Documents that Establish Identity and Employment Eligibility	List B Documents that Establish Identity	**and**	List C Documents that Establish Employment Eligibility
☐ 1. United States Passport ☐ 2. Certificate of United States Citizenship ☐ 3. Certificate of Naturalization ☐ 4. Unexpired foreign passport with attached Employment Authorization ☐ 5. Alien Registration Card with photograph	☐ 1. A State-issued driver's license or a State-issued I.D. card with a photograph, or information, including name, sex, date of birth, height, weight, and color of eyes. (Specify State)_____) ☐ 2. U.S. Military Card ☐ 3. Other (Specify document and issuing authority) _____		☐ 1. Original Social Security Number Card (other than a card stating it is not valid for employment) ☐ 2. A birth certificate issued by State, county, or municipal authority bearing a seal or other certification ☐ 3. Unexpired INS Employment Authorization Specify form # _____
Document Identification # _____	**Document Identification** # _____		**Document Identification** # _____
Expiration Date (if any) _____	**Expiration Date (if any)** _____		**Expiration Date (if any)** _____

CERTIFICATION: I attest, under penalty of perjury, that I have examined the documents presented by the above individual, that they appear to be genuine and to relate to the individual named, and that the individual, to the best of my knowledge, is eligible to work in the United States.

Signature	Name (Print or Type)	Title
Employer Name	Address	Date

Form I-9 (05/07/87)
OMB No. 1115-0136

U.S. Department of Justice
Immigration and Naturalization Service

ORGANIZING PERSONAL INFORMATION

The federal Forms W-4 and I-9 both ask for some of the same information. Each form also asks for specific information not on the other form. The lists below show some of the information required on each form.

Form W-4	Form I-9
name ———————————— name	
Social Security number	birth name
home address	home address
marital status	date of birth
number of tax allowances	Social Security number
additional money deducted from paycheck	citizenship status
exemption from withholding taxes	alien number
signature	admission number
date	signature
employer name	date

GUIDED PRACTICE

Compare the two lists above. Draw a line connecting information on Form W-4 to the matching information on Form I-9. Circle information in either column that *does not* have a match. The first two have been done for you as an example.

You should have circled each item except for *home address, signature,* and *date.* These were the only items that matched.

APPLIED PRACTICE 4: COMPLETING A PERSONAL DATA SHEET: STARTING A JOB

Use your own information to fill out the Personal Data Sheet on page 13. Put a question mark (?) in the spaces where you don't have the information. Ask your instructor for help with these spaces.

. . . .
Reading: Identifying similarities and differences in objects;
Writing: Entering appropriate information onto a form

PERSONAL DATA SHEET: STARTING A JOB

Name: _____ Birth Date: _____ / _____ / _____

       Last   First   Middle

Birth/Maiden Name: _____

Address: _____ Phone (_____) _____

       Street

_____

       City   State   Zip

SS# _____ - _____ - _____

Citizenship Status: ❏ U.S. Citizen or National
(check one box)

                  ❏ Alien: Permanent Resident

                  ❏ Alien: Work Permit

Marital Status: ❏ Married
(Check one box)

              ❏ Single

Spouse's Income: $1,000 or less   ❏ Yes

                                ❏ No

Number of Dependents (people you support financially): _____

Head of Household: ❏ Yes   ❏ No
(see definition on page 9)

Child-Care Expenses: Over $1,500 per year?   ❏ Yes

                                         ❏ No

COMPLETE A FORM W-4

On page 8, you decided how many allowances you would claim on the Personal Allowances Worksheet. Check your work. Read lines A through G below. Ask your instructor for help if you need it. When you've completed the worksheet, do your best to fill out the Employee's Withholding Allowance Certificate.

Directions and a blank Form W-4 are located on pages 161 and 162 in this book.

Personal Allowances Worksheet   For 1993, the value of your personal exemption(s) is reduced if your income is over $108,450 ($162,700 if married filing jointly, $135,600 if head of household, or $81,350 if married filing separately). Get Pub. 919 for details.

A Enter "1" for **yourself** if no one else can claim you as a dependent . . . . **A** _____

B Enter "1" if:
- You are single and have only one job; or
- You are married, have only one job, and your spouse does not work; or
- Your wages from a second job or your spouse's wages (or the total of both) are $1,000 or less.
. . **B** _____

C Enter "1" for your **spouse**. But, you may choose to enter -0- if you are married and have either a working spouse or more than one job (this may help you avoid having too little tax withheld) . . . . **C** _____

D Enter number of **dependents** (other than your spouse or yourself) whom you will claim on your tax return . . . . **D** _____

E Enter "1" if you will file as **head of household** on your tax return (see conditions under Head of Household, above) . **E** _____

F Enter "1" if you have at least $1,500 of **child or dependent care expenses** for which you plan to claim a credit . . **F** _____

G Add lines A through F and enter total here. Note: *This amount may be different from the number of exemptions you claim on your return* ▶ **G** _____

For accuracy, do all worksheets that apply.
- If you plan to **itemize or claim adjustments to income** and want to reduce your withholding, see the Deductions and Adjustments Worksheet on page 2.
- If you are **single** and have **more than one job** and your combined earnings from all jobs exceed $30,000 OR if you are **married** and have a **working spouse or more than one job,** and the combined earnings from all jobs exceed $50,000, see the Two-Earner/Two-Job Worksheet on page 2 if you want to avoid having too little tax withheld.
- If **neither** of the above situations applies, **stop here** and enter the number from line G on line 5 of Form W-4 below.

- - - - - - - - - - - - - - - - - Cut here and give the certificate to your employer. Keep the top portion for your records. - - - - - - - - - - - - - - - - -

Form **W-4**
Department of the Treasury
Internal Revenue Service

Employee's Withholding Allowance Certificate

▶ **For Privacy Act and Paperwork Reduction Act Notice, see reverse.**

OMB No. 1545-0010

19**93**

1 Type or print your first name and middle initial	Last name	**2** Your social security number

Home address (number and street or rural route)	**3** ☐ Single ☐ Married ☐ Married, but withhold at higher Single rate. **Note:** *If married, but legally separated, or spouse is a nonresident alien, check the Single box*
City or town, state, and ZIP code	**4** If your last name differs from that on your social security card, check here and call 1-800-772-1213 for more information . . . . ▶ ☐

5 Total number of allowances you are claiming (from line G above or from the worksheets on page 2 if they apply) . **5** [ ]

6 Additional amount, if any, you want withheld from each paycheck . . . . **6** $ [ ]

7 I claim exemption from withholding for 1993 and I certify that I meet **ALL** of the following conditions for exemption:
- Last year I had a right to a refund of **ALL** Federal income tax withheld because I had **NO** tax liability; **AND**
- This year I expect a refund of **ALL** Federal income tax withheld because I expect to have **NO** tax liability; **AND**
- This year if my income exceeds $600 and includes nonwage income, another person cannot claim me as a dependent.

If you meet all of the above conditions, enter "EXEMPT" here . . . . ▶ **7** [ ]

Under penalties of perjury, I certify that I am entitled to the number of withholding allowances claimed on this certificate or entitled to claim exempt status.

Employee's signature ▶ _____   Date ▶ _____ , 19 ____

8 Employer's name and address (Employer: Complete 8 and 10 only if sending to the IRS)	**9** Office code (optional)	**10** Employer identification number

Cat. No. 10220Q

TIME SHEETS

You've probably heard the saying "Time is money." Time is money on a job because for each hour you work, you help your company earn money. In return, your employer pays you money. If you are paid hourly, that payment is called a **wage**. If you are paid for a certain number of hours per week or month, that payment is called a **salary**.

To get paid, most employees must fill out a **time sheet** or punch a **time card**. It is important to complete time sheets accurately. Mistakes can cost you or your company time and money.

SKILL PREVIEW

Employers must keep track of employees' hours. Schools sometimes keep track of their students' hours as well. Test yourself. Can you account for your time spent at school this week?

Fill in the number of hours you spent in class each day this week.

DAY	HOURS SPENT IN CLASS
Monday	_____
Tuesday	_____
Wednesday	_____
Thursday	_____
Friday	_____
Saturday	_____

READING A TIME SHEET

Employers have several ways to track their employees' time. Some have their employees punch a card in a time clock. Others have the supervisors record employees' time. At many jobs, employees record their own hours on time sheets.

Look at Rhonda Kimmel's time sheet below. Notice that each day has two **In** columns and two **Out** columns. The first In and Out columns record time worked *before* lunch. The second In and Out columns record time worked *after* lunch. Employees at this company are not paid for their time at lunch, so their time schedules don't include lunch hours.

From: March 25
To: March 31

Name: Rhonda Kimmel

	In	Out	In	Out	Daily Total
Monday 3/25	8:00	12:00	1:00	5:00	8
Tuesday 3/26	8:30	12:00	1:00	5:00	$7\frac{1}{2}$
Wednesday 3/27	9:00	12:00	1:00	7:00	9
Thursday 3/28	7:30	12:30	1:45	5:00	$8\frac{1}{4}$
Friday 3/29					
Saturday 3/30					
Sunday 3/31	10:00	1:00	2:15	5:30	$6\frac{1}{4}$
				Weekly Total	

Employee's Signature _____

Supervisor's Signature _____

Look at the hours Rhonda has recorded for Monday:

- She started work at 8:00 and worked until 12:00.
- She took lunch from 12:00 to 1:00.
- Her afternoon work began at 1:00, and she left work at 5:00.

How many hours did Rhonda work between 8:00 A.M. and 12:00 noon? To find out, count the hours from 8:00 A.M. to 12:00 noon. There are four hours: 8:00 to 9:00, 9:00 to 10:00, 10:00 to 11:00, and 11:00 to noon. Rhonda worked for four hours.

Now answer these questions about the hours Rhonda worked on Monday.

1. How many hours did she work between 1:00 P.M. and 5:00 P.M.? _____

2. How much time did she take off for lunch? _____

3. How many total hours did Rhonda work on Monday? _____

You are correct if you answered 1. *4 hours*; 2. *1 hour*; 3. *8 hours*.

APPLIED PRACTICE 1: READING A TIME SHEET

Use the time sheet on page 16 to answer the questions below.

1. How many hours did Rhonda work on Tuesday? _____

2. On which day did Rhonda work the fewest hours? _____

3. On how many days did Rhonda take more than an hour off for lunch? _____

4. What time did Rhonda leave work for the day on Wednesday? _____

5. On which days did Rhonda not work? _____

6. Who signs this form? _____

WORKWISE

Discuss the reasons for using time sheets with a friend or a classmate. Why are time sheets important? Why is it important for employees to fill out a time sheet accurately? Why is it important for employers to read a time sheet accurately?

. . . .
Reading: Reading two- or more column charts to obtain information;
Computation: Perform computations of addition using whole numbers

CONVERTING NUMBERS AND ADDING DECIMALS

Employees don't always work whole hours. Rhonda, for instance, worked for 8 hours on Monday but $7\frac{1}{2}$ hours on Tuesday and $8\frac{1}{4}$ hours on Thursday. Rhonda wrote these hours as **fractions**. However, employers often prefer these hours to be written in **decimal** form. Look at the chart below.

Minutes	Words	Fractions	Decimals
15	a quarter hour	$\frac{1}{4}$ hour	.25 hour
30	a half hour	$\frac{1}{2}$ hour	.5 hour	← based on .50 hour
45	three-quarters of an hour	$\frac{3}{4}$ hour	.75 hour

decimal point ⌐

You can use this chart to change hours from fractions to decimals. For example, if you worked for 7 hours and 30 minutes, you worked for seven and a half hours. That is the same as writing $7\frac{1}{2}$ or 7.5 hours.

GUIDED PRACTICE

Mark worked for a half hour on the light machines. To write this time in decimals, he would convert $\frac{1}{2}$ hour into .5 hour. The chart provides this information.

Use the chart above to answer these questions.

1. Harold spent $8\frac{1}{4}$ hours putting siding on a house. How would he write this time in decimals?

2. Tao painted for $\frac{3}{4}$ hour. How many minutes did she work?

3. Leroy processed film for an hour and a half. How would he write his hours in decimal form?

4. Sonja worked for .25 hour on Wednesday. How many minutes did she work?

You were correct if you answered 1. *8.25 hours*; 2. *45 minutes*; 3. *1.50, or 1.5, hours*; 4. *15 minutes.*

Rhonda needs to figure out her **total hours** for the week. She followed these steps:

1. Change fractions and whole numbers to decimals.
2. Be sure to keep the decimal points in the same column.
3. Add zeros if needed to make an equal number of places after the decimal point.
4. Add the numbers.

Monday	8	←change numbers to decimals→	8.00←	⌐ keep decimal points in one column
Tuesday	$7\frac{1}{2}$		7.50	
Wednesday	9		9.00	add zeros to make an equal number of places after the decimal point
Thursday	$8\frac{1}{4}$		8.25	
Sunday	$6\frac{1}{4}$		+ 6.25	
TOTAL HOURS			39.00 or 39 ⌐ add the numbers

Notice that the decimal point in the answer is in the same column as in the numbers above it.

APPLIED PRACTICE 2: ADDING DECIMALS TO COMPUTE TOTAL HOURS

Find the total hours Rhonda worked for each week below. Remember to follow the same four steps that Rhonda followed above.

1. | Monday | $6\frac{1}{2}$ hours |
Wednesday	6.25 hours
Friday	6.75 hours
TOTAL HOURS	_____

3. | Monday | 4.50 hours |
Tuesday	$3\frac{1}{2}$ hours
Thursday	$4\frac{1}{4}$ hours
Friday	4 hours
TOTAL HOURS	_____

2. | Friday | 3.25 hours |
Saturday	4.50 hours
Sunday	4.25 hours
TOTAL HOURS	_____

4. | Wednesday | 8 hours |
Thursday	7.75 hours
Friday	7.75 hours
Saturday	8.25 hours
TOTAL HOURS	_____

CHECKING THE ACCURACY OF TIME SHEETS AND TOTAL PAY

Rhonda's workweek is finished. Before she can get paid, she needs to turn in an official time sheet. First, she changes her hours to decimal form. Then, she transfers them from her weekly time sheet to the official time sheet below.

Use One Time Sheet Per Pay Period

COMPLETED TIME SHEET REQUIRED FOR EMPLOYEE TO BE PAID

Pay Periods: 5th to 19th
          20th to 4th

Northgate
Store Location

Employee Name   *Rhonda Kimmel*

Job Title   *Sales Associate*

Social Security No.   *534-28-9900*

Month March		5	6	7	8	9	10	11	12	13	14	15	16	17	18	19
20	21	22	23	24	25	26	27	28	29	30	31	Month		1	2	3	4
					8.5	7.5	7	8.25	X	X	6¼						

| X | = Not Working Day/ Not an Activity Day | | H | = Holiday | | S | = Sick |

Employee's Signature _____   Total Hours _____

Supervisor's Signature _____   Date _____

ROUTING: **WHITE:** PAYROLL'S COPY   **YELLOW:** EMPLOYEE'S COPY   **PINK:** SUPERVISOR'S COPY

GUIDED PRACTICE

Rhonda needs to check her official time sheet for accuracy before she turns it in.

Turn to Rhonda's time sheet on page 16. Compare it to her official time sheet above. Did Rhonda transfer her hours correctly? If there are any mistakes, write the corrections below. Then, write these corrections on her official time sheet above.

1. On _____ , hours should be _____ .
       (date)   (number of hours)

2. On _____ , hours should be _____ .
       (date)   (number of hours)

3. On _____ , hours should be _____ .
       (date)   (number of hours)

You are correct if you wrote 1. *3/25, 8 hours*; 2. *3/27; 9 hours*; and 3. *3/31, 6.25 hours*. Be sure you have written these corrections on the time sheet above.

Rhonda is paid $10.25 per hour. She wants to know how much money she earned for her 8 hours of work on Monday. She needs to **multiply** her hours worked by her pay per hour. Look at the equation below.

$$8 \text{ hours} \times \$10.25 \text{ per hour} = \$82.00$$

hours worked   pay per hour   total pay for hours worked

Once Rhonda set up the problem, she used a calculator to find the answer.

GUIDED PRACTICE

Rhonda worked 7.5 hours on Tuesday. Set up a problem to find her total pay for Tuesday. Do not find the answer yet.

PROBLEM:

You know that Rhonda needs to multiply to find the answer. You were correct if you set up the problem as follows: *7.5 hours × $10.25 per hour.*

On a calculator, you'd find the answer by pressing these keys:

ON THE CALCULATOR

(7) (·) (5) (×)
(1) (0) (·) (2) (5) (=)
76.875

Rhonda earned $76.875 or $76.88.

APPLIED PRACTICE 3: CALCULATING PAY FROM A TIME SHEET

First, be sure that you've corrected the time sheet on page 20 as the Guided Practice on that page instructed. Next, use the corrected time sheet on page 20 to answer the questions below. Set up the problem, then find the answer. You can use a calculator if you wish.

1. How much money did Rhonda earn for her work on Thursday, March 28?

2. How much money did Rhonda earn for her work on Sunday, March 31?

3. How many total hours did Rhonda work from March 25 through 31?

4. How much money did Rhonda earn for her week of work?

Remember, Rhonda's check won't be made out for the entire amount that she earned. **Deductions** will have been made for taxes, insurance, and Social Security.

. . . .
Writing: Transferring dates and figures from written sources onto appropriate sections of forms;
Computation: Performing computations of multiplication using decimal fractions;
Reading: Reading two- or more column charts to obtain information

INTERPRETING A TIME SHEET

Rhonda's time sheet shows more information than just the hours she has worked. Look at the time sheet below. What other facts about Rhonda's job does it show?

Use One Time Sheet Per Pay Period

COMPLETED TIME SHEET REQUIRED FOR EMPLOYEE TO BE PAID

Pay Periods: 5th to 19th
20th to 4th

Northgate
Store Location

Employee's Name ___Rhonda Kimmel___

Job Title ___Sales Associate___

Social Security No. ___534-28-9900___

Month March					5	6	7	8	9	10	11	12	13	14	15	16	17	18	19
20	21	22	23	24	25	26	27	28	29	30	31 Month					1	2	3	4
8	5	X	X	X	8	7.5	9	8.25	X	X	6.25								

X	= Not Working Day/ Not an Activity Day		H	= Holiday		S	= Sick

Employee's Signature ___Rhonda Kimmel___   Total Hours ___52___

Supervisor's Signature _____   Date _____

ROUTING: **WHITE:** PAYROLL'S COPY   **YELLOW:** EMPLOYEE'S COPY   **PINK:** SUPERVISOR'S COPY

GUIDED PRACTICE

Can you find the following information on the time sheet? Put a check (✔) in each box below when you have found that information.

☐ Pay period   ☐ Letter code explanations

☐ Routing directions   ☐ Store location

You can find *pay period in the top left corner*, the *store location beneath the pay period*, the *letter code explanations above the employee's signature*, and the *routing directions at the bottom of the form.*

Use Rhonda's time sheet on page 22 to answer the following questions.

1. a. Who gets the white copy of the time sheet? _____

    b. Why does this department need the clearest copy? _____

    _____

2. What is Rhonda's second pay period in each month? _____

3. Which pay period does this time sheet cover? _____

4. What is Rhonda's store location? _____

5. What do you think might happen if Rhonda turns in the time sheet without her supervisor's signature?

    _____

6. Was Rhonda sick on any days during this pay period? _____

7. Did Rhonda have any holidays during this pay period? _____

8. From March 20 to March 31, on which dates did Rhonda not work? _____

WORKWISE

The time sheet asks employees to write an *X*, an *H*, or an *S* on the days they didn't work. Why do you think employers want this information? What do they do with it? Discuss these questions with a friend or a classmate.

. . . .
Reading: Using a completed form to locate information to complete a task

COMPLETE AND VERIFY A TIME SHEET

Fill in the time sheet below using the hours you attended school during one of the two pay periods covered. When you're finished, check the accuracy of your time sheet against your instructor's records of your attendance.

Use One Time Sheet Per Pay Period

COMPLETED TIME SHEET REQUIRED

Pay Periods: 5th to 19th
           20th to 4th

_____

Class Location

Student's Name _____

Areas of Study _____

Social Security No. _____

Month					5	6	7	8	9	10	11	12	13	14	15	16	17	18	19
20	21	22	23	24	25	26	27	28	29	30	31	Month				1	2	3	4

X	= Not Working Day/ Not an Activity Day		H	= Holiday		S	= Sick

Student's Signature _____   Total Hours _____

Supervisor's Signature _____   Date _____

        ROUTING: **WHITE:** PAYROLL'S COPY   **YELLOW:** STUDENT'S COPY   **PINK:** SUPERVISOR'S COPY

PAYCHECKS

Employers use **paychecks** to pay employees for their work. Paychecks are usually given out on certain days, such as every Friday, every other Tuesday, or the first and the 15th of each month.

These days, paychecks give much more information than the total amount of pay received. It is important that you understand exactly what your paycheck tells you. You also need to know how to deposit or cash your paycheck.

SKILL PREVIEW

Most paychecks have an attachment called a **paystub** or **pay statement**. This attachment gives information you may want to keep for your records. Do you recognize any of the paystub abbreviations and terms below? Put a check (✔) next to each one you recognize.

____ FICA	____ SSN
____ DED.	____ YTD
____ O.T.	____ REG. HRS.
____ HRS.	____ FED. WITH. TAX
____ HEALTH	____ PAY PERIOD

DIGITAL PRESS
1474 CONGRESS STREET
SAN DIEGO, CA 92110

PAY TO THE ORDER OF _____

_____

PAYABLE THROUGH: FIRST TRUST
494 E. CACTUS
SAN DIEGO, CA

P	Employee ID #	Name
A Y		
S T A T	Pay Period End	Regular Hours

ABC Company
1001 Cornella Street
New York, NY 10016

PAY DATE

Pay to the Order of Alexander Lew

Seven hundred six and 37/100

Payable through: Northern Bank
7 Wall Street
New York, NY 00571

57236
Employee #

2-4-93
Date

Employee Name Alexander Lew
Employee Number 57236

This Pay Period Earnings

Type	Hours	Amount
Regular	80	$820.00
OT	0	0.00

706.37
Amount

Marianne

Dollar

UNDERSTANDING PAYCHECK VOCABULARY

To understand a paycheck, you need to understand its vocabulary. The definitions below explain paycheck and paystub vocabulary.

Wage: payment for hours of work done

Salary: fixed amount of money paid at regular times for work done

Regular Hours (Reg. Hrs.): hours a person is regularly scheduled to work

Overtime Hours (O.T.): hours worked in addition to regular hours

Gross Pay: total amount of money earned, before deductions

Net Pay: actual amount of your paycheck, after deductions

Deductions (Ded.): money taken out of a paycheck to pay for certain things, including

a) **Federal Withholding Tax (Fed. With. Tax):** money deducted for income taxes paid to the federal government

b) **State Tax:** money deducted for income taxes paid to the state government

c) **Medical/Dental Benefits:** deductions related to medical or dental insurance

d) **Retirement:** money put into funds for payment back to you when you retire

e) **Vacation:** paid time off from work usually spent in recreation

f) **Sick Leave:** paid time off from work used when you are sick or caring for a sick family member

g) **FICA:** Federal Insurance Contributions Act, or Social Security. This is a nationwide insurance program for retired people and disabled people who can't work. Money deducted from each of your paychecks is deposited into Social Security accounts. When you retire, you should receive some of this money in monthly payments.

Year to Date (YTD): total amount paid or earned from January 1 through the current paycheck

Pay Period: period of time covered by a paycheck

Use the definitions on page 26 as you read the paycheck and paystub below.

ABC Company
1001 Cornelia Street
New York, NY 10016

57236	2-4-93
Employee #	Date

$\frac{2\text{-}10}{1903}$

Pay to the Order of ___ **Alexander Lew** ___

706.37
Amount

Seven hundred six and ³⁷/₁₀₀ _____ Dollars

Payable through: Northern Bank
7 Wall Street
New York, NY 00571

Marianne Rochester
Marianne Rochester, President

Employee Name ___ Alexander Lew ___   Pay Period ___ 1-15-93 to 1-31-93 ___
Employee Number ___ 57236 ___   SSN ___ 532-00-7329 ___

This Pay Period Earnings			Deductions		Year to Date	
Type	Hours	Amount	Type	Amount	Description	Amount
Regular	80	$820.00	Fed. With. Tax	80.00	Earnings	1,620.00
OT	0	0.00	FICA	8.00	Fed. With. Tax	162.00
			State With. Tax	20.00	FICA	17.25
			Union Dues	5.63	State With. Tax	42.00

1. Whom is the check made out to? _____

2. What company is the check from? _____

You are correct if you answered *Alexander Lew* and *ABC Company*.

APPLIED PRACTICE 1: INTERPRETING A PAYSTUB

1. How many hours did Alexander work during this pay period? _____

2. How much money has Alexander earned this year to date (YTD)? _____

3. How much did Alexander pay for union dues during this pay period? _____

4. Did Alexander work any overtime during this pay period? _____

5. What is Alexander's employee number? _____

. . . .
Reading: Recognizing task-related words with technical meanings; Using a completed form to locate information to complete a task

ADDING AND SUBTRACTING MONEY AMOUNTS

Our money system is based on **decimals**. If you need to add or subtract money amounts, you need to work with decimals. When you **add**, you find the total amount. When you need to add money amounts, follow these steps:

1. Line up the decimal points for each amount.
2. Bring down the decimal point for the answer.
3. Add the numbers.

GUIDED PRACTICE

Add $18.45 and $235.00.

```
            line up the decimal points
    18.45   for each amount
+  235.00
       .   ← bring down the decimal point
            for the answer
```

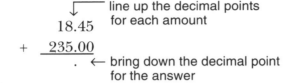

ON THE CALCULATOR

(1)(8)(·)(4)(5)(+)
(2)(3)(5)(·)(0)(0)(=)
(253.45)

You are correct if you answered *$253.45*.

APPLIED PRACTICE 2: ADDING MONEY AMOUNTS

Follow the three steps above to add these money amounts.

1. $37.00 plus $12.99

2. $40.00 plus $16.50

3. $690.50 plus $58.25

4. $807.95 plus $425.00 plus $65.05

5. $126.29 plus $365.45 plus $13.00

```
         add two zeros: $47.00
```
6. $47 plus $169.43

7. $20.99 plus $60

8. $98 plus $43.29

9. $62 plus $35.30

10. $14.99 plus $12

Subtracting means taking something away from the total. For instance, say you have $450 in your checking account, and you write a check for $300. You will need to take $300 from your total account balance. You'll need to subtract $300 from $450.

When you subtract money amounts, follow these steps:

1. Always put the total amount above the amount you're subtracting.
2. Line up the decimal points for each amount.
3. Bring down the decimal point for the answer.
4. Subtract the numbers.

GUIDED PRACTICE

Subtract $300.00 from $450.00.

```
                        ┌── line up the decimal
                        │   for each amount
put the total →   450.00
amount first    − 300.00
                   .   ←bring down the
                        decimal point for
                        the answer
```

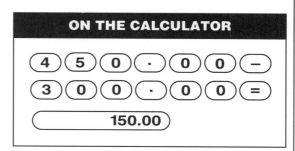

ON THE CALCULATOR

4 5 0 . 0 0 −
3 0 0 . 0 0 =
150.00

You are correct if you answered *$150.00*. You can check your answer by adding: $150.00 plus $300.00 = $450.00.

APPLIED PRACTICE 3: SUBTRACTING MONEY AMOUNTS

Follow the four steps above to subtract these money amounts. Be sure to check your answers by adding the answer to the amount subtracted. This should equal the total amount.

1. $98.00 minus $14.00

2. $465.99 minus $33.05

3. $124.75 minus $77.40

4. $239.75 minus $125.00

5. $900.00 minus $650.00

┌ add two zeros: $52.00

6. $52 minus $1.75

7. $29 minus $14.49

8. $360 minus $145.50

9. $35 minus $23.20

10. $132.00 minus $48

ENDORSING AND CASHING A PAYCHECK

To **endorse** means to sign your name. Banks require your signature before they will let you **deposit** or **cash** your paycheck. On the back of most checks there is a certain place for you to sign your name. Look at the back of the check below.

ENDORSE HERE:

X _Alexander Kerr_

DO NOT SIGN / WRITE / STAMP BELOW THIS LINE
FOR FINANCIAL INSTITUTION USAGE ONLY*

*FEDERAL RESERVE BANK REGULATION CC

Notice how Alexander endorsed his paycheck. He signed his name in cursive, not in print. He also signed his full name, exactly as it is typed on the front of the check. Finally, Alexander signed his name in the correct place.

GUIDED PRACTICE

List the three things that Alexander did when endorsing his paycheck. (*Hint*: Read the paragraph above.)

_____

He signed his name *in cursive*; *as it's typed on the front of the check*; and *in the correct place.*

APPLIED PRACTICE 4: ENDORSING A PAYCHECK

Using your own name, endorse the back of the paycheck below.

ENDORSE HERE:

X _____

DO NOT SIGN / WRITE / STAMP BELOW THIS LINE
FOR FINANCIAL INSTITUTION USAGE ONLY*

*FEDERAL RESERVE BANK REGULATION CC

Cashing a paycheck means getting **currency,** or dollars and cents, for the amount written on your paycheck. If you choose to cash your paycheck, there are a few things you should know.

First, you'll need to go to a bank, a currency exchange, or a supermarket or other store that cashes paychecks. Second, you'll need to endorse your paycheck. Third, you'll probably need to show the cashier some **identification** with your picture on it. This may include a driver's license, a passport, or a state ID card.

It's a good idea to wait until you're at the counter to endorse your paycheck. Someone who stole your wallet or purse might use your identification and cash your check if you'd already endorsed it.

GUIDED PRACTICE

Put a check (✔) next to the *three* things you should do when you cash a paycheck into dollars and cents.

_____ 1. go to a bank, a currency exchange, or a store that cashes paychecks

_____ 2. endorse your paycheck as soon as you get it

_____ 3. endorse your paycheck at the counter

_____ 4. show the cashier your identification

You are correct if you checked answers *1, 3,* and *4.*

APPLIED PRACTICE 5: CASHING A PAYCHECK

If Alexander cashes this paycheck, how much money will he receive? _____

ABC Company 1001 Cornelia Street New York, NY 10016	57236 Employee #	8-4-93 Date	2-10 ──── 1903

Pay to the Order of ___**Alexander Lew**_____ | **692.09** |

Amount

___**Six hundred ninety-two and** 09/100_____ Dollars

Payable through: Northern Bank
                7 Wall Street
                New York, NY 00571

Marianne Rochester
Marianne Rochester, President

Reading: Selecting parts of text or visual materials to complete a task

DEPOSITING A PAYCHECK

If you have a checking or savings account at a bank, you probably **deposit** some or all of your paycheck. To deposit a check means to turn it in to the bank. The bank then adds the check amount to your **account balance**, the amount of money you have in your bank account.

To deposit a check, you will need to fill out a **deposit slip**. Look at Mia's deposit slip below.

MIA MEJIA
140 W. HURON #2
CHICAGO, IL 60622

DATE October 4 19 93

CHECKS AND OTHER ITEMS ARE RECEIVED FOR DEPOSIT SUBJECT TO THE TERMS AND
CONDITIONS OF THIS FINANCIAL INSTITUTION'S ACCOUNT AGREEMENT.
DEPOSITS MAY NOT BE AVAILABLE FOR IMMEDIATE WITHDRAWAL.

Mia Mejia

SIGN HERE ONLY IF CASH RECEIVED FROM DEPOSIT

PYRAMID BANK
The Pyramid Bank of the Midwest
Chicago, IL 60601

743 000 1 3 002 24

CURRENCY		
COIN		
CHECKS LIST CHECKS SINGLY	480	00
TOTAL FROM OTHER SIDE	0	00
SUB-TOTAL	480	00
TOTAL ITEMS / LESS CASH RECEIVED	80	00
TOTAL DEPOSIT	400	00

3/47-10
BRANCH B

DEPOSIT
TICKET

PLEASE ITEMIZE
ADDITIONAL
CHECKS ON
REVERSE
SIDE

GUIDED PRACTICE

Mia's paycheck totals $480. She is depositing $400 in her checking account. She is asking the bank for the remaining $80 in cash.

Match the phrases from the deposit slip above with the amount Mia filled in. Write the letter of the amount on the line provided.

_____ 1. checks   a. $80.00

_____ 2. sub-total   b. $480.00

_____ 3. less cash received   c. $480.00

_____ 4. total deposit   d. $400.00

You are correct if you answered 1. *b* or *c*; 2. *b* or *c*; 3. *a*; 4. *d*.

Imagine that today is payday. Your paycheck is for $620. You need to deposit some of this money into your checking account. You need the rest of the paycheck amount in cash. Answer these questions.

1. How much is your paycheck? _____

2. How much of this amount do you want to deposit in your checking account?

   _____

3. How much of this amount do you want in cash? _____

Now check your answers. **Add** your answers to questions 2 and 3. When added together, do they equal your paycheck total of $620? If so, your answers are correct. If not, try again. Your deposit amount and your cash received, added together, should equal the amount of your paycheck.

APPLIED PRACTICE 6: FILLING OUT A DEPOSIT SLIP

Using your answers in the Guided Practice above, fill out this deposit slip.

Checking Deposit	For In-Bank Use Only	▲ PYRAMID BANK The Pyramid Bank of the Midwest Date _____ / _____ / _____ Credit Checking Account of: Print Name(s). _____ _____ Address. Please Print. (If new, use Change of Address form) _____ _____ Upon the terms and conditions of the account agreement and subject to detailed verification. ⫶2169 02 ▪ ⫶	Account Number		
				Dollars	Cents
			Cash		
			Checks (List Singly)		
			Total From Other Side		
			Sub-Total		
			Less cash received		
			Deposit		

Check your work. Do your deposit amount and your cash amount, added together, equal the total check amount?

Writing: Entering appropriate information onto a form;
Computing: Perform computations of addition and subtraction using decimal fractions

INTERPRET A PAYCHECK

Using the information below, calculate Luisa's net pay. Then fill in the paycheck and paystub.

Employee: Luisa Ortíz	Gross pay: $540.00
Employee Number: 9783	Fed. With. Tax: $54.00
Social Security Number: 450-90-8090	FICA: $5.40
Pay Date 12/15/93	Union Dues: $15.00
Pay Period End 12/12/93	State With. Tax: $16.50
Regular Hours: 72	Health Plan: $18.50
Overtime Hours: none	Net Pay: $430.60

DIGITAL PRESS
1474 CONGRESS STREET
SAN DIEGO, CA 92110

EMPLOYEE ID #	PAY DATE

PAY TO THE ORDER OF _____

_____ AMOUNT

_____ DOLLARS

PAYABLE THROUGH: FIRST TRUST
494 E. CACTUS
SAN DIEGO, CA

SIGNED *Baxter Jacobs*
BAXTER JACOBS, CFO

- -

PAY STATEMENT

Employee ID #	Name	Social Security Number		Pay Date

Pay Period End	Regular Hours	Overtime Hours	File Number	Department
			472417	43

This Pay Period Earnings	Deductions	Year to Date
Gross	Fed. With. Tax FICA State With. Tax	Earnings Fed. With. Tax FICA
Net	Union Dues Health Plan	State With. Tax

BENEFITS ON THE JOB

In many jobs today, full-time employees are offered more than just an hourly wage or a monthly salary. Employees often receive **benefits** in addition to their pay.

Different companies offer different employee benefits. Sometimes the benefits offered depend on what a company thinks is important or what the company can afford. For example, an employer might think that health insurance is very important. That employer may have a complete health care package as a benefit. Another employer might value extra vacation time and offer employees more vacation days.

SKILL PREVIEW

If you owned a company, what benefits would you offer your employees? What would your employees get besides an hourly wage or a salary? List as many benefits as you can think of on the lines below.

_____

_____

_____

_____

UNDERSTANDING BENEFITS

Chandra has a new job at Blue Sky Foods. Her manager has given her the company's **benefit package**, which describes all of the company's benefits.

Blue Sky Foods: Benefits

REQUIRED PAYROLL DEDUCTIONS

- **Federal Income Tax:** This is the income tax that the federal government requires be **deducted**, or taken out of your pay. This deduction is part of your yearly income tax.

- **FICA (Social Security):** This money is taken out of each paycheck. When you retire, the government should pay you some of this money back in monthly Social Security payments.

- **Retirement:** This money is deducted from each paycheck and invested in a retirement fund of your choice. When you reach retirement age, you can collect this money plus the interest it has earned.

- **Industrial Insurance (workers' compensation):** This money pays your wages and covers medical costs if you miss work due to an on-the-job accident.

INSURANCE

- **Health (medical costs):** Money is deducted from each paycheck to help cover health care costs. At Blue Sky Foods, this benefit covers the cost for employees only (employees' families are not covered).

- **Dental:** Money is deducted from each paycheck to help cover dental care costs, including one free dental visit per year.

- **Life (life insurance costs):** Money is taken from each paycheck to cover life insurance costs. Blue Sky Foods employees may choose to pay more to cover their families.

HOLIDAYS

Employees are paid for certain holidays during the year even though the company is closed on those days. Blue Sky Foods holidays are Memorial Day, July 4, Labor Day, Martin Luther King, Jr., Day, Thanksgiving Day, and December 25.

VACATION

Each Blue Sky Foods full-time employee has 10 paid vacation days a year.

SICK LEAVE

Each employee has six days per year for use when either the employee or a dependent is ill. Employees are paid their regular salary when using sick leave.

Using the benefits information on page 36, match each benefit below with the correct description. Write the letter of the description on the line provided.

	Benefit	Description
_____	1. health insurance	a. for on-the-job accidents
_____	2. sick leave	b. for employees' teeth
_____	3. vacation	c. for celebration days
_____	4. industrial insurance	d. for employees' health
_____	5. dental insurance	e. for days the employee is ill
_____	6. holidays	f. for use after the employee stops working permanently
_____	7. retirement	g. for employees' leisure time

You are correct if you matched 1. *d*; 2. *e*; 3. *g*; 4. *a*; 5. *b*; 6. *c*; 7. *f*.

APPLIED PRACTICE 1: EXPLAINING BENEFITS

In your own words, describe *when* you would use the following benefits.

1. vacation pay: _____

2. Social Security: _____

3. sick leave: _____

4. medical insurance: _____

5. workers' compensation: _____

6. life insurance: _____

. . . .

Reading: Recognizing common words and meanings; Selecting parts of text or visual materials to complete a task

DEFINING WORDS IN CONTEXT, FOLLOWING SEQUENTIAL INSTRUCTIONS

The law requires that many employers post notices like the one on page 39. The *upper* half of this notice describes **workers' compensation benefits**. The *lower* half tells what an employee should do if hurt on the job.

GUIDED PRACTICE

Read the notice on page 39. Look for the phrases listed below. Each time you find one of these phrases, put a check (✔) next to it, right on the notice.

occupational disease   wage replacement
disability pensions   vocational assistance

What do you think these phrases mean? Find the checks you put on the notice on page 39. Read the words before and after each check. Then use the hints below to define each phrase.

Example: occupational disease: disease caused by ___*something at your workplace*___

1. disability pension: pension for a person who is _____

2. wage replacement: replacing _____ lost because of a job injury

3. vocational assistance: help in finding a new _____

You are correct if you answered 1. *disabled*; 2. *wages*; 3. *job*.

APPLIED PRACTICE 2: FOLLOWING SEQUENTIAL INSTRUCTIONS

Read the lower half of the notice on page 39. If an employee at Blue Sky Foods is injured at work, what should he or she do? Write the three steps below:

1. _____

2. _____

3. _____

This is your official industrial insurance poster. You are required by law to post this notice.

NOTICE TO EMPLOYEES

If a job injury occurs...

Your employer is insured with the Washington State Fund. If you become injured on the job or suffer from an occupational disease, you are entitled to workers' compensation benefits. Benefits include:

Medical care. Medical expenses arising from your workplace injury or disease will be fully paid by the State Fund.

Disability income. If you can't work for more than three days because of your injury or illness, you may be eligible for wage-replacement benefits.

Pensions. Injuries that permanently keep you from returning to work may qualify you for a disability pension.

Partial disability benefits. You'll get a monetary award to compensate for the loss of certain bodily functions.

Death benefits for survivors. If a worker dies, the surviving spouse and children may receive a pension.

Vocational assistance. Under certain conditions, you may be eligible for help in returning to work.

In an emergency...

Report your injury. Tell the person listed to the right if you are injured, no matter how minor the injury seems.

Get medical care. You have the right to go to the doctor of your choice. All medical bills that arise from a workplace injury or occupational disease will be paid by the Washington State Fund.

Tell your doctor the injury is work-related. Your doctor will complete an Accident Report form and send it to us. This is the first step in opening your industrial insurance claim.

Report your injury to:

_____
(Employer fills in this space)

Helpful phone numbers:

_____
Ambulance

_____
Police

_____
Fire

WASHINGTON
INDUSTRIAL INSURANCE
STATE FUND

> **Important: Every worker is entitled to workers' compensation benefits. You cannot be penalized or discriminated against for filing a claim. For more information, call the department's toll-free hotline at 1-800-547-8367. Hearing-impaired, TDD customers, may phone (206) 586-4404.**

Department of Labor and Industries, Olympia, Washington, 98504. Toll free 1-800-547-8367.

F242-191-000 (6/89)

 3

UNDERSTANDING MEDICAL FORMS

On page 41 is the application for **medical coverage** for employees at Blue Sky Foods. An important part of this application is the bottom section, **Dependent Eligibility Information**. A **dependent** is a person you support financially—for example, a child or an elderly or disabled family member.

On page 41 is the application

GUIDED PRACTICE

Look at the section of the form on page 41 called **Dependent Eligibility Information**. There are four questions about your dependents over age 18. What are these questions really asking? Rewrite the questions in your own words on the lines below.

Example: Married? *Is your dependent married ?*

1. Income tax dependent? _____

2. Resides regularly as a member of your household?_____

    _____

3. Full-time student at an accredited school?_____

    _____

You are correct if you answered 1. *Is this person listed as a dependent on your income tax return?* 2. *Does your dependent live with you year-round?* and 3. *Does your dependent go to a licensed college, university, or vocational school full-time?*

APPLIED PRACTICE 3: COMPLETING A MEDICAL INSURANCE APPLICATION

Use your own information to fill out the application on page 41. Put a check (✔) next to any section for which you don't have the information. Your instructor can help you fill in these areas.

To fill in the column called **Medical Center**, you must choose a medical clinic from the list. Look under the area called **Medical Center Selection**. Choose any one. (If you were truly applying for medical coverage, you would have more information on each of these medical centers to help you choose.)

Watch out for the shaded areas on the insurance application. These areas are to be filled out by the medical insurance office when it receives your application.

. . . .

Reading: Recognizing task-related words with technical meanings; Making inferences from text
Writing: Entering appropriate information onto a form

Group Health Cooperative of Puget Sound

APPLICATION FOR GROUP COVERAGE

P.O. Box 19161
Seattle, WA 98109

EMPLOYER: PLEASE CHECK APPROPRIATE BOX.

☐ Open Enrollment
☐ New Employee
☐ Information Change
☐ Adding Dependent(s)

REASON FOR ADDING DEPENDENT(S):

☐ Terminate Coverage for:
☐ Subscriber and Dependents
☐ Dependent(s) only

☐ Transfer to COBRA
Start Date _____
☐ 18 months
☐ 36 months

EFFECTIVE DATE OF CHANGE: _____

Group Number _____
Group Name _____
Telephone Number _____

SHADED AREAS FOR GHC USE ONLY

Original Date of Hire ___/___/___
Date of Rehire ___/___/___
Date Transferred From Part to Full Time ___/___/___
Hours Worked Per Week _____

EMPLOYEE: COMPLETE THE FOLLOWING NON-SHADED AREAS. PLEASE PRINT.

Employee Name _____

Marital Status: ☐ Married ☐ Single Date Married ___/___

Resident Address _____
Home Phone _____
City _____ State _____ Zip _____ County _____ Work Phone _____
Former Name of Applicant or Spouse _____
Medicare Number _____

CONSUMER NUMBER	EFF. DATE	CHECK ONE ADD	CHECK ONE REMOVE	List Persons To Be Covered (Please Print) LAST	FIRST	M.	S.S. NO.	SEX	DATE OF BIRTH MO-DY-YR	RELATIONSHIP TO SUBSCRIBER	MEDICAL CENTER *	ENR-S
SUB				Employee					/ /			/ /
DEP				Spouse 1					/ /			/ /
DEP				Dependents (Please give address if different than Employee's) 2					/ /			/ /
DEP				3					/ /			/ /
DEP				4								/ /
DEP				5								/ /

*MEDICAL CENTER SELECTION

Please use this chart to pick the center each family member will use by putting the corresponding code into the column above marked "MEDICAL CENTER."

BAI—Bainbridge
BRN—Burien
DOW—Olive Way/Downtown
EPC—Eastside
EVC—Everett
FAC—Factoria

FED—Federal Way
FHC—Capitol Hill
FPR—Family Practice Res
GHU—University
LYN—Lynnwood
MAC—Madrona
NES—North Everett Satellite

NGT—Northgate
NSH—Northshore
OLY—Olympia
POR—Port Orchard
RVM—Rainier
RNT—Renton

SIL—Silverdale
TAC—Tacoma/Cushman
TAS—Tacoma South
VAS—Vashon
WCM—Whatcom/Skagit Div
WOL—Olympia West

DEPENDENT ELIGIBILITY INFORMATION

If you have listed a dependent child over the age of 18 years, please answer the questions below about your dependent:

1. Married? ☐ Yes ☐ No
2. Income tax dependent? ☐ Yes ☐ No
3. Resides regularly as a member of your household? ☐ Yes ☐ No
4. Full-time student at an accredited school? ☐ Yes ☐ No

If full-time student, give name of college, university or vocational school dependent is attending: _____

Your dependent's eligibility will be determined upon our receipt of your completed questionnaire. If your group medical contract specifies a limiting age for dependents, GHC reserves the right to request proof of school enrollment status. If your dependent is determined ineligible for medical coverage under your group contract, you will be notified in writing.

SUBSCRIBER'S SIGNATURE _____ DATE _____
(Coverage cannot be granted without signature)

Please notify GROUP HEALTH in writing of any changes to address or family status.

ARE YOU OR ANY OTHER PERSON NAMED ABOVE COVERED BY OTHER HEALTH INSURANCE OR MEDICARE?

☐ NO ☐ YES COVERED BY: _____

NAME OF INSURANCE COMPANY _____
INSURANCE COMPANY ADDRESS _____

POLICY HOLDER _____ POLICY NUMBER _____ EFFECTIVE DATE _____

THE OTHER INSURANCE IS:
☐ GROUP COVERAGE
☐ INDIVIDUAL COVERAGE

☐ MEDICARE-PART A
☐ MEDICARE-PART B

Subscriber's Medicare Number _____
Spouse's Medicare Number _____

SEND TO GHC

PA-1078 (08-00393) (2-92) GS-7332   ♻ PRINTED ON RECYCLED PAPER

UNDERSTANDING RETIREMENT BENEFITS

A **retirement plan** is a system in which your employer deducts money from each paycheck and invests it in one or more bank accounts. When you retire, you can collect all the money from your account, including the interest it has earned.

On page 43 is a retirement plan enrollment form. This form asks for information about you and about your **beneficiary.** A beneficiary is a person you choose to receive your money in case you die before you can collect it. There are two kinds of beneficiaries: *primary* and *contingent*.

A **primary beneficiary** will receive any money in your account at the time of your death. A **contingent beneficiary** will receive money from your account only if no primary beneficiary is still living. For example, say that your spouse is your primary beneficiary. If your spouse died, your contingent beneficiary would get the money.

GUIDED PRACTICE

To complete this enrollment form, you'll need to know some vocabulary. Match the vocabulary word with the definition you think is correct. Write the letter of the definition on the line provided.

Vocabulary Word	**Definition**
_____ 1. intended beneficiary	a. paying out
_____ 2. disbursing	b. identify by name
_____ 3. accumulated contributions	c. person you want to get money
_____ 4. designate	d. make a sworn statement
_____ 5. certify	e. money in a retirement fund

You are correct if you matched 1. *c*; 2. *a*; 3. *e*; 4. *b*; 5. *d*.

APPLIED PRACTICE 4: COMPLETING A RETIREMENT ENROLLMENT FORM

Complete sections 1 through 5 on the enrollment form on page 43. Be sure to write at least one primary and one contingent beneficiary in the space provided.

. . . .
Reading: Determining meaning of technical usage of terms;
Problem Solving: Differentiating;
Writing: Entering appropriate information onto a form

ENROLLMENT FORM

EMPLOYEE PORTION

①

TYPE OR PRESS FIRMLY	DATE OF BIRTH			SEX		SOCIAL SECURITY NO.
	MONTH	DAY	YEAR	MALE ☐ FEMALE ☐		– –

② **LAST NAME**

FIRST NAME

MIDDLE NAME **MAIDEN NAME**

③ **MAILING ADDRESS**

CITY	STATE	ZIP CODE (+4 OPTIONAL)
		–

NOTE: The beneficiary must be related by blood or law, or have an insurable interest in the life of the member. If you are unsure whether an intended beneficiary meets the above requirements, consult your personnel officer or the Department of Retirement Systems. A member may change the beneficiary or beneficiaries by requesting and completing the proper form issued by the Department of Retirement Systems.

FOR THE PURPOSE OF DISBURSING ANY ACCUMULATED CONTRIBUTIONS STANDING TO MY CREDIT IN THE EVENT OF MY DEATH PRIOR TO RETIREMENT, I HEREBY DESIGNATE THE FOLLOWING BENEFICIARY(S):

④

FULL GIVEN NAME OF BENEFICIARY	DESIGNATION	RELATIONSHIP	BIRTH DATE	ADDRESS		
	☐ PRIMARY ☐ CONTINGENT			street		
				city	state	zip
	☐ PRIMARY ☐ CONTINGENT			street		
				city	state	zip
	☐ PRIMARY ☐ CONTINGENT			street		
				city	state	zip
	☐ PRIMARY ☐ CONTINGENT			street		
				city	state	zip

I HEREBY CERTIFY THAT ALL OF THE INFORMATION I HAVE ENTERED ON THIS FORM IS TRUE AND COMPLETE.

⑤

_____ SIGNATURE OF EMPLOYEE

_____ DATE

EMPLOYER PORTION

EMPLOYER NAME

EMPLOYEE POSITION TITLE

FIRST DATE OF EMPLOYEE ELIGIBILITY

RETIREMENT SYSTEM—check one:

☐ **P**UBLIC EMPLOYEES   ☐ **S**TATE PATROL
☐ **T**EACHERS   ☐ **J**UDICIAL
☐ **L**AW ENFORC. OFF.   ☐ **F**IRE FIGHTER

PLAN—check one:

☐ PLAN 1   ☐ PLAN 2

AGENCY NO.

TYPE OR PRINT EMPLOYER NAME AND MAILING ADDRESS BELOW

I HEREBY CERTIFY THAT ALL OF THE INFORMATION ENTERED ON THIS FORM IS TRUE AND COMPLETE.

_____ PRINT NAME

_____ TITLE OF PERSONNEL OR PAYROLL REPRESENTATIVE

_____ PHONE

Social Security Number has been verified. _____ Initials

_____ SIGNATURE

IDENTIFY APPROPRIATE BENEFITS

Read each situation below. For each one, choose which benefit the Blue Sky Foods employee should use. Then explain why you chose that benefit.

sick leave	paid vacation days	paid holidays
life insurance	dental insurance	health insurance
workers' compensation	retirement fund	tax deductions

1. Betty Wilson, a Blue Sky truck driver, gets a call from the dispatcher that her son is sick at school. She must leave work to pick him up at school, and then stay home to take care of him.

   Which benefit will she use? _____

   Why? _____

2. Blue Sky Foods is sending its advertising director, José Olmos, to a conference in Dallas. While José is there, he wants to take two extra days to visit a friend.

   Which benefit will José use? _____

   Why? _____

3. Last Thursday, Leon Alexander broke his wrist while loading canned peas onto a truck. His doctor said he won't be able to drive the forklift until his wrist heals, probably in three to four weeks.

   What benefit will Leon use while he waits for his wrist to heal? _____

   Why? _____

4. Thelma Green, personnel director for Blue Sky Foods, and her husband were killed in an avalanche while on a ski trip. Thelma's husband was her primary beneficiary; her daughter was her contingent beneficiary.

   Which benefit will be used? _____

   Who will receive the money? _____

UNIT II

Personal Forms

Credit

Complete a Credit Card Application

Bills and Budgets

Create a Personal Budget

CREDIT

Shopping with **credit cards** means "buy now; pay later." Most businesses accept credit cards instead of cash. The business records your purchase. It sends the bill to your credit card company. Your credit card company pays the bill and sends you a monthly **statement** of the purchases you've made with your card. There are three main types of credit:

Retail credit cards are offered by department stores, gas companies, and other businesses. These cards can be used only in the store or company that issued them.

Major credit cards, sometimes called **bank cards**, are offered through banks. These credit cards, such as Visa or MasterCard, can be used in many different businesses.

Loans, offered by banks and other lending companies, don't involve cards. A loan is money you borrow. You pay it back on a schedule. You also pay back additional money called **interest**.

Interest is money charged to your account when you don't pay the entire amount due. Credit cards and loans have different **interest rates**. For example, a retail credit card may have a 20 percent interest rate. That means that for every $100 on your account balance each month you will owe $20 in interest. Interest is sometimes called a **finance charge**.

How do you get a credit card or a loan? Usually, you have to fill out an application form. You'll need to prove that you are creditworthy, or able to pay back the money you charge with your card or the money you borrow.

SKILL PREVIEW

Check your credit knowledge. Write *T* for true or *F* for false.

_____ 1. Credit card companies usually send out monthly statements.

_____ 2. It's OK to skip a few loan payments.

_____ 3. Credit cards add a finance charge if you don't pay the total amount you owe each month.

_____ 4. Retail credit cards can be used in many different stores and businesses.

UNDERSTANDING CREDIT VOCABULARY

Most credit applications ask for information on you, your family, your employment, and your finances. They also use certain words you'll need to know.

GUIDED PRACTICE

Look at the areas shaded in gray on the credit card application on page 49. Each shaded area is defined below. Next to each definition, write the number from the application where that word is located.

_____ **Applicant:** person who is applying for the credit card or loan

_____ **Dependents:** people you support financially

_____ **Gross Monthly Income (salary):** amount of your monthly paycheck, before deductions

_____ **Other Monthly Income:** amount of money you earn _not including_ your paycheck (for example, rent from tenants, retirement or disability payments)

_____ **Disclosure of Alimony, Separate Maintenance or Child Support Payment is Optional:** you may choose whether you want to write down any alimony or child support payments you receive

_____ **Credit References:** businesses or credit card companies with whom you have accounts and who can provide information about your credit status

_____ **Creditor:** person or business to whom you owe money

_____ **Estimated Texaco Monthly Purchases:** amount of money (in gasoline or other merchandise) you believe you'll charge on your Texaco card each month

_____ **Signature and Customer Agreement:** your signature is your agreement that all information is correct and that Texaco can contact your credit references about your credit standing. You understand and agree with the Texaco card agreement terms (see page 51).

You are correct if you answered, from top to bottom, _1, 2, 3, 4, 5, 6, 7, 8,_ and _9._

APPLIED PRACTICE 1: UNDERSTANDING CREDIT VOCABULARY

For many people, the key to building good credit is to start with one credit card and use it responsibly. Often this first card is a retail credit card. Think about the types of retail credit offered in your area. Which one might be a good one for you to apply for?

. . . .
Reading: Recognizing task-related words with technical meanings;
Problem Solving: Differentiating

STAR POWER

TEXACO CREDIT CARD APPLICATION
ALL APPLICABLE SECTIONS MUST BE COMPLETED (PLEASE PRINT)

TEXACO

① APPLICANT'S NAME — FIRST | MIDDLE | LAST | AGE | SOCIAL SECURITY NUMBER

CURRENT ADDRESS

STREET ADDRESS AND APARTMENT NO., IF APPLICABLE (NO P.O. BOX PLEASE) | HOME PHONE NUMBER AREA CODE ( ) | NO. OF DEPENDENTS (INCLUDING YOURSELF) ②

CITY & STATE | ZIP CODE | ☐ OWN/BUYING ☐ OTHER ☐ RENT | YEARS AT THIS ADDRESS

PREVIOUS ADDRESS

IF AT PRESENT ADDRESS LESS THAN ONE YEAR, GIVE PREVIOUS ADDRESS

CITY | STATE | ZIP CODE | YEARS AT THIS ADDRESS

EMPLOYMENT

PRESENT EMPLOYER | JOB TITLE (If military, give rank) | YEARS EMPLOYED

STREET ADDRESS

CITY | STATE | ZIP CODE | BUSINESS PHONE NUMBER AREA CODE ( )

GROSS MONTHLY INCOME (SALARY) ③ | OTHER MONTHLY INCOME ④ | DISCLOSURE OF ALIMONY, SEPARATE MAINTENANCE OR CHILD SUPPORT PAYMENT IS OPTIONAL ⑤

PREVIOUS EMPLOYER & ADDRESS (IF WITH PRESENT EMPLOYER LESS THAN 5 YEARS) | YEARS EMPLOYED

⑥ **CREDIT REFERENCES**

(Bank Card, Oil Card, Dept. Store, etc.) (If accounts given as references carried in another name, please indicate that name)

⑦ CREDITOR | ADDRESS | ACCOUNT NUMBER | For Texaco Use Only

O—

B—

D—

R—

F—

T—

BANK

BANK NAME | ACCOUNT NUMBER

ADDRESS | TYPE ACCOUNTS ☐ CHECKING ☐ SAVINGS ☐ LOAN

CO-USER INFORMATION

NOTE: A CREDIT APPLICANT, IF MARRIED, MAY APPLY FOR A SEPARATE ACCOUNT. IF ONLY ONE PERSON APPLIES FOR CREDIT, AND ONLY THAT PERSON WILL USE THE ACCOUNT, THEN THAT PERSON MAY CHOOSE NOT TO ANSWER ANY QUESTION WHICH WOULD REVEAL MARITAL STATUS.

WILL YOUR SPOUSE OR CO-APPLICANT USE THE ACCOUNT? ☐ YES ☐ NO IF ANSWERED YES, PLEASE COMPLETE THE FOLLOWING BLANKS

NAME—FIRST | MIDDLE | LAST | JOB TITLE OR OCCUPATION

EMPLOYER AND ADDRESS | BUSINESS PHONE NO. AREA CODE ( ) | GROSS MONTHLY INCOME | YEARS EMPLOYED

NAME & ADDRESS OF NEAREST RELATIVE NOT LIVING WITH YOU | RELATIVE'S PHONE NO. AREA CODE ( ) | RELATIONSHIP

CARD(S) WILL BE USED FOR ☐ CAR ☐ BOAT ☐ TRUCK ☐ PLANE | ESTIMATED TEXACO MONTHLY PURCHASES $ ⑧ | NO. CARDS DESIRED | DRIVER'S LICENSE NO. AND STATE

⑨ **SIGNATURE AND CUSTOMER AGREEMENT:** Everything I have stated in this application for credit is correct to the best of my knowledge. TEXACO is given permission to check my credit references or other information on this application and to obtain a consumer credit report to check my credit standing. The application is the property of TEXACO REFINING AND MARKETING INC. I have received a copy of the Texaco Credit Card Agreement, which is part of this application, and agree to be bound by its terms and conditions in the event this application is approved.

✓

SIGNATURE OF SPOUSE OR CO-APPLICANT (REQUIRED ONLY IF SPOUSE OR CO-APPLICANT WILL BE JOINTLY LIABLE)

SIGNATURE OF APPLICANT — (Commercial Applicants: Officer should sign and indicate title)
DATE OF APPLICATION

COMMERCIAL APPLICANTS: If credit applicant is a company, partnership, or corporation, processing of this application will be facilitated if accompanied by a letter on your firm's letterhead detailing your type of business, years in operation, names of your company's principals, or other information such as a recent financial statement normally furnished in connection with the extension of commercial credit. Also, please indicate estimated monthly charges.

S-86C (2-91)

LOCATING DETAILS

The Texaco Credit Card Agreement on page 51 is part of the credit card application. The agreement tells you the facts about this credit card: your legal rights, Texaco's rights, the types of accounts, and the finance charge for your state.

GUIDED PRACTICE

Read the three sentences on page 51 under the heading **Notice to Buyer**.

1. What should you do before you sign the credit application?

   _____

2. When can you pay the full amount on your account?

   _____

You are correct if you answered 1. *read the credit agreement and be sure all of the Texaco credit terms are typed in*; and 2. *at any time.*

APPLIED PRACTICE 2: IDENTIFYING DETAILS WITHIN A TEXT

Use the credit card agreement on page 51 to answer the questions below.

1. Look under the heading **Important Notice to Applicants**. If you let a friend use your credit card, are you responsible for the charge?

   _____

Find your state on the chart.

2. What is your balance subject to finance charge? _____

3. What is your periodic (monthly) rate? _____

4. What is your annual percentage rate? _____

5. What is the annual fee? _____

Texaco Credit Card Agreement

NOTICE TO BUYER
(1) DO NOT SIGN THIS AGREEMENT BEFORE YOU HAVE READ IT OR IF ANY OF THE SPACES INTENDED FOR THE AGREED TERMS ARE LEFT BLANK
(2) YOU ARE ENTITLED TO A COPY OF THIS AGREEMENT AT THE TIME YOU SIGN IT KEEP IT TO PROTECT YOUR LEGAL RIGHTS
(3) YOU MAY AT ANY TIME PAY OFF THE FULL BALANCE UNDER THIS AGREEMENT

IMPORTANT NOTICE TO APPLICANTS
FINANCE CHARGES will be made in amounts or at rates not in excess of those permitted by law in your state of residence.

A consumer report may be requested in connection with this application Upon request you will be informed whether a consumer report was requested, and if such report was requested, you will be informed of the name and address of the consumer reporting agency that furnished the report. Subsequent reports may be requested or utilized in connection with an update, renewal or extension of the credit you have requested No additional notice will be given to you if such subsequent reports are requested

Upon approval of this application mail order merchandise, insurance, Texaco Auto Club and travel club offerings may be mailed to you on a periodic basis unless you specifically request that they not be sent

Illinois Residents Residents of Illinois may contact the Illinois Commissioner of Banks and Trust Companies, 117 South Fifth Street, Room 100 Reisch Building, Springfield, Illinois 62701. phone (217) 782-7966, for comparative information on FINANCE CHARGES, fees and grace periods

Ohio Residents The Ohio laws against discrimination require that all creditors make credit equally available to all credit-worthy customers and that all credit reporting agencies maintain separate credit histories on each individual upon request. The Ohio Civil Rights Commission administers compliance with this law

Texas Residents This contract is subject in whole or in part to Texas law which is enforced by the Consumer Credit Commissioner, 2601 North Lamar Boulevard, Austin, Texas 78705-4207, phone (512) 479-1285, (214) 263-2016, (713) 461-4074

Wisconsin Residents Be advised that no provision contained in any marital property agreement, or in any unilateral statement under Wis Rev Stat S 766.59, or in any court decree under Wis Rev Stat S 766.70 will adversely affect Texaco's rights unless prior to the time it grants credit, Texaco is furnished a copy of said agreement, statement, or decree or unless Texaco has actual knowledge of an adverse provision in said agreement, statement, or decree when the obligation is incurred

By using or permitting another to use your Texaco Credit Card(s), you are agreeing to pay all amounts that will be owing in accordance with the terms and conditions explained under Texaco Credit Card Agreement section of this application

If your account is not paid according to terms, Texaco may declare the total balance of your account due and payable immediately and/or withdraw credit privileges

In case of loss, theft or unauthorized use of your Credit Card, notify Texaco promptly Your liability for unauthorized charges before notification shall not exceed $50

Should you have any questions about your account, you may contact Texaco at the address or phone number indicated on this brochure Under federal law and the laws of certain states, you should register any protest about your bill in writing in order to protect your rights

If you correspond with Texaco regarding your account, please indicate your Credit Card number

NOTICE
ANY HOLDER OF THIS CONSUMER CREDIT CONTRACT IS SUBJECT TO ALL CLAIMS AND DEFENSES WHICH THE DEBTOR COULD ASSERT AGAINST THE SELLER OF GOODS OR SERVICES OBTAINED PURSUANT HERETO OR WITH THE PROCEEDS HEREOF. RECOVERY HEREUNDER BY THE DEBTOR SHALL NOT EXCEED AMOUNTS PAID BY THE DEBTOR HEREUNDER

The information about the costs of the card described in this application is accurate as of January 1991. This information may have changed after that date. To find out what may have changed, call us at:

1-800-552-STAR (7827)

or write to us at

Texaco Refining and Marketing Inc., P.O. Box 2000, Bellaire, Texas 77402-2000.

REGULAR PURCHASES: Single purchases under $50, exclusive of mail order merchandise, are due and payable upon receipt of each monthly statement

TIME CHARGE PLAN: Single purchases of $50 or more for products and services are placed under Texaco's Time Charge Plan. The required monthly payment is 10% of the Time Charge balance or $20, whichever is greater. If the revolving purchase balance is less than $20, you must pay the full amount.

Payment for mail order merchandise is subject to the terms stated on each individual offer. The Time Charge purchase privilege is not available to Commercial or Government accounts

REVOLVING PURCHASES: For qualifying accounts, all purchases of goods and services except annual membership fees, auto club fees, mail order merchandise installments, and insurance premiums are eligible for our Revolving credit terms. You may pay your account in full every month or you may revolve your purchases in accordance with the schedule below.

Payment for mail order merchandise is subject to the terms stated on each individual offer. The Revolving purchase privilege is not available to Commercial or Government accounts

Revolving Balance	Minimum Payment*	
$0-$200	$20	PLUS
$200-$650	10%	FINANCE
Over $650	$65 plus all over $650	CHARGES

*The "Minimum Payment" includes all New Regular purchases, the current due portion of Revolving purchases, any installment amounts, FINANCE CHARGES and any past due amounts. The difference between the "New Balance" and the "Minimum Payment" due will represent the deferred balance of your Revolving and/or installment purchases

The total balance on your account, including Regular, Revolving and Installment purchases, appears on your statement as the "New Balance" You may pay your New Balance in full at any time. However, under our terms you must pay at least the "Minimum Payment Due" each month. We must receive your Minimum Payment Due within 25 days of the statement closing (billing) date

FINANCE CHARGE can be avoided if we receive payment of your New Balance within 25 days of the statement closing date. If your New Balance is not paid in full, a FINANCE CHARGE will be computed using the "Method of Computing the Balances for Purchases" described in the table below.

In case of loss, theft, or unauthorized use of your Credit Card, promptly notify Texaco at the address or phone number on this application. Your liability for unauthorized charges before notification shall not exceed $50.00

If you believe there is an error in your billing, notify Texaco promptly in writing at Texaco Refining and Marketing Inc. P.O. Box 2000, Bellaire, Texas 77402-2000 to protect your rights under the law. Be sure to include your account number. Telephoning will not preserve your billing error rights

STATE OF RESIDENCE	BALANCE SUBJECT TO FINANCE CHARGE	PERIODIC (MONTHLY) RATE (S)	ANNUAL PERCENTAGE RATE(S)	GRACE PERIOD OR FREE RIDE FOR PURCHASES (Requires payment of New Balance)	ANNUAL FEE	MINIMUM FINANCE CHARGE	METHOD OF COMPUTING THE BALANCE FOR PURCHASES
Colorado, Georgia, Indiana, New Jersey, New Mexico, Oklahoma, Wyoming	ALL	1.75%	21%	25 DAYS	NONE		
Arizona, Delaware, Illinois, Kentucky, Nevada, New Hampshire, New York, Oregon	ALL	1.80%	21.6%	25 DAYS	NONE		
Connecticut, Missouri, Pennsylvania	ALL	1.25%	15%	25 DAYS	NONE		
Minnesota	ALL	1.33%	16%	25 DAYS	NONE		
Michigan	ALL	1.70%	20.4%	25 DAYS	NONE		
Arkansas	ALL	.83%	10%	25 DAYS	NONE		
District of Columbia, Texas	0-$500 / OVER $500	1.50% / 1.00%	18% / 12%	25 DAYS	NONE	Any calculated FINANCE CHARGE of less than $.50 will be adjusted to a minimum of $.50 in all states except AR, CT, DC, HI, KY, MD, MT, NE, NV, NH, NM, NC, OR, ND, RI and WI	SEE DESCRIPTION OF METHOD BELOW**
California	0-$1,000 / OVER $1,000	1.50% / 1.00%	18% / 12%	25 DAYS	NONE		
Iowa, Vermont	0-$500 / OVER $500	1.50% / 1.25%	18% / 15%	25 DAYS	NONE		
Nebraska	0-$500 / OVER $500	1.75% / 1.50%	21% / 18%	25 DAYS	NONE		
Maryland	0-$700 / OVER $700	1.50% / 1.00%	18% / 12%	25 DAYS	NONE		
West Virginia	0-$750 / OVER $750	1.50% / 1.00%	18% / 12%	25 DAYS	NONE		
Kansas	0-$1000 / OVER $1000	1.50% / 1.20%	18% / 14.4%	25 DAYS	NONE		
Alaska	0-$1,000 / OVER $1,000	1.50% / .83%	18% / 10%	25 DAYS	NONE		
Mississippi	0-$800 / OVER $800	1.50% / 1.00%	18% / 12%	25 DAYS	NONE		
Alabama	0-$750 / OVER $750	1.75% / 1.50%	21% / 18%	25 DAYS	NONE		
Florida, Hawaii, Idaho, Louisiana, Maine, Massachusetts, Montana, North Carolina, North Dakota, Ohio, Rhode Island, South Carolina, South Dakota, Tennessee, Utah, Virginia, Washington, Wisconsin	ALL	1.50%	18%	25 DAYS	NONE		

**In the states of ME, MA, MN, MS, NE, NM, NC and RI we figure the FINANCE CHARGE on your account by applying the periodic rate to the "average daily balance" of your account excluding current purchases. To get the "average daily balance" we take the beginning balance of your account each day and subtract any payments, credits and unpaid FINANCE CHARGES. We do not add in any new purchases. This gives us the daily balance. Then, we add all the daily balances for the billing cycle together and divide the total by the number of days in the billing cycle. This gives us the "average daily balance."

In all other states we figure the FINANCE CHARGE on your account by applying the periodic rate to the "average daily balance" of your account including current purchases. To get the "average daily balance" we take the beginning balance of your account each day, add any new purchases and subtract any payments, credits and unpaid FINANCE CHARGES. This gives us the daily balance. Then, we add up and divide the total by the number of days in the billing cycle. This gives us the "average daily balance."

INTERPRETING CREDIT TERMS

The credit terms on page 53 describe the facts behind a Sears, Roebuck and Company credit card.

GUIDED PRACTICE

Read the **bold** type at the top of the agreement. If you receive this credit card but decide you don't want it after all, how much money do you owe?

_____

You are correct if you answered *none, unless you've used the card.*

APPLIED PRACTICE 3: INTERPRETING CREDIT TERMS

Use the credit terms on page 53 to answer the questions below.

1. If you live in Kansas, what is your annual percentage rate if you owe up to $1,000?

   _____

2. Look at the information across from the heading **Grace Period To Repay Balance**. If you receive a credit card bill dated July 1, when will your payment be due?

   _____

3. Look at the information across from the heading **Minimum Finance Charge**. If you live in Florida, what is your minimum monthly finance charge?

   _____

4. If you live in California, when will Sears charge a late payment fee?_____

5. Read the paragraph under the heading **Ohio residents only**. In your own words, what does the paragraph say?

   _____

   _____

. . . .
Reading: Determining meaning of technical usage of terms; Making inferences from text

IMPORTANT SEARSCHARGE CREDIT TERMS

The information below includes the costs associated with a SearsCharge Account. It is accurate as of May 1991, but may change after that date. To find out what may have changed write to: Sears Telemarketing Center, 2269 Village Mall Dr., Mansfield, OH 44906. A copy of the entire SearsCharge agreement for you to keep, with all terms applicable to your state of residence, will be sent to you with the credit card(s). You need not accept the card and are not required to pay any fee or charge disclosed unless the card is used.

Annual Percentage Rate	The annual percentage rate is 21% unless you reside in a state shown below:
	
	Alabama 21%
	  to $750, 18% on excess
	Alaska 18%
	  to $1000, 10.5% on excess (See
	  Variable Rate Information)
	Arkansas 10.5%
	  (See Variable Rate Information)
	California........................19.2%
	Connecticut 18%
	Florida 18%
	Hawaii 18%
	Iowa 19.8%
	Kansas 21%
	  to $1000, 14.4% on excess
	Maine 18%
	
	Massachusetts 18%
	Michigan,
	  Puerto Rico 20.4%
	Minnesota 18%
	Missouri 20.04%
	Nebraska 21%
	  to $500, 18% on excess
	No. Carolina 18%
	No. Dakota 18%
	Pennsylvania 18%
	Rhode Island 18%
	Texas........................... 18%
	Washington 18%
	W. Virginia 18%
	Wisconsin 18%

Variable Rate Information	(Arkansas Residents Only) Your Annual Percentage Rate may vary. The rate is determined by adding 5% per annum to the Federal Reserve Discount Rate on 90 day commercial paper in Arkansas. (Alaska Residents Only) Your Annual Percentage Rate may vary on balances in excess of $1,000. The rate is determined by adding 5% per annum to the rate charged member banks for advances by the 12th Federal Reserve District that prevails on the 25th day of the month preceding the calendar quarter in which charges are made.
Grace Period To Repay Balance	You have 30 days from your billing date to repay your balance before being charged a finance charge.
Balance Calculation Method For Purchases	The Average Daily Balance method (including new transactions) is used in all states except ME, MA, MN, MT, NM, and ND where the Average Daily Balance method (excluding new transactions) is used.
Minimum Finance Charge	A minimum monthly finance charge of 50¢ applies in all states except AR, CT, HI, MD, NE, NC, ND, RI, VA, DC and PR.
Late Payment Fees	In the states of AL, AZ, AR, CA, FL, GA, IL, IN, KS, LA, MO, MS, MT, NV, NY, OH, OK, OR, UT, VA, and WA, if I fail to make any required minimum monthly payment within 10 days after its due date, Sears may charge and I agree to pay a late payment charge. In AR, GA, MS, NV, NY, OK, OR, UT and WA, it will be $5.00. In AL, AZ, CA, FL, IL, IN, KS, LA, MO, MT, OH and VA, it will be 5% of the amount of the required minimum monthly payment or $5.00 ($3.00 in OH), whichever is less. In FL, no late charge will be imposed if it would be less than $1.00.
Annual Fees	None
Over-The-Credit-Limit Fees	None
Transaction Fees	None

Ohio residents only: The Ohio laws against discrimination require that all creditors make credit equally available to all creditworthy customers, and that credit reporting agencies maintain separate credit histories on each individual upon request. The Ohio Civil Rights Commission administers compliance with this law.

New York residents only: A consumer report may be ordered in connection with this application, or subsequently in connection with the update, renewal or extension of credit. Upon your request, you will be informed whether or not a consumer credit report was ordered, and if it was, you will be given the name and address of the consumer reporting agency that furnished the report.

Wisconsin residents only: Wisconsin law provides that no agreement, court order or individual statement applying to marital property will affect a creditor's interests unless prior to the time credit is granted the creditor is furnished with a copy of the agreement, court order, or statement, or has actual knowledge of the adverse provision.

May 1991

ORGANIZING PERSONAL FINANCIAL INFORMATION

Ernesto Gómez wants to apply for a loan. He has started to fill in the Personal Data Sheet on page 55 with his financial information. The rest of his information is below.

GUIDED PRACTICE

Use Ernesto's information below to complete the Personal Data Sheet on page 55.

current job:
chef, The Western Inn
32111 Merced Avenue
Bakersfield, CA 93312
555-7332
worked there for 10 months
salary: $2,130/month

married?
no

bank:
Great Coastal Savings Bank
670 Norman Avenue
Bakersfield, CA 93312
checking account #030-003993-6
savings account #031-5007-486-1

past job:
chef's assistant, Flannery's Deli
7928 Pershing Avenue North
Stockton, CA 95209
555-2019
worked there for 2 years
salary: $1,505/month

number and age of dependents:
1 son, age 11

credit references:
Bakersfield Auto Sales
6729 Rosedale Highway
Bakersfield, CA 93310
loan #0469
loan is paid in full

....

SELF-CHECK

Check your work. Did you transfer the correct information to the data sheet? Did you write the correct information after **Current Employer** and **Past Employer**?

....

APPLIED PRACTICE 4: COMPLETING A PERSONAL DATA SHEET: FINANCIAL

It's a good idea to organize your own financial information. Gather your information. Then fill out the blank Personal Data Sheet: Financial on page 166. If you prefer to keep some information private, fill it out at another time.

. . . .
Reading: Selecting parts of text to complete a task;
Writing: Entering appropriate information onto a form

PERSONAL DATA SHEET: FINANCIAL

PERSONAL INFORMATION

Name: __Gómez_____Ernesto_____S___ SS#: ___-___-___ Birth Date __3 / 18 / 59__
    Last   First   Middle Initial

Present Address: __5532 S 25th Street____Bakersfield____CA____93301__
          Street   City   State   Zip

How long at present address? __10 months_____

Past Address: __168 W. Vine____Stockton____CA____95202__
        Street   City   State   Zip

How long at past address? __2 years_____

Telephone Number: (home) __555-1872____ (work) __555-7332____

Number of Dependents: _____ Age of Dependents: _____

Citizenship Status: ____ U.S. Visa # __85-9741-5678____ Type _____

Spouse's Name: _____ SS#: ___-___-___
        Last   First   Middle Initial

Spouse's Employer: _____
        Employer Name   Employer Address   Phone

EMPLOYMENT INFORMATION

Current Employer: _____
        Employer Name   Employer Address   Phone

Job Title: _____ Length of time employed ____ years ____ months Monthly Salary: _____

Past Employer: _____
        Employer Name   Employer Address   Phone

Job Title: _____ Length of time employed ____ years ____ months Monthly Salary: _____

FINANCIAL INFORMATION

Bank: _____
    Bank Name   Bank Address

Account Type: __ Checking __Savings __Loan __Other Account Number_____

Bank: _____
    Bank Name   Bank Address

Account Type: __ Checking __Savings __Loan __Other Account Number_____

CREDIT REFERENCES

	Creditor	Address	Account #
1.			
2.			
3.			

COMPLETE A CREDIT CARD APPLICATION

In this unit, you have learned about personal credit: what it is and how to apply for it. Use what you've learned to fill out the SearsCharge application form below. If you wish to keep some information private, just put an *X* through that section. You can fill it in at a later time.

STORE #   I.D. CHECK: ☐ YES ☐ NO

DEPT #   ASSOCIATE #

SEARSCHARGE CREDIT ACCOUNT APPLICATION ID 91

Please indicate below name in which account is to be carried. Applicant, if married, may apply for a separate account.

(COURTESY TITLES ARE OPTIONAL)   FIRST NAME   MIDDLE INITIAL   LAST NAME

☐ MR. ☐ MRS. ☐ MISS ☐ MS

RESIDENCE ADDRESS   APT.   CITY   STATE   ZIP CODE

HOME TELEPHONE   BUSINESS TELEPHONE   SOCIAL SECURITY NUMBER   NO. OF DEPENDENTS (EXCLUDE YOURSELF)

( )   ( )

ARE YOU A U.S. CITIZEN?
☐ YES
☐ NO (IF NO, EXPLAIN IMMIGRATION STATUS)   HOW LONG AT PRESENT ADDRESS   ☐ YEARS ☐ MOS.

DO YOU   ☐ OWN ☐ BOARD   ☐ RENT ☐ L/W PARENTS   ☐ OTHER _____   MONTHLY RENT OR MORTGAGE $

PREVIOUS ADDRESS (IF LESS THAN 2 YEARS AT PRESENT ADDRESS)   APT.   CITY   STATE   ZIP CODE   HOW LONG? ☐ YEARS ☐ MOS.

EMPLOYER (RETIRED/STUDENT, INDICATE: HOW LONG/YEAR IN SCHOOL)   ADDRESS   CITY   STATE   ZIP CODE   HOW LONG? ☐ YEARS ☐ MOS.

OCCUPATION (FORMER OCCUPATION IF RETIRED)   NET INCOME (TAKE HOME PAY) $ ☐ PER MONTH ☐ PER WEEK   PREVIOUS EMPLOYER (IF LESS THAN 1 YEAR WITH PRESENT)   HOW LONG? ☐ YEARS ☐ MOS.

OTHER INCOME* $ ☐ PER MONTH ☐ PER WEEK   SOURCE OTHER INCOME   *Note: Alimony, child support or separate maintenance income need not be disclosed if you do not wish to have it considered as a basis for paying this obligation.

CHECK MAJOR CREDIT CARDS YOU HAVE: ☐ DISCOVER CARD ☐ MASTERCARD ☐ VISA   AUTO LOAN? ☐ YES ☐ NO   NAME OF LENDER   MO. PAYMENT $

CHECK OTHER CREDIT CARDS YOU HAVE: ☐ J C PENNEY ☐ MONTGOMERY WARDS ☐ OTHER (LIST)   PREVIOUS SEARS ACCOUNT? ☐ YES ☐ NO   ACCOUNT NUMBER

DO YOU HAVE A CHECKING ACCOUNT? ☐ YES ☐ NO   NAME OF BANK/FINANCIAL INSTITUTION   ACCOUNT NO. (OPTIONAL)   DO YOU HAVE A (MARK ALL THAT APPLY): ☐ SAVINGS ACCOUNT ☐ CD ☐ MONEY MARKET ☐ OTHER

Complete this section if you want cards issued to additional buyers on your account.

1. FIRST NAME   LAST   RELATIONSHIP   2. FIRST NAME   LAST   RELATIONSHIP

Complete this section if: (1) your spouse is an authorized buyer, (2) you reside in a community property state (AZ, CA, ID, LA, NV, NM, TX, WA, WI), or (3) you are relying on the income or assets of a spouse as a source for payment.

SPOUSE. FIRST NAME   MIDDLE INITIAL   LAST NAME   AGE

EMPLOYER   NET INCOME (TAKE HOME PAY) $ ☐ PER MONTH ☐ PER WEEK

I agree to pay Sears in accordance with the credit terms disclosed to me and to comply with all terms of the SearsCharge Agreement. A copy of the SearsCharge Agreement will be given to me to keep when my application is approved. Sears will retain a security interest where permitted by law under the Uniform Commercial Code on all merchandise charged to the account. Sears is authorized to investigate my credit, employment, and income references and to report to proper persons and credit bureaus my performance of the account. Finance charges not in excess of those permitted by law will be charged on the outstanding balance from month to month.

X _____

APPLICANT'S SIGNATURE   DATE   **SEE OTHER SIDE FOR IMPORTANT CREDIT TERMS.**

©1990 Sears, Roebuck and Co.   Rev. 6/90

BILLS AND BUDGETS

You get bills. Paying them and keeping track of them are part of daily life.

How do your bills relate to your work? You get paid for the work you do. But you need to manage your own finances. If you don't plan well, you could have money worries that affect the way you work.

It's important to know where your money goes. You should know how much you spend on food, housing, clothes, and other things. To do this, you will need to review your bills and create a **budget**. A budget is a plan for how you will use your money.

A strict budget is hard to keep. However, planning how to spend your money well will help you decide what you *can* and *can't* afford.

SKILL PREVIEW

What do you spend your money on? To get an idea, rank the following types of bills and expenses. Put a *1* next to the bill that costs you the most each month, a *2* next to the one that costs you second most, and so on. Rank only the types of expenses that *you* actually have.

_____ Housing/Rent

_____ Electricity/Heat/Water

_____ Child Care

_____ Car Payment/Transportation

_____ Entertainment

_____ Food

_____ Credit Cards/Loan Payment

YOUR NEW

Combined Utility Billing

In hope of serving you better we've changed our billing syst
sample that shows the new and different features on your

Account Number—All of your property's combined utility ac
transferred to this new number. Please refer to it when y

City of Seattle
Combined Utility Billing Statement

City of Seattle
Combined Utility Billing Statement

GENE SMITH
GENE SMITH, OWNER
847 NE 94TH ST
SEATTLE WA 98115

TOTAL A
DUE DATE
ACCOUNT N

METER NUMBE

SERVICE

INTERPRETING BILLING STATEMENTS

Billing statements tell you all about your account with a company. You may receive billing statements from credit card companies and **utilities** (water, gas, electric, sewer, garbage, or telephone companies).

Read the following explanation from the City of Seattle about reading its utility bill.

YOUR NEW

Combined Utility Billing Statement

In hope of serving you better we've changed our billing system and statement. Below is a sample that shows the new and different features on your statement.

Account Number—All of your property's combined utility account information has been transferred to this new number. Please refer to it when you call or write about the property's combined billing statement and include it on your check when making payments.

Phone—Our phone number is on the billing statement for your convenience.

Service Address—This shows the address of the property that receives the service listed on the billing statement.

Payments Received—We've added a new feature to show payments we received since the last billing statement.

Wastewater—Listed as "SEWER" on prior billing statements.

Solid Waste—Listed as "GARBAGE" on prior billing statements.

Water Usage—This new section compares your current water use to the same period a year ago. When customers change it takes a year before comparisons are shown.

Payment Stub—Please return this part of the billing statement with your payment. The amount due shows at both the top and bottom of the statement.

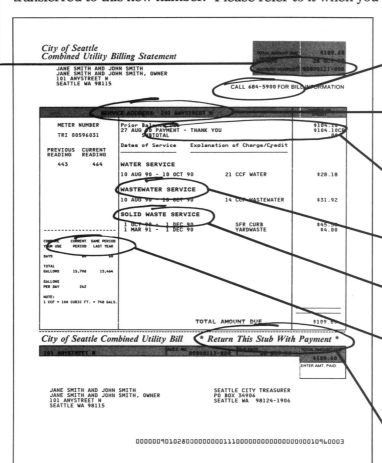

Based on the explanation of the billing statement, what is a **service address**?

_____

Look at the right side of the statement. A service address is defined as the *address of the property that receives the service listed.*

Use the utility billing statement on page 58 to answer the following questions.

1. What are the three utilities covered on this bill?

_____

2. What phone number is on the bill?

_____

3. Why is it useful to have this phone number?

_____

4. The new bill compares your current water usage with last year's usage. How could you use this information?

_____

5. If you have a problem and you need to call the city, how should you identify yourself?

_____

WORKWISE

If you have a problem with a utility bill, you'll probably call the utility company. You will need to identify yourself and describe the problem. These telephone skills are commonly used in the workplace as well. How do you conduct these conversations? Make a list of the approaches you use. For example, your list may use words such as *polite* or *firm*. When you're finished, compare your list with a friend's or a classmate's.

. . . .
Reading: Identifying factual details and specifications within text; Making inferences from text

READING BILLS

Personal **bills** may not all look the same. However, most bills include much of the same information. On almost any bill, you'll find the following:

Who:	who is sending the bill
	who should pay the bill
Dates:	when the bill was sent
	when the bill is to be paid
Description:	what the bill is for
Costs:	cost of each item
	total amount due
Account Number:	for identification

Before you can create a budget, you need to know how much money you owe for each bill you receive. You need to be able to read bills carefully.

GUIDED PRACTICE

Look at the utility bill from the City of Seattle on page 61.

What is the total amount of the bill? _____

You are correct if you answered *$70.59.*

APPLIED PRACTICE 2: READING A UTILITY BILL

Use the utility bill on page 61 to answer the following questions.

1. What is the service address? _____

2. How much does the customer owe for: Water Service _____

                                                        Wastewater Service _____

                                                        Solid Waste Service _____

3. What is the account number? _____

4. When is the payment due? _____

5. a. Has the City of Seattle received the previous balance? _____
   b. How do you know? _____

. . . .
Reading: Identifying factual details and specifications within text

City of Seattle
Combined Utility Billing Statement

TOTAL AMOUNT DUE:	**$70.59**
DUE DATE:	**02 DEC 93**
ACCOUNT NUMBER:	**00186620-005**

GENE SMITH
GENE SMITH, OWNER
847 NE 94TH ST
SEATTLE WA 98115

CALL 555-5900 FOR BILL INFORMATION

SERVICE ADDRESS: 847 NE 94TH ST	CHARGE OR CREDIT

METER NUMBER	Prior Balance Due		$83.58
	18 SEP 93 PAYMENT—THANK YOU		$83.58CR
HAY 17986418	SUBTOTAL		$ 0.00

PREVIOUS READING	CURRENT READING
0718	0731

Dates of Service	Explanation of Charge/Credit	
WATER SERVICE		
26 AUG 93 — 31 OCT 93	13 CCF WATER	$17.79
WASTEWATER SERVICE		
26 AUG 93 — 31 OCT 93	10 CCF WASTEWATER	$25.30
SOLID WASTE SERVICE		
1 NOV 93 — 1 JAN 94	1 CAN CURB/ALLEY	$27.50

WELCOME TO OUR NEW BILLING SYSTEM!
PLEASE READ THE ENCLOSED INFORMATION BROCHURE TO
LEARN MORE ABOUT YOUR NEW BILL.

WATER USAGE

COMPARE YOUR USE	CURRENT PERIOD	SAME PERIOD LAST YEAR
DAYS	66	58
TOTAL GALLONS	9,724	14,212
GALLONS PER DAY	147	245

NOTE:
1 CCF = 100 CUBIC FT. = 748 GALS.

TOTAL AMOUNT DUE	**$70.59**

MULTIPLYING AND DIVIDING MONEY AMOUNTS

You know that a budget is a plan for how you will use your money. A budget can help you avoid spending more money than you earn. Money that you earn is called **income**. Money that you spend is called **expenses**.

Cassandra Polk decided to create a monthly budget for herself. She is a single mother with a six-year-old son. She works full time (40 hours a week) as a carpenter. She makes $13 an hour. Cassandra gets paid twice a month. The first thing she needs to do is to figure out her monthly income.

MONTHLY INCOME

To find her monthly income, Cassandra multiplies the amount of her paycheck by two (because she gets paid two times a month).

$780 a paycheck × 2 paychecks

$780 dollars a paycheck
×   2 paychecks a month
$1,560 dollars a month

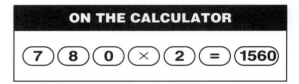

Cassandra now knows that she has $1,560 a month that she can spend. Next, she needs to know what her expenses cost.

MONTHLY EXPENSES

Many of Cassandra's expenses are *monthly* bills such as rent, utilities, and child-care bills. However, some of her expenses are *weekly* costs. Food is a weekly cost. If Cassandra wants to create a monthly budget, she needs to know how much she spends on food each month.

To find how much she spends on food in a month, Cassandra multiplied her weekly food bill by four (because there are about four weeks in a month).

$70 a week × 4 weeks

$70 dollars a week for food
×   4 weeks in a month
$280 dollars a month for food

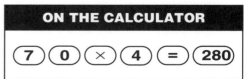

Cassandra spends $280 a month on food.

A few of Cassandra's expenses are *yearly* costs. Her renter's insurance, for instance, costs $120 a year. Cassandra needs to find out how much this costs each month.

To find how much she needs to save for renter's insurance each month, Cassandra divided her yearly bill by 12 (because there are 12 months in a year).

$120 a year ÷ 12 months

ON THE CALCULATOR

$$\frac{\$10}{12)\overline{\$120}}$$ dollars a month

months in a year — dollars a year

(1)(2)(0)(÷)(1)(2)(=)(10)

Cassandra needs to save $10 a month to pay for renter's insurance.

GUIDED PRACTICE

Cassandra spends about $50 a week on entertainment for her and her son. How would Cassandra figure out her monthly entertainment cost?

She would **multiply / divide** the weekly cost by **4 / 12**.
    choose one   *choose one*

You are correct if you answered that she would *multiply* the weekly cost by *4.*

Now complete this math problem to find Cassandra's monthly entertainment cost:

$50 a week × 4 weeks

The correct answer is $200. Cassandra spends about $200 a month on entertainment.

ON THE CALCULATOR
(5)(0)(×)(4)(=)( )

APPLIED PRACTICE 3: CALCULATING MONTHLY EXPENSES

Use the costs listed below to figure out Cassandra's monthly expenses. First, set up the math problem. Then, find the answer. You may use a calculator.

1. Car insurance ($600 a year)

2. Child care ($120 a week)

3. Transportation ($10 a week)

UNDERSTANDING A BUDGET CHART

The chart below shows Cassandra's monthly expenses.

MONTHLY BUDGET FORM			
Budget Category	**Paid How Often?**	**Amount**	**Monthly Amount**
Housing	Monthly	$500/month	$500
Food	Weekly	$70/week	$280
Child Care	Weekly	$120/week	$480
Entertainment	Weekly	$50/week	$200
Utilities water, sewer, electricity, gas, garbage	Monthly	$72/month	$72
Telephone	Monthly	$44/month	$44
Renter's Insurance	Yearly	$120/year	$10
Car Insurance	Yearly	$600/year	$50
Transportation	Weekly	$10/week	$40
Health Insurance	Monthly	$75/month	$75
Total Monthly Amount			$1,751

To read charts, you must look both *across* each row and *down* each column. For example, **Housing** is the heading of a row. **Paid How Often?** is the heading of a column. To find how often Cassandra pays her housing bill, look across from Housing and down from Paid How Often? She pays her housing bill monthly.

How would you find Cassandra's monthly budget for child care?

To find this answer, look across the row called **Child Care**. Then look down the column called **Monthly Amount**. Which amount is across from Child Care and down from Monthly Amount?

_____

If you found *$480*, you are correct.

Cassandra pays her transportation costs weekly. However, the chart shows her **monthly** budget for transportation. Why is it important for Cassandra to know her monthly transportation costs?

_____

You are correct if you answered *so that she knows how much she must budget each month to cover her transportation expenses.*

APPLIED PRACTICE 4: READING CHARTS FOR INFORMATION

Use the monthly budget chart on page 64 to answer the questions below.

1. a. What is Cassandra's largest monthly expense?_____

   b. How much is it? _____

2. How much does Cassandra pay each month for health insurance? _____

3. How often does Cassandra pay her utility bill? _____

4. What is Cassandra's total monthly expense amount? _____

5. Cassandra makes $1,560 per month. Does this income cover her expenses?

   _____

. . . .
Reading: Reading two- or more column charts to obtain information

CREATE A PERSONAL BUDGET

Chart your own monthly budget. First, circle the types of bills you have from the list below. Then, using these bills, fill in the Monthly Budget Form on page 167.

housing	child care	car payments
sewer	electricity	health insurance
garbage	entertainment	renter's or homeowner's insurance
food	education	loan payments
gas	car insurance	transportation (gas, public transportation fares)
water	telephone	credit card payments

Ask your instructor for help if you need to. If you feel that some of this information is private, leave those areas blank. You can fill them out in the privacy of your own home.

WORKWISE

Cassandra found that her income did not meet all of her expenses. She wants to pay all of her bills and still have money for a savings account for her and her son.

Cassandra has to make a choice. Should she ask her boss for a raise? Should she look for part-time work? Cut down on expenses? Find an apartment with lower rent? Should she find less expensive daycare for her son? Or should she look for a new full-time job that would pay her more money?

Discuss Cassandra's choices with a classmate. If you were in her shoes, what would you do?

UNIT III

Education and Certification Forms

Application and Training Forms
Complete a Training Application

Certification and Licensing Forms
Write a Letter to Request Information

APPLICATION AND TRAINING FORMS

A job you want may require more training or education than you have. To get that job, you will have to apply for training or education. You will need to fill out applications for **training** or **education** programs.

SKILL PREVIEW

Think about your career goals. What job do you want in the future? Think about that job, then answer the questions below.

1. What is your future job goal? _____

2. Are there training programs for this job? _____

3. If this job has training programs, what do you know about them?

   _____

   _____

4. How can you find out more about training programs for this job?

   _____

   _____

APPLICATION INFORMATION   PRINT LEGIBLY - USE BALLPOINT PEN
                                 DO NOT WRITE IN SHADED AREAS

MOUNTAIN TECHNICAL SCHOOL   STUDENT I.D. NO.   Will Complete When?
                                         083298   Month/Year

OCCUPATIONAL DESCRIPTION	COURSE NUMBER	EMPLOYMENT OUTLOOK	PAY WHEN HIRED	LENGTH OF PROGRAM	CO. PRO
NURSING ASSISTANTS Assist in the care of hospital patients under the direction of nursing and medical staff. They may make beds, serve meals, and bathe patients.	8174	Faster than Average 943 openings per year	$870– $1,625 per month	135 hours 3 months	$12
LICENSED PRACTICAL NURSES—Care for injured, convalescent, and handicapped persons in hospitals, clinics, private homes, and other settings. They work under the direction of a registered nurse, licensed physician, or dentist.	8164	Faster than Average 616 openings per year	$1,390– $2,160 per month	1,260 hours 11 months	$1,000.

MO   DAY   YEAR

NT NAME - LAST   FIRST

T ADDRESS   APT. NO.   CITY

ATE   SEX   U.S. CITIZEN   WHAT IS YC
                                       FOR ATTEN
       F___M   ___YES ___NO
    (CHECK ONE)   (CHECK ONE)

OU PREVIOUSLY ATTENDED THIS COLLEGE?

    IF YES: ___DAY ___EVE _____YEAR

FORMATION IS REQUESTED TO COMPLY WITH RE-   ETI
ENTS OF THE OFFICE OF CIVIL RIGHTS IN ITS IN-
ETATION OF TITLE VI OF THE CIVIL RIGHTS ACT OF
TITLE IX OF THE EDUCATIONAL AMENDMENTS OF

OF COURSE FOR WHICH YOU ARE APPLYING   IF
                                               T

                    • • • DO NOT WRIT

E NUMBER   DATE ENTERED CLASS

ORGANIZING PERSONAL EDUCATION RECORDS

Most education applications ask for the same information about you and your history in school. You can keep track of that information by writing it on a sheet of paper. Add to that sheet each time you take a class.

On page 71, Hoa Nguyen (pronounced "Wa Win") is keeping track of her training on a Personal Data Sheet. Each time she has to fill out a school application, she'll take this sheet with her and be able to copy it easily.

GUIDED PRACTICE

Complete the following information about the class you're in right now.

School Name City, State	Course	Will Complete When? Month/Year

You should have filled in all three boxes. If you're not sure what to write, ask your instructor.

APPLIED PRACTICE 1: INTERPRETING PERSONAL EDUCATION RECORDS

Read through Hoa's Personal Data Sheet on page 71. Find the answers to the following questions.

1. What is Hoa's Social Security number? _____ - _____ - _____

2. What is Hoa's highest grade completed? _____

3. Did Hoa graduate from high school? _____

4. What employer training has Hoa had? _____

APPLIED PRACTICE 2: COMPLETING A PERSONAL DATA SHEET: EDUCATION

Write your own education history on the blank Personal Data Sheet: Education on page 168. You will use the completed form later in this lesson.

....
Reading: Using a completed form to locate information to complete a task;
Writing: Entering appropriate information onto a form

PERSONAL DATA SHEET: EDUCATION

Name: _Nguyen_ _Hoa_ _Van_   SS# _821 - 47 - 9636_
    last   first   middle

Present Address: _3098 Martin Luther King, Jr., Parkway_
                 street

Beaumont,   _TX_   _77701_
      city   state   zip

Birth Date: _1 / 10 / 52_   Phone: _512-555-3994_

U.S. Citizen _X_ Yes ___ No   Visa # _____ Type _____

Highest grade completed _12_

	School Name City, State	Courses	Completed: Mo/Yr
High School	South City School Ho Chi Minh City, Vietnam	Favorite Study Areas: Science Biology	6/1970
GED	none	Favorite Study Areas:	
Technical or Trade School	none		
Community College	Beaumont Community College Beaumont, TX	English as a Second Language	2/1993
Military Training	none		
Employer Training	Resthaven Home Beaumont, TX	kitchen equipment industrial mixer commercial machines	3/1993

COMPARING CAREER CLUSTERS

Hoa wants to change jobs. At the nursing home, Hoa helps with the cooking and kitchen cleaning. Hoa wants to earn more money and to use her health and science skills.

She has watched other employees at the nursing home lately.

She watched the reception desk. The people there answer the telephones, take messages, use a computer, and do a lot of writing.

Hoa also watched the nurses. Some nurses give patients medication and meals. Other nurses and nursing assistants help keep the patients comfortable and clean.

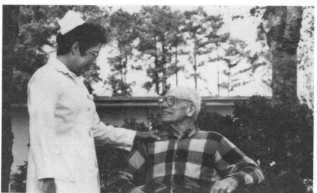

GUIDED PRACTICE

The jobs described above fit into larger categories called **career clusters**. For example, a person working as a truck driver would be in the **transportation** career cluster.

Draw a line from the job to the career cluster in which it belongs.

Job	Career Cluster
Nurse	Business and Office
Receptionist	Health

You are correct if you connected *Nurse* to *Health* and *Receptionist* to *Business and Office.*

Below are detailed descriptions of the two career areas Hoa watched at work: **Health**, and **Business and Office**. Read the career descriptions. Then answer the questions that follow.

HEALTH

People who are employed in health occupations provide care for the sick and injured and help people maintain their health. This field offers a great variety of occupations from service oriented to technical and administrative positions. The largest occupational fields are registered nurses, nurses aides, and licensed practical nurses.

Hospitals employ about half of all health workers. Others work in clinics, laboratories, pharmacies, nursing homes, mental health centers, and other public and private agencies. Because of the increase in the aging population and the move away from hospital to home-based health care, we can expect to see more physician's assistants, nurses and nurses aides/orderlies working out of the home setting. Employment in the health field is expected to grow much faster than average through the mid-1990's.

BUSINESS AND OFFICE

Workers in business and office occupations perform the many different jobs necessary to keep organizations running on a daily basis. These jobs range from bookkeeping, typing and operating business machines to solving problems and devising ways to provide better service. Administrative assistants, bookkeepers, accountants, receptionists, and typists are a few examples of the many different occupations in this group. The largest occupations are secretaries and typists.

Employment in this field is expected to increase slower than the average for all occupations through the mid-1990's. Because of the great influx of computer technology into the office place, knowing how to use a computer is a definite plus in getting a job in the business and office field. Secretaries and typists rely heavily on word processors.

1. Which career cluster requires experience with computers? (*Hint:* Read the last two sentences in each career description.)

_____

2. Which career cluster is expected to grow more quickly than average? (*Hint:* Read the second paragraph in each career description.)

_____

3. Which career cluster might be better for Hoa? _____

4. Give two reasons for your choice in number 3.

_____

_____

. . . .
Reading: Distinguishing between relevant and irrelevant information in text or visuals

IDENTIFYING TRAINING PROGRAMS

No matter what career area Hoa selects, she will probably need some training. There are four main ways to get training.

Workplace: Employers may offer training to teach employees new skills.

Technical or Trade Schools: These schools teach the skills people may need to enter a job, to keep up with changes at a job, or to enter a new field.

Community Colleges: These schools offer two-year programs for job training and general education; for example, computer training or beginning classes in education or dentistry. Students then transfer to a university to finish their degree.

University or Colleges: These schools offer four-year programs in occupations such as science, business, and education.

GUIDED PRACTICE

What kind of school or program would be the best place to get training for a certain skill? Match the skill on the left with the correct type of educational program. You may use a type of program more than once. Write the letter of the program on the line provided.

Skill

Example: _a_ teacher

_____ 1. auto mechanic

_____ 2. computer skills

_____ 3. basic writing skills

_____ 4. doctor

_____ 5. appliance repair

_____ 6. supervisory skills

Type of Educational Program

a. university

b. workplace

c. technical/trade school

d. community college

You are correct if you answered 1. *b* or *c*; 2. *b*, *c*, or *d*; 3. *d*; 4. *a*; 5. *c*; 6. *b*.

WORKWISE

What kind of training have you received on a job? Perhaps you entered a formal training program your employer offered. Or perhaps you learned a skill just by doing your job. Think for a few moments. Then list the job skills you've gotten from on-the-job training.

Read the two nursing program descriptions below. Then answer the questions that follow. Ask your instructor to explain any medical terms you do not know.

Nursing Assistant–Certified

This Nursing Assistant program meets both state and federal curriculum requirements for Nursing Assistant Certification. Those who successfully complete this program are eligible to take the State Certification Examination. The 135 hour course (60 hours of classroom/laboratory instruction and 75 hours in the clinic setting) is open to any person 16 years of age or older who has the interest and ability to pursue this occupational goal. Nursing Assistants, registered and certified, can work in long term care facilities, hospitals and home health care agencies. The clinical training includes full-day Saturday sessions in convalescent centers. Textbooks and uniforms are required.

Licensed Practical Nurse

This course approved by the State Board of Practical Nurse Examiners prepares students to perform the duties of a practical nurse and makes them eligible to take the state LPN Examination. The course is eleven months (two semesters, plus one summer session). Students will participate in classroom, laboratory and clinical experiences. Major units of study are anatomy and physiology, nursing process, pediatrics, obstetrics and gynecology. Students must be 18 years of age or older and pass a physical examination. Textbook and uniform costs are approximately $400. High School completion or GED is required to take the licensing examination.

1. How many hours is the Nursing Assistant–Certified course? (*Hint:* Read the third sentence.)

   _____

2. After taking either of these courses, how would a student become certified in that profession? (*Hint:* Read the beginning of both descriptions. What do both programs make you eligible to do?)

   _____

3. Which program requires Saturday hours? _____

4. Which training program requires that the student pass a physical examination?

   _____

5. How much education is required before you take the Licensed Practical Nurse exam?

   _____

6. Which program can a 16-year-old enter?_____

. . . .

Reading: Identifying factual details and specifications within text; Selecting parts of text or visual materials to complete a task

COMPARING AND CONTRASTING INFORMATION

OCCUPATIONAL DESCRIPTION	COURSE NUMBER	EMPLOYMENT OUTLOOK	PAY WHEN HIRED	LENGTH OF PROGRAM	COST OF PROGRAM
NURSING ASSISTANTS Assist in the care of hospital patients under the direction of nursing and medical staff. They may make beds, serve meals, and bathe patients.	8174	Faster than Average 943 openings per year	$870–$1,625 per month	135 hours 3 months	$125.00
LICENSED PRACTICAL NURSES—Care for injured, convalescent, and handicapped persons in hospitals, clinics, private homes, and other settings. They work under the direction of a registered nurse, licensed physician, or dentist.	8164	Faster than Average 616 openings per year	$1,390–$2,160 per month	1,260 hours 11 months	$1,000.00

Hoa must choose between the two nursing programs described in the chart above. She has $500 in savings. Hoa applied and qualified for student federal financial aid. This means that the government will pay for her school costs. She will pay the money back to the government when she finishes school.

Hoa would like to finish training as soon as possible. However, she wants a job that will lead to a promotion. She also wants to earn as much money as possible.

GUIDED PRACTICE

When you **compare**, you look for similarities, or things that are alike. To **contrast** is to find differences. Answer this question by comparing information in the chart.

What are three similarities between the two occupations described above?

_____

_____

You are correct if you answered any of the following: *both jobs deal with patients in hospitals; both work under qualified nursing and medical staff; both have faster-than-average employment growth; both jobs earn salaries;* and *both jobs require training programs.*

APPLIED PRACTICE 5: COMPARING AND CONTRASTING INFORMATION

Compare the following information on the chart on page 76.

Example: Employment Outlook

    a. Which is better? _nursing assistant_

    b. Why? _There are more openings per year._

1. Occupational Description

    a. Which occupation requires more skills? _____

    b. Why? _____

2. Pay When Hired

    a. Which is higher? _____

    b. Why? _____

3. Length of Training Program

    a. Which is shorter? _____

    b. Why? _____

4. Opportunity for Advancement

    a. Which job gives more opportunity for promotion? _____

    b. Why? _____

5. a. Based on what you've read about Hoa, which program do you suggest she register for?

    _____

    b. Why? _____

COMPLETE A TRAINING APPLICATION

Use your completed Personal Data Sheet: Education from page 167 to fill out the application form below. Or, if you prefer, use an application from a school in your area, especially one you may want to attend in the future.

APPLICATION INFORMATION | **PRINT LEGIBLY - USE BALLPOINT PEN**
DO NOT WRITE IN SHADED AREAS

MOUNTAIN TECHNICAL SCHOOL

STUDENT I.D. NO.
083298

TODAY'S DATE: ___/___/___
MO   DAY   YEAR

STUDENT NAME - LAST	FIRST	MIDDLE	SOCIAL SECURITY NO.

STREET ADDRESS   APT. NO.   CITY   STATE   ZIP CODE   TELEPHONE

BIRTHDATE	SEX ___F ___M (CHECK ONE)	U.S. CITIZEN ___YES ___NO (CHECK ONE)	WHAT IS YOUR LONG-TERM GOAL FOR ATTENDING THIS TECHNICAL SCHOOL?	EMERGENCY TELEPHONE

HAVE YOU PREVIOUSLY ATTENDED THIS COLLEGE?
___ YES
___ NO   IF YES: ___DAY ___EVE _____ YEAR

MILITARY SERVICE: (CHECK ONE)
_____ VETERAN
_____ IN SERVICE NOW   _____ HAVE NEVER BEEN IN THE MILITARY

THIS INFORMATION IS REQUESTED TO COMPLY WITH REQUIREMENTS OF THE OFFICE OF CIVIL RIGHTS IN ITS INTERPRETATION OF TITLE VI OF THE CIVIL RIGHTS ACT OF 1976 & TITLE IX OF THE EDUCATIONAL AMENDMENTS OF 1972.

ETHNIC BACKGROUND: (CHECK ONE)
___ BLACK   ___ ASIAN OR PACIFIC ISLANDER
___ HISPANIC   ___ NATIVE AMERICAN OR NATIVE ALASKAN
___ WHITE   ___ OTHER (SPECIFY): _____

TITLE OF COURSE FOR WHICH YOU ARE APPLYING

IF YOU ARE ENROLLED IN A HIGH SCHOOL WHILE ATTENDING THIS COLLEGE, GIVE NAME OF SCHOOL:

★ ★ ★ DO NOT WRITE BELOW THIS LINE ★ ★ ★

COURSE NUMBER	DATE ENTERED CLASS	NON-RESIDENT ALIEN ___YES ___NO (CHECK ONE)	HIGH SCHOOL CREDITS ___YES ___NO (CHECK ONE)

CLASS TITLE / DESCRIPTION	INSTRUCTOR	FEES	RECEIPT NO.
	REFUND AMOUNT / DATE	VISA _____ M/C _____ # _____	

WITHDRAWAL DATE	COMPLETED COURSE ___YES ___NO (CHECK ONE)	INSTRUCTOR'S SIGNATURE

PT. 1 - WHITE - STUDENT RECORDS - DATA ENTRY
PT. 2 - CANARY - DATA ENTRY
PT. 3 - PINK - INSTRUCTOR

MOUNTAIN TECHNICAL SCHOOL IS AN EQUAL OPPORTUNITY AND AFFIRMATIVE ACTION EMPLOYER, AND IS IN COMPLIANCE WITH SEX AND HANDICAP REGULATIONS.

CERTIFICATION AND LICENSING FORMS

Many jobs today require that you have a **certificate** or an occupational **license**. This certificate or license shows that you've had the training you need to perform a job well. To get a certificate or license, you often need to fill out certain forms and to take a test of some kind.

Government agencies usually control certification and licensing training. They regulate what is taught in the training programs. They name the qualifications needed for someone to work in that occupation. And these agencies issue the forms and tests you must complete to become licensed or certified.

SKILL PREVIEW

On the lines below, write three occupations that you believe require a license or certificate.

1. _____

2. _____

3. _____

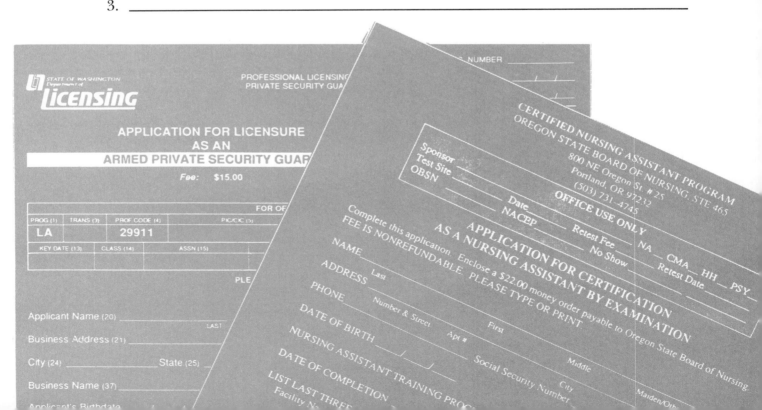

INTERPRETING REQUIREMENTS

Licensing: Certain jobs require you to be licensed by a local, state, or federal agency. These agencies want to be sure that you are experienced enough to do the job well. They want to be sure that you perform your work in a professional manner. Small-business owners often need to have a business license. Licensing is used to protect the public.

Licensing requirements differ from one job to another. They may include

- having certain levels of education,
- having on-the-job experience, and
- passing an examination.

Certification: Certificates prove that a student or a trainee has mastered certain skills. You may earn a certificate from your school, your training program, or your job. Sometimes a certificate is a step toward getting a license.

SOME OCCUPATIONS REQUIRING LICENSING OR CERTIFICATION

Accountant
Acupuncturist
Aeronautic/Astronautic Engineer
Airplane Pilot
Architect
Auctioneer
Barber
Bill Collector
Boilermaker
Chemical Engineer
Chiropractor
Civil Engineer
Construction Inspector
Cosmetologist
Counselor (Mental Health, School, Marriage and Family Counselor; Social Worker; or Hypnotherapist)
Court Reporter
Debt Adjuster
Dental Hygienist
Dentist
Detective
Dietitian
Dispensing Optician

Electrical and Electronics Engineer
Electrician
Elementary School Teacher
Emergency Medical Technician
Employment Agency Manager
Escrow Officer
Firearms Dealer
Funeral Director (Mortician)
General Contractor
Guard
Health Administrator (Nursing Home)
Health Care Assistant
Hearing Aid Fitter and Trainee
Industrial Engineer
Landscape Architect
Licensed Practical Nurse
Manicurist
Massage Therapist
Master, Mate, and Pilot
Naturopath
Mechanical Engineer

Metallurgical Engineer
Midwife
Mining Engineer
Notary
Nursing Assistant
Nutritionist
Occupational Therapist
Optometrist
Osteopath
Petroleum Engineer
Pharmacist
Physical Therapist
Physician
Physician Assistant
Plumber
Podiatrist
Psychologist
Radiologic Technician
Real Estate Agent
Real Estate Appraiser
Registered Nurse
Respiratory Therapist
Stockbroker
Surveyor
Veterinarian
Veterinary Technician

Read page 80. Then use your own words to complete the sentences below.

1. Licensing is meant to _____

2. Certificates prove _____

3. Licensing requirements differ from one occupation to another but may include

    _____

You are correct if you answered 1. *to protect the public*; 2. *that a student or trainee has certain skills*; 3. *education, experience, a test.*

APPLIED PRACTICE 1: INTERPRETING REQUIREMENTS

Use your own words to answer the questions below.

1. How do licensing requirements protect the public?

    _____

2. Why are licensing and certification requirements good for employers?

    _____

3. If you were in a job that required you to be certified (have a certificate), how would that protect you?

    _____

4. What do you think a government agency could do if someone who is licensed or certified does not perform the work as well as required?

    _____

WORKWISE

Read through the list of occupations on page 80. Do you recognize each job title? Look up any job you're curious about in a resource such as the *Dictionary of Occupational Titles* or the *Occupational Outlook Handbook.* You can ask a reference librarian at your library to help you find these books.

. . . .
Reading: Determining the main idea of a paragraph or section; Making inferences from text

APPLYING FOR CERTIFICATION

The application form on page 83 is for certification as a nursing assistant. You would fill out this application after finishing a training program and when you were ready to take the certification exam or test.

The application form on page 83

GUIDED PRACTICE

1. Read the application directions. What type of writing should the applicant use to fill out this form?

   _____

2. The application asks mainly for two kinds of information. Which of the following *two* words would best describe the application?

   ____ Personal   ____ Credit   ____ Employment   ____ Education

You are correct if you answered 1. *typewriting or print*; and 2. *Personal* and *Employment*.

APPLIED PRACTICE 2: INTERPRETING A CERTIFICATION APPLICATION

Use the application form on page 83 to answer these questions.

1. What agency will give this student his or her certification exam?

   _____

2. a. What two items must be attached or enclosed along with the application when you turn it in?

   _____

   b. Why does the agency ask for these two items? _____

3. Which employer should an applicant list first? _____

4. Does the applicant have to answer the survey questions at the bottom of the page?

   _____

. . . .
Reading: Selecting parts of text or visual materials to complete a task; Making inferences from text

CERTIFIED NURSING ASSISTANT PROGRAM
OREGON STATE BOARD OF NURSING, STE 465
800 NE Oregon St. # 25
Portland, OR 97232
(503) 731–4745

APPLICATION FOR CERTIFICATION
AS A NURSING ASSISTANT BY EXAMINATION

Complete this application. Enclose a $22.00 money order payable to Oregon State Board of Nursing. FEE IS NONREFUNDABLE. PLEASE TYPE OR PRINT.

NAME_____

       Last   First   Middle   Maiden/Other

ADDRESS _____

    Number & Street Apt #   City   State   Zip

PHONE_____ Social Security Number _____–_____–_____

DATE OF BIRTH _____/_____/_____

NURSING ASSISTANT TRAINING PROGRAM NAME _____

DATE OF COMPLETION _____/_____/_____   Attach copy of certificate of training.

LIST LAST THREE EMPLOYERS STARTING WITH CURRENT OR MOST RECENT.

Facility Name	Location	Dates of Employment	
		From	To
_____	_____	_____	_____
_____	_____	_____	_____
_____	_____	_____	_____

Have you ever been arrested, charged or convicted of a misdemeanor or a felony?

☐ YES ☐ NO   If you answered YES, attach an additional page and explain.

Include dates, places, charges, and results.

I hereby certify that I have read this application and the attached documents and I certify that the information they contain is true and correct. I authorize Oregon State Board of Nursing to conduct a criminal records check through the Law Enforcement Data System (LEDS)..

Signature_____   Date _____

Please complete the following optional survey questions:
    SEX: Female _____ Male _____

    RACE: Asian ___ Black ___ Hispanic ___ Native American ___ White ____ Other ____

8516001692

APPLYING FOR A LICENSE

The application form on page 85 is for a license to be an armed private security guard.

The application form on page 85 is for a license to be an armed private security guard.

GUIDED PRACTICE

1. Look at the directions at the top of the application. What type of writing should the applicant use on the form?

   _____

2. What two kinds of addresses does this application require?

   _____

You are correct if you answered 1. *typewriting or print*; 2. *home* and *business*.

APPLIED PRACTICE 3: INTERPRETING A LICENSING APPLICATION

Use the application form on page 85 to answer the following questions.

1. What agency grants this license? _____

2. Why do you think this application asks for a business address?

   _____

3. a. Is the applicant required to give a Social Security number? _____

   b. Why is it on this application? _____

4. Look at the list after the phrase *Applying for*. In what three ways can a person applying for a license have prior experience as a security guard?

   _____

   _____

5. What do you think the agency will do once it has evaluated the completed application? (*Hint*: Look at the upper right-hand corner of the application.)

   _____

. . . .

Reading: Selecting parts of text or visual materials to complete a task; Making inferences from text

STATE OF WASHINGTON
Department of
Licensing

PROFESSIONAL LICENSING SERVICES
PRIVATE SECURITY GUARD SECTION

TEMP. REG. NUMBER	
DATE OF ISSUE	/ /
EXPIRES ON (60 DAYS)	/ /

APPLICATION FOR LICENSURE
AS AN
ARMED PRIVATE SECURITY GUARD

Fee: $15.00

FOR VALIDATION ONLY   001-070-299-0011

Make remittance payable to: STATE TREASURER

FOR OFFICE USE ONLY

PROG (1)	TRANS (3)	PROF CODE (4)	PIC/CIC (5)		EXPIRATION DATE (9)	EXPT (10)	STAT (11)	TYP (12)
LA		29911						

KEY DATE (13)	CLASS (14)	ASSN (15)	BILLED AMOUNT (16)	SIGN	SPLIT	QRTD

PLEASE TYPE OR PRINT CLEARLY

Applicant Name (20) _____
                        LAST   FIRST   MI

Business Address (21) _____
                                   STREET

City (24) _____ State (25) _____ Zip Code (26) _____ County(27) _____ [ ]

Business Name (37) _____ Telephone ( ) _____

Applicant's Birthdate ___/___/___ Sex [ ] M [ ] F Social Security Number (40) _____
                                                   REQUESTED FOR IDENTIFICATION PURPOSES ONLY. ENTERING SSN
                                                   IS VOLUNTARY AND IS NOT REQUIRED FOR LICENSING APPROVAL.

Applicant Home Address (28) _____
                                         STREET

City (31) _____ State (32) _____ Zip Code (33) _____ County(34) _____ [ ]

Unarmed Private Security Guard License #29910- _____ Personal Ident. Code _____
                                                           12-DIGIT LETTER/NUMBER COMBINATION FROM LICENSE

Firearms Certification # _____ (Issued by CJTC).   [ ] U.S. Citizen   [ ] Resident Alien

Applying for: [ ] License based on current registration as an Unarmed Security Guard

               [ ] Endorsement of License in the State of _____.

               [ ] Licensure based upon having been employed as a Private Security Guard continuously since January 1,
                   1991 (Applying prior to June 30, 1992).

[ ] Employed by the above company   [ ] Offer of employment from above company

FOR OFFICE USE ONLY

Comments: _____
_____
_____
_____

CERT DATE (44) [| | | | |]

CERT NO. (45) [| | | | |]

PSG-690-014 ARMED PRIVATE SEC GUARD APP (N/10/91)M Page 1 of 3

USING A PHONE BOOK TO FIND INFORMATION

The applications on pages 83 and 85 are for specific jobs in Oregon and Washington. You will probably need to find your own applications to apply for licensing or certification for your job.

GUIDED PRACTICE

Look over the list of jobs on page 80. These jobs require a license or certificate. Below, list at least two of these occupations for which you'd like licensing or certification information. Put a check (✔) next to the job that interests you the most.

_____

_____

If you haven't yet discovered what some of the jobs involve, ask your instructor to help you research them.

APPLIED PRACTICE 4: GETTING INFORMATION

Now you will find out where to get information on licensing and certification. Using your local phone book, follow each step below.

1. Find the State Government section in your phone book. It's most likely at the beginning of the white pages.

2. In that section, look for the **Licensing Department** or **Division**. If there is no such listing, look for a **Professional Regulations Department**.

Note: If your phone book does not contain either of these headings, you can call the General Information number for your state. Ask for the name and address of the agency in charge of professional licensing and certification.

3. Under the **Licensing** or **Professional Regulations** heading, look for the job titles you listed above. Is your job interest listed? If so, continue on to step 4. If not, call the Licensing or Regulations Department. Ask for the name and address of the agency in charge of licensing for your job interest.

4. Use the information you've found to answer the questions on page 87.

1. What agency or person will you need to contact for licensing information about your job?

_____   _____
name   phone number

_____   _____
street address   city, state, zip

(*Note*: Some of this information may not be listed. You may need to call the agency to get the complete address.)

2. What do you want to know about getting a license in this occupation? Using each word in **bold** type below, write at least one other question you could ask to help you find this information.

    Example: Where can I get the licensing forms?

    <u>Where can I call for more information about this job? Where</u>
    <u>can I get training for this occupation?</u>

    a. **How** much does the license cost?

    _____

    _____

    b. **Why** does the state require the license?

    _____

    _____

    c. **When** should I apply for the license?

    _____

    _____

    •

    ### SELF-CHECK

    Review this page. Did you write at least one question for each **bold** type word? Is there anything else about this occupation or about licensing that you want to know?

    •

WRITE A LETTER TO REQUEST INFORMATION

To find answers to your questions about licensing, you will need to write a letter requesting information. You will use the information you found in the phone book as well as the questions you asked on page 87.

Organize your letter by writing your information and questions in the suggested areas. Try to write complete sentences, spell words correctly, and write clearly.

Write your home address and the date.

Write the person's name, the agency name, and the address of the agency you're writing to.

Write **Dear Madam or Sir:** if you don't know the person's name.

I would like information about licensing as a(n)_____.
(your job choice)

Add any questions about licensing you may have.

How would you like the agency to contact you? Give your preference; be sure to give your address and phone number.

Write **Sincerely,** then sign your name on the next line.

Print or type your name.

When your letter is approved by your instructor, and if you are interested in the occupation you chose, recopy your letter onto a clean sheet of paper. Then mail your letter to the agency. If you prefer, you can call and ask these questions.

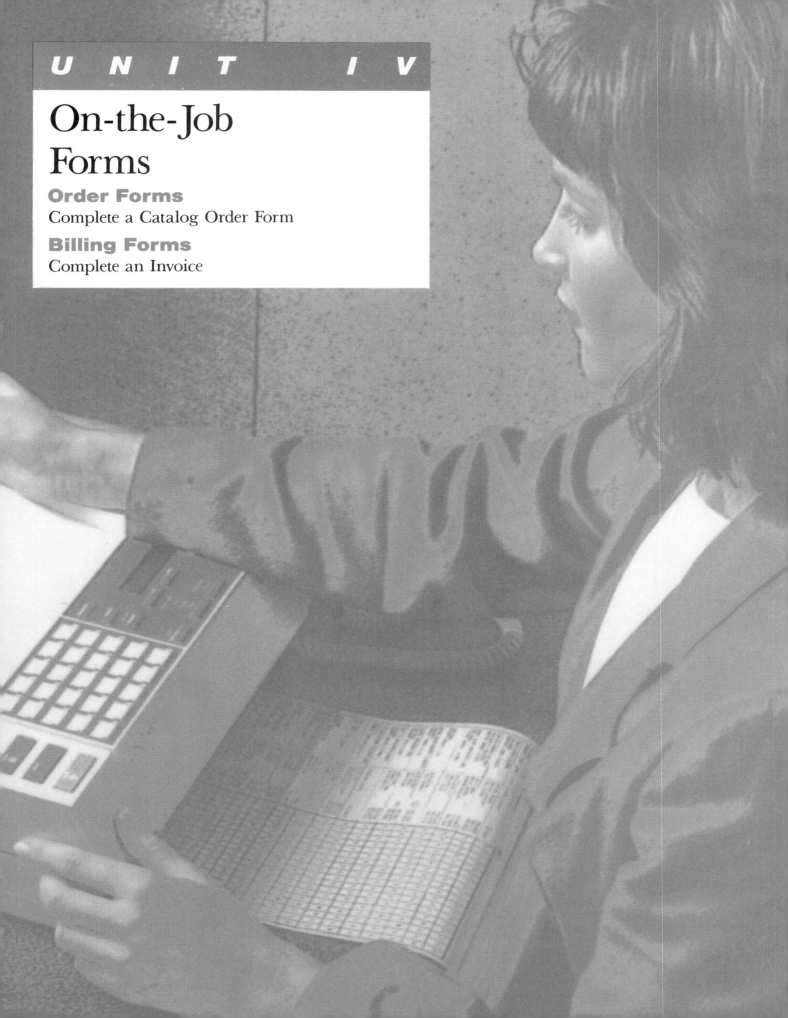

UNIT IV

On-the-Job Forms

Order Forms
Complete a Catalog Order Form

Billing Forms
Complete an Invoice

ORDER FORMS

Whenever you buy something, whether at work or on your own time, your purchase is recorded in some way. In a restaurant, for example, the waiter or waitress writes your order on an order pad. Someone may then enter it on a computerized order system. Even if your waiter can remember your order, he may need to write it down for the cook or the cashier.

SKILL PREVIEW

What does a waiter need to know about his customer's food? Food orders usually include

1. a main dish
2. two side dish choices (soup, salad, potatoes, vegetables)
3. dressings or toppings (salad dressing, catsup, etc.)
4. a drink
5. dessert

On the order form below, list the food you would like to eat right now. Use the food categories listed above.

DAD'S DINER

_____
main dish

_____
two side dishes

_____
dressing or topping

_____
drink

_____
dessert

CLARIFYING A VERBAL ORDER

In a restaurant, you speak to give your order to the waiter. This is a **verbal order**. When you give a verbal order, it is important to make eye contact and to face the person you're speaking to.

GUIDED PRACTICE

Read over your order on page 91.

- Did you forget anything?
- Do you want to change anything?

After you check your order, take it to your instructor or to a classmate. Ask this person to imagine that he or she is going to cook your food and that it must be cooked correctly.

Have this person ask you at least three questions to **clarify** (make clear) what you ordered. Write the questions on the lines below. The questions could begin with

"How . . . ?"
"What . . . ?"
"How many . . . ?"

1. _____

2. _____

3. _____

Your food order probably seemed clear to you. But another person may need to ask questions to do the job right.

On any job, ask questions if something isn't clear to you. Otherwise, you may waste time and money. What other problems could occur if you don't ask questions on the job?

1. _____

2. _____

You may have said something like *Other employees could get angry because I didn't do my work correctly* or *My employer may think that I can't do the job.*

Find two people to help you with this activity.

Imagine that you are a waiter or waitress. The two people helping you are customers. Ask each customer to think of a meal to order. Record each order, one at a time, on the order forms below. Be sure to ask questions if you need to.

Customer #1   **Customer #2**

* * *

SELF-CHECK

Look over the tickets carefully. Remember the categories of information usually on food order forms (listed on page 91).

As you look over the tickets, ask yourself these questions:

- Are these categories clear on your order?
- Did you ask any questions to clarify the orders?

* * *

APPLIED PRACTICE 2: CHECKING A VERBAL ORDER

Ask your customers any other questions you need to clarify their orders. Change your order forms as needed. Now, read the order back to your customers to make sure that each is complete and correct.

. . . .

Oral Communications: Using attentive posture and maintaining eye contact in listening; Receiving spoken instructions in the workplace;
Writing: Entering appropriate information onto a form

UNDERSTANDING AN ORDER FORM

At most workplaces, orders are not just spoken. They also have to be **written.** Perhaps the order includes many details—too many to remember. Or maybe you need written paperwork to **document** an order, to prove that the order took place.

At work, buying equipment and supplies is called **purchasing.** Some purchasing is done through catalogs. For example, your instructor may have ordered this book through the Contemporary Books catalog. Here is part of the **order form** for Contemporary Books:

CONTEMPORARY BOOKS, INC.
180 NORTH STETSON AVENUE, SUITE 1200
CHICAGO, ILLINOIS 60601-6790
PHONE: (800) 621-1918
FAX: (312) 540-4662

ORDER FORM

BILL TO _Accounting Department, RCC_   SHIP TO _RCC Learning Center_

ATTENTION _Leon Washington_   ATTENTION _Patricia Kelly, Instructor_

ADDRESS _4306 232nd Street W_   ADDRESS _4306 232nd Street W_

CITY _Rockford_ STATE _IL_ ZIP _61103_   CITY _Rockford_ STATE _IL_ ZIP _61103_

PURCHASE ORDER NO. _40463_   PHONE NO. _815-555-3608_

QUAN.	TITLE NO.	TITLE	PRICE 1-3	PRICE 4 OR MORE
	4190-0	**NUMBER SENSE: DISCOVERING BASIC MATH CONCEPTS** Complete Set (includes 1 copy of each of the 10 student texts, 1 copy of each of the 4 diagnostic tests, 1 answer key, and 1 teacher's guide)	42.95	42.95
10	4234-6	Whole Number Addition & Subtraction	5.00	3.75
10	4233-8	Whole Number Multiplication & Division	5.00	3.75
	4231-1	▶ Diagnostic/Placement and Mastery Tests: Whole Numbers (pack of 10)	15.00	11.25
	4230-3	Decimal Addition & Subtraction	5.00	3.75
	4228-1	Decimal Multiplication & Division	5.00	3.75
	4227-3	▶ Diagnostic/Placement and Mastery Tests: Decimals (pack of 10)	15.00	11.25
	4226-5	The Meaning of Fractions	5.00	3.75
	4225-7	Fraction Addition & Subtraction	5.00	3.75
	4224-9	Fraction Multiplication & Division	5.00	3.75
	4223-0	▶ Diagnostic/Placement and Mastery Tests: Fractions (pack of 10)	15.00	11.25
	4222-2	Ratio & Proportion	5.00	3.75
	4221-4	The Meaning of Percent	5.00	3.75
	4220-6	Percent Applications	5.00	3.75
	4219-2	▶ Diagnostic/Placement and Mastery Tests: Ratio, Proportion & Percent (pack of 10)	15.00	11.25
1	4191-9	Number Sense Answer Key	3.50	3.50
1	4218-4	Teacher's Resource Guide	7.25	7.25

Not all order forms look alike. However, most order forms have this information:

- who is ordering
- who will pay
- where to send the order form
- where to send the shipment

Using the information on the form on page 94, match the questions and answers. Write the letter of the answer on the line provided.

_____ 1. Who receives the shipment?   a. Leon Washington

_____ 2. Who receives the bill?   b. Patricia Kelly

_____ 3. Who receives the order form?   c. Contemporary Books

You are correct if you matched 1. *b*; 2. *a*; 3. *c*.

APPLIED PRACTICE 3: LOCATING INFORMATION ON A COMPLETED ORDER FORM

Use the order form on page 94 to answer the questions below.

1. In the series called *Number Sense: Discovering Basic Math Concepts,* what is the price of one copy of the book about multiplying and dividing fractions?

_____

2. What is the price of one copy of the book called *Ratio & Proportion?*

_____

3. a. What is the title number of the book called *Teacher's Resource Guide?*

_____

 b. Why do you think a title number is important?

_____

4. Why do you think the books cost less if you order four or more copies of each?

_____

5. How many copies of *Whole Number Addition & Subtraction* were ordered?

_____

. . . .

Reading: Using a completed form to locate information to complete a task; Reading two- or more column charts to obtain information

LOCATING SPECIFIC DETAILS

Often, instructors must fill out an order form to get books and other classroom materials. As you can see from the ads on page 97, instructors have many choices. The pencils have four lead sizes. The binders come both with and without label holders. The message pads come in different colors.

GUIDED PRACTICE

Imagine that you are ordering supplies. You need to order 36 pencils.

1. Look at the ads on page 97. What is the heading on the ads for pencils?

   _____

2. What do you need to specify when you order pencils?

   _____

3. If you need 36 pencils, how many dozen pencils should you order? (*Hint:* There are 12 pencils in a dozen.) _____

4. What will be the cost of 36 pencils? _____

5. The ad says, "as low as 84¢ per dozen." Will you pay this amount for 36 pencils? Why or why not?

   _____

   _____

You are correct if you answered 1. *Reliable Economy Pencils*; 2. *the lead*; 3. *3 dozen (36 pencils)*; 4. *$2.76 ($.92 × 3 dozen)*; 5. *No. The pencils cost 84¢ per dozen only if you buy 6 dozen or more.*

WORKWISE

If you've had to order supplies or equipment at a workplace, you know that keeping up-to-date records of your purchasing is very important. Discuss this issue with a friend or a classmate. What can happen if you don't keep good records of your orders?

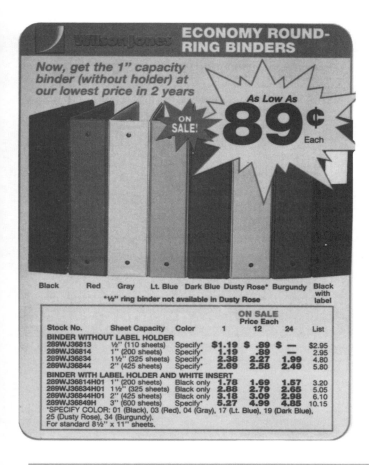

APPLIED PRACTICE 4: LOCATING INFORMATION IN ADS

Use the advertisements above to answer the following questions.

1. What is the stock number of the pencils? _____

2. How many color choices are there in binders? _____

3. How many sheets are on the "While You Were Out" message pads? _____

4. How many types of lead are available in the pencils? _____

5. In the binders without label holders, how many size choices are there? _____
(*Hint*: Look under the heading **Sheet Capacity**.)

COMPLETING AN ORDER FORM

Order forms often use special vocabulary as well as **abbreviations**, or shortened words. Look across the top row of the order form below. Make your best guess as to what each word means. Write the definition below each word.

Qty.	Unit (each, doz., etc.)	Reliable Stock #	Color (please specify)	Description	Unit Price	Total

Here are the definitions: *Qty.* means *a quantity, or number of units. Units* are *the number or amount of each product sold*; for example, order pads are sold in units of one dozen. *Reliable Stock #* means *the stock number for Reliable Office Supplies.* The *stock number* identifies *the specific product. Description* is *the name of the product.*

The *Unit Price* is *the cost per item.* To find the *Total,* multiply the unit price by the quantity. Look at the example below.

$1.55 × 2 = $3.10
for a dozen (unit price)   dozen units (quantity)   total cost

Once you've set up your problem, you can use a calculator to find the answer.

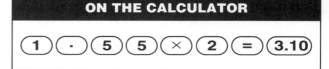

ON THE CALCULATOR

(1)(·)(5)(5)(×)(2)(=)(3.10)

Find the total cost of each item below. First set up the problem. Then multiply to find the answer. Use a calculator if you wish.

1. 12 binders that cost $.89 per binder

2. 5 message books that cost $3.99 per book

3. 6 dozen pads that cost $1.29 per dozen

4. 6 dozen pencil holders that cost $.84 per holder (*Hint:* How many holders are in one dozen?)

When you use ads like the ones in the Reliable catalog, it can be easy to make a costly mistake unless you

- work carefully
- proofread, or check, your work

Practice filling out this order blank for six dozen pink "While You Were Out" pads.

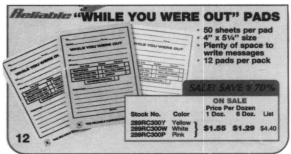

Qty.	Unit (each, doz., etc.)	Reliable Stock #	Color (please specify)	Description	Unit Price	Total

Your order form should look like this:

Qty.	Unit (each, doz., etc.)	Reliable Stock #	Color (please specify)	Description	Unit Price	Total
6	doz	289RC300P	Pink	"While You Were Out" pads	$1.29	$7.74

Proofread the order form below against the ad at the top of the page. The order should be for three dozen yellow pads. Are there any mistakes? If there are, correct them on this order form.

Qty.	Unit (each, doz., etc.)	Reliable Stock #	Color (please specify)	Description	Unit Price	Total
3	doz	289RC300W	Yellow	"While You Were Out" pads	$1.29	$3.87

. . . .
Reading: Recognizing task-related words with technical meanings;
Computation: Computing costs and cost savings

COMPLETE A CATALOG ORDER FORM

Use the catalog ads to fill out the order form below. Be sure to fill out the order form completely. Find the total price for each item you order. You should order

- five message books (200-set books)
- six dozen yellow "While You Were Out" pads

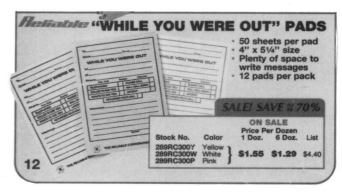

Reliable
The Office Supply People
P.O. Box 6383 · Chicago, IL · 60680-6383

CALL TOLL-FREE 24 HOURS A DAY—7 DAYS A WEEK
1-800-735-4000   **1-800-326-3233**
PHONE   FAX

SHIP TO:
Address: _____

City: _____ State: _____ Zip: _____

Attention: _____

Purchase Order No. ___4701A___

Your Name _____

Title _____

Phone (Required): (___) _____

Qty.	Unit (each, doz., etc.)	Reliable Stock#	Color (please specify)	Description	Unit Price	Total

Every effort is made for this catalog to be totally accurate. However, an occasional printing error may occur. Therefore, we reserve the right to bill at corrected prices.

©1990 THE RELIABLE CORPORATION
ALL RIGHTS RESERVED

Illinois, Georgia and Nevada residents include applicable Sales Tax. A $2.99 small order handling charge will be added to each order under $25. For all other orders a 99¢ handling charge will be added.

NOTE: Items with an "NS" prefix will have separate shipping charges.

Sub Total	
Handling Charge	.99
Sales Tax (IL, GA & NV residents apply applicable tax)	.94
TOTAL	

BILLING FORMS

When you go shopping, you buy **merchandise,** pay for it, and receive a **receipt** or sales slip. The sales slip is a written record of what you purchased. It shows the items you bought, what they cost, the tax, the date, and other information.

Businesses shop too. Offices order supplies. Department stores purchase the clothes they sell you. Auto manufacturers buy raw material like steel and fabric to make cars. As you learned on page 94, when businesses shop, it's called **purchasing**.

When businesses make a purchase, they receive a receipt or a bill called an **invoice**.

SKILL PREVIEW

Receipts often come in handy. When would you need to use a sales receipt? List all the reasons you can think of on the lines below.

_____

_____

_____

_____

INTERPRETING A SALES RECEIPT

```
              MARTHA'S GROCERY  #5

           ********************
                 emp. #16

     Cr. Mushroom                  .62
     Eggs Lg.                     1.09
     Ap. Juice                    1.22
     Cheese, Kraft                3.88
     Coffee, Hills Bro.           5.69
     Gum, Baz.                     .85
          SUBTOTAL               13.35

          TAX                     1.07
          TOTAL                  14.42

          CASH                   15.00
          CHANGE                   .58

     11/30/93       2:31 p.m.        #5574
```

GUIDED PRACTICE

What information can you find on the sales receipt above? Put a check (✔) next to each type of information below that you can find on the receipt.

☐ date   ☐ sale item

☐ time   ☐ description of items

☐ cost of each item   ☐ total cost

☐ type of payment   ☐ employee name

☐ tax   ☐ change given

☐ store identification   ☐ employee identification

You are correct if you checked everything except *employee name* and *sale item*.

Use the sales receipt from Martha's Grocery on page 102 to answer these questions.

1. How much did the eggs cost? _____

2. What date and time did this customer make her purchase? _____

3. How did she pay for her purchases? _____

4. What is the subtotal amount of the merchandise? _____

5. What is the total amount of the merchandise and the tax? _____

6. At what store did this purchase take place? _____

7. What is the employee's ID number? _____

8. What kind of juice did the customer buy? _____

9. How much change did the customer receive? _____

10. What brand of cheese did the customer buy? _____

WORKWISE

Receipts differ from one place to the next. Some are simpler than the one from Martha's Grocery. Some are more complex. Invoices can be very complicated.

Collect some sales receipts. Compare them. Do they all contain similar information?

Next, find someone who can show you invoices from his or her workplace. How are these invoices similar to your receipts? How are they different?

. . . .
Reading: Identifying factual details and specifications within text; Interpreting codes and symbols

INTERPRETING AN ORDER FORM

Business purchases are often made through catalogs. Businesses can place their catalog orders in three ways:

- over the phone (verbal)
- by mail (written)
- through a fax machine (written)

No matter which way an order is placed, purchasing follows the same steps. The diagram below shows the steps involved in purchasing.

> **Verbal order** is placed by customer over phone
> OR
> **Written order** form is completed by customer

⬇

> Office receives and records **order**
> Office begins **invoice**

⬇

> Warehouse fills **order** and completes **invoice**
> Warehouse ships **order**

⬇

> Customer receives **merchandise** and **invoice**

GUIDED PRACTICE

Use the diagram above to answer these questions.

1. Who begins the purchasing process? _____

2. Before the warehouse fills the order, where must the order be recorded?

_____

3. Where is the order shipped from? _____

You are correct if you answered 1. *the customer*; 2. *at the office*; 3. *the warehouse.*

ACE BUSINESS SUPPLY

FREE DELIVERY • FREE PARKING
NEXT DAY SERVICE

FAX 555-7032

FAX ORDER FORM

Customer Order No. _765232_   Date _9/3/93_

Name _Alberto's Auto_

Delivery Address _8376 Aurora Ave. N   Albuquerque, NM_

Buyer _Alberto Ramírez_   Phone _555-0439_   Fax _555-0438_

Instructions/Comments _____

QTY.	MANUFACTURER	STOCK NUMBER	DESCRIPTION
3	Loganite	LOG 23-225	Primo Citrus Hand Cleaner
1 case	Plus One	PLU 998	Single-Fold Paper Towels
1 case	Durahold	DUR 236A	Blue Cloth Shop Towels

Alberto Ramírez needed supplies for his automotive repair shop. He filled out the order form above. He then sent the order form by fax.

APPLIED PRACTICE 2: INTERPRETING AN ORDER FORM

Read over Alberto's order. Then answer the following questions.

1. What three items did Alberto order? (*Hint:* Look under the heading **Description**.)

   _____

2. From what company did Alberto order these items? _____

3. What is the date of Alberto's order? _____

4. Who is the manufacturer of the hand cleaner? _____

5. What is the stock number of the single-fold paper towels? _____

. . . .

Reading: Selecting parts of text or visual materials to complete a task; Using flowcharts to sequence events

TRANSFERRING INFORMATION

On this page, you'll find Alberto's completed order form and the catalog entry he's ordering from.

LOGANITE PRIMO CITRUS HAND CLEANER. Smooth lotion formula. Works fast, smells fresh, natural citrus power. Contains premium skin conditioners; aloe, lanolin, jojoba oil. Biodegradable. In an easy-to-use pump container. 14 oz.

LOG 23-225...........................NEW...........3.99 ea.

PLUS ONE PAPER TOWELS. White towels for use in C-Fold, Multi-Fold, and Single-Fold dispensers.

PLU 998 Single-Fold, 1-ply, 334/pkg., 12/case......51.95 cs.

PLU 231 C-Fold, 2-ply, 150/pkg., 16/case..........49.60 cs.

PLU 579 Multi-Fold, 1-ply, 334/pkg., 12/case.......51.15 cs.

Some items subject to carton minimum.

DURAHOLD BLUE WIPER. Strong, cloth-like shop towels. Size: 12 1/2" x 14 1/2". 20 per package, 10 packages per case.

DUR 236A..45.65 cs.

♠ **ACE BUSINESS SUPPLY**

FREE DELIVERY • FREE PARKING
NEXT DAY SERVICE

FAX 555-7032

FAX ORDER FORM

Customer Order No. _765232_ Date _9/3/93_

Name _Alberto's Auto_

Delivery Address _8376 Aurora Ave. N Albuquerque, NM_

Buyer _Alberto Ramírez_ Phone _555-0439_ Fax _555-0438_

Instructions/Comments _____

QTY.	MANUFACTURER	STOCK NUMBER	DESCRIPTION
3	Loganite	LOG 23-225	Primo Citrus Hand Cleaner
1 case	Plus One	PLU 998	Single-Fold Paper Towels
1 case	Durahold	DUR 236A	Blue Cloth Shop Towels

Ace Business Supply has sent Alberto the merchandise he ordered. Ace now needs to complete an **invoice** for this order.

Just like a sales receipt, Ace's invoice will list details about each item purchased. It will also list the name and address of the customer who must pay for the items and the place the order was **shipped** to. In Alberto's case, the name and address are the same for both.

Complete this part of the invoice. Because the order was shipped to the same place that must pay for it, you can write *same* under the heading **Shipped To**.

♠ ACE
BUSINESS SUPPLY

INVOICE NO.
3051

SOLD TO	SHIPPED TO
STREET & NO.	STREET & NO.
CITY STATE ZIP	CITY STATE ZIP

You should have entered the name and address of Alberto's Auto on the left side of the form and *same* under **Shipped To**.

Three lines on the invoice below have been started for you. Complete these three lines using the information from the order form and the catalog on page 106.

CUSTOMER'S ORDER #	SALESPERSON BB	PAYMENT Money Order	DATE	
QTY.	ITEM DESCRIPTION	STOCK NO.	UNIT PRICE	PRICE
3	Loganite Primo Citrus Hand Cleaner			11.97
	Plus One Paper Towels			
			SUBTOTAL	
			TAX	
			TOTAL	

WORKING WITH MONEY ORDERS

Alberto received the invoice from Ace Business Supply. He decided to pay the amount due with a **money order**.

A money order is a guarantee of payment. It's safer than cash (it's not as likely to be stolen), and it's safer than a personal check (it can't "bounce").

Say you need a money order for $10 to pay a phone bill. You can go to a bank, store, or post office where money orders are sold. You pay $10 plus a fee. The employee will write a $10 money order made out to the phone company. Only the phone company is able to cash your money order. The company is guaranteed to receive $10.

GUIDED PRACTICE

Here is a copy of the money order Alberto sent to Ace Business Supply. Look over the money order. Then answer the questions below.

```
                                          Money Order
                                          108 5954 570
TravelersExpress              TRAVELERS EXPRESS COMPANY, INC. - DRAWER
                              P.O. BOX 9476, MINNEAPOLIS, MN 55480
                                  DATE  9/3/93              75-53
                                                           919
PAY
TO THE    ACE BUSINESS SUPPLY
ORDER OF _____
                    = NOT VALID FOR OVER THREE HUNDRED U.S. DOLLARS =

                          MAPLE LEAF
AMOUNT   118.41          ◄ SUPER DELI ►                      DOLLARS

Payable thru
Norwest Bank
Minn. So. N.A.  SIGNATURE  Alberto Ramírez   ADDRESS  8371 Aurora Ave. North
Faribault, MN   BY SIGNING YOU AGREE TO THE SERVICE CHARGE AND OTHER TERMS ON THE REVERSE SIDE.

  ⑈091900533⑈:108  5954570⑈"   90
```

1. What is the amount of the money order? _____

2. Who can cash the money order? _____

3. Who signed the money order? _____

You are correct if you answered 1. *$118.41*; 2. *Ace Business Supply*; and 3. *Alberto Ramírez*.

① LIMITED RECOURSE:
This Money Order will not be paid if it has been forged, altered, or stolen, and recourse is only against the endorser. This means that persons receiving this Money Order should accept it only from those known to them and against whom they have effective recourse.

② Payee's Endorsement
For information concerning this Money Order, contact TRAVELERS EXPRESS COMPANY, INC.

③ PURCHASER'S AGREEMENT:
You, the purchaser, agree to immediately complete this Money Order by filling in the front of the Money Order, signing, and addressing it at the bottom. The terms of this Money Order bind you, your heirs, or others who receive this Money Order from you.

SERVICE CHARGE:
If this Money Order is not used or cashed (presented for payment) within three (3) years of the purchase date, there will be a non-refundable service charge where permitted by law. The service charge will be deducted from the amount of payment shown on the Money Order. The service charge is twenty-five (25) cents per month from the date of purchase, but not more than twenty-one (21) dollars.

RESTRICTIONS ON USE:
The business or person selling this Money Order cannot use it to pay personal or business obligations.

APPLIED PRACTICE 4: INTERPRETING A MONEY ORDER

Using the back of the money order above, answer the questions below.

1. Read the information under the heading **Limited Recourse**. Will Ace Business Supply receive its money if the money order has been **altered** in any way?

    _____ Yes   _____ No

2. Read the information under the heading **Purchaser's Agreement**. What three things should the purchaser do immediately after buying the money order?

    _____

3. How much time does Ace Business Supply have to use or cash this money order before the service charge is in effect?

    _____

4. If you worked for Ace Business Supply, the "payee" of this money order, you would need to endorse the money order before you deposit it. At which circled number would you endorse this money order?

    ① _____   ② _____   ③ _____

5. When you endorse this money order, you'll use the business's name instead of your own name. Endorse this money order now, writing **Ace Business Supply.**

. . . .
Writing: Entering appropriate information onto a form;
Reading: Identifying factual details and specifications within text

COMPLETE AN INVOICE

Fill out the invoice below for the order shipped to Alberto's Auto. Use Alberto's order form and the catalog information on page 106. Be sure to fill out the invoice completely. Look at the hints to fill out the subtotal and the tax.

♠ ACE BUSINESS SUPPLY

INVOICE NO. 3051

SOLD TO	SHIPPED TO
STREET & NO.	STREET & NO.
CITY STATE ZIP	CITY STATE ZIP

CUSTOMER'S ORDER #	SALESPERSON	PAYMENT	DATE

QTY.	ITEM DESCRIPTION	STOCK NO.	UNIT PRICE	PRICE

Add the prices. ⟶

SUBTOTAL	
TAX	8.84
TOTAL	

Add the tax to the subtotal to get the total. ⟶

INVOICE

SELF-CHECK

Before you turn your invoice in to your instructor, ask another student to check it over carefully for errors. Businesses usually have a person who double-checks an order before it is sent to the warehouse.

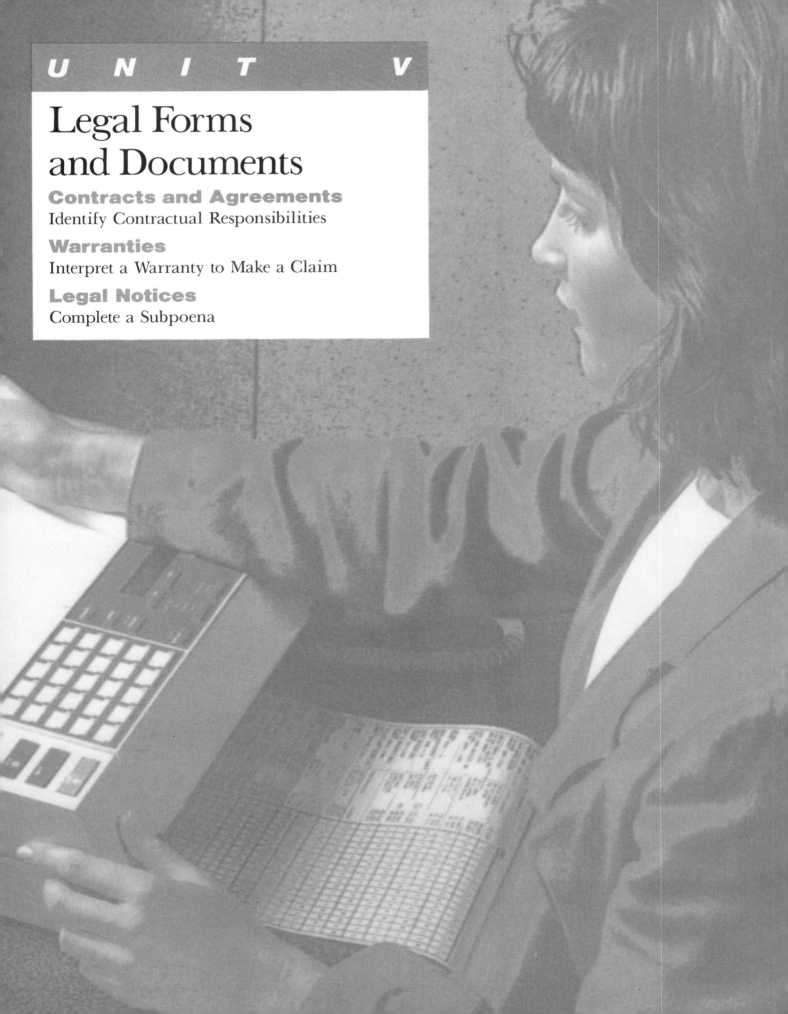

UNIT V

Legal Forms and Documents

Contracts and Agreements
Identify Contractual Responsibilities

Warranties
Interpret a Warranty to Make a Claim

Legal Notices
Complete a Subpoena

CONTRACTS AND AGREEMENTS

In our world today, **contracts** are a part of life. A contract is an agreement between people or organizations. A contract is meant to **bind,** or hold, people to the terms of their agreement. Each person who signs a contract is promising to uphold his or her end of the deal.

Contracts can be enforced in court. A person who decides to **breach** (break) a contract can be **sued**, or taken to court. The court may require this person to uphold the terms of the contract or to pay for **damages** (money lost because of the broken contract).

SKILL PREVIEW

Think of three times that you have or *could have* made a contract with someone. Your agreements may or may not have been put in writing. List these contracts below.

1. _____

   _____

2. _____

   _____

3. _____

   _____

Articles of Agreement

Between

and

The party of the first part, in consideration of

agrees to

Employment Contract

1. *Parties to Contract.*
   This contract is made between _AA Hardware, Inc._ (e
   and _Stanley R. Evans_ (employee).

2. *Date of Contract.*
   This employment contract is effective _September 2, 19_

3. *Base Salary.*
   The employer shall pay the employee $ _28,8_
   full-time work, payable in equal installme
   of each month.

4. *Commission.*
   The employee shal
   For each
   will

UNDERSTANDING CONTRACTS

Contracts are also called **agreements**. Contracts can be either written or oral (spoken). Oral, or "handshake," agreements are **valid**, or legal, in most circumstances. However, in most cases it is safer to put the contract in writing. This helps ensure that each **party**, or person, understands his or her obligations under the agreement.

There are five parts to a valid contract:

1. An **offer** is the invitation to exchange goods or services.

2. The offer must be expressed in definite **terms**. Terms are the specific details of the contract. These can include *who, what, what price, what time,* and the *place*.

3. **Acceptance** is when the person receiving the offer agrees to its terms.

4. **Consideration** is the exchange of promises to do (or not to do) something.

5. There must be no **defenses** to the contract. Defenses are things that make a contract invalid. Defenses can be a contract's **illegal purpose** (such as selling drugs) or a person's **incapacity** (mental illness or not being of legal age).

GUIDED PRACTICE

Mario owns a transmission repair shop. His friend Bill paints cars. Mario tells Bill that he will fix the transmission on Bill's car for free and will pay for parts *if* Bill will paint Mario's car and pay for the paint. Mario also asks that they both finish the work by the end of the month. Bill thinks about the offer. He agrees to the terms.

Answer these questions about Bill and Mario's agreement.

1. Was an offer made? _____ yes _____ no

2. Did the offer include definite terms? _____ yes _____ no

3. Was the offer accepted? _____ yes _____ no

4. Was there consideration for the contract? (Did both parties promise to do or not to do something? _____ yes _____ no

5. Are there any defenses that would make the contract invalid? (incapacity? illegality?) _____ yes _____ no

You are correct if you answered 1. *yes*; 2. *yes*; 3. *yes—Bill agreed to Mario's terms*; 4. *yes—both Mario and Bill have promised to do something*; 5. *no (as far as we can tell from the story).*

On page 113, you listed some contracts you have had or could have had. For instance, you may have listed a **lease** to rent an apartment. Choose one of the contracts you listed to write about. Then fill in the following blanks.

1. What contract did you choose to write about?

   _____

2. Who made the **offer**? _____

3. What **terms** were included in the offer?

   a. goods or services involved _____

   b. dates or times involved _____

   c. price or payment involved _____

4. Was the offer accepted? _____ If so, by whom? _____

5. a. There was **consideration**. I promised _____

   _____

   b. The other party promised _____

   _____

6. There were no **defenses** to forming the contract.

   a. It was created for a legal purpose.   _____ yes   _____ no

   b. All parties were of **sound mind** and **legal age**.   _____ yes   _____ no

7. Look over your answers.

   a. Was your example a valid contract?   _____ yes   _____ no

   b. If not, why wasn't it? _____

. . . .
Reading: Recognizing task-related words with technical meanings; Identifying similarities and differences in objects

IDENTIFYING PARTS OF A CONTRACT

Look over the **employment contract** on page 117. Each paragraph in the contract relates to one of the contract areas listed below. Match the paragraph number with the contract area it relates to. The first one has been done for you.

Paragraph Number	Contract Area
_*a*_ **Example**: title, Employment Contract	a. offer
_____ 1. paragraph 1, Parties to Contract	b. terms
_____ 2. paragraph 2, Date of Contract	c. acceptance
_____ 3. paragraph 3, Base Salary	d. consideration
_____ 4. paragraph 5, Vacation	
_____ 5. paragraph 8, Termination	
_____ 6. paragraph 9, Agreed To	

You are correct if you answered 1. *b*; 2. *b*; 3. *d*; 4. *b*; 5. *b*; 6. *c*.

APPLIED PRACTICE 2: FINDING AND EXPLAINING PARTS OF A CONTRACT

Answer these questions about the contract on page 117.

1. What is the offer about? _____

2. How do you know the offer has been accepted? _____

3. What consideration (promise) does the employer make? _____

   _____

4. What consideration does the employee give? _____

5. Who are the parties named in the contract? _____

6. Are there any defenses to the contract? _____

. . . .
Reading: Using a completed form to locate information to complete a task;
Writing: Recording essential information in phrases or simple sentence form accurately and precisely

Employment Contract

1. *Parties to Contract.*
   This contract is made between __AA Hardware, Inc.__ (employer)
   and __Stanley R. Evans__ (employee).

2. *Date of Contract.*
   This employment contract is effective __September 2, 1993__.

3. *Base Salary.*
   The employer shall pay the employee $ __28,800.00__ per year for
   full-time work, payable in equal installments on the first and fifteenth days
   of each month.

4. *Commission.*
   The employee shall be entitled to a commission based on the following:
   __For each $1,000.00 of merchandise Stanley Evans sells, he__
   __will receive 10% of that amount, equaling $100.00.__

5. *Vacation.*
   The employee shall be entitled to __10__ days of paid vacation per year.

6. *Health and Sick Leave Benefits.*
   The employee shall be entitled to the following health and sick leave
   benefits:
   __Blue Shield Health Plan and 8 sick days__
   __yearly__.

7. *Other Benefits.*
   __AA Hardware provides truck and pays for__
   __gasoline.__

8. *Termination.*
   Either party may terminate this agreement on not less than __14__ days'
   notice.

9. *Agreed To:*
   AA Hardware __Jesse Clark__ __8/28/93__
   EMPLOYER   DATE
   __Stanley R. Evans__ __Sept. 1, 1993__
   EMPLOYEE   DATE

ASKING QUESTIONS FOR CLARIFICATION

Read these stories about people who believe they have valid contracts.

1. AA Hardware, Inc., wants to buy hammers from Bam Bang Hammers Manufacturing. The two companies agree to work together. Bam Bang Hammers will make 100 hammers per month for AA Hardware at $4 a hammer. AA Hardware will pay Bam Bang $400 each month for the hammers, even if AA doesn't sell all of the hammers each month.

2. Elsie Washington lives in Garden Villa Nursing Home. Her daughter takes care of her legal matters because Elsie is not mentally sound. Elsie still owns her old house. Her former neighbors, the Colemans, want to buy it. The Colemans make Elsie an offer in a written contract, and she signs the contract.

3. Maria promises her friend Louisa that if she wins the lottery, she will give Louisa one-third of the winnings. Louisa accepts the offer.

4. Two car thieves write a contract. They agree to evenly divide the money they get when they sell three stolen cars.

GUIDED PRACTICE

On page 119, you will evaluate these stories to see if the contracts are valid. You will need to ask questions about the five parts of a legal contract. Create these questions below. Use each word in **bold** type as a clue to what each question should ask.

Example: offer   Has an ___offer___ been made?

1. **terms**   Are the _____ clear and definite?

2. **acceptance**   Has the offer been _____ ?

3. **consideration**   Have both parties given _____ to the offer by promising something?

4. **defenses**   Are both parties of sound _____ ?

Is the contract about a _____ activity?

You are correct if you answered 1. *terms*; 2. *accepted*; 3. *consideration*; 4. *mind*; *legal*.

Reread the four stories on page 118. Evaluate them by asking the questions from the Guided Practice on page 118. Does each story answer each of the five questions?

Use the chart below to help you evaluate. Put a check (✔) in the areas you think each story covers. Put an X in the areas you think each story does not cover.

	Offer	Terms (who, what, when, where, price)	Acceptance	Consideration	Defenses (sound mind, legal activity)
1. AA Hardware/ Bam Bang Hammers					
2. Elsie Washington/ the Colemans					
3. Maria/ Louisa					
4. Car Thieves					

DEVELOPING A CONTRACT

Read over the **Articles of Agreement** on page 121. This is a contract. Decide where you would fill in the following information on the Articles of Agreement.

Example: The **names** of the people involved belong after the word _between._

1. **Acceptance** of the contract belongs after the phrase _____

    _____

2. The **consideration** (promise) of each person belongs after the phrase _____

    _____ (*Hint:* This phrase appears two times.)

3. The **terms** of the offer belong after the phrase _____
    (*Hint:* This phrase appears two times.)

You are correct if you answered 1. *Sealed and delivered in the presence of*; 2. *in consideration of*; 3. *agrees to.*

APPLIED PRACTICE 4: CONSTRUCTING A WRITTEN CONTRACT

Ask a classmate or your instructor to help you construct a contract based on the format on page 121. Then follow these steps:

1. Decide what the contract will be about. Will it be about a service or some goods?
2. Decide who will be the **party of the first part** and who will be the **party of the second part**.
3. Decide what terms each of you wants.
4. Fill out the agreement on page 121. Be sure your offer is legal and be sure both of you sign your names.

SELF-CHECK

Read your contract aloud once it's finished. Is the information clear? Is each area on the contract completed? Did you sign and date the contract?

Communication: Interacting with co-workers to accomplish a task;
Reading: Identifying factual details and specifications within a text; Organizing information from multiple sources into a series;
Writing: Recording essential information in phrases or simple sentence form accurately and precisely

Articles of Agreement,

Between

of the first part,

and

of the second part.

The party of the first part, in consideration of

agrees to

The party of the second part, in consideration of

agrees to

This instrument may not be changed orally.

In Witness Whereof, the parties hereunto have set their hands and seals the
day of   in the year one thousand nine
hundred and

Sealed and delivered in the presence of   _____

_____

IDENTIFY CONTRACTUAL RESPONSIBILITIES

Look at the completed contract on page 169. Read this contract carefully, asking the questions about each part of a standard contract. Then answer the questions below.

1. Given that both parties are of sound mind and are of legal age, is this a valid contract? Why or why not?

   _____

   _____

2. Who is the party of the first part? _____

3. What are the responsibilities of the first party?

   _____

   _____

4. Who is the party of the second part? _____

5. What are the responsibilities of the second party?

   _____

   _____

WORKWISE

Many jobs today involve oral agreements between the employee and the employer. These verbal agreements usually cover terms such as job duties, salary, and work schedule. Sometimes, employees aren't sure what the terms of their employment really are. If this happens to you, you should *ask questions* and, if necessary, *get these terms in writing*. This will protect you. It may even save your job!

WARRANTIES

Many of the products and services you buy today come with a **warranty.** This warranty is a promise that the product or service meets a certain standard of quality. Sometimes, we compare the warranties on similar products before deciding which one to buy.

These days, we expect warranties when we buy brand-new things such as appliances and cars. That's why you need to understand warranties: what they say, what they mean, and what you can do if something goes wrong with the product.

SKILL PREVIEW

You may already have some experience with warranties. Perhaps you've bought something that broke soon after you bought it. When you buy a product or pay for a service, what do you expect the warranty to cover?

_____

_____

_____

_____

A *limited warranty* means that the customer must share some of the cost of replacement or repair. A *full warranty* would mean that the manufacturer paid all costs.

Limited Warranty

Braun Inc. warrants this Braun Appliance to be free of de
in material and workmanship for a period of one year fr
date of original purchase.
If the appliance exhibits such a defect, Braun Inc. will,
option, repair or replace it, provided the consumer:

Returns the appliance postpaid and insured to
Service Department, Braun Inc., 66 Broadway,
Route 1, Lynnfield, MA 01940,
or one of its authorized service centers.

Submits proof of date of original purchase

eed assistance*...
ool Consumer Assistance Center
number. Dial free from anywhere in

1-800-253-1301
th one of our trained consulta
can instruct you in how to ob
y operation from your applian
necessary, recommend a qua
mpany in your area.

r, write to:

am Clark
er Assistance Representative
ol Corporation
63
Harbor, MI 49022

lude a daytime phone numbe
dence.

uesting assistance, please p
mber, serial number, date of

10. WARRANTY INFORMATION
5 YEAR LIMITED WARRANTY
Maple Chase Company's warrants to the original consumer purc
new Smoke Alarm to be free from defects in material and w
under normal use and service for a period of five (5) years
purchase. Maple Chase Company agrees to repair or replace
any defective Smoke Alarm provided, that it is returned
prepaid and with proof of purchase date to Maple Chase
warranty does not cover damage resulting from accident,
or lack of reasonable care of the product. This warranty is
express warranties, obligations or liabilities. THE IMPLI
OF MERCHANTABILITY AND FITNESS FOR A PARTI
ARE LIMITED TO A PERIOD FOR FIVE (5) YEARS FRO
Some states do not allow limitations on how long an in
so the above limitations may not apply to you. IN NO
CHASE COMPANY BE LIABLE FOR ANY INCIDENTAL
DAMAGES FOR BREACH OF THIS OR ANY OTHER V
OR IMPLIED, WHATSOEVER, EVEN IF THE LOSS O
BY ITS NEGLIGENCE OR FAULT. Some states do r
limitation of incidental or consequential damage

WHIRLPOOL®
Microwave Oven Warranty

LENGTH OF WARRANTY
FULL ONE-YEAR WARRANTY
From Date of Purchase

LIMITED FOUR-YEAR WARRANTY
Second Through Fifth Year From
Date of Purchase

WHIR

WILL NOT PAY FOR

o:

stallation of the microwave oven.

3. If you need service*...

Whirlpool
SERVICE

Whirlpool has a nationwide
network of authorized
Whirlpool service compa-
nies. Whirlpool service
technicians are trained to fulfill
the product warranty and provide after-warranty
service, anywhere in the United States. To locate
the authorized Whirlpool service company in your
area, call our Consumer Assistance Company or
telephone number (see Step 2)
telephone directory Yel

WHIRLPOOL WILL PAY FOR
FSP® replacement parts and repair labor to correct defects in
materials or workmanship. Service must be provided by an
authorized Whirlpool® service company.
FSP® replacement magnetron tube on microwave ovens if
defective in materials or workmanship.

al, single-family household use.
ed in the home.
fire, flood, acts of G

APPLIANCES
MAJOR

UNDERSTANDING COMMON PARTS OF A WARRANTY

Imagine that the small company you work for has built a new lunchroom for employees. The lunchroom has several new appliances: a coffee maker, a microwave oven, and a smoke alarm. You are now responsible for keeping the information about these items and dealing with any problems they may pose.

Each item has an owner's manual with operating instructions, safety procedures, and warranty information. Here is the warranty for the coffee maker.

A *limited warranty* means that the customer must share some of the cost of replacement or repair. A *full warranty* would mean that the manufacturer paid all costs.

These *directions* tell you what to do if your appliance needs repairs or replacement.

This *legal language* tells you that the manufacturer won't pay for damage the product causes to other things and that different laws apply from state to state.

Limited Warranty

Braun Inc. warrants this Braun Appliance to be free of defects in material and workmanship for a period of one year from the date of original purchase.
If the appliance exhibits such a defect, Braun Inc. will, at its option, repair or replace it, provided the consumer:

1. Returns the appliance postpaid and insured to Service Department, Braun Inc., 66 Broadway, Route 1, Lynnfield, MA 01940, or one of its authorized service centers.

2. Submits proof of date of original purchase.

This warranty does not cover finishes, nor does it cover damage resulting from accident, misuse, dirt, water, tampering, unreasonable use, servicing performed or attempted by unauthorized service agencies or units that have been modified or used for commercial purposes.

ALL IMPLIED WARRANTIES, INCLUDING ANY IMPLIED WARRANTY OF MERCHANTABILITY OR FITNESS FOR ANY PARTICULAR PURPOSE, ARE LIMITED IN DURATION TO ONE YEAR FROM DATE OF ORIGINAL PURCHASE. IN NO EVENT WILL BRAUN INC. BE RESPONSIBLE FOR CONSEQUENTIAL DAMAGES RESULTING FROM THE USE OF THIS PRODUCT.

Some states do not allow the exclusion or limitation of incidental or consequential damages, so the above limitation may not apply to you.
This warranty gives you specific legal rights, and you may have other legal rights which vary from state to state.

Here you can find *what product* is covered by this warranty and *how long* the warranty is valid.

This paragraph tells you *what problems the warranty will not cover.*

The warranty on page 124 has six types of information that are found on most appliance warranties. The first type of information is **what kind of warranty it is—** limited or full. The second type of information is **what product is covered**. What are the four other types of information? List them below.

_____   _____

_____   _____

You are correct if you answered *how long it is covered, directions* for getting repairs or replacement, *what the warranty won't cover,* and *legal language* about damage to other products.

APPLIED PRACTICE 1: UNDERSTANDING COMMON PARTS OF A WARRANTY

Read through the warranty on page 124. Look carefully for the six types of information listed in the Guided Practice. Answer the questions below.

1. a. What kind of warranty is this? _____

   b. What does that mean? _____

2. For what period of time is this warranty valid? _____

3. What two things does the manufacturer ask you to send if the product needs repairs or replacement?

   a. _____

   b. _____

4. Name four things the warranty doesn't cover.

   a. _____

   b. _____

   c. _____

   d. _____

. . . .
Reading: Identifying factual details and specifications within text

USING A DICTIONARY TO DEFINE WORDS AND PHRASES

Warranties often use difficult words. To understand a warranty, you may need to look up word meanings in the dictionary. You'll need to know how to choose the right definition of a word. You'll also need to know how to define a **phrase** (several words put together).

Here is a dictionary entry for the word *warranty*.

> **war·ran·ty** \'wȯr-ənt-ē, 'wär-\ *n, pl* -ties [ME *warantie*, fr. ONF, fr. *warrantir* to warrant] (14c) **1** **a :** a real covenant binding the grantor of an estate and his heirs to warrant and defend the title **b :** a collateral undertaking that a fact regarding the subject of a contract is or will be as it is expressly or by implication declared or promised to be **2** : something that authorizes, sanctions, supports, or justifies : WARRANT **3 :** a usu. written guarantee of the integrity of a product and of the maker's responsibility for the repair or replacement of defective parts

GUIDED PRACTICE

As you can see, *warranty* has several definitions in this dictionary entry. How do you know which one is the one you need?

First, think about what you already know about warranties. Then, skim through the definitions again. Which definition looks right?

Write the number of that definition here: _____

You are correct if you answered definition number *3*. There are clue words within this definition that may have helped you. These clues are *guarantee, product, maker's responsibility, repair or replacement, defective parts.*

To decide which definition is correct, look for clue words that best fit with what you already know about a word or phrase.

The Braun coffee maker warranty contains this sentence:

In no event will Braun Inc. be responsible for consequential damages resulting from the use of this product.

What does this sentence mean? To understand this sentence, you must understand the phrase *consequential damages.* Here are the definitions of each word.

con•se•quence [kŏn'sĭ kwĕns'] *or* [-kwens] *n.*
1. Something that follows from an action or condition; an effect; result: *Have you considered the consequences of your decision?* **2.** Importance; significance: *a matter of no consequence.*

con•se•quent [kon'sĭ kwĕnt'] *or* [-kwent] *adj.*
Following as an effect or result: *heavy rains and the consequent flooding of the farmlands.*

con•se•quen•tial [kŏn'sĭ **kwen'**shəl] *adj.* **1.** Consequent. **2.** Important; signficant.

dam•age [dăm'ĭj] n. **1. a.** Harm or injury that causes loss or makes a thing less valuable or useful: *damage done to a car in an accident.* **b.** The loss caused or the cost of repair: *Did the damage amount to $100?* **2. damages. a.** In law, money to be paid to make up for an injury or loss: *sue for damages.* **b.** Individual injuries to property or persons: *repair all damages.* —*v.* **dam•aged, dam•ag•ing.** To harm, hurt, or injure: *Some insects damage plants.* —**dam'aged** *adj.: a damaged building.* —**dam'ag•ing** *adj.: Damaging gossip harmed her reputation.*

APPLIED PRACTICE 2: DEFINING AN UNFAMILIAR PHRASE

Read each definition and answer the questions below.

1. Which definition seems to belong in a warranty, *money to be paid to make up for an injury or loss* or *injuries to property or persons?*

   _____

2. There are two definitions for *consequential.* Check each definition for clue words that make sense in the sentence we're defining. Which definition seems to belong in a warranty?

   _____

3. What do you think *consequential damages* may mean? _____

   _____

4. Now try to define the entire sentence from the Braun warranty. Look up any unfamiliar words in the dictionary. On the lines below, write what you think the sentence means.

   _____

   _____

UNDERSTANDING WARRANTY VOCABULARY

Because you are in charge of the new lunchroom appliances, you read through the warranty for each product. You find several unfamiliar words and phrases in each warranty. You decide it's a good idea to look up the meanings of these unfamiliar words.

Below is the warranty for the new smoke alarm. Next to the warranty are words and phrases that may be unfamiliar to you. If you find any other unfamiliar words, add them to the list.

10. WARRANTY INFORMATION:

5 YEAR LIMITED WARRANTY

Maple Chase Company s warrants to the original consumer purchaser each new Smoke Alarm to be free from defects in material and workmanship under normal use and service for a period of five (5) years from date of purchase. Maple Chase Company agrees to repair or replace, at its option, any defective Smoke Alarm provided, that it is returned with postage prepaid and with proof of purchase date to Maple Chase Company. This warranty does not cover damage resulting from accident, misuse or abuse or lack of reasonable care of the product. This warranty is in lieu of all other express warranties, obligations or liabilities. THE IMPLIED WARRANTIES OF MERCHANTABILITY AND FITNESS FOR A PARTICULAR PURPOSE ARE LIMITED TO A PERIOD FOR FIVE (5) YEARS FROM PURCHASE DATE. Some states do not allow limitations on how long an implied warranty lasts, so the above limitations may not apply to you. IN NO CASE SHALL MAPLE CHASE COMPANY BE LIABLE FOR ANY INCIDENTAL OR CONSEQUENTIAL DAMAGES FOR BREACH OF THIS OR ANY OTHER WARRANTY, EXPRESS OR IMPLIED, WHATSOEVER, EVEN IF THE LOSS OR DAMAGE IS CAUSED BY ITS NEGLIGENCE OR FAULT. Some states do not allow the exclusion or limitation of incidental or consequential damages, so the above limitation or exclusion may not apply to you. This warranty gives you specific legal rights, and you may also have other legal rights which vary from state to state.

This Smoke Alarm's manufacture and distribution is licensed by the U.S. Nuclear Regulatory Commission.

This product meets all the requirements of U.L. Standard 217.

11. WHERE TO SEND YOUR SMOKE ALARM IF IT NEEDS SERVICE:

If repair or service is required, return the Smoke Alarm to Maple Chase Company in a well padded box. Ship it postage prepaid to:

MAPLE CHASE COMPANY
PRODUCT SERVICE DEPARTMENT
2820 Thatcher Road
Downers Grove, IL 60515

Warranty Vocabulary

defects in material and workmanship

postage prepaid

misuse

abuse

in lieu of

liabilities

implied

negligence

_____

_____

Remember to follow these steps when you're looking up words:

1. Change plural words to singular before you look them up (for instance, change *defects* to *defect*).

2. Read all definitions carefully.

3. Look for clue words that best fit your sentence.

4. Write down the definition for each word in a phrase, then work on making sense of the whole phrase.

Choose four words or phrases from the warranty vocabulary list on page 128. You will be defining these words. First, write the vocabulary words on the lines below. Then, decide if you need to change the word at all before you look it up.

warranty vocabulary word   **exact word to look up in the dictionary**

Example a. _defects_   b. _defect_

1. a. _____   b. _____

2. a. _____   b. _____

3. a. _____   b. _____

4. a. _____   b. _____

Be sure that you wrote the exact word to look up in the dictionary in list **b.**

APPLIED PRACTICE 3: DEFINING COMMON WARRANTY VOCABULARY

Copy your words from the **b.** list onto the chart below. Look up each word. Choose the correct definition, then decide what the word means within the warranty.

WORD/PHRASE IN WARRANTY	DEFINITION	MEANING
defect	an imperfection or a lack of something	flaw or problem

. . . .
Reading: Recognizing task-related words with technical meanings; Following sequential directions to complete a task;
Writing: Spelling task-related words and abbreviations correctly

USING A WARRANTY TO MAKE A CLAIM

The new appliances have worked well for five months. But on Thursday, there seems to be a problem with the microwave oven. You go to your files and pull out the warranty and the service information. This information is found on page 131.

GUIDED PRACTICE

After reading the information, you think you qualify for warranty service: the oven has not been misused; it's plugged in; the door is shut all the way. You follow all the directions, but the oven doesn't work. You decide to call for assistance.

Use the information on page 131 to answer the questions below.

1. What phone number will you call? _____

2. How much will this phone call cost? _____

3. What information will you need to have when you call? _____

The answers to these questions can be found under the heading **If you need assistance. . . .** You are correct if you answered 1. *1-800-253-1301*; 2. *nothing; 1-800 numbers are free*; 3. *model and serial numbers, date of purchase, description of the problem.*

APPLIED PRACTICE 4: MAKING A WARRANTY CLAIM

The service assistant on the phone agrees that you need service. You must use a service company recommended by Whirlpool to get the service free of charge. Look at the information on page 131 after the heading **If you need service**. Answer the questions below.

1. There are two ways to find the authorized Whirlpool service company in your area. What are they?

    a. _____

    b. _____

2. Look in the yellow pages to find the authorized Whirlpool service company in your area. When you find it, write the name, address, and phone number below.

Name	Address	Phone Number

. . . .

Reading: Cross-referencing within and across source materials to select information to perform a routine; Organizing information from multiple sources into a series

WHIRLPOOL®
Microwave Oven Warranty

LENGTH OF WARRANTY	WHIRLPOOL WILL PAY FOR
FULL ONE-YEAR WARRANTY From Date of Purchase	FSP® replacement parts and repair labor to correct defects in materials or workmanship. Service must be provided by an authorized Whirlpool℠ service company.
LIMITED FOUR-YEAR WARRANTY Second Through Fifth Year From Date of Purchase	FSP® replacement magnetron tube on microwave ovens if defective in materials or workmanship.

WHIRLPOOL WILL NOT PAY FOR

A. Service calls to:
   1. Correct the installation of the microwave oven.
   2. Instruct you how to use the microwave oven.
   3. Replace house fuses or correct house wiring.
   4. Replace owner accessible light bulbs.
B. Repairs when microwave oven is used in other than normal, single-family household use.
C. Pickup and delivery. This product is designed to be repaired in the home.
D. Damage to microwave oven caused by accident, misuse, fire, flood, acts of God or use of products not approved by Whirlpool.
E. Any labor costs during limited warranty.
F. Repairs to parts or systems caused by unauthorized modifications made to the appliance.

8-92

WHIRLPOOL CORPORATION SHALL NOT BE LIABLE FOR INCIDENTAL OR CONSEQUENTIAL DAMAGES. Some states do not allow the exclusion or limitation of incidental or consequential damages, so this limitation or exclusion may not apply to you. This warranty gives you specific legal rights, and you may also have other rights which vary from state to state.

Outside the United States, a different warranty may apply. For details, please contact your authorized Whirlpool distributor or military exchange.

---

2. If you need assistance*...
Call Whirlpool Consumer Assistance Center telephone number. Dial free from anywhere in the U.S.:
1-800-253-1301
and talk with one of our trained consultants. The consultant can instruct you in how to obtain satisfactory operation from your appliance or, if service is necessary, recommend a qualified service company in your area.

If you prefer, write to:

Mr. William Clark
Consumer Assistance Representative
Whirlpool Corporation
2000 M-63
Benton Harbor, MI 49022

Please include a daytime phone number in your correspondence.

*When requesting assistance, please provide: model number, serial number, date of purchase, and a complete description of the problem. This information is needed in order to better respond to your request.

---

3. If you need service*...

 Whirlpool has a nationwide network of authorized Whirlpool℠ service companies. Whirlpool service technicians are trained to fulfill the product warranty and provide after-warranty service, anywhere in the United States. To locate the authorized Whirlpool service company in your area, call our Consumer Assistance Center telephone number (see Step 2) or look in your telephone directory Yellow Pages under:

APPLIANCES – HOUSEHOLD – MAJOR – SERVICE & REPAIR
ELECTRICAL APPLIANCES – MAJOR – REPAIRING & PARTS
OR
WASHING MACHINES, DRYERS & IRONERS – SERVICING

WHIRLPOOL APPLIANCES
AUTHORIZED WHIRLPOOL SERVICE

SERVICE COMPANIES
XYZ SERVICE CO
123 Maple...............999-9999

INTERPRET A WARRANTY TO MAKE A CLAIM

Turn to the Emerson Limited Warranty on page 170. Read the warranty carefully. Then, decide whether each claim below is covered by the warranty.

A group of friends have a party. Rick brings his new Emerson tape player, and he and Lucas hook it up to some bigger amplifiers. Everything sparks and blows up. All of the equipment is ruined.

1. Can Rick make a warranty claim to replace his tape player? _____

2. Why or why not? _____

A department store has an unsupervised play area for children. The play area has a new Emerson tape player and several children's tapes. After one week, a tape gets stuck in the tape player. The staff gets the tape out, but the tape player won't work anymore.

3. Can the department store make a warranty claim? _____

4. Why or why not? _____

Miguel buys a tape player on March 15. On April 20, the antenna breaks off as Miguel is tuning the radio.

5. Can Miguel make a warranty claim? _____

6. Why or why not? _____

Miguel lives in the country, and there are no service agencies near him. If he were to make a claim, what would he have to do? List each step below. (*Hint:* This information is on the warranty.)

7. Step 1. _____

    Step 2. _____

    Step 3. _____

    Step 4. _____

LEGAL NOTICES

If you live in the United States, it is important to understand the forms and documents involved in the U.S. legal system. Someday you may decide to enter the legal system to let the court decide a case for you. Or you may be asked to go to court for someone else. At that time, you will need to understand legal notices and legal language.

SKILL PREVIEW

Legal notices are documents sent to people by the courts and by attorneys. Many different types of notices are involved with the U.S. legal system. Can you name a few? List as many as you can on the lines below.

_____

_____

_____

_____

Name: _____ Birth Dat

Last   First   Middle

Birth/Maiden Name: _____

2180 - Served
2280 - Not Served
2380 - Served By Mail
Subpoena - Subpoena Duces Tecum

IN THE CIRCUIT COURT OF COOK COUNTY, ILLINOIS   (Rev.

State of Illinois
County of Cook
City of Chicago

v.

Lyle Williams
1310 W. Roscoe
Chicago, IL 60657

No. 7632-3-93

rian Hernández

SUBPOENA

CONTESTED HEARING

Hearing Proc

nfraction is a determination that you have   The cor
uested a contested hearing because you   state must
s infraction.   fraction. A
                                                 you did cr
the following: If th
r expense.   be requi
examine witnesses in court.   court c
t from the prosecutor. You must do so at
the list should be given to you at least 7   Fail

STATE OF WASHINGTON
COUNTY OF SNOHOMISH
CITY OF LYNNWOOD

VS.

DEFENDANT'S NAME

IN THE NAME OF THE STATE OF WASHINGTON
REQUIRED TO APPEAR AT LYNNWOOD MU

ncluding the officer who issued the Notice.
must apply to the court in person at least

SUMMONS / SUBPOENA / NOTICE
LYNNWOOD MUNICIPAL COURT
Lynnwood, 19000 - 44th Ave. W. • P.O.
CITATION NO

Case Assigned To:

LYNNWOOD   MUNICIPAL COURT
SNOHOMISH COUNTY

19000 - 44th Ave. W. • P.O. Box 5008
Lynnwood, WA 98046-5008
775-1971 Ext. 342

Date

NO.

NOTICE OF HEARING

E 008
971 Ext. 342   Judge
E DATE

VIOLATION(S):   Courtroom

Black

Illinois on

s notification of the date for your _____ hearing.

MUST APPEAR ON _____ at _____ (am/pm).

(day of week)   (date)   (time)

OR

AIGNMENT

NG

CC.

Officer
Defense Atty.
Bondsman

UNDERSTANDING THE PROCESS OF LEGAL NOTICES

In many parts of the legal process, there are forms to be read and filled out. Read the following story about Lyle Williams. He decided to enter the legal system to let the court decide a case for him.

Lyle Williams was making a delivery with the company van. A police officer pulled him over for speeding and gave him a ticket. Lyle was upset for two reasons: first, he didn't think he had been speeding; and second, the ticket may cost him his job. His boss won't let drivers with tickets on their records drive the company van.

Lyle decided to **contest** (conTEST) the ticket, or to challenge it in court. He checked box number 3 on the back of the ticket and sent it in to the court.

Please check one, and only one, of the boxes below, sign your name, and return this notice to the court listed on the other side of this notice, in person or by mail within fifteen (15) days. A mailed response must be mailed not later than midnight on the day the response is due. If you send payment without checking one of the boxes, it will be assumed you choose #1. Checks should have the citation number written on them.

MY RESPONSE IS:

1. I CHOOSE TO PAY THE MONETARY PENALTY AND HAVE ENCLOSED FULL PAYMENT. You may pay the full amount of the penalty to the court indicated on the other side. If you must make time payments, appear in person at the court office. The amount of the penalty has been set by Supreme Court rule. This will close the case. A traffic infraction will go on your driving record.

2. I REQUEST A HEARING TO EXPLAIN THE CIRCUMSTANCES. If you agree that you committed the infraction, you still may explain the circumstances surrounding the infraction. The court will notify you in writing of the hearing date. You may not require witnesses to appear at the hearing but they may attend voluntarily. A traffic infraction will go on your driving record.

3. I REQUEST A HEARING TO CONTEST THIS INFRACTION NOTICE. If you believe you did not commit the infraction or have a defense to it, you may have a hearing to challenge the determination that you committed it. At the hearing the state must prove by a preponderance of the evidence (more likely than not) that you committed the infraction. You may require witnesses, including the officer who issued the notice, to appear at the hearing. The court will notify you in writing of the hearing date and how to request that witnesses be present.

ENCLOSE PAYMENT IN FULL (if box #1 is checked) or PROMISE TO APPEAR (if box #2 or #3 is checked)

Lyle Williams
(Signature)

When Lyle checked box number 3 on the ticket, what exactly did he agree to? Read section 3 on page 134 carefully. Then complete the sentences below in your own words.

1. Lyle requests a hearing to _____

_____

2. At the hearing, Lyle may require _____

_____

3. The court will write to Lyle about _____

_____

Your answers should say something like this: 1. *challenge the ticket in court*; 2. *witnesses to come and speak, including the officer who issued the ticket*; 3. *the hearing date and how to ask witnesses to come.*

APPLIED PRACTICE 1: ORDERING THE HEARING PROCESS

Section 3 on the ticket gives information about the hearing. Using this information, can you figure out the order of the hearing process?

Below are seven events that happen in the process of contesting a ticket. The list is out of order. Using the spaces on the right, write the events in the order they occur, from first to last. (*Hint*: Refer to section 3 on page 134 if you need help.)

Request witnesses   1. _____

Get notice of hearing   2. _____

Get ticket   3. _____

Prepare defense   4. _____

Judge decides case   5. _____

Have hearing   6. _____

Send ticket to court   7. _____

. . . .

Reading: Identifying factual details and specifications within text; Selecting parts of text to complete a task; Organizing information from multiple sources into a series

UNDERSTANDING LEGAL VOCABULARY

Some of the legal terms on the traffic ticket may be new to you. You would need to know this legal vocabulary before you went through a traffic hearing.

GUIDED PRACTICE

Read over the list of legal terms on page 137. Then read the back of the ticket on page 134. Add any unfamiliar words to the list.

WORKWISE

If you're involved in a legal procedure, you need to understand the legal words you come across. In the same way, when you're at work, you need to understand all the work-related terms you come across. Have you seen unfamiliar words on a job you've had? What did you do? Discuss this with a friend or classmate. What can you do if this occurs in the future?

APPLIED PRACTICE 2: DEFINING LEGAL VOCABULARY

Choose at least six words from the list on page 137 to define. Put a check (✔) in the box next to those words. Then use a dictionary to look up the meaning of each word. In your own words, write the meaning on the line next to the legal term.

Look at the example below.

> **subpoena**: a writ requiring a person
> to appear in court and give testimony

What is a *writ*? What is *testimony*? To understand the definition of *subpoena*, you might need to look up *writ* and/or *testimony* in the dictionary.

> **writ**: a formal written document

> **testimony**: a statement made by a witness
> under oath, usually in a court of law

When you understand all the words in the dictionary definition, write your own definition. For instance, you may have defined *subpoena* as:

subpoena   <u>*a document stating that you must testify in court*</u>

Now define the six legal terms you checked on page 137.

Legal Terms

☐ appeal _____

☐ arraignment _____

☐ atty. _____

☐ consideration _____

☐ contest(ed) _____

☐ defendant _____

☐ evidence _____

☐ examine _____

☐ hearing _____

☐ infraction _____

☐ issuance _____

☐ notification _____

☐ preponderance _____

☐ prosecutor _____

☐ sentencing _____

☐ subpoena _____

☐ summons _____

☐ warrant _____

_____   _____

_____   _____

. . . .

Reading: Cross-referencing within and across source materials to select information to perform a routine

INTERPRETING LEGAL NOTICES

Read the two forms on page 139. Then answer the following questions.

1. What are the titles of the two forms? _____

2. Look at the Notice of Hearing, under the heading **Hearing Procedures**. At the hearing, will there be a jury?

   _____

3. Look under the headings **Rights of Defendants** and **Hearing Procedures**. The Notice of Hearing mentions three things the defendant may have to pay for at the hearing. What are they?

   _____

4. What may happen if a person fails to obey the Summons/Subpoena/Notice?

   _____

You were correct if you answered 1. *Notice of Hearing* and *Summons/Subpoena/Notice*; 2. *no*; 3. *a lawyer, a monetary penalty, and court costs*; 4. *the person may be arrested.*

APPLIED PRACTICE 3: INTERPRETING TWO LEGAL NOTICES

Now that you've read the legal forms on page 139, can you figure out exactly what their purpose is? To find out, answer the questions below.

1. What is the purpose of the Notice of Hearing? _____

2. Who completes and sends the Notice of Hearing? _____

3. What is the purpose of the Summons/Subpoena/Notice? (*Hint*: Use the definition of *subpoena* on page 136 if you need to.)

   _____

4. Who would receive a subpoena? _____

. . . .
Reading: Identifying factual details and specifications within text; Determining the main idea of a paragraph or section

LYNNWOOD MUNICIPAL COURT

SNOHOMISH COUNTY

19000 - 44th Ave. W. • P.O. Box 5008
Lynnwood, WA 98046-5008
775-1971 Ext. 342

Date

NO.

NOTICE OF HEARING

This is notification of the date for your _____ hearing.

YOU MUST APPEAR ON _____ , _____ at _____ (am/pm).

(day of week)   (date)   (time)

FAILURE TO APPEAR ON THE ABOVE DATE
WILL RESULT IN THE NON-RENEWAL OF YOUR
DRIVER'S LICENSE UNTIL THE ORIGINAL
PENALTY PLUS $47.00 HAS BEEN PAID.

See Reverse Side for Instructions

NOTICE OF HEARING

12-001

CONTESTED HEARING

The issuance of your Notice of Infraction is a determination that you have committed the infraction. You have requested a contested hearing because you do not believe you have committed this infraction.

Rights of Defendants:

As defendant, you are entitled to the following:

The right to bring a lawyer, at your expense.

The right to present evidence and examine witnesses in court.

The right to request a witness list from the prosecutor. You must do so at least 14 days before the hearing and the list should be given to you at least 7 days before the hearing.

The right to subpoena witnesses, including the officer who issued the Notice. If you wish to subpoena a witness, you must apply to the court in person at least 5 days prior to your hearing.

Hearing Procedures:

The contested hearing will be heard before the court without a jury. The state must prove by a preponderance of evidence that you did commit the infraction. After consideration of the evidence, the court will determine whether you did commit the infraction.

If the court determines that you did commit the infraction, you may be required to pay a monetary penalty. You may also be required to pay court costs in addition to the monetary penalty.

You may appeal the court's decision that you did commit the infraction.

Failure to Appear:

Failure to Appear will result in a determination that you did commit the infraction.

Failure to Appear is a crime and could result in a criminal charge of Failure to Appear being filed against you and the issuance of a warrant for your arrest. The court will notify the Department of Licensing if you fail to appear and your driver's license will not be renewed until you have paid all the penalties and costs you owe.

STATE OF WASHINGTON
COUNTY OF SNOHOMISH
CITY OF LYNNWOOD

VS.

SUMMONS / SUBPOENA / NOTICE

LYNNWOOD MUNICIPAL COURT
19000 - 44th Ave. W. • P.O. Box 5008
Lynnwood, WA 98046-5008 Telephone 775-1971 Ext. 342

Case Assigned To:

Judge:

Courtroom

DEFENDANT'S NAME	CITATION NO.	CITATION DATE	NOTICE DATE	VIOLATION(S):

IN THE NAME OF THE STATE OF WASHINGTON, YOU ARE HEREBY SUMMONED AND REQUIRED TO APPEAR AT LYNNWOOD MUNICIPAL COURT ON THE DATE AND TIME BELOW.

DATE   AT   FOR   CC:

_____ARRAIGNMENT   Officer: _____
_____TRIAL   Defense Atty.: _____
_____SENTENCING   Bondsman: _____
_____HEARING   _____

FAILURE TO OBEY THIS SUMMONS MAY RESULT IN THE ISSUANCE OF A WARRANT FOR YOUR ARREST.

_____
JUDGE / COMMISSIONER / CLERK

12-002 (12/89)

DEFENDANT'S COPY

SKIMMING AND SCANNING FOR DETAILS

Lyle has decided to ask two witnesses to come to his hearing: the police officer who gave him the ticket and one eyewitness who saw him get the ticket. The **subpoena** on page 141 will be sent to the eyewitness.

GUIDED PRACTICE

Look over the subpoena carefully. Then answer the questions below.

1. Look at the upper left corner of the page. Was this subpoena served?_____

2. What two parties are involved in the hearing?

3. What is the name of the eyewitness? _____

4. Who signed this document to say that it is valid? _____

You are correct if you answered 1. *yes*; 2. *the State of Illinois and Lyle Williams*; 3. *Miriam Hernández*; 4. *Maka Elder, a notary public*.

APPLIED PRACTICE 4: INTERPRETING A COMPLETED SUBPOENA

Read the subpoena on page 141. Then answer the questions below.

1. What is the eyewitness being told to do? _____

   _____

2. What will happen if the eyewitness does not appear at the hearing? _____

   _____

3. Who is Gayle Tamvakis? _____

4. Why does the subpoena need to be signed by a notary public? _____

   _____

(Rev. 12-88) CCG-6

IN THE CIRCUIT COURT OF COOK COUNTY, ILLINOIS

State of Illinois
County of Cook
City of Chicago

v.

Lyle Williams
1310 W. Roscoe
Chicago, IL 60657

No. 7632-3-93

SUBPOENA

To: Miriam Hernández

YOU ARE COMMANDED to appear to testify before the Honorable Judge Alma Black
in Room 301, 17 N. State, Chicago Illinois on
September 30 19 93 at 2:00 p.m.

YOU ARE COMMANDED ALSO to bring the following:

in your possession or control.

YOUR FAILURE TO APPEAR IN RESPONSE TO THIS SUBPOENA WILL SUBJECT YOU TO PUNISHMENT FOR CONTEMPT OF THIS COURT.

WITNESS ...., 19...

Aurelia Pucinski
Clerk of Court

Atty No. 407936
Name Alice Beauchamp
Attorney for Lyle Williams
Address 902 N. Michigan Ave. Ste. 1340
City Chicago
Telephone 312-555-6043

I served this subpoena by handing a copy to Miriam Hernández
on September 14, 19 93 I paid the witness
$ 25.00 for witness and mileage fees.

Gayle Tamvakis

Signed and sworn to before me September 14, 19 93.

Maka Elder Notary public

AURELIA PUCINSKI, CLERK OF THE CIRCUIT COURT OF COOK COUNTY

COMPLETE A SUBPOENA

Lyle now must fill out a subpoena for the police officer who issued him the speeding ticket. Use the information below to fill out the subpoena on page 171 as Lyle would.

Police Officer: Philip Long

Police Station: District 7, 6120 S. Racine Avenue, Chicago IL 60636

What he should bring: a record of all speeding tickets given at the same intersection as the speeding ticket he gave Lyle. Lyle's ticket was number 510238.

Where to appear: Judge Alma Black
Room 301
17 N. State Street
Chicago, IL
September 30, 1993
2 p.m.

Complete these sections also. You can copy this information from the subpoena served to Miriam Hernández (page 141).

Case number
Parties involved
Attorney information

Since this subpoena has not been served, that part will be blank.

WORKWISE

Think of a job you have had or would like to have. What kind of legal forms might be involved with that job?

Where is your nearest court? Do the forms used there look like the ones used in this lesson? Call the court and ask if it's possible to observe in a courtroom.

ANSWER KEY

UNIT I: EMPLOYMENT-RELATED FORMS

STARTING A JOB

SKILL PREVIEW
Page 5

Responses may include federal tax forms, state tax forms, medical insurance form, retirement form, citizenship form, dental coverage form, union membership form, life insurance form.

APPLIED PRACTICE 1:
ASKING QUESTIONS ABOUT A TAX FORM
Page 7

Answers will vary. Have your instructor or another student read your questions aloud to be sure that they make sense.

APPLIED PRACTICE 2:
FINDING ANSWERS ON FORM W-4
Page 8

1. You would be exempt from income tax withholding if *all* of the following were true: (1) last year you owed no taxes; (2) this year you expect to owe no taxes; and (3) if you earned more than $600 this year and some of it was nonwage income (such as interest on bank accounts), no one can claim you as a dependent.
2. Answers will vary.

APPLIED PRACTICE 3:
FINDING ANSWERS ON FORM I-9
Page 10

1. A person is legally eligible if he or she is *one* of the following: (1) a U.S. citizen, (2) an alien with permanent residence status, or (3) an alien authorized by the Immigration and Naturalization Service to work in the United States.
2. An employee must show either *one* of the following from List A:
    > passport
    > foreign passport with work permit
    > certificate of U.S. citizenship
    > alien registration card with photo
    > certificate of naturalization

or *two* of the following (one from List B, one from List C):
    > driver's license
    > original Social Security card
    > state ID card
    > authorized birth certificate
    > U.S. military card
    > unexpired INS work permit
    > other ID card
3. the document identification number and the expiration date

APPLIED PRACTICE 4:
COMPLETING A PERSONAL DATA SHEET: STARTING A JOB
Page 12

Check with your instructor to be sure your Personal Data Sheet is correct.

SKILL MASTERY
Page 14

Check with your instructor to be sure your Form W-4 is correct.

TIME SHEETS

SKILL PREVIEW
Page 15

Answers will vary. Be sure you counted each hour you spent in class this week.

APPLIED PRACTICE 1:
READING A TIME SHEET
Page 17

1. $7\frac{1}{2}$
2. Sunday
3. 2; she took more than an hour for lunch on Thursday and Sunday
4. 7:00 P.M.
5. Friday and Saturday
6. Rhonda (the employee) and her supervisor

APPLIED PRACTICE 2:
ADDING DECIMALS TO COMPUTE TOTAL HOURS
Page 19
1. 19.50, or 19.5, hours
2. 12.00, or 12, hours
3. 16.25 hours
4. 31.75 hours

APPLIED PRACTICE 3:
CALCULATING PAY FROM A TIME SHEET
Page 21
1. 8.25 hours × $10.25 = 84.5625, or $84.56
2. 6.25 hours × $10.25 = 64.0625, or $64.06
3. 8.0 + 7.5 + 9.0 + 8.25 + 6.25 = 39.00, or 39, hours
4. 39 hours × $10.25 = 399.75

APPLIED PRACTICE 4:
INTERPRETING A TIME SHEET
Page 23
1. a. the Payroll Department
   b. so that it can issue a check reflecting the correct number of hours
2. the 20th to the 4th
3. the second
4. Northgate
5. she may not get a check
6. no
7. no
8. 3/22, 3/23, 3/24, 3/29, and 3/30

SKILL MASTERY
Page 24
Check with your instructor to be sure you filled the time sheet correctly.

PAYCHECKS
SKILL PREVIEW
Page 25
Answers will vary.

APPLIED PRACTICE 1:
INTERPRETING A PAYSTUB
Page 27
1. 80 hours
2. $1,620.00
3. $5.63
4. no
5. 57236

APPLIED PRACTICE 2:
ADDING MONEY AMOUNTS
Page 28

1. $49.99	6. $216.43
2. $56.50	7. $80.99
3. $748.75	8. $141.29
4. $1,298.00	9. $97.30
5. $504.74	10. $26.99

APPLIED PRACTICE 3:
SUBTRACTING MONEY AMOUNTS
Page 29

1. $84.00	6. $50.25
2. $432.94	7. $14.51
3. $47.35	8. $214.50
4. $114.75	9. $11.80
5. $250.00	10. $84.00

APPLIED PRACTICE 4:
ENDORSING A PAYCHECK
Page 30
You should have signed your name, in cursive, next to the X.

APPLIED PRACTICE 5:
CASHING A PAYCHECK
Page 31
$692.09

APPLIED PRACTICE 6:
FILLING OUT A DEPOSIT SLIP
Page 33
Check with your instructor to be sure you filled out your deposit slip correctly.

Page 34

The paycheck and stub should be filled out like this:

Page 34

DIGITAL PRESS 1474 CONGRESS STREET SAN DIEGO, CA 92110		9783 EMPLOYEE #	12/15/93 PAY DATE

PAY TO THE ORDER OF _Luisa Ortíz_ _430.60_ AMOUNT

Four hundred thirty and 60/100 _____ DOLLARS

PAYABLE THROUGH: FIRST TRUST
494 E. CACTUS
SAN DIEGO, CA

Baxter Jacobs
BAXTER JACOBS, CFO

P A Y	Employee ID #	Name	Social Security Number	Pay Date
	9783	Luisa Ortíz	450-90-8090	12/15/93
S T A T E	Pay Period End	Regular Hours	Overtime Hours	File Number	Department
	12/12/93	72		472417	43

M E N T	This Pay Period Earnings	Deductions		Year to Date
	Gross 540.00	Fed. With. Tax 54.00 FICA 5.40 State With. Tax 16.50		Earnings Fed. With. Tax FICA
	Net 430.60	Union Dues 15.00 Health Plan 18.50		State With. Tax

BENEFITS ON THE JOB

SKILL PREVIEW

Page 35

Answers will vary but may include any of the following: medical insurance, dental insurance, sick leave, retirement benefits, child-care benefits, vacation days, holidays, worker's compensation, union dues, company car, tuition reimbursement, family leave, maternity leave.

APPLIED PRACTICE 1:
EXPLAINING BENEFITS

Page 37

Your wording may vary, but answers should include the following information.

1. when I go on vacation or take several days off
2. When I retire, these payments will become part of my income.
3. when I'm too sick to go to work
4. when I need to go to the doctor or the hospital
5. if I get hurt on the job
6. If I die, my life insurance money will go to my family or other heirs.

APPLIED PRACTICE 2:
FOLLOWING SEQUENTIAL INSTRUCTIONS

Page 38

1. report the injury to the person listed on the notice
2. get medical care by the doctor of his or her choice
3. tell the doctor the injury is work-related

APPLIED PRACTICE 3:
COMPLETING A MEDICAL INSURANCE APPLICATION

Page 40

Check with your instructor to be sure your medical insurance application is correct.

APPLIED PRACTICE 4:
COMPLETING A RETIREMENT ENROLLMENT FORM

Page 42

Check with your instructor to be sure your enrollment form is correct.

1. sick leave
   She will use sick leave time because she's tending her son, who is ill.
2. paid vacation days
   While José is at the conference, he will be paid his regular amount. However, when he's visiting his friend, he will be on vacation.
3. workers' compensation
   Leon's injury occurred on the job. This benefit will pay both his medical costs and his lost wages.
4. life insurance
   Thelma's daughter, the contingent beneficiary, will receive Thelma's life insurance funds because Thelma's husband, the primary beneficiary, was also killed.

UNIT II: PERSONAL FORMS

CREDIT

SKILL PREVIEW
Page 47

1. T	3. T
2. F	4. F

APPLIED PRACTICE 1: UNDERSTANDING CREDIT VOCABULARY
Page 48

Answers will vary. You should have listed a department store, a gas company, or another business in your area that offers credit cards.

APPLIED PRACTICE 2: IDENTIFYING DETAILS WITHIN A TEXT
Page 50

1. yes
2–5. Answers will vary. Check with your instructor to be sure your answers are correct.

APPLIED PRACTICE 3: INTERPRETING CREDIT TERMS
Page 52

1. 21 percent
2. July 31
3. 50¢
4. if the required minimum monthly payment is not paid within 10 days after the due date
5. Your wording may vary, but answers should contain this information: In Ohio, it is illegal for creditors to discriminate against credit applicants if they are creditworthy. Credit reports must be kept on each applicant if the applicant requests it.

APPLIED PRACTICE 4: COMPLETING A PERSONAL DATA SHEET: FINANCIAL
Page 54

Check with your instructor to be sure your personal data sheet is correct.

SKILL MASTERY
Page 56

Check with your instructor to be sure your application is correct.

BILLS AND BUDGETS

SKILL PREVIEW
Page 57

Answers will vary.

APPLIED PRACTICE 1: INTERPRETING A UTILITY BILLING STATEMENT
Page 59

1. water, wastewater, and solid waste
2. the utility company's number: 684-5900
3. so that you can call if you have questions about your bill
4. to figure out ways to conserve water and keep your water bill down
5. you should use the account number assigned to you on your bill

APPLIED PRACTICE 2:
READING A UTILITY BILL
Page 60
1. 847 NE 94th Street
2. water: $17.79
   wastewater: $25.30
   solid waste: $27.50
3. 00186620-005
4. December 2, 1993
5. a. yes
   b. because under the words *Prior Balance Due* are the words *Payment—Thank You.* The prior balance of $83.58 was paid on September 18.

APPLIED PRACTICE 3:
CALCULATING MONTHLY EXPENSES
Page 63
1. $600 a year ÷ 12 months in a year = $50 a month
2. $120 a week × 4 weeks in a month = $480 a month
3. $10 a week × 4 weeks in a month = $40 a month

APPLIED PRACTICE 4:
READING CHARTS FOR INFORMATION
Page 65
1. a. housing
   b. $500
2. $75
3. monthly
4. $1,751
5. No. She spends $191 more than she earns. She earns $1,560, but she spends $1,751. $1751 − $1560 = $191

SKILL MASTERY
Page 66
If you'd like, check with your instructor to be sure your weekly budget chart is filled out correctly.

UNIT III: EDUCATION AND CERTIFICATION FORMS

APPLICATION AND TRAINING FORMS
SKILL PREVIEW
Page 69
Answers will vary.

APPLIED PRACTICE 1:
INTERPRETING PERSONAL EDUCATION RECORDS
Page 70
1. 821-47-9636
2. 12
3. yes
4. employer training at the Resthaven Home in kitchen equipment, the industrial mixer, and commercial machines.

APPLIED PRACTICE 2:
COMPLETING A PERSONAL DATA SHEET: EDUCATION
Page 70
Check with your instructor to be sure that your Personal Data Sheet is correct.

APPLIED PRACTICE 3:
COMPARING CAREER CLUSTERS
Page 73
1. Business and Office
2. Health
3. Answers will vary. However, Hoa wants a job that uses her health and science skills. Health may be the better career cluster for Hoa.
4. If you chose **Health**, you may have listed these reasons: Hoa could use her health and science skills; the health field is growing quickly, so there will be jobs both now and in the future; and Hoa works in a nursing home, so she is familiar with nursing health care.

   If you chose **Business and Office**, your reasons may include the following: Hoa could choose from many different jobs in this career cluster; she could find a job in a business of any type or size; and she will use a computer or a word processor.

Page 75

1. 135 hours
2. by taking and passing an examination
3. Nursing Assistant–Certified
4. Licensed Practical Nurse
5. a high school diploma or a GED, plus the 11-month Licensed Practical Nurse course
6. Nursing Assistant–Certified

APPLIED PRACTICE 5:
COMPARING AND CONTRASTING INFORMATION
Page 77

1. a. Licensed Practical Nurse
   b. LPNs must do more than make beds, serve meals, and bathe patients. They work with registered nurses, doctors, and/or dentists. They care for patients in several different settings.
2. a. Licensed Practical Nurse
   b. More skills and more training are required.
3. a. Nursing Assistant
   b. Nursing Assistants learn fewer job skills than Licensed Practical Nurses.
4. a. Licensed Practical Nurse
   b. Licensed Practical Nurses have more skills.
5. a. Answers will vary.
   b. Be sure you have given reasons for your suggestion.

SKILL MASTERY
Page 78

Check with your instructor to be sure your application is correct.

CERTIFICATION AND LICENSING FORMS
SKILL PREVIEW
Page 79

Answers will vary. You may have listed some of the jobs found on page 80.

APPLIED PRACTICE 1:
INTERPRETING REQUIREMENTS
Page 81

Answers will vary but should contain the following information:

1. Licenses are meant to ensure that people are qualified for their jobs and will serve the public well.
2. Employers can be sure that a person with a license or certificate will have the knowledge and skills to do the job well.
3. A certificate would protect you because you would know what duties were expected of you to perform your job well. You would also know how much you should get paid based on the current standards in your area.
4. If a government agency finds that a licensed person is not maintaining government standards, the agency can take the license or certificate away. The agency can force the person to quit that occupation.

APPLIED PRACTICE 2:
INTERPRETING A CERTIFICATION APPLICATION
Page 82

1. the Oregon State Board of Nursing
2. a. a $22.00 money order and a copy of the applicant's certificate of training
   b. The $22.00 fee probably pays for the costs of processing the application. The copy of the training certificate ensures that the applicant completed the required courses.
3. the applicant's current job (the job the applicant has now or the most recent job held)
4. no

APPLIED PRACTICE 3:
INTERPRETING A LICENSING APPLICATION
Page 84
1. the State of Washington Department of Licensing, Professional Licensing Services, Private Security Guard Section
2. The business address proves you are employed.
3. a. no
   b. for identification
4. current registration as an unarmed security guard, license in another state, or work experience (continuous employment as private security guard)
5. The agency will probably grant a temporary license. The box in the upper right-hand corner of the application tells you this.

APPLIED PRACTICE 4:
GETTING INFORMATION
Page 86
1. Answers will vary. Check with your instructor to be sure you have found the correct information.
2. Questions will vary, but may include the following:
   a. **how:**
      How can I get help finding more information?
      How can I get a job in the field, then request a license?
      How can I pay the fee—with check, charge, or cash?
      How do I decide what kind of training program is best?
      How does the agency decide on the licensing standards?
   b. **why:**
      Why do I have to pay to apply?
      Why does the state get money for this license?
      Why does the state tell schools what to provide in training?
      Why do I have to get a certificate before a license?
   c. **when:**
      When does the paperwork have to be in?
      When will you send me information?
      When will I be qualified for this job?
      When does the license have to be renewed?
      When is the training program offered?
      When will I get my temporary card?

SKILL MASTERY
Page 88
Check with your instructor to be sure your letter requesting information is correct and complete.

UNIT IV: ON-THE-JOB FORMS

ORDER FORMS
SKILL PREVIEW
Page 91
Answers will vary.

APPLIED PRACTICE 1:
TAKING A VERBAL ORDER
Page 93
Answers will vary.

APPLIED PRACTICE 2:
CHECKING A VERBAL ORDER
Page 93
Check with your instructor to be sure the orders you took are clear.

APPLIED PRACTICE 3:
LOCATING INFORMATION ON A COMPLETED ORDER FORM
Page 95
1. $5.00
2. $5.00
3. a. 4218-4
   b. The title number ensures that you order and receive the correct item.
4. because you may order more books if the price is cheaper
5. 10

APPLIED PRACTICE 4: LOCATING INFORMATION IN ADS

Page 97

1. 289WA800
2. eight
3. fifty
4. four
5. four

APPLIED PRACTICE 5: FINDING THE TOTAL COST

Page 98

1. $12 \times \$.89 = \$10.68$
2. $5 \times \$3.99 = \$19.95$
3. $6 \times \$1.29 = \$7.74$

Page 99

4. $72 \times \$.84 = \$60.48$. The unit price is cost *per holder*. There are 12 holders in a dozen, and you're ordering 6 dozen pencil holders. To find the total number of holders, multiply 6 (dozen holders) $\times$ 12 (holders in a dozen). $6 \times 12 = 72$. Next, multiply the total number of holders by the cost per holder. 72 (holders) $\times$ \$.84 (cost per holder) = \$60.48.

APPLIED PRACTICE 6: PROOFREADING YOUR WORK

Page 99

The order form should look like this:

Qty.	Unit (each, doz., etc.)	Reliable Stock #	Color (please specify)	Description	Unit Price	Total
		Y			$1.55	$4.65
3	doz	289RC300Y	Yellow	"White You Were Out" pads	$1.29	$3.87

SKILL MASTERY

Page 100

The order form should look like this:

Page 100

Reliable — The Office Supply People
P.O. Box 6383 · Chicago, IL · 60680-6383

CALL TOLL-FREE 24 HOURS A DAY—7 DAYS A WEEK
1-800-735-4000 PHONE   **1-800-326-3233** FAX

SHIP TO: (Your information here)
Address: _____
City: _____ State: _____ Zip: _____
Attention: _____

Purchase Order No. _____ 4701A _____
Your Name _____
Title _____
Phone (Required): ( ) _____

Qty.	Unit (each, doz., etc.)	Reliable Stock#	Color (please specify)	Description	Unit Price	Total
5	each	289RC700Z		200 set Telephone Message Book	$2.99	$14.95
6	dozen	289RC300Y	Yellow	"While You Were Out" pads	$1.29	$7.74

Every effort is made for this catalog to be totally accurate. However, an occasional printing error may occur. Therefore, we reserve the right to bill at corrected prices.

©1990 THE RELIABLE CORPORATION ALL RIGHTS RESERVED

NOTE: Items with an "NS" prefix will have separate shipping charges.

Sub Total	$22.69
Handling Charge	.99
Sales Tax (IL, GA & NV residents apply applicable tax)	.94
TOTAL	$24.62

150 · USING FORMS AND DOCUMENTS

BILLING FORMS

SKILL PREVIEW
Page 101
Answers will vary but may include the following: when you've been overcharged by the store and want a refund, when something you bought broke and needs repairs, when you want to return an item for a refund or an exchange, when you need to show proof of purchase.

APPLIED PRACTICE 1:
LOCATING INFORMATION ON A SALES RECEIPT
Page 103
1. $1.09
2. 11/30/93, 2:31 P.M.
3. cash
4. $13.35
5. $14.42

6. Martha's Grocery #5
7. 16
8. apple juice
9. $.58
10. Kraft

APPLIED PRACTICE 2:
INTERPRETING AN ORDER FORM
Page 105
1. hand cleaner, single-fold paper towels, blue cloth shop towels
2. Ace Business Supply
3. 9/3/93
4. Loganite
5. PLU 998

APPLIED PRACTICE 3:
TRANSFERRING INFORMATION
Page 107
Your invoice should look like this:

Page 107

CUSTOMER'S ORDER # 765232		SALESPERSON BB	PAYMENT money order		DATE (today's date)
QTY.	ITEM DESCRIPTION		STOCK NO.	UNIT PRICE	PRICE
3	Loganite Primo Citrus Hand Cleaner		LOG 23-225	3.99	11.97
1 case	Plus One Single-Fold Paper Towels		PLU 998	51.95	51.95
				SUBTOTAL	
				TAX	
				TOTAL	

1. no
2. fill in the front of the money order, sign the money order, and address the money order
3. 3 years from the purchase date

4. 2
5. You should have written *Ace Business Supply* on line 2.

SKILL MASTERY
Page 110

Your completed invoice should look like this:

Page 110

	♠ ACE BUSINESS SUPPLY				INVOICE NO.	
					3051	

SOLD TO				SHIPPED TO		
Alberto Ramírez				Alberto's Auto		
STREET & NO.				STREET & NO.		
8376 Aurora Ave. N				same		
CITY	STATE	ZIP		CITY	STATE	ZIP
Albuquerque, NM		87103				

CUSTOMER'S ORDER #	SALESPERSON	PAYMENT	DATE
765232	BB	money order	(today's date)

QTY.	ITEM DESCRIPTION	STOCK NO.	UNIT PRICE	PRICE
3	Loganite Primo Citrus Hand Cleaner	LOG 23.225	3.99	11.97
1 case	Plus One Single-Fold Paper Towels	PLU 998	51.95	51.95
1 case	Durahold Blue Cloth Shop Towels	DUR 236A	45.65	45.65
			SUBTOTAL	109.57
			TAX	8.84
			TOTAL	118.41

UNIT V: LEGAL FORMS AND DOCUMENTS

CONTRACTS AND AGREEMENTS
SKILL PREVIEW
Page 113

Answers will vary but may include the following: renting an apartment, getting a job, hiring someone, selling a car or other item, getting a loan, buying a car, buying a house.

APPLIED PRACTICE 1:
EVALUATING A CONTRACT
Page 115

Answers will vary. Check with your instructor to be sure your answers are correct.

APPLIED PRACTICE 2:
FINDING AND EXPLAINING PARTS OF A CONTRACT
Page 116

1. employment
2. the employee, Stanley R. Evans, has signed the contract
3. a salary of $28,800 plus commission
4. full-time work
5. AA Hardware, Inc. (Jesse Clark), and Stanley R. Evans
6. no

APPLIED PRACTICE 3:
ASKING QUESTIONS FOR CLARIFICATION
Page 119
Your completed chart should look like this:

Page 119

	Offer	Terms (who, what, when, where, price)	Acceptance	Consideration	Defenses (sound mind, legal activity)
1. AA Hardware/ Bam Bang Hammers	✓	✓	✓	✓	✓
2. Elsie Washington/ the Colemans	✓	✓	✓	✓	✗
3. Maria/ Louisa	✓	✗	✓	✗	✓
4. Car Thieves	✓	✓	✓	✓	✗

APPLIED PRACTICE 4:
CONSTRUCTING A WRITTEN CONTRACT
Page 120
Check with your instructor to be sure your written contract is correct.

SKILL MASTERY
Page 122
1. Yes. The contract is complete, and it is for a legal purpose.
2. Rosemary A. Cirelli
3. to deliver five healthy iguanas to Reptiles, Inc., by the second Monday of each month for a year, beginning July 1993.
4. Reptiles, Incorporated
5. to supply 20 wire cages at least 2' × 2' to Rosemary Cirelli for use for one year starting July 1993; to pay Rosemary Cirelli $50 per iguana ($250 per month for five iguanas) by cashier's check upon delivery of iguanas

WARRANTIES
SKILL PREVIEW
Page 123
Answers will vary.

APPLIED PRACTICE 1:
UNDERSTANDING COMMON PARTS OF A WARRANTY
Page 125
1. a. limited
   b. the customer must share the cost of replacement or repair
2. for one year from the date of the original purchase
3. a. the appliance (coffee maker), postpaid and insured
   b. proof of date of original purchase (for instance, the sales receipt or a credit card statement)

4. Answers may include any four of the following: finishes; damage from misuse, accident, dirt, water, tampering, unreasonable use, service by unauthorized agencies, or units modified or used for commercial purposes. This information is located in the paragraph that begins, "This warranty does not cover. . . ."

APPLIED PRACTICE 2: DEFINING AN UNFAMILIAR PHRASE
Page 127

1. individual injuries to property or persons. You can tell that this definition better fits a warranty because of the clue words injuries and property.

2. consequent, or following as an effect or result

3. damages that happen as the result of something

4. Your wording may vary, but answers should contain this information: Braun Inc. will not pay for damages to other products that result from using this Braun product.

APPLIED PRACTICE 3: DEFINING COMMON WARRANTY VOCABULARY
Page 129

If you defined any words other than those in the chart below, check with your instructor to be sure your definitions are correct.

Page 129

WORD/PHRASE IN WARRANTY	DEFINITION	MEANING
defect	an imperfection or lack of something	flaw or problem
defects in material and workmanship	defect: a flaw material: what something is made of or used for workmanship: the quality of a piece of work	a flaw in what the product is made of or the quality of the work
postage prepaid	paid in advance	postage paid in advance
misuse	not used in the best way	treated poorly
abuse	wrong use or treatment	treated badly
in lieu of	in place of	instead
liabilities	legal responsibility	manufacturer's legal responsibility to do something
implied	stated indirectly or by association	stated indirectly
negligence	neglect	bad treatment

APPLIED PRACTICE 4:
MAKING A WARRANTY CLAIM
Page 130
1. a. call the Consumer Assistance Center telephone number
   b. look in the yellow pages under the headings listed
2. Check with your instructor to be sure you have located the correct service franchise.

SKILL MASTERY
Page 132
1. no
2. The tape player was damaged because it was improperly connected to the equipment of other manufacturers.
3. no
4. The tape player was used in a commercial application and could have been misused by the unsupervised children.
5. yes
6. The antenna broke while being used under normal conditions, within 90 days from the date of original purchase.
7. Step 1: pack the tape player in a well-padded cardboard box.
   Step 2: enclose a $9.00 check made out to Emerson Radio Corp.
   Step 3: enclose the sales receipt to show proof of purchase.
   Step 4: pay for shipping; send package by UPS or other insured shipper.

LEGAL NOTICES
SKILL PREVIEW
Page 133
Answers will vary but may include the following: ticket (notice of infraction), warrant, notice of deposition, bail notice, notice of failure to appear, subpoena, summons, notice of hearing, jury duty notice.

APPLIED PRACTICE 1:
ORDERING THE HEARING PROCESS
Page 135
1. Get ticket
2. Send ticket to court
3. Get notice of hearing
4. Prepare defense
5. Request witnesses
6. Have hearing
7. Judge decides case

APPLIED PRACTICE 2:
DEFINING LEGAL VOCABULARY
Page 136
Your wording may vary slightly, but definitions should be similar to the definitions below. If any words you defined are not listed below, check with your instructor to be sure you defined them correctly.

appeal: the transfer or request for transfer of a case from a lower court to a higher court for a new hearing
arraignment: an accusation or charge
atty.: attorney
consideration: careful thought; deliberation
contested: disputed, challenged
defendant: the person against whom a legal action is brought
evidence: the statements and objects examined for judgment in a court of law
examine: to interrogate or question formally to obtain facts
hearing: a formal session for listening to testimony and arguments
infraction: a breach or violation of a law, rule, or regulation
issuance: the act of issuing (to put out; announce)
notification: a letter or other form that makes something known
preponderance: a clear superiority in weight, number, or importance
prosecutor: the person who begins a legal action, especially the public official who represents the state and the people in court
sentencing: the judgment of a court of law; the verdict
subpoena: an order requiring a person to appear in court and give statements
summons: a document ordering a defendant, witness, or juror to appear in court
warrant: a legal paper giving an officer the power to carry out the law

APPLIED PRACTICE 3:
INTERPRETING TWO LEGAL NOTICES
Page 138
1. to tell a person (a defendant) when and where his or her hearing will be
2. people who work at the municipal court
3. to summon a person to appear at court
4. a person who will testify at a hearing

APPLIED PRACTICE 4:
INTERPRETING A COMPLETED SUBPOENA
Page 140
1. to appear and testify at court

Page 142

2. he or she could be punished for contempt of court
3. the person who served, or handed over, the subpoena to Miriam Hernández
4. to guarantee that the subpoena was received by Miriam and that Miriam was paid by Gayle Tamvakis.

SKILL MASTERY
Page 142
The subpoena should look like this:

```
2180 - Served
2280 - Not Served
2380 - Served By Mail                                    (Rev. 12-88) CCG-6
Subpoena - Subpoena Duces Tecum
             IN THE CIRCUIT COURT OF COOK COUNTY, ILLINOIS

        State of Illinois
        County of Cook
        City of Chicago          }
                     v.              No.  7632-3-93
        Lyle Williams
        1310 W. Roscoe
        Chicago, IL 60657
                            SUBPOENA

To:  Philip Long

        YOU ARE COMMANDED to appear to testify before the Honorable  Judge Alma Black
in Room  301  17 North State, Chicago                           Illinois on
September 30        , 19 93 , at   2:00          p.m.
        YOU ARE COMMANDED ALSO to bring the following:
Record of all speeding tickets given at same intersection
as ticket given to defendant (ticket number 510238)
in your possession or control.
        YOUR FAILURE TO APPEAR IN RESPONSE TO THIS SUBPOENA WILL SUBJECT YOU TO
PUNISHMENT FOR CONTEMPT OF THIS COURT.
                            WITNESS                          , 19....
                               Aurelia Pucinski
Atty No. 407936                       Clerk of Court
Name     Alice Beauchamp
Attorney for Lyle Williams
Address  902 N. Michigan Ave. Ste. 1340
City     Chicago
Telephone 312-555-6043
        I served this subpoena by handing a copy to ...............................
..........................on......................, 19... I paid the witness
$............................for witness and mileage fees.
        ......................................
Signed and sworn to before me ............................., 19....
                            ............................Notary public
        AURELIA PUCINSKI, CLERK OF THE CIRCUIT COURT OF COOK COUNTY
```

GLOSSARY

abbreviation: shortened word

acceptance: in a contract, agreement by the person receiving the offer

account balance: the amount of money you have in your bank account

account number: the number a company gives to a customer's account

alien: someone who is not a U.S. citizen

appeal: to ask to bring a legal case from a lower court to a higher court for a new hearing

applicant: person who applies for something

arraignment: an accusation or charge

beneficiary: the person you choose to receive money from your life insurance policy or retirement plan, if you should die before you can collect it

benefit: something an employer provides employees in addition to pay, such as health insurance or paid vacation

benefit package: a list of all the benefits provided by an employer

bill: a piece of paper that shows the amount owed

billing statement: a piece of paper mailed out by a company that shows the amount owed and other information about a customer's account

bind: to hold to an agreement

breach: to break an agreement

budget: a plan for how a person will use his or her money

career cluster: a group of jobs that are related to one another

cash: to cash a paycheck is to receive money, or currency, for the amount written on the check

certificate: a piece of paper that proves that a person has acquired certain skills

clarify: explain something in more detail

consequential damages: damages that happen as a result of something

consideration: in a contract, the exchange of promises by both sides

contest: to challenge in court

contingent beneficiary: the person you name to be your beneficiary, if your primary beneficiary should die

contract: an agreement between people or organizations

credit: a way to buy something now and pay for it at a future date

credit reference: a business or credit card company that can provide information about a person's credit record

creditor: person or business to whom you owe money

currency: dollars and cents

damages: in a warranty, injuries to people or property; in a contract, money lost because of a broken contract

deduction (ded.): money taken out of a paycheck to pay for certain things, such as taxes or benefits

defect: an imperfection, flaw, or lack of something

defendant: the person against whom a legal action is brought

defenses: in a contract, things that make the contract illegal

dental benefits: an insurance plan offered by some employers to pay for dental costs; usually, the employee and the employer each pay a part of the cost (the employee's share is deducted from his or her paycheck)

dependent: a person you support financially, such as a child or spouse

deposit: to add money to a bank account

deposit slip: a form provided by the bank that is filled out to show how much money is being deposited

document (noun): paper or papers with written information about something

document (verb): to put something in writing

education program: a program offered by a school or an employer that teaches people certain knowledge or skills

employment forms: papers that workers must fill out when they start a new job

endorse: to sign your name to the back of a check in order to deposit or cash it

exempt or exemption: to be excused from paying part or all of your taxes

expenses: the amount of money that a person spends

federal withholding tax: money deducted from your paycheck for income taxes paid to the federal government

FICA (Federal Insurance Contributions Act): also known as Social Security, the amount deducted from your paycheck as part of a government insurance program, which is paid back to you after you stop working because of retirement or disability

finance charge: the fee you must pay to a credit card company if you don't pay the entire amount owed on your bill

Form I-9: a form new employees must fill out proving that it is legal for them to work in the United States

Form W-4: a tax form employers use to figure out how much income tax to withhold from an employee's paycheck

full warranty: a company's offer to pay the full cost of repairing or replacing a faulty item

grace period: the period of time before a person must make a payment on a loan or credit card bill

gross pay: total amount of money earned, before deductions

head of household: on Form W-4, a single person with dependents who pays more than one-half of the cost of keeping up a home

hearing: a formal session for listening to testimony and arguments

holiday: a day that companies are closed because of a special reason, such as New Year's Day or Labor Day

identification: a document (such as a driver's license) that proves you are who you say you are

in lieu of: instead of

income: the amount of money that a person earns

income tax withholding form: *see* Form W-4

industrial insurance (workers' compensation): money paid to an employee (in the amount of wages and medical costs) who misses work because of an on-the-job accident

infraction: a breach or violation of the law

interest rate: the percentage of your loan or credit balance that you must pay in addition to the amount borrowed

invoice: a bill given to a business when it makes a purchase

issuance: the act of issuing (to put forth; announce)

legal notice: a document sent by a court or an attorney

liability: something a person or company is legally responsible for

license: a piece of paper that proves that a person or business is capable of doing a certain job in a professional way

life insurance: an insurance plan that pays the beneficiary of the person holding the policy, if that person should die

limited warranty: a company's offer to pay part of the cost of repairing or replacing a faulty item

loan: money that you borrow

major credit card: a card offered by a bank that allows you to buy things at many different businesses and pay for them later

medical benefits: an insurance plan offered by some employers to pay for health care; usually, the employee and the employer each pay a part of the cost (the employee's share is deducted from his or her paycheck)

merchandise: things that are bought or sold

money order: a type of check that guarantees payment to the person or business that receives it

negligence: neglect, or failure to take care of something

net pay: actual amount of a paycheck, after deductions have been subtracted

notification: a letter or notice that makes something known

offer: in a contract, the invitation to exchange goods or services

order form: a form that is filled out when making a purchase

overtime hours (O.T.): hours worked in addition to regular hours

party: in legal terms, a person involved in a contract or court action

paycheck: a check given to an employee as payment for work completed

payment due date: the date a bill must be paid to avoid being charged a late fee

pay period: the amount of time covered by one paycheck

pay statement: an attachment to a paycheck which has information on earnings and deductions

pay stub: a small pay statement

postage prepaid: postage paid in advance

preponderance: a clear superiority in weight, number, or importance

primary beneficiary: the person you name to be your first beneficiary

purchasing: buying (at most workplaces, refers to buying equipment or supplies)

quantity: amount, or number or units

receipt: a written record of a purchase

regular hours (Reg. Hrs.): hours a person is normally scheduled to work

retail credit card: a card offered by a business that allows you to buy things from that business and pay for them later

retirement: the period of time after a person stops working, usually after age 65

retirement plan: a benefit that some employers offer their employees, in which money is deducted from your paycheck and invested in a special account, to be paid back to you with interest after you retire

salary: a regular payment for working a certain number of hours per week or per month

sales slip: receipt

sentencing: the judgment of a court of law; the verdict

service address: the address of a property receiving a utility service

sick leave: paid time off from work used when an employee is sick or caring for a sick family member

state tax: money deducted for income taxes paid to the state government

subpoena: an order requiring a person to appear in court and give statements

sue: to take someone to court

summons: a document ordering a defendant, witness, or juror to appear in court

term: in a contract, refers to a specific detail

testimony: a statement made by a witness under oath, usually in court

time card: a card that a worker punches into a time clock to show what time the worker starts and finishes work

time sheet: a piece of paper on which workers write down how many hours they have worked

training program: a program offered by an employer or school that teaches people certain skills or knowledge

unit: a single item

unit price: the cost per item

utility: a company that provides one of these services: water, gas, electricity, telephone, garbage pickup, or sewer service

vacation: paid time off from work usually spent in recreation

valid: legal

verbal order: to tell someone what you want them to do

wage: payment for work, figured by the hour

warrant: a legal paper giving an officer the power to carry out the law

warranty: a promise made by a company that its product meets a certain standard of quality

withholding allowances: reasons you can give for having less tax withheld from your paycheck

writ: a written legal order signed by a court officer

year to date (YTD): total amount paid from January 1 through the current paycheck

1993 Form W-4

Department of the Treasury
Internal Revenue Service

Purpose. Complete Form W-4 so that your employer can withhold the correct amount of Federal income tax from your pay.

Exemption From Withholding. Read line 7 of the certificate below to see if you can claim exempt status. *If exempt, complete line 7; but do not complete lines 5 and 6.* No Federal income tax will be withheld from your pay. Your exemption is good for one year only. It expires February 15, 1994.

Basic Instructions. Employees who are not exempt should complete the Personal Allowances Worksheet. Additional worksheets are provided on page 2 for employees to adjust their withholding allowances based on itemized deductions, adjustments to income, or two-earner/two-job situations. Complete all worksheets that apply to your situation. The worksheets will help you figure the number of withholding allowances you are entitled to claim. However, you may claim fewer allowances than this.

Head of Household. Generally, you may claim head of household filing status on your tax return only if you are unmarried and pay more than 50% of the costs of keeping up a home for yourself and your dependent(s) or other qualifying individuals.

Nonwage Income. If you have a large amount of nonwage income, such as interest or dividends, you should consider making estimated tax payments using Form 1040-ES. Otherwise, you may find that you owe additional tax at the end of the year.

Two-Earner/Two-Jobs. If you have a working spouse or more than one job, figure the total number of allowances you are entitled to claim on all jobs using worksheets from only one Form W-4. This total should be divided among all jobs. Your withholding will usually be most accurate when all allowances are claimed on the W-4 filed for the highest paying job and zero allowances are claimed for the others.

Advance Earned Income Credit. If you are eligible for this credit, you can receive it added to your paycheck throughout the year. For details, get Form W-5 from your employer.

Check Your Withholding. After your W-4 takes effect, you can use **Pub. 919,** Is My Withholding Correct for 1993?, to see how the dollar amount you are having withheld compares to your estimated total annual tax. Call 1-800-829-3676 to order this publication. Check your local telephone directory for the IRS assistance number if you need further help.

Personal Allowances Worksheet

For 1993, the value of your personal exemption(s) is reduced if your income is over $108,450 ($162,700 if married filing jointly, $135,600 if head of household, or $81,350 if married filing separately). Get Pub. 919 for details.

A   Enter "1" for **yourself** if no one else can claim you as a dependent . . . . **A** _____

B   Enter "1" if:
- You are single and have only one job; or
- You are married, have only one job, and your spouse does not work; or
- Your wages from a second job or your spouse's wages (or the total of both) are $1,000 or less.

. . **B** _____

C   Enter "1" for your **spouse.** But, you may choose to enter -0- if you are married and have either a working spouse or more than one job (this may help you avoid having too little tax withheld) . . . . **C** _____

D   Enter number of **dependents** (other than your spouse or yourself) whom you will claim on your tax return . . . . **D** _____

E   Enter "1" if you will file as **head of household** on your tax return (see conditions under **Head of Household,** above) . **E** _____

F   Enter "1" if you have at least $1,500 of **child or dependent care expenses** for which you plan to claim a credit . . **F** _____

G   Add lines A through F and enter total here. Note: *This amount may be different from the number of exemptions you claim on your return* ▶ **G** _____

For accuracy, do all worksheets that apply.
- If you plan to **itemize or claim adjustments to income** and want to reduce your withholding, see the Deductions and Adjustments Worksheet on page 2.
- If you are **single** and have **more than one job** and your combined earnings from all jobs exceed $30,000 OR if you are **married** and have a **working spouse or more than one job,** and the combined earnings from all jobs exceed $50,000, see the Two-Earner/Two-Job Worksheet on page 2 if you want to avoid having too little tax withheld.
- If **neither** of the above situations applies, **stop here** and enter the number from line G on line 5 of Form W-4 below.

-------- **Cut here and give the certificate to your employer. Keep the top portion for your records.** --------

Form **W-4**
Department of the Treasury
Internal Revenue Service

Employee's Withholding Allowance Certificate

▶ **For Privacy Act and Paperwork Reduction Act Notice, see reverse.**

OMB No. 1545-0010

1993

1 Type or print your first name and middle initial Last name	2 Your social security number

Home address (number and street or rural route)

City or town, state, and ZIP code

3 ☐ Single ☐ Married ☐ Married, but withhold at higher Single rate.
Note: *If married, but legally separated, or spouse is a nonresident alien, check the Single box.*

4   If your last name differs from that on your social security card, check here and call 1-800-772-1213 for more information ▶ ☐

5   Total number of allowances you are claiming (from line G above or from the worksheets on page 2 if they apply) .   **5** _____

6   Additional amount, if any, you want withheld from each paycheck . . . .   **6** $ _____

7   I claim exemption from withholding for 1993 and I certify that I meet **ALL** of the following conditions for exemption:
- Last year I had a right to a refund of **ALL** Federal income tax withheld because I had **NO** tax liability; **AND**
- This year I expect a refund of **ALL** Federal income tax withheld because I expect to have **NO** tax liability; **AND**
- This year if my income exceeds $600 and includes nonwage income, another person cannot claim me as a dependent.

If you meet all of the above conditions, enter "EXEMPT" here . . . . ▶ **7** _____

Under penalties of perjury, I certify that I am entitled to the number of withholding allowances claimed on this certificate or entitled to claim exempt status.

Employee's signature ▶   Date ▶   , 19 ___

8 Employer's name and address (Employer: Complete 8 and 10 only if sending to the IRS)	9 Office code (optional)	10 Employer identification number

Cat. No. 10220Q

Deductions and Adjustments Worksheet

Note: *Use this worksheet only if you plan to itemize deductions or claim adjustments to income on your 1993 tax return.*

1 Enter an estimate of your 1993 itemized deductions. These include: qualifying home mortgage interest, charitable contributions, state and local taxes (but not sales taxes), medical expenses in excess of 7.5% of your income, and miscellaneous deductions. (For 1993, you may have to reduce your itemized deductions if your income is over $108,450 ($54,225 if married filing separately). Get Pub. 919 for details.) **1** $ _____

2 Enter: { $6,200 if married filing jointly or qualifying widow(er)
$5,450 if head of household
$3,700 if single
$3,100 if married filing separately } **2** $ _____

3 **Subtract** line 2 from line 1. If line 2 is greater than line 1, enter -0- **3** $ _____

4 Enter an estimate of your 1993 adjustments to income. These include alimony paid and deductible IRA contributions **4** $ _____

5 **Add** lines 3 and 4 and enter the total **5** $ _____

6 Enter an estimate of your 1993 nonwage income (such as dividends or interest income) **6** $ _____

7 **Subtract** line 6 from line 5. Enter the result, but not less than -0- **7** $ _____

8 **Divide** the amount on line 7 by $2,500 and enter the result here. Drop any fraction **8** _____

9 Enter the number from Personal Allowances Worksheet, line G, on page 1 **9** _____

10 **Add** lines 8 and 9 and enter the total here. If you plan to use the Two-Earner/Two-Job Worksheet, also enter the total on line 1, below. Otherwise, **stop here** and enter this total on Form W-4, line 5, on page 1. **10** _____

Two-Earner/Two-Job Worksheet

Note: *Use this worksheet only if the instructions for line G on page 1 direct you here.*

1 Enter the number from line G on page 1 (or from line 10 above if you used the Deductions and Adjustments Worksheet) **1** _____

2 Find the number in **Table 1** below that applies to the **LOWEST** paying job and enter it here **2** _____

3 If line 1 is **GREATER THAN OR EQUAL TO** line 2, subtract line 2 from line 1. Enter the result here (if zero, enter -0-) and on Form W-4, line 5, on page 1. **DO NOT** use the rest of this worksheet **3** _____

Note: *If line 1 is **LESS THAN** line 2, enter -0- on Form W-4, line 5, on page 1. Complete lines 4-9 to calculate the additional withholding amount necessary to avoid a year-end tax bill.*

4 Enter the number from line 2 of this worksheet **4** _____

5 Enter the number from line 1 of this worksheet **5** _____

6 **Subtract** line 5 from line 4 **6** _____

7 Find the amount in **Table 2** below that applies to the **HIGHEST** paying job and enter it here **7** $ _____

8 **Multiply** line 7 by line 6 and enter the result here. This is the additional annual withholding amount needed **8** $ _____

9 Divide line 8 by the number of pay periods remaining in 1993. (For example, divide by 26 if you are paid every other week and you complete this form in December 1992.) Enter the result here and on Form W-4, line 6, page 1. This is the additional amount to be withheld from each paycheck **9** $ _____

Table 1: Two-Earner/Two-Job Worksheet

Married Filing Jointly		All Others	
If wages from **LOWEST** paying job are—	Enter on line 2 above	If wages from **LOWEST** paying job are—	Enter on line 2 above
0 - $3,000	0	0 - $6,000	0
3,001 - 8,000	1	6,001 - 11,000	1
8,001 - 13,000	2	11,001 - 15,000	2
13,001 - 18,000	3	15,001 - 19,000	3
18,001 - 22,000	4	19,001 - 24,000	4
22,001 - 27,000	5	24,001 - 50,000	5
27,001 - 31,000	6	50,001 and over	6
31,001 - 35,000	7		
35,001 - 40,000	8		
40,001 - 60,000	9		
60,001 - 85,000	10		
85,001 and over	11		

Table 2: Two-Earner/Two-Job Worksheet

Married Filing Jointly		All Others	
If wages from **HIGHEST** paying job are—	Enter on line 7 above	If wages from **HIGHEST** paying job are—	Enter on line 7 above
0 - $50,000	$350	0 - $30,000	$350
50,001 - 100,000	660	30,001 - 60,000	660
100,001 and over	730	60,001 and over	730

Privacy Act and Paperwork Reduction Act Notice.—We ask for the information on this form to carry out the Internal Revenue laws of the United States. The Internal Revenue Code requires this information under sections 3402(f)(2)(A) and 6109 and their regulations. Failure to provide a completed form will result in your being treated as a single person who claims no withholding allowances. Routine uses of this information include giving it to the Department of Justice for civil and criminal litigation and to cities, states, and the District of Columbia for use in administering their tax laws.

The time needed to complete this form will vary depending on individual circumstances. The estimated average time is: **Recordkeeping** 46 min., **Learning about the law or the form** 10 min., **Preparing the form** 69 min. If you have comments concerning the accuracy of these time estimates or suggestions for making this form more simple, we would be happy to hear from you. You can write to both the **Internal Revenue Service,** Washington, DC 20224, Attention: IRS Reports Clearance Officer, T:FP; and the **Office of Management and Budget,** Paperwork Reduction Project (1545-0010), Washington, DC 20503. **DO NOT** send the tax form to either of these offices. Instead, give it to your employer.

☆ **U.S. GOVERNMENT PRINTING OFFICE: 1993 315-082**

EMPLOYMENT ELIGIBILITY VERIFICATION (Form I-9)

1 **EMPLOYEE INFORMATION AND VERIFICATION:** (To be completed and signed by employee.)

Name: (Print or Type) Last	First	Middle	Birth Name
Address: Street Name and Number	City	State	ZIP Code

Date of Birth (Month/Day/Year)	Social Security Number

I attest, under penalty of perjury, that I am (check a box):

☐ 1. A citizen or national of the United States.

☐ 2. An alien lawfully admitted for permanent residence (Alien Number A _____)

☐ 3. An alien authorized by the Immigration and Naturalization Service to work in the United States (Alien Number A _____ ,
or Admission Number _____ , expiration of employment authorization, if any _____) .

I attest, under penalty of perjury, the documents that I have presented as evidence of identity and employment eligibility are genuine and relate to me. I am aware that federal law provides for imprisonment and/or fine for any false statements or use of false documents in connection with this certificate.

Signature	Date (Month/Day/Year)

PREPARER/TRANSLATOR CERTIFICATION (To be completed if prepared by person other than the employee). I attest, under penalty of perjury, that the above was prepared by me at the request of the named individual and is based on all information of which I have any knowledge.

Signature	Name (Print or Type)		
Address (Street Name and Number)	City	State	Zip Code

2 **EMPLOYER REVIEW AND VERIFICATION:** (To be completed and signed by employer.)

Instructions:
Examine one document from List A and check the appropriate box, **OR** examine one document from List B **and** one from List C and check the appropriate boxes.
Provide the **Document Identification Number** and **Expiration Date** for the document checked.

List A Documents that Establish Identity and Employment Eligibility	List B Documents that Establish Identity	**and**	List C Documents that Establish Employment Eligibility
☐ 1. United States Passport	☐ 1. A State-issued driver's license or a State-issued I.D. card with a photograph, or information, including name, sex, date of birth, height, weight, and color of eyes. (Specify State)_____)		☐ 1. Original Social Security Number Card (other than a card stating it is not valid for employment)
☐ 2. Certificate of United States Citizenship			
☐ 3. Certificate of Naturalization	☐ 2. U.S. Military Card		☐ 2. A birth certificate issued by State, county, or municipal authority bearing a seal or other certification
☐ 4. Unexpired foreign passport with attached Employment Authorization	☐ 3. Other (Specify document and issuing authority)		
☐ 5. Alien Registration Card with photograph	_____		☐ 3. Unexpired INS Employment Authorization Specify form # _____
Document Identification # _____	**Document Identification** # _____		**Document Identification** # _____
Expiration Date (if any) _____	**Expiration Date (if any)** _____		**Expiration Date (if any)** _____

CERTIFICATION: I attest, under penalty of perjury, that I have examined the documents presented by the above individual, that they appear to be genuine and to relate to the individual named, and that the individual, to the best of my knowledge, is eligible to work in the United States.

Signature	Name (Print or Type)	Title
Employer Name	Address	Date

Form I-9 (05/07/87)
OMB No. 1115-0136

U.S. Department of Justice
Immigration and Naturalization Service

Employment Eligibility Verification

> **NOTICE:** Authority for collecting the information on this form is in Title 8, United States Code, Section 1324A, which requires employers to verify employment eligibility of individuals on a form approved by the Attorney General. This form will be used to verify the individual's eligibility for employment in the United States. Failure to present this form for inspection to officers of the Immigration and Naturalization Service or Department of Labor within the time period specified by regulation, or improper completion or retention of this form, may be a violation of the above law and may result in a civil money penalty.

Section 1. Instructions to Employee/Preparer for completing this form

Instructions for the employee.

All employees, upon being hired, must complete Section 1 of this form. Any person hired after November 6, 1986 must complete this form. (For the purpose of completion of this form the term "hired" applies to those employed, recruited or referred for a fee.)

All employees must print or type their complete name, address, date of birth, and Social Security Number. The block which correctly indicates the employee's immigration status must be checked. If the second block is checked, the employee's Alien Registration Number must be provided. If the third block is checked, the employee's Alien Registration Number *or* Admission Number must be provided, as well as the date of expiration of that status, if it expires.

All employees whose present names differ from birth names, because of marriage or other reasons, must print or type their birth names in the appropriate space of Section 1. Also, employees whose names change after employment verification should report these changes to their employer.

All employees must sign and date the form.

Instructions for the preparer of the form, if not the employee.

If a person assists the employee with completing this form, the preparer must certify the form by signing it and printing or typing his or her complete name and address.

Section 2. Instructions to Employer for completing this form

(For the purpose of completion of this form, the term "employer" applies to employers and those who recruit or refer for a fee.)

Employers must complete this section by examining evidence of identity and employment eligibility, and:
- checking the appropriate box in List A *or* boxes in both Lists B and C;
- recording the document identification number and expiration date (if any);
- recording the type of form if not specifically identified in the list;
- signing the certification section.

NOTE: Employers are responsible for reverifying employment eligibility of employees whose employment eligibility documents carry an expiration date.

Copies of documentation presented by an individual for the purpose of establishing identity and employment eligibility may be copied and retained for the purpose of complying with the requirements of this form and no other purpose. Any copies of documentation made for this purpose should be maintained with this form.

Name changes of employees which occur after preparation of this form should be recorded on the form by lining through the old name, printing the new name and the reason (such as marriage), and dating and initialing the changes. Employers should not attempt to delete or erase the old name in any fashion.

RETENTION OF RECORDS.

The completed form must be retained by the employer for:
- three years after the date of hiring; or
- one year after the date the employment is terminated, whichever is later.

> Employers may photocopy or reprint this form as necessary.

U.S. Department of Justice
Immigration and Naturalization Service

OMB #1115-0136
Form I-9 (05/07/87)

PERSONAL DATA SHEET: STARTING A JOB

Name: _____ Birth Date: _____ / _____ / _____
       Last   First   Middle

Birth/Maiden Name: _____

Address: _____ Phone (___) _____
         Street

         _____
         City   State   Zip

SS# _____ - ____ - _____

Citizenship Status: ❏   U.S. Citizen or National
(check one box)

                         ❏   Alien: Permanent Resident

                         ❏   Alien: Work Permit

Marital Status: ❏   Married
(check one box)

                     ❏   Single

Spouse's income: $1,000 or less   ❏   Yes

                                     ❏   No

Number of Dependents (people you support financially): _____

Head of Household: ❏   Yes   ❏   No
(see definition on page 63)

Child-Care Expenses: Over $1,500 per year?   ❏   Yes

                                                ❏   No

PERSONAL DATA SHEET: FINANCIAL

PERSONAL INFORMATION

Name: _____ SS#: ____ - __ - ____ Birth Date __/__/__
       Last   First   Middle Initial

Present Address: _____
       Street   City   State   Zip

How long at present address? _____

Past Address: _____
       Street   City   State   Zip

How long at past address? _____

Telephone Number: (home) _____(work) _____

Number of Dependents: _____ Age of Dependents: _____

Citizenship Status: _____ U.S. Visa # _____ Type _____

Spouse's Name: _____ SS#: ____ - __ - ____
       Last   First   Middle Initial

Spouse's Employer: _____
       Employer Name   Employer Address   Phone

EMPLOYMENT INFORMATION

Current Employer: _____
       Employer Name   Employer Address   Phone

Job Title: _____ Length of time employed ___ years ___ months Monthly Salary: _____

Past Employer: _____
       Employer Name   Employer Address   Phone

Job Title: _____ Length of time employed ___ years ___ months Monthly Salary: _____

FINANCIAL INFORMATION

Bank: _____
       Bank Name   Bank Address

Account Type: __ Checking __Savings __Loan __Other Account Number _____

Bank: _____
       Bank Name   Bank Address

Account Type: __ Checking __Savings __Loan __Other Account Number _____

CREDIT REFERENCES

	Creditor	Address	Account #
1.	_____	_____	_____
2.	_____	_____	_____
3.	_____	_____	_____

MONTHLY BUDGET FORM			
Budget Category	**Paid How Often?**	**Amount**	**Monthly Amount**
Total Monthly Amount			

PERSONAL DATA SHEET: EDUCATION

Name: _____ SS# _____ - ___ - _____
last   first   middle

Present Address: _____
street

_____
city   state   zip

Birth Date: ____/____/____ Phone: _____

U.S. Citizen _____ Yes _____ No Visa # _____ Type _____

Highest grade completed _____

	School Name City, State	**Courses**	**Completed: Mo/Yr**
High School		Favorite Study Areas:	
GED		Favorite Study Areas:	
Technical or Trade School			
Community College			
Military Training			
Employer Training			

Articles of Agreement,

Between   Rosemary A. Cirelli
Route 3 Box 202A
Gaston, OR 97119

of the first part,

and   Reptiles, Incorporated
Jack Rusin, Owner
624 9th Ave SW
Portland, OR 97205

of the second part.

The party of the first part, in consideration of

     $50.00 per iguana

   agrees to

   supply 5 iguanas per month to the party of
the second part. The iguanas will be in good
health and delivered to Reptiles, Inc. by the
second Monday of each month for one year,
beginning in July, 1993.

The party of the second part, in consideration of

   supplying 20 wire cages at least 2'×2' to the
party of the first part for use for the duration
of this contract.

   agrees to

   pay the party of the first part $50.00 per
iguana, for a total of $250.00 per month.
Payment will be made by cashier's check and is
due upon delivery of the iguanas.

This instrument may not be changed orally.

In Witness Whereof, *the parties hereunto have set their hands and seals the*
twenty-first   *day of*   May   *in the year one thousand nine*
hundred and   ninety-three.

Sealed and delivered in the presence of

Rosemary A. Cirelli

Jack Rusin

```
**************** EMERSON LIMITED WARRANTY *****************
*                        AUDIO                                              *
*                                                                           *
*                                                                           *
*  Emerson Radio Corp. warrants this product to be free from defects in material and workmanship under  *
*  normal use and conditions for a period of 90 days from date of original purchase.  *
*                                                                           *
*  Should service be necessary under this warranty for any reason due to manufacturing defect or malfunc-  *
*  tion during this 90 day period, Emerson Radio Corp. will provide carry-in repair service at an Emerson  *
*  Authorized Service Agency at no charge.                                  *
*                                                                           *
*  There are Emerson Authorized Service Agencies located throughout the country. For the one nearest  *
*  you, DIAL TOLL FREE: 1-800-537-5373.                                     *
*                                                                           *
*  In the event there is no local Emerson Authorized Service Agency, you may return the unit to the  *
*  Emerson Factory Service Center* listed below.                            *
*        *   Pack the unit in a well-padded heavy corrugated box.           *
*        *   Enclose your check or money order payable to Emerson Radio Corp. in the amount of $9.00  *
*            to cover shipping and handling costs.                          *
*        *   Enclose proof of purchase.                                     *
*        *   Ship the unit prepaid via UPS or parcel post (insured)         *
*                                                                           *
*  Note: This warranty is void if the product is:                          *
*        (a)  Damaged through negligence, misuse, abuse, or accident.       *
*        (b)  Used in a commercial application or rentals.                  *
*        (c)  Modified or repaired by anyone other than an Authorized Emerson Radio Corp. Service  *
*             Agency or Factory Service Center.                             *
*        (d)  Damaged because it is improperly connected to the equipment of other manufacturers.  *
*                                                                           *
*  This warranty does not cover:                                           *
*        (a)  Damage to tape cartridge (if applicable)                      *
*        (b)  Damage to the equipment of other manufacturers not properly connected to the product.  *
*        (c)  Costs incurred in the shipping of the product to an Authorized Emerson Radio Corp. Service  *
*             Agency or Emerson Factory Service Center.                     *
*        (d)  Damage or improper operation of unit caused by customer abuse, misuse, negligence, or  *
*             failure to follow operating instructions provided with the product.  *
*        (e)  Ordinary adjustments to the product which can be performed by customer as outlined in the  *
*             owners manual.                                                *
*                                                                           *
*  THIS WARRANTY IS VALID ONLY IN THE UNITED STATES OF AMERICA.  IT IS NON-  *
*  TRANSFERABLE AND APPLIES ONLY TO THE ORIGINAL PURCHASER AND DOES NOT  *
*  EXTEND TO SUBSEQUENT OWNERS OF THE PRODUCT. ANY APPLICABLE IMPLIED WARRAN-  *
*  TIES, INCLUDING THE WARRANTY OF MERCHANTABILITY, ARE LIMITED IN DURATION TO A  *
*  PERIOD OF THE EXPRESS WARRANTY AS PROVIDED HEREIN BEGINNING WITH THE DATE OF  *
*  ORIGINAL PURCHASE AT RETAIL AND NO WARRANTIES, WHETHER EXPRESS OR IMPLIED  *
*  SHALL APPLY TO THIS PRODUCT THEREAFTER.                                  *
*                                                                           *
*  UNDER NO CIRCUMSTANCES SHALL EMERSON RADIO CORP. BE LIABLE FOR ANY LOSS,  *
*  DIRECT, INDIRECT, INCIDENTAL, SPECIAL, OR CONSEQUENTIAL DAMAGE ARISING OUT OF  *
*  OR IN CONNECTION WITH THE USE OF THIS PRODUCT.  (SOME STATES DO NOT ALLOW  *
*  LIMITATION ON IMPLIED WARRANTIES OR EXCLUSION OF CONSEQUENTIAL DAMAGE,  *
*  THEREFORE THESE RESTRICTIONS MAY NOT APPLY TO YOU.)                      *
*                                                                           *
*  THIS WARRANTY GIVES YOU SPECIFIC LEGAL RIGHTS, HOWEVER, YOU MAY HAVE OTHER  *
*  RIGHTS WHICH MAY VARY FROM STATE TO STATE                               *
*                                                                           *
*                        *EMERSON RADIO CORP                                *
*              STATE HIGHWAY #41 & COUNTY ROAD, 100W.                       *
*                        PRINCETON, IN 47670                                *
*************************************************************
                                                           P/N. AU589F
```

IN THE CIRCUIT COURT OF COOK COUNTY, ILLINOIS

v.   }   No. ....

SUBPOENA

To:

    YOU ARE COMMANDED to appear to testify before the Honorable ....

in Room ...., ... Illinois on

........................., 19...., at ....m.

    YOU ARE COMMANDED ALSO to bring the following:

in your possession or control.

    YOUR FAILURE TO APPEAR IN RESPONSE TO THIS SUBPOENA WILL SUBJECT YOU TO PUNISHMENT FOR CONTEMPT OF THIS COURT.

            WITNESS ...., 19....

           .... *Aurelia Pucinski* ....
                        Clerk of Court

Atty No.
Name
Attorney for
Address
City
Telephone

    I served this subpoena by handing a copy to ....

.............................on..............................., 19... I paid the witness

S..............................for witness and mileage fees.

                 ....

Signed and sworn to before me ....,19....

                        ....Notary public

AURELIA PUCINSKI, CLERK OF THE CIRCUIT COURT OF COOK COUNTY

Contents
Consonants

Long Vowels

UNIT 3

Theme: Let's Play

UNIT 4

Consonant Blends, Y as a Vowel

Theme: Everybody Eats

Endings, Digraphs, Contractions
Theme: Whatever the Weather

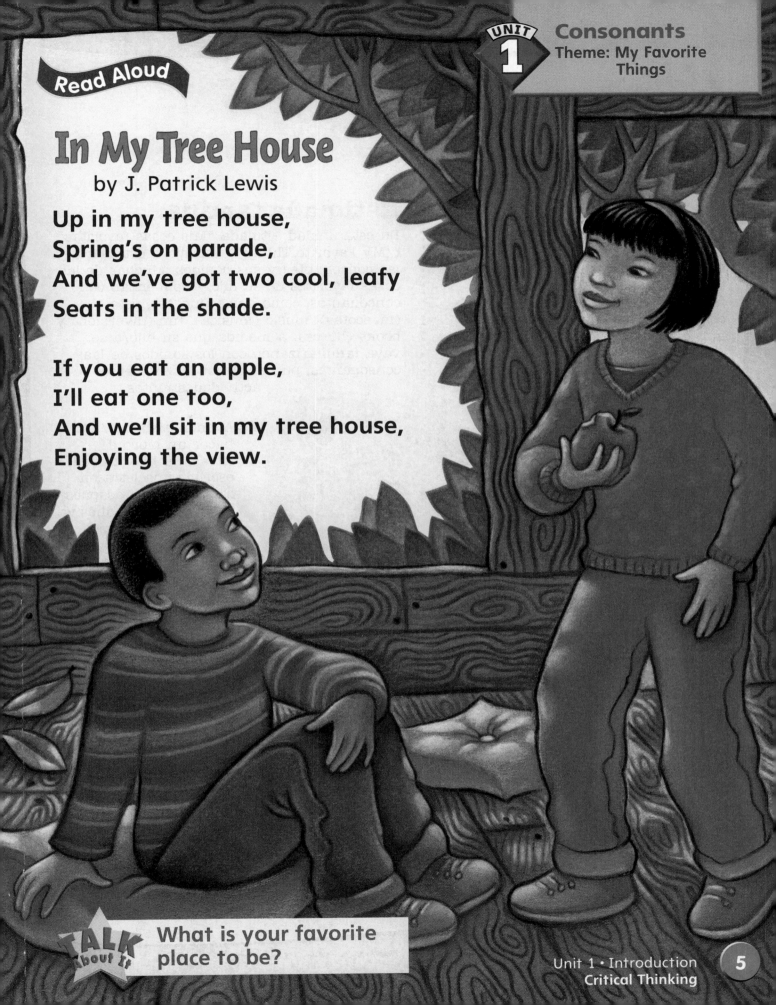

In My Tree House
by J. Patrick Lewis

Up in my tree house,
Spring's on parade,
And we've got two cool, leafy
Seats in the shade.

If you eat an apple,
I'll eat one too,
And we'll sit in my tree house,
Enjoying the view.

TALK About It What is your favorite place to be?

Dear Family,

In this unit about "My Favorite Things," your child will be learning about consonants and the sounds they make. Many of your child's favorite things begin with consonants, such as home, pets, music, fun, and books. As your child becomes familiar with consonant sounds, you might try these activities together.

▶ Help your child make a Letter Book. Your child can print a letter on each page, then tape or glue on pictures that begin with that letter.

▶ Read the poem on page 5 aloud. Help your child to identify the consonants at the beginning of words such as house and view.

▶ Your child might enjoy reading these books with you. Look for them in your local library.

The Very Hungry Caterpillar by Eric Carle

A Pocket for Corduroy by Don Freeman

Sincerely,

_____

Estimada familia:

En esta unidad, titulada "Mis cosas favoritas" ("My Favorite Things"), su hijo/a estudiará las consonantes y sus sonidos. Muchas de las cosas favoritas de su hijo/a comienzan con consonantes, como home (juegos), pets (mascotas), music (música), fun (diversión) y books (libros). A medida que su hijo/a se vaya familiarizando con los sonidos de las consonantes, pueden hacer las siguientes actividades juntos.

▶ Ayuden a su hijo/a a hacer un Libro de letras. Su hijo/a puede escribir una letra en cada página y después unir con cinta adhesiva o pegamento dibujos que comiencen con esa letra.

▶ Lean en voz alta el poema en la página 5. Ayuden a su hijo/a a identificar las consonantes al principio de palabras como house (casa) y view (vista).

▶ Ustedes y su hijo/a disfrutarán leyendo estos libros juntos. Búsquenlos en su biblioteca local.

The Very Hungry Caterpillar de Eric Carle

A Pocket for Corduroy de Don Freeman

Sinceramente,

_____

Name _____

Bb go together.
Bb are partner letters.

▶ **Color** **each ball that has partner letters on it.**

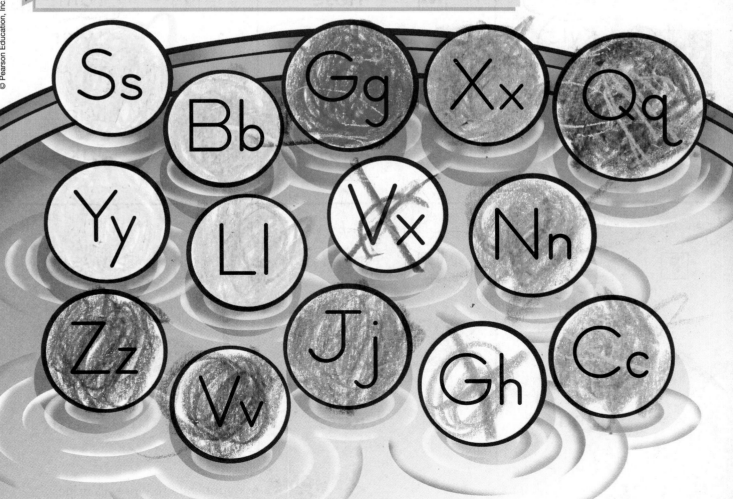

Look at the letter above each picture. Circle each word that begins with its partner letter.

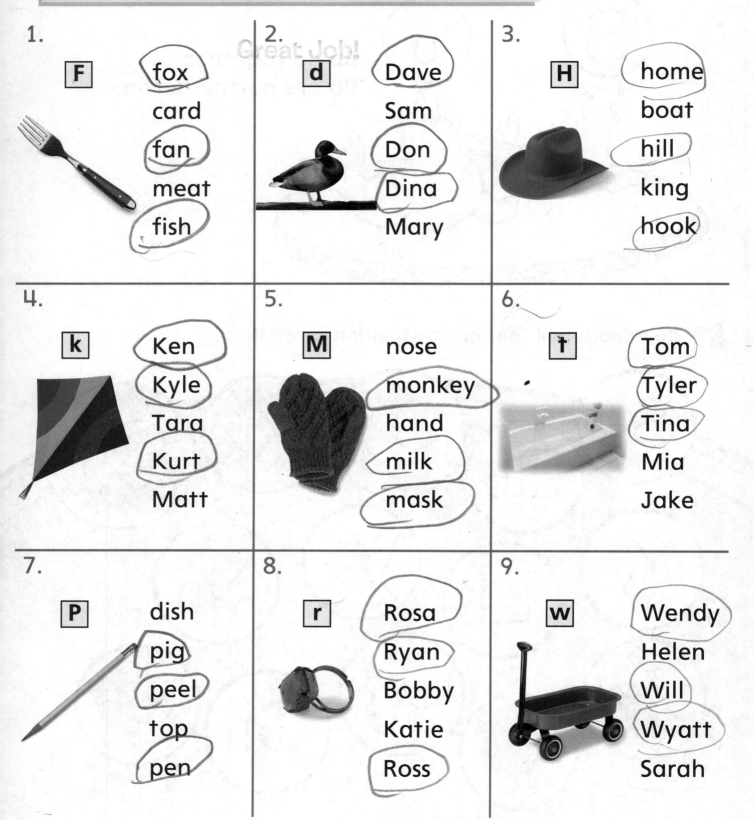

1. **F** — (fox), card, (fan), meat, (fish)

2. **d** — (Dave), Sam, (Don), (Dina), Mary

3. **H** — (home), boat, (hill), king, (hook)

4. **k** — (Ken), (Kyle), Tara, (Kurt), Matt

5. **M** — nose, (monkey), hand, (milk), (mask)

6. **t** — (Tom), (Tyler), (Tina), Mia, Jake

7. **P** — dish, (pig), (peel), top, (pen)

8. **r** — (Rosa), (Ryan), Bobby, Katie, (Ross)

9. **w** — (Wendy), Helen, (Will), (Wyatt), Sarah

 Ask your child to write his or her name, then write partner letters for each consonant.

Name _____

Suzy sat on the sand.
Suzy sat by the sea.
Suzy sat in the sun.
Suzy sat with me.

Sand begins with the sound of **s**. Circle each picture whose name begins with the sound of **s**.

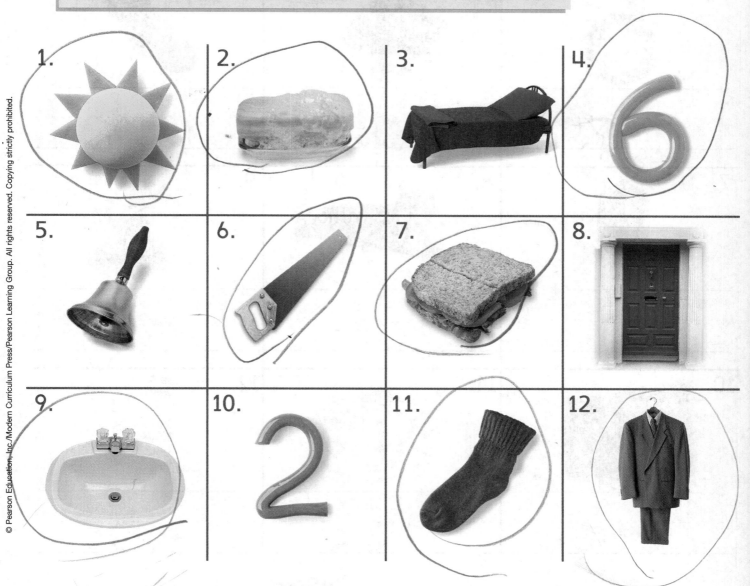

The sound of s: Phonemic awareness

Say the name of each picture. If it begins with the sound of **s**, print **s** on the line. Then trace the whole word.

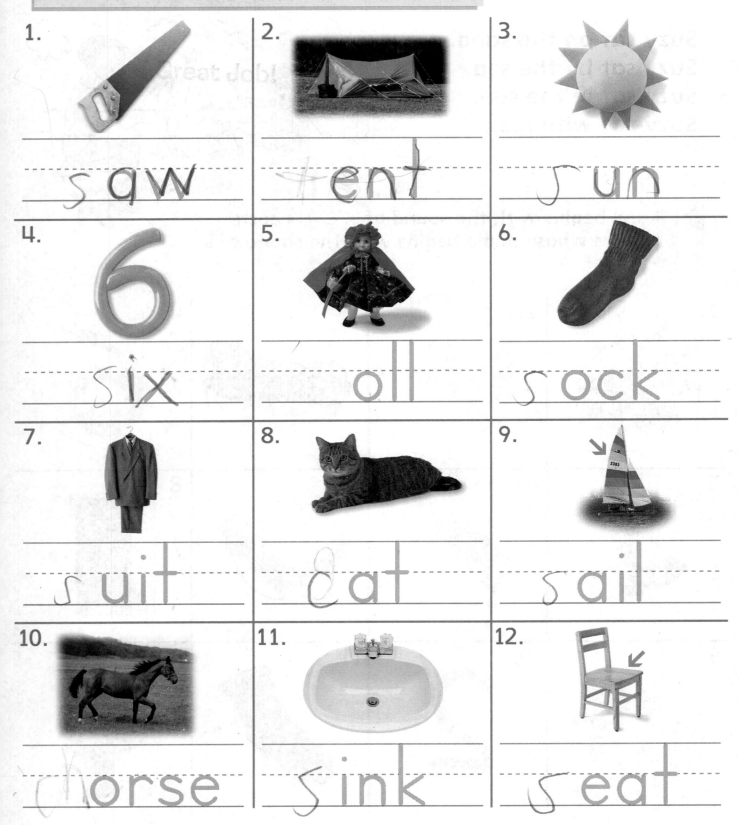

1. s a w

2. t ent

3. s un

4. s ix

5. oll

6. s ock

7. s uit

8. cat

9. s ail

10. horse

11. s ink

12. s eat

10   The sound of s: Sound to symbol

 HOME

Say, "Sister Sue sells ____." Ask your child to finish the sentence with words that begin with s.

Name_____

Ten toy tigers
Sat down for tea.
Ten tails tipped the table—
Oh, dear me!

> Tea **begins with the sound of t.** Circle **each
> picture whose name begins with the sound of t.**

Say the name of each picture. If it begins with the sound of **t**, print **t** on the line. Then trace the whole word.

1. top

2. tire

3. aw

4. tent

5. tape

6. bed

7. ten

8. Tack

9. tub

10. ose

11. toys

12. sun

Ask your child to name three objects in your home that begin with the sound of *t*.

Name _____

Let's bounce the ball high,
Let's bounce the ball low.
Let's bounce the ball fast,
Let's bounce the ball slow.

Great Job!

> **Ball** begins with the sound of **b**. **Circle** each picture whose name begins with the sound of **b**.

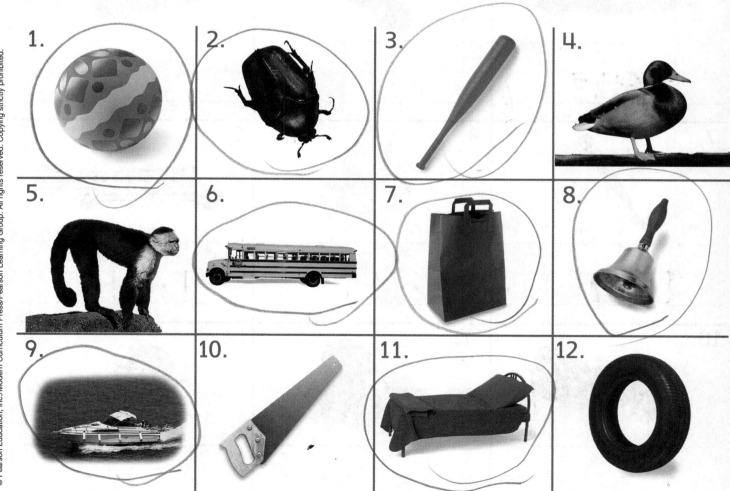

1.

2.

3.

4.

5.

6.

7.

8.

9.

10.

11.

12.

Say the name of each picture. If it begins with the sound of **b**, print **b** on the line. Then trace the whole word.

1. bag

2. boat

3. ball

4. belt

5. ock

6. box

7. bat

8. un

9. bus

10. bed

11. oys

12. bug

Say "Buddy bought a ___." Ask your child to add a word that begins with the sound of *b*.

Name _____

Say the name of each picture. If the name **begins** with the sound of the letter in the box, print it on the first line. If it **ends** with that sound, print it on the second line.

1. **b**

b | o

2. **t**

i | t

3. **s**

b | s

4. **b**

b

5. **t**

T

6. **b**

b

7. **s**

s

8. **b**

b

9. **b**

b | s

10. **s**

s

11. **t**

t

12. **s**

s

Say each picture name. Draw a line through the pictures in a row that begin with the same letter sound. Write the letter that wins in each game.

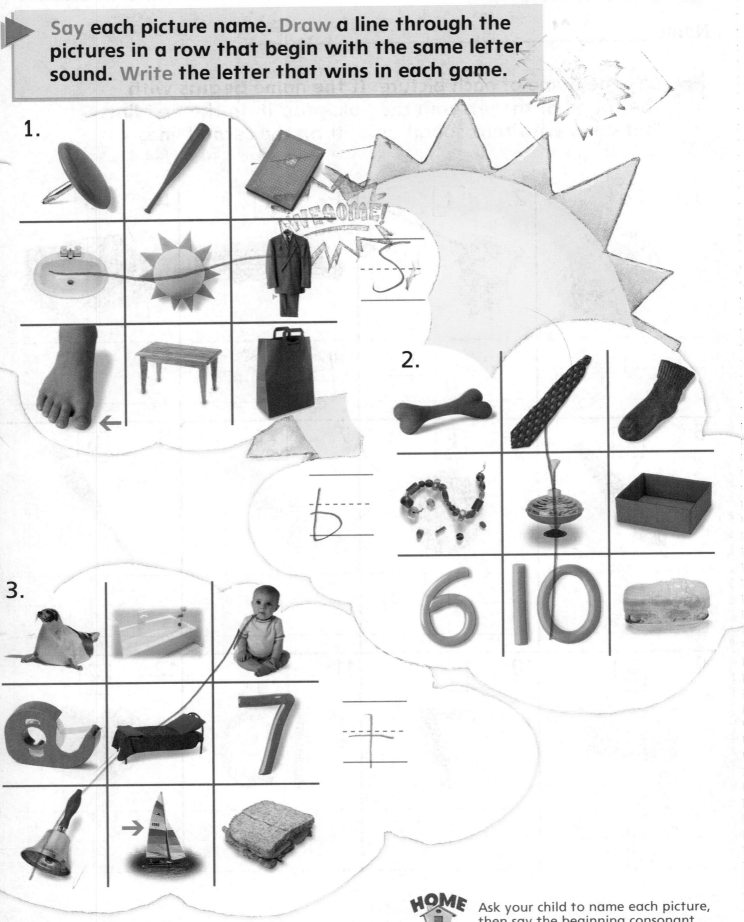

1.

2.

3.

Initial consonants s, t, b

HOME

Ask your child to name each picture, then say the beginning consonant for the picture name.

Name _____

My hamster has been running
On his wheel since half past five.
He's gone a hundred miles by now,
So when will he arrive?

> Hamster **begins with the sound of h.** Say **the name of each picture.** Circle **the beginning letter of the picture name. Then** circle **each picture whose name begins with the sound of h.**

1.
S
T
B
(H)

2.
T
B
(H)
S

3.
B
H
S
(T)

4.
(S)
H
T
B

5.
B
T
(H)
S

6.
T
(H)
S
B

Say the name of each picture. If it begins with the sound of **h**, print **h** on the line. Then trace the whole word.

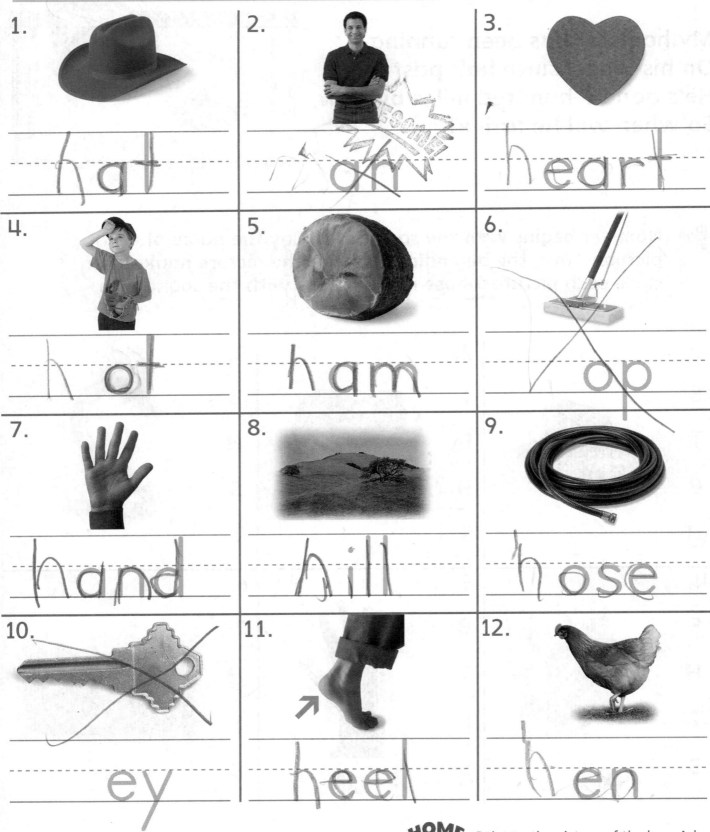

1. hat

2. an

3. heart

4. hot

5. ham

6. op

7. hand

8. hill

9. hose

10. ey

11. heel

12. hen

HOME

Point to the picture of the hen. Ask your child to think of other animals whose names begin with *h*.

Name _____

Mom gave me a muffin for lunch.
Mom gave me a muffin to munch.
The muffin I munched was yummy.
The muffin is in my tummy.

> **Mom begins with the sound of m.** Circle each picture whose name begins with the sound of **m.**

1. 	2. 	3. 	4. 
5. 	6. 	7. 	8. 
9. 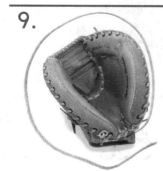	10. 	11. 	12. 

Say the name of each picture. If it begins with the sound of **m**, print **m** on the line. Then trace the whole word.

1.
moon

2.
mop

3.
mask

4.
all

5.
ix

6.
man

7.
mouse

8.
Map

9.
milk

10.
op

11.
eart

12.
meat

HOME
Point to a picture. Have your child say its name and then think of a word that begins with the same sound.

Name _____

Where's Katy's kite?
Where's Katy's key?
Where's Katy's kitty?
Katy has lost all three!

Kite begins with the sound of k. Say the name of each picture. Circle the beginning letter of the picture name. Then circle each picture whose name begins with the sound of k.

1.
H
M
Ⓚ
T
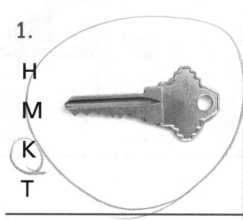

2.
M
Ⓚ
T
H

3.
K
T
Ⓗ
M
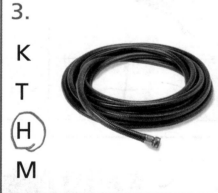

4.
T
Ⓚ
M
H

5.
H
Ⓜ
K
T

6.
T
H
M
Ⓚ

The sound of k: Phonemic awareness   **21**

Say the name of each picture. If it begins with the sound of **k**, print **k** on the line. Then trace the whole word.

1. Key

2. ike

3. King

4. ook

5. Kite

6. ork

7. ilk

8. Kitten

9. Kitchen

10. Ketchup

The sound of k: Sound to symbol

HOME Taking turns with your child, think of more words that begin with the sound of k, such as *keep* and *kind*.

Name _____

Say the name of each picture. Find the beginning letter of each picture name. Circle that letter.

1.
(H) M K

2.
M (K) H

3.
K H (M)

4.
H (M) K

5.
(K) M H

6.
M (H) K

7.
H K (M)

8.
(K) M H

9.
M (H) K

10.
H (K) M

11.
K M (H)

12.
(M) H K

Say the name of each picture. If the name **begins** with the sound of the letter in the box, print it on the first line. If it **ends** with that sound, print it on the second line.

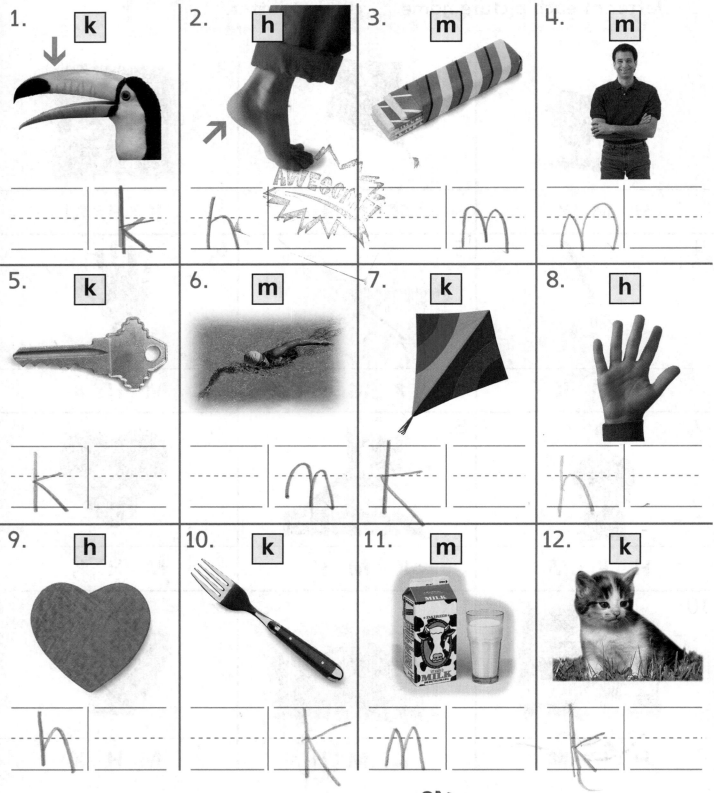

1. k — k

2. h — h

3. m — m

4. m — m

5. k — k

6. m — m

7. k — k

8. h — h

9. h — h

10. k — k

11. m — m

12. k — k

24   Initial/final consonants h, m, k

HOME Ask your child to name two pictures that begin with the same sound and two that end with the same sound.

Name _____

Joy can pick a prize.
It will be hers to keep.
Will she take the jacks or the jet,
The jump rope or the jeep?

> **Jeep begins with the sound of j. Circle each picture whose name begins with the sound of j.**

1.

2.

3.

4.
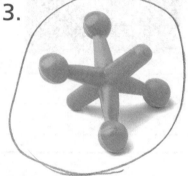

5.

6.

7.

8.

9.

Say the name of each picture. If it begins with the sound of **j**, print **j** on the line. Then trace the whole word.

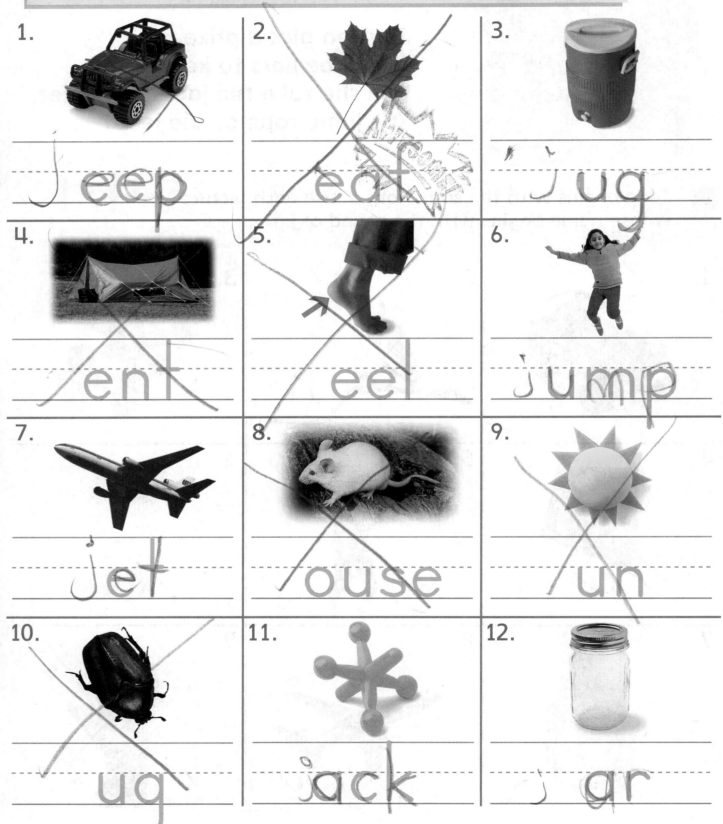

1. j eep

2. eaf

3. j ug

4. ent

5. eel

6. j ump

7. j et

8. ouse

9. un

10. ug

11. j ack

12. j ar

The sound of j: Sound to symbol

 HOME

Help your child think of sentences using words that begin with *j*, such as *Joe juggled the jacks.*

Name _____

Five furry foxes
Fanning in the heat.
They all run away
On furry fox feet.

> **Five** begins with the sound of **f.** Circle each
> picture whose name begins with the sound of **f.**

1.

2.

3.

4.

5.

6.

7.

8.

9.

10.

11.

12.

Say the name of each picture. If it begins with the sound of **f**, print **f** on the line. Then trace the whole word.

1. fish

2. _eaf

3. four

4. feet

5. five

6. fan

7. _ail

8. fork

9. fence

10. _amp

11. fox

12. fire

HOME

Make up riddles for your child to answer with words from the page, such as *What rhymes with box?* (*fox*)

Name _____

Get the gifts.
Do not be late.
Run to the garden,
And open the gate.

> **Garden** begins with the sound of **g**. Circle each picture whose name begins with the sound of **g**.

1.

2.

3.

4.

5.

6.

7.

8.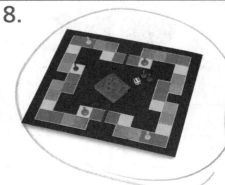

9.

The sound of g: Phonemic awareness **29**

Say the name of each picture. If it begins with the sound of **g**, print **g** on the line. Then trace the whole word.

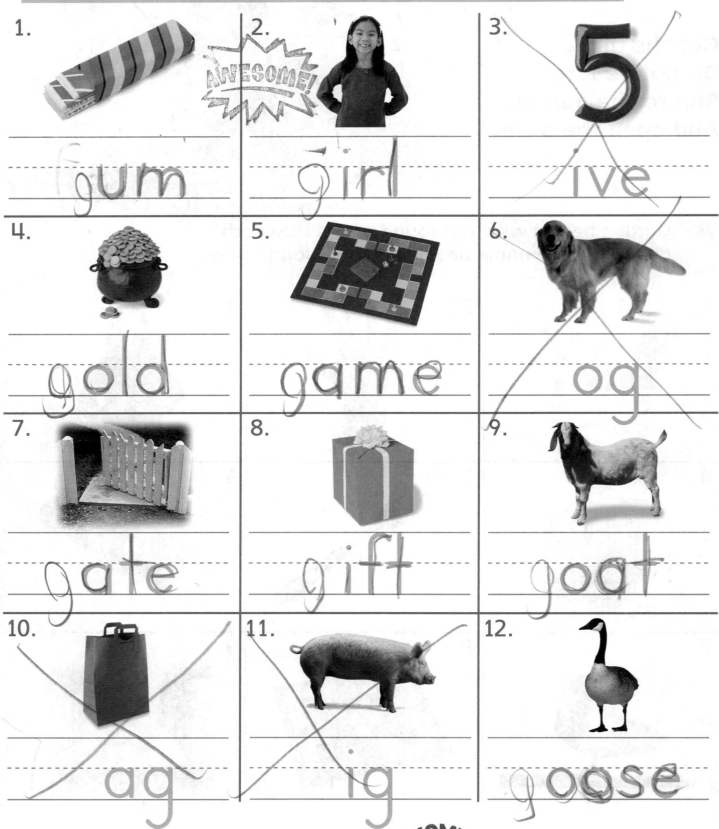

1. gum

2. girl

3. five

4. gold

5. game

6. og

7. gate

8. gift

9. goat

10. ag

11. ig

12. goose

The sound of g: Sound to symbol

Invite your child to think of more words that begin with *g* such as *go, get, good, give.*

Name _____

> Say the name of each picture. If the name **begins** with the sound of the letter in the box, print it on the first line. If it **ends** with that sound, print it on the second line.

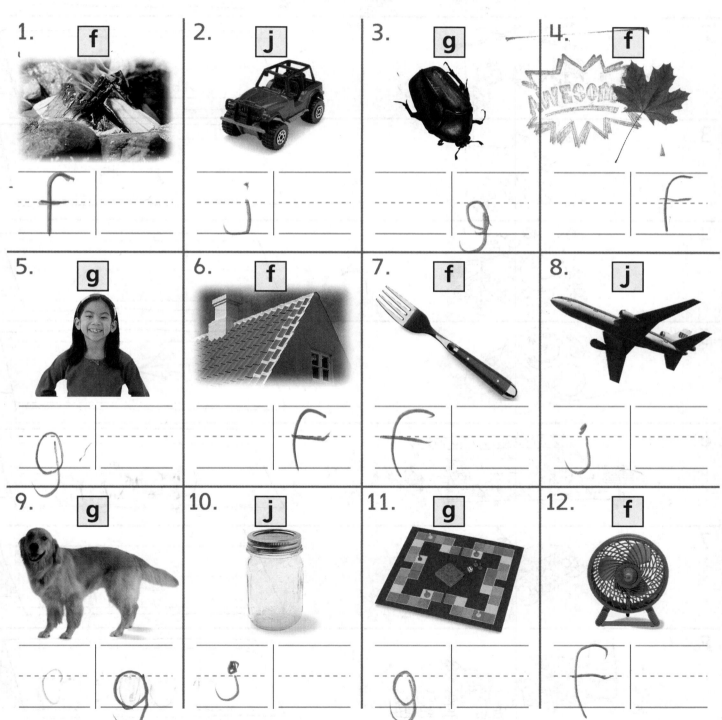

1. f — f

2. j — j

3. g — g

4. f — f

5. g — g

6. f — f

7. f — f

8. j — j

9. g — g

10. j — j

11. g — g

12. f — f

Say the name of each toy. Print a letter to finish the word on each sign. Then trace the word.

1. 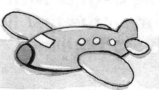 jet

2.  fish

3.  goat

4. bug

5. dog

6.  game

7. 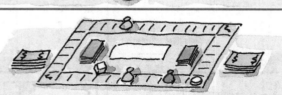 jeep

8.  farm

 HOME
Ask your child to finish sentences using words from the page, such as *Cows and ducks live on a _____. (farm)*

Name_____

Look, look, Lizzy!
Quick, come and see.
A lovely little ladybug
Just landed on me.

Ladybug begins with the sound of l. Circle each picture whose name begins with the sound of l.

1. 2. 3. 4.
5. 6. 7. 8.
9. 10. 11. 12.

Say the name of each picture. If it begins with the sound of l, print l on the line. Then trace the whole word.

1. l og

2. ell

3. ock

4. ill

5. l ips

6. l eaf

7. l amp

8. oll

9. ake

10. all

11. l id

12. l etter

Ask your child to use two of the *l* words in a sentence, such as *I saw a log in the lake.*

Name _____

Denny does the dishes.
Dori does them, too.
Dad feeds the dog,
And soon they are through.

AWESOME!

> **Dishes begins with the sound of d.** Circle **each picture whose name begins with the sound of d.**

1.
2.
3.
4.
5.
6.
7.
8.
9.
10.
11.
12.

The sound of d: Phonemic awareness   **35**

Say the name of each picture. If it begins with the sound of **d**, print **d** on the line. Then trace the whole word.

1. d oll

2. oot

3. d oor

4. id

5. ey

6. duck

7. dive

8. deer

9. dog

10. desk

11. dishes

12. arn

 HOME

Ask your child to name three objects in your home that begin with the *d* sound.

Name _____

No, no, Nellie.
No, no, Ned.
Do not jump up
On my nice neat bed.

▶ **No** begins with the sound of **n**. **Circle** each picture whose name begins with the sound of **n**.

Say **the name of each picture. If it begins with the sound of n,** print **n on the line. Then** trace **the whole word.**

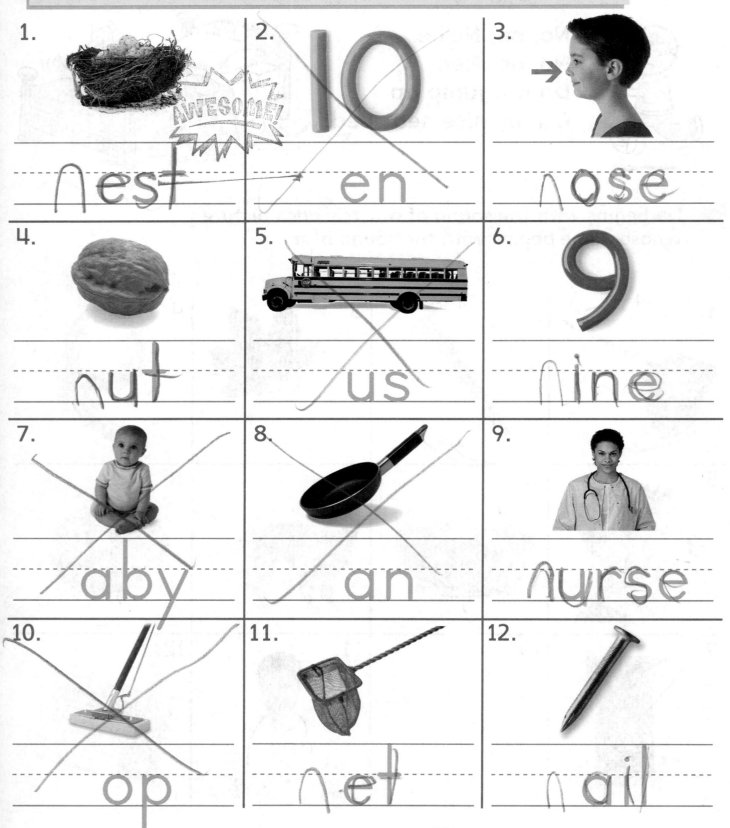

1. nest

2. ~~en~~

3. nose

4. nut

5. ~~us~~

6. nine

7. ~~aby~~

8. ~~an~~

9. nurse

10. ~~op~~

11. net

12. nail

With your child, take turns naming as many words that begin with *n* as you can.

Name_____

> **Say** the name of each picture. If the name **begins** with the sound of the letter in the box, print it on the first line. If it **ends** with that sound, print it on the second line.

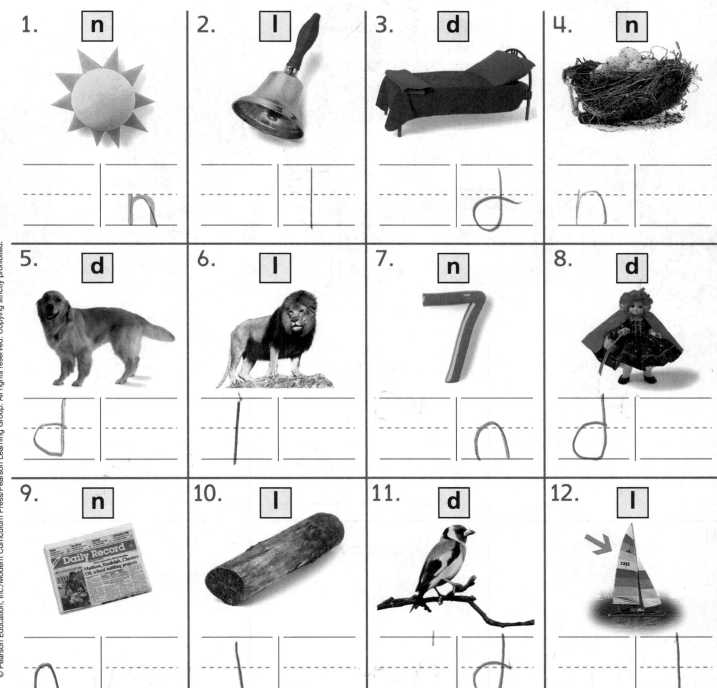

1. **n**   n

2. **l**   l

3. **d**   d

4. **n**   n

5. **d**   d

6. **l**   l

7. **n**   n

8. **d**   d

9. **n**   n

10. **l**   l

11. **d**   d

12. **l**   l

Say the names of the pictures in the boxes. Look for these pictures in the big picture. Circle each one. Write the letter of each beginning sound.

1.

dog

2.

Lock

3.

Leaf

4.

doLL

5.

nex

6.

nine

HOME

Make up riddles for your child to solve using picture names, such as *I have four legs and I bark.* (dog)

Name _____

We watch from the window
As winter winds blow.
We watch from the window,
And wish it would snow.

▶ Window **begins with the sound of w.** Circle **each picture whose name begins with the sound of w.**

1.

2.

3.

4.

5.

6.

7.

8.

9.

The sound of w: Phonemic awareness   **41**

Say the name of each picture. If it begins with the sound of **w**, print **w** on the line. Then trace the whole word.

1. wagon

2. eel

3. wing

4. watch

5. wave

6. og

7. ey

8. wallet

9. web

HOME Ask your child to choose two pictures whose names begin with the sound of *w* and use the words in a sentence.

Name _____

Carla has a cape.
She's carrying a cane.
Cory has her dad's coat
To play a dress-up game.

AWESOME!

> Cape **begins with the sound of c.**
> Circle **each picture whose name
> begins with the sound of c.**

1.

2.

3.

4.

5.

6.

7.

8.

9.
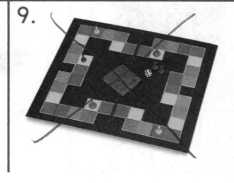

Say the name of each picture. If it begins with the sound of c, print c on the line. Then trace the whole word.

1. can

2. cap

3. atch

4. cane

5. og

6. ake

7. cow

8. car

9. cup

10. cage

11. um

12. comb

44   The sound of c: Sound to symbol

HOME

Ask your child to pick three words from the page that begin with c, then draw a picture showing them.

Name_____

The roses are red.
The ribbon is, too.
I ran over to bring
These red roses to you.

> Roses **begins with the sound of r.**
> Circle **each picture whose name**
> **begins with the sound of r.**

1.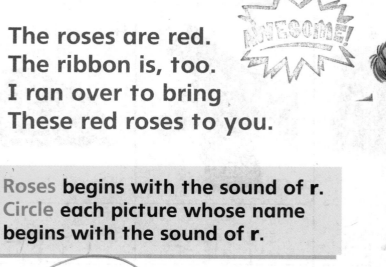

2.

3.

4.

5.

6.

7.

8.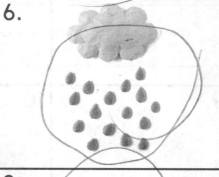

9.

Say the name of each picture. If it begins with the sound of **r**, print **r** on the line. Then trace the whole word.

1. ring

2. ~~ake~~

3. rip

4. rat

5. ~~at~~

6. ~~en~~

7. radio

8. ~~ips~~

9. rain

10. rug

11. rake

12. ~~eb~~

 HOME Point to the ring picture and ask your child, *What rhymes with king?* Repeat with rhymes for *rip*, *rat*, and *rug*.

Name _____

Penny passed the peach pie,
Peach pie, peach pie.
Penny passed the peach pie,
Till not a piece was left.

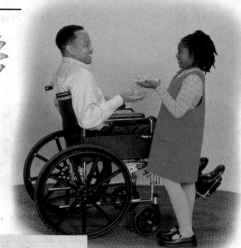

> **Peach** begins with the sound of **p**. Circle each
> picture whose name begins with the sound of **p**.

1.

2.

3.

4.

5.

6.

7.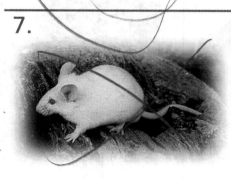

8.

9.

Say the name of each picture. If it begins with the sound of p, print p on the line. Then trace the whole word.

1. pot

2. up

3. pig

4. ine

5. oap

6. Pen

7. Purse

8. pin

9. Peas

10. ap

11. at

12. Pie

With your child, make up a silly sentence using three words from the page that begin with p.

Name _____

Quinn's toy duck said,
"Quack, quack, quack!"
"Quiet!" said Quincy.
But the duck quacked back!

> Quack **begins with the sound of qu.** Say **the name of each picture. If it begins with the sound of qu,** print **qu on the line.**

1. qu

2.

3.

4. qu

5. qu

6. qu

7.

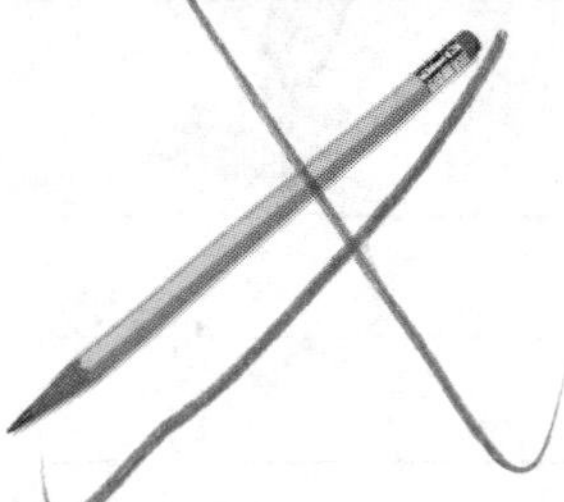

8. qu

Viv has a valentine.
Val has one, too.
Vic makes a valentine
To give to you.

Wonderful!

▶ **Valentine** begins with the sound of **v**. Say the name of each picture. If it begins with the sound of **v**, print **Vv** on the line.

1.

2.

3.

4.

5.

6.

7.

8.

9.

10.

11.

12.

With your child, make up a story using some of the words from the page that begin with *v*.

Name _____

> Say the name of each picture. Print the letter for its beginning sound on the first line. Then print the letter for its ending sound on the second line.

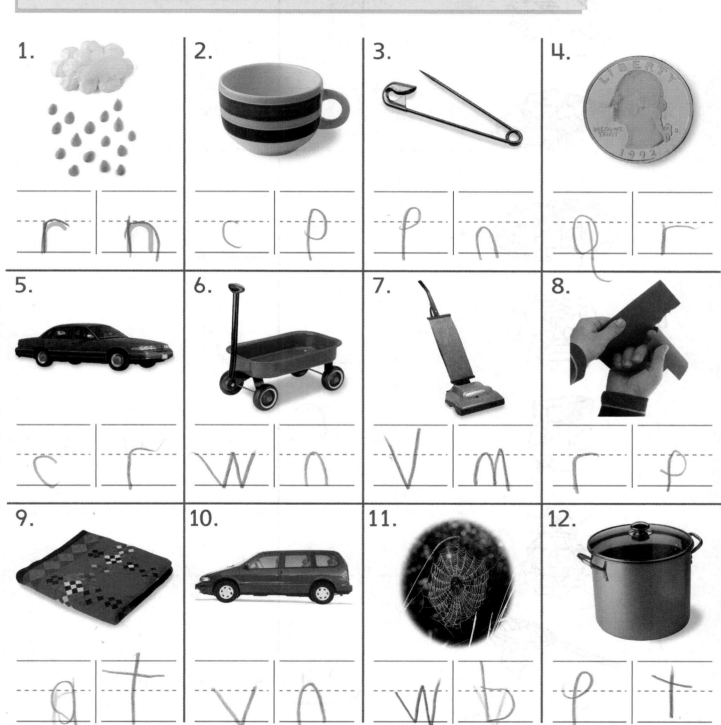

1. r n

2. c p

3. p n

4. q r

5. c r

6. w n

7. v m

8. r p

9. q t

10. v n

11. w b

12. p t

Say each picture name. Write the word that names each picture. What is the secret message?

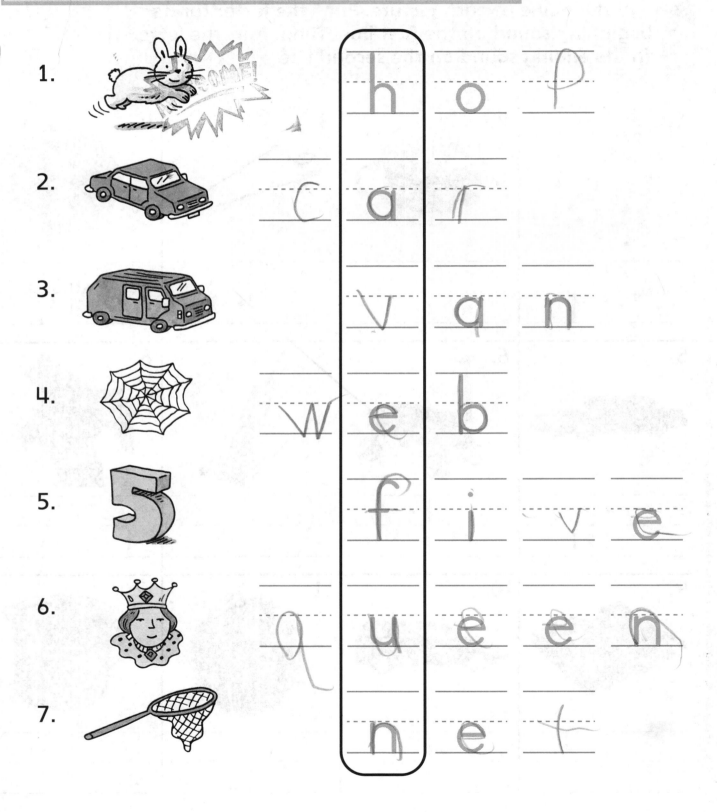

1. h o p

2. c a r

3. v a n

4. w e b

5. f i v e

6. q u e e n

7. n e t

Initial/final consonants w, c, r, p, q, v

 HOME Ask your child what the secret message is.

Name _____

Will Foxie Fox and Oxie Ox
Fit inside our big toy box?
Mix things up and push and pull.
Fox and Ox make the toy box full!

> **Box** ends with the sound of **x.** Say the name of each picture. If it ends with the sound of **x,** print **Xx** on the line.

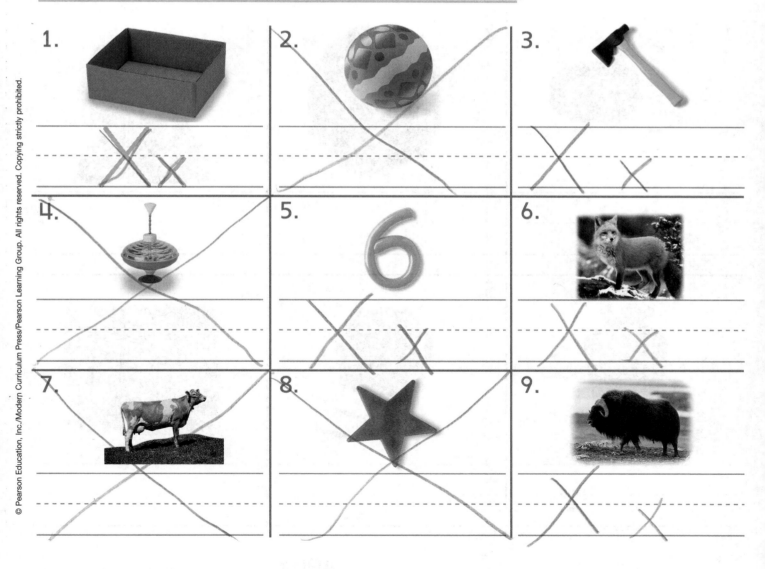

1.

2.

3.

4.

5.

6.

7.

8.

9.

Yesterday I went shopping
With my Grandma Lin.
I got a yellow yo-yo.
You can watch it spin.

> **Yo-yo** begins with the sound of **y**. Say the name of each picture. If it begins with the sound of **y**, print **Yy** on the line.

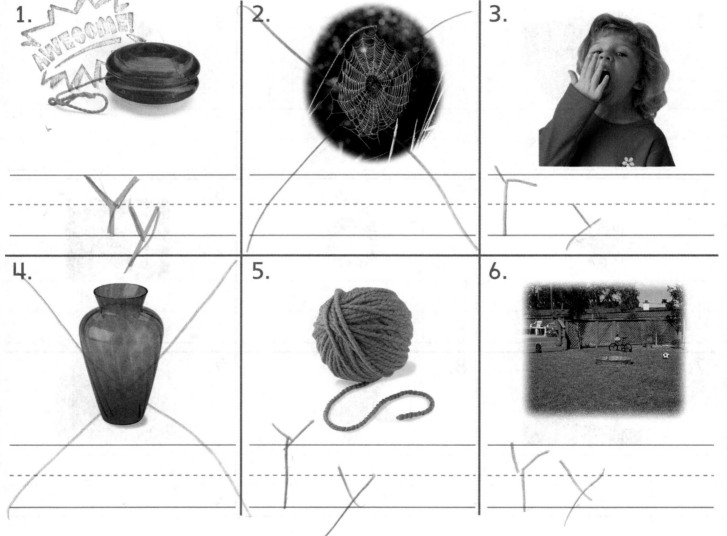

1. Yy

2.

3.

4.

5.

6. Yy

The sound of y: Sound to symbol

Say, "In my yard, I have a _____." Ask your child to finish the sentence with words that begin with y.

Name _____

Zelda and Zena
Went to the zoo.
There they saw zebras
And lions, too.

> **Zoo** begins with the sound of **z**. Say the name of each picture. If it begins with the sound of **z**, print **Zz** on the line.

1.

Zz

2.

Zz

3.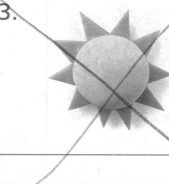

4.

Zz

5.

6.

Zz

Say the name of each picture. If the name begins with the sound of the letter in the box, print it on the first line. If it ends with that sound, print it on the second line.

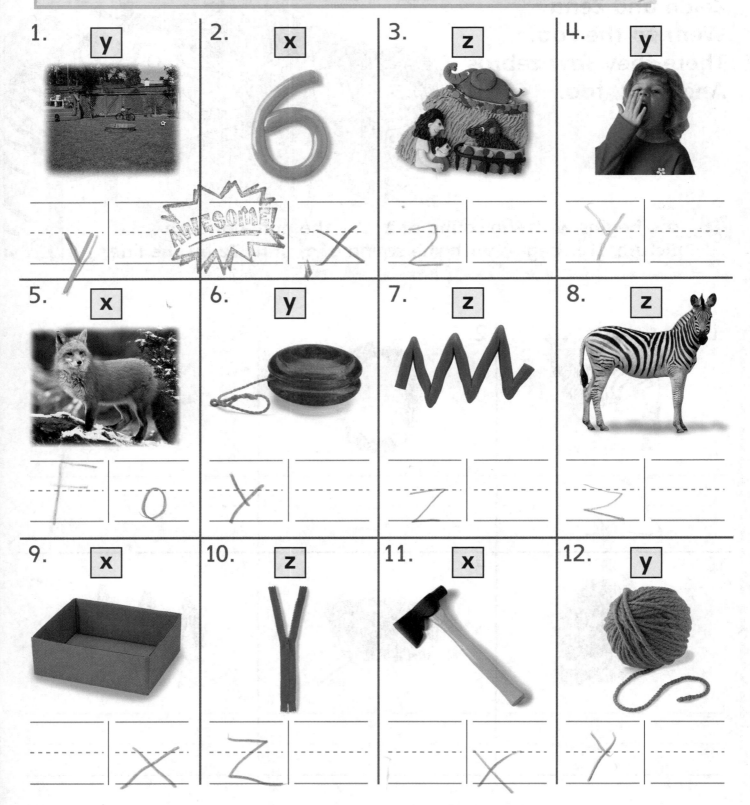

1. y

2. x

3. z

4. y

5. x

6. y

7. z

8. z

9. x

10. z

11. x

12. y

 HOME

Help your child to think of more words that begin or end with x, y, or z, such as *x-ray*, *play*, and *zip*.

Name _____

Say the name of each picture. Print the letter for its middle sound on the line.

1.

t

2.

l

3.

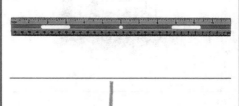

g

4.

n

5.

l

6.

d

7.

m

8.

p

9.

b

10.

m

11.

k

12.

t

Say the name of each picture. Print the letter for its middle sound on the line. Trace the whole word.

1. baby

2. pony

3. radio

4. wagon

5. ruler

6. lemon

7. seven

8. robot

9. tiger

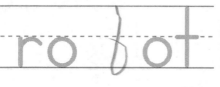

HOME Say each middle sound and ask your child to tell you which picture name or names have that sound.

Name _____

Phonics & Spelling

Say the name of each picture. Print the letter for its beginning sound. Then print the letter for its ending sound. The words in the box may help you.

bed	cat	fox	ham	jar	beak
pig	queen	tub	van	web	yard

1.

van

2.

pig

3.

fox

4.

tub

5.

bed

6.

cat

7.

jar

8.

web

9.

ham

10.

beak

11.

yard

12.

queen

Review consonants: Spelling **59**

Phonics & Writing

Draw a picture of yourself with your friends. Write a sentence about the picture.

Name _____

Camping Fun

It is fun to camp in a tent.

1

A dog can camp in a tent, too!

4

Review consonants: Take-home book   **61**

A tent can go in the woods or in a yard.

2

A tent can be big or little.

3

Name _____

> Say the name of each picture. Print the letter for the missing sound to finish each word. Trace the whole word.

1. yarn	2. bus	3. vase
4. hat	5. campfire	6. heart
7. jug	8. zebra	9. pen
10. queen	11. wagon	12. tub

Say the name of each picture. Fill in the bubble next to the letter or letters that stand for the beginning sound.

1.
○ y
○ d
● m

mit

2.
○ k
● r
○ w

rope

3.
● l
○ p
○ t

lemp

4.
● c
○ n
○ z

cow

5.
○ f
○ t
● qu

quortow

6.
○ v
● w
○ k

we mes

Say the name of each picture. Fill in the bubble next to the letter that stands for the ending sound.

7.
○ k
○ z
● x

fox

8.
● g
○ c
○ z

bog

9.
○ n
● p
○ r

maps

10.
○ f
● n
○ q

pan

11.
● d
○ t
○ j

brad

12.
● k
○ l
○ w

fork

Frogs Call

Little frogs call.
They sing a song.
Soon the rain will fall.
Tree frogs like wet places.
They hop and jump.
Some tree frogs are green.
Some are red.
Others are blue or yellow.
You can not touch some
tree frogs.
The wet skin can make you sick!

What can tree frogs do?

Dear Family,

In this unit about "Amazing Animals," your child will learn about the vowels **a, e, i, o,** and **u** and the sounds they make. Many animal names contain short vowels such as cat, hen, pig, fox, and duck. As your child becomes familiar with short vowel sounds, you might try these activities together.

▶ Make a collage of animals whose names have the same short vowel sound. With your child, draw pictures or cut pictures from magazines and glue them on paper, one sheet for each vowel.

▶ Your child might enjoy reading these books with you. Look for them in your local library.

Pet of a Pet by Marsha Hayles
How Chipmunk Got His Stripes by Joseph Bruchac

Sincerely,

_____

Estimada familia:

En esta unidad, que trata de "Animales asombrosos," su hijo/a aprenderá las vocales **a, e, i, o, u** y los sonidos que éstas hacen. Los nombres de muchos animales contienen vocales con sonidos breves, como por ejemplo, cat (gato), hen (gallina), pig (cerdo), fox (zorro), y duck (pato). A medida que su hijo/a se vaya familiarizando con las vocales de sonidos breves, podrían hacer las siguientes actividades juntos.

▶ Hagan un collage de fotos o dibujos de animales cuyos nombres contienen vocales con sonidos breves. Junto con su hijo/a dibujen o recorten fotos de revistas y péguenlos en hojas de papel—una hoja por vocal.

▶ Quizás a su hijo/a le gustaría leer con ustedes los siguientes libros que podrían buscar en su biblioteca local.

Pet of a Pet de Marsha Hayles
How Chipmunk Got His Stripes de Joseph Bruchac

Sinceramente,

_____

Name _____

An ant can dance.
An ant can sing.
An ant can do most anything.

Can you dance?
Can you sing?
Can you do most anything?

▶ Ant **has the short sound of a.** Circle **each picture whose name has the short sound of a.**

1. 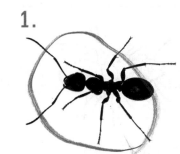	2. 	3. 	4. 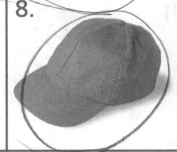
5. 	6. 	7. 	8. 
9. 	10. 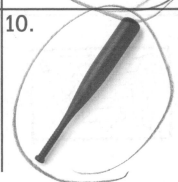	11. 	12. 

Say the names of the pictures in each row.
Color the pictures whose names rhyme.

1.

2.

3.

4.

      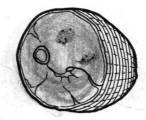   

5.

   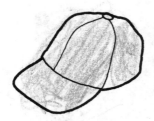      

HOME

Help your child use rhyming words from
the page to make up silly sentences
such as *The rat chased the cat.*

Name _____

> Say the name of each picture. Circle its name.

1.

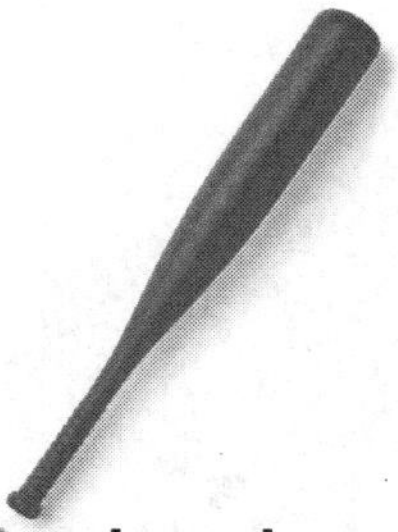

(bat)   bad   bag

2.

ant   wax   (ax)

3.

nap   (can)   cat

4.

cab   (cap)   nap

5.

man   bag   (band)

6.

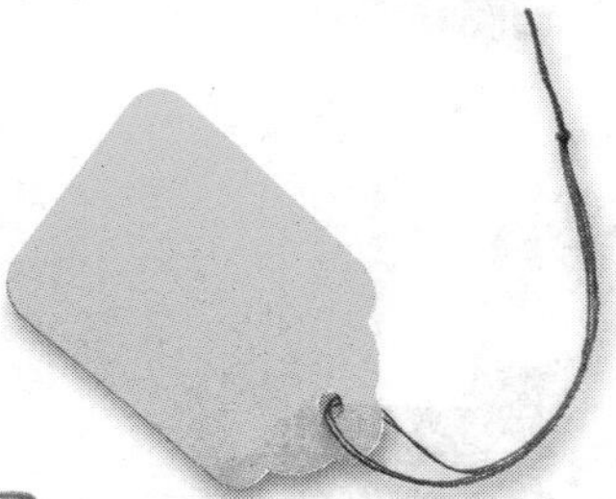

(tag)   rag   tap

7.

fat   (fan)   tan

8.

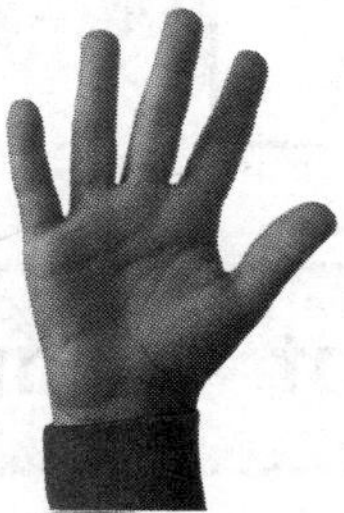

had   (hand)   land

9.

tap   lap   (lamp)

10.

(van)   had   ran

11.

(bad)   cab   dad

12.

pat   (pan)   ran

Read **the words in the blue box.** Print **a word in the puzzle to name each picture.**

Across →

2.

5.

6.

Down ↓

1.

3.

4.

1. g
2. m a p
t
3. h
4. p
5. b a g
6. h a t
n
b d

| bag | cat | hand | hat | map | pan |

Use **some of the words from the box to write a sentence.**

the cat is on the flor

The map is on the tobl

HOME Make up riddles using some of the words from the box. Ask your child to guess each word.

Name _____

 Blend the letter sounds together as you say each word. Then color the picture it names.

1.

v
a
n

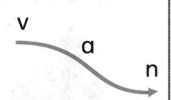  

2.

c
a
p

 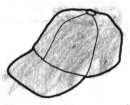 

3.

h
a
m

4.

b
a
t

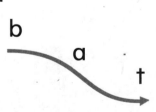   

5.

c
a
n

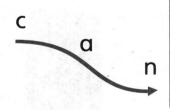   

Blend the letter sounds together as you say each word. **Print** the word on the line. **Draw** a line to the picture whose name rhymes.

1. m
   ap

   map

2. r
   at

   rat

3. h
   am

   ham

4. t
   ag

   tag

5. r
   an

   ran

6. s
   ad

   sad

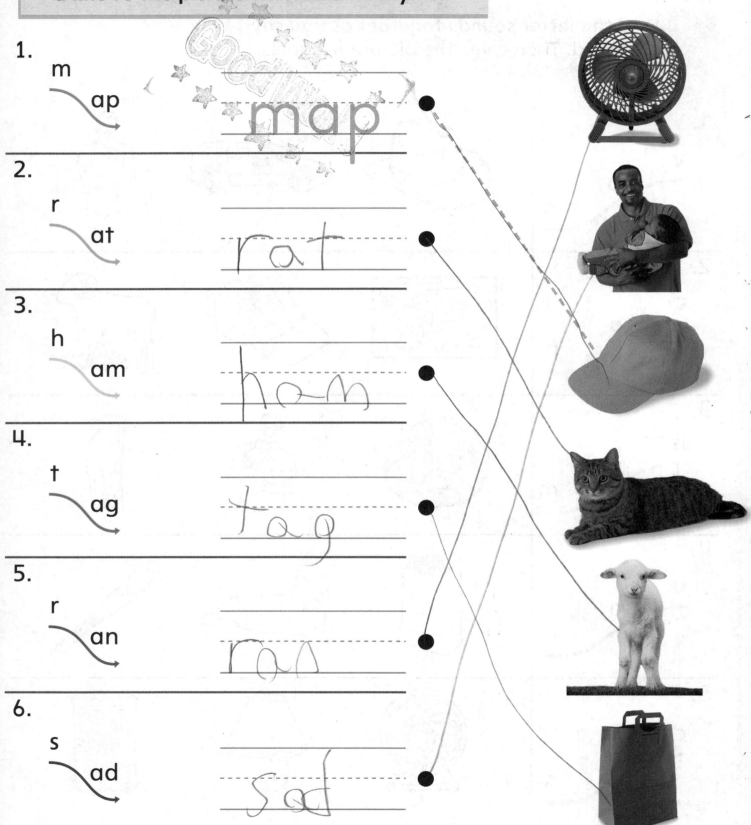

HOME

Invite your child to say a picture name and think of as many rhyming words as possible.

Name _____

> Say the name of each picture. Print the letter for its beginning sound. Then print the letter for its ending sound.

1.

cat

2.

pan

3.

tag

4.

han

5.

map

6.

bab

7.

ram

8.

rat

9.

hat

10.

bag

11.

can

12.

bat

13.

ma

14.

cab

15.

van

16.

fan

> Look **at the picture.** Circle **the word that will finish the sentence.** Print **it on the line.**

1. Max is my _cat_ .
   cat
   sat
   can

2. He licks my _hand_ .
   land
   hand
   ham

3. Max sits on my _lap_ .
   pad
   rap
   lap

4. He likes my _dad_ .
   sad
   dad
   bad

5. He plays with a _bag_ .
   bat
   rag
   bag

6. Max takes a _nap_ .
   nap
   cap
   cab

 Why does the girl like Max?

 Help your child think of sentences using words from the page to continue the story.

Name _____

Say the name of each picture. Print the name on the line. In the last box, draw a picture of a short **a** word. Print the word.

1.
fan

2.
cap

3.
bag

4.
bab

5.
rat

6.
can

7.
ram

8.
man

9.
han

10.
map

11.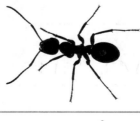
bnt

12.

Short vowel a: Spelling 75

Read **the sentences.** Circle **the word that will finish each sentence.** Print **it on the line.**

1. Jan got in the _____van_____.

can
~~van~~
cat

2. It was time to go to _____camp_____.

cap
lamp
~~camp~~

3. In the van, Jan had a _____sax_____.

tap
nap
~~sat~~

4. At camp, Jan made a name _____tag_____.

~~tag~~
rag
tan

5. Jan made a mask with a _____bag_____.

wag
bad
~~bag~~

6. Jan played in the _____band_____.

~~band~~
can
hand

 Do you think Jan had fun at camp? Why?

 Ask your child questions that can be answered with words on the page, such as *Jan was sleepy so she took a ____.* (nap)

76 **Short a: High-frequency words, critical thinking**

Name _____

Phonics & Reading

Read the story. Use short **a** words to finish the sentences.

Go, Ant!

The cat takes a nap.
The ant runs fast.
The ant is on the cat.
The cat is up!

The cat taps the ant.
Go, ant, go!
The cat can not get the ant.

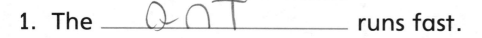

1. The _____ant_____ runs fast.

2. The ant is on the _____cat_____.

3. The cat _____awecs_____ the ant.

TALK About It

Why does the cat want to catch the ant?

Phonics & Writing

Use one of the letters to make a word with **an** or **ap**. Write each real word on the lines.

r y c m p

an

1. chman

2. ppn

3. Dacaa

4. ran

c l b n t

ap

5. nap

6. tap

7. lap

8. cap

Write a sentence using one of the words you made.

_____

_____

_____

Review short vowel a: Phonograms

HOME Invite your child to think of more words that end with *an* or *ap* such as *fan, tan, gap, map, rap, zap.*

Name _____

BATS

Written by **Jennifer Jacobson**

Photographs by **Dr. Merlin Tuttle**

A bat has fur.

1

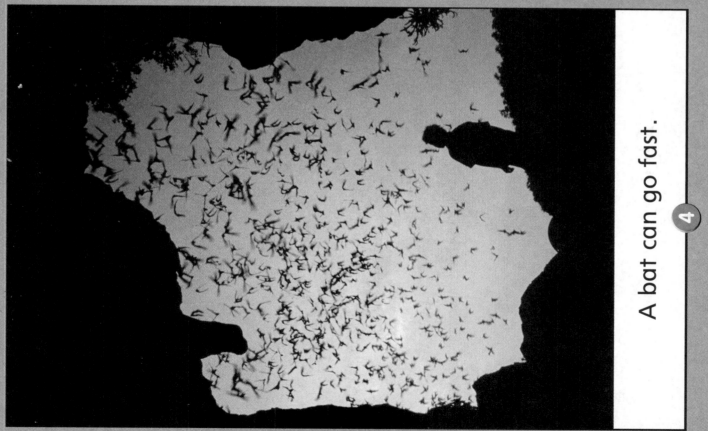

A bat can go fast.

4

2 This bat has a bug.

3 A bat can go far.

Name_____

> Read **the words in the box.** Write a word to finish each sentence.

I	the
My	with
here	said

1. Pal got ___the___ ball.

2. "Run," ___said___ Dan to Pal.

3. Pal ran ___with___ the ball.

4. "Now run ___here___, Pal," said Dan.

5. "___My___ dog runs fast," Dan said.

6. "___I___ like to play with my dog."

Unscramble **the letters to** write **a word from the box. The word shapes will help you print the words.**

1. asdi 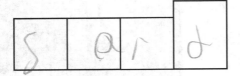 s a r d

here   my
said   with
the

2. eth 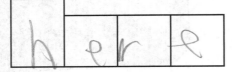 t h e

3. hree 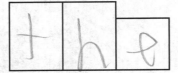 h e r e

4. hwit 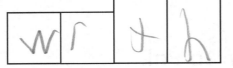 w r t h

5. ym 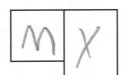 m y

CHECKING UP

Put a ✔ **next to each word you can read.**

☑ with   ☑ said   ☑ my   ☑ here   ☑ the   ☑ I

 HOME Using any two words on the page, help your child make up a sentence, then draw a picture to go with it.

Name _____

A big pink pig
Ate a big fig,
Put on a big wig,
And did a jig.

▶ **Pig has the short sound of i. Circle each picture whose name has the short sound of i.**

1. 	2. 	3. 	4. 
5. 	6. 	7. 	8. 
9. 	10. 	11. 	12. 

Say the names of the pictures in each row.
Color the pictures whose names rhyme.

1.

bib   scra

2.

 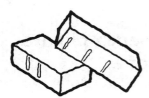  

3.

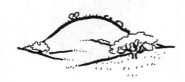   

4.

 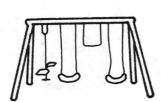  

5.

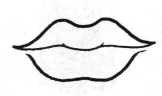   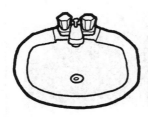

84   **Short vowel i: Phonograms/rhyme**

HOME

With your child, make up silly
sentences using the rhyming
words from each row.

Name _____

> **Say** the name of each picture. **Circle** its name.

1.
pin   wig   (pig)

2.
(six)   ax   mix

3.
hid   (lid)   did

4.
(bib)   bit   bad

5.
fin   (pin)   pan

6.
fill   (hill)   bill

7.
mix   mat   (mitt)

8.
sing   sank   (sink)

9.
will   (milk)   mitt

10.
win   (fin)   fan

11.
(fist)   fish   fast

12.
win   (wing)   ring

> Farmer Jill's pigs have short **i** words on them. Help Farmer Jill catch her pigs. **Circle** the short **i** words.

pin

cat

sink

hill

tag

lid

fan

big

> Use **some of the short i words on the pigs to write a sentence.**

_____

- -

_____

_____

- -

_____

With your child, take turns making up poems and rhymes for each short *i* word.

Name _____

> **Blend** the letter sounds together as you say each word. Then, **color** the picture it names.

1.

w
  i
    g

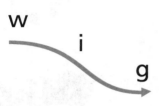  

2.

m
  a
    p

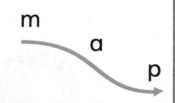  

3.

p
  i
    n

4.

b
  i
    b

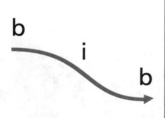   

5.

m
  a
    n

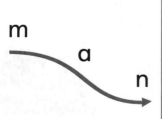   

Short vowels a, i: Blending phonemes   **87**

Blend the letter sounds together as you say each word.
Print the word on the line. **Draw** a line to the picture it names.

1.

p
ig
_____

2.

p
an
_____

3.

s
ix
_____

4.

c
ap
_____

5.

r
at
_____

6.

r
ip
_____

88   **Short vowels a, i: Blending phonograms**

Ask your child to think of a rhyming word for three of the picture names.

Name _____

> Say the name of each picture. Print the letters for its beginning and ending sounds. Trace the whole word.

1.

wig

2.

lit

3.

pig

4.

six

5.

pin

6.

lip

7.

bib

8.

gif

9.

sink

10.

milk

11.

lips

12.

ri

13.

fin

14.

sit

15.

is

16.

is

▶ Look at the picture. Circle the word that will finish the sentence. Print it on the line.

1.	I got a _gift_ .	gap gift gum
2.	Is it a _mitt_ ?	milk mitt tip
3.	Does it drink _milk_ ?	milk mitt mat
4.	Will it fit in a _dish_ ?	damp dig dish
5.	Can it swim in the _sink_ ?	sick sink sank
6.	It is a _fish_ !	fist fast fish

 Did you ever get a pet as a gift? Tell about it.

 With your child, pick a word on the page and take turns changing the first letter to make new words, such as *dish—fish*.

Name _____

Say the name of each picture. Print the name on the line. In the last box, draw a picture of a short **i** word. Print the word.

1.

lid

2.

six

3.

pig

4.

pin

5.

bib

6.

rip

7.

wig

8.

sink

9.

hill

10.

milk

11.

gift

12.

Read the sentences. Circle the word that will finish each sentence. Print it on the line.

1. Jim and Linda were going to _dig_.

dog
dig
pig

2. They went to the top of the _hill_.

bill
hit
hill

3. Jim saw a rock that was _big_.

rig
big
bag

4. He could just see the _r_.

tip
tap
rip

5. Linda's truck moved _____.

at
it
if

6. She was glad to help _____.

him
her
rim

What other things can be used to dig?

With your child, make up sentences with short *i* words such as "With a shovel, I can ___."

Short i: High-frequency words, critical thinking

Name_____

Fish Tale

The big fish has little fins.
The little fish has big fins.
The big fish likes to sing.
The little fish likes to swim.
The big fish sings to his friend.
The little fish waves a fin.

1. The ___big___ fish has little fins.

2. The big fish likes to ___sing___.

3. The little fish waves a ___fin___.

Why might the big and little fish be friends?

Review short i: Reading, critical thinking **93**

Use **one of the letters to make a word with ig or ing.** Write **each real word on a line.**

b c p f d   r s n k w

big

sing

1. _____

2. _____

3. _____

4. _____

5. _____

6. _____

7. _____

8. _____

▶ Write **a sentence using one of the words you made.**

_____

_____

_____

_____

Ask your child to guess these words as you say them aloud, stretching out the sounds: *j-ig, r-ig, w-ig, th-ing,* and *br-ing.*

Name _____

Fast Pig

This pig can run.

1

----- FOLD -----

The race ends.
The pig in pink wins.

4

Review short vowels a, i: Take-home book   **95**

2

The race has started.
The pig in pink is fast.

3

The pigs zip around the ring.
These pigs can not catch the pig in pink.

Name_____

Read the words in the box. Write a word to finish each sentence.

you	for
like	down
are	do

1. Min and Tim ____are____ playing in the sand.

2. Min says, "What did I ____do____ with my ring?"

3. "I will help look _____ it," Tim says.

4. Min and Tim look _____ in the sand.

5. "This looks _____ the ring," says Tim.

6. "Tim, _____ are my friend," says Min.

Write the letter to finish each word.
Then **print** the words on the lines.

down   are   for   do   like   you

1. d
2. d o w n
3. a r e
4. l i k e
5. y o u r
6. f o r u

1. down
2. do
3. are
4. like
5. you
6. for

Put a ✔ next to each word you can read.

☐ like   ☐ down   ☐ you   ☐ are   ☐ for   ☐ do

HOME Help your child make up sentences using the words on this page.

Name _____

Rub-a-dub-dub.
The cub is in the tub.
Rub-a-dub-dub.
The cub likes to scrub.

▶ **Cub has the short sound of u.**
Circle each picture whose name
has the short sound of u.

1.

2.

3.

4.

5.

6.

7.

8.

9.

10.

11.

12.

Say the names of the pictures in each row.
Color the pictures whose names rhyme.

1.
  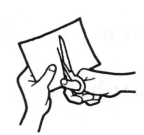 

2.

3.
 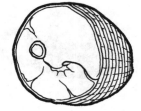  

4.

5.
 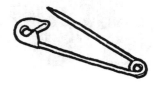  

100   Short vowel u: Phonograms/rhyme

Help your child think of more
words that rhyme with the ones
on this page.

Name _____

> Say the name of each picture. Circle its name.

1.

suds   sand   (sun)

2.

(gum)   mug   gust

3.

cut   cap   (cup)

4.

bun   (bus)   sun

5.

bag   bug   big

6.

but   tab   (tub)

7.

jug   jack   gum

8.

huts   mugs   (nuts)

9.

tuck   (duck)   luck

10.

mug   rug   rag

11.

cub   cup   club

12.

drum   dip   mad

> Help the cub get home. Draw a line from the cub to the first word with the short **u** sound. Draw a line to each short **u** word.

fun

dog

jug

bug

cat

jam

nut

fox

bed

rug

tub

> Use **some of the short u words from the puzzle** to write **a sentence.**

_____

- - - - - - - - - - - - - - - - -

_____

- - - - - - - - - - - - - - - - -

_____

HOME

With your child, take turns naming short _u_ words.

Name _____

▶ **Blend** the letter sounds together as you say each word. Then, **color** the picture it names.

1. b
 u
  g

2. c
 a
  n

3. p
 i
  n

 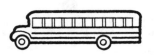 

4. t
 u
  b

5. r
 a
  t

6. w
 i
  g

► Blend the letter sounds together as you say each word. Print the word on the line. Draw a line to the picture it names.

1.

b
at

_____

2.

s
ix

_____

3.

r
ug

_____

4.

p
ig

_____

5.

p
an

_____

6.

c
ub

_____

Short vowels a, i, u: Blending phonograms

Help your child make up silly rhymes for these picture names, such as *a cub in a tub.*

Name _____

> Say the name of each picture. Print the letter for its beginning and ending sounds. In the last box, draw a picture of a short u word.

1. cup

2. sun

3. gum

4. bug

5. u

6. bus

7. rug

8. hug

9. but

10. u

11. u

12. u

13. run

14. cut

15. nut

16. u

Look at the picture. Circle the word that will finish the sentence. Print it on the line.

1. Gus sits on the _____ rug _____.

rub
rug
jug

2. He plays with his _____ pup _____.

pup
up
cup

3. Soon Gus sees the _____ bus _____.

bud
bug
bus

4. He jumps _____.

hug
up
cup

5. Gus has to _____ run _____.

rub
fun
run

6. The bus is stuck in the _____!

mud
mug
hum

 What do you think will happen next?

 Ask your child to raise a hand for the short *u* words as you say, *But the bus was just stuck in the mud for an hour.*

Name _____

Say the name of each picture. **Print** the picture name on the line. In the last box, **draw** a picture of a short **u** word. **Print** the word.

1.

tub

2.

3.

4.

5.

6.

7.

8.

9.

10.

11.

12.

Read the sentences. Circle the word that will finish each sentence. Print it on the line.

_____

- - - - - - - - - - - - - - - - - -

1. Our farm is _____.

fan
fin
fun

_____

- - - - - - - - - - - - - - - - - -

2. I look under trees for _____.

nuts
rugs
suns

_____

- - - - - - - - - - - - - - - - - -

3. Bugs buzz and _____.

hut
hand
hum

_____

- - - - - - - - - - - - - - - - - -

4. The pigs dig in the _____.

must
mud
mug

_____

- - - - - - - - - - - - - - - - - -

5. My dog jumps and _____.

runs
rings
cuts

_____

- - - - - - - - - - - - - - - - - -

6. He likes the warm _____.

gum
sun
hum

 TALK About It What are some things you might do at a farm?

 HOME Help your child to make up a sentence using the words *fun* and *sun*, then draw a picture to go with it.

Name _____

 **Phonics & Reading**

 Read the story. **Use** short **u** words to finish the sentences.

A Fuss in a Bus

The bug jumps in the bus.
The pup hums in the bus.
The cub runs in the bus.
"Sit down!" says the driver.
"Do not make such a fuss!"
The bug sits.
The cub sits.
The pup does not hum.
No more fuss in the bus!
Now it can go.

_____
- - - - - - - - - - - -

1. The _____ jumps in the bus.

_____
- - - - - - - - - - - - -

2. The pup hums in the _____.

_____
- - - - - - - - - - - -

3. The _____ runs in the bus.

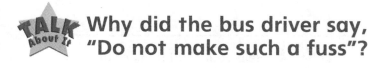 **TALK About It** Why did the bus driver say, "Do not make such a fuss"?

Review short u: Reading, critical thinking **109**

Phonics & Writing

Use **one of the letters to make a word with** **un** or **ug**. **Write each real word on a line.**

b r f s l

un

1. _____

2. _____

3. _____

4. _____

m b k j t

ug

5. _____

6. _____

7. _____

8. _____

Write a sentence using one of the words you made.

_____

_____

_____

110   **Review short vowel u: Phonograms**

HOME   Help your child think of other *un* and *ug* words.

Name _____

Lunch in a Jug

Make a jug bird feeder.

1

---- FOLD ----

Put nuts and seeds in the jug.
Watch the fun.

4

Review short vowel u: Take-home book   **111**

Scrub a milk jug.
Cut a hole in the jug.

2

Put a string on the jug.
Hang the jug up.

3

Name _____

My dog has lots of spots.
My dog's spots look like dots.
My dog's spots are on his hair.
My dog's spots are everywhere!

> **Spot** has the short sound of **o**. Circle each picture whose name has the short sound of **o**.

1.

2.

3.

4.

5.

6.

7.

8.

9.

10.

11.

12.

Say the names of the pictures in each row.
Color the pictures whose names rhyme.

1.

2.

3.

4.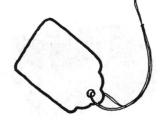

5.

 With your child, make up action rhymes using short *o* words from the page, such as *hop with a mop*.

Name _____

▶ **Say** the name of each picture. **Circle** its name.

1.

top pot pack

2.

box fox fog

3.

log dog lot

4.

nap map mop

5.

tap tip top

6.

hat hot hit

7.

dog dig dug

8.

bat box bug

9.

fill duck doll

10.

ox sock ax

11.

rip rack rock

12.

pop pup pat

Short vowel o: Sound to symbol   115

Color each short **o** word red.
What do you see?

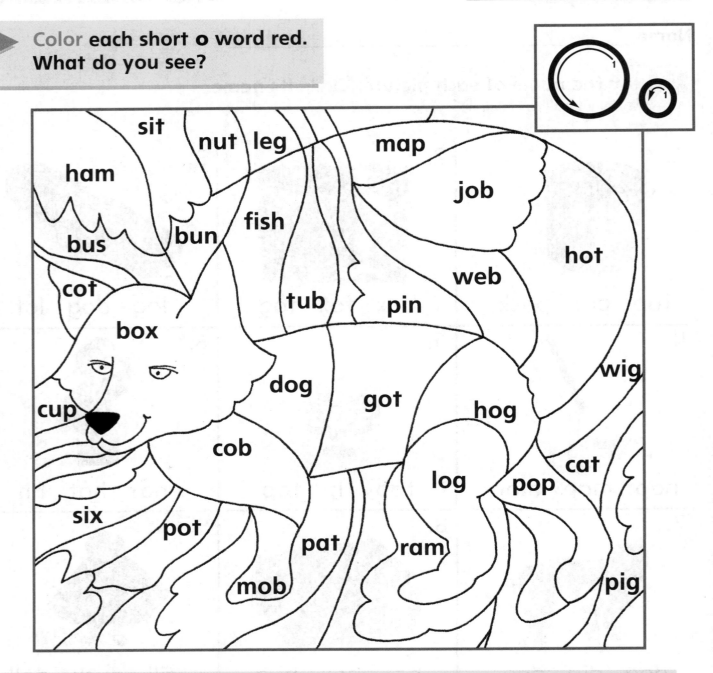

Use some of the short **o** words in the puzzle to write a sentence.

Short vowel o: Sound to symbol

Help your child make up a story
using some of the short *o* words
on the page.

Name_____

⮞ **Blend** the letter sounds together as you say each word. **Color** the picture it names.

1. l
   o
   g

2. b
   a
   t

3. c
   u
   b

4. f
   o
   x

5. p
   i
   n

6. r
   u
   g

Short a, i, u, o: Blending phonemes   **117**

Blend the letter sounds together as you say each word. **Print** the word on the line. **Draw** a line to the picture it names.

1.

b
ox

_____
- - - - - - - - - - - -
_____

2.

s
ix

_____
- - - - - - - - - - - -
_____

3.

c
up

_____
- - - - - - - - - - - -
_____

4.

m
an

_____
- - - - - - - - - - - -
_____

5.

d
og

_____
- - - - - - - - - - - -
_____

6.

b
us

_____
- - - - - - - - - - - -
_____

118   Short vowels a, i, u, o: Blending phonograms

HOME

Name the beginning letter of a word. Ask your child to say a word that starts with that letter.

> ► Say the name of each picture. Print the letters for its beginning and ending sounds. Trace the word. In the last box, draw a picture of a short o word. Print the word.

1. _____
mop

2. _____
bog

3. _____
log

4. _____
top

5. _____
fox

6. _____
pot

7. _____
box

8. _____
rock

9. _____
pop

10. _____
ox

11. _____
frog

12. _____

Look at the picture. Circle the word that will finish the sentence. Print it on the line.

1. Bob is _hot_ .

hot
got
hop

2. He sits on top of a _rock_ .

rock
rack
lock

3. He takes off his _soks_ .

sacks
socks
locks

4. The grass is _soft_ .

sack
lift
soft

5. He sees a frog in the _pond_ .

pond
pot
pod

6. The frog hops on a _log_ .

lock
lost
log

 What do you think Bob might do next?

 With your child, think of silly sentences using the short o words, such as *The frog took off its socks.*

Name _____

> Say the name of each picture. Print the picture name on the line. In the last box, draw a picture of a short o word. Print the word.

1.

_____

_ _ _ _ _ _ _ _ _ _ _ _ _ _ _ _

_____

2.

_____

_ _ _ _ _ _ _ _ _ _ _ _ _ _ _ _

_____

3.

_____

_ _ _ _ _ _ _ _ _ _ _ _ _ _ _ _

_____

4.

_____

_ _ _ _ _ _ _ _ _ _ _ _ _ _ _ _

_____

5.

_____

_ _ _ _ _ _ _ _ _ _ _ _ _ _ _ _

_____

6.

_____

_ _ _ _ _ _ _ _ _ _ _ _ _ _ _ _

_____

7.

_____

_ _ _ _ _ _ _ _ _ _ _ _ _ _ _ _

_____

8.

_____

_ _ _ _ _ _ _ _ _ _ _ _ _ _ _ _

_____

9.

_____

_ _ _ _ _ _ _ _ _ _ _ _ _ _ _ _

_____

10.

_____

_ _ _ _ _ _ _ _ _ _ _ _ _ _ _ _

_____

11.

_____

_ _ _ _ _ _ _ _ _ _ _ _ _ _ _ _

_____

12.

_____

_ _ _ _ _ _ _ _ _ _ _ _ _ _ _ _

_____

▶ Circle **the word that will finish the sentence.** Print **it on the line.**

1. Jill likes to _____.

job
jog
jug

2. She puts on shoes and _____.

sand
soft
socks

3. She jogs with her _____.

dot
dock
dog

4. She runs to the _____ of the hill.

top
tap
mop

5. It gets very _____.

hog
hit
hot

6. She _____ to rest.

sips
stops
steps

 TALK About It **What sports do you like? Why?**

 HOME Help your child think of sentences using words from this page to continue the story.

Name_____

 **Phonics & Reading**

Read the story. **Print** **short o** words to finish the sentences.

Foxes

Foxes live in many places.
Some foxes live where it is hot.
Some live where it is cold.
Foxes are like dogs.
They have soft fur.
A baby fox is called a cub or
a pup.

_____

1. _____ live in many places.

_____

2. Some foxes live where it is _____.

_____

3. Foxes are like _____.

 How is a fox like a dog?

Phonics & Writing

Use **one of the letters to make a word with** **ot** or **og**. Write **each real word on a line.**

l d v p n

ot

1. _____

2. _____

3. _____

4. _____

l m d h f

og

5. _____

6. _____

7. _____

8. _____

Write **a sentence using one of the words you made.**

_____

_____

_____

HOME   Help your child think of words that end in *on, od, ox,* and *ob.*

Name _____

In the Tub

A dog and a pup had a bath
in a tub.

1

FOLD

Then, the dog and the pup got out
and ran!

4

Review short vowels a, i, u, o: Take-home book   **125**

Six hot bugs said, "Can we hop in the tub?"
The dog said, "You can."

2

Six big pigs said, "Can we jump in the tub?"
The dog said, "You can."

3

Name _____

> **Read** the words in the box. **Write** a word to finish each sentence.

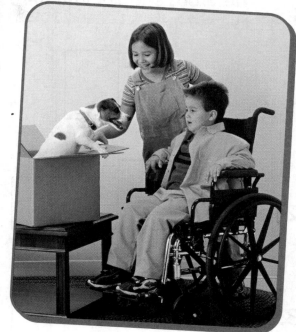

of	her
Our	have
one	come

1. __Our__ family has a pet.

2. We __have__ a dog.

3. Molly is __one__ name.

4. We could not find Molly __her__ day.

5. I said, "Molly, __come__ here!"

6. Molly jumped out __of__ a box!

Unscramble **the letters to write a word from the box. The word shapes will help you print the words.**

have	one	of
our	come	her

1. fo   O f

2. erh   h e r

3. uro   O v r

4. evha   h a v e

5. neo   o n e

6. moce   c o m e

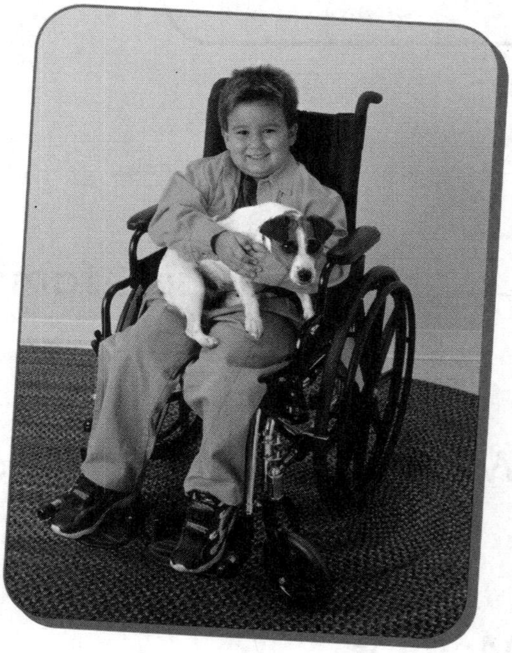

CHECKING UP

Put a ✔ next to each word you can read.

☑ one   ☑ come   ☑ have   ☑ of   ☑ our   ☑ her

HOME Use some of the words on this page to make up sentences with your child.

Name _____

"Red Hen, Red Hen,"
Jen said to her hen.
"Red Hen, Red Hen,
Get back to your pen!"

▶ **Hen has the short sound of e. Circle each picture whose name has the short sound of e.**

1.

2.

3.

4.

5.

6.

7.

8.

9.

10.

11.

12.

Say the names of the pictures in each row.
Color the pictures whose names rhyme.

1.

 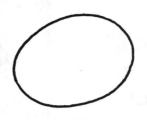  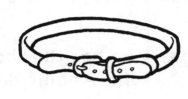

2.

3.

   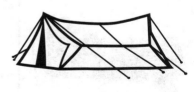

4.

5.

  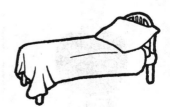 

130   Short vowel e: Phonograms/rhyme

Name a picture. Ask your child to
think of words that rhyme.

Name _____

Say **the name of each picture.** Circle **its name.**

1.

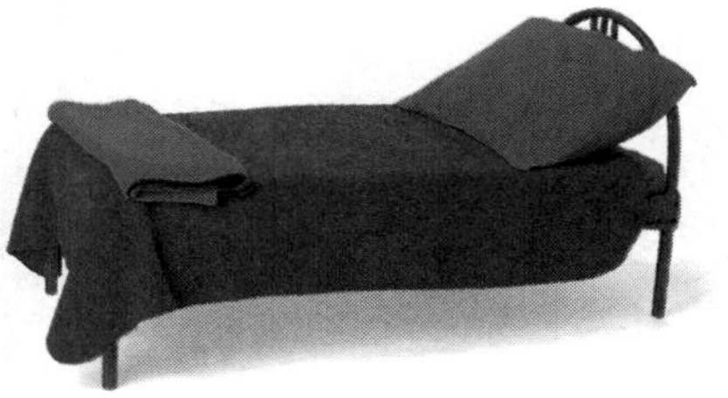

bed   fed   led

2.

bill   sell   bell

3.

tan   ten   tin

4.

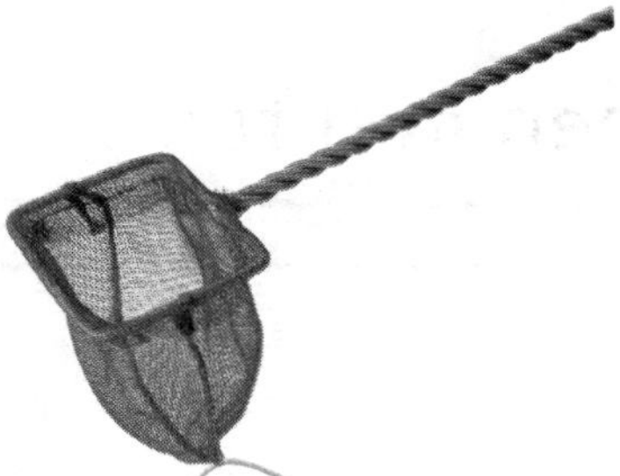

met   net   nut

5.

west   well   web

6.

jet   pet   wet

7.

went   man   men

8.

leg   egg   beg

9.

ten   tent   bent

10.

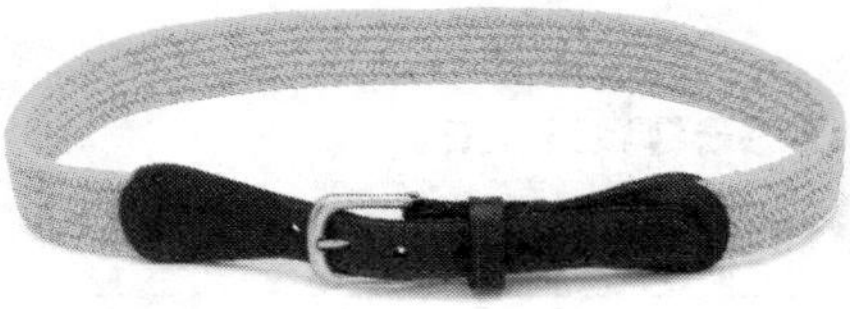

belt   bell   melt

11.

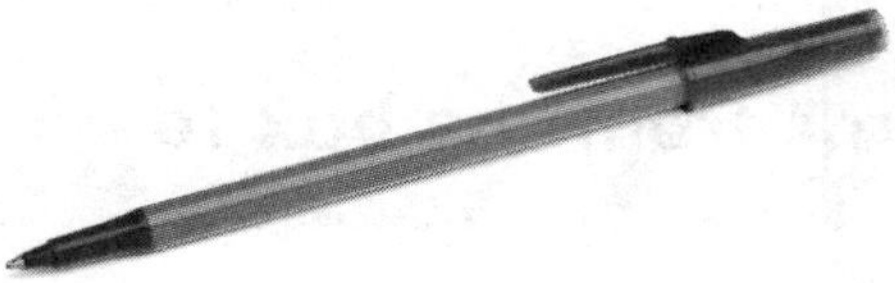

pin   pet   pen

12.

nest   not   just

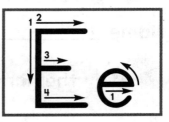

Four red hens are missing from their pen. Draw a **hen in each box.** Follow the directions **below.**

1.

Draw a hen in a bed.

2.

Draw a hen in a tent.

3.

Draw a hen on a sled.

4.

Draw a hen in a nest.

| hen | bed | tent | sled | nest |

Use some of the words from the box to write **a sentence.**

HOME

Make up riddles using some of the words from the box. Ask your child to guess each word.

Name _____

> **Blend** the letter sounds together as you say each word.
> **Fill in** the bubble under the picture it names.

1. r
   ug

   ○   ○   ○

2. t
   en

   ○   ○   ○

3. s
   ix

   ○   ○   ○

4. h
   at

   ○   ○   ○

5. t
   op

   ○   ○   ○

6. l
   eg

   ○   ○   ○

Blend the sounds together as you say each word. Print the word on the line. Draw a line to the picture it names.

1.

n
et
_____
- - - - - - - - - - - - - - -
_____

2.

m
op
_____
- - - - - - - - - - - - - - -
_____

3.

s
un
_____
- - - - - - - - - - - - - - -
_____

4.

w
ig
_____
- - - - - - - - - - - - - - -
_____

5.

c
at
_____
- - - - - - - - - - - - - - -
_____

6.

p
en
_____
- - - - - - - - - - - - - - -
_____

HOME

Name a vowel. Ask your child to read a word that has that vowel.

Name _____

► Say the name of each picture. Print the letter for its beginning and ending sounds. In the last box, draw a picture of a short e word.

1. net	2. web	3. bed	4. pen
5. leg	6. ten	7. hen	8. jet
9. tent	10. led	11. desk	12. belt
13. nest	14. men	15. ves	16. e

Short vowel e: Spelling   **135**

Look at the picture. **Circle** the word that will finish the sentence. **Print** it on the line.

1. Meg sits at her _desk_ .

mask
desk
duck

2. She picks up her _pen_ .

pen
pet
pig

3. Meg draws a _nest_ .

best
nest
net

4. Then she draws a big _egg_ .

leg
egg
beg

5. On the nest sits a _hen_ .

hen
ten
pen

6. Meg hangs it by her _bed_ .

belt
bell
bed

 What kinds of things do you like to draw?

 HOME Point to the picture of the pen and ask your child to name as many words that rhyme with *pen* as possible.

136   Short e: High-frequency words, critical thinking

Name_____

 Say the name of each picture. Print the picture name on the line. In the last box, draw a picture of a short e word. Print the word.

1.

bed

2.

ten

3.

4.

men

5.

web

6.

pen

7.

leg

8.

desk

9.

nest

10.

jet

11.

hen

12.

Short vowel e: Spelling   **137**

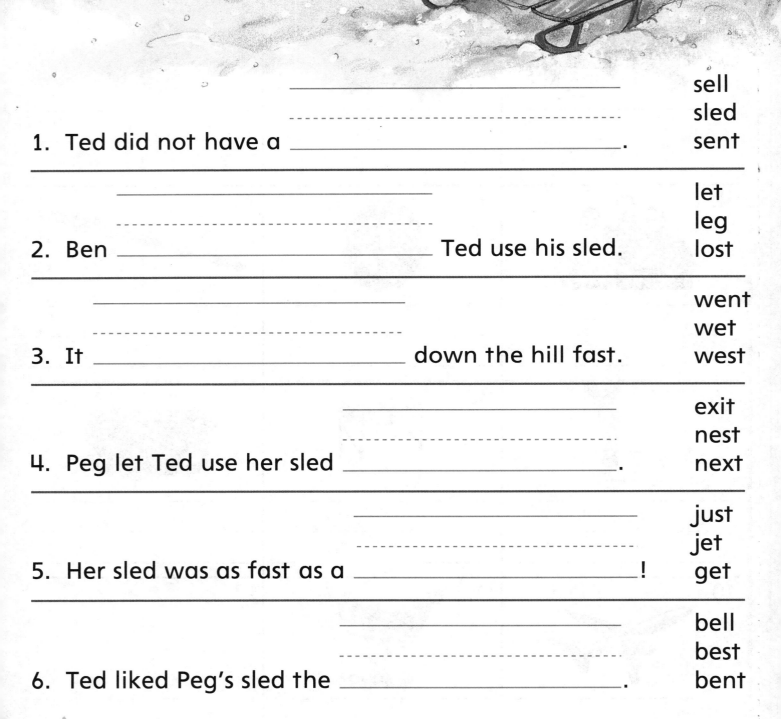

Circle **the word that will finish the sentence.** Print **it on the line.**

1. Ted did not have a _____.

sell
sled
sent

2. Ben _____ Ted use his sled.

let
leg
lost

3. It _____ down the hill fast.

went
wet
west

4. Peg let Ted use her sled _____.

exit
nest
next

5. Her sled was as fast as a _____!

just
jet
get

6. Ted liked Peg's sled the _____.

bell
best
bent

TALK About It
Which sled would you like to use? Why?

With your child, think of sentences to continue the story using some of the words on the page.

138   Short e: High-frequency words, critical thinking

Name _____

 **Phonics & Spelling**

Say the name of each picture. **Circle** the vowel you hear in its name. **Print** the word.

1.

a e i o u

bag

2.

a e i o (u)

cup

bag
bus
lid
map
pig
jet
cup
sock

3.

a e (i) o u

pig

4.

a (e) i o u

jet

5.

(a) e i o u

map

6.

a e i (o) u

sock

7.

a e i o (u)

bus

8.

a e (i) o u

lid

Phonics & Writing

Write a postcard to tell a friend about a trip. Some of the words in the box may help you.

cat	map	bed	top	bus
dog	six	jet	did	sun

TO:

My Friend
1 Happy Lane
Yourtown,
USA
12345

Review short vowels: Writing

HOME Ask your child to use as many of the words in the box as possible in a sentence.

Name _____

Fish Food

What do fish like to eat best?

1

FOLD

Some fish must hide to get away.
Can you spot a fish here?

4

This fish likes to eat lots of bugs.

2

----FOLD----

This fish can fish for small fish.

3

Review short vowels a, i, u, o, e: Take-home book

Name _____

> **Say** the name of each picture.
> **Print** the picture name on the line.

1. 	2. 	3. 
bed		

4. 	5.	6. 

7.	8. 	9.

10. 	11.	12. 

Short vowels: Assessment   **143**

 Fill in the bubble beside the sentence that tells about the picture.

1.
- ⬤ One pen is in a box.
- ○ One pin is in a bag.

2.
- ○ The gift is here in the bag.
- ⬤ The quilt is here on the bed.

3.
- ⬤ The man set up the tent.
- ○ The men are on the bus.

4.
- ○ Miss Beck runs with the dog.
- ○ Jeff hugs the cat on the bed.

Can you read each word? Put a ✔ in the box if you can.

☑ I   ☑ are   ☑ of   ☐ here   ☑ like   ☐ one

☑ for   ☐ my   ☑ her   ☑ with   ☑ down   ☑ come

☑ the   ☑ you   ☑ our   ☑ said   ☑ have   ☑ do

144   Short vowels and high-frequency words: Assessment

Play
by Frank Asch

Come play with me said the sun,
Come play with me said the earth,
Come play with me said the sky.
What shall we play said I?

Let's fly a kite said the sun,
Stand on me said the earth,
I'll bring the wind said the sky,
I'll hold the string said I.

What are other fun ways to play outdoors?

Dear Family,

In this unit called "Let's Play," your child will learn about the sounds of long vowels. Many words related to play contain long vowels, such as skate, feet, bike, boat, and flute. As your child becomes more familiar with vowel sounds, you might try these activities together.

▶ Look through old magazines and catalogs to find and cut out pictures of toys, games, musical instruments, sports events, or sports equipment whose names have long vowel sounds. Ask your child to group the pictures according to the long vowel sounds.

▶ Read the poem on page 145 with your child and help him or her to identify the words with long vowel sounds.

▶ Your child might enjoy reading these books with you. Look for them in your local library.

Ten Minutes Till Bedtime
by Peggy Rathmann

Lentil by Robert McCloskey

Sincerely,

Estimada familia:

En esta unidad, titulada "Juguemos" ("Let's Play"), su hijo/a estudiará los sonidos de las vocales largas en inglés. Muchas palabras relacionadas con actividades de entretenimiento contienen vocales con sonidos largos, como por ejemplo, skate (patín), feet (pies), bike (bicicleta), boat (bote), y flute (flauta). A medida que su hijo/a se vaya familiarizando con los sonidos de las vocales, pueden hacer las siguientes actividades juntos.

▶ Busquen y recorten en revistas y catálogos viejos ilustraciones de juguetes, juegos, instrumentos musicales, eventos o equipos deportivos cuyos nombres contengan vocales con sonidos largos. Pidan a su hijo/a que agrupe las ilustraciones de acuerdo a los sonidos largos de las vocales.

▶ Lean el poema en la página 145 con su hijo/a y ayúdenle a identificar las palabras que contengan vocales con sonidos largos.

▶ Ustedes y su hijo/a disfrutarán leyendo estos libros juntos. Búsquenlos en su biblioteca local.

Ten Minutes Till Bedtime
de Peggy Rathmann

Lentil de Robert McCloskey

Sinceramente,

Name _____

James wants to bake
a big birthday cake.
He plans to make
the cake for Jake.

> **Bake has the long sound of a.** Circle each picture whose name has the long sound of **a.**

1. 	2. 	3.	4. 
5.	6. 	7. 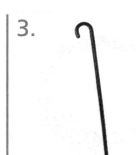	8.
9.	10. 	11. 	12. 

Say the names of the pictures in each row.
Color the pictures whose names rhyme.

1.

cake   rake   rain

2.

3.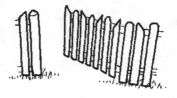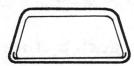

4.

5.

tape

148   Long vowel a: Phonograms/rhyme

HOME   With your child, make up short rhymes using the rhyming words in each row.

Name _____

Say **the name of each picture.** Circle **its name.**

1.
tape (tail) late

2.
late lake (rake)

3.
(nail) rail name

4.
case cap (cape)

5.
gave (game) name

6.
(pill) pail sail

7.
(gate) game date

8.
pain ran (rain)

9.
van save vase

10.
may (hay) way

11.
pail rain (Gail)

12.
play (pay) hay

Help **Jay get to the game. Read each word. Draw a line to join the long a words.**

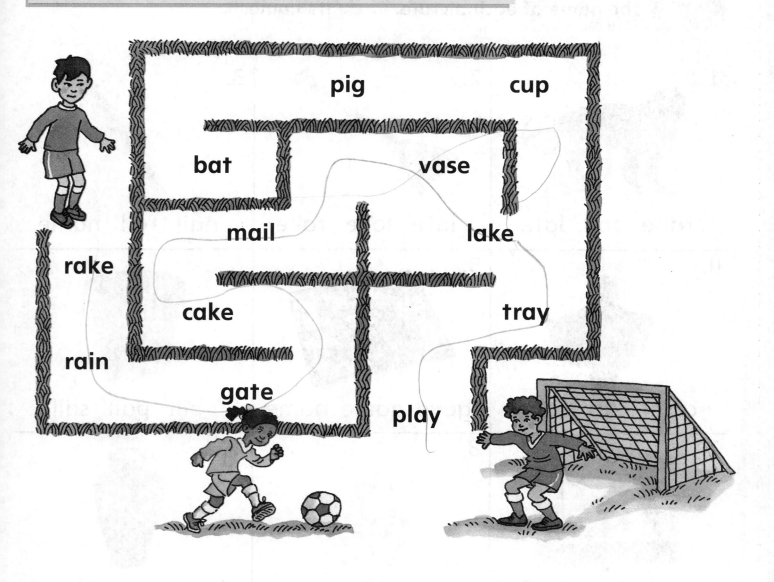

pig   cup

bat   vase

rake   mail   lake

cake   tray

rain

gate   play

▶ **Use some of the long a words to write a sentence.**

_____

- -

_____

- -

_____

HOME

With your child, make up a story using some of the words along the path that leads to the soccer game.

Name _____

> **Say** the name of each picture. If the vowel sound is short, color the box with the word **short**. If the vowel sound is long, color the box with the word **long**.

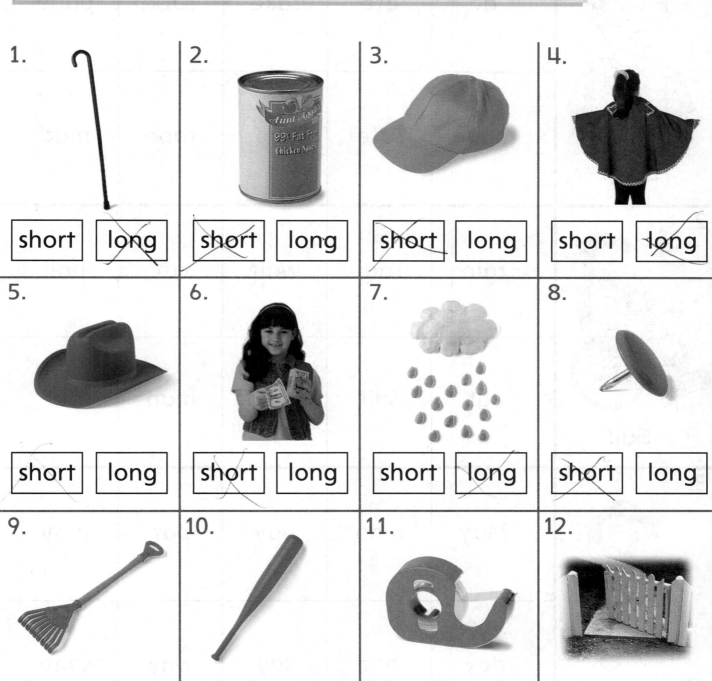

1. | short | ~~long~~

2. | ~~short~~ | long

3. | ~~short~~ | long

4. | short | ~~long~~

5. | short | long

6. | ~~short~~ | long

7. | short | ~~long~~

8. | ~~short~~ | long

9. | short | ~~long~~

10. | short | long

11. | ~~short~~ | long

12. | short | ~~long~~

▶ Help **Dave, Gail, and Ray** find the long **a** words.
Circle **each one you find.**

1.

Dave

at	ate	rake	rack	page
made	safe	tap	tape	mad

2.

Gail

rain	ram	wait	cat	pail
sat	sail	main	man	pal

3.

Ray

May	man	pay	pat	play
day	hat	say	way	sand

HOME

With your child, think of sentences using words that rhyme with *Dave, Gail,* and *Ray,* such as *Ray wants to play today.*

Name _____

> ▶ **Say** the name of each picture. **Circle** its name.

1.

rat   rate

2.

pain   pan

3.

tap   tape

4.

can   cane

5.

can   cane

6.

cape   cap

hate   hat

7.

cape   cap

8.

cape   cap

9.

ran   rain

10.

bat   bait

11.

hay   hat

12.

take   tack

Long and short vowel a: Sound to symbol   **153**

Color **each balloon that has three rhyming long a words.**

1. game tame name

2. take tape ape

3. cane lane mane

4. sail same rail

5. cake rake lake

6. gate date late

7. fade made make

8. cave wave cake

9. bake fake fame

10. nail mail pail

11. rain gain pain

12. hay day pay

HOME

Pick a balloon with three rhyming words. Ask your child to name another word that rhymes.

Name _____

 Say the name of each picture. **Print** the missing vowels on the line. In the last box, draw a picture of a long **a** word. **Print** the word.

1. c a p e

2. c __ n

3. r __ __ n

4. v __ s __

5. c __ k __

6. l __ k e

7. b __ g

8. n __ __ l

9. g __ m e

10. p __ l

11. g __ t

12.

> Look **at the picture.** Circle **the word that will finish each sentence.** Print **it on the line.**

1. _____

_____ and Ray go out to play.

Save
Dave
Sand

2. They go to the _____.

lake
make
late

3. They play a _____.

gate
name
game

4. Ray sits by a _____.

save
came
cave

5. Dave sees a boat with a _____.

save
sail
mail

6. They go in when it _____.

rains
cane
ran

 What are some things you might do at a lake?

 Ask your child to use the words circled on this page in sentences.

Name_____

> Say the name of each picture. Print the picture name on the line. In the last box, draw a picture of a long **a** word. Print the word.

1.
_____
- - - - - - - - - - - - - - - -
_____

2.
_____
- - - - - - - - - - - - - - - -
_____

3.
_____
- - - - - - - - - - - - - - - -
_____

4.
_____
- - - - - - - - - - - - - - - -
_____

5.
_____
- - - - - - - - - - - - - - - -
_____

6.
_____
- - - - - - - - - - - - - - - -
_____

7.
_____
- - - - - - - - - - - - - - - -
_____

8.
_____
- - - - - - - - - - - - - - - -
_____

9.
_____
- - - - - - - - - - - - - - - -
_____

10.
_____
- - - - - - - - - - - - - - - -
_____

11.
_____
- - - - - - - - - - - - - - - -
_____

12.
_____
- - - - - - - - - - - - - - - -
_____

Circle **the word that will finish the sentence.**
Print **it on the line.**

1. The bus was _____.

lane
late
lake

2. Mom had to _____.

wait
wade
wake

3. Then, she ran home in the _____.

rate
rake
rain

4. Mom came in by the _____.

gain
gate
game

5. She _____ me a big hug.

gave
gain
gate

6. I gave her the _____.

made
mail
make

Do you think Mom was glad to be home? Why?

With your child, continue the story using some of the words printed on this page.

Name _____

Read the story. **Use** long **a** words to finish the sentences.

Hooray For Ray!

It was the day of the big game.
Ray was at bat.
The ball came at him.
Ray gave the ball a big whack!
Ray raced around the bases.
He came to home plate.
"Safe!"
"Hooray for Ray!"

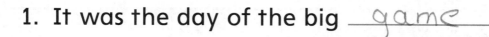

1. It was the day of the big ___game___.

2. Ray raced around the ___bases___.

3. He was ___came___ at home ___plate___.

How do you think Ray felt as he raced around the bases? Why?

Phonics & Writing

Use **one of the letters to make a word with** **ay** or **ail**. **Write** **each real word on the lines.**

d s p h v

ay

1. _____

2. _____

3. _____

4. _____

p m s y n

ail

5. _____

6. _____

7. _____

8. _____

▶ **Write a sentence using one of the words you made.**

_____

_____

_____

160   **Review long vowel a: Phonograms**

HOME Help your child think of other long vowel *a* words, such as *race* and *grape*.

Name _____

Make a Face

It is fun to make a clown face.

---- FOLD ----

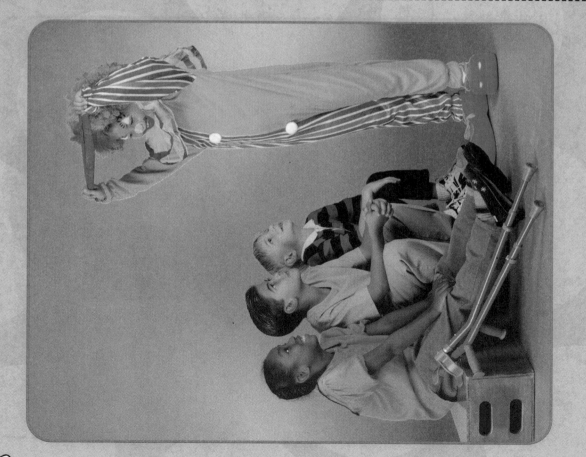

Now you can play!

4

Review long vowel a: Take-home book **161**

2 You will need some face paint.

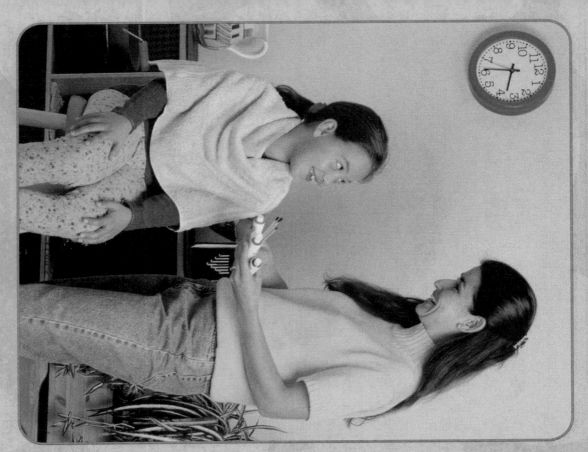

- - - - FOLD - - - - - - - -

3 Start by making shapes.

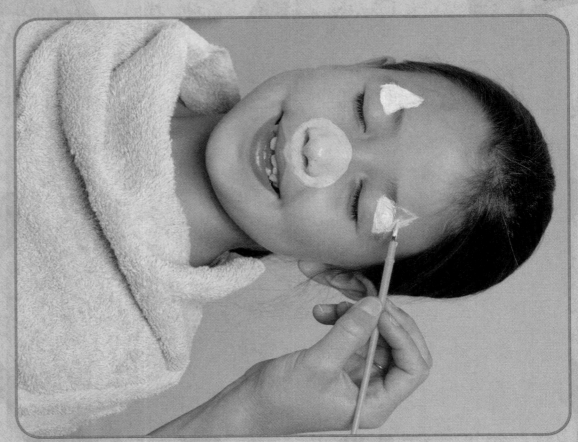

Name _____

▶ Read **the words in the box.** Write **a word to finish each sentence.**

They	~~Where~~
~~out~~	~~two~~
were	your

1. Kate and Jay ___were___ at the beach.

2. Dad took them ___out___ to play in the waves.

3. "I see ___two___ fish," said Kate.

4. "___where___ are the fish?" Jay said.

5. Dad said, "They are by ___your___ feet."

6. ___They___ jumped in the waves all day.

Look at the picture. Then, print words from the box to finish the story. The word shapes will help you.

They	were	two
out	Where	your

1. Where did the cat and dog go to play?

2. They went to the beach.

3. Soon the two friends were hot.

4. The dog went to swim out in the waves.

5. "Do not shake your waves on me!" said the cat.

CHECKING UP

Put a ✔ next to each word you can read.

☐ they ☐ were ☐ where ☐ out ☐ two ☐ your

164 High-frequency words

HOME Help your child retell the story, using some of the new words.

Name _____

I ride my bike.
I fly a kite.
I take a hike.
Then, I say good night!

> **Ride** has the long sound of **i**. **Circle** each picture whose name has the long sound of **i**.

1.

Kite

2.

3.

4.

5.

6.

7.

8.

9.

10.

11.

12.

Say the names of the pictures in each row. Color the pictures whose names rhyme.

1.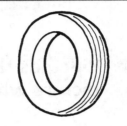

2.

3.

4.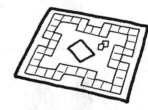

5.

6.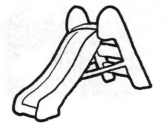

166 Long vowel i: Phonograms/rhyme

Point to a picture and ask your child to name it. Taking turns, try to say as many rhyming words as you can.

Name _____

> Say the name of each picture. Circle its name.

1.

mine (nine) vine

2.

dive   dine   (dime)

3.

pin   pie   pine

4.

(ride)   hide   ripe

5.

bite   (bike)   kite

6.

fine   fire   (five)

7.

tie   ride   (tire)

8.

bite   tide   bike

9.

like   (kite)   tile

10.

vine   wine   (line)

11.

dive   dime   five

12.

(hide)   ride   hit

Read the words in the box. Print a word in the puzzle to name each picture.

Sound to Symbol
Across

1.

3.

4.

7.

8.

| tie | bike | ride | ice |
| kite | mice | pie | dime |

Down

2.

5.

6.

1. b i k e
2. (k)
3. t i e
4. r i d e
5. (d e)
6. (i)
7. m i c e
8. p i e

Use **some of the words from the box to write a sentence.**

168   Long vowel i: Sound to symbol

HOME

Help your child make up a short poem using some of the long *i* words.

Name _____

 Say the name of each picture. If the vowel sound is short, color the box with the word **short**. If the vowel sound is long, color the box with the word **long**.

1.

| short | ~~long~~ |

2.

| ~~short~~ | long |

3.

| short | ~~long~~ |

4.

| ~~short~~ | long |

5.

| ~~short~~ | long |

6.

| ~~short~~ | long |

7.

| short | ~~long~~ |

8.

| ~~short~~ | long |

9.

| short | long |

10.

| ~~short~~ | long |

11.

| ~~short~~ | long |

12.

| short | ~~long~~ |

Say the name of each picture. Circle its name.

1.

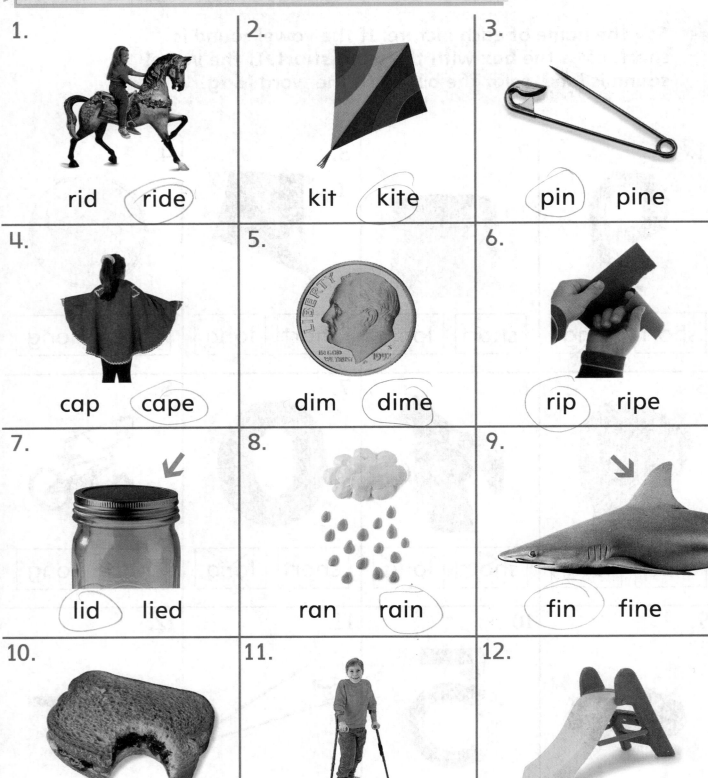

rid (ride)

2.

kit (kite)

3.

(pin) pine

4.

cap (cape)

5.

dim (dime)

6.

(rip) ripe

7.

(lid) lied

8.

ran (rain)

9.

(fin) fine

10.

bit (bite)

11.

(Tim) time

12.

slid (slide)

170 Long and short vowels a, i: Sound to symbol

With your child, make up sentences using the short and long vowel words, such as *The shark's fin is fine.*

Name _____

 Say **the name of each picture. Print the missing vowels on the line. Trace the whole word.**

1.

r i d e

2.

p i g

3.

d i m e

4.

f i r e

5.

l i n e

6.

h i v e

7.

l i d

8.

k i t e

9.

f i v e

10.

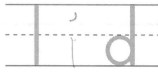

b i k e

11.

d i v e

12.

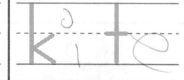

s i x

> Look at the picture. Circle the word that will finish the sentence. Print it on the line.

1. **5** Jim has _____ dimes.

fine
file
five

2. He will not get a _____.

kite
bite
bake

3. He will not get a _____.

lie
pie
pile

4. First, Jim waits in _____.

like
lied
line

5. He has fun on the _____.

rise
ripe
ride

6. He rides home on his _____.

take
bike
bite

 Why do you think Jim chose the ride?

 Help your child think of sentences using words from the page to continue the story.

Name _____

Spelling

> Say the name of each picture. Print the name on the line. In the last box, draw a picture of a long i word. Print the word.

1.

bike

2.

3.

4.

5.

6.

7.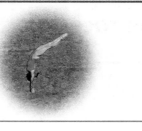

8.

9.

10.

11.

12.

▶ Circle **the word that will finish the sentence.**
Print it on the line.

1. Mike likes his _____.

bite
bike
bake

2. It has a nine on the _____.

side
sale
sand

3. It is the same size as _____.

miss
mine
mitt

4. Mike will _____ it in the race.

ride
ripe
rake

5. The race is six _____ long!

miss
mills
miles

6. Last time it ended in a _____.

tie
tide
tip

 How does it feel when you win a race?

 Help your child make up a sentence that uses any two circled words, then draw a picture that goes with it.

Name_____

Read the story. Use long **i** words to finish the sentences.

Flying a Kite

Children in many places like to fly kites.
In Japan, children fly kites on New Year's day.
The kites can come in many shapes and sizes.
Children tie on a string.
The kites dive and glide.
Hold on to the line!

_____

- -

1. Children in many places like to fly _____.

_____

- - - - - - - - - - - - - - - - - - - -

2. Children _____ on a string.

_____

- - - - - - - - - - - - - - - - - - - -

3. The kites _____ and glide.

TALK About It Can you think of more shapes and sizes for kites?

Use one of the letters to make a word with ide or ine. Write each real word on the lines.

r s w h y

_____
ide

1. _____

2. _____

3. _____

4. _____

n m b f l

_____
ine

5. _____

6. _____

7. _____

8. _____

Write a sentence using one of the words you made.

_____

_____

_____

Review long vowel i: Phonograms

HOME Help your child make up a sentence using as many long vowel *i* words as you can.

Name _____

Di Tries

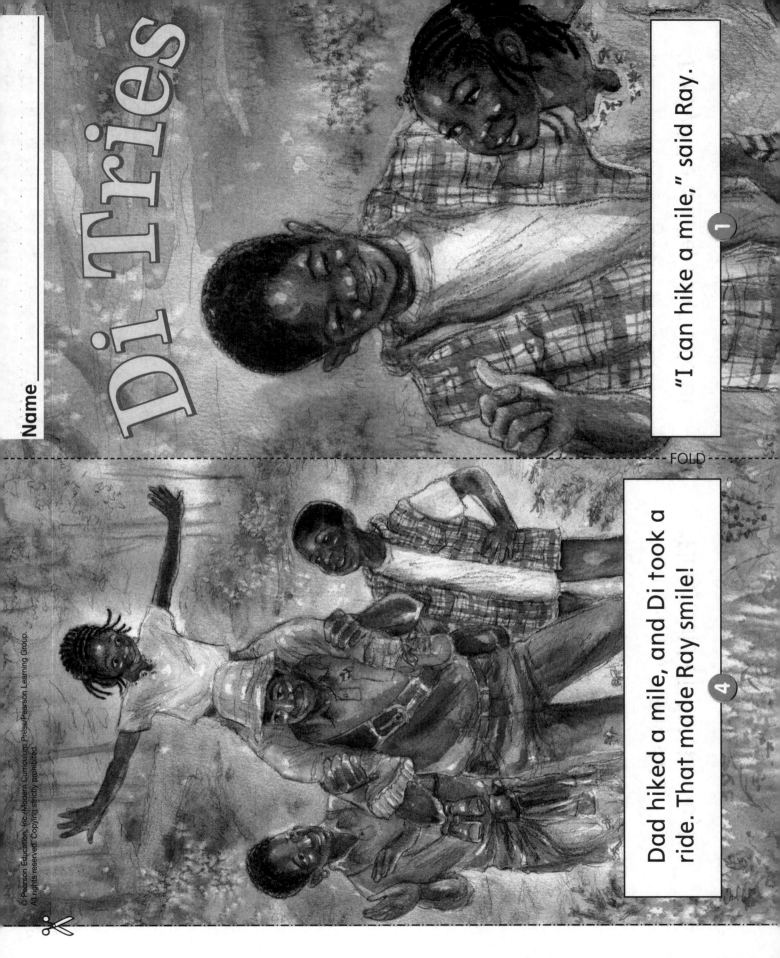

"I can hike a mile," said Ray.

1

Dad hiked a mile, and Di took a ride. That made Ray smile!

4

© Pearson Education, Inc./Modern Curriculum Press/Pearson Learning Group.
All rights reserved. Copying strictly prohibited.

Review long vowels a, i: Take-home book   **177**

"I may hike a mile, too," said Di.

2

"You can try," Ray said.
"Fine," said Di. "Make way!"

3

Name _____

 Read the words in the box. Write a word to finish each sentence.

long	there
Why	little
could	about

_____

1. _____ was Maya smiling?

2. She was thinking _____ her pets.

3. She had two _____ white mice.

4. The mice had _____ tails.

5. Maya _____ hold them in her hands.

6. The mice liked to be _____.

▶ **Look at the picture. Then, print words from the box to finish the story. The word shapes will help you.**

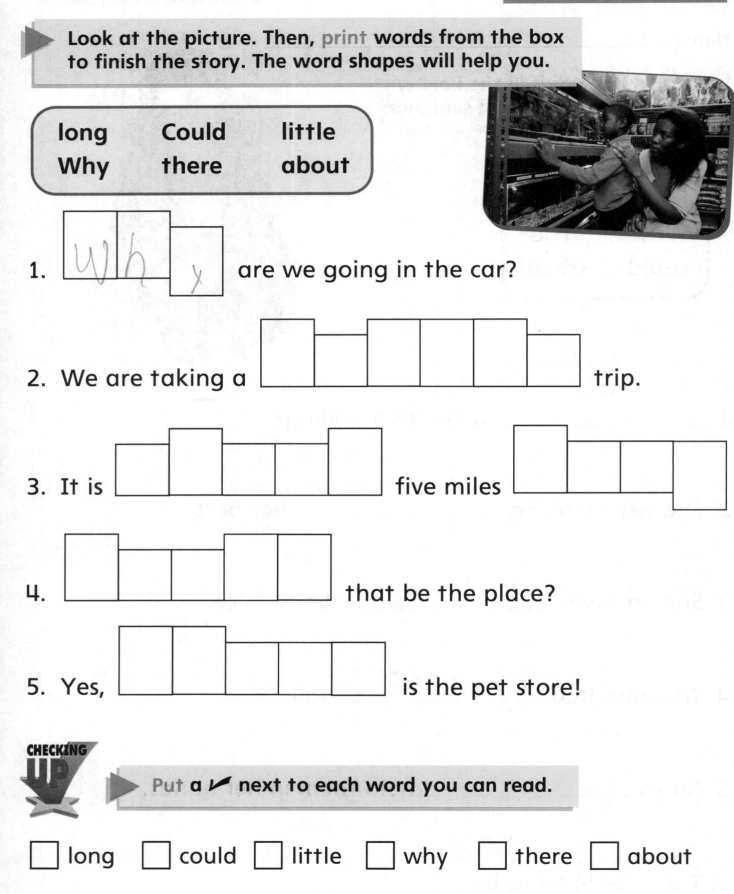

> long   Could   little
> Why   there   about

1. W h __ y   are we going in the car?

2. We are taking a ⬜⬜⬜⬜⬜ trip.

3. It is ⬜⬜⬜⬜⬜ five miles ⬜⬜⬜⬜ .

4. ⬜⬜⬜⬜⬜ that be the place?

5. Yes, ⬜⬜⬜⬜⬜ is the pet store!

CHECKING UP

▶ **Put a ✔ next to each word you can read.**

☐ long   ☐ could   ☐ little   ☐ why   ☐ there   ☐ about

HOME

Help your child use the boxed words to make up sentences, such as *The little mouse is nice.*

Name _____

Lu used a tube
Of strong white glue
To paste her cube
On top of Sue's.

> **Tube has the long sound of u. Circle each picture whose name has the long sound of u.**

1.	2. 	3. 
4. 	5. 	6. 
7. 	8. 	9. 
10. 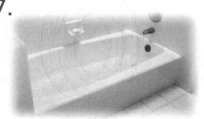	11. 	12. 

Say the names of the pictures in each row.
Color the pictures whose names rhyme.

1.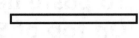

2.

3.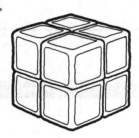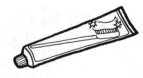

4.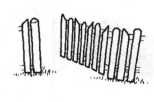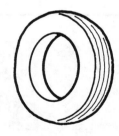

5.

182   Long and short vowel u: Phonograms/rhyme

 HOME

With your child, make up a sentence
that rhymes for each row of rhyming
pictures, such as *I sang a tune in June.*

Name _____

> Say the name of each picture. Circle its name.

1.

rule   mule   rude

2.

cup   cube   cub

3.

cute   cube   cub

4.

tub   tube   tug

5.

tune   tube   tub

6.

Sue   due   fuss

7.

use   sit   suit

8.

June   tune   nuts

9.

use   sun   suit

10.

tune   tube   tuck

11.

run   bun   rude

12.

fun   suit   fruit

Read **each sentence.** Use **the code to make each pair of words.** Print **them on the lines. Then,** circle **the word that finishes the sentence.**

1 = a	2 = e	3 = i	4 = u	5 = b	6 = c
7 = f	8 = l	9 = m	10 = r	11 = s	12 = t

1. June plays the

tuba
12 4 5 1

_____ .
10 4 8 2

2. Luke will feed his

_____
7 8 4 12 2

_____ .
9 4 8 2

3. Sue likes to eat

_____
6 4 5 2

_____ .
7 10 4 3 12

4. Ben got a new

_____
11 4 3 12

_____ .
6 8 4 2

DUKE

5. Duke's house is

_____
12 10 4 2

_____ .
5 8 4 2

HOME

Make up riddles using the long vowel *u* words from the page. Ask your child to guess each word.

Name _____

> Say the name of each picture. If the vowel sound is short, color the box with the word **short**. If the vowel sound is long, color the box with the word **long**.

1.

| short | long |

2.

| short | long |

3.

| short | long |

4.

| short | long |

5.

| short | long |

6.

| short | long |

7.

| short | long |

8.

| short | long |

9.

| short | long |

10.

| short | long |

11.

| short | long |

12.

| short | long |

Color the bubble blue if it has three long u words in it.

1.
rude
Sue
tune

2.
suit
tune
fruit

3.
mule
use
cube

4.
fire
tire
ride

5.
blue
rule
Sue

6.
cute
mute
cube

7.
pail
sail
tail

8.
mile
file
pile

9.
rug
tug
mug

 Use some of the long vowel u words on this page to write a sentence.

_____

- -

_____

_____

- -

_____

186 Long vowel u: Phonemic awareness

HOME

Point to a bubble and say the words inside. With your child, take turns naming other words with the long or short vowel sound.

Name _____

> Say **the name of each picture.** Circle **its name.**

1.

tub   tube

2.

tub   tube

3.

pin   pine

4.

dim   dime

5.

cub   cube

6.

cub   cube

7.

ran   rain

8.

cut   cute

9.

rid   ride

10.

hat   hate

11.

cape   cap

12.

kit   kite

Look at the picture. **Circle** the word that will finish the sentence. **Print** it on the line.

1. Luke will _____ a box.

us
use
tune

2. The box looks like a _____ _____ .

cute
cube
cub

3. He got it from _____ _____ .

rule
Sue
due

4. Luke has a _____ _____ of glue in it.

tune
tub
tube

5. He will put a _____ _____ in it, too.

ruler
rude
rubs

6. Luke will take it on the _____ _____ .

suit
bun
bus

 TALK About It
Where do you think Luke is taking the box?

 HOME
Help your child to think of a sentence that uses some of the long *u* words on the page.

188 Long and short vowel u: High-frequency words, critical thinking

Name_____

 Say the name of each picture. Print the missing vowels on the line. Trace the whole word.

1.

c __ b

2.

t __ l

3.

J __ n

4.

f __ v

5.

__ l __ k

6.

t __ b

7.

k __ t

8.

s __ t

9.

g __ m

10.

c __ p

11.

m __ l

12.

__ l __ t __ n

**Circle the word that will finish the sentence.
Print it on the line.**

1. Sue has a _____.

mule
mile

2. Is a mule a _____ pet?

cube
cut

3. Will she ride it in _____?

tune
June

4. Does the mule like to eat _____?

fruit
rule

5. I do not have a _____.

clue
cuts

6. I want to ask _____.

Sue
suit

 **Where do you think Sue lives?
Why do you think that?**

 Help your child to continue the
story using some of the circled
words on the page.

190   Long vowel u: High-frequency words, critical thinking

Name _____

> Say the name of each picture. Print the name on the line. In the last box, draw a picture of a long u word. Print the word.

1.

cube

2.

3.

4.

5.

6.

7.

8.

9.

10.

11.

12.

Circle the long a, long i, and long u words in the puzzle. The words in the box will help you.

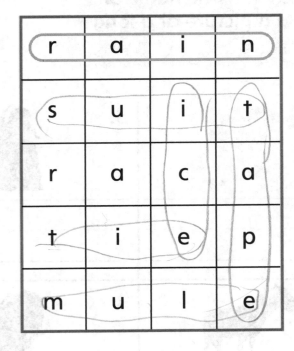

r	a	i	n
s	u	i	t
r	a	c	a
t	i	e	p
m	u	l	e

rain	ice	tape
suit	tie	mule

Print the word from the box that names each picture.

1. rain
2. ice
3.  mule
4. suit
5.  tie
6. tape

 HOME Ask your child to use three of the words from the box in a sentence.

Name _____

Read **the story.** Use **long u words to finish the sentences.**

The Blue Suit

A cute cub saw some fruit.
The fruit was blue.
"This fruit looks good,"
said the cub.
He ate the fruit.
He hummed a tune.
Blue juice got all over him.
"Look!" said the cub's dad.
"You have a new blue suit!"

1. The _____ was blue.

2. Blue _____ got on the cub.

3. The cub had a new _____ _____.

What kind of fruit did the cub eat?

Use **one of the letters to make a word with une** or **ule. Write each real word on the lines.**

j d b t

_____
_____ une

1. _____

2. _____

3. _____

m l r v

_____
_____ ule

4. _____

5. _____

▶ **Write a sentence using one of the words you made.**

_____

_____

_____

HOME Ask your child questions that can be answered with long *u* words, such as "What word means song?" *(tune)*

Name _____

Hand Games

You can use your hands to make pictures. Shine a light on a wall.

1

---- FOLD ----

Hold up two hands and move them. Make a bird that can fly!

4

Review long vowels a, i, u: Take-home book   **195**

Make a cute rabbit. Hold up one hand this way.

2

Make a huge white swan. Hold up two hands like this.

3

Name_____

Turn the jump rope,
High, low, fast, slow!
Put on a show!
Come on, let's go!

 Rope **has the long sound of o.** Circle **each picture whose name has the long sound of o.**

1. 	2. 	3. 	4. 
5. 	6. 	7. 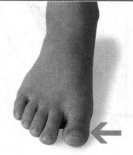	8. 
9. 	10. 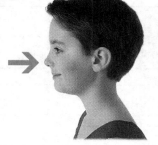	11. 	12. 

Say the names of the pictures in each circle. Color the parts of the circle that have pictures with long **o** names.

1.

2.

3.

4.

Use **some** of the long **o** words to write a sentence.

_____

- -

_____

- -

_____

HOME With your child, take turns saying all the long o words you can name.

Name _____

> Say the names of the pictures in each row.
> Color the pictures whose names rhyme.

1.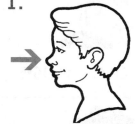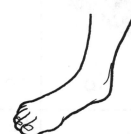

2.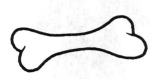

3.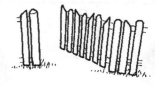

4.

5.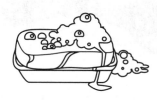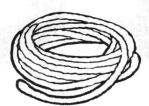

Say **the name of each picture.** Circle **its name.**

1.

coat   cat   coal

2.

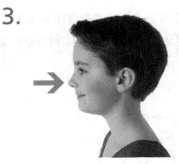

ripe   rope   rip

3.

name   rose   nose

4.

sap   soap   sop

5.

boat   bat   toad

6.

robe   rob   bone

7.

rain   cone   cane

8.

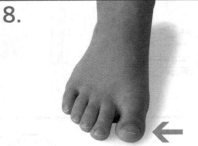

doe   hoe   toe

9.

gate   goat   got

10.

row   bow   toe

11.

hose   hope   hot

12.

cone   boat   bone

Help your child think of other words that rhyme with the names of the pictures on this page, such as *nose, rose, toes.*

Name _____

> Say the name of each picture. Circle the letters that make the long sound of **o**.

1.

g(oa)t

2.

b(ow)

3.

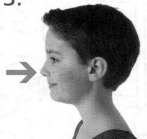

n(o)s(e)

4.

c o n e

5.

r o p e

6.

b o a t

7.

n o t e

8.

r o w

9.

s o a p

10.

h o s e

11.

coat

12.

b o n e

> **Look at the picture. Then, follow the directions below.**

Directions

1. Color the hose green.
2. Color the boat blue.
3. Circle the girl who will row.
4. Draw a toad on the stone.
5. Make an X on the hoe.
6. Color the roses red.
7. Draw a hole for the mole.
8. Draw a rope on the goat.

With your child, make up a story about the picture using the long o words.

Name _____

> Say the name of each picture. If the vowel sound is short, color the box with the word **short**. If the vowel sound is long, color the box with the word **long**.

1.

| short | long |

2.

| short | long |

3.

| short | long |

4.

| short | long |

5.

| short | long |

6.

| short | long |

7.

| short | long |

8.

| short | long |

9.

| short | long |

10.

| short | long |

11.

| short | long |

12.

| short | long |

Long and short vowel o: Phonemic awareness   **203**

Say the name of each picture. Circle the words in the boxes that rhyme with the picture name.

1.

bone	cane	loan	moan	can
Joan	tone	run	zone	coat

2.

got	boat	coat	note	vote
rate	cute	tote	gate	moat

3.

snow	doe	tip	top	slow
go	tube	row	foe	tail

4.

rope	slow	blow	rip	snow
low	ride	bow	tow	rock

204   Long vowel o: Sound to symbol

HOME

Help your child to make up sentences using the rhyming words, such as *I wore a coat in the boat.*

Name_____

Say **the name of each picture.** Circle **its name.**

1.

cat (coat)

2.

not (note)

3.

mop mope

4.

kit kite

5.

bat (boat)

6.

rob (robe)

7.

got (goat)

8.

cub (cube)

9.

sap (soap)

10.

(rat) rate

11.

moan (man)

12.

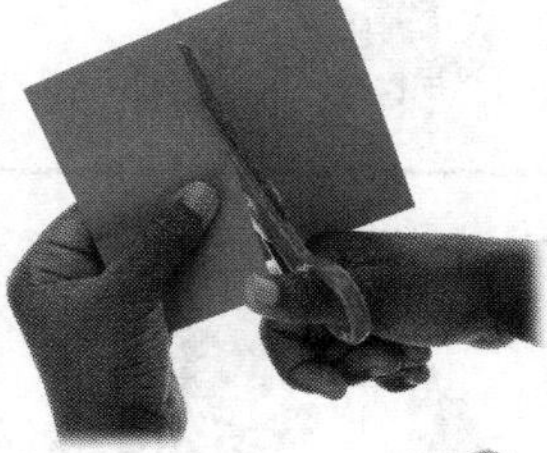

cute (cut)

Look **at the picture.** Circle **the word that will finish the sentence.** Print **it on the line.**

1. A mole hides in a _hole_ .

hose
hole
hope

2. A fish swims in a _bowl_ .

box
bone
bowl

3. A goat eats a _cone_ .

bone
cone
cane

4. A cat goes up a _pole_ .

poke
pole
loan

5. A dog begs for a _bone_ .

bone
robe
boat

6. A fox cleans its _coat_ .

cone
coal
coat

 Which animals make good pets? Why?

 Ask your child to use the words circled on this page in sentences.

Name _____

 Say the name of each picture. Print the missing vowels on the line. Trace the whole word.

1. c o n e

2. h o s e

3. r o b e

4. t _ p

5. r o p e

6. c o a t

7. n o t e

8. n o s e

9. s o a p

10. p o t

11. m o p

12. b o a t

Circle **the word that will finish the sentence.** Print **it on the line.**

_____

----

1. The store is up the _____ .

road
robe
role

_____

----

2. Joan goes in and smells the _____ .

song
soak
soap

_____

----

3. It gets on her _____ .

not
nose
hope

_____

----

4. Joan sees a red _____ .

boss
bow
row

_____

----

5. She sees a blue _____ , too.

robe
rob
ripe

_____

----

6. She will pay and take them _____ .

hose
hole
home

What kind of store did Joan visit?

With your child, think of other sentences using these long o words.

Name _____

> **Say** the name of each picture. **Print** the name on the line. In the last box, **draw** a picture of a long **o** word. **Print** the word.

1.

bone

2.

soap

3.

rope

4.

_____

5.
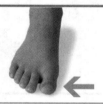

hose

6.

toe

7.

coat

8.

cone

9.

boat

10.

_____

11.

nose

12.

_____

Say each picture name. Draw a line through the three pictures in a row that have the same long vowel sound.

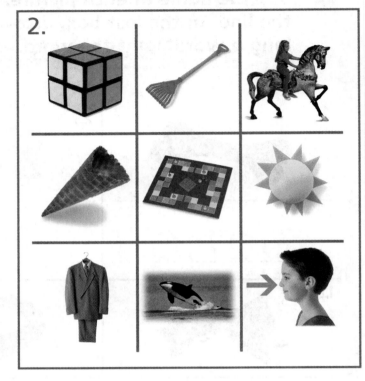

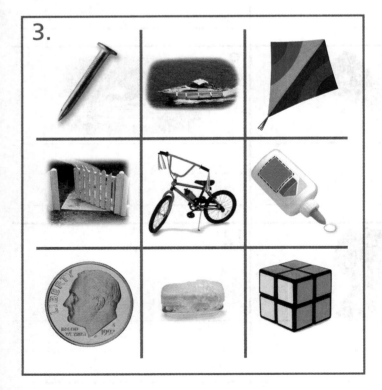

Review long vowels a, i, u, o: Sound to symbol

 Ask your child to think of more words using the long vowel *a, i, u,* or *o* that "won" in each puzzle.

Name_____

 **Phonics & Reading**

Read the story. Use long o words to finish the sentences.

Joe's Show

Joe wanted to put on a show.
"My dog Bo will be in the
show," he said.
"Bo can catch a bone."
Joe's friend Rose came by.
"Can my dog Moe be in your
show?" Rose asked.
"He knows how to roll over,"
she said.
"Yes," said Joe.
Moe and Bo were stars!

_____

1. Joe wanted to put on a _____.

_____

2. Bo can catch a _____.

_____

3. Moe knows how to _____ over.

 TALK About It **What other tricks can pets do?**

Review long vowel o: Reading, critical thinking **211**

Phonics & Writing

Use **one of the letters to make a word with ose or old.** Write **each real word on the lines.**

r h n f p   g s c p h

_____
_ _ _ _ _ _ _ _ _ _ _ _ _ _
ose

1. _____

2. _____

3. _____

4. _____

_____
_ _ _ _ _ _ _ _ _ _ _ _ _ _
old

5. _____

6. _____

7. _____

8. _____

➤ Write **a sentence using one of the words you made.**

_____

_____

_____

212   **Review long vowel o: Phonograms**

Ask your child to put two thumbs up for a rhyming pair; then, say word pairs such as *rose–hose* or *sold–stop*.

Name _____

Games Around the Globe

Children around the globe like to play games.

1

FOLD

Children in many places like to jump rope. What kind of games do you like to play?

4

Some children play ball games. They must know the rules of the game.

2

---- FOLD ----

Some children like to play clapping games. They can clap and sing a tune.

3

Name _____

▶ **Read** the words in the box. **Write** a word to finish each sentence.

from	which
them	because
Their	want

_____

1. Joe could not go out _____ of the rain.

_____

2. "Do you _____ to call Cody or Flo?"
Mom said.

_____

3. Joe did not know _____ friend to call.

_____

4. Mom said Joe could call both of _____.

_____

5. They played a game _____ Mexico.

_____

6. _____ game was fun!

Look at the picture. Then, print words from the box to finish the story. The word shapes will help you.

from   their   because
them   Which   want

1. Lin and Lola know Joel them school.

2. They _____ him to be _____ friend.

3. Joel used to say, " _____ twin is which?"

4. Now he can tell _____ apart.

5. He knows because Lin has a gold cap.

CHECKING UP

Put a ✔ next to each word you can read.

☐ them ☐ want ☐ because ☐ which ☐ from ☐ their

216   High-frequency words

HOME   Help your child to make up a sentence using some of the words in the box.

Name_____

Here in my tree
Is the best place to be.
I can see down,
But the green leaves
Hide me!

> Tree **has the long sound of e.** Circle **each picture whose name has the long sound of e.**

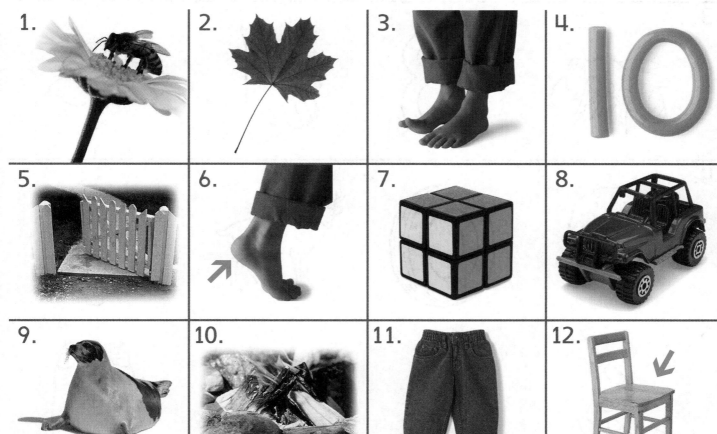

1.

2.

3.

4.

5.

6.

7.

8.

9.

10.

11.

12.

Long vowel e: Phonemic awareness   **217**

Say the names of the pictures in each row.
Color the pictures whose names rhyme.

1.

 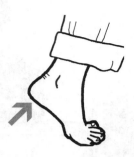  

2.

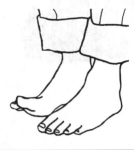   

3.

  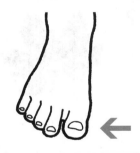 

4.

 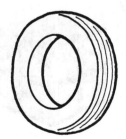  

5.

218 Long vowel e: Phonograms/rhyme

 With your child, take turns naming the first picture in a row and saying a new word that rhymes, such as *wheel, feel.*

Name _____

> Say **the name of each picture.** Circle **its name.**

1.

beet   feed   (feet)

2.

(leaf)   lead   feel

3.

meat   (seat)   seed

4.

feel   (heel)   heat

5.

see   tea   (bee)

6.

real   seat   (seal)

7.

(jeep)   Jean   peep

8.

beep   (peel)   reel

9.

beam   seem   (team)

10.

bead   jeans   (bean)

11.

need   (seed)   seal

12.

beads   bean   beep

Help **Jean and Lee find the seals at the zoo.** Read each word. Draw a line to join the long e words.

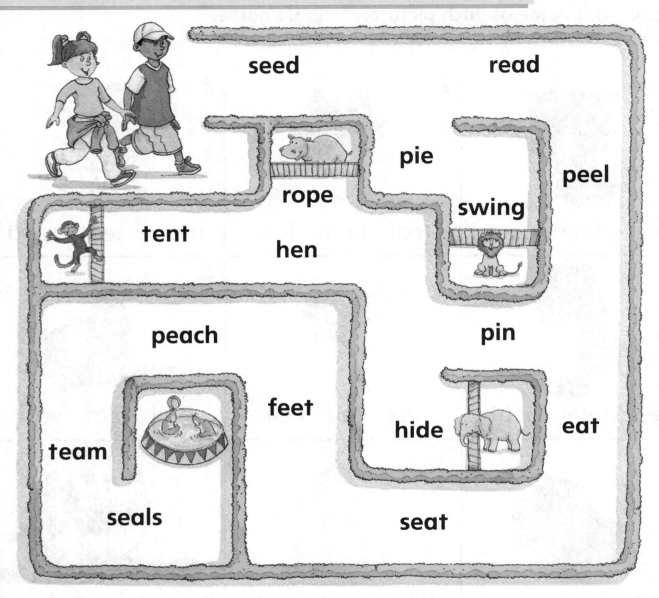

seed

read

pie

peel

rope

swing

tent

hen

peach

pin

feet

hide

eat

team

seals

seat

Use **some of the long e words to write a sentence.**

HOME

Help your child to use some of the words along the path to make up a short story.

Name _____

> Say the name of each picture. If the vowel sound is short, color the box with the word **short**. If the vowel sound is long, color the box with the word **long**.

1.

| short | long |

2.

| short | long |

3.

| short | long |

4.

| short | long |

5.

| short | long |

6.

| short | long |

7.

| short | long |

8.

| short | long |

9.

| short | long |

10.

| short | long |

11.

| short | long |

12.

| short | long |

Long and short vowels a, i, e: Phonemic awareness   **221**

Say the name of each picture. Circle the words in the boxes that rhyme with the picture name.

1.

me	team	see	met	bean
he	we	fee	tea	seed

2.

feel	seal	sell	deep	deal
men	meal	real	leaf	help

3.

feet	beat	bet	heat	set
seat	net	neat	peat	wet

4.

please	pegs	feet	meats	fleas
seals	teas	begs	deep	team

HOME

Ask your child to clap for a rhyming pair; then, say word pairs from the page, such as *me, see* and *tea, met*.

Name _____

> Say the name of each picture. Circle its name.

1.

(bed)   bead

2.

met   (meat)

3.

neat   net

4.

(kite)   kit

5.

(ten)   teen

6.

set   (seat)

7.

mean   (men)

8.

(cube   cub)

9.

beds   beads

10.

(cape)   cap

11.

bit   (bite)

12.

(eat)   at

Long and short vowels a, i, u, e: Sound to symbol   **223**

Look at the picture. Circle the word that will finish the sentence. Print it on the line.

1. I sit in my _____.

seal
seed
seat

2. It feels nice to rest my _____.

feet
feel
feed

3. Dean heats up the _____.

met
team
meat

4. Mom piles on more _____.

peak
peas
pens

5. Can I eat a heap of _____?

beds
beans
beads

6. After I eat I brush my _____.

teeth
team
ten

 What food do you like best? Why?

 Help your child make up a story using some of the circled words on the page.

Name _____

> Say the name of each picture. Print the missing vowels on the line. Trace the whole word.

1.
feet

2.
hen

3.
seal

4.
bed

5.
net

6.
seat

7.
team

8.
meat

9.
jeep

10.
w b

11.
leaf

12.
heel

Circle the word that will finish the sentence. Print it on the line.

jeans
jeep
1. We rode to Lee's game in the _____ . peep

seats
seals
2. We sat in a row with many _____ . seems

well
week
3. The Seals beat the Bees last _____ . keep

lead
leap
4. The Bees are in the _____ . leak

neat
need
5. The Seals _____ to win. seed

tent
tame
6. Will Lee's _____ win the game? team

 Which team do you think will win?

 With your child, make up a silly sentence using some of the circled words.

Name _____

 Say the name of each picture. Print the name on the line. In the last box, draw a picture of a long e word. Print the word.

1. heel

2. bee

3. leaf

4. bed

5. seed

6. team

7. seat

8. men

9. feet

10. pea

11. jeep

12.

Long and short vowel e: Spelling   **227**

Look at the vowel sound. Color the pictures in each row whose names have that vowel sound.

1. Long a

2. Long i

3. Long u

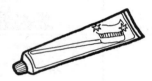   

4. Long o

5. Long e

228 Review long vowels a, i, u, o, e:
Phonemic Awareness

 Ask your child to think of rhyming words for three of the picture names.

Name _____

> **Blend** the letter sounds together as you say each word. Then **color** the picture it names.

1. c a n e

2. h o s e

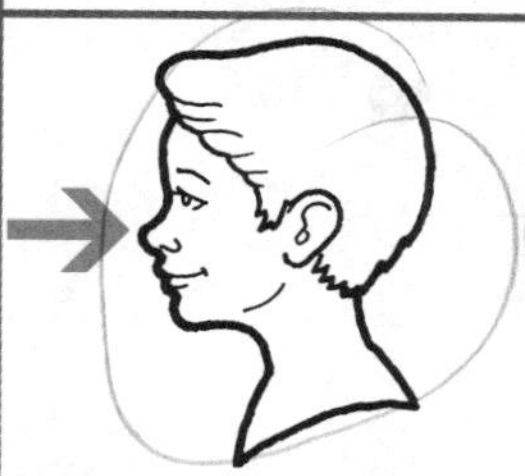

3. t u b

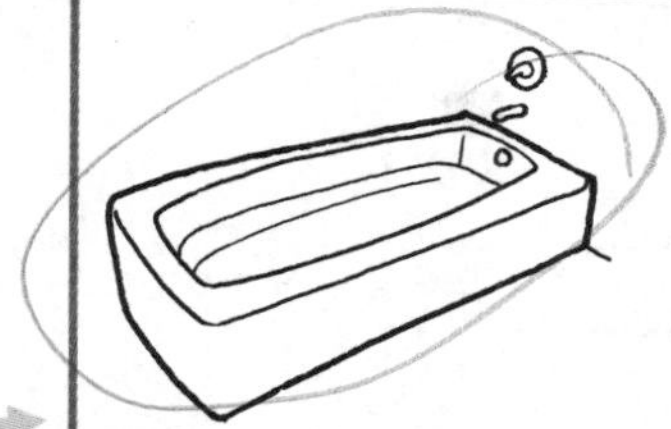

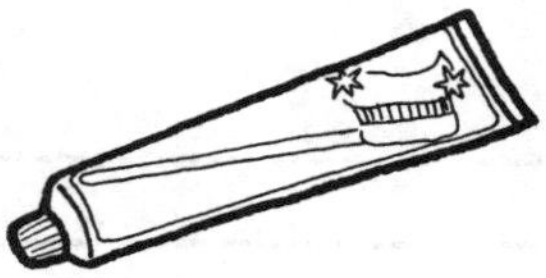

4. s e a t

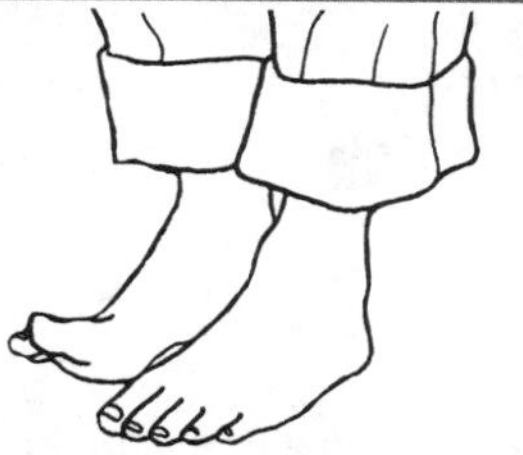

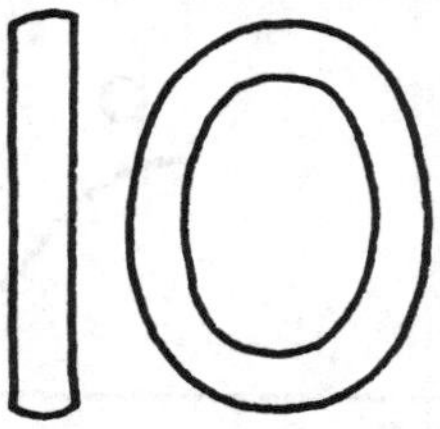

5. p i n

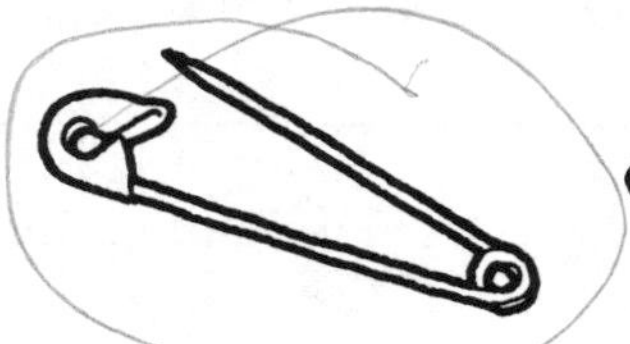

6. d o g

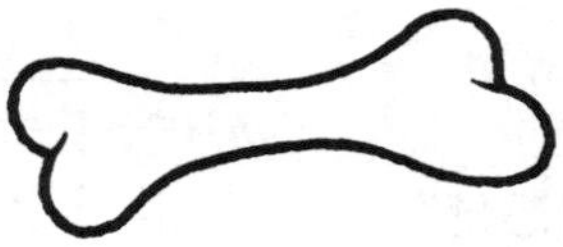

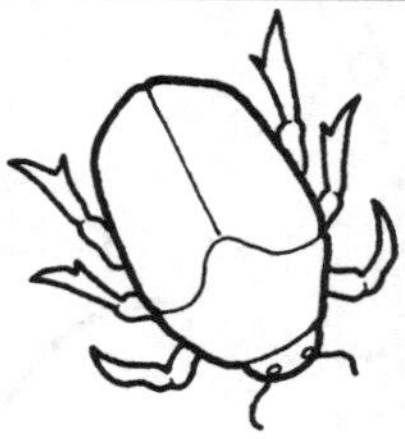

Review long and short a, i, u o, e: Blending phonemes   **229**

▶ **Blend** the letter sounds together as you **say** each word.
Print the word on the line. Draw a line to the picture it names.

1.

c
ub
_____
- - - - - - - - - - - - - - - - - -
_____   ●

2.

m
eat
_____
- - - - - - - - - - - - - - - - - -
_____   ●

3.

r
ain
_____
- - - - - - - - - - - - - - - - - -
_____   ●

4.

p
ig
_____
- - - - - - - - - - - - - - - - - -
_____   ●

5.

m
op
_____
- - - - - - - - - - - - - - - - - -
_____   ●

6.

t
ube
_____
- - - - - - - - - - - - - - - - - -
_____   ●

230   **Review vowels: Blending phonograms**

HOME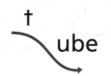

Help your child make up silly rhymes for picture names, such as *Hop on a mop.*

Name _____

 Say the name of each picture. Print the missing vowels on the lines. Trace the whole word.

1. coat

2. tire

3. feet

4. r _ b _

5. tube

6. b _

7. dime

8. h _

9. l _ af

10. cake

11. suit

12. nail

Read the word in the box. Add an e to make a long vowel word. Write it on the first line. Then change the vowel of the word in the box to make a short vowel word. Write it on the second line.

	Long Vowel	**Short Vowel**
1. tap	tape	top
2. pin		
3. cut		
4. hop		
5. not		
6. pan		
7. hid		

HOME Help your child think of sentences using short and long vowel word pairs, such as *I did not get a note.*

Name _____

Say and spell each long vowel word.
Print each word on a line in the box
that shows its long vowel sound.

fruit	rain	pie	bean	bike
bone	hay	soap	seal	glue

Long a

_____ _____

_____ _____

Long i

_____ _____

_____ _____

Long u

_____ _____

_____ _____

Long o

_____ _____

_____ _____

Long e

_____ _____

_____ _____

Phonics & Writing

Write a letter to a friend. Tell about a game, sport, or hobby you like. The words in the box may help you.

kite	rope	feet
bike	flute	day

Dear _____ ,

Your friend,

234   Review long vowels a, i, u, o, e: Writing

HOME   You may want to help your child address an envelope and mail the letter to a friend.

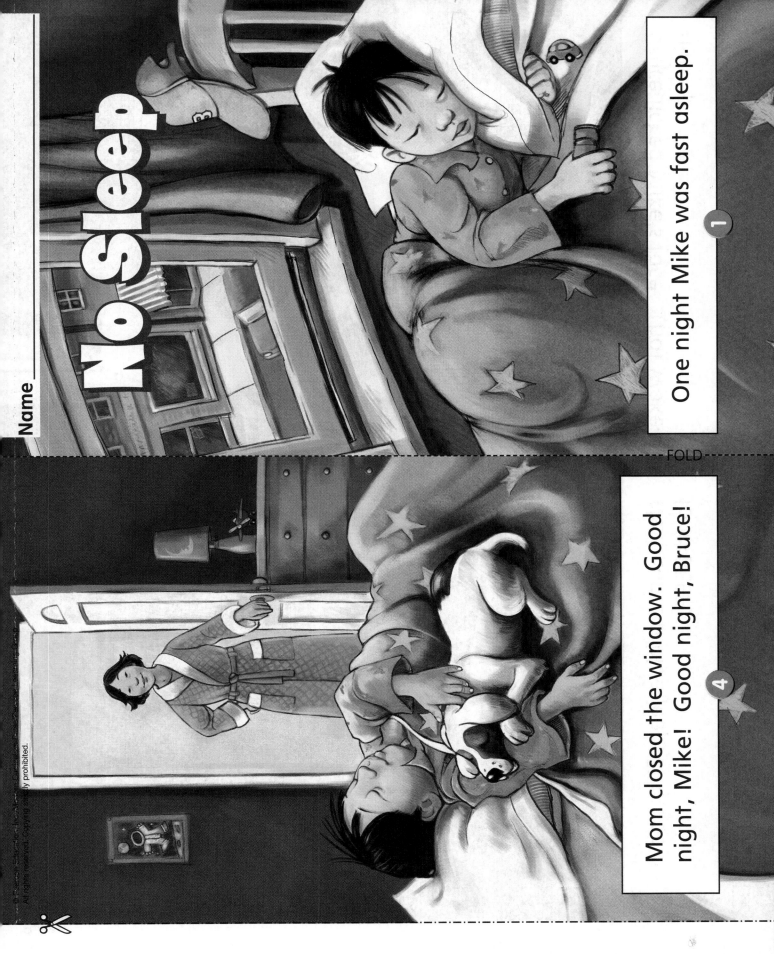

No Sleep

1 One night Mike was fast asleep.

- - - - - FOLD - - - - -

4 Mom closed the window. Good night, Mike! Good night, Bruce!

Bruce licked Mike's face. That woke him up.

2

Next came a blue jeep. It made a loud BEEP.

3

Name _____

Say **the name of each picture.** Fill in **the bubble beside the picture name.**

1.
- ● cake
- ○ rake
- ○ coat
- ○ keep

2.
- ○ mile
- ○ mail
- ○ ruler
- ● mule

3.
- ○ wave
- ○ vase
- ● five
- ○ dive

4.
- ○ bone
- ● cone
- ○ cane
- ○ tune

5.
- ○ jeans
- ● jeep
- ○ deep
- ○ game

6.
- ○ sail
- ○ seem
- ○ rose
- ● suit

7.
- ● tie
- ○ toe
- ○ lie
- ○ tire

8.
- ○ rail
- ○ road
- ○ read
- ● rain

9.
- ○ bait
- ○ goat
- ● boat
- ○ toad

10.
- ○ tile
- ● tube
- ○ tape
- ○ time

11.
- ○ mate
- ○ moat
- ○ boat
- ● meat

12.
- ● rope
- ○ soap
- ○ pole
- ○ robe

 Circle the word that will finish the sentence. Print it on the line.

1. Sue had a _____ blue kite.

   net
   neat

2. The kite did _____ have a tail yet.

   not
   note

3. Joe _____ up rags to make a tail.

   cut
   cute

4. Then they sailed the _____ .

   kit
   kite

Can you read each word? Put a ✔ in the box if you can.

☐ long   ☐ their   ☐ where   ☐ want   ☐ out   ☐ little

☐ your   ☐ could   ☐ about   ☐ two   ☐ from   ☐ why

☐ they   ☐ which   ☐ them   ☐ were   ☐ there   ☐ because

Read Aloud

Everybody Eats Bread

People came to America from all over the world. They brought many ways to make bread.

French Americans make long, skinny loaves. The crust is crisp and brown. Mexican Americans wrap a flat bread around beans and meat. Jewish Americans bake bread with eggs and milk. They twist the loaf into a braid.

It does not matter what shape bread is. Every shape tastes good!

TALK about It

What kind of bread do you like best?

Dear Family,

In this unit called "Everybody Eats," your child will learn about words that begin and end with consonant blends and words with **y** as a vowel. Many food names, such as **gr**apes, **pl**um, **str**awberr**y**, mi**lk**, and che**rry**, begin or end with consonant blends or end with **y** as a vowel. As your child becomes familiar with consonant blends and words with **y** as a vowel, you might try these activities together.

▶ Talk with your child about a favorite food. Have him or her draw a picture of the food. Then, help him or her to write a sentence about the food.

▶ Read the article on page 239 together. Ask your child to identify words with consonant blends and **y** as a vowel.

▶ Your child might enjoy reading these books with you. Look for them in your local library.

The Giant Carrot by Jan Peck
Blueberries for Sal by Robert McCloskey

Sincerely,

_____

Estimada familia:

En esta unidad, titulada "Todos comemos" ("Everybody Eats"), su hijo/a estudiará palabras en inglés que comienzan y terminan con combinaciones de consonantes y palabras con y como una vocal. Muchos nombres de alimentos, como por ejemplo, **gr**apes (uvas), **pl**um (ciruela), **str**awberr**y** (fresa), mi**lk** (leche) y che**rry** (cereza), comienzan o terminan con grupos de consonantes o terminan con **y** como una vocal. A medida que su hijo/a se vaya familiarizando con los grupos de consonantes y las palabras con **y** como una vocal, pueden hacer las siguientes actividades juntos.

▶ Conversen con su hijo/a sobre una comida favorita. Pídanle que haga un dibujo de dicha comida y después, con su ayuda, que escriba una oración que describa la comida.

▶ Lean juntos el artículo en la página 239. Pidan a su hijo/a que identifique palabras con combinaciones de consonantes e **y** como una vocal.

▶ Ustedes y su hijo/a disfrutarán leyendo estos libros juntos. Búsquenlos en su biblioteca local.

The Giant Carrot de Jan Peck
Blueberries for Sal de Robert McCloskey

Sinceramente,

_____

Name_____

I love to munch
Fresh fruit for brunch
And have a bunch
Of grapes with lunch.

▶ **Say** the name of the first picture in the row.
Circle each picture in the row whose name begins
with the same blend.

1.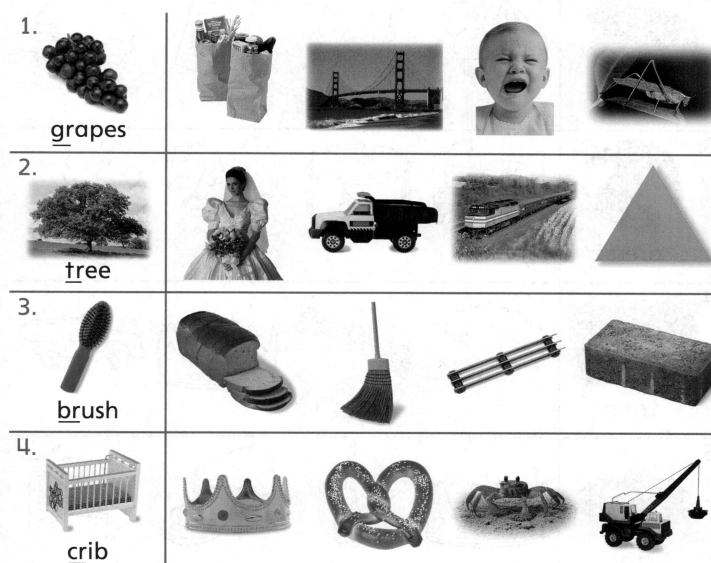

grapes

2.

tree

3.

brush

4.

crib

Say the name of the first picture in the row.
Color each picture in the row whose name begins with the same blend.

1.  prize

2.  frog

3.  dress

4.  train

5.  crab

242   R blends: Sound to symbol

HOME Ask your child to say the name of each picture and name the first two letters of each word.

Name _____

> **Say** the name of each picture. **Circle** its name.

1.

free (tree)

2.

trick (brick)

3.

(prize) cries

4.

(frog) frame

5.

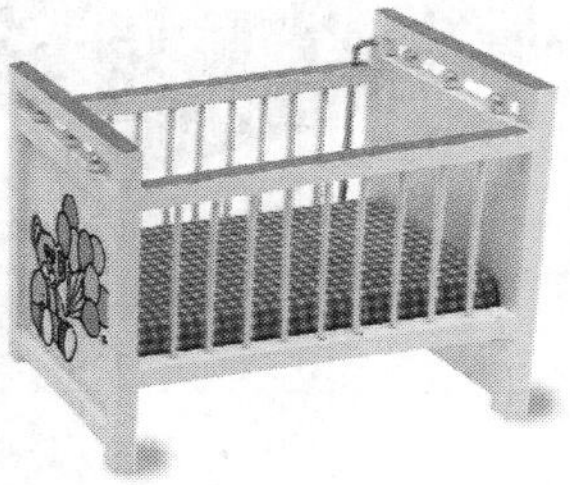

crab (crib)

6.

drive (dress)

7.

braid (bride)

8.

(grapes) grass

9.

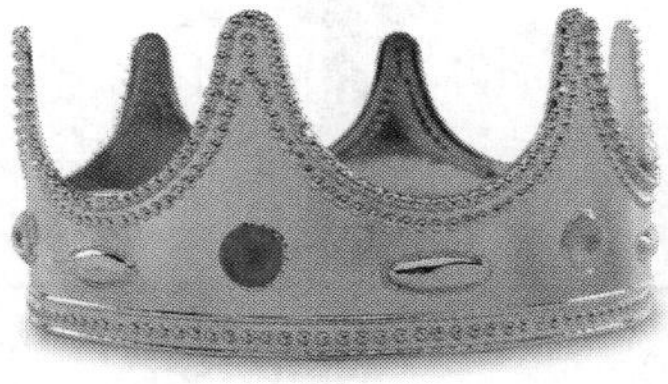

crane (crown)

10.

(drum) drip

11.

frown (frame)

12.

(grass) grab

Say the name of each picture. Print its beginning blend on the line. Trace the whole word.

1. crab

2. train

3. bride

4. fruit

5. brick

6. dress

7. prize

8. _ane

9. tree

10. drum

11. crib

12. frog

 Point to a picture and ask your child to think of another word that begins with the same sound.

Name _____

Slice the plum.
Place it on a plate.
You take some.
I'll be glad to wait.

Say the name of the first picture in the row.
Circle each picture in the row whose name begins with the same blend.

1. <u>pl</u>ug

2. <u>bl</u>ock

3. <u>cl</u>ub

4. <u>fl</u>ag

5. <u>gl</u>ass

Say **the name of each picture.** Circle **its name.**

1. (block)   flock

2. grape   (plate)

3. (class)   glass

4. drag   (flag)

5. clue   (glue)

6. (plug)   plum

7. crack   (clock)

8. (plant)   plan

9. (flat)   float

10. grass   (glass)

11. (club)   clap

12. (fly)   cry

HOME
Play a word game with your child by saying, "I say *fly*, you say fl___." Your child supplies a word with the blend.

Name_____

> Say the name of each picture. Print its beginning blend on the line. Trace the whole word.

1. club

2. plant

3. flag

4. plate

5. clock

6. fly

7. flat

8. glove

9. block

10. globe

11. plug

12. glue

L blends: Spelling **247**

Say the name of each picture. Circle the word that will finish the sentence. Print it on the line.

1. Take a peek into my

class .

clap
class
grass

2. Bruce draws a funny

clown .

clock
clown
frown

3. Fran makes a clock from a paper

plate .

plate
prank
plum

4. Mr. Glen lets us grow

plant .

plans
plates
plants

5. We play with clay and

blocks .

braids
drives
blocks

6. We look at the

globe .

globe
glass
grape

 Would you like to do what Bruce and Fran did in school? Why?

 Point to the words *Bruce, Fran, Glen, grow, play, clay* and ask your child to think of more words that begin with the same sounds.

Name _____

Spice smells nice,
And tastes good, too.
But too much spice
Can spoil the stew.

▶ **Say** the name of the first picture in the row. **Circle** all the pictures in the row whose names begin with the same blend.

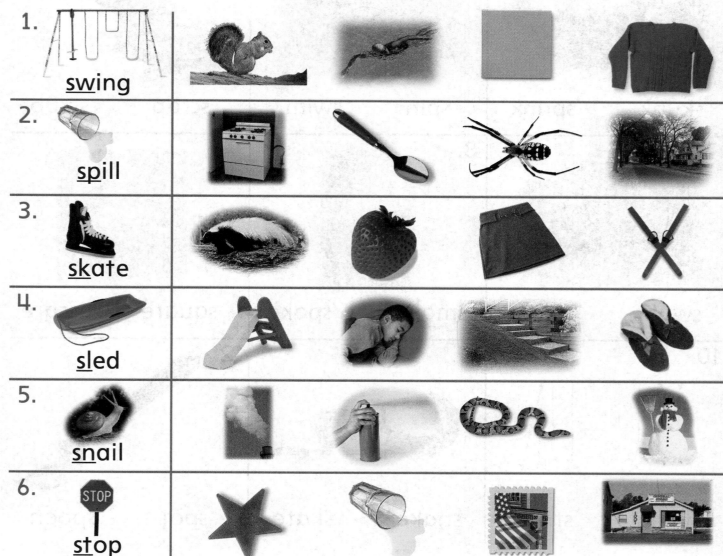

1. <u>sw</u>ing

2. <u>sp</u>ill

3. <u>sk</u>ate

4. <u>s</u>led

5. <u>sn</u>ail

6. <u>st</u>op

Say the name of each picture. Circle its name.

1. sled   slide

2. stops   steps

3. spill   spade

4. skunk   spunk

5. spin   swim

6. scrap   scrub

7. sweet   street

8. smoke   spoke

9. square   scare

10. swing   string

11. snake   skate

12. spot   spoon

HOME

Say "s-l, sl." Ask your child to name a word that begins with the sl sound. Repeat for st, sp, sk, sw, sm.

Name _____

 Say the name of each picture. Print its beginning blend on the line. Trace the whole word.

1. skate

2. sled

3. scrub

4. star

5. snail

6. stop

7. smoke

8. shirt

9. spill

10. swing

11. square

12. swim

Say the name of the picture. Circle the word that will finish the sentence. Print it on the line.

1. Be sure to __stop__ and read each rule!

spill
stop
star

2. Take turns on the __slide__.

slide
sling
slip

3. Do not run near the __swing__.

sting
swing
swim

4. Please do not pet the __snake__.

snake
spoke
snail

5. Look before you cross the __stree__.

steps
street
stamp

6. Always __swim__ with a pal.

sweep
snake
swim

 What other safety rules do you know?

 HOME Help your child to think of new sentences using some of the circled words.

Name_____

I'd like to be in a marching band,
With a shiny gold trumpet in my hand.
I'd look my best in my hat and coat,
And I'd never, ever miss a note!

Say the name of the first picture in the row. Circle each picture in the row whose name ends with the same blend.

1. jump

2. desk

3. sink

4.  list

5. hand

Say the name of each picture. Print its ending blend on the line. Trace the whole word.

1. trunk

2. lamp

3. desk

4. milk

5. list

6. wi__

7. nest

8. sink

9. mask

10. belt

11. jump

12. hand

254 Final blends: Spelling

HOME

Ask your child to point to a picture, name a word that rhymes, and then name the letters in the final blend.

Name _____

> ▶ Blend **the letter sounds together as you say each word.** Color **the picture it names.**

1.

sl → e → d

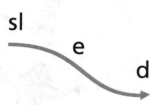  

2.

cr → i → b

3.

pl → u → g

4.

fl → a → g

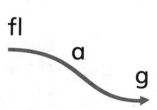  

5.

dr → u → m

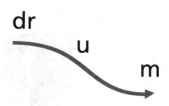  

Blend the letter sounds together as you say each word. Then **print** the word on the line. **Draw** a line to the picture it names.

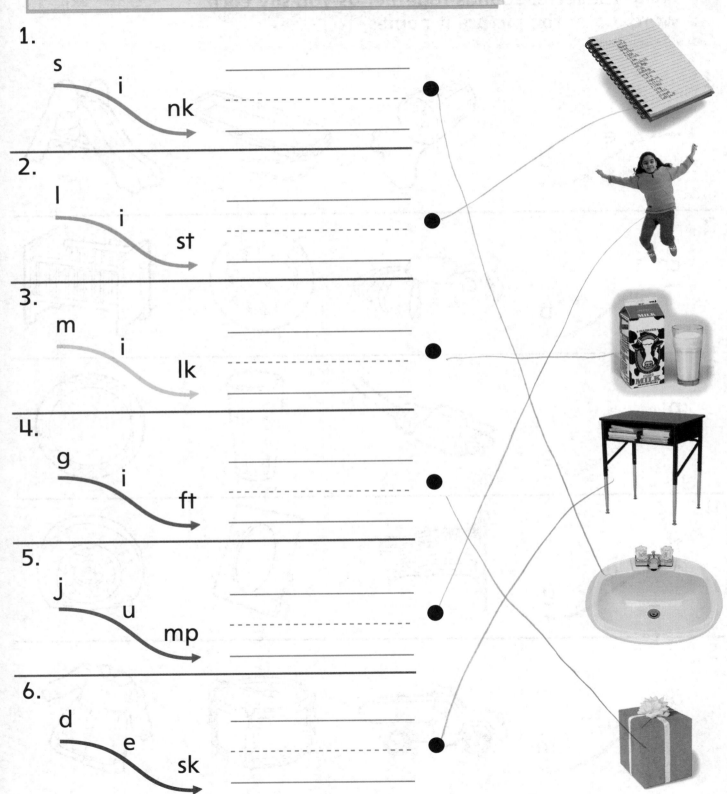

1.

s
i
nk

2.

l
i
st

3.

m
i
lk

4.

g
i
ft

5.

j
u
mp

6.

d
e
sk

Point to a word. Ask your child to name the final blend, then say a word with the same final blend.

Name_____

Fred's Bread

Fred made some bread.
He mixed flour, water,
and too much yeast.
The bread grew and grew.
Now Fred had too much bread!
He asked his friends to stop by.
They sliced the soft bread and made toast.
Then they spread jam on the toast.
They had a feast!

_____
- -

1. Fred made some _____.

_____
- -

2. Fred asked his friends to _____ by.

_____
- -

3. He and his friends had a _____.

 Why did Fred end up
with so much bread?

Add the word part to each of the blends in the boxes. Say the word. If it is a real word, write it on the line.

| tr | sm | br | cl | sl |

| pl | gr | gl | cl | st |

ick

ay

1. _____

2. _____

3. _____

4. _____

5. _____

6. _____

7. _____

8. _____

Write a sentence using two of the words you made.

_____

_____

_____

Ask your child to make up a sentence using two more of the words he or she wrote.

Name _____

Won't you try my berry pie?
The crust is flaky, my, oh my.
Come on, have some.
Don't be shy.
If you won't try it, I may cry!

▶ **Say** the name of the picture. **Circle** the words in the boxes with the same sound of **y** as the picture name. Then, **circle** the pictures whose names have the vowel sound of **y**.

1.

by	lazy	yellow	dry	yet
my	sky	yoke	cry	yarn

2.

yes	fry	you	yard	funny
yellow	puppy	sly	yell	windy

3.

20

fly	candy	yams	lady	penny
pry	fairy	baby	try	pony

Say the name of each picture. Circle its name.

1. puppy   buggy

2. fry   fly

3. lady   baby

4. funny   penny

5. pony   penny

6. cry   try

7. spy   sky

8. fifty   twenty

9. sly   fry

HOME
Point to each picture and help your child think of a word or name that rhymes, such as *puppy-guppy*.

Name _____

 Say the name of each picture. Circle the word that will finish the sentence. Print it on the line.

1. Wendy can not ride a
   _____
   POnY .

   bony
   pony
   penny

2. She is too small to feed a
   _____
   PUPPY .

   puffy
   poppy
   puppy

3. She can not draw the
   _____
   SKY .

   sky
   sly
   spy

4. Mom will not let her eat
   _____
   Candy .

   sandy
   candy
   funny

5. I feel sad if she starts to
   _____
   Cry .

   my
   cry
   try

6. Wendy is only a
   _____
   baby .

   bunny
   baby
   buggy

TALK About It **What can a baby do?**

Y as a vowel: High-frequency words, critical thinking **261**

Say the name of each picture. Print the picture name on the line. In the last box, draw a picture of a word in which **y** is a vowel. Write the word.

1.

baby

2.

fly

3.

pony

4.

penny

5.

sky

6.

fry

7.

candy

8.

cry

9.

Ask your child to say the name of his or her picture and spell the word.

Name _____

Read the sentences. Use the mixed-up letters to make a word from the box. Print the word on the line to finish the sentence.

| grapes | try | bread | fresh | smell |

1. "The fruit looks ___fresh___ ," Clare said.   **s h r e f**

2. "Let us buy some ___grapes___ ," said Greg.   **a r p e g s**

3. "I will ___try___ to find green ones."   **r t y**

4. "Just ___smell___ the plums!" Clare said.   **e l l s m**

5. "Now all we need is ___bread___ ."   **e a d b r**

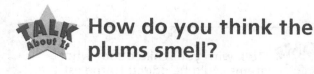 **How do you think the plums smell?**

Review consonant blends and y as a vowel:
Words in context, critical thinking   **263**

Phonics & Writing

Write a shopping list for your family's next trip to the store. List things to buy. Look at the words in the box for help.

bread	drink	sweet	fruit
plums	grapes	milk	berry

SHOPPING LIST

_____

- -

_____

- -

_____

- -

_____

- -

_____

- -

_____

- -

_____

- -

_____

HOME Talk with your child about what items could be added to the list.

Name _____

PIZZA FEAST

Did you ever try to make a pizza?
First, you make the crust.

1

------ FOLD ------

Bake the pizza till it is crisp. Then,
put it on a plate. It will taste great!

4

Review consonant blends and y as a vowel: Take-home book   **265**

Press the crust in a pan. Make it round and flat.

2

Spread the sauce and cheese all over.

3

Name _____

▶ Say **the name of each picture. Fill in** the bubble beside the picture name.

1.

- ◯ trip
- ◯ prize
- ◉ train
- ◯ drain

2.

- ◯ snail
- ◉ snake
- ◯ skate
- ◯ string

3.

- ◯ clock
- ◯ braid
- ◯ blouse
- ◉ block

4.

- ◯ crab
- ◯ grab
- ◯ club
- ◉ crib

5.

- ◉ flag
- ◯ glass
- ◯ flat
- ◯ blank

6.

- ◯ green
- ◉ dress
- ◯ drum
- ◯ desk

7.

- ◯ deck
- ◯ drive
- ◉ desk
- ◯ jump

8.

- ◯ clap
- ◉ plant
- ◯ plug
- ◯ plate

9.

- ◉ stamp
- ◯ steps
- ◯ stop
- ◯ spill

10.

- ◯ glue
- ◉ globe
- ◯ drive
- ◯ glove

11.

- ◉ frame
- ◯ lamp
- ◯ fly
- ◯ frog

12.

- ◯ glass
- ◯ spot
- ◉ spoon
- ◯ smoke

Circle **the word that will** finish **each sentence.** Print **it on the line.**

1. __Start__ the day with a good meal.

Stop
Start
Star

2. Corn __flakes__ and milk are great.

flags
frames
flakes

3. _____ adding some fruit.

Fry
Try
Why

4. __Drink__ a glass of juice.

Drink
Trunk
Dress

5. Some __toast__ is good, too.

float
test
toast

6. Stay away from _____ things.

sweet
smoke
square

Read Aloud

Let it Snow!

In a blizzard, the wind blows very hard. Snow falls faster and very heavily. The temperature is close to zero. The heavy snow and blowing wind make it hard to see.

Once, a big blizzard hit Chicago. Schools and offices were closed for days. There was so much snow that some of it was sent by train to Florida. Children in Florida had never seen snow!

TALK About It

How do you find out what the weather will be each day?

Dear Family,

In this unit, "Whatever the Weather," your child will learn about contractions, words ending with **ed** and **ing,** and consonant digraphs. A consonant digraph is formed with two letters that stand for one sound. For example, the **sh** in sheep and the **th** in thermometer are digraphs. As your child becomes familiar with these concepts, you might try these activities together.

▶ Help your child to create a weather chart. For each day of the week, he or she can draw a picture of that day's weather. At the end of the week, ask your child to tell you what the weather was each day.

▶ With your child, read the article on page 269. Help him or her to identify the words with consonant digraphs and contractions and words that end in **ed** or **ing.**

▶ Your child might enjoy reading these books with you. Look for them in your local library.

The Snowy Day
by Ezra Jack Keats

Let's Count the Raindrops
by Fumi Kosaka

Sincerely,

Estimada familia:

En esta unidad, titulada "Pronósticos del tiempo" ("Whatever the Weather"), su hijo/a estudiará en inglés contracciones, palabras que terminan en **ed** y en **ing** y digramas de consonantes. Un digrama de consonantes está formado por dos letras que representan un sonido. Por ejemplo, la **sh** en sheep (oveja) y la **th** en thermometer (termómetro) son digramas. A medida que su hijo/a se vaya familiarizando con estos conceptos, pueden hacer las siguientes actividades juntos.

▶ Ayuden a su hijo/a a crear un mapa meteorológico. Para cada día de la semana, su hijo/a puede hacer un dibujo sobre el tiempo que hubo ese día. Al final de la semana, pídanle que les explique cuál fue el tiempo en cada día.

▶ Lean juntos el artículo en la página 269. Ayuden a su hijo/a a identificar las palabras con contracciones, los digramas de consonantes y las palabras que terminan en **ed** o en **ing.**

▶ Ustedes y su hijo/a disfrutarán leyendo estos libros juntos. Búsquenlos en su biblioteca local.

The Snowy Day de Ezra Jack Keats

Let's Count the Raindrops de Fumi Kosaka

Sinceramente,

Name_____

It rained and poured all week.
Now it's raining again.
The puddles are growing so big!
I'm jumping and playing in them.

> **Say** the name of each picture. **Print** the ending you see in the corner of the box to finish its name. **Trace** the whole word.

1. ed
spilled

2. ed
melted

3. ing
eating

4. ing
raining

5. ed
boiled

6. ing
fishing

7. ed
rowed

8. ed
peeled

9. ing
crying

Read the word below each picture. Each picture name has a base word and an ending. Trace the circle around the base word. Then, read the words beside each picture. Circle each base word.

1. jumped

| asked | yelled | fixed | played |
| mixed | rocked | bumped | rained |

2. reading

| going | telling | sailing | mixing |
| asking | waiting | resting | boating |

3. melted

| waited | seated | heated | landed |
| mailed | loaded | floated | ended |

4. cooking

| rowing | crying | flying | fishing |
| picking | saying | eating | melting |

 HOME

With your child, hunt for words with endings in favorite storybooks.

Name _____

> Circle **the word that will finish the sentence.** Print **it on the line.**

_____

1. We were _____ to eat.

| | waiting |
| | waited |

_____

2. Dad was _____ the ham.

| | cooking |
| | cooked |

_____

3. Mom was _____ for help.

| | asking |
| | asked |

_____

4. She and I _____ the baby.

| | dressing |
| | dressed |

_____

5. Sandy _____ the fruit.

| | peeling |
| | peeled |

_____

6. I _____ the most!

| | helping |
| | helped |

How does this family help each other?

Inflectional endings -ed and -ing:
High-frequency words, critical thinking   **273**

► **Circle the word that will finish the sentence.**
Print it on the line.

1. Dad was _____ fishing.

	go
	going

2. I _____ him to take me
   to Mary's home.

	asking
	asked

3. We were _____ a ball
   to each other.

	kicked
	kicking

4. Then we _____ to get wet.

	started
	starting

5. It was _____ cats and dogs.

	rain
	raining

6. We _____ for the rain
   to stop.

	waiting
	waited

7. Then we _____ on Mary's
   swing set.

	played
	playing

**What does "raining
cats and dogs" mean?**

274 Inflectional endings -ed and -ing:
High-frequency words, critical thinking

Using words with endings, take turns
telling what you did today.

Name _____

My soft mittens are thick, not thin.
My fingers and thumbs stay warm in them.
When the thermometer says thirty-three,
Outside with my mittens is where I'll be.

> **Thumb** begins with the sound of **th**. Circle each picture whose name begins with the sound of **th**.

1.

2. 3

3. 2

4. (tiger)

5. (rose)

6. (girl thinking)

7. 30

8. (thermometer)

9. (train)

10. (thread)

11. (tie)

12. 13

Say the name of each picture. Print **th** or **t** to finish each word. Trace the whole word.

1. thick

2. thin

3. tire

4. ink

5. thirty

6. tie

7. tiger

8. tape

9. tree

10. tumb

11. orn

12. ten

276 Discriminating between th and t: Spelling

HOME

Help your child to make up a sentence using words with *t* and *th*, such as *Thirty tigers had thick tails*.

Name_____

The wind whines and whistles.
It whips through the tree.
It whirls around wildly,
And takes my white cap from me!

> **White begins with the sound of wh. Circle each picture whose name begins with the sound of wh.**

1.

2.

3.

4.

5.

6.

7.

8.

9.

10.

11.

12.

Say the name of each picture.
Print **wh** or **th** to finish each word.
Trace **the whole word.**

1. wh eel

2. th umb

3. th ick

4. th orn

5. wh eat

6. th ink

7. wh ale

8. th in

9. wh ite

10. th ree

11. th read

12. wh istle

Ask your child: *What comes after two and before four?* Take turns making up riddles for other picture names.

Name_____

Shannon is in the sunlight.
What does she see?
A shiny, shimmering shadow.
She says, "You can't catch me!"

▶ **Shadow begins with the sound of sh.**
Circle each picture whose name begins
with the sound of sh.

1. 	2. 	3. 	4. 
5. 	6. 	7. 	8. 
9. 	10. 	11. 	12. 

Consonant digraph sh: Phonemic awareness **279**

Say the name of each picture.
Print **sh** or **s** to finish each word.
Trace the whole word.

1. ___ell

2. ___ail

3. ___ade

4. s ix

5. sh oe

6. ___elf

7. ___ip

8. ___eep

9. s eat

10. ___irt

11. s ock

12. ___out

 Ask your child to make up sentences using some of the words on the page.

Name_____

Outside it was chilly.
Chen's pets chose to stay indoors.
Chen sat in a chair with Lily,
While Chip chased yarn on the floor.

> **Chair** begins with the sound of **ch**. Circle each picture whose name begins with the sound of **ch**.

1.

2.

3.

4.

5.
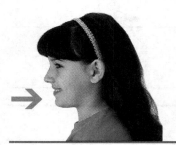

6.

7.

8.

9.

10.

11.

12.

Say the name of each picture. **Print ch or c** to finish each word. **Trace** the whole word.

1.

ch in

2.

ch eck

3.

c oat

4.

ch eese

5.

c ube

6.

ch ick

7.

ch alk

8.

c at

9.

ch ain

10.

ch erry

11.

c ow

12.

ch air

282   **Discriminating between ch and c: Spelling**

 HOME Ask your child to identify common household items whose names begin with *ch* or *c*, such as *chair* and *comb*.

Name _____

Knock, knock, knock.
Who's knocking at the door?
We know who it is—
The wind, and nothing more!

Knock begins with the letters **kn.** You only hear the sound of **n.** Say the name of each picture. Trace the whole word. Then, circle the pictures whose names begin with **kn.**

1. knee

2. think

3. knot

4. knob

5. knife

6. whale

7. chin

8. knock

9. knit

▶ **Circle the sentence that tells about the picture.**

1.
The tire is black and white.

Chad tied a knot in the rope.

2.
Randy did not skin his knee.

Kelly kneels down on the mat.

3.
Did you hear a knock at the door?

Did Nick knock over the vase?

4.
I fed the bread to the chicks.

I used a knife to slice the cheese.

5.
Chuck knows where his watch is.

Kate turned the knob to the left.

6.
Susan knits a sweater for her sister.

Jenny ties a knot with her shoe strings.

7.
The knight does not ride a horse.

The knight rides a horse with spots.

Ask your child to point to and read each *kn* word.

Name _____

▶ **Circle the word that will finish the
sentence. Print it on the line.**

1. Chuck _____ about a sunny beach.

knows
knob
knock

2. We catch the bus at _____.

thick
three
thorn

3. Beth puts a _____ sheet down.

white
wheat
whip

4. Chuck finds _____ in the sand.

sheets
shades
shells

5. I _____ Beth a new game.

teach
reach
cheat

6. Then we sit and look at the _____.

shape
ships
shake

**What else can people do
at the beach?**

Review consonant digraphs:
High-frequency words, critical thinking   **285**

Read **each clue.** Print **the answer to each** riddle on the line. Use **the cloud pictures** if you need help.

three	sheep	wheel	cherry
ship	chick	whale	knife

1. My hair is called wool.
   I can be white, brown, or black.

   _____

   I am a _____.

2. I hatch out of an egg.
   My mother is a hen.

   _____

   I am a _____.

3. I live in the sea.
   I am much bigger than a fish.

   _____

   I am a _____.

4. I sail across the sea.
   People ride in me.

   _____

   I am a _____.

5. I come after two
   and before four.

   _____

   I am _____.

6. I am round. I help
   cars and bikes go.

   _____

   I am a _____.

7. I am round and red.
   I am good to eat.

   _____

   I am a _____.

8. I am very sharp. People
   use me to cut things.

   _____

   I am a _____.

286 Review consonant digraphs:
High-frequency words

HOME Ask your child to read the riddles to you so you can guess the answers.

Name _____

> **Blend** the letter sounds together as you say each word. **Print** the word on the line. **Draw** a line to the picture it names.

1. ch
   i n

2. th
   i n k

3. kn
   o b

4. sh
   e l f

5. wh
   e a t

6. kn
   e e

Look at the picture. Then follow the directions.

1. Color the ship black.

2. Circle the shell on the beach.

3. Write a three on the flag.

4. Color the wheel brown.

5. Color the thick rope yellow.

6. Draw a whale in the water.

7. Draw a box around each knot.

8. Color the sky blue but keep the cloud white.

With your child, make up a story to go with the picture.

288   **Review consonant digraphs: Reading**

Name_____

© Pearson Education, Inc./Modern Curriculum Press/Pearson Learning Group. All rights reserved. Copying strictly prohibited.

Read the story. **Use** words in which two letters stand for one beginning sound and words with endings to finish the sentences.

Looking for Chuck

Where was Chuck?
Shari and Shane looked all over.
They knew Chuck did not like storms.
Now thunder was booming.
Lightning flashed.
Chuck was hiding.
After a while Shari sat down.
She said, "I give up."
Just then Shane said, "There's Chuck!
He's chewing his toy under your chair!"

_____
----

1. _____ was Chuck?

_____
- -

2. _____ was booming.

_____
- -

3. Chuck was _____ his toy.

Why was Chuck hiding?

Review endings, digraphs: Reading, critical thinking   **289**

Phonics & Writing

Add the word part to each of the letter pairs in the boxes. Say the word. If it is a real word, write it on the line.

| th | ch | kn | wh | sh |

in

1. _____

2. _____

3. _____

| th | ch | wh | sh | kn |

ip

4. _____

5. _____

6. _____

▶ Write a sentence using two of the words you made.

_____

_____

_____

HOME Ask your child to think of more words that begin with *th*, *wh*, *sh*, *ch*, and *kn*.

Name _____

CLOUDS

Clouds come in many shapes and colors. Did you know they can tell you about the weather?

1

- FOLD - - - - - - - -

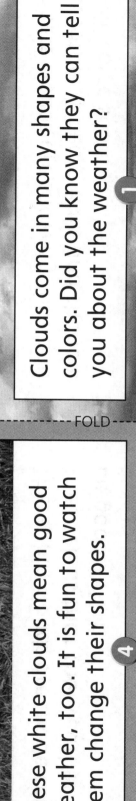

Cumulus Clouds

These white clouds mean good weather, too. It is fun to watch them change their shapes.

4

Review endings, consonant digraphs: Take-home book   **291**

These clouds are showing that bad weather is near. Rain and thunder will come soon.

2

---- FOLD ----

Cirrus Clouds

These thin clouds are made of ice. They tell us that the weather will be good.

3

Name _____

They'll slide down the hill.
They will go very fast.
I'll slide down, too.
I will be the last.

I will = I'll	you will = you'll	they will = they'll
he will = he'll	she will = she'll	we will = we'll
	it will = it'll	

▶ **They'll** is a short way to say **they will.** Read each sentence. Circle the short way to write the <u>underlined words</u>.

1.	<u>It will</u> be fun to go for a ride on a sled.	You'll It'll
2.	<u>I will</u> get on the sled.	We'll I'll
3.	<u>You will</u> get on the sled with me.	You'll She'll
4.	<u>They will</u> all get on the sled, too.	They'll It'll
5.	Oh, no! Get off or <u>we will</u> fall!	he'll we'll

 What are some other things to do outside when the weather is cold?

She's **is a short way to say she is.** Look **at each picture.** Read **the sentence. Print the short way to write the** <u>underlined words</u>. Use **the words in the box to help you.**

she is = she's   it is = it's   he is = he's

1. <u>It is</u> a nice day to play in the park.

_____

_____ a nice day to play in the park.

2. <u>He is</u> going down the slide.

_____

_____ going down the slide.

3. <u>She is</u> having fun in the water.

_____

_____ having fun in the water.

4. <u>He is</u> playing on the swings.

_____

_____ playing on the swings.

5. <u>It is</u> full of things to do!

_____

_____ full of things to do!

 TALK About It **What else can you do at the park?**

 HOME Ask your child what words form the contractions *they'll*, *we'll*, and *you'll*.

294   Contractions with is: Words in context, critical thinking

Name _____

▶ **I'm** is a short way to say **I am.** Look at each picture. Read the sentence. Print the short way to write the <u>underlined words</u>. Use the words in the box to help you.

> **I am = I'm**   **we are = we're**
> **you are = you're**   **they are = they're**

1.  <u>You are</u> going to the zoo.

   _____

   - - - - - - - - - - - - - - - - - -

   _____ going to the zoo.

2. I am going with you.

   <u>I am</u> going with you.

   _____

   - - - - - - - - - - - - - - - - - -

   _____ going with you.

3. <u>We are</u> going to see the seals.

   _____

   - - - - - - - - - - - - - - - - - -

   _____ going to see the seals.

4.  <u>They are</u> fun, and the cubs are, too.

   _____

   - - - - - - - - - - - - - - - - - -

   _____ fun, and the cubs are, too.

5.  I think <u>we are</u> going to love the zoo!

   _____

   - - - - - - - - - - - - - - - - - -

   I think _____ going to love the zoo!

 **What other animals
can you see at the zoo?**

Contractions with am and are:
Words in context, critical thinking   **295**

Can't is a short way to say **can not**. Read the sentences. Circle the short way to write the <u>underlined words</u>. Use the words in the box to help you.

| can not = can't | does not = doesn't |
| will not = won't | is not = isn't |

1. Wags <u>is not</u> clean. He is a muddy mess!	can't doesn't isn't
2. Mom says he needs a bath. Wags just <u>will not</u> get into the tub.	won't isn't doesn't
3. Wags <u>does not</u> like baths. He runs away.	isn't can't doesn't
4. I <u>can not</u> catch him. Mom will help me.	can't doesn't won't
5. Wags <u>is not</u> muddy now. I am the one who needs a bath!	isn't can't doesn't

TALK About It
Who needs a bath now and why?

HOME
Using the contractions, take turns making up other sentences about Wags.

Name _____

> **Circle** the sentence that tells about the picture.

1.

I'll eat the hot dog.

I'm going to read the book.

2.

It's in the bag.

She'll sleep in the tent.

3.

We won't go on the ride.

We're on the ride.

4.

She's going to play on the swing.

They're going to like my painting.

5.

You're going to rake the yard.

We'll drive up to the lake.

6.

I can't skate very well on the ice.

He doesn't like ice cream on his cake.

Fill in the bubble beside the sentence that tells about the picture.

1.
- ○ It's a dog.
- ○ It can't be a dog.
- ○ They're dogs.

2.
- ○ He's on a bike.
- ○ She's in a jet.
- ○ I'm on the bus.

3.
- ○ It won't rain today.
- ○ It'll rain all day.
- ○ I'll play in the rain.

4.
- ○ We don't like bugs.
- ○ She'll eat a hot dog.
- ○ We're eating the fruit.

5.
- ○ They'll go for a ride.
- ○ We'll go for a swim.
- ○ You're up a tree.

6.
- ○ She can't find her shoes.
- ○ He doesn't want to ride his bike.
- ○ She's trying to catch a fish.

HOME Ask your child to use contractions such as *I'll, I'm,* and *won't* to tell about himself or herself.

Name _____

Phonics & Spelling

Say and spell the words below. Print the words on the lines where they belong.

fishing	can't	melted	I'm	peeled	ship
think	knot	chin	whale	rowing	spilled

Words that have **ed** endings

1. _____ 2. _____ 3. _____

Words that take the place of two small words

4. _____ 5. _____

Words whose beginning sound is made up of two letters

6. _____ 7. _____ 8. _____

9. _____ 10. _____

Words that have **ing** endings

11. _____ 12. _____

Phonics & Writing

What kind of weather do you like best? Write a description of your favorite kind of weather. Use describing words to tell about what you see, hear, or feel. The words in the box may help you.

| know | I'm | playing | walking |
| rained | what | that | it's |

_____

- -

_____

- -

_____

- -

_____

- -

_____

- -

_____

- -

_____

HOME Ask your child to forecast tomorrow's weather.

Name _____

It's Raining

Chad and Trina looked out.
"It's raining," Trina said. "We
can't play out there."

1

- - - - - - - - - - - - - - - - - FOLD - - - - - - - - - - - - - -

"It isn't raining," said Trina.
"It's Dad! He's making it rain!"

4

Review endings, digraphs, contractions: Take-home book   **301**

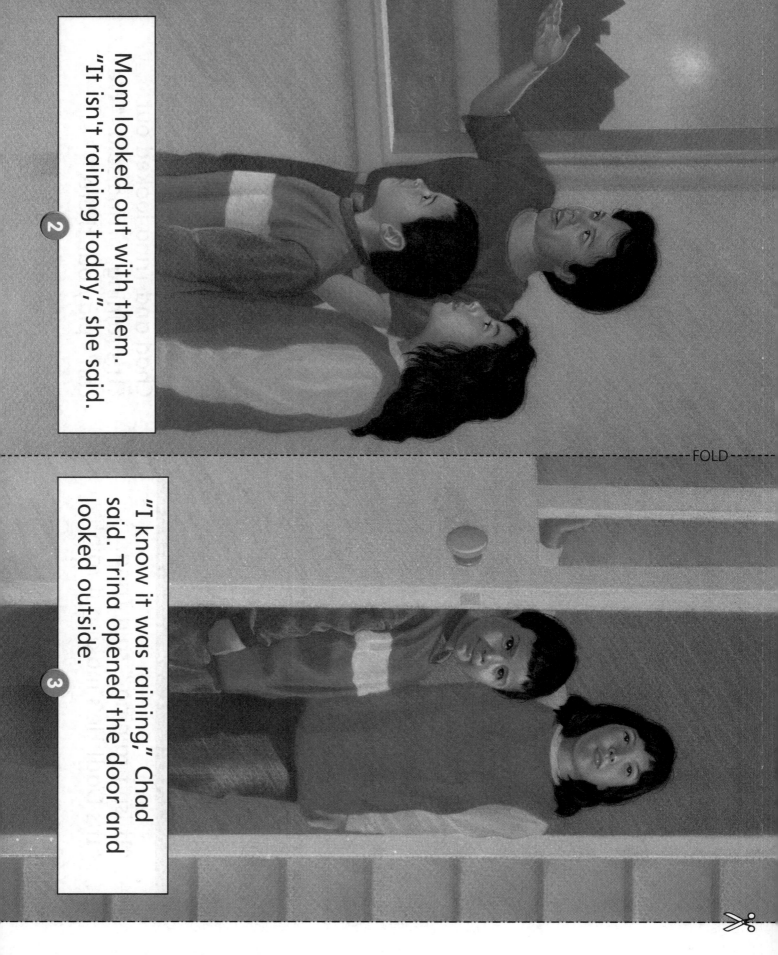

Mom looked out with them.
"It isn't raining today," she said.

2

"I know it was raining," Chad
said. Trina opened the door and
looked outside.

3

Name _____

Say the name of each picture. Fill in the bubble beside the picture name.

1.

○ knee
○ knob
○ knife

2.

○ wheel
○ whip
○ white

3.

○ chain
○ thin
○ chin

4.

○ sheep
○ ship
○ chip

5.

○ thin
○ cherry
○ three

6.

○ knit
○ knot
○ knock

7.

○ chair
○ shame
○ chat

8.

○ while
○ throat
○ whale

9.

○ throne
○ thumb
○ shade

Look **at the picture.** Circle **the word that will finish the sentence.** Print **it on the line.**

1.

_____

How deep do you _____ it is?

think
knew
chase

2.

_____

She's _____ to find out.

rowing
spilled
trying

3.

_____

It's up to his _____!

knot
chin
whale

4.

_____

She _____ get it out.

isn't
don't
can't

5.

_____

_____ happy that it snowed.

They're
I'll
It's

6.

_____

The snow has all _____!

peeled
spilled
melted

---

304   Endings, digraphs, contractions: Assessment

Introduction to Audiologic Rehabilitation

RONALD L. SCHOW
Idaho State University

MICHAEL A. NERBONNE
Central Michigan University

Website Design
Jeff E. Brockett

Allyn and Bacon
Boston ■ *London* ■ *Toronto* ■ *Sydney* ■ *Tokyo* ■ *Singapore*

Vice President: Paul A. Smith
Executive Editor, Publisher: Stephen D. Dragin
Editorial Assistant: Barbara Strickland
Marketing Manager: Amy Cronin
Editorial Production Service: Bernadine Richey Publishing Services
Manufacturing Buyer: Chris Marson
Cover Administrator: Linda Knowles
Text Design: Carol Somberg Design
Electronic Composition: Omegatype Typography, Inc.

Library of Congress Cataloging-in-Publication Data

Introduction to audiologic rehabilitation / Ronald L. Schow, Michael A. Nerbonne [editors].
    p. cm.
    Includes bibliographical references and indexes.
    ISBN 0-205-31946-7 (hardcover)
      1. Deaf—Rehabilitation. 2. Audiology. I. Schow, Ronald L. II. Nerbonne, Michael A.

RF297 .I56 2001
617.8′063—dc21

                                                2001045081

Printed in the United States of America

10 9 8 7 6 5 4   RRD-VA   06   05   04

■ CONTENTS

3 **Cochlear Implants and Other Rehabilitative Areas** 81
Alice E. Holmes

4 Auditory Stimuli in Communication 101

Michael A. Nerbonne
Ronald L. Schow

5 Visual Stimuli in Communication 139

Nicholas M. Hipskind

6 Language and Speech of the Deaf and Hard of Hearing 183

Deborah N. Seyfried Culbertson
Patricia B. Kricos

8 Audiologic Rehabilitation Services in the School Setting 247
Kris English

PART TWO: Comprehensive Approaches to Audiologic Rehabilitation 275

9 Audiologic Rehabilitation for Children: Assessment and Management 277
Mary Pat Moeller
Ronald L. Schow
Dorothy Johnson

12 Case Studies: Adults and Elderly Adults 435

Michael A. Nerbonne
Jeff E. Brockett
Dan F. Konkle
Alice E. Holmes

■ CONTRIBUTORS

JEFF E. BROCKETT, M.S.
Assistant Clinical Professor
Department of Speech Pathology and Audiology
Idaho State University
Pocatello, ID 83209

ANNE STROUSE CARTER, PH.D.
VA Medical Center
Audiology (126)
Mountain Home, TN 37689

DEBORAH N. SEYFRIED CULBERTSON, PH.D.
Associate Professor of Audiology
Department of Communication Sciences and Disorders
Radford University
Radford, VA 24112

KRIS ENGLISH, PH.D.
Assistant Professor
Department of Speech-Language Pathology
Duquesne University
Pittsburgh, PA 15282

KATHY PICHORA-FULLER, PH.D.
Associate Professor of Audiology
School of Audiology and Speech Sciences
University of British Columbia
Vancouver, BC

NICHOLAS M. HIPSKIND, PH.D.
Associate Dean of the College of University Division, and
*   Associate Professor of Audiology*
Indiana University
Bloomington, IN 47401

ALICE E. HOLMES, PH.D.
Associate Professor of Audiology
Department of Communicative Disorders
University of Florida Health Science Center
Gainesville, FL 32610

DOROTHY JOHNSON, M.S.
SKI-HI Institute
Department of Communicative Disorders
Utah State University
Logan, UT 84321

DAN F. KONKLE, PH.D.
Professor of Audiology
Department of Communication Disorders
Central Michigan University
Mt. Pleasant, MI 48859

PATRICIA B. KRICOS, PH.D.
Professor of Audiology
Department of Communication Sciences and Disorders
University of Florida
Gainesville, FL 32611

MARY PAT MOELLER, PH.D.
Director: Center for Childhood Deafness
Boys Town National Research Hospital
Omaha, NE 68181

H. GUSTAV MUELLER, PH.D
Senior Audiology Consultant: Siemens Hearing Instruments, USA
Faculty Appointments: Central Michigan University, Vanderbilt University

MICHAEL A. NERBONNE, PH.D.
Professor of Audiology
Department of Communication Disorders
Central Michigan University
Mt. Pleasant, MI 48859

RONALD L. SCHOW, PH.D.
Professor of Audiology
Department of Speech Pathology and Audiology
Idaho State University
Pocatello, ID 83209

■ PREFACE

This new edition of *Introduction to Audiologic Rehabilitation* comes at an exciting time in the history of audiology. There are wonderful new developments in digital hearing aid technology and cochlear implants, for example, that are making hearing rehabilitation more challenging and more rewarding. It is simply a fact that we are living in a time when it is possible to provide functional hearing to the deaf and those of us working in this field have seen miracles before our very eyes. The most successful results associated with audiologic rehabilitation, however, do not usually come without a lot of work and a lot of skill on the part of the professionals involved. Consequently, students need to be well prepared. We hope the updating and changes in our text help in this regard.

At Idaho State University we have surveyed the status of audiologic rehabilitation (AR) among ASHA audiologists every decade since 1980. The most recent findings for the year 2000 are just in (see resource web site) and they show that the most important rehabilitative activities are still associated with hearing aid fitting. According to this survey, fully 79% of ASHA audiologists are involved in hearing aid dispensing. Not surprisingly, hearing instrument orientation (HIO) is frequently given on an individual basis even in places where dispensing does not occur, and 85% of the audiologists report this type of activity. Also, counseling is still a prominent focus for audiologists with 86% to 92% involved in various types of counseling. Outcome measures continue to be a crucial issue in rehabilitation. There were 72% of audiologists who reported using real ear measures, 82% reported use of sound field measures, and the increasing utility of self report has resulted in a 25% increase in the past decade in their use (from 33% to 58%).

Accordingly, in this new edition we have refined our previous model for AR so that it is particularly applicable for those who fit hearing aids. Included in this revised model is the new function and disability terminology that comes from the World Health Organization. Self report measures have always been given prominent treatment in this text, but we now have included software within the resource web sites that accompany this book so students can enter hearing data and determine representative self report outcome measures. In order to provide readers an opportunity to practice AR and see day-to-day applications of the text material, we have added a variety of activities and materials (see note below). In addition, we have developed new supportive materials for HIO and other handouts to help the audiologist as they counsel the new hearing aid user.

In our new survey data there were notable increases from our previous AR surveys in the areas of post-surgery cochlear implant therapy and tinnitus management.

Percentages for these areas doubled or nearly doubled between 1990 and 2000. Two other important emerging rehabilitative activities were found to be vestibular disorder therapy, which 29% of audiologists now report that they perform, and 37% report recommending forms of CAPD therapy. The developing interest in new rehabilitation activities prompted us to add a new chapter (Chapter 3) for this edition, which focuses mainly on cochlear implants but also provides some treatment of tinnitus and vestibular therapy. CAPD was covered in previous editions and continues to receive treatment in Chapters 8 and 9.

We want to thank the authors of the various chapters and our colleagues, secretaries, and students who have helped us with the task of updating and completing this new edition. Special thanks are due to Jeff Brockett who helped us bring our text into the new technological age with companion web sites. We feel certain these web resources will help make this text more user friendly and will be of great value to students and to our colleagues who teach AR coursework. We also want to thank the following reviewers: Linda I. Rosa-Lugo, University of Central Florida; Teresa R. Boemio, Teachers College, Columbia Univeristy; and Peter J. Ivory, California State University, Northridge.

We both have a continuing passion for audiologic rehabilitation and hope that this revised text will spark a similar reaction from the audiologists of tomorrow.

■ NOTE ON WEB SITES

A resource web site has been produced along with this book and will provide supplementary information that should be helpful to students and instructors using this text for academic coursework. The site is maintained by Allyn and Bacon. Another web site has also been developed at Idaho State University, which will be available as long as this edition is in print. It should provide ongoing resource material to the owner of this text during any coursework and, subsequently, when the student has become a working professional doing audiologic rehabilitation (AR). These web site resources include handouts, diagrams, position paper links, interactive Shockwave activities and other useful documents. The companion web site at Idaho State University is at the following address (http://www.isu.edu/spchpath/rehab/).

Fundamentals of Audiologic Rehabilitation

Overview of Audiologic Rehabilitation

Ronald L. Schow
Michael A. Nerbonne

C O N T E N T S

■ INTRODUCTION

Most of us have had occasion to converse with someone who has a hearing problem. Unless the person had received proper help for the hearing difficulties it probably was a frustrating experience for both parties. When the person with hearing loss is a family member or close friend, we become aware that the emotional and social ramifications of this communication barrier can be substantial as well.

Providing help to address all these hearing problems is the focus of this book. Help is possible, but often not utilized. This chapter gives an overview of a process that is crucial for the welfare of persons who suffer from hearing impairment and, in turn, for those who communicate with them.

Definitions and Synonyms

Simply stated, we may define *audiologic habilitation/rehabilitation* as those professional efforts designed to help a person with hearing loss. These include services and procedures for lessening or compensating for a hearing impairment and specifically involve facilitating adequate receptive and expressive communication (ASHA, 1984; WHO, 2000). A key consideration in this rehabilitation process involves assisting the person with hearing impairment to attain full potential by using personal resources to overcome difficulties resulting from the hearing loss. Two kinds of important service that are closely related but distinct from the audiologic habilitation/ rehabilitation process are *medical intervention* and *teaching academic subjects to the deaf.*

Several terms have been used to describe this helping process. *Audiologic habilitation* refers to remedial efforts with children having a hearing loss at birth, since technically it is not possible to restore (rehabilitate) something that has never existed. *Audiologic rehabilitation,* then, refers to efforts designed to restore a lost state or function. In the interest of simplicity, the terms *habilitation* and *rehabilitation* are used interchangeably in this text, technicalities notwithstanding. Variations of the *audiologic rehabilitation* term include *auditory and aural rehabilitation, hearing rehabilitation,* and *rehabilitative audiology.* Terms used to refer to rehabilitative efforts with the very young child include *parent advising/counseling/tutoring* and *pediatric auditory habilitation. Educational* (or *school*) *audiology* is sometimes used to refer to auditory rehabilitative efforts performed in the school setting.

Audiologic habilitation is sometimes used to refer to those efforts to assist children with hearing loss, since we cannot rehabilitate something that was never there in the first place. Nevertheless, for simplicity's sake, audiologic rehabilitation (AR) is used throughout this text.

Providers of Audiologic Rehabilitation

Audiologic rehabilitation (AR), then, is referred to by different names and is performed in a number of different settings. All aspects of assisting the client in the audiologic rehabilitation process are not performed by one person. In fact, professionals from several different disciplines are often involved, including educators, psychologists, social workers, and rehabilitation counselors. Nevertheless, the audiologist in particular, and in some circumstances the speech–language pathologist or the educator of those with impaired hearing, will assume a major AR role. These professionals provide overall coordination of the process or act as advocates for the person with impaired hearing. Audiologic rehabilitation is not something we *do* to a person following a strict "doctor-knows-best" medical model. It is a process designed to counsel and work with persons who are deaf and hard of hearing so that they can actualize their own resources in order to meet their unique life situations. This text has been written with the hope of orienting and preparing such "counselors" or "advocates for the hearing-impaired" so that they can be effective in a problem-solving process.

Education Needs of Providers

Currently there is a transition in audiology centered around establishing a professional doctorate in audiology as the minimum educational requirement to practice as an audiologist. Along with other professional bodies, the Academy of Rehabilitative Audiology (ARA) adopted a position statement that emphasizes the need for future Au.D. students to be well prepared in audiologic rehabilitation. The ARA provides a list of relevant content areas in AR that should be incorporated into any Au.D. program to ensure adequate preparation in this all-important area of audiology. This statement and other documents along similar lines are available on a resource website that goes with this text (see ARA, ASHA, and AAA statements on competencies for AR).

Regardless of academic background, those from the different professions mentioned in the previous section who successfully perform AR must, like competent audiologists, possess an understanding of and familiarity with several areas of knowledge. These include (1) characteristics of hearing impairment, (2) effect of hearing loss on persons, and (3) the previously noted competencies needed for providing audiologic rehabilitation. For purposes of the present treatment, it is assumed that other coursework or study has brought the reader familiarity with the various forms of hearing impairment, as well as procedures used in the measurement of hearing loss. These procedures, referred to as *diagnostic audiology*, serve as a preliminary step toward rehabilitative audiology. The task at hand, then, is to review briefly some characteristics of hearing loss, to explore the major consequences of hearing impairment, and finally to discuss the methods and competencies needed to help with this condition.

■ HEARING LOSS CHARACTERISTICS

Important characteristics of hearing loss as they relate to audiologic rehabilitation include (1) degree and configuration of impairment, (2) time of onset, (3) type of loss, and (4) auditory speech recognition ability.

Degree of Hearing Impairment and Configuration

One major aspect of hearing impairment or loss is the person's hearing sensitivity or degree of loss (see Table 1.1). The amount of loss will vary across the frequency range, leading to different configurations or shapes of hearing loss, including the most common patterns of flat, sloping, and precipitous. (Practice in degree and configuration interpretation is provided on the website.) The category of hearing impairment includes both the hard of hearing and the deaf. Persons with limited amounts of hearing loss are referred to as being *hard of hearing*. Those with an extensive loss of hearing are considered deaf. Generally, when hearing losses, measured by pure tone average (PTA) or speech recognition threshold (SRT), are poorer than 80 to 90 dB HL, a person is considered to be *audiometrically deaf*. However, deafness can also be described functionally as the inability to use hearing to any

TABLE 1.1

Degree of Hearing Impairment Descriptions, Based on Pure Tone Findings

DEGREES OF HEARING IMPAIRMENT	PTA IN dB BASED ON 0.5, 1, 2 Kᵃ Hzᵇ		
	Children		Adults
Slight to Mild	21–40		26–40
Mild to Moderate	—	41–55	—
Moderate	—	56–70	—
Severe	—	71–90	—
Profound	—	91 plus	—

ᵃK = 1000.

ᵇThe three frequencies of 0.5, 1, and 2K are used for interpreting audiograms and comparing to SRTs. Higher frequencies, including 3K and 4K, should be considered in hearing aid fitting decisions and compensation cases.

meaningful extent for the ordinary purposes of life, especially for verbal communication. This latter way of defining deafness is independent of the findings from audiometric test results.

The prevalence of hearing impairment may be considered for all persons combined and for children and adults separately. In the United States the prevalence of hearing impairment is estimated to be from 14 to 40 million, depending on whether conservative or liberal figures are used (Goldstein, 1984; Schow et al., 1996). These estimates vary depending on the definition of loss; the loss may be self-defined or involve different decibel fence levels, some as low as 15 dB HL, but most are higher, commonly 20 to 25 dB HL. Authorities have suggested that a different definition of loss should be applied for children, because in a younger person the consequences are greater for the same amount of loss. The prevalence of loss also varies depending on whether the conventional pure tone average (500, 1000, 2000 Hz) is used or whether some additional upper frequencies (like 3000 and 4000 Hz) are included. In this book we recommend that different pure tone average fences be used for children and adults at the "slight-to-mild" degree of loss level, although the degree designation is similar at most levels. In addition, we recommend that either 3000 or 4000 Hz be used in evaluating loss, although the usual three-frequency pure tone average will typically be used in analyzing audiograms. Table 1.1 indicates that a hearing loss is found in children at a lower (better) decibel level than in adults; this is consistent with ASHA screening levels for schoolchildren that define normal hearing up to and including 20 dB HL (ASHA, 1997). A reasonable estimate from recent prevalence studies would be that at least 10% of the population has permanent, significant impairment of hearing (28 million in the United States). Approximately one-third of 1% of the total U.S. population is deaf (about 0.7 million). Thus, the remaining 27.3 million are in the hard-of-hearing group (Schow et al., 1996).

A reasonable estimate is that 10% of the population have hearing loss. In the United States this would be about 28 million persons, but this includes only the most serious problems and not minor hearing difficulties.

Audiometric Patterns of Hearing Loss
Using Degree and Configuration

In rehabilitating adults, audiologists may use degree and configuration of loss to group those who are hard of hearing, thus focusing on the most common audiometric patterns. While a focus on the audiogram alone involves a simplification of the many variables discussed in this chapter, it nevertheless allows us to group persons in a useful way for treatment. The Songbird approach to hearing aid fitting proposes that nine common audiometric categories of flat, sloping and precipitous configurations constitute the great bulk of all those who are usually fit with hearing aids (McCandless, Sjursen, & Preeves, 2000). The data summarized here categorize loss, similar to the songbird approach, and show a large sample of adult hearing losses (based on the better ear) involving more than 1200 persons. This sample shows eight exclusive groups of hearing loss: two flat, (N=286) two sloping, (N=248), two precipitous (N=304), and two groups with loss only at 4000 Hz (N=362). The two 4K loss groups are seldom fit with hearing aids. These eight categories constitute the entire range of hearing losses usually encountered by an average audiologist but only six show the classic flat, sloping, or precipitous patterns which are usually amplified. For these six when we look at the configuration (shape) of the loss between 1000 and the average of 2000, and 4000 Hz, almost equal sized groups show a flat pattern, a sloping pattern, and a precipitous pattern (see Figure 1.1).

Flat 1 = 248*	Sloping 1 = 199*	Precipitous 1 = 250*	Total N = 838*
Flat 2 = 38*	Sloping 2 = 49*	Precipitous 2 = 54*	(*6 categories)

See Figure 1.1 and the resource website where the reader may enter better ear thresholds on any client for 1000, 2000 and 4000 Hz to categorize the loss into an exclusive audiometric pattern.

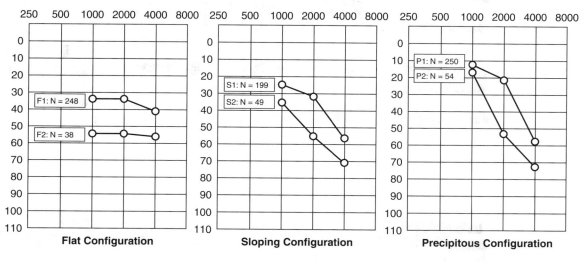

FIGURE 1.1

Six categories showing flat, sloping, and precipitous hearing configurations on 838 ears tested at health fairs. (Brockett & Schow, 2001).

Children form a subpopulation of the total group of 28 million individuals with impaired hearing. It is estimated that about 3 million U.S. children are deaf and hard of hearing, and even more fit in this category if high-frequency and conductive losses are included (Shepherd et al., 1981; see Chapter 9). Of these 3 million (2 million in school; 7 million younger), about 50,000 of school-age are deaf (American Annals of the Deaf, 2000). As with children, most adults with impaired hearing are considered to be hard of hearing, and only a small minority are deaf (Schow et al., 1996).

Degree (sensitivity), however, is only one of several important dimensions of a hearing loss. Even though it is often the first measure available and provides useful evidence of the impact of the loss, there are exceptions to this generalization. Some children with a profound impairment of 90 dB HL outperform, in language and academic areas, average children who have a loss of only 70 dB HL.

Table 1.2 contains a description of deafness and hard of hearing categories in terms of typical hearing aspects, use of hearing, use of vision, language development, use of language, speech, and educational needs. Prevalence estimates are also shown.

Time of Onset

Cochlear implant recipients are increasingly avoiding the full effects from various kinds of deafness and are an exception to the rule that sensorineural losses cannot be helped medically.

Most hard of hearing youngsters are thought to have hearing loss beginning early in life, but mild losses may not be detected, so prevalence data on young children are scarce and somewhat uncertain (Lundeen, 1991). With youngsters who are deaf or have more severe impairment, the time when a hearing loss is acquired will determine, in part, the extent to which normal speech and language will be present. Severe hearing loss (deafness) may be divided into three categories (*prelingual, postlingual, deafened*) depending on the person's age when the loss occurs (see Tables 1.2 and 1.3). *Prelingual deafness* refers to impairment present at birth or prior to the development of speech and language. The longer during the crucial language development years (up to age 5) that a person has normal hearing, the less chance there is that language development will be profoundly affected. *Postlingual deafness* means that loss occurs after about age 5; its overall effects are therefore usually less serious. However, even though language may be less affected, speech and education will be affected substantially (see Chapters 6 and 8). *Deafened* persons are those who lose hearing after their schooling is completed (i.e., sometime in their late teen years or thereafter). Normal speech, language, and education can be acquired by these individuals, but difficulty in verbal communication and other social, emotional, and vocational problems may occur (see Table 1.3).

Type of Loss

The type of loss may be *conductive* (damage in the outer or middle ear), *sensorineural* (impairment in the inner ear or nerve of hearing), or *mixed* (a combination of conductive and sensorineural). Generally, conductive losses are amenable to medical intervention, whereas sensorineural losses are primarily aided through audiologic rehabilitation. Other less common types of loss are possible as well, such as *functional* (nonorganic) problems and *central auditory processing* (CAP or AP)

TABLE 1.2

Categories and Characteristics of Hearing Impairment

Characteristic	CATEGORY OF DEAFNESS			
	Hard of Hearing (27,300,000)[a]	Prelingual (80,000)[a]	Postlingual (160,000)[a]	Deafened (460,000)[a]
Hearing impairment	*Sensitivity:* mild, moderate, or severe; *Recognition:* fair to good (70%–90%)	*Sensitivity:* severe or profound degree of loss; *Recognition:* fair to poor		
Use (level) of hearing	Functional speech understanding (lead sense)	Functional signal warning and environmental awareness (hearing minimized)		
Use of vision	Increased dependence		Increased dependence	
Language and speech development	Dependent on rehabilitation measures (e.g., amplification)	Dependent on amplification and early intervention	Dependent on amplification and school rehabilitation	Normal
Use of language	May be affected	Almost always affected	May be affected	Usually not affected
Use of speech	May be affected	Always affected	Usually affected	May be affected
Educational needs	Some special education	Considerable special education	Some special education	Education complete

[a]United States prevalence data for these categories, based on Schow et al. (1996); and Davis (1994), incidence figures.

TABLE 1.3

Definitions of Hearing Impairment

Persons with hearing impairment have been divided into the following groups:

Prelingually deaf persons were either born without hearing (congenitally deaf) or lost hearing before the development of speech and language: 3–5 years (adventitiously deaf). Both speech and language are affected to varying degrees and, because they usually are acquired formally instead of naturally, may be stilted, mechanical, and difficult to understand. The prelingually deaf person communicates primarily through fingerspelling, signs, and writing, but may possess enough speech and speechreading ability for basic social expression.

Postlingually deaf persons are those who became profoundly deaf after the age of 5–10 years and, although possessing no hearing for practical purposes, had normal hearing long enough to establish fairly well developed speech and language patterns. While speech generally is affected (more for the 5- than for the 10-year-old), communication may be through speech, signs, fingerspelling, and writing. Once the counselor becomes accustomed to their speech, it may be quite understandable. Speechreading, however, may be more haphazard and not always dependable.

Deafened refers to those people who suffer hearing loss after completing their education, generally in their late teens or early twenties and upward. Such people usually have fairly comprehensible, nearly normal speech and language, but they need instruction to acquire useful speechreading. Frequently, they face problems of adjustment because of the late onset of their hearing loss.

Hard of hearing persons may have been born thus or subsequently experienced a partial loss of hearing. While they have acquired speech normally through hearing and communicate by speaking, speech may be affected to some extent; for example, the voice may be too soft or too loud. They understand others by speechreading, by using a hearing aid, or by asking the speaker to raise his or her voice or enunciate more distinctly.

Source: Adapted from Moores, 1996, and Vernon and Andrews, 1990.

disorders (which arise from the processing centers throughout the auditory system, but chiefly in the brainstem or the brain). In the latter type of loss the symptoms may be very subtle. In cases of sensorineural loss, auditory speech recognition or hearing clarity is usually affected. This is also the case in difficult listening situations for those with CAP problems.

Auditory Speech Recognition Ability

Auditory speech recognition or identification ability (clarity of hearing) is another important dimension of hearing loss. The terms *speech recognition, speech identification,* and *speech discrimination* will be used interchangeably throughout this text, and all are included under the general category of speech perception or comprehension (see Chapter 4). *Speech discrimination* has been used for many years to describe clarity of hearing as measured in typical word intelligibility tests, but *speech recognition* and *identification* have now replaced *discrimination* since they more precisely describe what is being measured. *Discrimination* technically implies only the ability involved in a same–different judgment, whereas *recognition* and *identification* indicate an ability to repeat or identify the stimulus. *Recognition* is commonly used by diagnostic audiologists, but *identification* meshes nicely with the nomenclature of audiologic rehabilitation procedures as discussed further in Chapter 4. All these terms will at times be used due to historical precedents and evolving nomenclature.

The speech recognition ability in an individual who is hard of hearing typically is better than in a person who is deaf. Persons who are deaf are generally considered unable to comprehend conversational speech with hearing alone, whereas those who are hard of hearing can use their hearing to a significant extent for speech perception. However, some minimal auditory recognition may be present in persons who are deaf even if verbal speech reception is limited, since a person may use hearing for signal warning purposes or simply to maintain contact with the auditory environment (see Table 1.2). Nevertheless, auditory recognition ability and degree of loss are somewhat independent.

In a person of advanced age, a mild degree of loss sometimes may be accompanied by very poor speech recognition. This is referred to as *phonemic regression* and is not unusual in hearing losses among elderly persons who evidence some degree of central degeneration. Disparity in degree of loss and speech recognition ability is also possible in young persons with hearing impairment. For example, a child may be considered deaf in terms of sensitivity, but not in terms of auditory recognition or educational placement. Some children with a degree of loss that classifies them as audiometrically deaf (e.g., PTA = 90+ dB) may have unexpectedly good speech recognition. Thus, speech recognition also is an important variable in describing a hearing loss.

> The degree of loss alone is not adequate to define whether a person is deaf or hard of hearing and to determine a rehabilitation plan. Many other factors, including time of onset and clarity of hearing (word recognition), must be considered.

CONSEQUENCES OF HEARING LOSS: ■ PRIMARY AND SECONDARY

Communication Difficulties

The primary and most devastating effect of hearing loss is its impact on verbal communication. Children with severe to profound hearing loss do not generally develop speech and language normally, because they are not exposed to the sounds of language in daily living. In instances of a lesser degree of loss or if the loss occurs in adult years, the influence on speech and language expression tends to be less severe. Nevertheless, affected individuals still experience varying degrees of difficulty in receiving the auditory speech and environmental stimuli that allow us to communicate and interact with other humans and with our environment. For children, the choice of a communication (educational) system relates directly to this area of concern. If the educational setting and methods are chosen and implemented appropriately, according to the abilities of the child, the negative impact of the loss can be minimized. Secondary consequences and side effects of hearing loss include educational, vocational, psychological, and social implications (see Chapters 5 and 7 for a discussion of communication systems and their psychosocial implications).

Variable Hearing Disability

A health condition, such as a hearing disorder, can be described by a newly revised classification system within the World Health Organization (WHO, 2000), which standardizes terminology throughout the world. If hearing is not "functioning" normally, the umbrella term *disability* is used, and three dimensions are involved within this: (1) *impairment* or problems in body structure and function, (2) *activities*, in this case chiefly communication, and (3) *participation* within life situations. Besides these three dimensions, environmental and personal factors influence the disability. This provides an excellent framework for the provision of audiologic rehabilitation, and these terms have been incorporated into the rehabilitation model discussed later in the chapter. Activity (especially communication) limitations can be thought of as the primary consequence of hearing loss, whereas participation restrictions involve secondary consequences of the loss that affect social, vocational, and other life situations.

The WHO term disability has been changed to activity limitation. This refers to the primary consequence of hearing impairment.

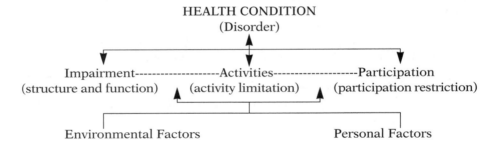

HEALTH CONDITION
(Disorder)

Impairment----------------------Activities----------------------Participation
(structure and function)   (activity limitation)   (participation restriction)

Environmental Factors   Personal Factors

A useful method for measuring the activity limitations and participation restrictions is through self-assessment of hearing, wherein persons make personal estimates about their hearing difficulties. This procedure has been applied with both children and adults. Both the person with impaired hearing and significant others can complete questionnaires independently to provide a more complete picture of the communication, psychosocial, and other effects from the loss (see Chapter 10, Schow and Smedley, 1990).

The WHO term handicap has been changed to partici-pation restriction. This refers to the secondary conse-quences of hearing impairment, includ-ing restrictions in the social, emo-tional, educational, and vocational areas.

In preparing to deal with the broad consequences of hearing loss, we must recognize that the impact of a hearing disorder will vary considerably depending on a number of personal and environmental factors. Several of the most important personal factors are presented in Table 1.2. Although not included there, other variables are also important. For example, certain basic characteristics of the individual may have considerable impact on the primary consequences in verbal communication and the secondary effects in education, social, emotional, and vocational areas. The presence of other serious disabilities like blindness, physical limitations, or mental retardation will complicate the situation. A person's native

When the eight categories of hearing loss are used, it is possible to develop profiles for *activity limitation* and *participation restriction* for each group using self-report. In this way, expectations for the consequences of hearing loss can be anticipated, and the measurement of rehabilitation success can be compared through the use of outcomes measures. The figures show the eight groupings when activity limitation and participation restriction self-report findings are compared. As can be seen, some configuration categories, such as F2 and S2, tend to produce more activity limitations and participation restrictions than other configuration categories.

Health Fair Self-report Data (Brockett & Schow, 2001)

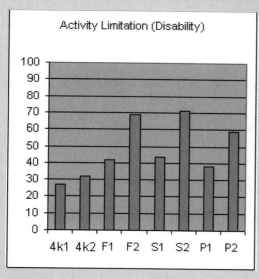

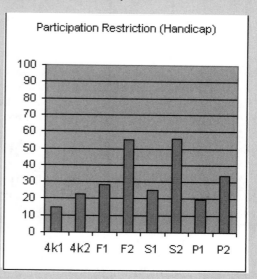

intelligence can also have a tremendous impact in conjunction with a hearing loss. Naturally, basic intelligence will vary from person to person regardless of whether or not he or she is hearing impaired. However, Vernon (1968) reported on 50 years of research showing that, as a group, persons with hereditary deafness demonstrate a normal range of IQs as measured by performance scales. Whatever the native intellectual ability, it will influence the resultant primary and secondary consequences of hearing loss.

Environmental factors include barriers and facilitators that function with the environment that make things harder or easier for communication to occur.

■ REHABILITATIVE ALTERNATIVES

Little can be done to change basic, innate IQ or native abilities. Nevertheless, a number of AR procedures may have a profound effect on the personal and environmental factors relevant to hearing loss. For example, it is estimated that about 80%

of Americans who could benefit from hearing aids are not using amplification (Smith, 1991). In addition, there are babies and young children who have hearing loss requiring amplification, but whose losses have not been identified; school-children whose aids are not in good condition; teenagers and young adults who, because of vanity or unfortunate experiences with hearing aids, are not getting the necessary help; adults and elderly individuals who have not acquired hearing aids because of pride or ignorance; and others whose instruments are not properly fitted or oriented to regular hearing aid use. Adults also have been found to be using many poorly functioning hearing aids (Schow et al., 1993a). All of these cases represent a need for audiologic rehabilitation. Identifying those who need amplification, persuading them to obtain and use hearing aids or cochlear implants, adjusting them for maximum benefit, and orienting the new user to the instruments are all tasks in the province of AR that may reduce the negative effects of a hearing loss.

Audiologic rehabilitation also includes efforts to improve communication, as well as addressing a variety of other concerns for the hearing impaired person. Before discussing procedures and the current status of audiologic rehabilitation, however, a brief review of the history of AR is in order.

Historical Background

Although audiologic rehabilitative procedures are common today, they have not always been utilized for individuals with hearing loss. For centuries it was assumed that prelingual deafness and the resultant language development delay and inability to learn were inevitable aspects of the impairment. The deaf were thought to be retarded, so for many years no efforts were made to try to teach them. The first known teacher of persons with severe to profound hearing loss was Pedro Ponce de León of Spain, who in the mid- to late 1500s demonstrated that persons who are deaf can be taught to speak and are capable of learning. Other teachers, including Bonet and de Carrion in Spain and Bulwer in England, were active in the 1600s, and their methods gained some prominence. During the 1700s, Pereira (Pereire) introduced education of the deaf to France, and the Abbé de L'Epée founded a school there. Schools were also established by Thomas Braidwood in Great Britain and by Heinicke in Germany. De L'Epée employed fingerspelling and sign language in addition to speechreading, whereas Heinicke and Braidwood stressed oral speech. Beginning in 1813, John Braidwood, a grandson of Thomas Braidwood, tried to establish this oral method in America, but he was unsuccessful because of his own ineptness and poor health. Thomas Gallaudet went to England in 1815 to learn the Braidwood oral method, but was refused help because it was feared that he would interfere with John Braidwood's efforts. Consequently, Gallaudet learned de L'Epée's manual method in Paris through contact with Sicard and Laurent Clerc. He returned to the United States and opened his own successful school. (See additional details in Moores, 1996.)

The manual approach to teaching persons who were deaf remained the major force in America until the mid-1800s, when speechreading and oral methods were promoted and popularized by Horace Mann, Alexander Graham Bell, and others. The stress on the use of residual hearing had been suggested earlier, but it began to receive strong emphasis with the oral methods used during the 1700s and 1800s. Until electric amplification was developed in the early 1900s, the use of residual hearing required ear trumpets and *ad concham* (speaking directly in the ear) stimulation. More vigorous efforts in the use of hearing followed the introduction of electronic hearing aids in the 1920s (Berger, 1988).

Also in the early 1900s, between 1900 and 1930, several schools of lipreading were started and became quite prominent. Although these institutions were directed principally toward teaching adults with hearing impairment how to speechread, considerable public recognition also was gained for this method of rehabilitating the hearing impaired. (*Speechreading* and *lipreading* will be used interchangeably in this text, although *speechreading* is the more technically accurate term; see Chapter 5 for details.)

BIRTH OF AUDIOLOGY. During World War II, the need to rehabilitate servicemen with impaired hearing resulted in the birth of the audiology profession. The cumulative effect of electronic amplification developments, adult lipreading courses, and the World War II hearing rehabilitation efforts gradually led to the recognition of audiologic rehabilitation as separate from education for persons who are deaf. Eventually, audiologists were recognized as the professionals responsible for providing such services to adults, and soon it was also realized that audiologists could provide crucial. help to youngsters who are deaf or hard of hearing.

In the military rehabilitation centers a number of methods were developed to help those with impaired hearing, including procedures for selecting hearing aids. Hearing aid orientation methods requiring up to 3 months of coursework were developed. Considerable emphasis was also placed on speechreading and auditory training.

In the late 1940s and 1950s, as audiology moved into the private sector, the approach to hearing aids changed. Whereas hearing aids were freely dispensed in government facilities, in civilian life people bought amplification exclusively from hearing aid dealers. Methods evolved wherein audiologists would perform tests and recommend hearing aids, but dealers would sell and service the instruments. At that time, the American Speech–Language–Hearing Association (ASHA) maintained that audiologists could not sell hearing aids because this would compromise their professional objectivity. Thus, strict rules were written into the ASHA Code of Ethics, and, except in military facilities, audiologists were excluded from hearing aid sales and follow-up.

In audiologic rehabilitation, audiologists performed preliminary hearing aid work (hearing aid evaluations), but concentrated on providing speechreading and auditory training. These two methods were promoted and used in certain places. For example, speech and hearing centers often set up speechreading and auditory training classes, and adult community education programs using these methods were sponsored. With newer and better hearing aids, however, the magic and motivation of the lipreading schools dissipated, and the ideas worked out in the leisurely 3-month military rehabilitation programs were found to be economically unfeasible in the "real world." In one center it was reported that everything had been tried to attract clients for audiologic rehabilitation therapy except "dancing girls" (Alpiner, 1973).

The name *audiology* was first used to describe this new profession in 1946, and Raymond Carhart, who pioneered in the audiologic rehabilitation of World War II servicemen, not only helped name audiology but started the first training program at Northwestern University in 1947.

Because of these setbacks, the 1960s and 1970s were years of examination and reflection for audiologists committed to AR. Such self-examination revealed that the potential clientele for auditory rehabilitation is large and most are not receiving help.

INFANTS. Beginning in the 1960s many audiologists recognized the need for early identification of hearing loss so that management could be initiated during the critical language development years. The incidence of hearing loss in newborns was found to be about 1 per 1000 children, a higher prevalence than for other disabilities screened routinely in the newborn. Identification methods were subsequently developed and recommended during this time, and programs evolved to provide early auditory rehabilitation. The advent of cochlear implantation in young children who are deaf during the past decade has provided another important avenue for management of these youngsters.

CHILDREN. School-age youngsters with hearing impairment were also found to be in need of assistance. Many children who were hard of hearing were (and still are) educated in the regular schools, and several studies indicated that these children were not receiving the specialized support that they needed. Compared to youngsters with normal hearing, children with 15- to 45-dB losses showed delays of 15 to 19 months in reading skills and arithmetic (Ling, 1972). In addition, educational lags

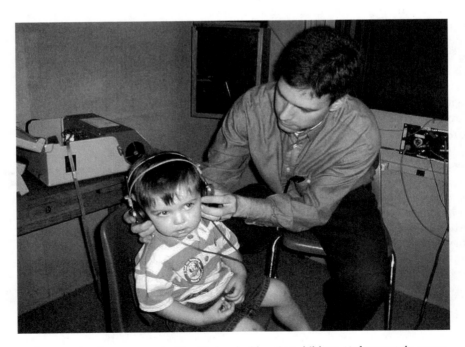

Basic screening is necessary to identify hard-of-hearing children. Unfortunately, many hard-of-hearing children are not receiving AR.

of 1 to 2 years were common with children with hearing impairment, and many of them repeated grades (Kodman, 1963). Even children with mild temporary losses from otitis media showed serious delays in academic progress (Holm & Kunze, 1969). As of 1972–1973 it was estimated that only 21% of the 440,000 hard of hearing school-age youngsters (40 to 90 dB) in the United States received any of the special education assistance that they needed (Marge, 1977). The actual number of school children who are hard of hearing is probably much greater; these are only the ones identified (see Chapter 9). Recent reports indicate that these children are still being underserved (Bess, 1986; Blair et al., 1985). Hearing aid procurement for these children has been deficient, because an estimated 15% to 75% (depending on degree of loss) do not use hearing aids (Matkin, 1984; Shepherd et al., 1981). There is little reason to believe this has changed in the last few years and, in fact, there is some evidence that the prevalence of high-frequency loss is increasing due to noise exposure (Chermak & Peters-McCarthy, 1991). Even with the advent of promising sound field amplification in classrooms, recent progress reports indicate that we are still in the early stages of implementation for those and other AR services in the schools (Flexer, 1992). Thus, rehabilitation for school-age children has become an important priority, and there is an acute need for the rehabilitative or educational audiologist in this setting nationwide.

ADULTS. Among adults, the needs for hearing rehabilitation are also apparent. Ries's (1994) data revealed that hearing problems are reported by 4% of the population from 25 to 34 years of age. This figure rises dramatically with age, so that for those 75 years and older 38% of the population report problems. In addition, it is estimated that there are between 5 and 6 million hearing aid users in this country, but conservative estimates suggest that another 15 to 20 million should be using hearing aids. Also, about one-fourth of the aids being used by adults have been shown to be in poor working condition (Schow et al., 1993a).

DIFFICULTIES IN ACCEPTANCE OF AUDIOLOGIC REHABILITATION. When audiologists reflected on the limited acceptance of audiologic rehabilitation, it became apparent that, despite the subject's importance, many in the profession lacked interest. In 1966, the Academy of Rehabilitative Audiology was organized to help audiologists with rehabilitative interests direct their efforts toward reversing these trends. This organization and its members have had an important influence on the emergence of AR as a viable part of audiology.

One reason for the noted neglect of rehabilitation in the past was the hearing aid situation. Primarily because of the success of aggressive sales practices by hearing aid dealers and the ASHA policy that prevented heavy audiologic involvement, 70% to 90% of all hearing aids in this country were for many years being sold without active involvement of medical or audiological consultants. Because audiologists did not dispense hearing aids until the 1970s, they were for many years deprived of close contact with clients during the postfitting period. In contrast, the hearing aid dealers were intimately involved in the most crucial rehabilitation process. This situation began to change in the mid- to late 1970s because of relaxation in the ASHA policy prohibiting audiologists from dispensing hearing aids. Finally, due to a

Audiologists were not totally free to dispense hearing aids until 1979 because their national association, ASHA, prohibited it.

Supreme Court decision, ASHA removed these restrictions in 1979. This decision has had a profound effect on AR and the role of the audiologist in working with persons who are deaf and hard of hearing.

Current Status

Fortunately, audiologists generally have begun to recognize the opportunities for rehabilitation through early intervention and the provision of services in schools and in neglected adult and geriatric settings. This awareness has been reflected within ASHA, as evidenced in a series of policy statements on rehabilitative audiology issued by special ASHA subcommittees (ASHA, 1984, 1992, 1997). Similar supportive statements on rehabilitation issues have emerged from another major professional organization for audiologists, the American Academy of Audiology (AAA, 1988, 1993, 2000). The Americans with Disabilities Act also created an increased awareness of the need for hearing services (ADA, 1990).

In the past 25 years, a number of alternative audiologic rehabilitation approaches have been developed and the profession has gradually moved away from an emphasis on speechreading and auditory training toward a major focus on hearing aid fitting and orientation, with considerable attention to communication patterns and the environment. This change in emphasis has continued and become more widespread, based on recent surveys (Schow et al., 1993b; Millington, 2001).

A common factor in all new approaches is the recognition that successful hearing aid fitting and orientation and general communication help are the central issues in most audiologic rehabilitation. In most cases now, the focus in AR is on amplification, whereas extensive speechreading and auditory training have become occasional, ancillary procedures. Heavy emphasis on these methods is warranted only in certain instances.

The 1980s and 1990s have seen the emergence of a new breed of audiologists, more aware of the millions of children and adults in need of audiologic rehabilitation. Results of recent surveys show that approximately 75% to 80% of all ASHA audiologists are involved in direct dispensing of hearing aids. According to our most recent survey conducted in 2000, 85% to 92% of all audiologists are involved in hearing aid evaluation orientation and in rehabilitation counseling. A smaller number (12–23%) reported being involved in communication rehabilitation, including speechreading and auditory training (Millington, 2001).

PROCEDURES IN AUDIOLOGIC REHABILITATION: ■ AN AR MODEL

This section will describe important procedures and elements of audiologic rehabilitation in order to provide a framework for the remainder of this text.

The audiologic rehabilitation model used here emerged in 1980 when the first edition of this text appeared. It has been slightly revised with each new edition of the text, based on the work of Goldstein and Stephens (1981) and other trends in

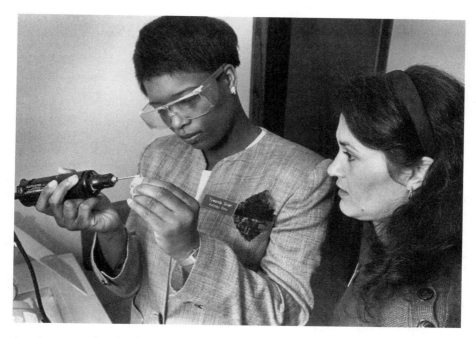

A major aspect of AR involves ensuring that hearing aids are working properly for the patient.

audiology (Stephens, 1996). In its current form it is in harmony with the World Health Organization's (2000) International Classification of Functioning and Disability. The model is intended to encompass all types and degrees of hearing impairment as well as all age groups.

Entry and discharge are considered peripheral to the central aspects of the model. The model consists of two major components: assessment and management. Each component has four divisions and associated subsections. The model is shown in Table 1.4 and Figure 1.2.

REHABILITATION ASSESSMENT PROCEDURES. Following the initial auditory diagnostic tests that indicate the need for audiologic rehabilitation, it is necessary to perform more in-depth workups to determine the feasibility of various forms of audiologic rehabilitation. These assessment procedures should focus on Communication status, Overall participation variables, Related personal factors, and Environmental factors (which are collectively abbreviated as CORE).

> The CORE assessment issues help audiologists consider relevant factors that should be evaluated before treatment starts.

COMMUNICATION STATUS. Within the area of *communication* status, which includes impairment and activity, both traditional audiometric tests and questionnaires may be used to assess auditory abilities and self-reported consequences of hearing loss. Visual abilities assessment should include a simple screening and measurement of speechreading abilities. Any evaluation of communication must also consider language, because it is at the heart of verbal communication. If the patient

TABLE 1.4

Audiologic Rehabilitation Model Used in This Text

(ENTER THROUGH DIAGNOSTIC–IDENTIFICATION PROCESS)

Assessment (CORE)	**C**ommunication status: Impairment and activity limitations	Auditory Visual Language Manual Communication self-report Previous rehabilitation Overall
	Overall participation variables	Psychological (emotional) Social Vocational Educational
	Related personal factors	Types I, II, III, IV Personality IQ Age Race Gender
	Environmental factors	Services Systems Barriers Facilitators Acoustic conditions
Management (CARE)	**C**ounseling and psychosocial (modifying personal attitude)	Interpretation Information Counseling and guidance Acceptance Understanding Expectations and goals

	Audibility and impairment	Hearing aid fitting
		Cochlear implants
		Assistive devices
		    Assistive listening
		    Alerting and warning
		    Tactile
		    Communication
		Instruction and orientation

	Remediate communication activity	Tactics to control situation Philosophy based on realistic expectations Personal skill-building
	Environmental/coordination/ participation improvement	Situation improvement Vocational Educational Social Communication partner Community context

(Discharge)

Note: This model is based on Goldstein and Stephens (1981), Stephens (1996), and the current WHO (2000) terminology.

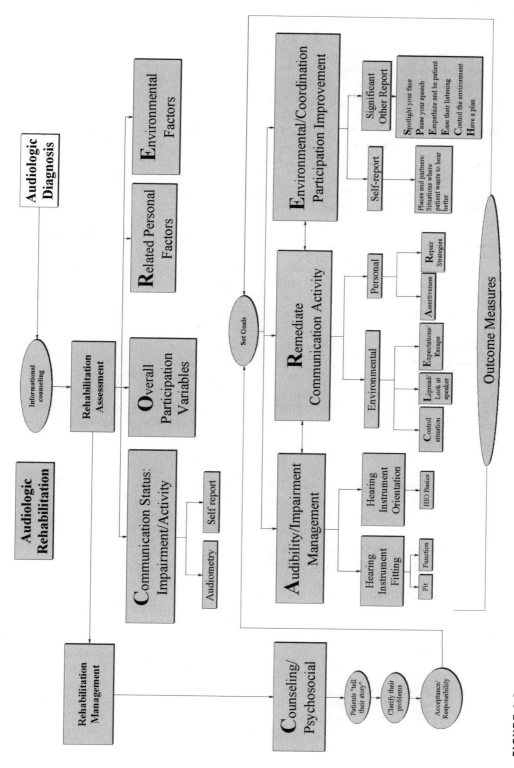

FIGURE 1.2

Model for audiologic rehabilitation.

(Schow, 2001; Brockett and Schow, 2001).

understands a manual–gesture system, this needs to be evaluated, as does any prior treatment. Included in *overall communication* are combined sensory abilities, such as audiovisual and tactile–kinesthetic capacities. Expressive and receptive communication skills should both be considered.

OVERALL PARTICIPATION VARIABLES. Included in this area are participation aspects of hearing loss, including psychological, social, vocational, and educational factors. Social factors such as family and significant others, social class, and life-style are to be considered according to the Goldstein and Stephens model. The vocational domain includes position, responsibility, and competence. In addition, the patient's level and form of education must be considered.

RELATED PERSONAL FACTORS. These include the person's attitude, which is considered a crucial aspect of rehabilitation. Goldstein and Stephens (1981) suggested that rehabilitation candidates can be categorized into four types according to attitude. Type I candidates have a strongly positive attitude toward management and are thought to comprise two-thirds to three-quarters of all patients. Most of the remaining candidates fit into Type II: Their expectations are essentially positive, but slight complications are present such as hearing loss that is difficult to fit with amplification. Persons with Type III attitudes are negative about rehabilitation, but show some willingness to cooperate, and those in Type IV reject hearing aids and the rehabilitation process altogether. In the latter two categories, management cannot proceed in the usual fashion until some modification of attitude is achieved. [We consider it important to evaluate attitude prior to rehabilitation.] In the WHO (2000) system, personal factors listed also include age, race, gender, education, personality and character style, aptitude, other health conditions, fitness, life-style, habits, upbringing, coping styles (assertiveness), social background, profession, and past and current experiences.

ENVIRONMENTAL FACTORS. These include individual aspects, services, and systems. The individual issues include the physical features of the environment as well as direct personal contacts. The services include social structures and services in the work environment, socially, communication-wise, and transportation-wise. Systems refer to laws, regulations, and rules, both formal and informal. Finally, the acoustic environmental conditions confronted by the hearing-impaired person should be evaluated.

MANAGEMENT PROCEDURES. Once a thorough, rehabilitation-oriented assessment has been completed, management efforts should be initiated. These may take the form of short- or long-term therapy and may involve individual or group sessions. The four aspects of management included here are those detailed in the previous edition of this book. They are also prominently featured in the Goldstein–Stephens model as well as in the WHO (1999) terminology. These include (1) Counseling and psychosocial aspects, (2) Audibility or amplification aspects, (3) Remediation of communication activity, and (4) Environmental coordination/participation improvement (abbreviated as CARE).

CARE defines a management approach that includes four critical components of AR.

Though all four management components are listed sequentially, they may occur simultaneously or in a duplicative and interactive fashion. For example, information about communication is generally introduced early in the counseling phase. However, additional information on how we hear, basics of speech acoustics, visible dimensions of speech, and how to maximize the use of conversational cues may be further emphasized later in the remediation of communication.

COUNSELING/PSYCHOSOCIAL. Counseling/psychosocial includes interpretation of audiologic findings to the client and other significant persons. In addition, pertinent information, counseling, and guidance are needed to help these individuals understand the educational, vocational, psychosocial and communicative effects of hearing impairment. Considerable understanding and support are necessary in dealing with children who are deaf and hard of hearing, their parents, adults of all ages with hearing impairment, and their families. If the clinician is a good listener, in this process he will allow the clients to "tell their own story," and this will in turn help clients to clarify their problems, accept responsibility, and set appropriate goals. This process should bring acceptance and understanding of the conditions along with appropriate expectations for management. It is at this stage that good-attitude (Types I and II) patients must set goals to improve audibility with amplification, whereas clients with poor attitudes (Types III and IV), if not modified toward acceptance and understanding, may not be ready and will resist this type of goal.

AUDIBILITY IMPROVEMENT USING AMPLIFICATION AND ASSISTIVE DEVICES.

Amplification fitting. This phase is sometimes referred to as *hearing-aid evaluation,* but it needs to be broader in scope. Here we must consider all forms of amplification, not just hearing aids. For example, cochlear implants, signal warning devices, and other assistive devices like telephone amplifiers should be considered in this phase. In many cases, accurate fitting of these devices will go a considerable way toward resolution of the hearing problem. In most cases, the fitting of hearing devices should be followed by adjustment, modification, and alteration of the basic controls and coupler arrangement until satisfactory amplification is achieved. Effort should be made to ensure that no other amplification arrangements are substantially superior to the ones being used.

Hearing Instrument Orientation (HIO Basics). Individuals need to learn about the purpose, function, and maintenance of hearing aids and other assistive devices used by themselves or their child or other family member to avoid misunderstanding and misuse. Amplification units are relatively complex, and this instruction must be given more emphasis than a 5-minute explanation or a pamphlet.

Hearing instrument orientation (HIO), as defined throughout this text, includes basic elements that should be included to help new hearing aid users. Chapter 2 will explain these HIO basics.

REMEDIATE COMMUNICATION ACTIVITY. The major impact of hearing loss lies in the area of communication activity. Communication deficits often manifest themselves in educational difficulties for children and in vocational difficulties for adults. In most cases, amplification is considered the most important tool in combating this problem, but some basic communication training and related strategies are recommended for all new amplification users. These involve both environmental and personal adjustments and may provide the basis for more extensive therapy if the client selects goals in this area.

Although a basic overview is adequate in most cases of hearing aid fitting, cochlear implants require more extensive skill building wherein the patient learns methods to facilitate communication in conjunction with this new device. Speechreading and improvement of auditory listening strategies are included here, as are related speech and language rehabilitation efforts. Specific communication skills are identified in this phase of therapy and then, through such things as assertiveness training and incorporation of anticipatory and repair strategies, clients may learn to cope better with communication challenges.

ENVIRONMENTAL COORDINATION: PARTICIPATION IMPROVEMENT. Self-reports provide a useful method to help clients select a few situations (places and partners) wherein they would like to improve their hearing and communicating. With the therapist they can identify strategies for improvement. Pre- and post-self-report measures can help determine the success of these efforts. Also in this phase of treatment we include coordination with other sources of help. Disability is not an individual attribute, but rather a collection of conditions, and many of these are created by the social and physical environment. It is a collective responsibility for all elements of society to help make necessary modifications. Although referrals in all areas are not usually necessary, they should be considered. Liaison among client, family, and other agencies is included as are reassessment and modification of the intervention program.

> Self-report outcome measures have become a key element to help measure the communication improvement results of AR for different environments and situations (places and partners).

Coordination and teamwork are a useful concept in audiologic rehabilitation. Particularly in the case of the hearing impaired youngster, many persons may work with or need to work with the child. The parents should be at the center of the rehabilitative process. Also, physicians, social workers, hearing aid dispensers, teachers, school psychologists, and other school personnel need to be coordinated to assist the child and family. For adults, much depends on the particular setting in which the rehabilitation occurs. Sometimes physicians, psychologists, or social workers function in the same clinical setting. In these cases, involvement of another professional may occur naturally and easily. In other situations, the AR therapist can make referrals, when indicated, and encourage the adult to follow up. Sometimes persons are resistant to obtaining medical care or seeing a rehabilitation counselor. Often, parents or adults resist social services, psychiatric assistance, or hearing aid devices. When a client refuses to accept advice, the audiologist must provide whatever insight and help possible, based on the audiologist's background and training, but must respect the rights of the client or the parents. Nevertheless, the audiologic rehabilitation process demands that referrals be made when indicated, and overall coordination within the relevant context is an important dimension that should not be neglected.

Additional clarification and details on this AR model can be found in Goldstein and Stephens (1981) and WHO (2000).

■ SETTINGS FOR AUDIOLOGIC REHABILITATION

Audiologic rehabilitation may be conducted in a variety of settings with children, adults, or the elderly who are either deaf or hard of hearing. A review of these settings may help to demonstrate the many applications of AR (see Table 1.5).

TABLE 1.5		
Summary of Audiologic Rehabilitation Settings for Children, Adults, and Elderly Persons		
CHILDREN	ADULTS	ELDERLY ADULTS
Early intervention	University and technical schools	(Most settings listed under Adults)
Preschool	Vocational rehabilitation	Community programs
Parent groups	Military-related facilities	Nursing homes and long-term care facilities
Regular classrooms	ENT Clinic–Private practice	
School conservation program follow-up	Community, hospital, and university hearing clinics	
School resource rooms	Hearing aid specialists and dispensers	
Residential school classrooms		

Children

Very young children with hearing impairment and their parents may be recipients of early intervention efforts through home visits or clinic programs. Parent groups are also an important rehabilitation option. As children enter preschool and other school settings, audiologic rehabilitation takes on a supportive, coordinative function with teachers of youngsters with impaired hearing managing the classroom learning. Specifically, children in resource rooms, in residential deaf school classrooms, and in regular classrooms can be helped with amplification (both group and individual), communication therapy, and academic subjects. Important help and insights can also be given to the child's parents and teachers, and other professionals may be involved as needed. Hearing conservation follow-up for youngsters who fail traditional school screenings represents another type of rehabilitative work carried out with children.

Adults

Adult AR services are needed for individuals with long-standing hearing loss, as well as for persons who acquire loss during adulthood. Such traumatic or progressive hearing disorders may be brought on by accident, heredity, disease, or noise.

Adults may be served in university or technical school settings, through vocational rehabilitation programs, in military-related facilities, in the office of an ear specialist, or in the private practice of an audiologist. In addition, many adults are served in community, hospital, or university hearing clinics or through hearing aid dealers and dispensers. A variety of rehabilitative services may be provided in all these settings.

Elderly Adults

The vast majority of elderly clients are served through the conventional programs previously described for adults. A substantial proportion of clients seen in these settings for hearing aid evaluations and related services are 65 years of age or older.

The full array of hearing aid and communication rehabilitation services may be provided for the elderly in these clinics, including hearing aid evaluation, orientation, and group and individual therapy. Aside from conventional clinical service, rehabilitation may be provided to the elderly in community screening and rehabilitation programs in well-elderly clinics, retirement apartment houses, senior citizen centers, churches, and a variety of other places where senior citizens congregate. Nursing homes or long-term care facilities also provide opportunities for audiologic rehabilitation since so many residents in these settings have substantial hearing loss and are required to have hearing screening under Medicare law (Bebout, 1991). Nevertheless, rehabilitation personnel should be realistic and anticipate less than 100% success with the elderly who are residents in health care facilities (Schow, 1992). Audiologic rehabilitation will be better accepted if it can be applied before persons enter such a facility.

SUMMARY

Audiologic habilitation and rehabilitation involve a variety of assessment and management efforts for the person who is deaf or hard of hearing, coordinated by a professional with audiologic training. Audiology's commitment to this endeavor has waxed and waned during the past 50+ years, but recently a resurgence of interest has been spurred by a variety of factors.

A model of rehabilitation has been presented here to provide a framework for assessment and management procedures in audiologic rehabilitation as described in the remaining chapters of this book. Professionals who intend to engage in AR must be familiar with the characteristics of hearing loss reviewed in this chapter if they are to perform effective rehabilitation.

SUMMARY POINTS

- Audiologic rehabilitation (AR) is defined as those professional efforts designed to help someone with hearing loss achieve better communication and minimize the resulting problems. It does not include closely related medical intervention or the teaching of academic subjects to the deaf.
- Audiologists are the chief providers of AR, but speech pathologists and teachers of the deaf also do a great deal of this work. In addition, other professionals such as social workers and rehabilitation counselors may provide key rehabilitative assistance to those with hearing loss.
- AR providers need some background in diagnostic audiology, and they need an understanding of hearing loss and its effect on both children and adults.

- Hearing impairment can be defined in terms of degree of loss, time of onset, type of loss, and word recognition ability. Those with milder forms of hearing loss are called hard of hearing; those with extensive hearing loss who cannot use hearing for the ordinary purposes of life are considered deaf.

- The deaf may be divided into three groups: the prelingually deaf, who are born deaf or acquire it in the first 5 years of life; the postlingually deaf, who acquire hearing loss after age 5 through the school years; and the deafened, who acquire hearing loss after their education is completed.

- The most serious and primary consequence of hearing impairment is the effect on verbal communication, and this is often referred to as disability. The secondary consequences of hearing impairment may be referred to as a handicap and include social, emotional, educational, and vocational issues. The World Health Organization (WHO) now suggests that communication *activity limitation* be used instead of disability and that we speak of *participation restriction* instead of handicap. In connection with these new terms, WHO also suggests that personal factors and environmental factors are key issues in the provision of AR hearing services. These terms and factors help us properly understand the consequences of hearing impairment and provide the basis for a model of AR.

- Both children and adults are underserved and many more should receive AR help. Only 20% of those who should be using hearing aids obtain them. Even those who have hearing aids can often be shown how to get more effective help from amplification and can benefit from other services to assist them in their communication breakdowns.

- The early history of AR is essentially the history of efforts to help the deaf, beginning in the 1500s. Audiology came into being as a profession in the mid-1940s in connection with World War II, and both audiologic diagnosis and audiologic rehabilitation (AR) are considered key elements within this profession. In recent years, audiologists have become more involved in hearing aid fitting, and new developments such as cochlear implants, assistive listening devices, wider support for disabilities, and the emerging use of outcome measures have helped revitalize AR.

- The model for AR includes assessment and management; rehabilitation assessment includes four elements defined by the acronym CORE. These elements include an assessment of **C**ommunication and impairment through audiometry and self-report; **O**verall participation variables, including psychological, social, educational, and vocational factors; **R**elated personal factors; and **E**nvironmental factors.

- Management includes four elements also and these are summarized by the acronym CARE. These elements include **C**ounseling, which includes an effort to help clients accept the hearing loss and set reasonable goals; **A**udibility improvement by using hearing aids and assistive devices; **R**emediation of communication; and **E**nvironmental coordination and participation goals.

- Children receive AR services in a variety of settings, including early intervention and school programs. Adults and elderly adults are usually served in settings that dispense hearing aids; these include private practice, medical or ENT offices, hearing aid specialists, military or VA service centers, and community hearing clinics.

■ The first eight chapters in this book are organized to provide an overview of the fundamentals in AR, including hearing aids (Chapter 2), cochlear implants and other emerging AR methods (Chapter 3), auditory and visual stimuli (Chapters 4 and 5), speech and language issues (Chapter 6), psychosocial issues (Chapter 7), and educational alternatives (Chapter 8). Two chapters provide comprehensive explanations to illuminate AR for children (Chapter 9) and for adults (Chapter 10). Finally, two case study chapters illustrate how this work is done with children (Chapter 11) and with adults (Chapter 12).

RECOMMENDED READINGS

Alpiner, J. G., & McCarthy, P A. (2000). *Rehabilitative audiology: Children and adults* (3rd ed.). Baltimore: Williams & Wilkins.

DeConde Johnson, C., Benson, P. V., and Seaton, J. B. (1997). *Educational audiology handbook.* San Diego: Singular.

Gagne J. P. and Jennings, M. B. (2000) Audiological rehabilitation intervention services for adults with acquired hearing impairment. In: M. Valente, Hosford-Dunn and Roesser (Eds.) *Audiology treatment.* New York: Thieme Medical Publishers.

Tye Murray, N. (1998). *Foundations of aural rehabilitation.* San Diego: Singular.

RECOMMENDED WEB SITES

www.who.int/icidh/
www.audiology.org/professional/positions/
www.asha.org

REFERENCES

Alpiner, J. G. (1973). The hearing aid in rehabilitation planning for adults. *Journal of the Academy of Rehabilitative Audiology, 6,* 55–57.

American Academy of Audiology (AAA). (1988). Early identification of hearing loss in infants and children. *Audiology Today, 2,* 8–9.

American Academy of Audiology (AAA). (1993). Audiology: Scope of practice. *Audiology Today, 5*(1).

American Academy of Audiology (AAA). (2000). Principles and guidelines for early hearing detection and intervention programs. Year 2000 position statement from the joint committee on infant hearing. www.audiology.org/professional/positions/

American Annals of the Deaf. (2000). Annual survey of hearing-impaired children and youth. *American Annals of the Deaf, 139*(2), 239–243.

Americans with Disabilities Act (ADA) of 1990 (Public Law 101-336), 42 USC Sec. 12101. Equal opportunity for the disabled. Washington, D.C.

ASHA (American Speech–Language–Hearing Association). (1984). Definition of and competencies for aural rehabilitation. A report from the committee on rehabilitative audiology. *Asha, 26,* 37–41.

ASHA (American Speech–Language–Hearing Association). (1992). Spotlight on special interest division 7: Audiologic Rehabilitation. *Asha, 34,* 18.

ASHA, (American Speech Language Hearing Association). (1997). Guidelines for audiologic screening. Rockville, MD.

Bebout, J. M. (1991). Long term care facilities: A new window of opportunity opens for hearing health care services. *Hearing Journal, 44*(11), 11–17.

Berger, K. W. (1988). History and development of hearing aids. In M. C. Pollack (Ed.), *Amplification for the hearing-impaired* (3rd ed., pp. 1–20). New York: Grune & Stratton.

Bess, F. H. (1986). Unilateral sensorineural hearing loss in children. Special issue. *Ear and Hearing, 7*(1), 3–54.

Blair, J. C., Peterson, M., & Viehweg, S. H. (1985). The effects of mild hearing loss on academic performance among school-age children. *The Volta Review, 87,* 87–94.

Brockett, J., and Schow, R. L. (2001) Web site profiles common hearing loss patterns and outcome measures. *Hearing Journal 54*(8) 20.

Chermak G., & Peters-McCarthy, E. (1991). The effectiveness of an educational hearing conservation program for elementary school children. *Language, Speech, and Hearing Services in Schools, 22,* 308–312.

Davis, A. (1994). *Public health perspectives in audiology.* 22nd International Congress of Audiology. Halifax, NS, Canada.

Flexer, C. (1992). FM classroom public address systems. In M. Ross (Ed.), *FM auditory training systems: Characteristics, selection and use.* Parkton, MD: York Press.

Goldstein, D. P. (1984). Hearing impairment, hearing aids, and audiology. *Asha, 25*(9), 24–38.

Goldstein, D. P., & Stephens, S. D. G. (1981). Audiological rehabilitation: Management Model I. *Audiology, 20,* 432–452.

Holm, V. A., & Kunze, L. H. (1969). Effect of chronic otitis media on language and speech development. *Pediatrics, 43,* 833–839.

Kodman, F., Jr. (1963). Educational status of hard-of-hearing children in the classroom. *Journal of Speech and Hearing Disorders, 28,* 297–299.

Ling, D. (1972). Rehabilitation of cases with deafness secondary to otitis media. In A. Glorig & K. S. Gerwin (Eds.), *Otitis media* (pp. 249–253). Springfield, IL: Charles C Thomas Publisher.

Lundeen, C. (1991). Prevalence of hearing impairment among school children. *Language, Speech and Hearing Services in Schools, 22,* 269–271.

Marge, M. (1977). The current status of service delivery systems for the hearing impaired. *Asha, 19,* 403–409.

Matkin, N. D. (1984). Wearable amplification. A litany of persisting problems. In J. Jerger (Ed.), *Pediatric audiology: Current trends* (pp. 125–145). San Diego, CA: College Hill Press.

McCandless, G., Sjursen, W., and Preves, D. (2000). Satisfying patient needs with nine fixed acoustical prescription formats. *Hearing Journal. 53*(5), 42–50.

Millington, D. (2001). Audiologic rehabilitation practices of ASHA audiologists: Survey 2000. MS Thesis. Idaho State University.

Moores, D. (1996). *Educating the deaf—psychology, principles, practices* (4th ed.). Boston: Houghton Mifflin.

Ries, P. W. (1994). *Prevalence and characteristics of persons with hearing trouble: United States*. National Center for Health Statistics, *Vital Stat, 24,* 188.

Schow, R. L. (1992). Hearing assessment and treatment in nursing homes. *Hearing Instruments, 43*(7), 7–11.

Schow, R. L. (2001). A standardized AR battery for dispensers. *Hearing Journal.* 54(8) 10–20.

Schow, R. L., & Smedley, T. C. (1990). *(Special Issue) Self assessment of hearing. Ear and Hearing, 11*(5) (Suppl.), 1–65.

Schow, R. L., & Maxwell, S., Crookston, G., & Newman, M. (1993a). How well do adults take care of their hearing instruments? *Hearing Instruments, 44*(3), 16–20.

Schow, R. L., Balsara, N. R., Smedley, T. C., & Whitcomb, C. J. (1993b). *American Journal of Audiology, 2*(3), 28–37.

Schow, R. L., Mercaldo, D., & Smedley, T. C. (1996). *The Idaho hearing survey.* Pocatello, ID: Idaho State University Press.

Shepherd, N., Davis, J., Gorga, M., & Stelmachowics, P. (1981). Characteristics of hearing impaired children in the public schools: Part 1—Demographic data. *Journal of Speech and Hearing Disorders, 46,* 123–129.

Smith, M. (1991). The role of age and ageism in the "80% barrier." *Asha, 33*(11), 36–37.

Stephens, D. (1996). Hearing rehabilitation in a psychosocial framework. *Scandinavian Audiolgy* 25 (Suppl 43) 57–66.

Vernon, M. (1968). Fifty years of research on the intelligence of the deaf and hard-of-hearing. A survey of literature and disscussion of implications. *Journal of Rehabilitation of the Deaf, 1,* 1–11.

Vernon, M., & Andrews, J. (1990). *The psychology of deafness.* White Plains, NY: Longman Press.

World Health Organization (WHO). (2000). International classification of functioning, disability and health. Geneva: World Health Organization.

Hearing Aids and Assistive Devices

H. Gustav Mueller
Anne Strouse Carter

CONTENTS

■ INTRODUCTION

In nearly all cases, audiologic rehabilitation involves working with individuals who can benefit from the use of hearing aids or other assistive listening devices. Although all forms of auditory rehabilitation are important, reliance on visual and situational cues is inversely related to the quality of the hearing aid fitting. A critical first step for most patients, therefore, is to provide amplification that makes speech and environmental sounds of various inputs audible, optimizes intelligibility and sound quality, and assures that loud inputs are not uncomfortable or distorted. This might sound like a fairly straightforward task; however, hearing aids are sometimes fitted in a haphazard manner, without careful consideration of these underlying principles. Getting the right hearing aids on a patient and adjusting them precisely for that patient's listening needs can facilitate significantly many of the other aspects of auditory rehabilitation.

Twenty years ago, many master's degree training programs in audiology lumped the study of hearing aids together with speech audiometry (and other assorted topics) to create a single three-credit hour course. Today, at many universities, two or more courses are devoted solely to the selection and fitting of hearing aids. Why the change? The selection, fitting, and verification of hearing aids have become increasingly complex, and dispensing hearing aids has become an integral part of the scope of the practice of audiology. To do it right, extensive training is necessary.

In recent years, several factors have had a significant impact on the way that we select and fit hearing aids, which indirectly has influenced the amount of training required for proficiency. As you read this chapter, it is important to keep these issues in mind, because they are shaping the way that we do our job.

Programmable: A hearing aid, either digital or analog, that is programmed digitally using a PC or remote control device.

- *Advanced circuit design.* Each year new hearing aid circuits are introduced that provide a variety of new signal processing algorithms; today, some hearing aids have several separate channels of signal processing, each requiring patient-specific adjustments of several processing features.
- *Programmable hearing aids.* These instruments are programmed through the use of a personal computer, and the audiologist must be familiar with the software and the thousands of fitting options in order to obtain the optimum fit for the patient.

Digital: A hearing aid that uses digital processing of the signal.

Probe-mic measures: Using a tiny silicone tube placed near the tympanic membrane, which is attached to a miniature microphone, the gain and output of the hearing aid are assessed in the patient's ear.

- *Digital hearing aids.* True digital hearing aids are now common, and in some clinics or offices they comprise over 50% of the fittings. The "digital" buzz word is attractive to many consumers, but expectations also often are raised to unrealistic levels.
- *Probe-microphone measurements.* The ability to measure reliably the output of hearing aids at the patient's tympanic membrane allows for the use of precise verification protocols. Additionally, the performance of many other hearing aid features can be evaluated and quantified. The equipment is available today that would allow us to do all our testing and fitting in ear canal sound pressure level (SPL). Are we ready for this?
- *Computerization.* Hearing aid specifications, prescriptive fitting methods, automated testing procedures, hearing aid selection algorithms, and self-assessment inventories are now all available from computer software. Combine this with

digital and programmable hearing aids and PC-based probe-microphone measurements and the personal computer becomes the work station for audiometric testing and hearing aid selection, adjustment, fitting, and validation.

■ *Miniaturization.* Hearing aids continue to be made smaller and placed deeper in the ear canal. Evaluation and fitting techniques need to be modified for these smaller instruments. This trend also encourages more individuals with mild hearing loss to use amplification.

■ *Delivery system.* Twenty-five years ago it was considered unethical for audiologists to sell hearing aids for profit. Today, the majority of hearing aids are dispensed by audiologists, and the percentage increases annually.

■ *Internet.* Prospective hearing aid users now use the Internet to learn about hearing aids at manufacturers' Web sites, have their hearing aid questions answered through audiology discussion groups, and, in some cases, even purchase their hearing aids online.

In this chapter, we will cover a wide range of information about hearing aids, beginning with simple descriptions of how they work and how they are tested and eventually discuss the latest details concerning automated fitting procedures and programmable instruments. We will also review other important assistive listening and rehabilitative devices that can be used as an alternative to hearing aids.

■ HEARING AIDS

A successful hearing aid fitting, which should lead to a happy hearing aid user, depends on the audiologist's understanding of hearing aid technology and how to apply this technology to different types of hearing losses, loudness growth functions, and listening needs.

To get things started, the following is a simplified description of what makes a hearing aid work. Later in this chapter we will provide a more detailed description of some of these components.

Basic Components

The purpose of a hearing aid is to amplify, or make sounds louder, and to accomplish this with respect to the input signal and the patient's hearing loss configuration. You don't have to be an electrical engineer to understand how a hearing aid works. There are certain basic components, common to all types of hearing aids (see the block diagram in Figure 2.1). Here is a step by step walk-through of how things work:

1. Sound waves enter the hearing aid through the *microphone.*
2. The *microphone* converts the sound waves into an electrical signal.
3. The *amplifier* increases the strength of the electrical signal.
4. A smaller loudspeaker called a *receiver* functions to convert the amplified signals back into sound waves.
5. The amplified sound is channeled from the *receiver* directly to the ear canal. For hearing aids that fit behind the ear, the receiver sends the amplified sound into a clear plastic tube attached to a custom-made earmold. For hearing aids that

FIGURE 2.1

Basic components of a
hearing aid.

From M. Pollack (1988).
Electroacoustic charac-
teristics. In M. Pollack (Ed.),
*Amplification for the
Hearing Impaired* (3rd ed.).
Orlanda, FL: Grune &
Stratton.

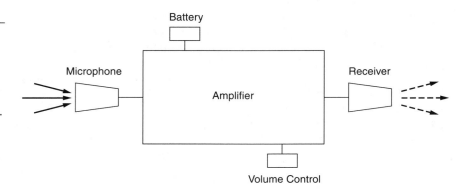

fit into the ear, the amplified sound is channeled into the ear canal by a small piece of tubing within the instrument.

6. The *battery* provides electrical energy to power the hearing aid and enable the amplification process to occur.

Pretty simple, huh? But this is just the basic framework. The typical hearing aid of today has many other features. And you will see that there are variations of each one of these basic components. These variations, along with other controls and features, allow us to customize each hearing aid for the individual patient.

Controls and Features

In addition to the basic components that we have just described, many hearing aids include additional controls or circuits. The following is a listing of the most common of these features:

1. *On–off switch.* Allows the user to turn the hearing aid off when not in use. In some hearing aids, this switch also activates the telecoil (see below). Generally, the **M** position indicates that the microphone is on, **O** turns the aid off, and **T** (if present) activates the telecoil. For custom-made instruments, the on–off switch (if present) is usually part of the volume control wheel.

Individuals with mild to moderate hearing loss often can do quite well on the telephone using the hearing aid in traditional microphone mode.

2. *Telecoil.* A special circuit designed to enhance the use of the hearing aid with the telephone. A telecoil switch may be incorporated into a toggle on–off switch, or exist as a separate control. Electromagnetic signals are picked up by the telecoil from the receiver of the telephone (leakage), amplified, and transduced to acoustic energy before entering the ear. Thus, the telecoil takes the place of the hearing aid microphone as the input component of the hearing aid system. Although proved beneficial for many users, there is substantial variability in the performance of the telecoil within each individual hearing aid, particularly in custom-made instruments, due to size and placement restrictions, making it necessary to carefully evaluate the performance characteristics of each device. Telecoils are not available on some smaller custom-made hearing aids due to space limitations. Often, hearing aids with multiple memories will devote one memory to the telecoil. In these instances, it can be accessed through a programming button on the hearing aid or by the use of a remote control device.

3. *Volume control.* A rotating wheel that allows the user to select a preferred listening level for a specific listening situation. The volume control functions by adjusting the amount of amplification of the input signal. In some smaller hearing aids, the volume control also acts as an on–off switch. For older individuals with poor dexterity, the volume control wheel can be raised for ease of use.

Many programmable instruments (both digital and analog) do not employ a volume control wheel; the notion is that the hearing aid is programmed to automatically adjust the volume for different input signals. Additionally, for the very small completely in the canal instruments, there usually is no volume control wheel due to space limitations. For these instruments, the volume is screw-set by the audiologist.

Even though research has shown that, when the hearing aids are programmed correctly, many patients do not *need* a volume control, it is *desired* by most patients, especially if they are previous users of hearing aids equipped with volume controls.

4. *Tone control.* A circuit designed to provide high- or low-frequency reduction, such as treble and bass adjustments on a stereo. Using a screwdriver-controlled potentiometer or a digitally controlled programmable system, the audiologist can make an adjustment so that there is greater or lesser amplification in certain frequency regions. For example, a patient's hearing loss may involve only the frequencies above 2000 Hz. The hearing aid, by manipulation of the tone control, can be adjusted so that it will not amplify substantially any frequencies below 2000 Hz. Conversely, a patient with an upward-sloping hearing loss might need some reduction of amplification in the higher frequencies. Today's programmable hearing aids have precise gain control in multiple frequency bands, allowing for appropriate adjustment of the frequency response for any type of hearing loss configuration.

5. *Output limiting.* All hearing aids use some form of output limiting, and many have an automatic gain control (AGC) circuit. Output-limiting potentiometers allow the audiologist to control the maximum output of the hearing aid; the purpose of this adjustment is to assure that loud sounds are not uncomfortably loud to the user. If a hearing aid is not limited using compression, peak clipping is the method utilized. Modern hearing aids often have two circuits for output limiting: one prior to the amplifier (to prevent overload) and one after the amplifier (to prevent listener discomfort).

Peak-clipping. In a peak-clipping linear system, increases in input level result in an equivalent increase in output. There is a limit, however, to the maximum output level that can be produced. When this point is reached, the output will not increase with further increases in input level, the system is forced into non-linearity when peak-clipping occurs, and the hearing aid is said to be in saturation. As the name implies, peaks of the signal that exceed a given voltage within the circuit are clipped off. Thus, hearing aid output is limited by means of distorting the signal and can result in poor sound quality and lack of clarity; hence, it is nearly always wise to use hearing aids that employ some type of compression. As with peak-clipping hearing aids, the audiologist adjusts the maximum output for the compression instruments as well, so that it does not exceed the patient's loudness discomfort level (LDL) (we will describe LDL measurements in a later section).

Compression. Given that most individuals fitted with hearing aids have a non-linear hearing loss and need the output of the hearing aid limited with minimal distortion, some form of compression is usually an appropriate feature. Compression can be *input* or *output* controlled (see comparative block diagrams in Figure 2.2). If input controlled, monitoring of the signal level takes places *before* the volume control. In this case, volume control adjustments do affect output levels, and the user has direct control over maximum output levels. If compression is output controlled, monitoring of the signal level occurs *after* the volume control. Thus, changes in the position of the volume control will not affect maximum output of the hearing aid, and the audiologist has direct control of output levels. For both types of compression, however, precise adjustments of compression parameters can be made by the audiologist at the time of the fitting to tailor the compression activation to the loudness growth function of the individual patient. In summary, compression is used to accomplish two fitting goals: (1) repackage "the world" so that it fits into the patient's residual dynamic range (AGCi) and (2) limit the output just below the patient's LDL without introducing distortion (usually AGCo).

6. *Directional microphone technology.* A desirable option, available for many hearing aids, is the use of a directional microphone. Directional amplification can be obtained using a single directional microphone or by using two omnidirectional microphones that have been electronically designed to produce a directional effect. Using directional amplification, the patient can improve the signal-to-noise (S/N)

> Most of today's hearing aids, especially the digital ones, have more than one compression circuit, often both input controlled *and* output controlled.

> Most patients fitted with directional microphone amplification also desire omnidirectional (equal amplification from all directions) for some listening situations. Most directional hearing aids are equipped with a button that allows the patient to switch to omnidirectional when needed.

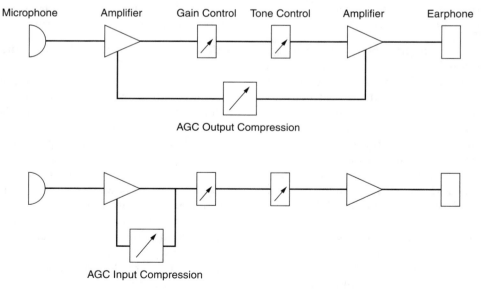

FIGURE 2.2

Block diagram of output compression hearing aid and input compression hearing aid.

From W. Olsen (1986). Physical characteristics of hearing aids. In W. Hodgson (Ed.), *Hearing Aid Assessment and Use in Audiologic Habilitation* (3rd ed.). Baltimore: Williams & Wilkins.

ratio of a listening situation by assuring that the desired speech signal is arriving from directly in front of the user; the surrounding noise signal will then receive less amplification, improving the S/N ratio by as much as 6 dB or more for some listening environments. Nearly all patients will benefit from directional hearing aids, although presently this feature is not available on the smaller custom-made instruments (see Mueller and Ricketts, 2000, for review).

As stated earlier, all types of hearing aids include the microphone, amplifier, receiver, and power source. The additional controls and circuitry that we have discussed may or may not be a part of the hearing aid system. It should be noted that the basic features described thus far are not the only options available. We will discuss more specialized features, including different types of compression and the features of digital hearing instruments, later in this chapter.

Optional controls and circuitry must be selected depending on the needs of the user. As an example, for the patient who wants a very small hearing aid and seldom uses the telephone, it might not be necessary to include a telecoil in the hearing aid.

On smaller instruments it is not always possible to obtain several features because of space limitations. If a person needs several of the features we have discussed, there might need to be a trade-off: a larger instrument for more features. Thus, in selecting the appropriate device for a patient, we must consider the type of hearing loss and the special needs of the user. This information will then guide the audiologist in choosing the most appropriate style of hearing aid, which we discuss next.

Hearing Aid Styles

Currently, six styles of hearing aids are available: (1) body aid; (2) eyeglass aid; (3) behind-the-ear (BTE) aid; (4) in-the-ear (ITE) aid; (5) in-the-canal (ITC) aid; and, (6) completely-in-the-canal (CIC) aid. (Examples of the different hearing aid styles are illustrated in Figure 2.3 and 2.4.) Why so many choices? First, technological advances have resulted in the increased sophistication and miniaturization of hearing aid components, which was not possible when the large body style of aid was developed several decades ago. Market statistics show that smaller hearing aids become more popular each year. Second, a certain style of hearing aid may not be appropriate for the degree and configuration of the patient's hearing loss. Larger-style hearing aids are capable of providing a greater amount of amplification as compared to smaller devices. Third, the need for additional controls and/or circuit types may influence the style of hearing aid selected. Before we go any further, let's take a look at each style individually, to give you a better idea of the need for different styles of hearing aids and the reasons why each style may or may not be selected for a particular patient.

THE BODY AID. Body-style hearing aids have larger microphones, amplifiers, and power supplies enclosed in cases that can be carried in a pocket, attached to clothing, or placed on the body in a harness. The external receiver attaches directly to a custom-made earmold and is powered through a flexible wire from the amplifier. Although not as popular as other hearing aid styles because of their size and poor

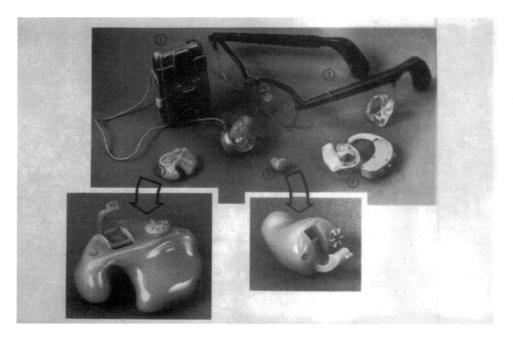

FIGURE 2.3

The different types of hearing aids. (1) body aid; (2) eyeglass; (3) in-the-ear; (4) in-the-canal; and (5) behind-the-ear.

From F. Bess and L. Hume (1995). *Audiology: The Fundamentals* (2nd ed.). Baltimore: Williams & Wilkins.

microphone placement (off the ear), body aids are very powerful and can be beneficial for those with very severe hearing losses. Due to the larger-size controls, they may also be indicated for patients with dexterity problems.

Because of the importance of placing the hearing aid microphone at the ear and of binaural amplification, body hearing aids usually are only used in those rare instances when behind-the-ear or in-the-ear models are not practical.

Who is a candidate for the body-style hearing aid? We have already mentioned two or three examples. The following is a summary of reasons why the audiologist may or may not choose the body style hearing aid for a particular patient.

WHY?

- High levels of amplification are available without feedback as compared to ear-level hearing aids because there is more distance between the microphone and receiver.
- Larger-size controls and battery are easier to manipulate for patients with dexterity problems.
- Due to its size and the possibility of secure placement, there may be less chance of loss or damage.

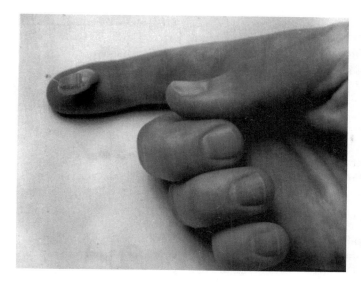

FIGURE 2.4

A completely-in-the-canal (CIC) hearing aid.
Courtesy of Siemens Hearing Instruments, Inc.

WHY NOT?

- Importance of binaural amplification; difficult to place two body aids on small children.
- Acoustic advantages of having microphone of hearing aids at ear level.

  Body aids subject to clothing noise.

  Frequency response of body aid is influenced by the baffle effect produced by the body, which reduces high-frequency amplification.
- Many special circuits and digital processing technology are not available for this style.
- Not cosmetically appealing.

THE EYEGLASS AID. It was once thought that combining hearing aids and eyeglasses would be a good idea, (because many people who need hearing aids already wear eyeglasses). Although sounding logical, we will discuss why this style is rarely selected today.

In the eyeglass-style hearing aid, the microphone, amplifier, and receiver are built into the temple portion of the eyeglass. Sound is channeled into the ear from the hearing aid through plastic tubing connected to a custom-made earmold. Eyeglass hearing aids can be fit monaurally or binaurally and can generally accommodate mild to moderately severe hearing losses. Once occupying a 20% or more market share, the popularity of the eyeglass style hearing aid has dramatically decreased (less than 0.5% of total annual sales). Even if the user needs to wear glasses and a hearing aid, it is rather impractical to have these two sensory devices tied together. Let's look at some reasons why the audiologist may or, in most cases, will not choose the eyeglass hearing aid.

WHY?

- Some previous eyeglass hearing aid users might demand to be fitted with the same style of hearing aid that they have been using for many years.
- Some special applications of CROS and BICROS fittings (discussed later) are easily accomplished using eyeglasses.

WHY NOT?

- They tend to be heavy, uncomfortable, and difficult to fit, adjust and repair.
- Unless the user wears eyeglasses at all times, there is a loss of amplification every time the glasses are removed. A hearing aid repair means loss of eyeglasses.
- It is difficult to find manufacturers who build and repair eyeglass hearing aids; because of limited demand, sophisticated circuitry is not available in this style.

Small versions of BTEs are available for children, with nearly the same amount of power as the larger models.

THE BTE. Behind-the-ear (BTE) hearing aids are housed in small curved cases, which, as the name implies, fit behind the ear. The microphone, amplifier, and receiver are all housed in the hearing aid case that is connected to a custom-made earmold by a flexible plastic tube. This hearing aid style can be worn monaurally or binaurally and has about a 20% market share of total hearing aid sales. BTE hearing aids usually are larger in size than the small in-the-ear custom-made instruments and thus can accommodate a greater range of additional controls and circuitry. Figure 2.5 shows a modern BTE that is digitally programmable and also

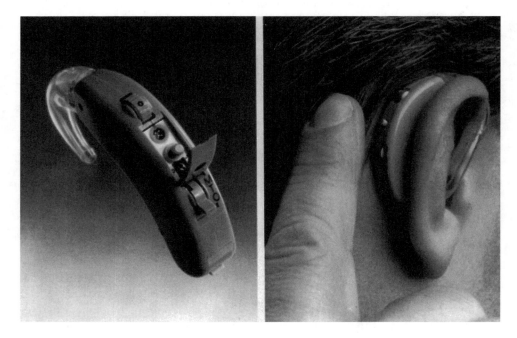

FIGURE 2.5

A digitally programmable behind-the-ear (BTE) hearing aid.
Courtesy of Siemens Hearing Instruments, Inc.

has multiple memories (storage of different electroacoustic settings for different listening conditions). The button shown in the middle of the back of the instrument is for changing memories. The opening between the button and the volume control wheel is for the computer adapter for programming the settings.

Because of their flexibility, the majority of hearing aid users could be successfully fit with BTE aids. Why aren't they? Here are the "why's" and "why not's" for selecting a BTE-model hearing aid.

WHY?

- Can achieve greater gain and maximum output than with a custom instrument.
- Telecoil circuitry is more powerful than can be obtained with smaller custom-made instruments.
- For children with rapidly growing ears, only the earmold needs to be replaced when fitting becomes lose; with custom-made hearing aids, the aid needs to be recased.
- Direct audio input is routinely available.
- If there is a medical reason why the ear canal should not be occluded, BTE hearing aids can be fit with open earmolds.

WHY NOT?

- The smaller custom-made hearing aids are less noticeable.
- The consumer considers BTE instruments to be old-fashioned.
- BTE hearing aids tend to be less secure than custom instruments (e.g., tend to fall off the ear during strenuous work or recreation).
- More difficult to insert, remove, and adjust volume control than for a custom instrument.

THE ITE. In-the-ear (ITE) hearing aids fit directly in the external ear. The circuitry is housed primarily in the concha area, and thus this model has no external wires or tubes. Because of its larger size, as compared to the ITC or CIC discussed later, the ITE can accommodate additional controls and larger circuitry when indicated. The ITE is the most commonly dispensed hearing aid in United States because its flexibility makes this style useful for all but the most severe cases of hearing loss (as discussed earlier, we would probably fit these severely hearing impaired patients with BTE hearing aids). Let's summarize additional reasons why we may or may not select the ITE style aid.

WHY?

Compared to BTEs
- Considered more modern and cosmetically acceptable.
- Better microphone placement for obtaining high-frequency gain.
- More secure fit.
- Easier to insert and remove and to adjust volume control.

Compared to ITCs
- More gain and output can be attained.
- Telecoil and direct audio input available.
- Directional microphone features are available.

- Volume control and battery are larger in size and therefore easier to manipulate.
- Less expensive.

WHY NOT?

Compared to BTEs

- For very severe losses, ITE hearing aids are more prone to feedback due to the closer proximity of the microphone and receiver.
- User might require the greater power of a BTE telecoil.
- For younger children, rapidly changing size of ear might make the use of a custom-made instrument impractical.

Compared to ITCs

- If all necessary features and functions can be placed in a more cosmetically acceptable hearing aid, then why not do it?

THE ITC. In-the-canal (ITC) hearing aids are a variation of the ITE, only smaller in size. Importantly, this style of hearing aid is not really totally in-the-canal, but is partially in-the-concha. ITC hearing aids, in contrast to the ITE style, occupy the ear canal, but only part of the concha, leaving a portion free for natural resonance and diffraction effects. Because of its smaller size, there may or may not be room for several controls or switches, depending on the size of the user's ear canal. ITC hearing aids can generally accommodate mild to moderate and some severe hearing losses. The following summarizes reasons why we would or would not select the ITC-style hearing aid for a particular patient.

WHY?

- More cosmetically appealing than the ITE.
- A portion of the concha is left free, allowing for natural resonance and diffraction effects, resulting in an increase in high-frequency amplification.
- Users often experience less difficulty with feedback when using the telephone versus the larger ITE style.
- Users experience less wind noise due to a deeper-seated microphone.

WHY NOT?

- Unable to obtain necessary gain and output.
- Telecoil typically not available.
- Directional microphone technology not available.
- May not be room for more than one external control (patient may have to choose between memory button or volume control).
- Because of the smaller size, there often is not room for more than one screwdriver-controlled adjustment (potentiometer).
- Smaller battery size and volume control may be difficult for individuals with dexterity problems.
- More expensive than ITE.

THE CIC. Completely-in-the-canal (CIC) hearing aids are the smallest type of hearing aid available to date. In addition to the obvious cosmetic appeal, they offer many acoustic advantages (see Mueller, 1994, for a review). As the name implies, these devices fit completely within the ear canal and thus are practically invisible when worn (see Figure 2.4). In general, these hearing aids also fit deeper in the ear canal than the ITE or ITC styles. This hearing aid, however, is easily inserted if the ear canal is relatively straight. It is removed using a short transparent cord. Because of its small size, external volume control wheels, tone controls, and other features are not a routine option on the CIC. CIC hearing aids generally are suitable for patients with mild to moderate hearing losses. The pros and cons of selecting the CIC-style hearing aid are similar to those listed for ITC aids.

> Manufacturers report that CICs account for over 50% of digital hearing aid sales.

WHY?

- An obvious cosmetic advantage over other custom instruments.
- Deep microphone placement and reduced residual ear canal volume (deeper fit) result in a significantly increased output and high-frequency amplification.
- Deep fitting helps to reduce the occlusion effect.
- Easy to insert and remove.
- Reduces wind noise since the microphone is seated within the ear canal.

> Occlusion effect: Patients note that their voice sounds "hollow" because their ear canal is plugged with the hearing aid.

WHY NOT?

- Cannot achieve desired gain and output, especially when substantial low-frequency gain is necessary.
- Telecoil and directional microphone are not available.
- The small battery and hearing aid size require reasonably good dexterity.
- The hearing aid cannot be built for some individuals because of the size or geography of the ear canal.
- More expensive than the ITC hearing aid.

Summary

Matching the right hearing aid style to the patient is an important first step in the hearing aid fitting procedure, although it is not always an easy task. Sometimes a little trial and error must be applied. We have listed several whys and why nots for various styles, and there are probably more. In most situations, one of the six styles described will be fitted binaurally, but in some instances a monaural arrangement will be used. However, in some cases more specialized types of hearing aid fittings may be more appropriate.

■ SPECIALIZED FITTING OPTIONS

CROS and BICROS

For the individual who has an unaidable hearing loss in one ear and normal hearing or an aidable hearing loss in the other ear, contralateral routing of signal (CROS) or bilateral contralateral routing of signal (BICROS) amplification may be the most appropriate hearing aid arrangement. A CROS hearing aid is used when there is good hearing in one ear and the opposite ear cannot benefit from amplification. This device places a microphone on the side of the poor ear with its receiver directed to the normal ear, so the good ear can receive sound from the opposite side of the head. We have made the person a "two-sided" listener, but, importantly, *not* a "two-eared" listener.

Somewhat different than the CROS fitting, BICROS hearing aids are used in cases where one ear is unaidable, but there is some degree of aidable hearing loss in the other. This device has two microphones, one near the better ear and the other near the poorer ear. The acoustic signals from both sides are delivered to a single amplifier and receiver, and the output is then directed into the best ear.

There are basically two types of CROS or BICROS fittings:

1. Hardwired: ITE, BTE, and eyeglass
2. Frequency modulated (FM)

In the *hardwire* system, the signal is carried from one side of the head to the other by wires concealed within the eyeglass frame or by a tube or cord around the back of the neck as in the ITE and BTE styles. If an *FM system* is utilized, signals are transferred across the head by an FM transmitter and picked up by an FM receiver positioned near the better ear. The signal is then converted back to acoustic energy and presented to the better ear. A more detailed description of FM systems is provided later in this chapter when we discuss assistive listening devices.

There is also a fitting arrangement referred to as a *transcranial* CROS. In this case, a powerful hearing aid is fitted to the unaidable ear (BTEs, ITEs, and CICs have all been used), with the hope that sound crosses over to the normal ear via bone conduction. There has been some limited success with this approach, but it requires that the bone conduction thresholds of the good ear be well within normal limits.

Bone Conduction and Implantable Hearing Aids

We receive sound in two ways, by air conduction via the ear canal, eardrum, and ossicles and by bone conduction, whereby sound is transmitted directly through the jaw and skull bones, bypassing the middle ear. Conventional hearing aids usually are designed to utilize an air conduction receiver, and, thus far, we have described the various styles of air conduction aids that are placed inside the ear canal or behind the ear. Some individuals with hearing loss, however, are unable to use conventional air conduction devices. They may have congenital atresia (missing or incomplete ear canals) or chronic infection of the middle or outer ear that is made worse when a hearing aid or earmold is worn. In these cases, bone conduction hearing aids are a practical solution.

TRADITIONAL BONE CONDUCTION DEVICES. In traditional bone conduction devices, amplified sound is delivered through a vibrator placed behind the ear and over the mastoid bone. These devices are most commonly integrated into body- or eyeglass-style hearing aids. In the body aid, a vibrating device is held against the mastoid process by a metal headband. In the eyeglass hearing aid, the vibrator is mounted into the stem of the eyeglass that extends behind the ear. Sound is picked up by the microphone and amplified, causing the bone conduction device to vibrate, which in turn sets the skull into vibration, resulting in the transmission of sound to the cochleae.

Traditional bone conduction devices have a number of drawbacks. They can be uncomfortable and rather cumbersome (recall that the bone conductor is kept in place either by a metal headband over the top of the head or by the spring-loaded arm of a pair of glasses). Additionally, headaches and soreness of the skin caused by pressure from the bone vibrator against the skull are common problems.

IMPLANTABLE HEARING AIDS. An implantable hearing aid is an electronic device that is surgically implanted in the temporal bone or middle ear space. If the device is implanted in the temporal bone, it is called a *bone-anchored hearing aid*; if the device is implanted in the middle ear cavity it is called a *middle ear implant*. Let's look at each device separately.

BONE-ANCHORED HEARING AIDS. The device you are probably more familiar with is the bone-anchored hearing aid (BAHA). In general, the BAHA is a replacement for the traditional bone conduction hearing aid, the difference being that instead of placing a vibrator over the temporal bone behind the ear the BAHA is surgically attached either magnetically or directly to the temporal bone. Because of the many drawbacks of the traditional bone conduction device, a patient often will choose a surgically implanted bone-anchored device over a conventional bone conduction device.

When a patient is fitted with a BAHA, a titanium screw is surgically implanted into the temporal bone behind the ear. After a 3-month healing period, an external mount is connected to the implanted screw, and the BAHA is attached to the mount (Figure 2.6). Once in place, the bone-anchored system works similarly to traditional bone conduction devices. The BAHA that is attached to the external mount vibrates in response to the incoming sound signal, and the sound is transmitted directly via the titanium fixture. The temporal bone acts as a pathway for the sound to travel to the cochlea without involving the ear canal or middle ear. Because of this design, the BAHA is used primarily in patients with a conductive or mixed hearing loss that either cannot be treated surgically or has not responded well to medical intervention. Such patients may present with otologic problems that include (1) a chronically draining ear that does not allow use of an air conduction aid (e.g., external otitis, draining mastoid cavity); (2) a congenital malformation of the middle/external ear, or microtia; or (3) ossicular disease. In these patients, the BAHA offers an advantage over the traditional bone conduction hearing aid. For example, in patients with middle ear infections the ear canal is left open, allowing the infection to heal. For patients with an incomplete or missing ear canal, the BAHA works without any pressure on the skin, thus avoiding the drawbacks of the conventional bone conductor.

> Bone-anchored hearing aid: a hearing instrument that is coupled either magnetically or directly to the temporal bone.

MIDDLE EAR IMPLANTS. A second type of implantable hearing aid being developed is the middle ear implant (MEI). This is a hearing aid that is either wholly or partially implanted within the middle ear cavity. Unlike the BAHA, for which a significant conductive component exists that prevents optimal use of an air conduction hearing aid,

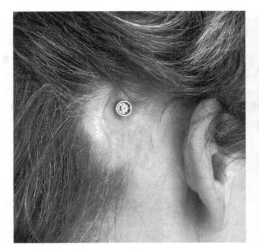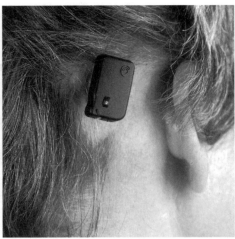

FIGURE 2.6

A bone-anchored hearing aid (BAHA). The left view shows the external mount, and the right view shows the electronic portion of the BAHA system attached.

Courtesy of Entific Medical Systems.

Middle ear implant: a hearing instrument that is either wholly or partially implanted in the middle ear.

an MEI may be used in patients with both conductive and/or sensorineural hearing losses. However, its main application is with sensorineural loss.

There are two major MEIs currently undergoing clinical trials: electromagnetic and piezoelectric. An electromagnetic MEI is partially implanted in the middle ear, meaning that it has an external and an internal portion. The external portion remains outside the body. Typically, it contains the microphone, battery, and electronics to convert sound to a signal that can be transmitted to the internal portion of the hearing aid. The internal portion contains a receiving magnet that is affixed to the ossicular chain. Depending on the design of the implant, the receiving magnet can be crimped onto the ossicular chain, drilled into a small hole in the incus, placed at the incudostapedial joint, or placed on the round window. How does the MEI work? Simply put, sounds in the environment are picked up by the external microphone and converted into an electrical signal. In turn, a magnetic field is set up, which is picked up by the implanted receiving magnet. The receiving magnet converts the signal to vibrations that move the bones of the middle ear similarly to the way that normal sounds move them.

The piezoelectric implant works in a manner similar to the electromagnetic MEI, except that, instead of using a receiving magnet, the electric current is transduced from the external microphone to a piezoelectric crystal located on the ossicular chain. The crystal bends in response to the incoming signal and causes the ossicular chain to vibrate the sound directly to the cochlea. Two manufacturers offer a totally implantable piezoelectric MEI. In one device, the tympanic membrane serves as the microphone and transduces vibration to the piezoelectric crystal attached to the ossicular chain. A second device places the microphone in the posterior wall of the ear canal.

USEFUL WEB SITES

Bone-anchored hearing aids: www.entific.com

Middle-ear implants: www.symphonix.com and www.stcroixmedical.com

■ THE EARMOLD

We have mentioned the term *earmold* numerous times, so now let's take a closer look at its characteristics. The earmold serves a variety of important functions. As you may recall, the earmold couples the hearing aid to the user's ear via a tube, as in the case of the BTE- and eyeglass-style hearing aids (or with wire cord and external receiver, as in the body-style hearing aid). As such, the earmold provides support for the BTE hearing aid and, most importantly, directs and modifies the amplified sound that reaches the ear canal.

As with custom hearing aids, custom earmolds come in various styles, ranging from large models that fill the entire concha of the outer ear to models in which only a small piece of tubing extends into the ear canal. In general, the greater the hearing loss, the larger the earmold needed. Figure 2.7 shows samples of many of the available earmold styles.

BTE AND EYEGLASS TUBE TYPE

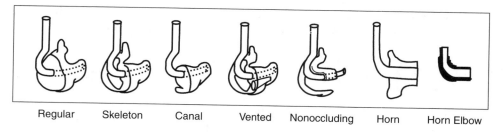

| Regular | Skeleton | Canal | Vented | Nonoccluding | Horn | Horn Elbow |

BODY WORN

Receiver

CUSTOM MOLDED

In the canal   In the ear

FIGURE 2.7

Basic types of earmolds.

From W. Staab & S. Lybarger (1994). Characteristics and use of hearing aids. In J. Katz (Ed.), *Handbook of Clinical Audiology* (4th ed.). Baltimore: Williams & Wilkins.

Once the earmold is coupled to the hearing aid, the properties of the sound reaching the user's ear are changed. The acoustic properties of the earmold itself and the length and diameter of the connecting tube play an important part in the final acoustical characteristics of the hearing aid system.

Acoustic Effects of Earmolds

The most important characteristic of the earmold is that it can be modified to alter the amplified signal delivered to the user's ear. As we will discuss later, it is important that the real-ear frequency response be tailored for each patient. By utilizing the following techniques, the audiologist can modify one or more portions of the frequency response of the hearing aid in order to deliver the acoustic signal more appropriately. While this section is geared toward earmolds, it is important to remember that many of the same damping and in particular venting principles and techniques applied to earmolds can also be used with custom-made hearing aids.

LOW-FREQUENCY MODIFICATION

THE VENT. The most common modification is called a vent, which is a small hole drilled into the canal portion of the earmold. The vent is usually parallel to the sound bore, although in some instances a diagonal vent is used (see Figure 2.8). Earmolds (and custom-made hearing aids) are vented for three primary reasons:

1. To allow unwanted amplified low frequencies to escape from the ear canal.
2. To release pressure to avoid a plugged-ear sensation.
3. To allow the normal input of unamplified sound.

Vents can be drilled to various diameters, depending on the results desired. The diameter of an earmold vent may vary from a small pressure-equalization vent to

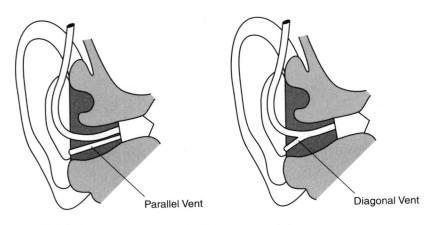

Parallel Vent   Diagonal Vent

FIGURE 2.8

Diagrams of parallel and diagonal vents.

From S. Lybarger (1985). Earmolds. In J. Katz (Ed.), *Handbook of Clinical Audiology* (3rd ed.). Baltimore: Williams & Wilkins.

an open earmold, in which the vent has been enlarged until nothing remains but the outermost portion of the earmold. In general, the larger the vent, the greater the low-frequency attenuation. Variable vents are also available that use small plastic plugs or different sizes of tubing that can totally occlude an existing vent or provide smaller openings of various diameters.

"Select-A-Vent" is a common term used to identify the small plastic plugs of various vent diameters.

MID-FREQUENCY MODIFICATION

DAMPER. Acoustic dampers are placed within the tubing or earhook of BTE-style hearing aids and in the receiver tubing of custom-made instruments. They are small inserts that act as resistors, altering the acoustic dimensions of the hearing aid system. In general, dampers will smooth out peaks of the frequency response and reduce the overall output. Metal pellets, mesh screens, cotton, and lamb's wool have all been used for this purpose. Without the use of dampers, some hearing aids produce a strong output peak in the mid-frequency range, typically near 1500 Hz, which can cause discomfort to the user. The effects of acoustic dampers on the hearing aid response depend on the value of the acoustic resistance of the dampers. Commercially available dampers are color coded (e.g., gray = 330 ohms, white = 680 ohms, etc.). Higher ohm values (acoustic resistance) cause more flattening of peaks and reduction in overall output. The location and number of dampers used will also influence the frequency response of the hearing aid.

HIGH-FREQUENCY MODIFICATION

ACOUSTIC HORN. An acoustic horn is produced by progressively increasing the internal diameter of the earmold tubing (e.g., 2 mm to 3 mm to 4 mm). The effect is an enhancement of high-frequency gain, especially in the important 3000- to 4000-Hz region. Not all ear canals are large enough to accommodate 4-mm-diameter tubing, and the use of a 3-mm-diameter horn is common. The use of horn tubing was advanced by Killion and Libby in the 1970s. (See Mueller and Grimes, 1987, for a review of this work.)

The acoustic horn approach cannot be used effectively with custom-made instruments.

Through the use of venting, damping, and horning, it is possible to shape the hearing aid's frequency response to a variety of different desired gain characteristics. It is important to remember that any modification to the hearing aid–earmold system can change the output delivered in the ear canal, and many of these alterations cannot be predicted from 2-cc coupler measurements. We therefore recommend measuring real-ear output (using probe microphone measurements) whenever alterations in the earmold are made.

The Earmold Impression

No matter which type of earmold is chosen, all must be made from an impression of the user's ear so that the exact shape can be replicated to ensure a proper fit (the same holds true when ordering a custom-made instrument). To make the ear impression, the audiologist follows these general steps:

1. The patient's ear canal is thoroughly inspected using an otoscope.
2. A cotton or foam rubber eardam is carefully inserted to a point beyond the second bend of the ear canal. The eardam allows the impression material to

fill the entire canal area and at the same time helps to protect the eardrum from injury.

3. Once the eardam is in place, impression material can be injected into the ear by use of a syringe. Material is injected into the ear canal starting from the position of the eardam and working outward until the entire concha and helix areas are filled.

4. The material is allowed to harden and is then removed by gently pulling outward and upward. If imperfections are observed, the ear impression must be remade.

5. Following removal, the audiologist again inspects the patient's ear canal to assure that remnants of impression material or the eardam are not present.

6. The finished impression is then mailed to an earmold laboratory (or custom-made hearing aid manufacturer) for fabrication.

■ BATTERIES

Although at one time both mercury and silver oxide batteries were used in hearing aids, today hearing aid batteries are zinc–air. Rechargeable batteries are also available. These can be removable batteries or built-in types that cannot be removed except by the manufacturer. Rechargeable batteries are not commonly used because of the need for frequent recharging and the relatively low cost of the replaceable batteries.

In general, body hearing aids use a common AA battery, such as that used in a Walkman-type pocket radio. BTE and eyeglass hearing aids usually require a 675 size hearing aid battery; however, smaller models will use size 13. ITE hearing aids will use either the 13 battery or the next smaller size 312, depending on the size of the aid itself. Most ITC hearing aids use a size 312, and CIC hearing aids require a size 10A or 5A battery.

Hearing aid batteries typically produce 1.3 to 1.5 volts. Battery life varies considerably from hearing aid to hearing aid, although manufacturers usually specify the expected battery performance for a given hearing aid. Battery life may vary depending on (1) the type of battery, (2) type of hearing aid, (3) hours per day of continuous use, (4) circuitry contained within the hearing aid, and (5) volume control setting during use. Generally, batteries may last anywhere from several days for high-output BTE hearing aids to several weeks for the some of the low-gain instruments.

■ ELECTROACOUSTIC PROPERTIES

Electroacoustic properties are used to describe hearing aid characteristics and are important when selecting the appropriate hearing aid for a particular patient. This applies when the hearing aid is ordered and again during the initial verification procedure. Hearing aid manufacturers also rely heavily on standardized electroacoustic testing for promotional specifications, quality control, repair, and to satisfy many FDA regulations.

Commonly considered electroacoustic characteristics are defined in Table 2.1. Such measures are made within acoustical isolation boxes where the input and output levels can be reliably measured and controlled. Thus, these electroacoustic measures are basically measures of input–output functions (test systems are available from several different manufacturers. Figure 2.9 shows an example of one type).

In a hearing aid test box, a regulating microphone monitors the input level and determines the appropriate compensation to maintain a constant sound level. Either a continuously variable sweep-frequency tone or a series of discrete frequencies is generated, generally ranging from 100 to 10,000 Hz. The input level can be selected from 50 to 100 dB SPL, depending on the specific parameter being measured.

Hearing aid output is measured within a standard *2-cc coupler* that attempts to imitate some of the acoustic conditions of the aided ear. While we know that the residual volume (after the hearing aid or earmold has been inserted) of the human ear canal is not 2 cc, this standard has been in place for many years, and it is unlikely that it will change soon. For quality control purposes, it is not really a disadvantage that the volume is larger than the volume of the real ear.

There are different coupler types for the various hearing aid styles. The *HA-1 coupler* has a large opening into which any tubing, earmold, or custom instrument

TABLE 2.1

Electroacoustic Properties Describing Hearing Aid Function

Gain	The difference between the output sound pressure level (SPL) in the earphone coupler and the input SPL; describes how much the input signal is amplified. Maximum or "full-on gain" is measured with the volume control full on. Reference or "use gain" usually is measured with the volume control set at approximately half-on, which generally represents the typical user setting.
Frequency response	Describes the available gain at each frequency; obtained by changing the frequency of the input signal and holding the input level constant.
Frequency range	Describes the useful range of the frequency response. It is expressed by two numbers that represent the low- and high-frequency limit of amplification.
Output sound pressure level (OSPL)	Sound pressure level developed in a 2-cc coupler when the input SPL is 90 dB and the volume control is in the full-on position; describes the maximum output that the hearing aid is capable of producing.
Harmonic distortion	The percentage of total output SPL that is a result of harmonics generated by the hearing aid. Total harmonic distortion is typically reported for 500, 800, and 1600 Hz.
Equivalent input noise	The level of internal noise generated by the hearing aid.

FIGURE 2.9

A hearing-aid analyzer for making electroacoustic measures of hearing-aid performance.
Courtesy of Frye Electronics.

can be mounted using a puttylike substance to ensure a tight acoustic seal. The
original form of the *HA-2 coupler* was designed to test button-type receivers on body
aids. A second type of HA-2 coupler includes an earmold simulator via entrance
through a tube and is designed to test BTE aids when an earmold is not included.
The hearing aid coupler is attached to a measuring microphone, allowing input–
output measures to be graphically displayed.

The various hearing aid measurements, as described in Table 2.1, are specified
by the American National Standards Institute (ANSI) in their 1996 ANSI Standard
S3.22 and provide a standardized system for comparing different hearing aids
among manufacturers. In accordance with these standards, hearing aid manufacturers provide specification sheets for each hearing aid to describe how the device
is designed to operate. Let's take a specific example and discuss the information
that is shown in Figure 2.10.

1. As you will recall, OSPL90 is the maximum output that the hearing aid is capable of producing. The upper-left graph shows the maximum output available for
this hearing aid across frequencies, the upper curve for a 90-dB input. Observe that
in general the maximum output in around 110 dB SPL. Because the real ear is

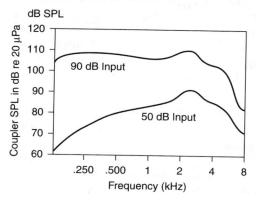

Saturated Output
OSPL 90 / Full-on Gain 40/06/110

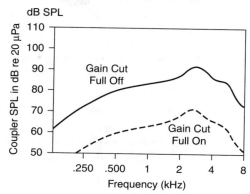

Frequency Response and Effect
of Full-on Gain (50-dB Input)

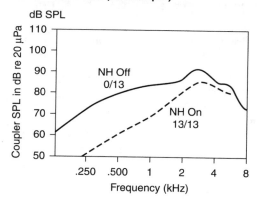

Frequency Response and Effect
of the N-H Control (50-dB Input)

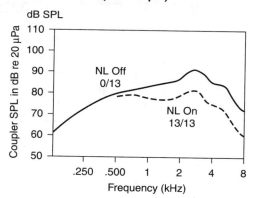

Frequency Response and Effect
of the N-L Control (50-dB Input)

FIGURE 2.10

Hearing-aid performance specifications from the manufacturer.
Courtesy of Siemens Hearing Instruments, Inc.

smaller than the 2-cc coupler, the hearing aid output will be greater than this when placed in the ear. In selecting an appropriate hearing aid, it is necessary that this output level not exceed the patient's loudness discomfort level. This is extremely important in assuring that the hearing aid will not produce uncomfortably loud sounds and still be able to provide enough output to amplify sound adequately for the user.

   2. The upper-right graph of Figure 2.10 shows the available gain at each specific frequency for this particular hearing aid, referred to as the frequency response curve. As described in Table 2.1, gain is the difference, in decibels, between the input level to the microphone of the hearing aid and the output at the level of the receiver, as measured in the hearing aid test box. This testing was conducted with a 50-dB input; hence, the gain for a given frequency is the value shown on the graph minus 50 dB. For example, observing the upper curve (solid line), the coupler output for 2000 Hz is 88 dB; the gain for this frequency would be 38 dB (88 dB output minus the input of 50 dB). Notice that this hearing aid is designed to produce more gain in the higher frequencies than in the low. This is a common design, as most hearing losses are downward sloping.

3. The two bottom graphs of Figure 2.10 show the changes in the frequency response for this hearing aid that the audiologist can make at the time of the fitting (either using screwdriver controls or through a computerized programmable feature). Notice that the original frequency response can be altered to accommodate a wide variety of hearing losses and amplification needs. Prescriptive formula fitting methods, which we will discuss later, provide guidance regarding the setting that is best for a given patient.

■ THE SELECTION AND FITTING OF HEARING AIDS

To this point in this chapter, we have provided some general information concerning how hearing aids are constructed, how they work, the variety of styles that is available, and how we can measure their performance on a standard coupler. Now comes the hard part: getting the right hearing aids on the right person!

Many prescriptive fitting methods are available today, with no specific procedure identified as superior. Whatever method is used, however, we believe that it must be approached systematically, *using appropriate verification tools*, and we have outlined a five-step protocol for selecting and fitting hearing aids. Although it is tempting to grab a couple of hearing aids out of a box and go directly to Step 4, you will find that the key to successful fittings is directly related to the time and thought expended during steps 1, 2, and 3.

Step 1: Selecting the Hearing Aid Candidate

Several issues must be considered when an individual is selected as a hearing aid candidate. Three of the most important factors are degree of hearing loss, amount of communication difficulty, and motivation to use hearing aids. Frequently, these three factors interrelate, and it is difficult to make a fitting decision based on information from only one or two of these categories.

DEGREE OF HEARING LOSS. Usually, the first step in determining hearing aid candidacy is to examine the pure tone thresholds. If the patient has a profound hearing loss (with accompanying poor word recognition), it might be that the hearing impairment is too severe to be helped with conventional hearing aids. It is then appropriate to consider the alternative amplification devices that we discuss later in the chapter.

A more common decision that needs to be made is to determine if the hearing loss is severe enough to warrant amplification. There are no strict rules for this determination, but most audiologists agree that if hearing is normal (thresholds of 20–25 dB or better) for 4000 Hz and below it is unlikely that hearing aids will be beneficial. As hearing loss starts to effect the higher speech frequencies of 3000 and 4000 Hz, which is the typical pattern, the patient will need to be considered for amplification. Many successful hearing aid users today have normal or near normal hearing through the frequencies of 2000 to 3000 Hz.

One method to assess the effects of the pure tone impairment is to calculate an audibility index, that is, the percent of average speech that is audible to the patient. The chart shown in Figure 2.11, developed by Mueller and Killion (1990), can be used for this purpose. Simply plot the audiogram on the chart and count the dots that are not audible (above the threshold line). Subtract this from 100% and you have the audibility index. Anyone with an audibility index below 85% could probably benefit from hearing aids, *but* only if the criteria of the next two categories are met.

DEGREE OF COMMUNICATION DISABILITY. A patient can have a significant hearing loss based on pure tone findings, yet might not believe that he has a hearing disability (or at least a hearing disability that needs to be treated). This can be influenced

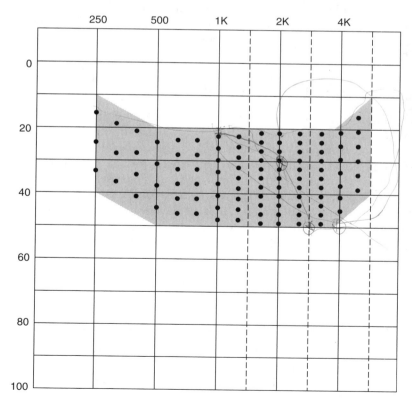

FIGURE 2.11

The count-the-dot audiogram form for calculation of the Articulation Index.

From G. Mueller & M. Killion (1990). An easy method for calculating the Articulation Index. *The Hearing Journal,* 45 (9), 14–17.

by the patient's life-style, occupation, and the amount of time that they spend communicating with others. In some cases it is denial or simply a lack of awareness of their problem—"I can hear fine, it's just that my family members mumble."

A standardized self-assessment inventory is an excellent way to survey each individual's communication problems. Although much of the same information could be gleaned from an extensive case history, a standard inventory is a more reliable and efficient method of collecting this information. Several self-assessment inventories are available, some specific to communication, some related to personality traits and expectations, and others related to social and emotional issues (see Chapter 10 for a review). Two useful Web sites for information on computerized self-assessment inventories are www.ausp.memphis.edu/harl and www.ihr.gla.ac.uk.

MOTIVATION TO USE HEARING AIDS. A final area concerning hearing aid candidacy is related to the motivation of the patient to use hearing aids. A person might have a significant hearing loss, admit having communication problems, and yet not be willing to use hearing aids. Logic suggests that these patients probably won't be happy hearing aid users, and it is tempting to simply tell them "Come back when you're ready." There is some evidence to suggest, however, that if we somehow can get these people to start using hearing aids they might become very successful hearing aid users, sort of a "Try it, you'll like it" approach.

Certainly, as with other health care providers, it is our responsibility to firmly tell the patient what we believe is the best treatment for him or her. Given that no one *really* wants to use hearing aids, a lukewarm recommendation is often viewed as no recommendation. Obviously, the final decision to purchase lies in the patient's hands.

Step 2: Preselection Measurements

Once it has been established that the patient meets the criteria for hearing aid candidacy, it is time to conduct preselection testing. Some of this testing might have been conducted previously as part of the audiologic diagnostic evaluation.

Before describing some specific audiologic measurements, it is important to first discuss prescriptive fitting procedures. This is because the prescriptive method that you select could determine the prefitting testing that is necessary. It is important to formalize the method we are using so that we have a gold standard for our hearing aid ordering and verification procedures.

Four different computerized fitting methods are commonly used with today's hearing aids:

1. Desired Sensation Level (DSL): 4.1 (dsl@audio.hhcru.uwo.ca)
2. National Acoustic Laboratories (NAL): v.NL1 (www.nal.gov.au)
3. FIG6 (www.etymotic.com)
4. Visual Input/Output Locator Algorithm (VIOLA): (www.ausp.memphis.edu/harl)

In addition to the above, various manufacturers have developed their own prescriptive methods. In some cases these algorithms are made known to the audiologists fitting the products; in other cases the algorithm is proprietary.

Once you have selected the prescriptive method that you believe is best, which might be different for different patients, the necessary prefitting testing can be conducted. Some methods only require pure tone thresholds; others require more extensive testing.

PURE TONE THRESHOLDS. You might already have the pure tone thresholds available from the auditory diagnostic testing. If not, thresholds are needed for all frequencies of interest (e.g., 250 to 6000 Hz, including 1500 and 3000 Hz.) For many prescriptive methods, these thresholds will be used to calculate the hearing aid gain requirements and in some instances to predict the patient's LDLs. It is also important to know if there is a conductive component to the hearing loss, because this might alter your gain requirements.

LOUDNESS DISCOMFORT LEVEL (LDL). One of the leading reasons that hearing aids are rejected is that the maximum output was placed too high. Obtaining the data that will assist in getting the output right, therefore, is one of the most important preselection measurements. This measurement, sometimes referred to as the uncomfortable level (UCL) or threshold of discomfort (TD), rather than LDL, is conducted using pure tones (or very narrow bands of noise) at two or three key frequencies (e.g., 500, 1500, and 3000 Hz). We recommend using the chart shown in Table 2.2; a rating of "Loud, but OK" is the value used for specifying the hearing aid's maximum output (see Mueller and Bright, 1994, for a review).

LOUDNESS CONTOUR TESTING. Although it is usually adequate to predict a patient's loudness function based on his thresholds and LDLs, it is sometimes helpful to establish an entire loudness growth function through actual measurement. This can be especially useful when selecting different types of compression and automatic signal processing parameters. Loudness contour testing, using the chart shown in Table 2.2, can be used with the VIOLA fitting software and the fitting modules of

---

TABLE 2.2

Categories of Loudness

Uncomfortably loud

Loud, but OK

Comfortable, but slightly loud

Comfortable

Comfortable, but slightly soft

Soft

Very soft

Source: R. M. Cox, (1995). Using loudness data for hearing aid selection: The IHAFF Approach. *The Hearing Journal 48*, 2; 10, 39–44.

In situ, meaning "in the original position," is a term also sometimes used to describe probe-mic testing.

some manufacturers. Many of today's hearing aids allow for abbreviated loudness testing using signals presented by the hearing aids. This often is referred to as *in situ* testing.

Step 3: Hearing Aid Selection

There are several important aspects of the hearing aid selection procedure, ranging from the style of the hearing aid, to the type of signal processing, to whether the hearing should be analog or digital, to whether the hearing aid should be remotely controlled. Many of these decisions require input from the patient, because a mistake in any one area potentially could lead to hearing aid rejection.

HEARING AID STYLE. Earlier in this chapter we summarized the pros and cons of different hearing aid styles. Using the information obtained from the preselection testing, it is now time to find the best style for your patient. In addition to the audiometric information available and necessary features for the patient (e.g., telecoil, directional microphone), you must also consider such aspects as the patient's dexterity, the pinna and ear canal geography, and the need for a cosmetically acceptable product. Financial resources cannot be overlooked; the small CIC hearing aids can be two to three times the cost of the larger ITE models.

GAIN AND FREQUENCY RESPONSE. Hearing aid specifications are based on measurements in a 2-cc coupler. Hence, it is important that when the hearing aids are ordered the preselection measurements be converted to this standard. The precise values that are selected, for the most part, are based on the prescriptive method utilized. After desired real-ear gain is calculated, reserve gain and coupler corrections are applied to derive desired 2-cc coupler values. This information then can be used to select a hearing aid that matches these specifications.

MAXIMUM OUTPUT. Recall that LDL testing was part of the preselection evaluation. These pure tone LDL values also need to be converted to 2-cc coupler values (see Mueller and Bright, 1994, for specific procedures). A hearing aid that matches these derived 2-cc coupler output specifications then can be selected. It is best to select a product that allows for adjustment of the maximum output so that the best level can be selected at the time of verification.

AUTOMATIC SIGNAL PROCESSING (ASP). Several types of automatic signal processing (ASP) circuits are available. In a few cases, a linear peak-clipping circuit will be your first choice, but for 90% or more of fittings, one of the following six types of ASP will be selected.

1. *Limiting compression.* This type of ASP has linear processing for the majority of inputs. It differs from peak clipping in that there is less saturation-induced distortion.
2. *Dynamic range compression.* Using AGC-I circuitry, this type of ASP is based on the notion that someone with a nonlinear loudness growth function should

be fitted with a hearing aid that also is nonlinear. The hearing aid usually begins compression for inputs of 50 to 70 dB.

3. *Wide dynamic range compression (WDRC)*. A variation of AGC-I instruments, this designator suggests that the hearing aid has a low kneepoint (e.g., around 40 dB SPL or lower). The design is based on the philosophy that speech should always, or nearly always, be in compression.

4. *Expansion.* Often used in conjunction with WDRC, this circuit reduces gain for inputs that are below the kneepoint, which usually is around 35 to 40 dB SPL. The goal is to reduce gain for unwanted noises (e.g., ambient room noise, hearing aid microphone noise) that fall below the level of soft speech.

5. *Bass increase for low levels (BILL).* A special type of AGC-I, BILL processing is based on the theory that background noise is primarily low frequency and that it should only be minimally amplified when it reaches high inputs.

6. *Treble increase for low levels (TILL).* Somewhat the opposite of BILL processing, TILL circuits vary high-frequency gain as a function of the input; the softer the input, the greater the high-frequency gain (low frequencies also increase, but not by as much).

We have described six different types of ASP, each of which has advantages. Selection of the best type of ASP for a given patient must be carefully considered.

PROGRAMMABLE HEARING AIDS. The majority of hearing aids fitted today are programmable; that is, the parameters of the hearing aid are adjusted digitally using a PC, remote control, or hand-held device.

Programmable hearing aids can have numerous channels or bands (discrete regions for adjustment of gain, output, and signal processing) and can have multiple memories (each memory can be programmed with different fitting parameters for different listening conditions). Programmable hearing aids that have multiple channels can be adjusted to provide the ASP strategies (e.g., BILL, TILL) discussed earlier. The different memories can be accessed by a remote device or by a button on the hearing aid.

Although the advantages of programmable products are numerous and significant, nearly 50% of hearing aids sold in the United States are nonprogrammable. It is perhaps useful, therefore, to review some of the many benefits of these programmable instruments (modified from Mueller and Hall, 1998):

- Greater flexibility and more precise adjustments than a nonprogrammable product; the equivalent of ten or more conventional adjustment trim pots.
- Ability to make fine tuning adjustments for compression parameters to control and shape input-specific gain and the maximum output.
- Ability to make precise adjustments for shaping the frequency response.
- Ease of adjustments and a greater fitting range for a fluctuating or progressive hearing loss.
- Provide different signal processing and maximum output for different frequency regions (requires a multichannel instrument).
- Provide a different frequency response and/or signal processing strategy for different listening conditions (requires a multiple-memory instrument).

While programmable hearing aids only account for about 50% of total hearing aid sales nationally, many clinics dispense nearly 100% programmable products.

DIGITAL SIGNAL PROCESSING. A subcategory of programmable is digital processing hearing aids. When digital hearing aids are selected, some additional features are available that often provide benefit for the patient (see Mueller, 2000, for review). These features include the following:

- *Automatic noise reduction:* The incoming signal is analyzed in several different channels, and if the signal is determined to be noise, an automatic gain reduction occurs in that channel.
- *Speech enhancement:* The incoming signal is analyzed, and areas that appear to be low-intensity speech consonants are identified and given a gain boost.
- *Adaptive feedback reduction:* When transient acoustic feedback occurs (such as when a telephone receiver is placed at the ear), the hearing aid automatically identifies the frequency and employs a frequency-specific temporary gain reduction to eliminate or reduce the feedback.
- *Directional microphone control:* The hearing aid will automatically change the strength and pattern of the directional amplification based on the intensity and azimuth of the noise source.
- In-situ *measures:* Signals generated from the hearing aid can be used to detect potential feedback, measure hearing and loudness growth, or present identification and warning signals (e.g., identify program selection, provide low-battery warning).

BINAURAL FITTINGS. Like shoes, gloves, and eyeglasses, hearing aids are usually fitted in pairs. It was once thought that a single hearing aid was satisfactory for someone with an aidable hearing impairment in both ears, but fortunately few professionals continue to hold this outdated belief. There are many advantages of a binaural fitting over a monaural one, and binaural is nearly always the fitting of choice. Some of these advantages include increased gain, improved localization, better sound quality, and improved speech understanding in background noise (see Mueller and Hall, 1998, for a complete review of the benefits of binaural).

OTHER CONSIDERATIONS. We have discussed many of the most important features of hearing aid selection. Other decisions that might need to be made include the need for a telecoil, direct audio input, directional microphone, or other special circuits. It is important to review all the features that we mentioned earlier in this chapter to assure that everything has been considered when the hearing aids are ordered.

Another consideration for audiologists concerns what is referred to as *starter* hearing aids. These are relatively inexpensive models, primarily designed for people who want to try out hearing aids, but do not want the expense of the traditional models. These products usually are not custom fit and do not have the sophisticated circuitry or programmability of conventional hearing aids. One company, in fact, promotes a disposable hearing aid. When the battery goes dead, you throw it away (the cost is around $40 and the life expectancy is about 1 month).

Starter hearing aids can be useful in encouraging hearing impaired people to try using hearing aids and, after trying out these low-end models, they can search out and purchase better products). On the other hand, if these low-end products do not fit well and the gain and output are not well matched to the person's hearing loss, their use can *discourage* the purchase of more sophisticated products. These products are helpful, however, for people who might only need hearing aids for a short period of time, for special listening situations, or for emergency backup for the patient's other hearing aids.

Step 4: Verification

The first verification procedure is to measure the performance of the hearing aids in the 2-cc coupler, as discussed earlier in this chapter. The gain, frequency response, OSPL90, and distortion of the hearing aid are checked to assure that it matches specifications and is consistent with the electroacoustic characteristics that were ordered. Additionally, an input–output function is conducted to evaluate the automatic signal processing that you requested.

If the hearing aid is programmable, or even if it has the more traditional screwdriver-controlled adjustments, changes can be made during the 2-cc coupler testing to facilitate the verification measurements that will be conducted when the patient arrives. For example, if preselection testing revealed that the patient's LDL was 105 dB SPL when corrected to the 2-cc coupler, adjustments to the output can be made at this time to obtain this value. Likewise, compression parameters can be adjusted to match the patient's loudness growth characteristics.

The most important verification procedures are conducted when the patient is wearing the hearing aids (if prefitting testing and coupler verification were conducted carefully, there should be few surprises).

In general, four different methods are used to verify if the hearing aids being fitted have the correct gain, frequency response, and signal processing characteristics. Some audiologists might use different methods for different patients, or combine methods for a single patient.

INFORMAL RATING OF SPEECH QUALITY AND INTELLIGIBILITY. "So, how does that sound?" This is perhaps the most popular question posed to a new hearing aid user. Although this question is commonly asked, opinions vary concerning how much emphasis should be placed on the patient's answer. Can patients reliably select what is best for them? Can they hear the difference between small but important changes in the frequency response? Is the frequency response that *sounds the best* necessarily the one that will result in the *best understanding of speech?* Probably not. It is, of course, always important to listen to the comments from the patient, but we believe that this only should be used as an adjunct to more structured verification protocols.

SPEECH RECOGNITION OR INTELLIGIBILITY TESTING. Because the patient usually sought amplification because of difficulty understanding speech, it seems logical that the verification procedure should measure his or her ability to understand aided speech. A speech testing approach can be used fairly successfully to compare *unaided* to *aided*; however, it is difficult to use speech testing for selecting the best frequency response or signal processing strategy, because of the inherent unreliability of available speech material and the time constraints of the hearing aid fitting procedure (patients do not like to sit in a booth while you deliver thousands of words). So clinical speech testing can be used successfully to determine if hearing aids are better than no hearing aids, but not for determining which set of hearing aids is best.

If speech testing is used, we suggest using tests that employ sentences in background noise. Two tests that work well for assessing hearing aid performance are the following:

1. Hearing In Noise Test (HINT): Available from House Ear Institute (www.hei.org)
2. Speech In Noise (SIN) test: Available from Auditec of St. Louis (www.auditec.com)

A self-assessment inventory, the Profile of Aided Loudness (PAL), can be used to determine if the patient has normal aided loudness perceptions of everyday sounds in the real world.

LOUDNESS SCALING. If part of your fitting goal is to restore normal loudness perceptions, then some type of aided loudness verification is warranted. This can be conducted using frequency-specific signals, but usually connected-speech testing is adequate. An example protocol would be as follows (using the chart shown in Table 2.2):

- Present connected speech at 45 dB SPL. A #2 rating is desired; #1 or #3 rating is acceptable.
- Present connected speech at 65 dB SPL. A #4 rating is desired; #3 or #5 rating is acceptable.
- Present connected speech at 85 dB SPL. A #6 rating is desired; #5 rating is acceptable.

When a desired or acceptable rating is not obtained, make adjustments to gain, compression, and/or output and repeat the protocol.

Probe microphone assessment often is referred to as real-ear testing.

PROBE MICROPHONE MEASUREMENTS. Perhaps the most reliable method to verify the performance of hearing aids is to measure the output of the hearing aid at the tympanic membrane of the hearing aid user. This is accomplished by placing a small silicone tube in the ear canal that is attached to a measurement microphone. A loudspeaker is used to present a variety of test signals, and the output from the hearing aid in the user's ear is analyzed using computerized equipment. The results are displayed on a monitor and can be printed for the patient's file. Figure 2.12 shows a typical probe microphone system.

There are few reasons *not* to use probe microphone measurements as part of the verification procedure. Although there is an initial outlay of funds to purchase this equipment, the long-term payoff is well worth the investment. In addition to verification of gain and frequency response, this equipment has a variety of other uses in the evaluation of hearing aids and assistive listening devices.

Using probe microphone measurements, the real-ear gain of the hearing aid can be compared to the gain specified by a prescriptive fitting protocol. Additionally, varied inputs can be presented to the hearing aid to evaluate the effects of different automatic signal processing strategies. The hearing aid's directional microphone, noise reduction, telephone coil, and other special features also can be reliably assessed using this equipment.

Step 5: Postfitting Counseling, Orientation, and Outcome Measures

Even the best hearing aid, with the best circuitry, adjusted precisely for the patient's hearing loss can be a failed fitting if appropriate counseling and follow-up are not conducted.

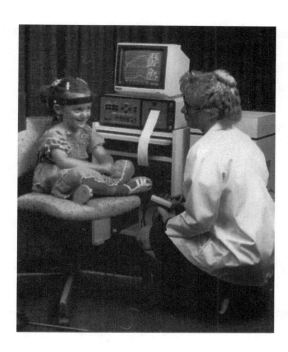

FIGURE 2.12

A probe microphone system for making real-ear measurements of hearing-aid outputs.
Courtesy of Frye Electronics.

POSTFITTING COUNSELING AND INSTRUMENT ORIENTATION. After the verification procedure is completed, it is time to sit down with the patient and walk through the use and care of the instruments. This is not something that can be rushed through. If possible, include significant others who spend time with the hearing aid user. It is good to have a hand-out that includes all the information that you will be presenting verbally (the user guide furnished by the manufacturer will have some of the information). Here is a basic list of things that you will want to discuss at the time of the hearing aid orientation. The acronym to help you remember the nine topics is HIOBASICS (Hearing Instrument Orientation BASICS) (Schow, 2001).

1. *H = Hearing expectations:* Unfortunately, hearing aids do not work just like eyeglasses. Everything will not be perfectly clear once they are put in place. Additionally, adjustment to amplification requires days, weeks, and even months for some patients. The patient needs to know this.

2. *I = Instrument operation:* The patient should be able to turn the hearing aid on and off, change programs (if necessary), adjust volume, activate telecoil (if present), and use with the telephone; demonstrate the use of the hearing aid on the telephone, and discuss assistive telephone listening devices.

3. *O = Occlusion effect:* Have the patient talk with the hearing aids in their ears, *but turned off,* to see if an occlusion effect is present. If so, and if it is bothersome, conduct treatments for reducing the occlusion effect (e.g., increase venting, lengthen canal) or explain why you cannot make it go away.

4. *B = Batteries:* Discuss different battery types and sizes, what batteries to use, how to obtain batteries, how long a battery lasts, and what to do with those funny sticky tabs (don't put them back on the battery!). Have the patient

demonstrate proficiency in opening and closing the battery door and inserting and removing the battery.

5. *A = Acoustic feedback:* Demonstrate what acoustic feedback sounds like (if the patient can hear it), what causes it, when it is OK and when it is not.

6. *S = System troubleshooting:* Provide the patient with a troubleshooting chart (see Table 2.3).

7. *I = Insertion and removal:* Demonstrate insertion and removal on an artificial ear; then have the patient practice in front of a mirror.

8. *C = Cleaning and maintenance:* Show the patient where wax accumulates in the receiver tubing, demonstrate the wax cleaning tool, and show how the hearing aid itself can be wiped clean. Talk about taking the battery out when storing the instrument; using a dry-aid kit if moisture is a problem; keeping the instrument away from water, excessive heat, and hair spray; avoiding dropping the hearing aid on a hard surface; and other potential hazards.

TABLE 2.3

Troubleshooting of Common Problems with Hearing Aids

PROBLEM	CAUSE	POSSIBLE SOLUTION
Instrument has no sound or sound is weak	Battery polarity reversed	Make sure battery is inserted correctly
	Low or dead battery	Replace with fresh battery
	Instrument not turned on	Rotate volume control
	Clogged wax guard	Clean wax guard
	Volume turned down	Turn up volume control
Instrument whistles	Improper seating in ear	Reinsert the instrument until it fits securely
	Volume control too high	Turn down volume control
	Clogged wax guard	Clean wax guard
	Excessive wax in the ears	Consult your hearing health care professional
Sound is distorted or intermittent	Low battery	Replace battery
	Battery compartment is not completely closed	Gently close the battery compartment
Buzzing sound	Low battery	Replace battery
Swelling or discharge in ear		Check with your physician

9. S = *Service, warranty, and repairs:* Explain warranty and repair policies, give patient the warranty card, and explain how repairs are handled in your office (do you allow walk-ins?).

A thorough orientation will also present material on effective communication. This will include discussion of listening styles (passive, aggressive, assertive), material on family communication dynamics (spouse, family members), information on using repair and anticipatory strategies, and the effective use of vision. In short, there are personal and environmental adjustments that the hearing aid user should try to utilize to complement the audibility improvements derived from amplification.

FOLLOW-UP VISITS AND OUTCOME MEASURES. On follow-up visits, it is useful to recheck some of the verification procedures that were conducted at the time of the fitting. Some general postfitting verification procedures might be the following:

- Present average level speech to the patient (e.g., 65 dB SPL). Determine if the programmed gain continues to be appropriate.
- With the volume control wheel set for speech at MCL, present loud speech (e.g., 85 dB SPL) to assure that it is not uncomfortably loud (you can use the chart in Table 2.2). If loud speech is only judged #5, it might be appropriate to reduce compression or raise the output to provide the patient with more headroom.
- Many manufacturers have *fitting assistant modules* in their software that will help make adjustments for other specific problems that the patient might report.

This is also a good time to repeat the self-assessment inventories that you gave the patient before the hearing aids were fitted in order to derive additional outcome measures regarding benefit. The patient can now respond to the questions relative to his or her performance with hearing aids, including use, benefit, and satisfaction measures. At this time it is also appropriate to consider providing other audiologic rehabilitation in addition to hearing aids, which is designed to further facilitate communication for the patient. Both short- and long-term forms of AR are discussed in detail in the chapters to follow.

Hearing aid outcome measures can relate to handicap, benefit, or satisfaction.

Two things to consider during your postfitting testing, adjustments, and counseling are the following:

ACCLIMATIZATION. Some research has suggested that it takes several weeks or even several months for the brain to adjust to a new acoustic input, that is, the new speech spectrum delivered by the hearing aid. It is possible, therefore, that maximum performance or improvement in performance from a previous hearing aid will not occur until acclimatization is complete.

Acclimatization can occur for a variety of hearing aid-related factors: for example, hearing new environmental sounds, soft speech, or a different speech spectrum.

AUDITORY DEPRIVATION. It is common to fit a person binaurally who has been a long-time monaural user. Research has suggested that for a person who has previously been aided monaurally, the ear that has not been aided for a period of time possibly will show a decline in performance for understanding speech. Can this decline be reversed? Possibly. Hence, speech understanding for this previously unaided ear, after some hearing aid use, might be better than predicted based on standard testing prior to the fitting of the hearing aids.

■ CONSIDERATIONS FOR THE PEDIATRIC PATIENT

In many respects, fitting hearing aids to infants and young children is the same as for adults; the goals of maximizing intelligibility and quality and making soft speech audible, average speech comfortable, and loud speech loud, but not too loud, are equally important for this population. However, some additional factors, must be considered as well as some procedural variations (see Bentler, 2000, for a review).

Prefitting Testing

For infants and young children it often is not possible to obtain precise pure tone thresholds or loudness growth functions. However, in many cases pure tone thresholds for different frequency regions can be estimated from auditory electrophysiologic testing. Methods are available to estimate loudness discomfort levels for children based only on thresholds data. Because precise threshold and loudness data often are not available, two factors are important: (1) the child should be reevaluated frequently so that changes in the fitting can be made as additional audiometric information becomes available, and (2) the child should be fitted with hearing aids that are highly adjustable (digital or digitally programmable when appropriate) so that alterations in the gain or output can be made easily.

Fitting Considerations

Different types of assistive listening technology rely on bypassing the hearing aid's microphone, either through direct auditory input (DAI) or through the hearing aid's telecoil. For children who are developing speech and language, this becomes even more critical. This reason alone might dictate the hearing aid style that is selected; for example, the telecoil of an ITE might not provide enough gain and output. As with adults, binaural amplification should be the standard fitting whenever there are two aidable ears.

When fitting infants and children, it is important to use probe microphone measures to assess the increased output of the hearing aid due to the smaller ear canal residual volume.

Prescriptive fitting approaches are available that are specifically designed for children. The most commonly used today is the Desired Sensation Level (DSL) 4.1 method. In particular, this selection procedure takes into account the need to deliver extended high-frequency information to the child, to consider the small residual ear canal volume of the child, and to limit the output to safe levels. Other methods, such as the NAL-NL1 also have been used successfully with the pediatric population.

Verification of Fitting

Because the infant or young child cannot provide subjective reports of the hearing aid performance, objective verification strategies are essential. The prescriptive fitting method can be verified easily using probe microphone measurements. With even the somewhat uncooperative child, this testing can be reliably conducted with a little patience. On occasion, young children are sedated for the electrophysiology measures; some audiologists also conduct their probe microphone measurements at this opportune moment.

Probe microphone measurements will reveal the amount of gain that is present throughout the frequency range. Importantly, this testing will also determine the maximum output that is delivered in the child's ear canal. Because the child's ear canal is much smaller than an adult's, the real-ear output often is 10 to 15 dB higher than shown in the 2-cc coupler. A hearing aid gain and output that are too high can result in discomfort for the child and possibly noise-induced hearing loss. As the child becomes older (e.g., 3 to 4 years of age), it is possible to conduct reliable loudness behavioral testing using specially designed charts (see Mueller and Bright, 1994). Just because a child says that sounds are not uncomfortably loud, however, does not guarantee that the hearing aid output is not damaging the ear; this is why objective ear-canal SPL measurements are essential.

Postfitting Procedures

Extensive parent counseling following the fitting is very important. The parents must know how to adjust and care for the hearing aid. Several practical accessories for children's hearing aids are available (e.g., "huggies," devices to help hold BTE hearing aids on the ear); a list of these accessories can be reviewed with the parents.

Follow-up visits for children need to be scheduled more frequently than for adults:

1. The hearing loss needs to be monitored to assure that it is not progressive, to verify previous findings, and to obtain additional information for hearing aid adjustment.
2. The fit of the hearing aid or earmold in the ear must be monitored. Because of the rapid ear growth of children, an earmold might become loose in a few months, causing acoustic feedback.
3. The electroacoustic characteristics of the hearing aids should be monitored. Children's hearing aids are subject to many bumps and bruises; it is important to ensure that the hearing aid maintains its appropriate gain and frequency response and that excessive distortion is not present.
4. Parent counseling and training is ongoing.

ASSISTIVE AND ALTERNATIVE ■ REHABILITATION DEVICES

Although hearing aids are designed to assist the hearing impaired individual in almost all listening environments, some patients, because of their age, degree of hearing loss, or other factors, might not derive significant benefit from hearing aids. Additionally, many hearing aid users will encounter difficult situations in which hearing aids may not provide optimal speech intelligibility. For instance, it might be difficult to listen in a noisy restaurant or in a business meeting where the speaker is at a distance from the listener. A hearing impaired child may have difficulty hearing the teacher when extraneous noise is present in the classroom or other children are talking in the hallways or on the playground outside. When watching a television program or using the telephone, a hearing aid may not provide necessary amplification. Being able to hear doorbells or safety alarms are other areas where special assistance might be helpful, especially for the severely hearing impaired.

You will recall that the microphone, the amplifier, and the receiver of the conventional hearing aid are located at the ear of the listener. We have previously discussed the advantages of this arrangement; however, in one respect this is a disadvantage to the hearing impaired listener since all incoming signals, both speech and noise, are amplified before being sent to the listener's ear. Thus, an unfavorable signal-to-noise ratio remains unfavorable. Assistive listening devices (ALDs) help to overcome this problem by increasing the loudness of the speech signal without significantly amplifying the background noise. This is accomplished by placing the microphone of the system close to the sound source and the receiver at the listener's ears so that the signal is transferred directly to the ear canal.

> **Assistive listening device:** class of hearing instruments with a remote microphone for improving signal-to-noise ratio.

Several broad categories of ALDs are available:

Personal and group amplification devices

Television amplification devices

Telephone devices

Signaling devices

We will take a look at each category throughout this section. For a more detailed discussion of ALDs, the reader is referred to Compton (1989) and Ross (1994).

Personal and Group Amplification Devices

Listening in groups, meetings, theaters, or classrooms can be adversely affected by interference from noise, room reverberation, and the distance from the speaker. Even individuals with only a mild degree of hearing loss may find it difficult to understand speech in such environments. Assistive listening devices are available that will increase the loudness of the person talking without significantly amplifying the background noise and can be used for listening one-to-one as well as in large groups.

A simple version of a personal or group amplification device consists of an amplifier with microphone input and a wire leading to an earphone. More elaborate systems are wireless, in which the signal is transmitted from the microphone and amplifier directly to the listener via infrared light or FM radio wave signals. Another system uses an induction loop, in which an electromagnetic signal is picked up by the telecoil in the listener's hearing aids. There are several important factors in examining how these systems work, where they may be used, and the advantages and disadvantages of each system type.

HARDWIRE SYSTEMS. Hardwire systems consist of a direct wire connection from a microphone to an amplifier and finally to a receiver. The receiver can be either the personal hearing aids, receiving the signal by direct audio input, or earphones. An example of a hardwire ALD is shown in Figure 2.13. Hardwire systems are most commonly used for listening to the television or radio. Let's take a look at the advantages and disadvantages of this type of listening system:

ADVANTAGES

- Portable
- Lightweight and inexpensive

DISADVANTAGES

- Limited by length of wire
- Sound quality may not be good

INDUCTION LOOP SYSTEMS. Induction loop systems (ILS) offer an advantage over hardwire systems in that they are wireless, thus avoiding the need for a cord between the sound source and listener. This system consists of a microphone, an amplifier, and a length of wire that surrounds (or "loops") a designated area, such as a theater or a classroom (see Figure 2.14 for an example of an induction loop for a large-area listening system). Typically, the wire loop is positioned around the ceiling of the room. A microphone is placed near the sound source, transmitting the signal via hard-wire coupling or FM radio waves to a receiver–amplifier that transforms the signal into electrical energy. This electric current flows through the wire

FIGURE 2.13

An example of a basic hardwire assistive listening device (ALD).
Courtesy of Williams Sound Corp.

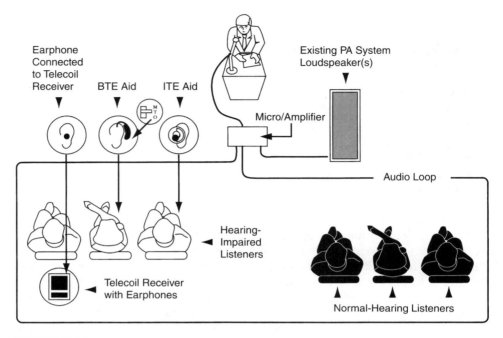

FIGURE 2.14

Use of an induction-loop large-area listening system. A coil of wire (loop) is added to existing sound system. Listeners with hearing impairment pick up sound using telecoil circuits contained in hearing aids or special receivers.

Reprinted with permission from C. Compton (1991). *Assistive devices: Doorways to Independence.* Annapolis, MD: Van Comp Associates.

loop, creating a magnetic field that can be picked up by a hearing aid telecoil or a specially designed induction receiver. Induction loop systems work well in the home and in rooms where the listeners have telecoil-equipped hearing aids. The advantages and disadvantages of the induction system include the following:

ADVANTAGES

- Wireless transmission
- Relatively inexpensive
- Separate receiver not needed if listener is wearing telecoil-equipped hearing aids

DISADVANTAGES

- Limited portability
- Strength of the magnetic signal decreases sharply with distance
- Possibility of electromagnetic interference
- Electromagnetic energy can travel through solid surfaces, causing spillover into adjacent rooms
- Affected by orientation of hearing aid telecoil
- Requires use of a hearing aid with a strong telecoil

As you can see from this list, a number of disadvantages are associated with the induction loop system. Many of these problems, however, have been minimized with the emergence of the three-dimensional (3-D) loop system. The 3-D system consists of a wireless microphone, a loop processor box, and one or more undercarpet floor mats. In a large room setting, then, the speaker's voice is sent from the wireless microphone to the 3-D loop processor box and then to the undercarpet floor mats. The floor mats contain several induction loops that create a 3-D magnetic field above the mat that transmits the auditory signal to the listener's telecoil-equipped hearing aids. Importantly, with the 3-D loop system, reception is unaffected by the characteristics and orientation of the telecoil, and adjacent rooms can be effectively looped without signal spillover. Induction loop systems work relatively well in classrooms and in small meeting rooms where the listeners have telecoil-equipped hearing aids.

INFRARED SYSTEMS. In the infrared system, a microphone picks up acoustic energy from the sound source, converts it to electrical energy, and transmits it to an infrared converter. The converter changes the electrical energy to light energy and transmits it on an infrared carrier beam. The listener wears a receiver that picks up the light energy and converts it back to acoustic energy. The typical receiver consists of lightweight earphones with an adjustable volume control, although direct audio input or an induction neck loop (for use with a hearing aid telecoil) can also be used (see Figure 2.15 for examples of different infrared use with the television). Infrared technology is popular in large areas, as well as for home television use.

ADVANTAGES

- Wireless transmission
- High-quality signal
- Uses various types of receivers
- Can be used simultaneously in adjacent rooms without interference
- Not affected by outside radio transmission

DISADVANTAGES

- Limited portability
- Person confined to a certain area for listening
- Receiver must be in direct line with transmitter for maximum sound quality
- Cannot be used outside because it is subject to interference from sunlight
- Signal is reflected by solid surfaces, which degrades sound quality

FM SYSTEMS. The function of the FM system is similar to that of the infrared system except that FM radio waves are used to transmit the signal, rather than infrared light waves. FM systems can be used in virtually any listening environment, ranging from one-to-one to large-group situations. In this system, a microphone–transmitter is placed at the sound source and the signal is transmitted via FM radio waves to a receiver worn by the listener. The receiver is typically a telecoil-equipped hearing aid that receives the signal via a silhouette adapter or induction loop or via direct audio input. The FM receiver can also be used with headphones for use without a hearing aid (see Figure 2.16). Two receiver options not pictured in Figure 2.16 can also be used with FM systems. The first is a loudspeaker, used in sound field

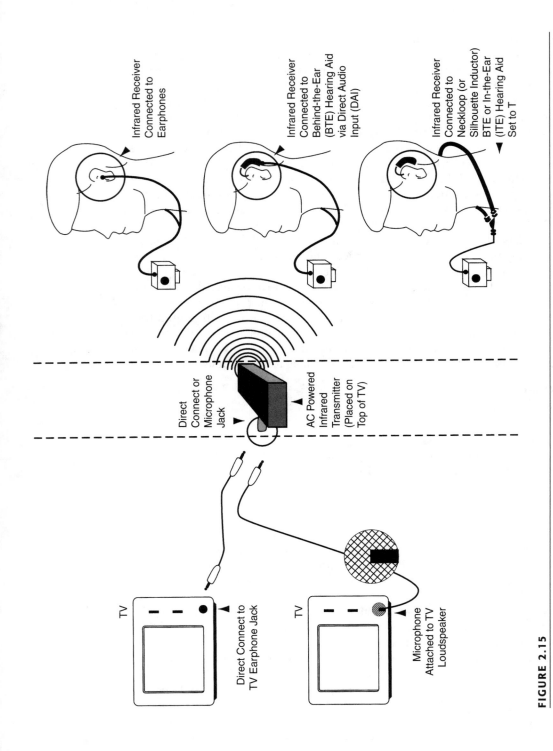

FIGURE 2.15

Use of infrared system with television.

Reprinted with permission from C. Compton (1991). *Assistive devices: Doorways to Independence*. Annapolis, MD: Van Comp Associates.

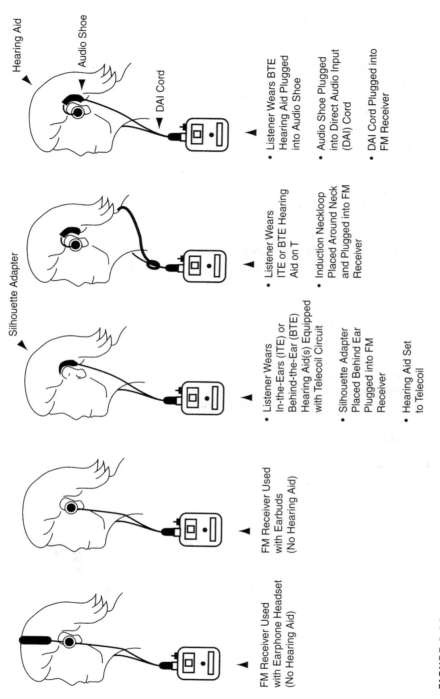

FM Receiver Used
with Earphone Headset
(No Hearing Aid)

FM Receiver Used
with Earbuds
(No Hearing Aid)

- Listener Wears
  In-the-Ears (ITE) or
  Behind-the-Ear (BTE)
  Hearing Aid(s) Equipped
  with Telecoil Circuit

- Silhouette Adapter
  Placed Behind Ear
  Plugged into FM
  Receiver

- Hearing Aid Set
  to Telecoil

- Listener Wears
  ITE or BTE Hearing
  Aid on T

- Induction Neckloop
  Placed Around Neck
  and Plugged into FM
  Receiver

- Listener Wears BTE
  Hearing Aid Plugged
  into Audio Shoe

- Audio Shoe Plugged
  into Direct Audio Input
  (DAI) Cord

- DAI Cord Plugged into
  FM Receiver

Silhouette Adapter

Hearing Aid

Audio Shoe

DAI Cord

FIGURE 2.16

Methods of sound pickup from an FM receiver.

Reprinted with permission from C. Compton (1991). *Assistive devices: Doorways to Independence*. Annapolis, MD: Van Comp Associates.

amplification. In sound field amplification systems, the audio signal is transmitted through a wireless FM microphone to several loudspeakers mounted on the walls or ceiling. Such systems are typically utilized in the classroom and offer an advantage over personal FM systems in that they provide an improved signal for all students in the classroom without requiring use of a specialized receiver. A second receiver option is the ear-level (BTE) FM receiver–hearing aid combination, as shown in Figure 2.17. This unit provides the user with a personal hearing aid and allows FM reception while eliminating the cords, neck loops, and body-worn receivers inherent in conventional FM systems. To achieve this, a microphone picks up the speech signal directly at the source, and the signal is transmitted via radio waves directly to the receiver attached to the hearing instrument. The options of hearing aid only, hearing aid with FM, and FM only accommodate the listener in a magnitude of listening environments. The BTE–FM system is ideal for listeners whose amplification needs require both a conventional hearing aid and the improved signal-to-noise ratio of an FM system.

As you can see from this description, an advantage of the FM system is that the signal may be received by the listeners in a number of ways. There are a number of additional advantages to using FM systems as compared to other listening systems.

ADVANTAGES

- Wireless transmission
- High-quality signal
- Most flexible system
- Uses various types of receivers
- Indoor and outdoor use possible
- Can be used simultaneously in adjacent rooms
- Electromagnetic interference not a problem
- Does not require that receiver be in direct line with transmitter

DISADVANTAGES

- Radio interference possible

FIGURE 2.17

A behind-the-ear hearing aid with an FM receiver.
Courtesy of Phonak.

In summary, remember that the principal advantage of any personal or group amplification system relates to the ability to selectively amplify the desired signal without amplifying background noise. Hardwire systems accomplish this by physically connecting the listener to the sound source. The induction loop system utilizes an electromagnetic field, the infrared system employs an invisible light beam, and the FM system connects the sound source and the listener via a frequency modulated radio wave. All the systems are effective in eliminating or reducing the negative impact of noise, reverberation, and distance to improve speech perception for hearing impaired listeners. The choice of which system to use depends on the needs of the individual listener and on the environment in which it will be used.

Television Amplification Devices

Listening to television is a major concern for the hearing impaired person, second only to the telephone when considering assistive listening devices (Ross, 1994). Typically, we turn up the volume on the television when we want to hear better. For the hearing impaired listener, however, simply turning up the volume does not greatly improve the ability to understand what is being said. Added to that, turning up the volume may interfere with another person's ability to enjoy the television. These difficulties can be minimized or eliminated by using one of the many television listening devices available. With the use of such devices, the hearing impaired listener can maintain control over the loudness that they receive, while the volume on the television is set to a level comfortable for others. The four basic amplification systems (hardwire, induction loop, infrared, FM) described in the previous discussion on personal and group listening systems can also be used in conjunction with television. Television listening systems work in a similar manner to personal and group listening devices, just on a smaller scale.

For deaf and severely hearing impaired individuals, closed-captioned decoders provide television access by inserting subtitles onto the screen of the television, thus allowing the user to understand the audio portion of the television program by reading the subtitles. Closed-captioned capability is now required on all new televisions with screens larger than 13 inches in accordance with the Television Decoder Circuitry Act of 1993.

Telephone Devices

People with hearing impairment often complain about problems using the telephone. Many hearing aids have a built-in telecoil that, when activated, helps to eliminate background noise and the acoustic feedback that occurs when the telephone receiver is held near the hearing aid microphone. Unfortunately, telecoils are not available on all hearing aids and are not equally efficient with all telephones. Moreover, there is often substantial variability in the performance characteristics of hearing aid telecoils depending on the type of hearing aid and the manufacturer. As an alternative, telephone amplifiers are available that function to increase the loudness of the telephone signal. These units may be portable and attach directly over the earpiece of the telephone, or they can be built into the receiver of the telephone.

Most models have a volume control so that the user can adjust the signal to a comfortable listening level.

Deaf and profoundly hearing impaired individuals must rely on nonauditory means of telephone communication, the telecommunication device for the deaf (TDD). This device is also referred to as a text telephone. TDDs are computerized systems that allow the user to directly call another person having similar equipment. Messages are typed and transmitted to the other individual's telephone and TDD, and the typed message is visually displayed on a screen. Calls from a TDD user can be placed indirectly with individuals not having a TDD through a relay system, available throughout the United States. Although TDDs are used mostly by deaf people, they are also used by individuals with less severe hearing losses and by speech impaired people who experience difficulty communicating over the telephone.

Signaling Devices

A hearing aid generally enables a person to hear most sounds, but if a person is not wearing a hearing aid, is in another room, or is using an assistive device to listen to the television, some sounds may go unnoticed. To address these situations, signaling devices can be set up to monitor the telephone, alarm clock, doorbell, smoke alarm, and even a crying baby. Most of these devices automatically flash a light or activate a wrist-worn vibrator to alert the person to the sound source. Other devices increase the intensity of the sound source or change the frequency to make it audible to the hearing impaired listener. Still other types of alerting devices are capable of activating a bed vibrator or fan to awake a sleeping person. These devices can be very important for hearing impaired individuals as they carry out their daily routines.

ALD WEB SITES

www.harcmercantile.com

www.phonicear.com

www.williamssound.com

www.sinuscarecenter.com/hrastaao.html

www.earaces.com/ald.htm

www.betterhearing.org/newtech.htm

Other Alternative Devices for the Deaf

The majority of hearing impaired individuals can benefit from conventional amplification and/or some type of assistive listening device. For totally deaf or profoundly hearing impaired people, however, conventional amplification devices may provide only limited or virtually no benefit at all. Other alternatives are available, including *cochlear implants, auditory brainstem implants,* and *vibrotactile devices.* Implant devices, especially cochlear implants, are playing an ever-increasing role in the habilitation and rehabilitation of children and adults with severe to profound hearing loss. A thorough review of implants is provided in Chapter 3.

- The basic components of a hearing aid are the microphone, amplifier, receiver, and battery. Behind-the-ear (BTE) instruments also require an earmold to channel the sound into the ear canal.
- The majority of today's hearing aids are programmable, meaning that the method in which the hearing aid processes sound can be adjusted and tailored for the patient using computer software.
- Hearing aid circuits can be either analog or digital. Digital processing, introduced in 1995, is rapidly becoming the standard. Two key components, the microphone and receiver, however, are the same for both digital and analog technology.
- Hearing aid compression and peak clipping are two forms of output limiting. Most modern hearing aids have both input and output compression on board the digital chip, but peak clipping is used occasionally.
- Hearing aid compression can be used to prevent loud sounds from being too loud and uncomfortable (usually accomplished with output compression) or can be used to repackage the wide intensity range of speech into the patient's reduced dynamic range (accomplished using input compression).
- A popular category of compression is termed wide dynamic range compression (WDRC). It is available in all the current digital products and is especially useful for providing audibility of soft speech.
- Common hearing aid styles include the behind-the-ear (BTE), in-the-ear (ITE), in-the-canal (ITC), and completely-in-canal (CIC). Essentially, the same technology can be obtained in each, and of the four styles the ITC and CIC are becoming the most popular, primarily because of cosmetic advantages.
- BTE hearing aids require coupling to an earmold. Earmolds can be modified through venting (low frequencies), the use of damping (mid-frequencies), or the use of horn tubing (high frequencies).
- Hearing aids are assessed, both at the manufacturer and in the clinic, using 2-cc coupler measures. These results are used to determine if the hearing aid meets a set of preestablished specifications. These results do *not* assure that the hearing aid is appropriate for a given patient.
- Whenever possible, it is recommended that individuals with hearing loss in both ears be fitted with binaural amplification. Some of the advantages include increased gain, improved localization, better sound quality, and improved speech understanding in noise.
- Verification of the hearing aid fitting can include informal patient judgments of quality and intelligibility, measures of speech understanding, loudness scaling, and probe microphone measurements. When prescriptive fitting procedures are used, probe microphone measures are the preferred method for determining if desired gain and output values have been achieved.
- After the fitting, it is important to remember HIOBASICS: Hearing expectations, Instrument operation, Occlusion effect, Batteries, Acoustic feedback, System trouble shooting, Insertion and removal, Cleaning and maintenance, and Service, warranty, and repairs.

- When fitting hearing aids to infants and children, it is important to remember that, because of their small ear canals, the output of the hearing aid will be greater than with adults. Probe microphone measures can be used to determine this difference value.
- In addition to hearing aids, many individuals can benefit from assistive devices, which can be used for special listening situations (e.g., amplifier for the telephone or an FM or infrared device for listening to the TV).

RECOMMENDED READING

Bentler, R. A. (2000). Amplification for the hearing-impaired child. In Alpiner J. G., & McCarthy, P. A. (Eds.). *Rehabilitative audiology* (pp. 106–139). New York: Lippincott Williams & Wilkins.

Berg, F. S. (1993). *Acoustics and sound systems in schools.* San Diego, CA: Singular Publishing Group.

Chasin, M. (1997). Current trends in implantable hearing aids. *Trends in Amplification, 2*(3), 84–107.

Mueller, H. G., & Hall, J.W. (1998). *Audiologists' desk reference*, Volume II. San Diego, CA: Singular Publishing Group.

Mueller, H. G., Hawkins, D. B., & Northern, J. L. (1992). *Probe microphone measurements.* San Diego, CA: Singular Publishing Group.

Palmer, C. V., & Mueller, H. G. (2000). Hearing aid selection and assessment. In Alpiner J. G., & McCarthy P. A. (Eds.). *Rehabilitative audiology* (pp. 332–376). New York: Lippincott Williams & Wilkins.

Ross, M. (1994). *Communication access for persons with hearing loss.* Baltimore: York Press.

Tyler, R. S., & Schum, D. J. (1995). *Assistive devices for persons with hearing impairment.* Boston: Allyn and Bacon.

Valente, M., Hosford-Dunn, H., & Roeser, R. (Eds.). (2000). *Audiology: treatment.* New York: Thieme.

REFERENCES

Bentler, R. A. (2000). Amplification for the hearing-impaired child. In Alpiner, J. G., McCarthy, P. A. (Eds.). *Rehabilitative audiology* (pp. 106–139). New York: Lippincott Williams & Wilkins.

Chasin, M. (1997). Current trends in implantable hearing aids. *Trends in Amplification, 2*(3), 84–107.

Compton, C. L. (1989). *Assistive devices: Doorways to independence.* Washington, DC: Assistive Device Center, Gallaudet University.

Cox, R. M. (1995). Using loudness data for hearing aid selection: The IHAFF approach. *The Hearing Journal 48*(2), 10, 39–44.

Mueller, H. G. (1994). Small can be good too! *The Hearing Journal, 47*(10), 11.

Mueller, H. G. (2000). What's the digital difference when it comes to patient benefit? *The Hearing Journal, 53*(3), 23–32.

Mueller, H. G., & Bright, K. E. (1994). Selection and verification of maximum output (pp. 38–63). In Valente, M. (Ed.), *Strategies for selecting and verifying hearing aid fittings.* New York: Thieme Medical Publishers.

Mueller, H. G., & Grimes, A. M. (1987). Amplification systems for the hearing impaired. In J. G. Alpiner & P. A. McCarthy (Eds.), *Rehabilitative audiology: Children and adults* (pp. 115–160). Baltimore: Williams & Wilkins.

Mueller, H. G., & Hall J. W. (1998). *Audiologists' Desk Reference,* Volume II. San Diego, CA: Singular Publishing Group.

Mueller, H. G., & Killion, M. C. (1990). An easy method for calculating the articulation index. *The Hearing Journal, 43*(9), 14–17.

Mueller, H. G., & Ricketts, T. A. (2000). Update on directional microphone hearing aids. *The Hearing Journal, 53*(5), 10–17.

Ross, M. (1994). *Communication access for persons with hearing loss.* Baltimore: York Press.

Schow, R. L. (2001). A standardized AR battery for dispensors. *Hearing Journal,* 54(8), 10–20.

Cochlear Implants and Other Rehabilitative Areas

Alice E. Holmes

C O N T E N T S

■ INTRODUCTION

New breakthroughs in audiology now allow us to assist persons in ways never thought of 20 years ago. Persons with profound sensorineural loss now have the potential to receive sound information through the use of cochlear implants. Treatment plans are now available for tinnitus sufferers and dizzy patients. This chapter will provide an overview of these new advances in audiology.

Most persons who are diagnosed with a sensorineural hearing loss are fit with hearing aids and can receive varying amounts of benefit from these devices. Unfortunately, for some individuals with severe to profound hearing loss these traditional amplification devices may offer only limited or no help, even with extensive experience and audiologic rehabilitation. Even the most powerful amplifiers are unable to provide meaningful information for environmental sound awareness or speech perception for persons with little or no residual hearing. Cochlear implant technology has offered many of these individuals an alternative means to receive some important information from their impaired auditory systems.

A cochlear implant is a device that electrically stimulates the auditory nerve of patients with severe to profound hearing loss to provide them with sound and speech information. It is not an amplifier that increases the level of the acoustic signal, but a surgically implanted device that bypasses the peripheral auditory system to directly simulate the auditory nerve. The cochlear implant does not restore normal hearing. Cochlear implant recipients vary in the amount of benefit that they receive from the device. Some individuals are provided with auditory awareness, detection of environmental sounds, and improvement in their speechreading abilities; other patients are able to achieve open-set speech perception without visual cues. Many individuals are able to conduct conversations over the telephone.

■ HOW DOES A COCHLEAR IMPLANT WORK?

A number of cochlear implant systems are available worldwide. Each has unique characteristics, advantages, and disadvantages, but all operate using the same basic principles. All cochlear implant systems commonly in use consist of an externally worn headset connected to a speech processor, with a battery source and a surgically implanted internal receiver stimulator attached to the electrode array.

The cochlear implant surgery is completed under general anesthesia. Typically, the surgeon makes an incision behind the ear and drills a small area in the mastoid bone for the placement of the receiver stimulator and the insertion of the electrode array. The electrode array is then threaded through the mastoid and the middle ear cavity and then inserted in the scala tympani of the cochlea through the round window. Insertion depths can range up to 30 mm depending on the implant system being used. The operation normally ranges from 1 to 3 hours and often is done on an outpatient basis.

Figure 3.1 shows one of the commercially available cochlear implant systems with a body processor. The headset consists of a microphone (1) and transmitter coil (5). The transmitter coil has a magnet that adheres to the head over the skin where the receiver stimulator (6) is placed. The microphone picks up the sound wave, converts it into an electrical signal and sends it to an externally worn speech processor (3) via a cord (2). The speech processor codes the information using a device-specific strategy and sends it to the external transmitter coil (5). The coil sends the information through the skin via FM radio waves to an internal receiver (6), which in turn sends the information to the implanted electrodes (7) that stimulate the available auditory nerve fibers (8). The auditory nerve then sends the information to the brain so that the person can perceive sound stimulation. This all occurs in a matter of microseconds.

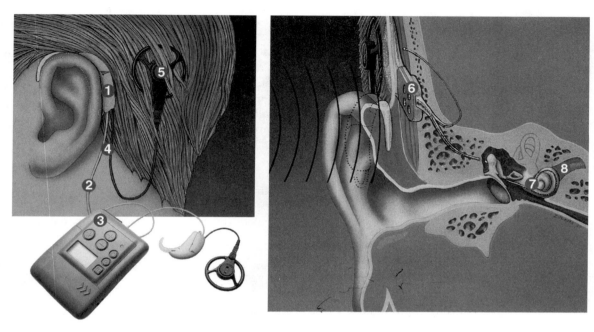

FIGURE 3.1

Components of a cochlear implant system and how it works.

Courtesy of Cochlear Corporation, Englewood, CO.

■ HISTORY OF COCHLEAR IMPLANTS

In 1972, the first wearable cochlear implant was implanted in an adult at the House Ear Institute. The House/3M device consisted of a single electrode implanted in the basal end of the cochlea with a ground electrode placed in the Eustachian tube. This device was capable of providing the patient with information on the presence or absence of sound, durational cues, and intensity cues. Even with this limited information, many individuals had improved speechreading abilities and were able to learn to identify many environmental sounds with training. Over 1000 persons received this commercially available device. In 1980 the device became available for use in children over the age of 2 years (Wilson, 2000).

Multielectrode devices came into wide use in the 1980s. With these systems, limited frequency cues became available to the patients, and many patients, were achieving some open-set speech understanding without the use of visual cues. In 1985, the U.S. Food and Drug Administration (FDA) approved the use of the Nucleus 22-Channel Cochlear Implant System for adults with postlingual profound deafness. In 1990, the FDA also approved the use of the device in children over the age of 2 years.

Continued development of cochlear implant systems and the speech processing strategies over the past two decades have resulted in marked improvements. The 1995 National Institute of Health Consensus Statement on Cochlear Implants reported that the majority of adults with recent processors achieve over 80% correct on high-context open-set sentence materials in an auditory-only condition. Cosmetic improvements have included a reduction in the size of the body-worn speech processors and the development of totally ear-level devices.

Currently, the FDA has granted approval for the cochlear implant systems submitted by two companies. The Nucleus 22 and the Nucleus 24 systems from Cochlear Corporation (Figure 3.2) and the Clarion systems from Advanced Bionics (Figure 3.3) are approved for general use with both children and adults. A third company, Med EL, is currently conducting investigational trials on their COMBI 40 systems (Figure 3.4) in the United States with both children and adults. Worldwide over 30,000 persons have received cochlear implants from these companies as of October 2000.

■ THE COCHLEAR IMPLANT TEAM

A multidisciplinary team is necessary for a successful cochlear implant program. These team members should be involved in the entire process from the evaluation for candidacy through the habilitation or rehabilitation process. The team must

FIGURE 3.2

Nucleus 24 body-worn SPrint and ear-level ESPrit cochlear implant systems.

Courtesy of Cochlear Corporation, Englewood, CO.

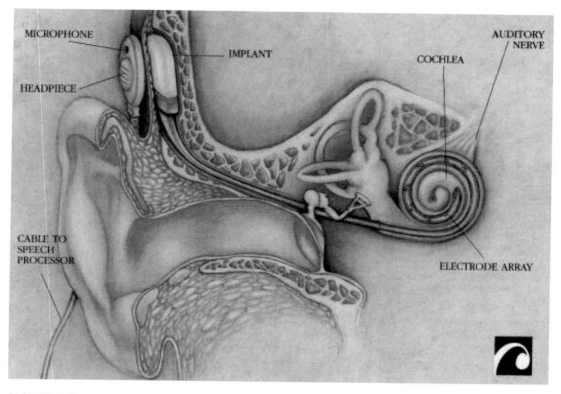

FIGURE 3.3

Clarion S-Series cochlear implant system.
Courtesy of Advanced Bionics, Sylmar, CA.

include both an otolaryngologist and an audiologist, who serve as the team leaders. The otolaryngologist makes the medical decisions and performs the surgery. The audiologist determines audiologic candidacy and programs the speech processor. He or she also develops the audiologic rehabilitation plan in conjunction with the other team members, which may include the following:

- Speech–language pathologists
- Psychologists
- Teachers of the hearing impaired
- Social workers
- Parents

Communication among team members is vital to success with a cochlear implant for any recipient.

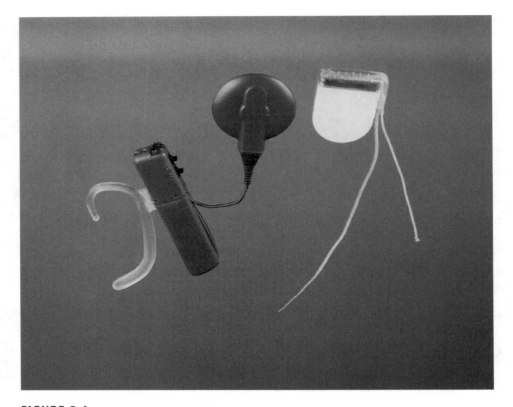

FIGURE 3.4

Med EL ear-level cochlear implant processor.
Courtesy of Med EL, Durham, NC.

■ WHO IS A CANDIDATE?

Not everyone is a candidate for a cochlear implant. Candidacy evaluations generally consist of a number of evaluations with several team members. With the improved outcomes, the criteria for implantation have vastly expanded since the 1980s when only adults with profound postlingual hearing impairments were eligible. Each of the implant companies in the United States has different criteria currently approved by the FDA (Zwolan, 2000). These criteria are changing rapidly, and it is important for professionals to remain current. Table 3.1 shows the candidacy guidelines for each of the companies distributing implants in the United States as of November 2000.

Formal evaluations should include standard audiometric unaided test batteries, otoacoustic emissions, aided speech perception testing, and aided speechreading evaluations. Speech and language evaluations should be completed on all children

TABLE 3.1

Candidacy Guidelines Associated with Degree of Hearing Loss as of November 2000

COMPANY	IMPLANT SYSTEM	AGE	HEARING LOSS	FDA APPROVAL STATUS
Advanced Bionics	Clarion S-Series Clarion S-Series	18 months–17 years ≥ 18 years	Profound (≥90 dB HL) Moderate to profound in the low frequencies; profound in the mid to high frequencies	Approved Approved
	Clarion Platinum Clarion Platinum	18 months–17 years ≥ 18 years	Profound (≥90 dB HL) Moderate to profound in the low frequencies; profound in the mid to high frequencies	Approved Approved
	Clarion Platinum	≥ 18 years	Moderate to profound in the low frequencies; severe to profound in the mid to high frequencies (≥70 dB HL)	Investigational
	Clarion Platinum BTE Clarion Platinum BTE	18 months–17 years ≥ 18 years	Profound (≥90 dB HL) Moderate to profound in the low frequencies; severe to profound in the mid to high frequencies (≥70 dB HL)	Investigational Investigational
Cochlear	Nucleus 22 Nucleus 22	18 months–17 years ≥ 18 years	Profound (≥90 dB HL) Moderate to profound in the low frequencies; profound in the mid to high frequencies	Approved Approved
	Nucleus 24 Nucleus 24	18 months–17 years ≥ 18 years	Profound (≥90 dB HL) Moderate to profound in the low frequencies; severe to profound in the mid to high frequencies (≥70 dB HL)	Approved Approved
	Nucleus 24-Countour Nucleus 24-Countour	12 months–17 years ≥ 18 years	Profound (≥90 dB HL) Moderate to profound in the low frequencies; severe to profound in the mid to high frequencies (≥70 dB HL)	Approved Approved
Med EL	COMBI 40+ COMBI 40+	18 months–17 years ≥ 18 years	Profound (≥90 dB HL) Moderate to profound in the low frequencies; profound (≥90 dB HL) in the mid to high frequencies	Investigational Investigational

(Zwolan, 2000; www.cochlear.com)

CT scan: computerized tomography scans of the temporal bone provide information on the surgical anatomy of the cochlea.

and all adults with prelingual hearing loss. Otologic–medical evaluations are done by the physician. CT scans are necessary to determine if the device can be implanted.

In addition to the audiometric guidelines for sensorineural hearing loss listed in Table 3.1, several other criteria are required prior to a person receiving a cochlear implant. There should be no medical contraindications such as the absence of the VIII nerve. The person must be free of active middle ear infections and be able to undergo surgery and anesthesia.

Patients and their families also should be counseled on the costs of cochlear implantation, and insurance reimbursement information needs to be provided. The cost of the cochlear implant system, surgery, and rehabilitative program ranges from $40,000 to $60,000. Most major insurance carriers (e.g., Blue Cross/Blue Shield), Medicare, and, in some states, Medicaid cover the procedure. Vocational Rehabilitation Services in some states also will pay for the cochlear implant. Several studies on the cost–utility of the procedures have shown the cochlear implant to be a cost-effective procedure that often results in less expensive educational training for the recipient and more employability.

Candidacy for Adults

Adults must have had at least a 3- to 6-month trial period with appropriate amplification and show limited benefit from the hearing aids as defined by less than 40% auditory-only speech recognition performance with open-set sentences. Individuals must have a strong support system and be motivated to undergo the rehabilitative process of speech processor programming and audiologic rehabilitation. They must have realistic expectations. Honest counseling about the range of benefits that people receive is necessary. The limitations of the device need to be covered. Potential candidates need to be told that not everyone is able to use the telephone even after training. Some individuals may only receive enhancement of their speechreading abilities and awareness of environmental sounds. It is helpful to have them contact other patients who have the cochlear implant. Caution should be taken not to have them talk only to the highest-functioning users, as this often leads to unrealistic expectations. The team leaders may make the appropriate referrals for further evaluations to other team members such as the psychologist if it is suspected that there may be problems with the patient's or family members' expectations.

Individuals must also want to be part of the hearing world. Adults with prelingual hearing loss have poorer prognoses for success with a cochlear implant. Although speechreading abilities may be improved in these individuals, very few have achieved any open-set speech perception without visual cues. This is particularly true in those individuals who lack oral communication skills. Referrals for psychological and speech–language pathology consultations are often necessary in this population.

There is no upper age limit for cochlear implantation. As long as the person meets all other criteria, he or she is a candidate. The issue is quality of life, not longevity. An 89-year-old who was implanted in our facility had relied on his wife for all communications for 2 years prior to receiving his implant. At the time of his evaluation, his wife had been diagnosed with Alzheimer's disease. About 1 year after he received his implant, his wife's condition had declined enough that their roles were reversed and he became her caregiver. Due in part to the benefits derived from the implant, both were able to remain in their home together and neither had to be institutionalized.

Candidacy for Children

Candidacy for children is sometimes very difficult to determine and should be done by the entire team of professionals listed previously. Children must have at least a 6-month trial period with appropriate and consistent binaural hearing aid use and must be receiving auditory training during that period (see Chapter 4). Limited benefit from amplification in young children is defined as lack of development in simple auditory skills over a 3- to 6-month period. In older children, when speech perception tests can be completed, limited benefit is defined as scores of less than 20% with open-set material.

Motivation and expectations of the family must be assessed, and they must be counseled to have appropriate expectations. Both the psychologist and the social worker on the team are helpful in assessing the family situation and assisting with compliance after the child receives the implant. Many families hope that the cochlear implant will correct the child's hearing. They must be told that the implant is not a cure and will not give the child normal hearing. As with adult recipients, these children's parents should be given the opportunity to talk with other families that have gone through the process with their child. They need to understand that intensive therapy will be a very important part of the child's audiologic and communication development. It is important to have all members of the team, including the teacher of the hearing impaired and the speech–language pathologist, active in the process. They can provide much of the support needed in training the child and family members.

The communication mode that the child uses does not determine candidacy, but the child's educational program must emphasize the development of auditory skills. Children trained in an auditory–verbal or auditory–visual mode of communication do progress more rapidly with their implants. Children placed in total communication programs do receive benefit from the implant if audition and speech are also encouraged along with signing (Meyer et al., 1998).

Teenagers pose an additional challenge when determining candidacy. Well-meaning relatives and friends who want the child to be part of the hearing world make the referrals. If the teen has some oral speech and language skills and wants the implant, then he or she may be a candidate. However, many teenagers have no desire or motivation to get a cochlear implant. In addition, the plasticity of the auditory system appears to decline rapidly after about 6 years of age. Therefore, congenitally deafened teens have poorer prognoses for success with an implant, much like that of prelingual adults. They also may have made the choice to enter the Deaf community and do not have an interest in hearing.

■ DEAF CULTURE AND COCHLEAR IMPLANTS

The Deaf community defines Deafness with a capital D as a culture rather than a disability. It is characterized by having its own language, American Sign Language (ASL). Some individuals within the Deaf community have expressed strong opinions against the use of cochlear implants, especially in children. They resent anyone who is trying to "fix a deaf child." They have likened cochlear implants to foot binding in ancient China, by trying to shape the child into actively using hearing. Many of their feelings stem from years of professionals forcing oral programming for all children with hearing loss and their own frustrations with traditional hearing aids.

Over the past 10 years the National Association of the Deaf (NAD) has softened its criticisms of cochlear implants. In 1990 the organization came out in strong opposition to the FDA approval of cochlear implants in children, stating that the research being conducted on children had no regard for the child's quality of life as a deaf adult. In their 2000 Position Statement on Cochlear Implants, the NAD recognized the technology of cochlear implants as a tool for use with some forms of communication. They asserted that the parents have the right to choose the cochlear implant, but emphasized that parents must be given all the options, including the option of sign language and the choice to be part of the Deaf World instead of the Hearing World. They continue to assert that young prelingually deafened children do not have the auditory foundation to learn spoken language easily, and therefore cochlear implants in these children may have less than favorable results. This is in direct conflict with data by Miyamoto et al. (1993) and Waltzman and Cohen (1998), which demonstrated that children implanted at a young age received significant speech perception benefits.

Implant teams must make parents aware of the Deaf culture issues. The parents do need to make informed decisions with knowledge of all options. Implants teams should be cognizant of the Deaf Culture issues and be prepared to address them when counseling parents. It is also important to provide information to Deaf clubs on the current status of cochlear implants and the possible benefits and limitations of the devices.

TREATMENT PLANS FOR COCHLEAR ■ IMPLANT RECIPIENTS

Once the evaluation and patient counseling have been completed and the decision has been made to proceed with the cochlear implant, the implant team may suggest that the patient go through some pretraining. With adults and older children the pretraining may include speechreading therapy and training in the use of communication strategies for communication breakdowns (Chapters 4 and 9). For children the pretraining may include conditioning for play audiometry using tactile or visual stimulation, which then will allow for more accurate assessment of hearing sensitivity with and without the implant.

After surgery the patient must wait approximately 4 to 6 weeks before the external headset and speech processor can be fit. This waiting period allows for healing of the incision area prior to placing the magnet on the sensitive surface where the external transmitter is placed.

Hook-up

The initial fitting and programming of the cochlear implant, commonly called the hook-up, usually takes 1.5 to 2 hours. During the hook-up or fitting of the headset and speech processor, the audiologist must program the speech processor using a specific manufacturer-designed diagnostic programming system interfaced with a personal computer.

All current generation implants have the capability of testing the integrity of the internal device by using a technique called telemetry (Abbas & Brown, 2000). Electrode voltages and impedances can be measured when current is supplied through the system. In this manner the audiologist can check the internal device prior to programming the system. If any of the electrodes are found to be out of compliance with standard values they will not be programmed for use. In some implant centers, telemetry is also completed by the audiologist in the operating room at the time of surgery to ensure proper device functioning before surgical closure.

To create the program, or MAP, for the speech processor, the audiologist must determine the electrical dynamic range for each electrode used. The programming system delivers an electrical current through the cochlear implant system to each electrode in order to obtain the electrical threshold (C-level) and comfort (C-level) measures. T-level or minimum stimulation level is the softest electrical current that produces an auditory sensation by the patient 100% of the time. The C-level is the

> MAP: cochlear implant program that encodes the acoustic signal and translates it into electrical stimulation levels based on the measured T- and C-levels. The programming of the CI processor is referred to as mapping.

The sound processor of the cochlear implant is programmed initially at the hook-up.

loudest level that can be listened to comfortably for a long period of time. The speech processor is then programmed or "mapped" using one of the several encoding strategies so that the electrical current delivered to the implant will be within this measured dynamic range between T-and C-levels. Obviously, T- and C-levels are much easier to obtain on adults and older children with postlingual hearing loss. Techniques for testing the T-levels in young children are similar to testing pure tone hearing thresholds, ranging from observational testing to conditioned play audiometry. Using a team approach with two audiologists is very helpful when programming or mapping the cochlear implants of young children. Obtaining the C-levels in children is a challenging task, with the audiologist often relying totally on behavioral observation. With children, audiologists will often evaluate only a limited number of electrodes spaced throughout the electrode array during the initial hook-up and either estimate the levels for the other electrodes or only include the tested electrodes in the initial program.

After T- and C- levels are established and the MAP is created, the microphone is then activated so that the patient is able to hear speech and sounds in the environment. The initial reaction to speech varies among patients. Most adults describe speech as sounding mechanical and cartoonlike. Children often react with tears. This is understandable considering that they may have no concept of what sound and hearing is and may find the stimulation frightening. Often they are hearing their own voice, including their crying, for the first time. As they are calmed down, they often realize that when they stopped crying the stimulation stopped. This can be the first step to auditory awareness.

Acclimatization to sound: adaptation to sound stimulation that changes the measured T- and C-levels, allowing the individual to tolerate higher levels.

Most current generation systems have multiple memories that allow the audiologist to save more than one MAP in the speech processors. This is very helpful to the audiologist because, due to acclimatization to sound, the initial T-and C-levels are often not the final values. Higher current values can be used to make alternative MAPs, which can be saved into the processor's multiple memories so that patients have the option of increasing the power between clinic visits.

The patient and family should also be instructed on the daily care and maintenance of the system. They must know how to place the headset, change batteries, manipulate the controls, and troubleshoot the unit. Parents need to be shown how to check the system prior to putting it on the child. Spare cords or cable should be supplied. Suggestions on wearing the units using belts, harnesses, or clips should be given. Accessories should be explained and demonstrated. Warnings on the dangers of electrostatic discharge (ESD) should be given, as well as any other safety factors. Static electricity can corrupt stored programs or, in rare cases, cause damage to the internal unit when the external device is being worn. Parents are told to remove the device when their child plays on plastic slides or on other static-generating materials. Warranty and loss and damage insurance information should be covered.

Electrostatic discharge (ESD): occurs when static electricity (accumulation of electrical charge) transfers between two objects charged to different levels.

The patients or the parents of young users are asked to keep a diary or log of their listening experiences. They are asked to record both positive and negative experiences. Significant others are also asked to keep a record of their observations when they are with the implant user. This helps in reprogramming the units on subsequent visits and also in developing the most appropriate treatment plans.

Follow-up Programming and Therapy

The second programming session is usually performed within 1 week of the initial hook-up. Review of the patient diary and experiences with the implant are helpful in determining if the programs provided sufficient power for sound awareness and detection or if any sounds were uncomfortably loud, indicating that the C-levels were set too high. During this visit, the T- and C-values are reevaluated and new MAPs are placed in the processor.

During this session, an initial screening of the patient's abilities should be completed. Table 3.2 contains examples of tests commonly used for patients with cochlear implants. Children should be tested using various age-appropriate auditory training screening material. These results will help guide the treatment plan. Auditory training programs developed for aided children with hearing loss can be used with cochlear implant users as well. Excellent reviews of screening devices and suggestions for treatment plans can be found in Nevins and Chute (1996) and Estabrooks (1998).

For adults, several programmed therapy plans have been developed for implant users. These include screening tests to help the clinician in determining the starting point in the plans (Cochlear, 1998; Wayner & Abrahamson, 1998). Auditory training methods such as speech tracking are extremely helpful in both treatment and monitoring progress with the device.

The amount and length of therapy with the cochlear implant depend on the patient. In many cases, the implant user will receive device programming and monitoring at the cochlear implant center and other audiologic habilitation or rehabilitation and speech–language therapy through their schools or local audiologists and therapists. A coordinated effort on the part of all professionals and parents is very important in developing and implementing the treatment plans. Face to face meetings, teleconferencing, written reports, and email are all means of maintaining

Speech tracking: a therapeutic procedure in which subjects are presented with prose and asked to repeat verbatim what they hear (De Filippo & Scott, 1978).

TABLE 3.2
Examples of Tests Commonly Used for Patients with Cochlear Implants

AGE GROUP	TESTS
Preschool	Early Speech Perception Test (Moogs & Geers, 1990) Meaningful Auditory Integration Scale (MAIS; Robbins et al., 1991)
School age	Craig Lip-reading Inventory (Craig, 1992) Lexical Neighborhood Test (LNT; Kirk et al., 1995) Multisyllabic Lexical Neighborhood Test (MLNT; Kirk et al., 1995) NU-Chips (Elliott & Katz, 1980) Phonetically Balanced Kindergarten Test (PBK; Haskins, 1949)
Adults	CID Everyday Sentence Test (Silverman & Hirsh, 1955) Hearing in Noise Test (HINT; Nilsson et al., 1994) Minimal Auditory Capabilities Battery (MAC; Owens et al., 1981) NU-6 Monosyllabic Word Test (Tillman & Carhart, 1966)

Post-implant therapy is a key to successful cochlear implant use.

contact with all parties involved. Parent-maintained notebooks, which all professionals may use, are also excellent. By having the parent in charge of a notebook that has records and communications to be shared by professionals, the parent can be empowered to be part of the process. Teachers and therapists who are not familiar with implants need to be provided with literature on cochlear implants and given instructions on how to check and troubleshoot the devices. They need to understand that the cochlear implant is designed to give the child more auditory information. They can still use similar teaching techniques with these children as they used prior to the implant, but they need to raise their expectations concerning what the child can accomplish using audition.

Programming follow-ups for adult patients with postlingual hearing loss usually consist of approximately six visits in the first 2 months of use, then at 3 months, 6 months, and annually thereafter. For young children the programming schedule suggested is weekly visits for 2 months, then at 6 months, 9 months, and every 6 months thereafter. These schedules can be modified to include more or less visits depending on the person's adaptation to the implant, auditory responsiveness, and ease of programming.

■ VARIABLES AFFECTING PERFORMANCE

Patient performance varies greatly among cochlear implant users. Many users are able to achieve open-set speech recognition even in the presence of background noise, whereas some patients receive only improvement in their speechreading abilities and awareness of environmental sounds. Age of onset, length of deafness, age of implantation, length of implant use, etiology of the hearing loss, nerve survival, mode of communication, cochlear implant technology, surgical issues, audiologic habilitation and rehabilitation methods, and motivation are examples of variables that affect success with the implant. Some of these are known factors, such as age of onset and length of deafness. Others are unknown quantities, such as the amount of nerve survival. Patients, parents, and significant others need to be made aware of the many variables that can affect performance.

Nerve survival: the amount of VIII nerve fibers that are available for stimulation.

■ FUTURE TRENDS IN COCHLEAR IMPLANTS

Advances in cochlear implants are occurring rapidly in design, programming techniques, coding strategies, and determining candidacy. Both internal and external devices are becoming smaller. The introduction of behind-the-ear speech processors has provided cosmetic advantages that are particularly attractive to adolescent and young adult users.

The Nucleus 24 system has incorporated neural response telemetry (NRT) technology to help in programming difficult to test patients. NRT is a means of testing an electrically evoked action potential without the use of additional equipment. Although this technique is available to the clinician, at this time the information is currently only providing an estimate of T- and C-levels (Abbas & Brown, 2000). Further development of this technique has the possibility of greatly enhancing the programming of young children and those patients who are unable to give accurate behavioral responses.

Currently, the standard procedure is to implant one ear only. Research into the possible benefits of implanting binaurally is being done in both the United States and Europe. Whereas the initial results seem promising, caution needs to be taken, especially with children. Outcome measures need to show that there is a favorable cost–benefit advantage of doing the procedure in both ears. This cost is not only monetary. One must consider the possibility that some future device may be developed that could only be used in an ear that had never had an implant. With the rapid changes in technology, if the child only has the implant in one ear, the other ear would be available so that the new procedure could be performed.

Neural response telemetry (NRT): allows the implant system to function as a miniature evoked potential system by sampling and recording action potentials generated by electrical stimulation.

■ AUDITORY BRAINSTEM IMPLANT

An auditory brainstem implant (ABI) has been developed for individuals with neu-rofibromatosis who are deafened from bilateral VIII nerve tumors. The implant is placed on the cochlear nucleus of the brainstem during the surgery to remove the tumor. To date, over 100 patients have received the ABI, and in early November 2000 the Nucleus 24 ABI was approved by the USFDA for use in cases of neurofi-bromatosis for patients over the age of 12 years (Cochlear, 2000). Results with this implant are similar to early generation multielectrode implants and show promise to those who have not been able to benefit from cochlear implants because they lack functioning VIII nerves.

■ VESTIBULAR REHABILITATION

Vestibular rehabili-tation: treatment techniques to aid in the recovery from vestibular weakness or dizziness.

Vertigo or dizziness is a common problem, particularly among the older adult pop-ulation. Twenty million Americans have vestibular problems, with about 12 million of these being over age 65. The traditional medical method of treatment has been primarily through medications or surgery. Unfortunately, these approaches have not been found to be effective in the majority of cases. Many patients are counseled that they may just have to live with the problem, which can significantly affect the quality of their lives. Vestibular rehabilitation is a new and promising area for those patients who suffer from balance problems, and an increasing number of au-diologists have become involved in providing some forms of this type of rehabili-tation in recent years.

The goals of vestibular rehabilitation include reducing symptoms, increasing mobility and independence, and minimizing the risk of falls. A variety of vestibu-lar rehabilitation (VR) therapy approaches is currently used. Adaptation therapy is often used in cases of unilateral vestibular dysfunction. Physical exercises are given to the patient to help rebalance the vestibular system. In the case of bilateral vestibular dysfunction, substitution therapy can help the person use alternative sen-sory inputs, such as vision, to compensate for the balance problem. The exercises used in the treatment plans can range from doing head movements to manipulat-ing through obstacle courses. For cases diagnosed with a condition called benign paroxymal positional vertigo (BPPV), simple head–body maneuvers, termed cana-lith repositioning procedures, are often used successfully to minimize or eliminate dizziness (Desmond, 2000).

■ TINNITUS REHABILITATION

Tinnitus: a ringing or buzzing sound in the ear that is not caused by external sound simulation.

Another common problem is tinnitus or ringing in the ear. The American Tinnitus Association estimates that there are approximately 50 million tinnitus sufferers in the United States. The amount of handicap that tinnitus causes varies greatly across the population. Some persons who have constant ringing are able to deal with it

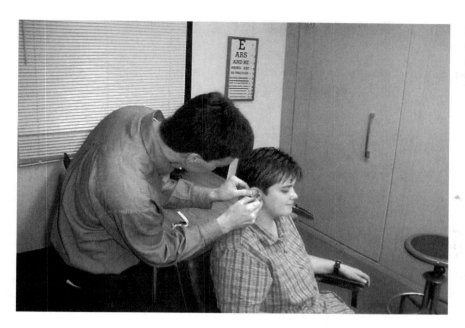

A tinnitus masker can be an effective option for some individuals experiencing excessive tinnitus.

quite well and do not let it interfere with their lives. On the other hand, tinnitus can become so handicapping that it can lead to suicide. Tinnitus is not a disorder in itself, but a symptom. Causes include hearing loss, medications, noise exposure, trauma, or illness. In about half the cases of severe tinnitus the etiology is unknown.

As with vestibular problems, medical treatments have not proved successful in alleviating the majority of cases of severe tinnitus. Again patients have often been counseled that they must learn to live with the problem. Nonmedical treatments such as the use of tinnitus maskers and habituation therapy are now being used successfully in many of these cases. A tinnitus masker can be used alone or in combination with a hearing aid. A simple masker device generates a noise that can be controlled by the patient. The masker signal can be white noise, broadband noise, or narrowband noise, and the patient is able to adjust the level of the sound until his or her tinnitus cannot be heard. When used in conjunction with amplification, the masking generator is built into the hearing aid.

Habituation therapy has also been found to be successful in many patients. In tinnitus retraining therapy the patient is taught to habituate to the tinnitus, whereby the tinnitus becomes part of his or her subconscious. Sound generators are used in this approach. The intensity level of the noise is set where the patient perceives it just below the level of the tinnitus. It is recommended that the patient use these generators for at least 8 hours a day. The patient can then learn to habituate to noise, with the goal of learning to habituate to the tinnitus. This therapy is long term in most cases and can take as much as 18 to 24 months. Appropriate directive counseling is also a necessary part of this program (Sandlin & Olsson, 2000).

Habituation: to make part of the subconscious by repetition.

- The scope of audiologic rehabilitation has increased dramatically in the past two decades, and now includes cochlear implants and other areas such as tinnitus and vestibular management.
- Cochlear implants offer a promising alternative for sound stimulation to individuals of all ages who receive limited benefits from traditional amplification.
- Worldwide, over 30,000 persons have been implanted with CIs.
- Candidacy for a cochlear implant involves a number of important issues, including the motivation and attitude of the individual or family regarding the role of hearing.
- Successful cochlear implant programs include an extensive amount of post-surgical training and follow a multidisciplinary approach.
- Vestibular problems such as balance or vertigo are experienced by millions of individuals.
- In addition to surgical and medical treatment strategies, persons with balance problems are being treated through a variety of therapy approaches referred to as vestibular rehabilitation (VR).
- Canalith repositioning often has been used successfully in cases suffering from vertigo.
- Tinnitus rehabilitation has become a viable alternative for millions of individuals afflicted with severe tinnitus.

R E C O M M E N D E D   R E A D I N G

Estabrooks, W. (1998). *Cochlear implants for kids.* Washington, DC: Alexander Graham Bell Association for the Deaf.

Nevins, M. E., & Chute, P. M. (1996). *Children with cochlear implants in educational settings.* San Diego, CA: Singular Publishing Group.

Niparko, J. K. (2000). *Cochlear implants: Principles and practices.* Philadelphia: Lippincott Williams & Wilkins.

Waltzman, S. B., & Cohen, N. L. (2000). *Cochlear implants.* New York: Thieme Medical Publishers.

Wayner, D. S., & Abrahamson, J. E. (1998). *Learning to hear again with a cochlear implant: An audiologic rehabilitation curriculum guide.* Austin, TX: Hear Again.

R E C O M M E N D E D   W E B   S I T E S

Nucleus Cochlear Implant Systems
http://www.cochlear.com.html

Advanced Bionics Cochlear Implant Systems
http://www.cochlearimplant.com/index.html

Med EL Cochlear Implant Systems
http://www.medel.com/intro.html

National Association of the Deaf (NAD)
http://www.nad.org/infocenter/newsroom/papers/CochlearImplants.html

R E F E R E N C E S

Abbas, P. J., & Brown, C. J. (2000). Eeltrophysiology and device telemetry. In Waltzman, S. B., & Cohen, N. L. (Eds.). *Cochlear implants*. New York: Thieme.

Cochlear Corporation (1998). *Rehabilitation manual*. Englewood, CO: Author.

Cochlear Corporation (2000). *Nucleus24ABI: the multichannel auditory brainstem implant*. Englewood, CO: Author.

Craig, W. N. (1992). *Craig lip-reading inventory: Word recognition*. Englewood, CO: Resource Point.

DeFilippo, C. L., and Scott, B. L. (1978). A method for training and evaluating the reception of ongoing speech. *Journal of the Acoustical Society of America, 63,* 1186–1192.

Desmond, A. L. (2000). Vestibular rehabilitation. In Valente, M., Hosford-Dunn, H. & Roeser, R. J. (Eds). *Audiology Treatment*. New York: Thieme.

Elliott, L. L., & Katz, D. (1980). Development of a new children's test of speech discrimination (technical manual). St. Louis, MO: Auditec.

Estabrooks, W. (1998) *Cochlear implants for kids*. Washington DC: Alexander Graham Bell Association for the Deaf.

Haskins, H. A. (1949). A phonetically balanced test of speech discrimination for children. Masters thesis. Evanston, IL: Northwestern University.

Kirk, K. I., Pisoni, D. B., & Osberger, M. J. (1995). Lexical effects on spoken word recognition by pediatric cochlear implant users. *Ear & Hearing, 16,* 470–481.

Meyer, T., Svirsky, M., Kirk, K., & Miyamoto, R. (1998). Improvements in speech perception by children with profound prelingual hearing loss: Effects of device, communication mode, and chronological age. *Journal Speech Hearing Research, 41,* 846–858.

Miyamoto, R., Osberger, M., Robbins, A., Myres, W., & Kessler, K. (1993). Prelingually deafened children's performance with the Nucleus multichannel cochlear implant. *American Journal of Otology, 14,* 437–445.

Moogs, J. S., & Geers, A. E. (1990). *Early speech perception test for profoundly hearing-impaired children*. St. Louis, MO: Central Institute for the Deaf.

National Association of the Deaf. (October 6, 2000). *NAD position statement on cochlear implants*.

National Institutes of Health. (May 15–17, 1995). *Cochlear implants in adults and children national institutes of health, consensus development conference statement*.

Nevins, M. E., & Chute, P. M. (1996). *Children with cochlear implants in educational settings*. San Diego, CA: Singular Publishing Group.

Nilsson, M. J., Soli, S. D., & Sullivan, J. A. (1994). Development of the Hearing in Noise Test for the measurement of speech reception in quiet and in noise. *Journal of the Acoustical Society of America, 95,* 1085–1099.

Owens, E., Kessler, D. K., Tellen, C. C., & Shubert, E. D. (1981). Minimal Auditory Capabilities Battery (MAC) battery. *Hearing Aid Journal, 9,* 32.

Robbins, A. M., Renshaw, J. J., & Berry, S. W. (1991). Evaluating meaningful auditory integration in profoundly hearing-impaired children. *American Journal of Otolaryngology, 12* (Suppl.), 144–150.

Sandlin, R. E., & Olsson, R. T. (2000). Subjective tinnitus: Mechanisms and treatment. In Valente, M., Hosford-Dunn, H., & Roeser, R. J. (Eds.). *Audiology treatment.* New York: Theime.

Silverman, S. R., & Hirsh, I. J. (1955). Problems related to the use of speech in clinical audiometry. *Annals Otology Rhinology Laryngology, 64,* 1234–1244.

Tillman, T. W., & Carhardt, R. (1966). An expanded test for speech discrimination utilizing CNC monosyllabic words. Northwestern University test No. 6. Brooks Air Force Base, TX: USAF School of Aerospace Medicine Technical Report.

Waltzman, S. B., & Cohen, N. L. (1998). Cochlear implantation in children younger than 2 years old. *American Journal of Otology, 19,* 1083–1087.

Wayner, D. S., & Abrahamson, J. E. (1998). *Learning to hear again with a cochlear implant: An audiologic rehabilitation curriculum guide.* Austin, TX: Hear Again.

Wilson, B. S. (2000). Cochlear implant technology. In Niparko, J.K., et al. (Eds.). *Cochlear implants principles and practices.* Philadelphia: Lippincott Williams & Wilkins.

Zwolan, T. A. (2000). Selection criteria and evaluation. In Waltzman, S. B., & Cohen, N. L. (Eds.). *Cochlear implants.* New York: Theime.

Auditory Stimuli in Communication

Michael A. Nerbonne
Ronald L. Schow

■ INTRODUCTION

As humans, the importance that communication plays in our lives cannot be overstated. Communication can take a variety of forms and involves one or more of our sensory modalities. The form of communication most often used to express oneself, oral communication, involves utilization of speech. This creates an extraordinary dependence on the sense of hearing in order to receive and perceive accurately the complex network of auditory stimuli that comprise speech. The sense of hearing, therefore, is crucial to the process of oral communication.

The onset of a significant auditory impairment in an individual can seriously impede the ability to communicate. Although a hearing loss may trigger other difficulties of a psychosocial, educational, or vocational nature, the inability of the person with hearing impairment to communicate normally serves as a fundamental cause of these other problems. Based on the critical role of audition in communication, audiologic rehabilitation represents an extremely important process whereby an individual's diminished ability to communicate as the result of a hearing loss can, it is hoped, be sharpened and improved. One area of audiologic rehabilitation that has traditionally been included in this process is auditory training. This procedure generally involves an attempt to assist the child or adult with a hearing impairment in maximizing the use of whatever degree of residual hearing remains.

This chapter will provide information regarding auditory training with patients with hearing impairment, including objectives and applications, assessment of auditory skills prior to therapy, and exposure to some of the past and present approaches to providing auditory training. Because of the conviction that the professional providing auditory training must be familiar with the basic aspects of oral communication, information is also provided about the oral communication process. This includes the introduction of a communication model, information regarding auditory perception and the acoustics of speech, and a discussion of the possible effects of hearing loss on speech perception.

■ A COMMUNICATION MODEL

Although a portion of the communication that normally takes place between individuals is nonverbal, we remain heavily dependent on our ability to receive and interpret auditory stimuli presented during oral communication. Successful oral communication involves a number of key components that deserve elaboration so that the reader may gain an appreciation of the basic process. All oral communication must originate with a *source* or *speaker* who has both a purpose for engaging in communication and the ability to properly encode and articulate the thought to be conveyed. The actual thought to be expressed is termed the *message*. The message is made up of auditory stimuli organized in meaningful linguistic units. Visual cues are also provided by the speaker in conjunction with the production of the auditory message. Another critical component of the process is *feedback* of speech, which then provides an opportunity for any needed adjustments or corrections to occur. The communication situation in which the message is conveyed is referred to as the *environment*. Factors associated with the environment, such as the presence of competing background noise, can drastically alter the amount and quality of the communication that takes place. The final major component of the communication process is the *receiver* or *listener*, who is charged with the responsibility of receiving and properly decoding and interpreting the speaker's intended thought. The listener also provides additional feedback to the speaker about how the message is being received.

These basic components of the oral communication process and their sequence are found in Figure 4.1. All the major components are equally important in accomplishing the desired end—communication. Disruption or elimination of any one part may result in partial or complete failure of the communication process. Proper application of this communication model is of concern to us throughout the chapter and the entire book.

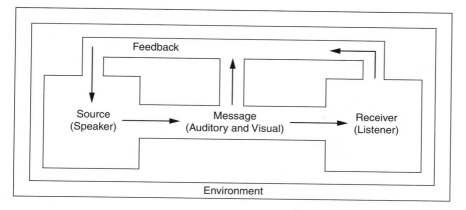

FIGURE 4.1

A simple model of the oral communication process.

■ AUDITORY PERCEPTION

Our ability to communicate verbally with others depends to a great extent on the quality of our auditory perception of the various segmental (individual speech sounds) and suprasegmental (rate, rhythm, intonation) elements that comprise speech. The following sections will focus on the basic aspects of auditory perception; the intensity, frequency, and duration components of speech; and transitional cues. The impact of hearing loss on speech perception is also discussed.

Development of Auditory Skills

It is both important and amazing to realize that the unborn infant possesses a functional auditory system that allows the child to begin perceiving auditory stimuli several weeks prior to birth. This is followed by further development and refinement in the neonate's auditory-processing skills in the days and weeks immediately following birth. As a result, the newborn infant not only is capable of detecting auditory stimuli, but also can make gross discriminations between various auditory signals on the basis of frequency and intensity parameters. This process of selective listening is extended to speech stimuli within a few weeks following birth. The rather rapid emergence of auditory skills, as described by Northern and Downs (1991), is crucial for the development of speech processing abilities, as well as the emergence of speech and language in the infant. Without the benefit of a normal-functioning auditory system and extensive exposure to auditory stimuli, however, the development of auditory and speech–language skills may be seriously affected.

Basic Perception Abilities

Although the human auditory system has sophisticated perceptual capabilities, it is limited, to some extent, in terms of the signals it can process. Optimally, the normal

Detection simply involves knowing that a sound is present, whereas discrimination is the ability to distinguish when two separate sounds are different.

human ear is capable of perceiving auditory signals comprising frequencies ranging from about 20 to 20,000 Hz. Stimuli made up entirely of frequencies below and above these limits cannot be detected. Intensity limits, as shown in Figure 4.2, vary as a function of the frequency of the auditory stimulus. The maximum range of intensity we are capable of processing occurs at 3000 to 4000 Hz and varies from about 0 to 130 dB SPL. Signals with intensity of less than 0 dB SPL are generally not perceived; in contrast, signals in excess of 130 dB SPL produce the sensations of feeling and pain rather than hearing.

In addition to the detection of acoustic signals, the human ear is also able to discriminate different stimuli on the basis of only minor differences in their acoustical properties. Our ability to discriminate changes in the frequency, intensity, or duration of a signal is influenced by the magnitude of each of the other factors. Stevens and Davis (1938) estimated that the normal ear is capable of perceiving approximately 340,000 distinguishable tones within the audible range of hearing. This total number was based only on frequency and intensity variations of the stimuli, and it suggests that our auditory system possesses amazing discrimination powers.

Acoustics of Speech

Knowledge about the acoustical properties of speech is important for understanding how speech is perceived. Therefore, basic information relevant to this process will be covered in the following sections.

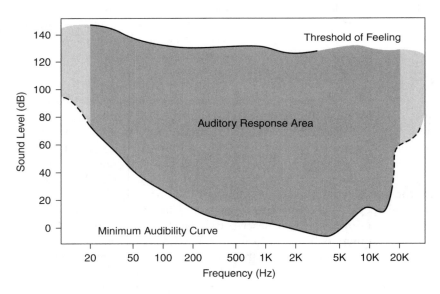

FIGURE 4.2

The auditory response area for persons with normal hearing.

Source: Durrant J. D. & Lovrinic J. H. (1995), *Bases of Hearing Science* (3rd ed.). Baltimore, MD: Williams & Wilkins. Reprinted by permission.

INTENSITY PARAMETERS OF SPEECH. The human ear is capable of processing signals within an intensity range approaching 130 dB; however, the range of intensity normally found in speech is relatively small. Fletcher (1953) reported that the average intensity of speech, when measured at a distance of approximately 1 meter from the speaker, approximates 65 dB SPL. This corresponds to a value of about 45 dB HL when expressed audiometrically. The average shout will approach 85 dB SPL (65 dB HL), and faint speech occurs at about 45 dB SPL (25 dB HL). Thus, a potential range of about 40 dB exists between the average intensities found with the softest and loudest speech that we are exposed to in common communication situations. Factors such as distance between the speaker and listener can influence the intensity levels for a given communication situation.

Considerable variability also exists in the acoustical energy normally associated with individual speech sounds. Table 4.1 lists the relative phonetic powers of the phonemes, as reported by Fletcher (1953). As illustrated, the most powerful phoneme, /ɔ/, possesses an average of about 680 times as much energy as the weakest phoneme, /θ/, representing an average overall difference in intensity between the two speech sounds of approximately 28 dB. Since a considerable amount of variability also exists in the intensity of individual voices, Fletcher estimated that, collectively, different speakers may produce variations in the intensity of these two phonemes as great as 56 dB. The relative power of vowels, according to Fletcher, is significantly greater than that of consonants, with the weakest vowel, /i/, having more energy than the most powerful consonant or semivowel, /ɝ/. Further, typical male speakers produce speech with an overall intensity that is about 3 dB greater than that of female speakers.

FREQUENCY PARAMETERS OF SPEECH. The overall spectrum of speech, as seen in Figure 4.3, is composed of acoustical energy from approximately 50 to 10,000 Hz (Denes & Pinson, 1993). Closer examination of this figure also reveals that the greatest amount of energy found in speech generally is associated with frequencies

TABLE 4.1

Relative Phonetic Power of Speech Sounds as Produced by an Average Speaker

ɔ	680	l	100	t	15
ɑ	600	ʃ	80	g	15
ʌ	510	ŋ	73	k	13
æ	490	m	52	v	12
ʊ	460	tʃ	42	ð	11
ɛ	350	n	36	b	7
u	310	dʒ	23	d	7
ɪ	260	ʒ	20	p	6
i	220	z	16	f	5
r	210	s	16	θ	1

Source: Speech and Hearing in Communication by H. Fletcher, 1953. Princeton, NJ: D. VanNostrand.

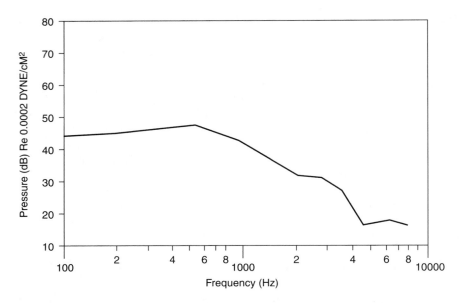

FIGURE 4.3

Long-interval acoustic spectrum of male voices. Measurement made with microphone 18 inches from speaker's lips.

Source: Miller, G. A. *Language and Communication.* New York: McGraw-Hill, p. 87. (1951).

below 1000 Hz. Above this frequency region, the energy of speech decreases at about a 9-dB/octave rate. The concentration of energy in the lower frequencies can be largely attributed to the fundamental frequency of the adult human voice (males, 130 Hz; females, 260 Hz) and the high intensity and spectral characteristics associated with the production of vowels. It should be noted that the fundamental frequency of children is substantially higher than that of adults, around 400 Hz (Hegde, 1995). As a result, the major energy concentration for this age group occurs higher on the frequency scale than for adults.

A key aspect of speech production and perception is the information associated with the segmental elements of speech. The segmental components consist of the numerous features associated with the individual vowel and consonant phonemes of the language. The vowels in English are composed mainly of low- and mid-frequency energy and, as indicated earlier, contribute most of the acoustic power in speech. Specifically, the frequency spectrum of each vowel contains at least two or three areas of energy concentration that result from the resonances that occur in the vocal tract during phonation. These points of peak amplitude are referred to as *formants,* and their location and pattern on the frequency continuum are unique for each vowel. Figure 4.4 illustrates the approximate location of the major formants associated with the vowels, as spoken by adult males. Formants provide important acoustic cues for the identification of vowels. However, it is important to note that even though each of the vowels has several formants, we need only hear the first two or three to be able to perceive accurately the vowel spoken (Peterson & Barney, 1952).

Formant refers to a band of frequencies that are resonated, or boosted in energy, by the vocal tract.

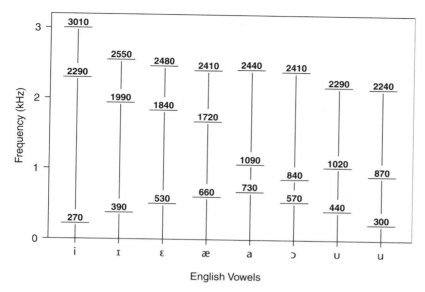

FIGURE 4.4

Mean values of formant frequencies of vowels of American English for adult males.

Source: Peterson, G. E., & Barney, H. L. (1952). Control methods used in the study of the vowels. *Journal of the Acoustical Society of America, 32,* 693–703.

The consonants in English display a broader high-frequency spectral composition than do vowels. This is particularly true for those consonants for which voicing is not utilized and whose production involves substantial constriction of the articulators. Although they contain relatively little overall energy, or intensity, when compared with vowels, consonants are extremely important in determining the intelligibility of speech. Consequently, accurate perception of consonants is vital.

Figure 4.5 contains estimates of the combined intensity and frequency values generally associated with the individual speech sounds in English. Specifically, the vertical axis presents the intensity levels in dB HL of the major components of each sound (if a particular sound has more than one major frequency component, each is noted by the same phonetic symbol), while the horizontal axis expresses the general frequency region associated with each speech sound. A close inspection of this figure discloses, as indicated earlier, that the vowels can generally be characterized as having considerable acoustic energy, for the most part confined to the low- and mid-frequency range. On the other hand, the consonants demonstrate decidedly less intensity overall and a much more diffuse frequency distribution as a group. The voiced consonants generally possess a greater amount of low- and mid-frequency energy, while the unvoiced consonants are made up of mid- and high frequencies. All consonants appear in the upper portion of the figure, reflecting their weaker intensity values.

In addition to the spectral properties associated with each of the consonants, it is important to identify the frequency characteristics related to the distinctive features associated with the production of these phonemes. Miller and Nicely's (1955) classification system includes five features: voicing, nasality, affrication, duration, and place of articulation. The voiced–voiceless distinction, as well as cues for nasality and affrication, are primarily carried by low-frequency energy. Information about place of articulation, on the other hand, is contained in the higher frequencies.

FIGURE 4.5

Intensity and frequency distribution of speech sounds in the English language. The values given should be considered only approximations, and are based on data reported by Fletcher (1953) and Ling & Ling (1978). Sounds with more than one major component appear in more than one location in the figure.

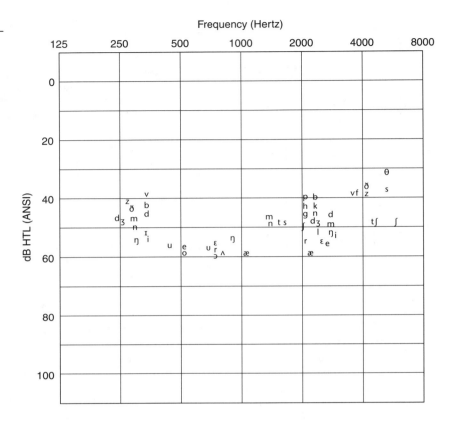

The segmental components of speech are the features associated with the individual speech sounds. The suprasegmental components (rhythm and prosody, pitch, rate) are overall features of speech that are superimposed on phonemes and words.

Table 4.2 categorizes each consonant phoneme by its place and manner of articulation and voicing features.

Another major component of speech is the suprasegmentals. The suprasegmental aspects are those features that are present in speech but are not confined to any single segment or phonemic element. Suprasegmental features, such as intonation, rhythm, stress, and pitch, are superimposed throughout speech as overall features. The suprasegmentals convey important information for speech perception, and this information is conveyed primarily in the low frequencies through acoustic cues associated with the fundamental frequency and other related aspects of speech.

TEMPORAL PARAMETERS OF SPEECH. The duration of individual speech sounds in our language covers a range from about 30 to 300 msec (Lehiste, 1976). A number of factors can significantly influence the duration of a given phoneme, making the direct comparison of duration among phonemes difficult. Yet the research of Crandall (1925), as cited by Fletcher (1953), suggests that vowels generally have a longer duration than consonants. Fletcher considered vowels to have average durations of between 130 and 360 msec, while the duration of consonants ranges from 20 to 150 msec. In spite of variations in absolute durational properties, in-

TABLE 4.2

Categorizing Consonants on the Basis of Manner and Place of Articulation and Voicing

Manner of Articulation	PLACE OF ARTICULATION						
	Bilabial	Labiodental	Linguadental	Alveolar	Palatal	Velar	Glottal
Plosives or Stops	p b			t d		k g	
Fricatives		f v	θ ð	s z	ʃ ʒ		h
Affricates					ʧ ʤ		
Nasal	m			n		ŋ	
Liquid				l,r			
Glide	w				j		

Note: Voiceless consonants are listed first, with voiced consonants underneath.

dividual phoneme duration does contribute toward speech perception. For instance, Minifie (1973) pointed out that the duration of stop consonants (examples: /p/ and /b/) varies systematically in a vowel-consonant-vowel context, with correct perception of the speech sound depending, to a degree, on the durational property of the phoneme produced.

As we all know, the overall rate of speech differs considerably from speaker to speaker. The research of Goldman-Eisler, as discussed by Lehiste (1970), demonstrates that the average rate of speech used during connected discourse ranges from about 4.4 to 5.9 syllables per second. The normal rate of speech, as expressed in phoneme output, averages about 12 phonemes per second, but can approach 20 phonemes when the speaker is excited (MacKay, 1987). Thus, the articulatory process is swift and capable of producing a flood of speech sounds and words that must be processed as effectively by the receiver, or listener, as they were produced by the speaker. Both of these are challenging tasks!

TRANSITIONAL CUES. The acoustic properties of a given phoneme spoken in isolation are altered significantly when the phoneme is produced with other phonemes conversational speech. In conversational speech the dynamic movements of the articulators in the production of adjacent phonemes produce acoustical byproducts, termed *transitional cues*. These cues make up a large portion of the total speech signal and are very important in the perception of speech, since they contain valuable information related to individual phoneme perception, especially for diphthongs and consonants.

For example, the second and third formants of vowels often contain transitions in frequency produced by the flowing movement of the articulators that signal the

Transitional cues result from the influences of coarticulation of individual speech sounds when combined into words, phrases, and so on.

presence of particular consonants that immediately follow. These formant transitions occur as the vocal resonances shift during articulation of vowels and consonants, which are combined in speech. Likewise, the durational aspects of vowels in connected speech can be altered to convey information regarding the phoneme to follow. For example, a voiced consonant in the final position is often accompanied by increased duration of the vowel immediately before it. The prolonged vowel duration contributes to our perception of voicing in the consonant which follows. This is an example of why formant transitional cues are a vital part of the speech signal and are quite important for speech perception.

Speech Perception and Comprehension

Our discussion has emphasized the segmental and suprasegmental aspects that constitute speech. The organization and production of these crucial elements into a meaningful oral message by the speaker and the accurate reception of this dynamic signal by the listener represent a highly complex, sophisticated process. However, mere reception of the segmented and suprasegmental elements of speech by a listener does not ensure proper perception of the message. Perception of speech implies understanding and comprehension, and the reception of speech by the auditory mechanism is only a first step in its perception.

In its most basic form, the perception of speech may be thought of as involving a number of important components. Among these are the following:

Detection. This basic aspect of auditory perception involves being aware of sound. Our ability to detect speech is influenced by our hearing acuity and the intensity level of the speech signal.

Discrimination. Speech discrimination refers to the ability to distinguish among the individual speech stimuli (phonemes, syllables, etc.) of our language.

Identification. The ability to identify or label what one has heard by pointing to, or naming.

Attention. A fundamental ingredient in the perception of speech relates to attending to or focusing on the speaker and the message being conveyed. The degree and quality of the listener's attention will influence how well speech is perceived.

Memory. A key component in speech perception is the ability to retain or store verbal information for relatively brief periods or, in some instances, extended lengths of time. Memory is also fundamental to other components of speech perception and enables us to combine individual speech units for the purpose of deriving meaning from an entire verbal message, rather than from each individual unit of the message.

Closure. The perceived speech elements must be brought together into a meaningful whole. This process, termed closure, helps a person to recognize speech even when some cues are absent, as with hearing loss.

Comprehension. Full perception and understanding of the meaning of an auditory message.

Our task in audiologic rehabilitation should be to take into consideration what is currently known concerning speech perception as we work with individuals with hearing impairments.

Speech Perception and Hearing Loss

Our success in processing speech is closely related to a number of important factors, and some of these will be discussed in the next section.

PHYSICAL PROPERTIES. Information concerning the physical properties of speech is most relevant when considering the relationship between the perception of speech and hearing loss, for the degree of our success in processing speech appears closely related to our ability to receive the coded acoustical information which makes up the signal.

The normal ear is well equipped to receive and process speech in most situations. Since speech is normally presented at average intensity levels of around 45 dB HL, it is well within the sensitivity range of the normal human ear. Also, although we are capable of hearing auditory signals ranging in frequency from about 20 to 20,000 Hz, only a portion of the entire range is required for the reception of speech, since speech contains energy from roughly 50 to 10,000 Hz. Consequently, in most listening conditions, those with normal hearing will have no difficulty in adequately hearing the speech sounds found in oral communication.

The same does not hold true for persons with hearing impairment. No longer are the intensity and frequency ranges of the impaired ear always sufficient to provide total perception of the speech signal. One or both of these stimulus parameters may be limited such that it becomes difficult to hear specific speech sounds adequately for identification purposes. For example, a person with 50-dB thresholds from 2000 to 8000 Hz would have considerable difficulty perceiving the phonemes with spectral compositions that primarily involve those higher frequencies. The information in Figure 4.5 regarding the relative frequency and intensity characteristics of individual speech sounds as spoken at a typical conversation level helps in understanding why this occurs.

While factors such as type of hearing loss and test materials can influence the outcome of investigations concerning hearing loss and the perception of phonemes, some general patterns of speech-perception difficulties have been observed for persons with hearing loss. For instance, most hearing-impaired listeners experience only minimal difficulty in vowel perception (Owens, Benedict, & Schubert, 1971). Specifically, in their research the vowel phonemes /ɛ/ and /o/ were found to have the highest probability of error. Only when the degree of impairment is severe to profound does the perception of vowels become significantly altered (Erber, 1979). Consonant perception, however, presents a far more difficult listening task for those with hearing impairment. Owens (1978) found phonemes such as /s/, /p/, /k/, /d/, and /θ/ to be among the most frequently missed by adults with sensorineural hearing loss. He also found misperceptions to be more frequent for phonemes in the final position of words than in the initial position. The most common errors in consonant phoneme perception occur with the place of articulation feature, followed by manner of articulation. Errors in the perception of nasality and voice among consonants are generally far less frequent.

Owens and his colleagues conducted a series of investigations regarding the perception of consonants. In one such study Owens et al. (1972) examined the relationship between the configuration of the audiogram and the specific consonant perceptual errors made by a group of hearing-impaired individuals. The /s/, /ʃ/, /ʧ/, /ʤ/ and the /t/ and /θ/ in the initial position only were found to be difficult for listeners with sloping configurations on the audiogram. The authors noted that these phonemes became increasingly difficult to hear accurately as the steepness of the sloping high-frequency hearing loss increased. Correct recognition of /s/ and the initial /t/ and /θ/ were found to be closely related to hearing sensitivity above 2000 Hz, while perception of /ʃ/, /ʧ/, and /ʤ/ was very dependent on sensitivity between 1000 and 2000 Hz. These findings point out the crucial role which hearing in this frequency region plays in the perception of several consonant phonemes. A similar study by Sher and Owens (1974) with listeners having high-frequency impairments confirmed that individuals with normal hearing to 2000 Hz and a sharp-sloping sensitivity loss for frequencies above that experience difficulty in adequately hearing a number of consonant phonemes. These authors pointed out that information concerning specific phoneme errors is useful in establishing audiologic rehabilitation strategies for persons with hearing losses of this type.

As can be seen, the actual overall degree of difficulty in speech perception imposed on an individual is related to the intensity and frequency features of the hearing loss found on the conventional audiogram. However, difficulty with speech perception can also be influenced by other related variables, which will be discussed elsewhere in this chapter and throughout the text. Therefore, while the audiogram usually is our most useful single predictor of a person's speech perception abilities, other factors to be discussed in the next section must be considered as well.

REDUNDANCY AND NOISE. The perception of speech is a highly complex process that involves more than the acoustics of speech or the hearing abilities of the listener, even though these are important variables, to be sure. Ultimately, for oral communication to be successful, sufficient information must be present in the message of interest for it to be perceived. The amount of information available for a given communication situation is closely associated with the concepts of redundancy and noise.

Conversational speech generally can be described as being highly redundant. That is, it contains information from a variety of sources which is available for a listener to use in comprehending a message, even though portions of the communication may not have been heard. The degree of redundance in oral communication varies from one expression to the next, so the extent to which a listener can predict what was said will also vary. Basically, the more redundant a message, the more readily it can be perceived by the listener, especially in difficult listening situations. A number of factors present in a given communication situation can influence the amount of redundancy present, and Table 4.3 provides a list of some of these.

Among the many factors associated with the redundancy, or predictability, found in conversational speech for the listener to use for perception are structural,

> The redundancy of speech relates to its predictability; the greater the redundancy, the better the odds will be that a listener can guess what was said, even when he or she did not hear the entire message.

TABLE 4.3

A Partial List of Factors That Can Influence the Amount of Redundancy in Speech

Within the speaker	Compliance with the rules of the language
	Use of appropriate articulation, intonation, stress
	Size and appropriateness of the vocabulary used to convey the message
Within the message	Number of syllables, words, etc.
	Amount of context
	Frequency composition of the speech signal
	Intensity of the speech signal
Within the communication environment	Amount of acoustic noise
	Degree of reverberation
	Number of situational cues present that are related to the message
Within the listener	Familiarity with the rules of the language
	Familiarity with the vocabulary of the message
	Knowledge of the topic of conversation
	Hearing abilities

Source: Adapted from Sanders, 1971.

semantic, and situational constraints (see Table 4.4). Structural constraints relate to the predictable manner in which linguistic units are chained together according to the rules associated with acceptable English. The selection and use of phonemes and words in an utterance are strongly influenced by these rules, making it easier for the listener to predict what is to follow after having heard only the initial portion of the sentence. Such syntactic clues can be used in conjunction with another factor related to redundancy, namely semantic constraints, which allow the listener to predict the type of vocabulary and expressions to be used based on the general semantic content of the expression. When the topic of conversation is food, for example, the listener can expect to hear a rather restricted range of vocabulary peculiar to that particular topic. Use of this small range of words will increase the redundancy of the message, making it easier to predict what is said. Situational constraints also create redundancy. Our conversational partner, the location of the conversation, the time of day it takes place, and other similar factors all influence what we say and how we say it, which also can make conversational speech more predictable. All these types of constraints, along with other factors listed in Table 4.3, collectively produce the redundancy that makes the perception of speech easier for us all.

Noise in oral communication refers to a host of factors that can actually reduce the amount of information present for the listener to use. In this context, "noise" refers to a variety of variables that can be counterproductive to communication, not just competing auditory noise. Table 4.5 provides a partial list of the potential sources of noise associated with oral communication with which the listener must contend. Each of these factors may reduce the amount of information in a spoken

TABLE 4.4
Levels of Linguistic Constraints Available to Enhance Speech Perception

Phonological constraints: Refers to the fact that rules govern how speech acts (e.g., phonemes) can be grouped together to produce words. For example, within any English word, the phoneme /z/ is not likely to be preceded by the phoneme /t/.

Lexical constraints: Refers to the fact that in any given language, the number of words that exist is finite. Moreover, some words are more familiar than others and some words are used more frequently than others. For example, during a conversation the word *telephone* is more likely to be uttered than the word *xylophone*.

Syntactic constraints: Refers to the fact that every language is governed by a set of grammatical rules that specifies the relationship between words used to communicate. For example, adjectives may be used to qualify nouns (as in "the *blue* shoes"); adjectives are not used to qualify verbs (as in "he *blue* ran").

Semantic constraints: Refers to the fact that the words used in a sentence are usually related to each other in a meaningful way. For example, although the sentence "Put the salt on the cloud" is syntactically correct; semantically, it is highly improbable.

Topical constraints: Refers to the fact that language usually takes place within a physical and social context. Generally, the use of language bears some relationship with the context in which it is used. For example, in a stadium, during a football game, it is more likely that the topic of discussion will center around sports-related activities than around religious beliefs and values.

Pragmatic constraints: Refers to the fact that language is governed by social norms that determine how it is used within a given community or situation. These rules are used to make the use of language more efficient for the purpose of exchanging ideas and to avoid confusion. For example, during a conversation, generally only one person talks at a time and there are rules that govern turn-taking.

Source: Adapted from Gagne & Jennings (2000).

TABLE 4.5
Some Potential Sources of Noise in Oral Communication

Within the speaker	Poor syntax Abnormal articulation Improper stress or inflection
Within the communication environment	Abnormal lighting Competing or distracting visual stimuli Competing or distracting auditory stimuli Reverberation
Within the listener	Lack of familiarity with the rules of the language Inability to identify the topic of the message Poor listening skills

Source: Adapted from Sanders, 1971.

message, thus reducing the amount of redundancy, or predictability, which is available for the listener to use in perceiving speech.

Thus, the degree of information available for the listener to use in perceiving a message is influenced in a positive or negative manner by a number of related variables that are part of oral communication. For the listener, particularly one with hearing impairment, the importance of each of these variables to the process of speech perception cannot be overstated.

■ THE AUDITORY TRAINING PROCESS

Traditionally, auditory training has been considered a major component of the audiologic rehabilitation process. Thus, its potential in assisting those with hearing loss has been expressed in major textbooks within the field of audiology, both in the past (Davis & Silverman, 1960; Oyer, 1966; Davis & Hardick, 1981) and recently (Alpiner & McCarthy, 2000; Tye-Murray, 1998).

The intent of the next major section of this chapter is to familiarize the reader with both the traditional and the current forms of auditory training and how they fit into the entire audiologic rehabilitation process.

Definition and Application of Auditory Training

Numerous attempts have been made to define auditory training in the past. Though similar in some respects, these definitions vary considerably according to the orientation of the definer and special considerations dictated by factors associated with hearing loss, such as its degree and time of onset.

Probably the most commonly referred to definition of auditory training is attributed to Carhart (1960), who considered auditory training a process of teaching the child or adult with hearing impairment to take full advantage of available auditory clues. As a result, Carhart recommended an emphasis in therapy on developing an awareness of sound, gross discrimination of nonverbal stimuli, and gross and fine discrimination of speech.

Later, in discussing the use of auditory training with children, Erber (1982) described it as "the creation of special communication conditions in which teachers and audiologists help hearing-impaired children acquire many of the auditory perception abilities that normally hearing children acquire naturally without their intervention" (p. 1). Erber stated further that "Our intent is to help the hearing-impaired child apply his or her impaired auditory sense to the fullest capacity in language communication, regardless of the degree of damage to the auditory system. Usually progress is achieved through careful application of amplification devices and through special teaching techniques" (p. 29).

The hearing abilities that a person with hearing loss has left are often referred to as residual hearing.

When considering auditory training for adults, two general objectives are usually relevant: (1) learning to maximize the use of auditory and other related cues available for the perception of speech and (2) adjustment and orientation to facilitate the optimum use of amplification, including cochlear implants and tactile devices.

Inherent in the various views of auditory training, as well as those of other professionals in audiologic rehabilitation, is the notion that persons with hearing impairment can be trained to maximize the use of whatever amount of hearing they possess. The ultimate aim of auditory training is, therefore, to achieve maximum communication potential by developing the auditory sensory channel to its fullest. In a sense, auditory training is often designed to improve one's listening skills, which will result in improved speech perception. Although the primary goal of auditory training is usually to maximize receptive communication abilities, it is important to point out that achieving this basic goal can result in other important accomplishments as well, including acquisition of more proficient speech and language skills, educational and vocational advancement, and successful psychosocial adjustment. As indicated earlier, if the communication skills of persons with hearing impairment can be improved, other areas of concern, such as educational progress, will be facilitated as well.

Early Efforts in Auditory Training

The earliest efforts in auditory training date back to the 18th century. Individuals in Europe used auditory training with the hearing impaired throughout the 1800s, with some success noted. Impressed with their accomplishments, Goldstein (1939) introduced a similar approach to auditory training in the United States in the late 1890s and early 1900s. Known as the Acoustic Method, this approach centered around systematic stimulation with individual speech sounds, syllables, words, and sentences to improve speech perception and to aid deaf persons in their own speech production. The Acoustic Method was utilized in a number of facilities throughout the country, including the Central Institute for the Deaf in St. Louis, Missouri, which Goldstein founded. Goldstein exerted a significant influence on the thinking of many professionals over the years regarding the potential of auditory training with persons with hearing impairment.

Until World War II, the primary focus of auditory training was its use with severely/profoundly deaf children in an effort to facilitate speech and language acquisition and increase their educational potential. However, the activities that occurred at VA audiology centers during World War II served to demonstrate on a large scale that adults with mild to severe hearing impairments could profit from auditory training as well. Led by Raymond Carhart, personnel in these centers developed and applied auditory training exercises with large numbers of adults, most with noise-induced hearing loss. Carhart (1960) later authored a book chapter that influenced the thinking of audiologists regarding auditory training with children and adults for years to come.

Raymond Carhart made many contributions to the profession of audiology and is considered by many to be the Father of Audiology.

CARHART. Carhart's approach to auditory training for prelingually impaired children was based on his belief that since listening skills are normally learned early in life, the child possessing a serious hearing loss at birth or soon after will not move through the normal developmental stages important in acquiring these skills. Likewise, when a hearing loss occurs in later childhood or in adulthood, some of the person's auditory skills may become impaired even though they were intact prior to the onset of the hearing loss. In each instance, Carhart believed that auditory training was warranted.

CHILDHOOD PROCEDURES. Carhart outlined four major steps or objectives involved in auditory training for children with prelingual deafness:

1. Development of awareness of sound
2. Development of gross discriminations
3. Development of broad discriminations among simple speech patterns
4. Development of finer discriminations for speech

Development of an awareness of auditory stimuli and the significance of sound involves having the child acknowledge the presence of sound and its importance in his or her world. The development of gross discrimination initially involves demonstrating with various noisemakers that sounds differ. Once the child can successfully discriminate grossly different sounds, he or she is exposed to finer types of discrimination tasks that include variation in the frequency, intensity, and durational properties of sound. When the child is able to recognize the presence of sound and can perceive gross differences with nonverbal stimuli, Carhart's approach calls for the introduction of activities directed toward learning gross discrimination for speech signals. The final phase consists of training the child to make fine discriminations of speech stimuli in connected discourse and integrating an increased vocabulary to enable him or her to follow connected speech in a more rapid and accurate fashion. Carhart also felt that the use of vision by the child should be encouraged in most auditory training activities.

ADULT PROCEDURES. Because adults who acquire a hearing loss later in life retain a portion of their original auditory skills, Carhart recommended that auditory training with adults focus on reeducating a skill diminished as a consequence of the hearing impairment. Initially, Carhart felt that it was important to establish "an attitude of critical listening" in the individual. This involves being attentive to the subtle differences among sounds and can involve a considerable amount of analytic drill work on the perception of phonemes that are difficult for the adult with hearing impairment to perceive. Lists of matched syllables and words that contain the troublesome phonemes, such as she–fee, so–tho, met–let, or mash–math, are read to the individual, who repeats them back. Such training should also include phrases and sentences, with the goal of developing as rapid and precise a recognition of the phonetic elements as is possible within the limitations imposed by the person's hearing loss. Speechreading combined with a person's hearing was also encouraged by Carhart during a portion of the auditory training sessions.

Because we often communicate under less than ideal listening circumstances, Carhart advocated that auditory training sessions for adults be conducted in three commonly encountered situations: (1) relatively intense background noise, (2) the presence of a competing speech signal, and (3) listening on the telephone. This emphasis on practice in speech perception under listening conditions with decreasing amounts of redundancy has been emphasized more recently by Sanders (1993) and numerous other audiologic rehabililationists.

According to Carhart, the use of hearing aids is vital in auditory training, and he recommended that they be utilized as early as possible in the auditory training program. These recommendations were consistent with Carhart's belief that systematic exposure to sound during auditory training was an ideal means of allowing a person to adequately adjust to hearing aids and assist in using them as optimally as possible.

Persons interested in more specific information concerning Carhart's auditory training strategies should review his chapter in the second edition of Davis and Silverman's *Hearing and Deafness* (1960).

■ CURRENT APPROACHES TO AUDITORY TRAINING

The basic intent of more recent methods of auditory training remains the same, that is, to maximize communication potential by developing to its fullest the auditory channel of the person with hearing impairment. This next section will discuss how this form of audiologic rehabilitation currently is being applied with the hearing impaired.

Candidacy for Auditory Training

In recent times, auditory training therapy has been utilized routinely with certain types of patients, but only occasionally with most others. Its most common use is with children with prelingual sensorineural hearing impairment, especially those with moderate to profound degrees of loss with congenital onset. Another targeted population for auditory training in recent times has been cochlear implant recipients, both children and adults. There is strong evidence that a structured program of listening training enhances the benefits derived from a cochlear implant. Although extensive auditory training typically is not utilized with hard of hearing adults, certain factors, such as exceptionally poor speech perception and/or a severe to profound degree of loss, may result in its application on a selective basis.

Assessment of Auditory Skills

An integral part of a comprehensive auditory training program is the assessment of individual auditory skills. Before, during, and at the conclusion of auditory training the clinician should attempt to evaluate the auditory abilities of the person with hearing impairment. Information of this nature is important for several reasons, including:

1. Determining whether or not auditory training appears warranted.
2. Providing a basis for comparison with posttherapy performance, to assess how much improvement in auditory performance, particularly speech perception, has occurred.
3. Identifying specific areas of auditory perception to concentrate on in future auditory training.

The nature of the auditory testing that takes place will vary considerably depending upon a number of variables, such as the age of the client, his or her language skills, and the type and degree of the hearing loss. The clinician must exercise care in selecting test materials for the individual patient, particularly with regard

Informal assessment of auditory awareness/localization skills.

to the language levels required for a given test. This requires that a variety of tests of auditory perception, both formal and informal, be available for assessment purposes so that the particular needs of each individual can be met adequately.

EVALUATING CHILDREN. Both the degree and the sophistication of testing appropriate for young children are limited by their physical and cognitive development. Therefore, informal testing and observation are relied upon heavily with this age group. For the infant, the initial goal of assessment for auditory training purposes may not center on speech perception. Rather, an effort may be made to identify the extent to which auditory skills have emerged, such as gross discrimination and localization of a variety of stimuli. Once this information is known, a specific program for developing auditory skills, such as that described in Chapter 9, can be implemented in conjunction with therapy related to development of speech and language.

For older children, more formal, in-depth assessment of overall speech perception abilities generally is possible. Specifically, materials have been developed that require the child to respond in a prescribed manner to individual words or phonemes presented at a comfortable listening level. Some of the commonly used formal tests of this type that have been designed for assessing speech perception in children with hearing impairment include the following:

Tests use either a closed-set or open-set format. A closed-set format for a test of speech perception involves presenting a test item (e.g., a word) and having the listener choose the correct response from a limited set of options (multiple choice). In an open-set format, the listener can respond with any word he or she feels is correct.

1. *Word Intelligibility by Picture Identification (WIPI) by Ross and Lerman (1970).* The authors of the WIPI modified an existing test for children (Myatt & Landes, 1963) to include only vocabulary appropriate for children with hearing impairment. The WIPI includes four lists that each contain 25 monosyllabic words. The child provides a picture-pointing response in a closed-set format. According to the authors, the test is suitable for use with hearing handicapped children with limited receptive and expressive language abilities.

2. *Northwestern University Children's Perception of Speech (NU-CHIPS) by Katz and Elliott (1978).* This test consists of 50 monosyllabic nouns that have been scrambled to form four individual lists. Like the WIPI, the NU-CHIPS uses a response format that requires that the child point to the one picture from several options which best represents the test items. Because of the basic vocabulary included and the nonverbal response format, use of the NU-CHIPS with many children with hearing loss appears appropriate.

3. *Five Sound Test by Ling (1976, 1989).* Five isolated phonemes (/a/, /u/, /i/, /s/, and /ʃ/) are spoken to the child at a normal conversational level. Those with usable residual hearing up to 1000 Hz should be able to detect the vowels. Children with some residual hearing up to 2000 Hz should detect /ʃ/, and those with residual hearing up to 4000 Hz (not worse than 90 dB HL at 4000 Hz) should detect /s/. In certain instances, Ling (1989) has advocated the use of a sixth sound, /m/, to obtain more information concerning the perception of low-frequency stimuli.

Additional test batteries are designed to assess varied aspects of auditory skills development in children. Examples include the following:

Figure–ground refers to the ability to perceive a target signal that is presented simultaneously with other competing signals.

1. *Test of Auditory Comprehension (TAC), developed through the Audiologic Services of the Los Angeles County Schools (Trammel, 1981).* Designed for children ages 4 to 12 years with moderate to profound hearing losses, the TAC is the evaluation part of a comprehensive auditory skills instructional plan. The instrument has 10 subtests that assess several areas of auditory perception, including speech discrimination, memory sequencing, figure–ground discrimination, and story comprehension. Results of TAC subtests are used to establish baseline performance and direction for the companion auditory training curriculum.

2. *Glendonald Auditory Screening Procedure (GASP), developed at the Glendonald Auditory School for the Deaf in Australia (Erber, 1982).* GASP is based on a model of auditory perception described in the next section of this chapter (see Figure 4.6). The basic test battery associated with GASP consists of three subtests of speech perception: (1) phoneme detection, (2) word identification, and (3) sentence comprehension. The GASP phoneme detection subtest is similar in format to the Five Sound Test developed by Ling (1976). According to Erber, the results from

Speech Stimulus

	Speech Elements	Syllables	Words	Phrases	Sentences	Connected Discourse
Detection	1					
Discrimination						
Identification			2			
Comprehension					3	

Response Task

FIGURE 4.6

An auditory stimulus–response matrix showing the three GASP subtests: Phoneme Detection (1), Word Identification (2), and Sentence (Question) Comprehension (3).

Source: From N. Erber (1982). *Auditory Training.* Washington, DC: Alexander Graham Bell Association for the Deaf. Reprinted by permission.

GASP can aid in planning auditory training because the child's performance on the subtests is predictive of other, related auditory tasks.

3. *Developmental Approach to Successful Listening (DASL) Test, by Stout and Windle (1994).* This comprehensive test of auditory skills evaluates numerous aspects of sound awareness, phonetic listening, and auditory comprehension. Children from 3 years of age can be evaluated with the DASL Test, and some normative information is available for children with varying degrees of hearing loss.

These tests all attempt to take into account the limitations of hearing-impaired youngsters' receptive vocabulary level and their ability to respond orally. However, the variability observed in the receptive and expressive communication skills of these children makes it unwise to draw any firm generalizations about the specific age range of children for whom any of these tests are suited. Vocabulary age rather than chronological age is a key consideration in selecting the appropriate test to use.

EVALUATING ADULTS. A number of formal tests of speech perception also are available for use with adults. Any of the traditional monosyllabic word lists, such as the CID W-22s (Hirsh et al., 1952) or the Northwestern University Auditory Test No. 6 (Tillman & Carhart, 1966), may be employed to evaluate overall word-recognition abilities.

Other tests allow for more in-depth assessment of the perception of consonants, which can be especially difficult for persons with hearing impairment to perceive accurately. For example, Owens and Schubert (1977) produced a 100-item, multiple-choice consonant perception test called the California Consonant Test (CCT).

Word recognition testing typically involves presenting a 25- or 50-word list of monosyllabic words at a comfortable intensity level for the listener. A percent correct score is calculated.

Thirty-six of the test items assess consonant perception in the initial word position, while 64 items test perception in the final position. Each of the 100 items is presented to the listener in a closed-set, multiple-choice format, as shown in Figure 4.7. Research by Schwartz and Surr (1979) demonstrated that, compared to the NU-6's, the CCT is more sensitive to the speech recognition difficulties experienced by individuals with high-frequency hearing loss. Consequently, the CCT is often relied on in assessing the speech recognition abilities of adult patients.

Tests which employ sentence-type stimuli also can be informative. Kalikow, Stevens, and Elliott (1977) developed a test called Speech Perception in Noise, or SPIN. This test is unique in that it attempts to assess a listener's utilization of both linguistic and situational cues in the perception of speech. Sentence material is presented against a background of speech babble, with the listener's task being to identify the final word in the sentence. Ten 50-item forms of SPIN have been generated, each version containing sentences with either high or low predictability relative to the final word in each sentence. Examples of each are shown in Table 4.6. Bilger and colleagues (1979) have revised the forms to make them more equivalent to each other. The SPIN test can provide important information concerning how effectively a given listener makes use of contextual information in the perception of speech, in addition to providing insight regarding how the listener perceives the acoustical properties of speech.

The Central Institute for the Deaf (CID) Everyday Speech Sentences (Davis & Silverman, 1978) have been used extensively to evaluate a listener's ability to perceive connected discourse. They consist of ten 10-sentence sets, as shown in Table 4.7. The sentences vary in length and form and possess several characteristics associated with typical conversation.

Results of these tests, as well as others, such as the Modified Rhyme Test, should provide the clinician with specific information concerning a client's consonant perception in a word and/or sentence context, as well as the ability to comprehend speech in sentence form.

Speech babble is a recording of several people talking at once.

ROBE _____	MAP _____	BAIL _____
RODE _____	MATCH _____	JAIL _____
ROSE _____	MATH _____	DALE _____
ROVE _____	MAT _____	GALE _____

LASS _____	DIES _____	LEAF _____
LAUGH _____	DIED _____	LEASE _____
LATCH _____	DIVE _____	LEACH _____
LASH _____	DINE _____	LEASH _____

FIN _____	PEAK _____	RAISE _____
PIN _____	PEACH _____	RAID _____
KIN _____	PEAT _____	RAGE _____
TIN _____	PEEP _____	RAVE _____

FIGURE 4.7

Examples of multiple-choice test items for the California Consonant Test. (Owens & Schubert, 1977).

TABLE 4.6

Examples of Low- and High-Predictability Sentences from the SPIN Test

SENTENCE	LEVEL OF PREDICTABILITY
The honey bees swarmed round the *hive*.	High
The girl knows about the *swamp*.	Low
The cushion was filled with *foam*.	High
He had considered the *robe*.	Low

Source: Kalikow, Stevens, & Elliott (1977).

TABLE 4.7

Examples of a 10-Sentence Set of CID Everyday Speech Sentences. From Davis & Silverman (1978).

1. *It's time* to *go.*
2. *If* you *don't want these old magazines, throw them out.*
3. *Do* you *want to wash up?*
4. It's a *real dark night so watch your driving.*
5. *I'll carry* the *package* for *you.*
6. Did *you forget* to *shut off* the *water?*
7. *Fishing* in a *mountain stream* is my *idea* of a *good time.*
8. *Fathers spend* more *time* with their *children than* they *used to.*
9. *Be careful not to break your glasses!*
10. *I'm sorry.*

Source: Davis & Silverman, 1978.

Additional information about speech perception can be gained by introducing competing noise to the test situation and varying the degree of redundancy in the test material. Also, addition of visual cues via speechreading during administration of these tests in a bisensory condition can provide useful information regarding a person's overall integrative skills (see Chapters 5 and 10).

Owens and coworkers (1985) developed a comprehensive set of tests, the Minimal Auditory Capabilities (MAC) Battery, for assessing auditory and visual skills of patients with severe to profound hearing impairment. The level of difficulty of the MAC is suitable for individuals for whom conventional speech perception tests may be too challenging, such as with persons having profound hearing loss. Included in the MAC battery are 14 subtests that evaluate both basic and more complex auditory perception abilities involving a variety of listening tasks with speech. One of the subtests also assesses speechreading skills. The battery is presently being widely used in the evaluation of cases considered for a cochlear implant (see Chapter 12). Another assessment battery developed for this purpose is the Iowa Cochlear Implant Battery (Tyler, Preece, & Lowder, 1983). The Cochlear Corporation (1998) has combined portions of the MAC and Iowa batteries for use with cochlear implant candidates and recipients.

Bisensory refers to using hearing and vision together.

Methods of Auditory Training

The more current approaches to auditory training vary considerably. According to Blamey and Alcantara (1994), it is possible to categorize them into one of four general categories, based on the fundamental strategy stressed in therapy:

1. *Analytic:* attempts to break speech into smaller components (phoneme, syllable) and incorporate these separately into auditory training exercises. Examples include exercises that emphasize same–different discrimination of vowel or consonant phonemes in syllables (e.g., /bi–ba/) or words (e.g., /kIp–kIt/) or require the listener to identify a word within a closed-set response format (e.g., run–money–bat).

2. *Synthetic:* emphasizes a more global approach to speech perception, stressing the use of clues derived from the syntax and context of a spoken message to derive understanding. Training synthetically involves the use of meaningful stimuli (words, phrases, sentences). This might involve practicing sentence perception based on prior information about context (e.g., having lunch, a classroom discussion on government) or having the clinician name a topic and present related words or phrases that the individual must repeat back.

3. *Pragmatic:* involves training the listener to control communication variables, such as the level of speech, the signal-to-noise ratio, and the context or complexity of the message, in order to obtain the necessary information via audition for understanding to occur. For example, the person with hearing impairment practices how to effectively use conversation repair strategies, like asking questions or requesting that a statement be repeated or clarified, to comprehend a paragraph read by the clinician. A similar activity centers around the use of QUEST?AR (Erber, 1996). Here, the patient is given a series of questions related to a specified topic, such as those listed in Table 4.8. The patient asks the clinician each question. The clinician answers each question and the patient then must correctly repeat the answer given before moving on to the next question. This conversationlike therapy strategy can be done in an auditory-only or auditory-visual mode.

4. *Eclectic:* includes training that combines most or all of the strategies previously described.

> Signal-to-noise ratio refers to comparing the intensity of the signal you wish to hear with all the other auditory signals present in that listening situation.

While the auditory training programs to be described all have analytic, synthetic, or pragmatic tendencies, most would best be described as eclectic, since more than one general strategy for the training of listening skills typically is used with a given child or adult.

ERBER. A flexible and widely used approach to auditory training designed primarily for use with children has been described by Erber (1982). This adaptive method is based on a careful analysis of a child's auditory perceptual abilities through the use of the GASP assessment battery (described briefly in the earlier portion of this chapter devoted to assessment). Recall that GASP's approach to evaluating a child's auditory perceptual skills takes into account two major factors: (1) the complexity

TABLE 4.8

Topics and Questions from QUEST?AR[a]

Where did you go? museum, restaurant, post office, shopping camping, doctor, zoo, beach, airport, swimming, mountains, picnic, music lesson, Mars, supermarket, and so forth

Questions:

1. Why did you go there?
2. When did you go?
3. How many people went with you?
4. Who were they? (names)
5. What did you take with you?
6. Where is (the place where you went)?
7. How did you get there?
8. What did you see on the way?
9. What time did you get there?
10. What did you do first?
11. What did you see?
12. How many? What colour? etc.
13. What happened at (the place where you went)?
14. What else did you do?
15. What were other people doing at (the place where you went)?
16. What was the most interesting thing that you saw?
17. What was the most interesting thing that you did?
18. What did you buy?
19. What kind? What flavour? What colour? etc.
20. How much did it cost?
21. Did anything unusual happen? What?
22. How long did you stay?
23. What did you do just before you came home?
24. When did you leave?
25. How did you get home?
26. What happened on the way home?
27. What time did you get home?
28. How did you feel then?
29. When are you going back?
30. Do you think that I should go sometime? Why?

[a]QUESTions for Aural Rehabilitation.
Source: Erber, 1996.

of the speech stimuli to be perceived (ranging from individual speech elements to connected discourse) and (2) the form of the response required from the child (detection, discrimination, identification, or comprehension). Several levels of stimuli and responses are involved, as shown in Figure 4.6. The GASP test battery evaluates only the three stimulus–response combinations indicated in the figure. However, Erber encourages the use of other available test materials to evaluate other stimulus–response combinations from the matrix in Figure 4.6, when appropriate.

Once the child's auditory capabilities are determined, an auditory training program is outlined using the same stimulus–response model as discussed for GASP assessment, when establishing goals and beginning points for therapy. Those stimulus–response combinations found not to be processed well during the GASP assessment phase logically become the same combinations targeted in auditory training activities that follow. Erber's approach is flexible and highly adaptable to children with a wide variety of auditory abilities, since the stimulus and response combinations range from the simplest (phoneme detection) to the most complex (sentence comprehension) perceptual tasks.

Erber also described three general styles which the clinician may use during auditory training, depending on the communication setting. These styles differ in specificity, rigidity, and direction, and are described in Table 4.9. Adaptive procedures, where the child's responses to speech stimuli are used to determine the next

TABLE 4.9
Three General Auditory Training Approaches

Natural conversational approach	1. The teacher eliminates visible cues and speaks to the child in as natural a way as possible, while considering the general situational context and ongoing classroom activity.
	2. The auditory speech perception tasks may be chosen from any cell in the stimulus–response matrix, for example, sentence comprehension.
	3. The teacher adapts to the child's responses by presenting remedial auditory tasks in a systematic manner (modifies stimulus and/or response), derived from any cell in the matrix.
Moderately structured approach	1. The teacher applies a closed-set auditory identification task, but follows this approach activity with some basic speech development procedures and a related comprehension task. Thus, the method retains a degree of flexibility.
	2. The teacher selects the nature and content of words and sentences on the basis of recent class activities.
	3. A few neighboring cells in the stimulus–response matrix are involved (for example, word and sentence identification and sentence comprehension).
Practice on specific tasks	1. The teacher selects the set of acoustic speech stimuli and also the child's range of responses, prepares relevant materials, and plans the development of the task, all according to the child's specific needs for auditory practice.
	2. Attention is directed to a particular listening skill, usually represented by a single cell in the stimulus–response matrix (e.g., phrase discrimination).

Source: Auditory Training by N. Erber, 1982. Washington, D.C.: Alexander Graham Bell Association for the Deaf. Reprinted by permission.

activity, can be employed with any of these styles. In attempting to develop a child's auditory abilities, Erber (1982) stated:

> Auditory training need not follow a developmental plan where, for instance, you practice phoneme detection first and attempt comprehension of connected discourse last. Instead, you might use the "conversational approach" during all daily conversation, and apply the "moderately structured approach" as a follow-up to each class activity. During each activity, you will note consistent errors. Later, you might provide brief periods of specific practice with difficult material. In this way, you can incorporate auditory training into conversation and instruction, rather than treat listening as a skill to be developed independently of communication. (p. 105)

Erber's emphasis on integrating the development of auditory skills into all activities with children with hearing impairment is shared by many, including Sanders (1993) and Ling and Ling (1978), who recommend that auditory training "be viewed as a supplement to auditory experience and as an integral part of language and speech training" (p. 113). Thus, therapy directed toward the development of auditory and language skills can and should be done in an integrated, mostly seamless manner.

As mentioned earlier, Erber's levels of perception model (detection, discrimination, identification, and comprehension) is widely used with both children and adults in rehabilitation therapy involving the development and improvement of auditory and visual perceptual skills for speech perception.

DASL II. Stout and Windle (1994) have developed a sequential, highly structured auditory-training program called the Developmental Approach to Successful Listening II, or DASL II. Like Erber's (1982) approach, the DASL II consists of a hierarchy of listening skills that are worked on in relatively brief, individualized sessions.

The DASL II curriculum can be used with persons of any age, but mainly has been utilized with preschool and school-age youngsters using either hearing aids or cochlear implants. Three specific areas of auditory skill development are focused on:

1. *Sound awareness:* deals with the development of the basic skills of listening for both environmental and speech sounds. The care/use of hearing aids and cochlear implants are also included.
2. *Phonetic listening:* includes exposure to fundamental aspects of speech perception such as the duration, intensity, pitch, and rate of speech. The discrimination and identification of vowels and consonants in isolation and in words are included in this area.
3. *Auditory comprehension:* emphasizes the understanding of spoken language by the child with hearing impairment. Includes a wide range of auditory processing activities from basic discrimination of common words to comprehension of complex verbal messages in unstructured situations.

The authors have developed a placement test that enables the clinician to evaluate the child's auditory skills relative to each of these three main areas. Specific subskills are tested, making it possible to determine the particular listening skills which a child has or has not acquired. As with the GASP approach, information from the DASL II placement test enables the clinician to determine the appropriate placement of the child within the auditory skills curriculum. The test's developers provided numerous activity suggestions for the clinician. These address each of the many subskills of the three main areas of listening which make up DASL II. These are organized from the simplest to the most difficult listening task. The following example is a list of subskills related to sound awareness that are included in the DASL II. Similar subskill lists and related activities are provided by the developers for all components of DASL II.

DEVELOPING SOUND AWARENESS SUBSKILLS

1. Responds to the presence of a loud, low-frequency gross environmental sound. (Example: loud banging on a hard surface)
2. Responds to the presence of a loud speech syllable or word.
3. Responds to the presence of a variety of different gross environmental sounds.
4. Indicates when ongoing environmental sounds stop.
5. Indicates when a sustained speech syllable or word stops.
6. Indicates when teacher or parent turns both hearing aids (or processor) on or off.
7. Discriminates between presence of spoken syllable or word and silence.
8. Discriminates between a variety of familiar environmental sounds in a set of two choices.
9. Discriminates between a variety of familiar environmental sounds in a set of three choices.
10. Discriminates between a variety of environmental sounds in a set of four choices.
11. If the student is amplified binaurally, locates the direction of sound on the same plane.
12. If the student is amplified binaurally, locates the direction of sound on different planes.
13. Identifies common environmental sounds.
14. If the student is amplified binaurally, he/she can detect when one aid is on vs. both aids on in a structured situation.

A team approach is encouraged with DASL II, with the audiologist, speech–language pathologist, classroom teacher and parents working in a coordinated fashion on relevant subskills. This makes it vital that frequent communication occurs among the team members.

Home intervention involves guiding the parents as they carry out important components of an early audiologic rehabilitation program in the home for an infant diagnosed with a hearing loss.

SKI-HI. Clark and Watkins (1985) developed this comprehensive identification and home intervention treatment program for infants with hearing impairment and their families, and it is in wide use nationally (see Chapter 9 for more details). One of the major components of SKI-HI's treatment plan is a developmentally based auditory stimulation–training program. It is utilized in conjunction with language–speech stimulation and consists of 4 phases and 11 general skills, which are listed in Table 4.10. Although these phases and skills are organized developmentally, infants may not always move sequentially from one phase or skill on the list to the next higher one in a completely predictable manner. SKI-HI provides an extensive description of activities which the clinician and parent or caregiver may utilize in working on subskills related to each of the specific general skills included in each

TABLE 4.10

The Four Phases and Eleven Skills of the SKI-HI Auditory Program

The approximate time line indicates the estimated amount of time spent by a profoundly deaf infant in each phase. The age of the child upon entry into the program and the amount of hearing loss are among the factors which will affect the time needed to progress through the four phases.

PHASES	SKILLS
Phase I (4–7 months)	1. *Attending:* child aware of presence of home and/or speech sounds but may not know meanings; stops, listens, etc.
	2. *Early vocalizing:* child coos, gurgles, repeats syllables, etc.
Phase II (5–16 months)	3. *Recognizing:* child knows meaning of home and/or speech sounds but may not be able to locate; smiles when hears Daddy home, etc.
	4. *Locating:* child turns to, points to, locates sound sources.
	5. *Vocalizing with inflection:* high/low, loud/soft, and/or, up/down
Phase III (9–14 months)	6. *Hearing at distances and levels:* child locates sounds far away and/or above and below
	7. *Producing some vowels and consonants*
Phase IV (12–18 months)	8. *Environmental discrimination and comprehension:* child hears differences among and/or understands home sounds
	9. *Vocal discrimination and comprehension:* child hears differences (a) among vocal sounds, (b) among words, or (c) among phrases and/or understands them
	10. *Speech sound discrimination and comprehension:* child hears differences among and/or understands distinct speech sounds
	11. *Speech use:* child imitates and/or uses speech meaningfully

Source: Watkins and Clark, 1993.

phase of the auditory training program. The structure and completeness of SKI-HI's auditory training component make it user friendly for parents under the guidance of clinicians. Table 4.11 provides a summary of an example of listening activities which are part of SKI-HI's comprehensive auditory stimulation program.

SPICE. Moog, Biedenstein, and Davidson (1995) developed the Speech Perception Instructional Curriculum and Evaluation (SPICE) to provide a guide for clinicians in evaluating and developing auditory skills in children with severe to profound hearing loss. It contains goals and objectives associated with four levels of speech perception. The first level, *detection,* is intended to establish an awareness and responsiveness to speech. The second and third levels, *suprasegmental* and *vowel and*

TABLE 4.11

A Lesson in SKI-HI's Auditory Stimulation and Training Program

Recognition of objects and events from sound source (Phase II, Skill 3, Subskill 6)

Parent objective	Parent will provide repeated meaningful opportunities for their child to associate environmental and speech sounds with their source.
Child objective	Child will demonstrate recognition of environmental and speech sounds by realizing their source.
Lesson	Review with the parents the sounds and activities that you have been utilizing for previous work on attending. Continue these activities, ensuring that the child is aware of the source of the sound and that the sounds are relevant to the child.
Materials	Naturally occurring environmental sounds and voice.
Activities	1. Ask everyone who comes to visit to knock several times, pause, and knock again. When someone knocks, take your child to the door and say, "listen," etc.
	2. Encourage the child to discover different sounds that toys make by providing him or her play time with several different sound toys.
	3. Stimulate the child to produce sounds by manipulating objects or toys (banging pans, squeezing toy, etc.) and stimulate vocalization by making sounds as you play with the toys.
	4. Imitate the child's actions, such as shaking a rattle, and imitate all vocalizations.
	5. Associate speech with all major movements (e.g., saying "roll" each time you roll the child over and "up" when you pick him or her up).
	6. Stimulate association of particular voices with particular people by having siblings/relatives use voice as they play with the child.

Source: Adapted from Clark and Watkins, 1985; Watkins and Clark, 1993.

---

consonant perception, are worked on in tandem. In the suprasegmental section, children work on differentiating speech based on gross variations in duration, stress, and intonation. In the vowel and consonant section, children begin to make perceptual distinctions among individual word stimuli with similar duration, stress, and intonation features, but with different vowels and consonants. With progress, the child is introduced to the fourth level, *connected speech.* Now the emphasis is the perception of words in a more natural environment (phrases and sentences). Activities for SPICE are done with combined auditory–visual presentation, as well as auditory-only listening situations. Much of these activities are carried out in short, structured therapy sessions that concentrate on specific listening skills. As the child progresses, the newly acquired skills can be refined further in more nat-

Connected or running speech is natural or conversational speech.

ural, informal conversation. Recently, SPICE has been used extensively with children using cochlear implants as an approach to developing listening skills in conjunction with their expanded auditory input.

CONSONANT RECOGNITION TRAINING. This approach to auditory training mainly has been used with adults and relies primarily on an analytic approach to facilitate improved speech perception. In addition to its use in auditory training, consonant recognition training frequently incorporates speechreading into a combined auditory–visual training approach. Walden et al., (1981) originally described consonant recognition training as it was utilized initially at Walter Reed Army Medical Center. Briefly, a large number of training exercises were developed and each exercise concentrates on a select number of consonants presented in a syllable context. The listener's task is to make same–different judgments between syllable pairs and to identify the nonsense syllables presented individually. The position of the consonants within the syllable is varied between exercises. The person with hearing impairment receives immediate feedback regarding the correctness of his or her response. This general procedure allows for intense drill to occur for a select number of consonants during a relatively short therapy session.

Walden and others presented data to support the efficacy of this approach to auditory training. They noted an 11.6% average improvement in consonant recognition. More impressively, a 28.2% average improvement was found in perception of sentences presented in a combined auditory–visual mode. A follow-up study (Montgomery et al., 1984) utilized a similar training protocol for consonant recognition which combined work on speechreading and auditory training. Using sentence material to assess performance, they noted a substantial improvement in speech recognition for adults with hearing impairment.

Another investigation (Rubenstein & Boothroyd, 1987) also examined the effectiveness of consonant recognition training as part of a larger study comparing analytic and synthetic therapy approaches to improving speech perception. Rubenstein and Boothroyd found that consonant recognition training did produce modest improvement in speech perception for a group of adults with hearing impairment, but the amount of improvement observed was not any greater than was achieved with a synthetic approach to auditory training.

More research needs to be focused on the relative merits of consonant-recognition training as it is used in attempting to improve auditory perception. Also needed is further clarification of the basic roles played by auditory and visual speech perception, both individually and when utilized in a combined manner, in the processing of speech by persons with hearing impairment (Walden & Grant, 1993; Gagne, 1994). In the meantime, interest in using consonant-recognition training continues, and its use has been extended in recent years to include computer-based programming as well (Tye Murray et al., 1990; Lansing & Bienvenue, 1994). Clinicians also can access a wealth of therapy materials useful in this type of analytic approach from Analytika (Plant, 1994).

COMMUNICATION TRAINING AND THERAPY. This common form of audiologic rehabilitation emphasizes the role of communication strategies and pragmatics to facilitate successful communication. The hearing impaired adult is coached regarding those factors in conversational situations that the listener can control or exercise that can maximize the opportunity to perceive what is spoken. Many of these factors are classified as being either anticipatory or repair strategies for the listener to use. Anticipatory strategies refer to things the listener can do to better prepare for communication or ensure that it will be successful. Some examples of anticipatory strategies that can be helpful are listed in Table 4.12.

Repair strategies involve techniques used to overcome a breakdown in communication that has already occurred. The person with hearing loss (and the speaker as well) can use one or more of these strategies to help with perceiving a given message. Examples of common repair strategies are also given in Table 4.12.

Table 4.13 demonstrates further how repair strategies can be used for specific communication problems. Persons with hearing impairment are encouraged to employ these communication strategies when necessary, which does require some degree of assertiveness on their part as they communicate with others. Successful use of communication strategies also requires that they be used in a diplomatic manner as well.

DeFilippo and Scott (1978) developed a technique called *speech tracking*, which can be used in therapy to provide practice in utilizing communication repair strategies in a conversation context. As it is used in therapy centered on improving auditory-speech perception, speech tracking involves having a listener repeat a phrase or sentence presented by a clinician in an auditory-only condition. To assist in perceiving 100% of the message, the listener can use various repair strategies, such as requesting that the entire sentence, or portions, be repeated or rephrased, until the complete utterance is comprehended. Visual cues may be added for bisensory

---

TABLE 4.12

Examples of Anticipatory and Repair Strategies the Person with Hearing Loss Can Use to Enhance the Extent to Which Hearing Contributes to Speech Perception

Anticipatory Strategies

Minimizing the distance from the speaker

Optimizing the hearing aid volume setting

Reducing the level of competing signals (stereo, TV)

Using situational cues to anticipate topics and words

Repair Strategies

Asking the speaker to repeat all or part of a message

Asking the speaker to rephrase or simplify the message

Asking a follow-up question to either confirm the content of a previous message or to elaborate on it

TABLE 4.13	

Some Communication Problems Commonly Experienced by Hearing Impaired People, and Associated (Specific) Requests for Clarification

WHAT WAS THE COMMUNICATION PROBLEM?	HOW YOU CAN ASK FOR HELP
You understood only part of the message.	Repeat the part you understood; ask for the part you didn't understand (e.g., "You flew to *Paris*?").
You couldn't see the speaker's mouth.	"Please put your hand down."
The person was speaking too fast.	"Please speak a little slower."
The person's speech was too soft.	"Please speak a little louder."
The sentence was too long.	"Shorter, please."
The person's speech was not clear.	"Speak a little more clearly, please."
The sentence was too complicated.	"Please say that in a different way."
You don't know what the problem was.	"Please say that again."

Source: Erber, 1993.

training as well. Performance in the speech tracking procedure is monitored by calculating the number of words or sentences correctly repeated by the listener per minute over a set period of time. An example of the tracking method as applied in a therapy session is provided below. (The topic of the sentence is fishing.)

Clinician: Dry flies float on the surface.
Listener: Dry . . . on the . . . ? Please repeat it.
Clinician: Dry flies float on the surface.
Listener: Dry flies . . . on the . . . ? Please repeat the word after "flies."
Clinician: Float.
Listener: Float?
Clinician: Yes.
Listener: Dry flies float on the water.
Clinician: No. On the surface of the water.
Listener: Oh. Dry flies float on the surface.
Clinician: Yes.

In recent years, audiologists have frequently included condensed variations of communication training and counseling as an important aspect of audiologic rehabilitation for adults at the time they are fitted with new hearing aids (Beyer & Northern, 2000). Many think that sharing information with the patient about the role of hearing and vision and the use of communication strategies in communicating is a timely and appropriate adjunct to the hearing aid orientation process, and audiologists have begun to do this on a more frequent basis (Schow et al., 1993). In a recent article, Montgomery (1994) discussed the rationale for providing a brief exposure to auditory rehabilitation at the time the patient who is hard of hearing is fitted with a hearing aid. Montgomery uses the acronym WATCH for his program, which includes the following key elements of AR: W: Watch the talker's mouth

CLEAR is another program designed for this purpose (see Chapter 10).

(lipreading); **A:** Ask specific questions (conversation-repair strategies); **T:** Talk about your hearing loss (admission of hearing loss); **C:** Change the situation (situation control); and **H:** Health care knowledge (consumer education and awareness). The program, which takes about one hour to share with the new hearing-aid user, is designed to provide important tips for successful communication, as well as to "encourage or empower the hearing-impaired patient to take charge of his or her communication behavior and take responsibility for its success." Audiologists are encouraged to consider providing this brief, but valuable, form of AR more routinely as they work with adults who are hard of hearing.

SUMMARY POINTS

- Basic oral communication involves five key components: the speaker, a message (often with auditory and visual forms), a listener, feedback to the speaker, and the environment in which the communication takes place.
- Both the segmental and suprasegmental components found in speech contribute to speech perception.
- Hearing impairment results in the loss of varying degrees of segmental and suprasegmental information, which leads to problems with speech perception.
- Speech has quite a bit of built-in redundancy, making it possible to figure out what was said even though the listener did not perceive all the acoustical information produced by the speaker.
- Auditory training is intended to facilitate auditory perception in the listener with impaired hearing.
- Long-term auditory training therapy is not done routinely with a majority of cases with hearing loss. However, it can be a key component of audiologic rehabilitation for cochlear implant recipients, those with prelingual onset of hearing loss, and those with severe to profound impairments.
- Assessment of auditory skills can provide valuable information regarding candidacy for therapy, can help in identifying areas in need of work in therapy, and can be useful in outcomes assessment.
- Analytic, synthetic, and pragmatic approaches to auditory training currently are employed in a variety of forms for children and adults.

RECOMMENDED READING

Blamey, P., & Alcantara, J. (1994). Research in auditory training. In J.-P. Gagne and N. Tye-Murray (Eds.), Research in audiological rehabilitation [Monograph]. *Journal of the Academy of Rehabilitative Audiology, 27,* 161–192.

Erber, N. (1982). *Auditory training.* Washington, DC: Alexander Graham Bell Association for the Deaf.

Erber, N. (1996). *Communication therapy for hearing-impaired adults.* Abbotsford, Vic. 3067/Australia: Clavis Publishing.

Gagne, J.-P., & Jennings, M. (2000). Audiological rehabilitation intervention services for adults with acquired hearing impairment. In M. Valente, H. Hosford-Dunn, and R. Roeser (Eds.). *Audiology treatment.* New York: Thieme.

Kricos, P. (Ed.) (2000). Contemporary models of aural rehabilitation. *Seminars in Hearing, 21*(3).

Tye-Murray, N. (1994). Communication strategies training. In J. Gagne & N. Tye-Murray (Eds.), Research in audiological rehabilitation [Monograph]. *Journal of the Academy of Rehabilitative Audiology, 27,* 193–208.

REFERENCES

Alpiner, J., & McCarthy, P. (Eds.). (2000). *Rehabilitative audiology: Children and adults* (3rd ed.). Baltimore: Williams and Wilkins.

Beyer, C., & Northern, J. (2000). Audiologic rehabilitation support programs: A network model. *Seminars in Hearing, 21*(3), 257–266.

Bilger, R., Rzcezkowski, C., Nuetzel, J., & Rabinowitz, W. (November, 1979). Evaluation of a test of speech perception in noise (SPIN). Paper presented at the convention of the American Speech–Language–Hearing Association, Atlanta, GA.

Blamey, P., & Alcantara, J. (1994). Research in auditory training. In J.-P. Gagne & N. Tye-Murray (Eds.), Research in audiological rehabilitation [Monograph]. *Journal of the Academy of Rehabilitative Audiology, 27,* 161–192.

Carhart, R. (1960). Auditory training. In H. Davis & R. Silverman (Eds.), *Hearing and deafness* (2nd ed.). New York: Holt, Rinehart & Winston.

Clark, T., & Watkins, S. (1985). *Programming for hearing impaired infants through amplification and home visits* (4th ed.). Logan, UT: Utah State University.

Cochlear Corp. (1998). *Rehabilitation manual.* Englewood, CO: Author.

Crandall, I. (1925, October). Sounds of speech. *Bell System Technical Journal,* 586–626.

Davis, J., & Hardick, E. (1981). *Rehabilitative audiology for children and adults.* New York: Wiley and Sons.

Davis, H., & Silverman, R. (1960). *Hearing and deafness* (2nd ed.). New York: Holt, Rinehart & Winston.

Davis, H., & Silverman, R. (1978). *Hearing and deafness* (4th ed.) New York: Holt, Rinehart & Winston.

DeFilippo, C., & Scott, B. (1978). A method for training and evaluating the reception of ongoing speech. *Journal of the Acoustical Society of America, 63,* 1186–1192.

Denes, P., & Pinson, E. (1993). *The speech chain* (2nd ed.). New York: Freeman & Co.

Durrant, J., & Lovrinic, J. (1995). *Bases of hearing science* (3rd ed.). Baltimore: Williams & Wilkins.

Erber, N. (1979). Speech perception by profoundly hearing-impaired children. *Journal of Speech and Hearing Disorders, 122,* 255–270.

Erber, N. (1982). *Auditory training.* Washington, DC: Alexander Graham Bell Association for the Deaf.

Erber, N. (1993). *Communication and adult hearing loss.* Abbotsford, Victoria: Clavis Press.

Erber, N. (1996). Communication therapy for hearing-impaired adults. Melbourne, Australia: Clavis Publishing.

Fletcher, H. (1953). *Speech and hearing in communication.* Princeton, NJ: D. VanNostrand Co.

Gagne, J.-P. (1994). Visual and audiovisual speech perception training: Basic and applied research needs. In J.-P. Gagne & N. Tye-Murray (Eds.), Research in audiological rehabilitation [Monograph]. *Journal of the Academy of Rehabilitative Audiology, 27,* 133–160.

Gagne, J.-P., & Jennings, M. (2000). Audiological rehabilitation intervention services for adults with acquired hearing impairment. In M. Valente, H. Hosford-Dunn, and R. Roeser (Eds.), *Audiology treatment.* New York: Thieme.

Goldstein, M. (1939). *The acoustic method of the training of the deaf and hard of hearing child.* St. Louis: Laryngoscope Press.

Hegde, M. (1995). *Introduction to communicative disorders* (2nd ed.). Austin, TX: Pro-Ed.

Hirsh, I., Davis, H., Silverman, S. R., Reynolds, E., Eldert, E., Bensen, R. (1952). Development of materials for speech audiometry. *Journal of Speech and Hearing Disorders, 17,* 321–337.

Kalikow, D., Stevens, K., & Elliott, L. (1977). Development of a test of speech intelligibility in noise using sentence materials with controlled word predictability. *Journal of the Acoustical Society of America, 61,* 1337–1351.

Katz, D., & Elliott, L. (1978, November). Development of a new children's speech discrimination test. Paper presented at the convention of the American Speech–Language–Hearing Association, Chicago.

Lansing, C., & Bienvenue, L. (1994). Intelligent computer-based systems to document the effectiveness of consonant recognition training. *Volta Review, 96,* 41–49.

Lehiste, I. (1970). *Suprasegmentals.* Cambridge, MA: The MIT Press.

Lehiste, I. (1976). Suprasegmental features of speech. In N. J. Lass (Ed.), *Contemporary issues in experimental phonetics* (pp. 225–242). New York: Academic Press.

Ling, D. (1976). *Speech and the hearing-impaired child: Theory and practice.* Washington, DC: Alexander Graham Bell Association for the Deaf.

Ling, D. (1989). *Foundations of spoken language for hearing-impaired children.* Washington, DC: Alexander Graham Bell Association for the Deaf.

Ling, D., & Ling, A. (1978). *Aural rehabilitation.* Washington, DC: Alexander Graham Bell Association for the Deaf.

Mackay, I. (1987). *Phonetics: The science of speech production* (2nd ed.). Austin, TX: Pro-Ed.

Miller, G. (1951). *Language and communication.* New York: McGraw-Hill.

Miller, G., & Nicely, P. (1955). Analysis of perceptual confusions among some English consonants. *Journal of the Acoustical Society of America, 27,* 338–352.

Minifie, F. (1973). Speech acoustics. In F. Minifie, T. Hixon, & F. Williams (Eds.), *Normal aspects of speech, hearing and language.* Englewood Cliffs, NJ: Prentice Hall.

Montgomery, A. (1994). WATCH: A practical approach to brief auditory rehabilitation. *The Hearing Journal, 47*(10), 53–55.

Montgomery, A., Walden, B., Schwartz, D., & Prosek, R. (1984). Training auditory–visual speech recognition in adults with moderate sensorineural hearing loss. *Ear and Hearing, 5,* 30–36.

Moog, J., Biedenstein, J., & Davidson, L. (1995). *The SPICE.* St. Louis: Central Institute for the Deaf.

Myatt, B., & Landes, B. (1963). Assessing discrimination loss in children. *Archives of Otolaryngology, 77,* 359–362.

Northern, J., & Downs, M. (1991). *Hearing in children* (4th ed.). Baltimore: Williams & Wilkins.

Owens, E. (1978). Consonant errors and remediation in sensorineural hearing loss. *Journal of Speech and Hearing Disorders, 43,* 331–347.

Owens, E., & Schubert, E. (1977). Development of the California Consonant Test. *Journal of Speech and Hearing Research, 20,* 463–474.

Owens, E., Benedict, M., & Shubert, E. (1971). Further investigation of vowel items in multiple-choice discrimination testing. *Journal of Speech and Hearing Research, 14,* 814–847.

Owens, E., Benedict, M., & Shubert, E. (1972). Consonant phoneme errors associated with pure tone configurations and certain types of hearing impairment. *Journal of Speech and Hearing Research, 15,* 308–322.

Owens, E., Kessler, D., Telleen, C., & Shubert, E. (1985). The Minimal Auditory Capabilities (MAC) battery. *Hearing Journal, 34*(9), 32–34.

Oyer, H. (1966). *Auditory communication for the hard of hearing.* Englewood Cliffs, NJ: Prentice Hall.

Peterson, G. E., & Barney, H. L. (1952). Control methods used in the study of the vowels. *Journal of the Acoustical Society of America, 32,* 693–703.

Plant, G. (1994). *Analytika.* Somerville, MA: Audiological Engineering Corp.

Ross, M., & Lerman, L. (1970). A picture identification test for hearing impaired children. *Journal of Speech and Hearing Research, 13,* 44–53.

Rubenstein, A., & Boothroyd, A. (1987). Effect of two approaches to auditory training on speech recognition by hearing-impaired adults. *Journal of Speech and Hearing Research, 30,* 153–160.

Sanders, D. (1971). *Aural rehabilitation.* Englewood Cliffs, NJ: Prentice Hall.

Sanders, D. (1993). *Management of hearing handicap* (3rd ed.). Englewood Cliffs, NJ: Prentice Hall.

Schow, R., Balsara, N., Smedley, T., & Whitcomb, C. (1993). Aural rehabilitation by ASHA audiologists: 1980–1990. *American Journal of Audiology, 2,* 28–37.

Sher, A., & Owens, E. (1974). Consonant confusions associated with hearing loss above 2,000 Hz. *Journal of Speech and Hearing Research, 17,* 669–681.

Stevens, S., & Davis, H. (1938). *Hearing: Its psychology and physiology.* New York: Wiley & Sons.

Stout, G., & Windle, J. (1994). *Developmental Approach to Successful Listening II.* Englewood, CO: Resource Point, Inc.

Tillman, T., & Carhart, R. (1966). An expanded test for speech discrimination utilizing CNC monosyllabic words. Northwestern University Auditory Test No. 6 (Technical Report No. SAM-TR55). Brooks Air Force Base, TX: USAF School of Aerospace Medicine.

Trammel, J. (1981). Test of auditory comprehension (TAC). North Hollywood, CA: Foreworks.

Tye-Murray, N. (1998). *Foundations of aural rehabilitation.* San Diego, CA: Singular Publishing Group.

Tye-Murray, N., Tyler, R., Lansing, C., & Bertschy, M. (1990). Evaluating the effectiveness of auditory training stimuli using a computerized program. *Volta Review, 92,* 25–30.

Tyler, R., Preece, J., & Lowder, M. (1983). *The Iowa cochlear implant tests.* Iowa City, Iowa: University of Iowa Press.

Walden, B., & Grant, K. (1993). Research needs in rehabilitative audiology. In J. Alpiner & P. McCarthy (Eds.), *Rehabilitative audiology: Children and adults.* Baltimore: Williams & Wilkins.

Walden, B., Erdman, I., Montgomery, A., Schwartz, D., & Prosek, R. (1981). Some effects of training on speech recognition by hearing-impaired adults. *Journal of Speech and Hearing Research, 24,* 207–216.

Watkins, S., & Clark, T. (1993). *SKI-HI resource manual: Family-centered home-based program for infants, toddlers & school-aged children with hearing impairment.* Login, VT: Hope, Inc.

Visual Stimuli in Communication

Nicholas M. Hipskind

C O N T E N T S

■ INTRODUCTION

When engaged in conversation, we tend to rely primarily on our hearing to receive and subsequently comprehend the message being conveyed. In addition, given the opportunity, we often look at the speaker in order to obtain further information related to the topic of conversation. The speaker's mouth movements, facial expressions, and hand gestures, as well as various aspects of the physical environment in which the communication takes place, are all potential sources of useful information. Humans learn to use their vision for communication to some extent, even though most of us enjoy the benefits of normal hearing and find it unnecessary in most situations to depend on vision to communicate effectively.

The hearing impaired person, on the other hand, is much more dependent on visual cues for communication. The degree to which the hearing impaired need visual information when conversing with someone is proportional to the amount of information that is lost due to hearing impairment. In other words, a person with a severe hearing loss is likely to be more dependent on visual information to communicate than an individual with a mild auditory impairment.

Visual information may be transmitted by means of a manual or an oral communication system. In oral communication, the listener uses visual cues by observing the speaker's mouth, facial expressions, and hand movements to help perceive what is being said. This process is referred to by such terms as lipreading, visual hearing, visual communication, visual listening, or speechreading. Among lay persons the most popular of these terms is lipreading. The term implies that only the lips of the talker provide visual cues. However, because the use of vision for communication involves more than merely watching the speaker's mouth, most professionals prefer the term *speechreading*. Thus, speechreading is used in the remainder of this chapter to refer to visual perception of oral communication.

> Speechreading involves attempting to perceive speech by using visual cues to supplement whatever auditory information is available.

Manual communication, or *signing,* also relies on a visual system. Manual communication is transmitted via special signs and symbols made with the hands and is received and interpreted visually. This complex form of communication allows for transfer of information via the visual channel when both the sender and the receiver are familiar with the same set of symbols.

The intent of this chapter is to discuss the advantages and limitations of vision as part of the audiologic rehabilitation process. Emphasis will be given to the factors that affect speechreading, as well as to a discussion of manual communication methods. The reader is reminded that the hearing impaired comprise two populations: the hard of hearing and the deaf. Although frequently classified under the generic term hearing impaired, these groups have different communication needs and limitations. Therefore, it is unrealistic to expect that a single rehabilitation method can satisfy all their communication needs. Ultimately, it is the clinician's responsibility to select appropriate strategies that will enable the hard of hearing and the deaf to use vision to effectively enhance their communicative skills, to achieve educational and vocational success, and to mature emotionally and socially.

■ FACTORS RELATED TO SPEECHREADING

The variables that affect the speechreading process usually fall in four general areas: the speaker, the signal code, the environment, and the speechreader. While research has contributed to a better understanding of how speech is processed visually, some of the findings are equivocal and have been found to be difficult to duplicate in the clinical setting. This is not to imply that professionals should ignore available laboratory findings; rather, they must realize the significance of these findings in order to provide individualized patient programming. The following section presents selected experimental evidence regarding factors that have been reported to influence the efficacy of speechreading. Figure 5.1 provides a summary of these factors.

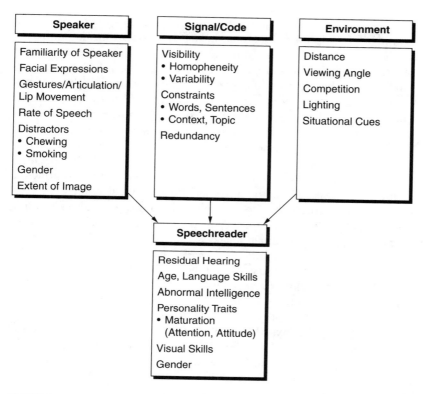

FIGURE 5.1

Summary of various factors related to speechreading performance. Arrows have been drawn from the Speaker, Signal/Code, and Environmental lists to Speechreader to signify that all these factors influence the speechreader's performance, in addition to those variables that are directly related to the speechreader.

Speaker

Differences among speakers have a greater effect on speechreading than on listening. Over 50 years ago a positive correlation was shown to exist between speaker–listener familiarity and the information received from speechreading. That is, speechreading performance improves when the speaker is familiar to the receiver (speechreader). Speakers who use appropriate facial expressions and common gestures and who position themselves face to face or within a 45-degree angle of the listener also facilitate communication for the speechreader (Berger, 1972a).

The rate of normal speech results in as many as 15 phonemes per second. Evidence suggests that the eye may be capable of recording only 8 to 10 discrete movements per second. Thus, at times a speaker's speaking rate may exceed the listener's visual reception capabilities. Although normal rate of speech may be too fast for optimal visual processing, extremely slowed and exaggerated speech production does not assure improved comprehension. It has been reported that speakers who use a slightly slower to normal speech rate accompanied by precise, not exaggerated, articulation are the easiest for the speechreader to understand. Recently, Montgomery and Houston (2000) noted that the rapidity of speech may not be as limiting a factor in determining speechreading success as was once thought, because each phoneme does not have a discrete visual image as speech is produced. Thus, the speechreader actually may not have to process as many visual stimuli per second as once thought. In addition, the speaker also should avoid simultaneous oral activities, such as chewing, smoking, and yawning, when conversing with a hearing impaired person. Other potentially counterproductive postures include holding a hand near the mouth while talking and wearing sunglasses. While the masking effects of these coincidental activities have not been documented, they seem likely to complicate an already trying task. With respect to the gender of speakers, Daly, Bench and Chappell (1996) were the most recent to demonstrate that female speakers are easier to speechread than are male speakers. Related to this finding, little evidence exists concerning the potential influence that gender-related variables associated with the speaker, such as a moustache or the use of lipstick, may have on speechreading success.

The speaker may enhance conversational efficiency by complementing speechreading with appropriate facial expressions and gestures (Sanders, 1993). From infancy, we learn that the spoken word "no" is accompanied by a stern facial expression and shaking of the head and/or index finger from side to side. Salutations are made in conjunction with a smile and the extension or wave of the hand, opening of the arms, and/or puckering of the lips. Similarly, shrugging of the shoulders has become a universal gesture that augments the verbal phrases "I don't know" or "I don't care." Consequently, appropriate nonverbal communication is closely associated with the verbal message and is used simultaneously with speech to provide emphasis and redundancy. This means that situations where the speechreader can observe both the head and body of the speaker generally will be more productive for the speechreader. Nitchie (1912) was one of the first teachers of speechreading to stress that the hearing impaired must learn to be cognizant of nonverbal cues, such as gestures, when attempting to understand speech.

Signal and Code

Distinctive features are unique characteristics of a given phoneme that distinguish one phoneme from another.

Speech consists of acoustic information that is efficiently received and effectively interpreted by the normal auditory mechanism. It possesses physical characteristics that are compatible with the receptive capabilities of the normal ear. The basic units of speech are consonants and vowels, classified as phonemes. A phoneme has distinctive acoustic features that enable the listener to distinguish it from all other speech sounds.

Vowels embody the major concentration of acoustic energy found in speech and are termed resonated phonemes. Vowel production is accomplished by directing vocalizations through the oral cavity, which is altered in shape and size by different tongue and lip positions. These subtle alterations are responsible for providing each vowel with specific acoustic features.

Consonants, which are primarily responsible for the intelligibility of speech, are termed articulated phonemes, because their production involves the manipulation of the various articulators: lips, tongue, and teeth. As pointed out in Chapter 4, these phonemes possess *distinctive features* that permit a listener to recognize them. Miller and Nicely (1955) classified these features as voicing, nasality, affrication, duration, and place of articulation. Except for place of articulation, the identifying characteristics of consonants are perceived well on the basis of acoustic information. Although difficult to distinguish acoustically, the place of articulation may be processed to some extent visually due to the visibility of the articulators.

Because many of the 40 or more phonemes used in English demonstrate ambiguous or very limited visible features, an individual who relies solely on vision to understand speech faces much uncertainty. Knowledge of the visual components of speech depends, for the most part, on research using small speech units, that is, consonant–vowel combinations or monosyllabic words (e.g., Jackson, 1988; Owens & Blazek, 1985).

VISEMES. The number of distinctive visual features of vowels and consonants is reduced to the shape of the mouth for vowels and the place of articulation for consonants. Because the perception of phonemes is primarily an auditory function based on acoustic features, Fisher (1968) coined the term *viseme* to indicate the distinguishable visual characteristics of speech sounds. A viseme, therefore, is a speech sound (phoneme) that has been classified by its place of articulation or by the shape of the mouth. This creates a major limitation for the observer of speech compared to that of the listener. Whereas combinations of auditory distinctive features are unique to each phoneme, several phonemes yield the same viseme, thus limiting the speechreader to the conclusion that one of a group of sounds was uttered.

> A viseme is a group of phonemes in which each looks alike when spoken.

Because groups of consonants are produced at the same points of articulation, the phonemes within these groups cannot be differentiated visually without grammatical, phonetic, or lexical information. These visually confusable units of speech are labeled *homophemes*, different speech sounds that look the same. Similarly, words that look alike are referred to as homophenous words. Look in the mirror and say aloud or have a friend utter the syllables /p/, /b/, and /m/. As you watch and listen simultaneously, the syllables sound so different that you may not notice their visual similarities. However, when these same syllables are formed without voice, you will note that their visual characteristics are indistinguishable. This same type of confusion often occurs among word groups (e.g., pet, bed, and men; tip, limb, and dip; and cough and golf). However, it has been demonstrated that talkers significantly influence the number of visemes produced (Kricos & Lesner, 1982). That is, some talkers are easier to speechread than are other talkers because they produce more distinctively different viseme groups. It has been estimated that, regardless of the number of viseme categories reported by various authors, in conversational speech nearly 50% of the words are indistinguishable visually; that is, they look like other words (Berger, 1972b).

> Homophenes are words that look alike when spoken, even though they sound different. Homophones are words that sound and look the same but are spelled differently.

CONSONANT VISEMES. A number of studies have been conducted to determine the number of visemes in spoken English. Woodward and Barber (1960) were the first to classify consonants into four visually contrastive groups based on their place of articulation: bilabials, rounded labials, labiodentals, and nonlabials. Fisher (1968) later tested for confusion among these same consonants when they occurred in the initial and final positions of words. In general, his results were in agreement with Woodward and Barber's classification of homophenous groupings; however, his viseme classes resulted in five clusters, rather than four, for both the initial and final positions. Others, such as Binnie, Jackson, and Montgomery (1976) and Lesner, Sandridge, and Kricos (1987), found that their viewers were able to recognize from five to nine distinct groups of consonants. Table 5.1 lists the homophenous classifications proposed by several authors. Table 5.1 also illustrates the chance for error that a listener has when required to interpret phonemes visually. Except for the *independent visemes* of /l/, /h/, /r/, and /w/ reported by Erber (1974), Binnie et al. (1976), Walden et al. (1977), Owens and Blazek (1985), and Lesner et al. (1987) and the /j/ reported by Jeffers and Barley (1971), all viseme clusters contain at least two phonemes. Consequently, on the average, the speechreader has at best a 50% chance of correctly identifying a specific isolated phoneme within any group when relying solely on vision.

VOWEL VISEMES. Although vowels are not considered articulated phonemes, Jeffers and Barley (1971) suggested that vowels can be visually recognized by their movements, that is, by "a recognizable visual motor pattern, usually common to two or more speech sounds" (p. 42). These authors observed seven visually distinct movements when the vowels were produced at a slow rate accompanied with pronounced

TABLE 5.1

Visemes for English Consonants Determined by Various Researchers

	VISEME GROUPS			
Jeffers and Barley (1971)	Fisher (1968)			Binnie et al. (1976)
	Initial[a]	Final[b]		
1. /f, v/	1. /f, v/	1. /f, v/		1. /f, v/
2. /w, r/	2. /p, b, m, d/	2. /p, b/		2. /p, b, m/
3. /p, b, m/	3. /hw, w, r/	3. /ʃ, ʒ, dʒ, tʃ/		3. /w/
4. /θ, ð/	4. /ʃ, t, n, l, s, z,	4. /t, d, n, θ, ð,		4. /l, n/
5. /ʃ, ʒ, tʃ, dʒ/	dʒ, j, h/	s, z, r, l/		5. /ʃ, ʒ/
6. /s, z/	5. /k, g/	5. /k, g, ŋ, m/		6. /r/
7. /j/				7. /θ, ð/
8. /t, d, n, l/				8. /t, d, s, z/
9. /k, g, ŋ/				9. /k, g/

[a]Observed in the initial position.

[b]Observed in the final position.

The order of the visemes is based on Binnie and coworkers (1976) rank-ordering of the visual clustering of these phonemes.

movement and normal rhythm. When the same phonemes were produced in conversational speech, the number of different movements was reduced to four. The distinctive visible characteristics of vowels as determined by Jeffers and Barley (1971) and Jackson et al. (1976) are shown in Table 5.2.

In general, it has been demonstrated that there are consistent visual confusions among vowels, frequently with vowels that have similar lip positions and movement (Jackson et al., 1976; Montgomery & Jackson, 1983). Furthermore, there are vowels that are seldom recognized visually and, as might be expected, the vowels that are perceived correctly in isolation are not necessarily comprehended visually in conversational speech.

In summary, most of the individual phonemes in our language are not unique visually, as they are produced orally, resulting in considerable confusion and misperception on the part of the speechreader.

VISIBILITY. In addition to the fact that a number of speech sounds and words look similar, another related problem for the speechreader is that many speech sounds are not very visible as they are produced. While phonemes like /p/ or /f/ can be seen quite well, other phonemes like /k/ or /t/ are produced in a far less visible manner. In addition, other features like *voicing* are not visible at all. It has been estimated that as many as 60% of the English phonemes are not readily visible (Woodward & Barber, 1960).

TABLE 5.2

Visemes for English Vowels, as Determined by Two Separate Studies

VISEME GROUPS

Jeffers and Barley (1971)	Jackson, Montgomery, and Binnie (1976)	
Ideal Viewing Conditions	Dimension 1	Lip Shape—from Lips Extended to Lips Rounded—/aɪ, æ, a, eɪ, ɛ, ʌ/ vs. /u, ʊ, ɚ, aʊ, oʊ, ɔɪ/
1. Lips Puckered, Narrow Opening—/u, u, o, oʊ, ɚ/		
2. Lips Back, Narrow Opening—/i, ɪ, eɪ, e, ʌ/		
3. Lips Rounded, Moderate Opening—/ɔ/	Dimension 2	Vertical Dimension of the Lips—/i, ɪ, ɛ/ vs. /aɪ, æ, a/
4. Lips Relaxed, Moderate Opening to Lips Puckered, Narrow Opening—/aU/		
5. Lips Relaxed, Moderate Opening—/ɛ, æ, a/	Dimension 3	General Size of Mouth Opening—Small vs. Large—/u, ʊ, ɚ, i/ vs. /æ, a, ɛ/
6. Lips Rounded, Moderate Opening to Lips Back, Narrow Opening—/ɔɪ/		
7. Lips Relaxed, Moderate Opening to Lips Back, Narrow Opening—/aɪ/	Dimension 4	Size of Movement from Nucleus 1 to Nucleus 2 in Diphthong Production—/aɪ/ vs. /eɪ/
Usual Viewing Conditions		
1. Lips Puckered, Narrow Opening—/u, ʊ, o, oʊ, ɚ/		
2. Lips Relaxed, Moderate Opening to Lips Puckered, Narrow Opening—/aʊ/	Dimension 5	Size of Lip Opening for Nucleus 2 in Dipthong Production—/aʊ/ vs. /aɪ/
3. Lips Rounded, Narrow Opening—/ɔ, ɔɪ/		
4. Lips Relaxed, Narrow Opening—/i, ɪ, eɪ, ʌ, E, æ, a, aɪ/		

VISUAL INTELLIGIBILITY OF CONNECTED DISCOURSE. Researchers have determined the visemes that viewers can identify at the syllable and word levels, but they are less certain about what is visibly discernible when these speech elements are portions of lengthier utterances. The visual properties of isolated speech units change when placed in sentence form, as does the acoustic waveform itself. Unless there is a visible pause between words, a speechreader presumably perceives an uninterrupted series of articulatory movements of varying degrees of inherent visibility. This sequence is broken only when the speaker pauses, either deliberately or for a breath. As a result, the written message "There is a blue car in our driveway," is spoken /ðɛrɪzəblukarɪnaʊɚdraɪvweɪ/. Connected speech contains numerous articulatory positions and movements that occur in a relatively short period of time. Consequently, the majority of phonemes in conversational speech occur in the medial position. The example just given contains an initial consonant /ð/, a final vowel /eɪ/, with numerous sounds (positions and movements) between these phonemes. Ironically, researchers have not determined the number of visemes that are identifiable when phonemes occur in the medial position.

The nature of grammatical sentence structure imposes constraints on word sequences that are not present when the words are used in isolation. These word arrangement rules change the probabilities of word occurrence. Thus, the receiver's task is altered (theoretically made easier) because of the linguistic information and redundancy provided by connected discourse. Language is structured in a way that provides more information than is absolutely necessary to convey a given meaning or thought. Even if certain fragments of the spoken code are missed, cues or information inherent in the message may assist the receiver in making an accurate prediction of the missing parts. That is, oral language is an orderly process that is governed by the rules of pragmatic, topical, semantic, syntactic, lexical, and phonological constraints that are the sources for linguistic redundancy (Boothroyd, 1988). This redundancy creates the predictability of conversational speech. Table 4.4 summarizes several types of linguistic constraints that contribute to this.

Briefly, the pragmatic constraints of language allow for two or more individuals to share thoughts and information orally. Similarly, the topical constraints, which are also referred to as contextual and situational constraints, limit conversation to a specific topic, which, in turn, governs the vocabulary that is appropriate to describe the topic. We use this rule consistently, even though we frequently introduce it in a negative manner. For example, how many times have you said, "Not to change the subject," and then promptly deviated from the original topic of conversation? You are engaging the rule of contextual information and, regardless of how it is initiated, it provides your receiver with a preparatory set that allows her or him to expect a specific vocabulary concerned with a specific event. The situation or environment determines the manner in which the speaker will describe a certain event. Comedians are masters at using this rule; they alter the language of their "stories" based on the makeup of their audience. Contextual and situational constraints are closely allied and are used interchangeably by some authors. For example, during a televised sporting event, when a coach disputes a decision by a referee, have you noticed how well you perceive what the coach says, even though you only have limited auditory and visual cues available? Contextually, you perceive an

Redundancy determines the predictability of a spoken message. The more redundancy present, the easier speechreading will be.

argument while the situation causes the coach to express himself by using a rather limited and heated vocabulary that enables you to predict the words being used. As illustrated in this instance, the situation in which the conversation occurs provides information that otherwise you may not have been able to obtain by relying solely on the articulatory features of the message for perception.

Redundancy, the result of these constraints, contributes significantly to the information afforded by oral language. Thus, redundancy allows the receiver to predict missed information from the bits of information that have been perceived. To illustrate, "Dogs going" means the same as "The dogs are going away." The latter is grammatically correct and contains redundant information. Plurality is indicated twice (dogs, are), present tense twice (are, going), and the direction twice (going, away). Consequently, it would be possible to miss the words "are" and "away" while comprehending the message ("dogs are going"). If we miss part of a message, linguistic redundancy can enable us to synthesize correctly what we missed. However, as will be mentioned in the discussion of perceptual closure, a minimum amount of information must be perceived before accurate predictions can be made. In the preceding example, the words "dogs" and "away" would have to be processed visually in order for the speechreader to conceptualize the message "The dogs are going away."

Although the constraints of language do not enhance the physical visibility of oral sentences, they assist the receiver in visually understanding or speechreading what has been said. Albright, Hipskind, and Schuckers (1973) demonstrated that speechreaders actually obtain more total information from the redundancy and linguistic rules of spoken language than from phoneme and word visibility. Clouser (1976) concluded that the ratio between the number of consonants and vowels did not determine the visual intelligibility of sentences; rather, he found that short sentences were easier to speechread than longer sentences. In another study related to visual perception of speech, Berger (1972b) determined that familiar and frequently used words were identified visually more often than were words used infrequently. Additional information on redundancy is provided in Chapter 4 (see Tables 4.3 and 4.4).

Environment

Circumstances associated with the environments in which the speechreader must communicate can influence the speechreading process considerably. For example, investigators have demonstrated that such factors as distance and viewing angles between the speaker and receiver affect speechreading performance. Erber's (1971) study regarding the influence of distance on the visual perception of speech revealed that speechreading performance was optimal when the speaker was about 5 feet from the speechreader. Although performance decreased beyond 5 feet, it did not drop significantly until the distance exceeded 20 feet. Similarly, there is evidence that simultaneous auditory and visual competition can have an adverse effect on speechreading under certain conditions (O'Neill & Oyer, 1981). Although the amount of lighting is not an important factor in speechreading, provided a reasonable amount of light is present, Erber (1974) suggested that, for optimal visual reception of speech, illumination should provide a contrast between the background and the speaker's face.

Garstecki (1977) concluded that speechreading performance improved when the spoken message was accompanied by relevant pictorial and auditory cues. This finding was given further support by Garstecki and O'Neill (1980), whose subjects had better speechreading scores when the CID Everyday Sentences were presented with appropriate situational cues. In essence, environmental cues provide speechreaders with contextual and situational information, thereby increasing their ability to predict what is being conveyed verbally.

Speechreader

Reduction of a person's ability to hear (auditory sensitivity) auditory stimuli is only one of several parameters that contribute to the disabling effects of hearing impairments. Other factors, such as auditory perception abilities (recognizing, identifying, and understanding), age of onset of the hearing loss, site(s) of lesions, and the educational and therapeutic management followed, all contribute toward making the hearing impaired population extremely heterogeneous. This heterogeneity appears to extend to speechreading, because hearing impaired individuals demonstrate considerable variability in their ability to use vision to speechread. Individual differences in speechreading abilities are large. This body of research is summarized by Dodd and Campbell (1987). Some persons possess amazing speechreading abilities, while others are able to perceive very little speech through the visual channel. Ever since speechreading has been included in audiologic rehabilitation, clinicians and researchers have attempted to determine what personal characteristics of the speechreader account for success or failure in speechreading, including variables such as age, gender, intelligence, personality traits, and visual acuity (O'Neill & Oyer, 1981). In general, it is impossible to totally clarify the characteristics associated with success in speechreading. The following is a sampling of the research that has been conducted in this area related to the speechreader.

AGE. There appears to be some interactions between a speechreader's age and other attributes that contribute to speechreading ability. Specifically, evidence suggests that speechreading proficiency tends to develop and improve throughout childhood and early adulthood and appears to be closely associated with the emergence of language skills. Even though their speechreading abilities are not fully developed, younger children, even infants, may use speechreading to some extent (Pollack, 1985).

Some older people demonstrate phonemic regression, that is, severe inability to understand speech via hearing, that is not consistent with their audiometric profiles (Gaeth, 1948). This same type of phenomenon may account, in part, for the finding that older individuals do less well in speechreading than their younger counterparts even when visual acuity is controlled. Hefler (1998) suggested that the elderly perform more poorly on experimental speechreading tasks because of the inability to process temporally changing visual information. Finally, it is important to note that decreased visual acuity may also contribute to reduced speechreading skill in the aged.

GENDER. This variable has been investigated thoroughly (Dancer et al., 1994). Overall, adult females consistently achieve higher speechreading scores than do males.

INTELLIGENCE. An abundance of research describes the relationship between speechreading and mental abilities. Generally, no demonstrable positive correlation has been found between understanding speech visually and intelligence, assuming intelligence levels in or above the "low normal" range (Lewis, 1972). However, a study conducted by Smith and his colleagues (1964) with a population of mentally impaired individuals revealed that much reduced intelligence levels did result in significantly poorer speechreading performance.

PERSONALITY TRAITS. As may be expected from the preceding discussion, investigators have not been able to ferret out specific personality traits that differentiate among levels of speechreading proficiency. While motivation is tenuous to assess, most clinicians intuitively concur that highly motivated (competitive) clients tend to speechread more effectively than do unmotivated clients. However, it is apparent that good and poor speechreaders generally cannot be stereotyped based on personality patterns (Giolas, Butterfield, & Weaver, 1974; O'Neill, 1951).

VISUAL SKILLS. Since speechreading is a visual activity, the acuity of vision is critical in the decoding process. As discussed in the Visual Assessment section of this chapter, vision has received meager attention from researchers in audiologic rehabilitation.

VISUAL ACUITY. In 1970, Hardick, Oyer, and Irion determined that they could rank order successful and unsuccessful speechreaders based on their visual acuity. Furthermore, these authors observed a significant relationship between eye blink rate and speechreading ability, with poorer speechreaders demonstrating higher eye blink rates. Just prior to this research, Lovering (1969) demonstrated that even slight visual acuity problems (20/40 and poorer) had an appreciable, negative effect on speechreading scores. Most recently, Johnson and Snell (1986) showed that distance and visual acuity have a significant effect on speechreading. These authors report that children with visual acuity of 20/80 or better should be able to speechread at 5 feet with an adequate degree of accuracy. When the speechreader is positioned 22 feet from the talker, then it is necessary that the speechreader have visual acuity no poorer than 20/30. If, however, the speechreader has one eye of 20/30 or better, then he or she should be able to speechread at a comparable level to those individuals with normal binocular vision under similar viewing conditions.

In support of the argument that good visual acuity is important for successful speechreading performance, Romano and Berlow (1974) concluded that visual acuity must be at least 20/80 before speech can be decoded visually. Recently, a line of research has compared visually evoked responses and speechreading ability. According to the results of this research, a viewer's ability to process speech visually is, in part, a function of the rapidity (latency) with which physical visual stimuli are transduced to neural energy for interpretation at the cortical level (Samar & Sims, 1983, 1984; Shepard, 1982; Shepard et al., 1977; Summerfield, 1992). While the clinical applicability of this research has not yet been fully realized, visually evoked responses can assist the clinician in understanding a client's ability to process visually oriented information. Potentially, visually evoked responses may provide audiologic rehabilitationists with information regarding a viewer's ability to speechread various types of oral stimuli.

VISUAL PERCEPTION. Based on Gibson's (1969) definition of perception, our eyes receive visual stimuli that are interpreted at a cortical level and provide us with visual information. This information, in turn, enables us to make a selective response to the original stimuli. Thus, when interpreting speech visually, the speechreader first "sees" the movement of the lips, which the cortex classifies as speech. The accuracy of the speechreader's response to these stimuli is partially a function of how well the peripheral-to-central visual process enables her or him to discriminate among the speaker's articulatory movements.

At present, explanations of the way in which the perceptual process develops are theoretical. However, two strategies appear relevant in connection with obtaining information from the environment. The first, figure–ground patterning, is achieved by identifying a target (meaningful) signal that is embedded in similar, but ambient, stimuli. Observe the following letters:

> W A B R I O D R A Z
>
> O P A I B L O H Y E
>
> L I P R E A D I N G
>
> I R A C R A X O L
>
> M U A L Y O C E P L

Figure–ground patterning involves an ability to focus on and perceive a target stimulus, or figure, from a background of other stimuli, or ground.

The letters within this rectangle are of the same case (capitals) and are placed in an order that meets the criterion of structural ordering. That is, all the letter combinations are possible and probable in written English. As noted, however, there is only one string of letters that creates a meaningful word, LIPREADING (see line 3). Thus, this sequence of printed symbols is the figure while all the other letters are merely spurious background stimuli. The development of figure–ground patterning permits the hearing impaired to separate meaningful visual and auditory events from ambient stimuli.

As early as 1912, Nitchie claimed that successful speechreaders are intuitive and able to synthesize limited visual input into meaningful wholes. Since then professionals have concurred that successful speechreaders possess the ability to visually piece together fragmented pictorial and spoken stimuli into meaningful messages. This ability, termed *closure,* is yet another strategy used to obtain information from environmental events. Before this strategy can be used effectively, a person must receive at least minimal stimulation and, more importantly, must have had prior experience (familiarity) with the whole. Both of the following sentences require that the reader use closure to obtain accurate information.

Being able to combine or pull bits of information together in order to figure out what was said is termed closure.

1. Humpty _____ _____ _____ _____ wall.
2. When you _____ time, you murder _____ .

In all probability you had little difficulty supplying the four words, *Dumpty sat on a,* to the first sentence. The second sentence may have been more difficult unless you are familiar with the adage, "When you kill time, you murder opportunity."

The first sentence provides considerably fewer physical cues than does the second; but experience with and exposure to nursery rhymes permitted you to perceive the whole expression. Effective visual closure skills are essential for the hearing impaired, because, due to their disorder and the limited visual cues afforded by speech, they receive fragmented or distorted auditory and visual stimuli. In trying to understand the role of prediction or predictability, it is paramount to realize that we do not merely get some information by perception (processing the stimuli) and some from the context (prediction), and then add the two. If we did, the total information received would be equal to, or less than (because of redundancy or correlation), the sum of what we can get from either channel alone. The fact that the total is greater than the sum of both channels (as measured above) implies a facilitating or feedback effect from one to the other: the aural information facilitates visual processing, and the visual information enhances auditory processing.

HEARING. Unfortunately, the hearing impaired generally are not any better at speechreading than are those with normal hearing. Among the hearing impaired, however, there is a mild relationship between speechreading proficiency and the degree of hearing loss present. Those persons with significant amounts of residual hearing have the potential to speechread more successfully than those with very limited hearing. This occurs because speechreading is enhanced by the availability of simultaneous auditory cues contained in speech. This is especially apparent in persons beginning to use either a cochlear implant or tactile device, where speechreading performance often improves dramatically relative to what it was previously; because of the increased input provided by these devices, speechreading becomes easier.

It is apparent that numerous factors have an impact on speechreading success. The successful clinician will be familiar with these and take each into account when assisting the hearing impaired in effectively using visual information for communication.

■ SPEECHREADING AND THE HEARING IMPAIRED

Assessing speechreading ability and providing effective speechreading instruction to the hearing impaired are two primary responsibilities of the aural rehabilitationist. The next section outlines some of the ways in which a person's visual communication ability can be evaluated. It also describes several traditional and current approaches to speechreading instruction.

Assessment of Speechreading Ability

Because of the complexities associated with the process, accurate evaluation of speechreading performance is difficult. Professionals have attempted for several decades to develop a means of reliable and valid measurement, but to date no universally acceptable test or battery of tests has emerged for this purpose. Nevertheless, clinicians recognize the importance of assessing speechreading ability to determine if visual communication training is warranted for a particular individual, as well as to evaluate the effectiveness of speechreading training. Consequently, a number of formal and informal approaches for measuring speechreading ability are currently in use.

FORMAL SPEECHREADING TESTS. Since the mid 1940s, speechreading tests have been developed, published, and used. These tests, designed specifically to measure the speechreading abilities of adults or children, may consist of syllables, words, sentences, stories, or a combination of these stimuli. Speechreading tests are presented either in a vision-only condition without acoustic cues or in a combined visual–auditory test condition in which the stimuli are both seen and heard by the speechreader. These formal tests sometimes are presented via prerecorded videotape, but often are administered in a live, face to face situation, where the clinician presents the test stimuli. Although the test contents remain constant, the manner of presentation may vary considerably among clinicians when tests are administered live, which can make interpretation of the results less secure due to the variability created by using different speakers to present the test stimuli (Montgomery et al., 1984). Some of these tests are listed in Table 5.3 and in the appendixes of this chapter. It should be noted that several tests originally developed to assess auditory speech perception have also been used frequently to evaluate speechreading skills.

Vision-only refers to attempting to perceive speech via visual cues (without voice).

INFORMAL SPEECHREADING TESTS. Informal tests are developed by the clinician, who selects stimulus materials of her or his choosing. Contents should vary as a function of the client's age and the information sought by the rehabilitationist. Clinicians use a variety of speech forms, including lists of words presented in isolation or in sentences. Sentence items may include statements like "What is your name?" or "Show me a toothbrush." Informal assessment allows the tester to select stimuli that are more pertinent for a particular client than items on formal speechreading tests. However, as a result of the loose format and the intent of these tests, the obtained results do not lend themselves well to comparative analysis.

Whether using formal or informal speechreading tests, it is important that the stimuli not be so difficult that they discourage the client nor so easy that test scores reflect a ceiling effect (100% correct for each viewer). Materials should be selected so that they approximate various types of stimuli encountered by the individual in everyday situations. For children and certain adults (such as those with severe speech or writing problems), the response mode should involve pointing with a multiple-choice format; most adults are capable of responding to (writing or repeating) open-set tests. Because of the various shortcomings of existing speechreading tests, these instruments cannot be expected to provide completely valid measures of speechreading ability, but may yield data of some clinical usefulness.

The use of live, face-to-face presentation, although widespread, should be conducted carefully with optimal consideration for distance (5 to 10 feet), lighting (no shadows), and viewing angle (0 to 45 degrees). Even following these precautions, speaker variability will introduce uncertainty into the test situation. Not only will two speakers produce the same speech stimuli differently, but a single talker, producing the same stimuli twice, will not do so in precisely the same manner each time. Therefore, it is difficult to compare a person's skills from one testing to an-

TABLE 5.3

Formal Speechreading Tests for Adults and Children

TITLE OF TESTS	AUTHOR(S)	CONTENT FORMAT
	Adults	
How Well Can You Read Lips?	Utley (1946)	Words Sentences Stories
Semi-Diagnostic Test	Hutton, Curry, & Armstrong (1959)	Words
Barley CID Sentences	Barley (1971)	Sentences
Lipreading Screening Test	Binnie, Jackson, & Montgomery (1976)	CV-Syllables
Denver Quick Test of Lipreading Ability[a]	Alpiner (1978)	Sentences
Assessment of Adult Speechreading Ability	New York League for the Hard of Hearing (1990)	Sentences Paragraphs
Iowa Sentence Test	Tyler, Preece, & Tye-Murray (1986)	Sentences
	Children	
Craig Lipreading Inventory[a]	Craig (1964)	Words Sentences
Butt Children's Speechreading Test	Butt and Chreist (1968)	Questions Commands
Diagnostic Test of Speechreading	Myklebust & Neyhaus (1970)	Words Phrases Sentences
The Children's Visual Enhancement Test	Tye-Murray & Geers (1997)	Words

[a]See Appendix 5B and 5C.

other (pre- and posttherapy) or to directly compare the performance of two individuals. Scores obtained through face to face test administration, although useful, need to be interpreted carefully.

Assessment of speechreading can involve the presentation of visual stimuli without any associated acoustic cues. Although this yields meaningful information regarding the basic skill of speechreading, additional testing of speechreading ability in a combined auditory–visual fashion is also advocated by many, because it more closely resembles ordinary person to person communication. Such testing provides a relevant measure of how well a person integrates visual and auditory information, which is how speech perception occurs in most real communication situations.

Speechreading abilities can also be assessed informally with speech tracking.

Visual Assessment and Speechreading Evaluation

It is important that assessment of speechreading skills be preceded by a measure of visual acuity. As discussed, there is clear evidence that even mild visual acuity problems can have adverse effects on speechreading performance. It is amazing, therefore, that audiologic rehabilitationists have given only limited attention to measuring basic visual abilities in connection with the assessment and instruction of speechreading with hearing impaired persons. Concern for this is further reinforced by research on visual disorders among those with hearing loss. Evidence indicates that the incidence of occular anomalies among hearing impaired students is greater than for normally hearing children of the same age. Campbell and her associates (1981) surveyed the literature and found that 38% to 58% of the hearing impaired reportedly have accompanying visual deficiencies. Even more alarming are data from the National Technical Institute for the Deaf showing that, of the total number of students entering in the past, 65% demonstrated defective vision (Johnson et al., 1981). Basic visual skills associated with the detection, recognition, resolution, and localization of visual stimuli are fundamental when assessing a person's visual acuity. Each of these measurements uses static stimuli; that is, the viewer describes specific characteristics of stationery targets that measure a certain aspect of the viewer's visual acuity. Although research on the relationship between visual acuity and speechreading has concentrated on visual *recognition* (commonly referred to as far visual acuity), at least for some clients it may be prudent to determine their ability to *detect, resolve,* and *localize* visual test stimuli prior to initiating speechreading therapy.

Hearing Impairment and Dependence on Vision

The degree to which the hearing impaired depend on vision for information is related to the extent of their hearing loss. To paraphrase Ross (1982), there is a world of difference between the deaf, who must communicate mainly through a visual mode (speechreading or manual communication), and the hard of hearing, who communicate primarily through an auditory mode (albeit imperfectly).

DEAF. The deaf, who receive quite limited meaningful auditory cues, must rely more on their vision to keep in contact with their environment. The deaf, by the nature of their disorder, use their vision projectively and are visually oriented. However, as stated throughout this chapter, vision generally is less effective than audition when used to decode spoken language. Furthermore, for the congenitally deaf, English usually is *not* their native language. Therefore, these individuals must learn to decode a foreign language without the benefit of auditory cues. English competency, which is most effectively and efficiently developed via the auditory channel, is essential to communication in our society. By definition, "speechreading is an inherently linguistic activity" (Boothroyd, 1988). The deaf therefore are further handicapped in that, before they can gain meaning from speechreading English, they must have developed the linguistic rules of English, which, in turn, are most naturally acquired through aural stimulation. In summary, to benefit from speechreading the listener–viewers must have a fairly extensive language background. Without this they are not able to fill in the gaps providing them with information that cannot be obtained through speechreading or hearing (Bevan, 1988). Thus, the deaf face the monumental challenge of having to speechread words that they may never have conceptualized.

HARD OF HEARING. Hard of hearing individuals, by definition, possess functional residual hearing, which permits them to receive and ultimately perceive more auditory stimuli within their environment. This enhanced ability would suggest that they are less dependent on their vision than are the deaf when perceiving speech. Even so, the hard of hearing, who employ their vision to supplement distorted and reduced acoustic stimuli, receive considerably more information from the spoken code than is provided solely by their auditory channel.

Various investigators have assessed the advantages that audition, vision, and a combination of these sensory modalities afford the receiver when decoding spoken stimuli (CHABA, 1991; Massaro, 1987). Few would disagree that using these two senses simultaneously produces better speech reception than using either alone. Likewise, it is clear that vision can provide information to the receiver when decoding speech in the absence of auditory cues. More importantly, however, even limited auditory input allows the listener to establish a referent from which additional information can be gained visually. Thus, the contributions made by these sensory mechanisms as receptors of speech fall into a hierarchy. That is, when both residual hearing and speechreading are available, the impaired listener tends to do better on a communicative task. For example, if a person achieves a speech recognition score of 50% with hearing alone and a speechreading score of 20% using similar test material, this individual might achieve a combined auditory–visual score that could approach 80% to 90%. In other words, there is more than a simple additive effect from the combination of auditory and visual information. Therefore, the utility of vision in decoding speech should be exploited in audiological communication training.

Traditional Speechreading Methods

During the early 1900s, four methods of teaching speechreading were popularized in the United States (O'Neill and Oyer, 1981). Three of these methods were nurtured by individuals who had normal hearing until adulthood, at which time they acquired significant hearing losses. Initially, they sought assistance to overcome the limitations placed on them by their sensory deprivation. Subsequently, they became interested in assisting other hearing impaired persons in developing speechreading skills, eventually establishing methods that bear their names: the Bruhn method (1929), the Kinzie method (Kinzie & Kinzie, 1931), and the Nitchie method (1912). Later Bunger (1944) wrote a book describing a speechreading method developed by Brauckman in Jena, Germany, the Jena method. Although these original four speechreading methods are seldom used now as they were originally conceived, it is recommended that the interested reader refer to French-St. George and Stoker (1988) for a historical chronicle of speechreading.

ANALYTIC AND SYNTHETIC APPROACHES. Each of the above original methods for teaching speechreading, as well as the recent approaches used currently, primarily makes use of one of two general approaches (analytic or synthetic) for speechreading instruction. However, for the most part, these incorporate the same general strategies as the analytical and synthetic approaches described in Chapter 4 for auditory training. The analytic approach to speeechreading is based on the concept that, before an entire word, sentence, or phrase (the whole) can be identified, it is necessary to perceive visually each of its basic parts. That is, because a word is constructed by placing phonemes in a given sequential order and sentences (thoughts) are constructed by correctly ordering words, it is essential that the viewer initially identify phonemes visually in isolation before attempting to perceive words. Likewise, we must be able to identify individual words before attempting to recognize strings of words (sentences or phrases). Said differently, this approach to speechreading considers the phoneme and syllable to be the key units for visual perception; therefore, these units must be recognized in isolation before comprehension of the whole is probable.

> Analytic speech-reading centers around visually perceiving the *details* found in speech.

Conversely, the synthetic approach to speechreading emphasizes that the perception of the whole is paramount regardless of which of its parts is perceived visually. Consequently, the speechreader is encouraged to comprehend the general meaning of oral utterances, rather than concentrating on accurately identifying each component within the oral message. As noted earlier, a considerable number of English phonemes are not visible or distinguishable on the speaker's lips; thus, the receiver must predict and synthesize information from fragmented visual input and also use available contextual cues. The synthetic approach therefore considers speechreading key words and the sentence and phrase to be the basic units and backbone of visual speech perception.

> Synthetic speech-reading involves grasping the general thought of the speaker through intuitive thinking.

A procedure known as Continuous Discourse Tracking (CDT) developed by De-Filippo and Scott (1978) is being used in speechreading assessment and therapy. Tracking requires the hard of hearing listener to speechread verbatim passages presented by the clinician either in a vision-only or in a combined auditory–visual manner. A performance score is derived by counting the number of words per minute (wpm) the listener–viewer correctly identifies. An example of how tracking is applied in a therapy session is presented in Chapter 4, and a tracking activity is available via website.

Table 5.4 contains examples of general speechreading therapy activities focused on emphasizing analytic and synthetic speechreading skills.

Recent Trends in Speechreading Instruction

The improvements in hearing aids, assistive listening devices (ALDs), vibrotactile devices, and cochlear implants that have occurred during the past two decades have made it possible for the hearing impaired, especially those with moderate to severe losses, to more effectively use their hearing than in the past in an integrated manner with speechreading. In a sense, this increased potential to greatly improve the communication abilities of those with hearing loss through hearing aids has, in part, led to much less emphasis on long-term speechreading therapy in rehabilitation

---

TABLE 5.4

Examples of Analytical and Synthetic Speechreading Therapy Activities

ANALYTIC ACTIVITIES

1. Present syllable pairs with initial consonants that are the same or different (e.g., /ba/ and /ba/, or /la/ and /ba/) and ask the speechreader to discriminate if the initial consonant in the syllable pair is the same or different.
2. Present three or four words (e.g., talk, tool, mop) and have the speechreader determine which word has /m/ in the initial position.
3. Present single words and ask the speechreader to identify each word from a short list of printed words that the speechreader has in front of him.

SYNTHETIC ACTIVITIES

1. Show the speechreader a picture and ask her to provide 4 to 6 words that logically could be used by someone talking about the picture.
2. Name a topic (e.g., popular television shows) and have the speechreader identify the name of each show that you present.
3. Present a short paragraph and then ask the speechreader to answer 3 to 4 questions based on the content of the paragraph.

---

programs for many individuals than in the past, particularly those with mild to moderate hearing impairments. Instead, what is done routinely with these individuals is to remind them of the importance of attending visually while communicating and encourage them to utilize this potentially helpful information as much as possible as another way, in addition to using hearing aids, to maximize overall speech perception. However, speechreading is still viewed as a useful component of audiological rehabilitation, and long-term therapy designed to facilitate speechreading skills still is recommended on a selective basis for some persons with hearing impairment. The next two sections briefly discuss some of the more recent ways in which speechreading has been incorporated into rehabilitation strategies for both children and adults.

CHILDREN. There has been a dearth of information available concerning speechreading strategies for this population (Yoshinaga-Itano, 1988). One probable explanation for this is that some therapeutic approaches used with hearing impaired children have focused almost exclusively on maximizing the use of the auditory channel (Wedenberg, 1951; Pollack, 1964, 1985), with little if any attempt made to teach speechreading skills. This auditory-only unisensory philosophy of management for the hearing impaired is sometimes referred to as the aural approach. Despite the unisensory orientation of these approaches, children trained in this manner often emerge with effective speechreading skills. Although this approach clearly focuses on processing and using auditory input, speechreading appears to develop synergistically with the acquisition of auditory and language skills (Pollack, 1964).

Other professionals believe that speechreading therapy has some relevance to a comprehensive plan for audiologic rehabilitation for children. Yoshinaga-Itano

In the aural approach, auditory abilities are developed to the fullest extent possible. Consequently, formal speechreading training is not incorporated into a child's overall program, and speechreading actually is prevented in some therapy activities.

Analytic drill emphasizing visual cues associated with a consonant.

(1988) suggests using what she terms a *holistic approach* when teaching hard of hearing children to speechread. This method differs from the traditional approaches to speechreading in that, rather than using a single technique for all young clients, it focuses on each individual child's motivation, tolerance, and sense of responsibility for communicating. Goals include building the child's knowledge base concerning the speechreading process and having the child develop an appreciation of the benefits that speechreading can provide in perceiving speech. Consequently, the stimuli used are client oriented, and therapy is based on each client's capabilities and needs in real-life situations, rather than just in canned exercises. Therefore, clinical activities must address the individual needs of each child. In addition, the speechreading activities must be interesting and give the child the opportunity to experience frequent success by correctly perceiving what is being presented. Figure 5.2 is an example of an activity that may be appropriate for *some* hard of hearing children. The child is given a worksheet with a picture on it and asked to speechread the key words presented by the clinician or by other children if it is being used

Space Patrol

FIGURE 5.2

Example of an exercise used in speechreading therapy with children.

space suit   space helmet

sky   sun

stop   stars

Here is a space ship. Lets take a ride in it. Put on your _____ and your _____ . Step in and sit down. We will see the _____ and the _____ in the _____ . We will not _____ for a long time.

in a group session. Beyond providing contextual and situational information, the picture has the potential to stimulate client motivation and interest. As a reward, the clinician may ask the child to color the picture. The clinician is reminded that this is only an example and the idea and format should be adapted to meet the needs and interests of her or his clients.

Children born with severe to profound hearing losses or who acquire the hearing loss prelingually become potential recipients of speechreading therapy if an oral or total communication approach to management is followed. These children are fit as early as possible with hearing aids binaurally or cochlear implants. As part of an overall management approach, they also are encouraged to use vision and speechreading therapy, along with auditory training. Both analytic and synthetic training activities are used to develop visual as well as auditory skills. Although a portion of speechreading and auditory skill development is done in vision-only or auditory-only conditions, many professionals currently advocate using both vision and audition together. Expressions with visual and auditory stimuli presented simultaneously are more natural and provide an opportunity to integrate the auditory and visual cues that are available. More information on the application of speechreading with hearing impaired children can be obtained in the publications by McCaffrey (1995), Tye-Murray (1993a, 1993b), or Haspiel (1987).

ADULTS. In the past, speechreading training was often provided to hearing impaired adults in an intensive manner over a lengthy period of time, which sometimes extended for weeks and even months. This approach is still used selectively in some instances, such as with adults with severe, progressive hearing losses or some cochlear implant recipients. For these individuals, speech perception is challenging at best, and attempting to maximize the use of visual cues through extensive speechreading therapy is sometimes warranted, even if the benefits derived are limited.

Long-term speechreading therapy typically includes both analytic and synthetic training activities. In addition, clinicians are encouraged to use both visual-only and visual–auditory sensory modalities throughout the therapy program. The level of difficulty for the speechreader can be varied by degrading either the visual or auditory stimulus. For example, increasing the distance between the speechreader and the clinician will increase the level of difficulty for the speechreading task. Focused speechreading therapy of this nature can be done in either an individualized or group setting. However, group sessions afford an opportunity for the participants to interact and learn from one another. In some instances, clinicians elect to conduct programs that combine both individual and group sessions for the participants to gain the benefits of each format. Guidance in this application of speechreading, including useful information regarding therapy activities, can be obtained from Wayner and Abrahamson (1996), Feehan, Samuelson, and Seymour (1982), and Tye-Murray (1997). Finally, it should be noted that research (Walden et al., 1977) suggests that much of the improvement in speechreading that many individuals derive from therapy may occur in the first several sessions, making long-term involvement in speechreading therapy something that only should be done on a selective basis.

Long-term speechreading therapy generally is used only in isolated situations, but there has been a growing interest in including limited speechreading instruction as part of a general orientation to effective communication skills. This approach is comparatively short term and typically emphasizes a number of key components of effective communication, including the importance of speechreading in communicating, as well as providing basic information about how to enhance speechreading performance in a variety of communicative situations. The intent here is not to engage the person with a hearing loss in therapy and drill-like activities in an attempt to improve visual perception of speech. Rather, it is to highlight to the individual the importance and benefits of using the visual skills that they already have in order to maximize speech perception abilities. This strategy has generally taken two different forms. In one of the approaches, clinicians organize small (6 to 12 members) groups of adults with hearing impairments. These groups typically meet once a week for 4 to 6 weeks, with each session devoted to a general topic related to enhancing overall communication skills. Among the more common topics included are the following:

Understanding hearing loss

Effective use of hearing aids and assistive listening devices

Speechreading

Communication strategies

The session devoted to speechreading often includes general information about the speechreading process, as well as tips for effective speechreading (Table 5.5).

Another approach used is to provide a streamlined and condensed version of the same type of communication-related information and helpful hints. This can be done in one session, often when the individual is fit with hearing aids. One example of this is the CLEAR program described in Chapter 10, and Montgomery's (1994) WATCH program is another example of this brief form of audiologic rehabilitation. WATCH includes an emphasis on the use of vision (W stands for "Watch the talker's mouth"). In this manner, the person is informed about the benefits of speechreading and encouraged to use it as much as possible.

INNOVATIVE OPTIONS. Speechreading training can occur in formats other than the traditional face to face approach. For example, individuals can use videotapes as self-instructional programs to improve speechreading skills. Examples include *I See What You're Saying*, a two-volume series produced by the New York League for the Hard of Hearing (1990) and the National Technical Institute for the Deaf (NTID) Speechreading Videotapes (1987).

Another innovative approach to speechreading training is referred to as computer-assisted interactive video (CAIV) instruction. The use of computers with computer-driven video and laser disc players has received considerable attention and

---

TABLE 5.5

Tips for Speechreading

Be relatively close to the person(s) with whom you are communicating.

Watch the speaker's mouth, facial expressions, and hand gestures as much as possible.

Be aware of the topic of conversation and contextual cues.

Maximize your hearing (hearing aids and assistive listening devices at optimum volume and minimize background noise).

Let the talker know that you have a hearing loss and request that she or he face you as much as possible.

application in hearing rehabilitation during the past decade. Mahshie (1987) defines interactive video as a "video program that can be controlled by the person using it." However, for this methodology to be useful, it must be capable of controlling complex protocols tailored to the rehabilitative needs of individual students or clients. Therefore, CAIV must incorporate a variety of teaching strategies and client response formats. The advantage of laser videodisc is the rapidity and accuracy with which specific stimuli can be accessed from the videodisc. Fifteen years ago the first interactive video for speechreading was developed at the NTID by Cronin and his colleagues (1979). This system was known as DAVID (Dynamic Audio Video Interactive Device). Since the initiation of this technology, researchers and clinicians have used interactive video systems to determine the benefits of cochlear implants and vibrotactile devices on speechreading. In 1986, laser videodisc technology was introduced as a speechreading training protocol (Kopra et al., 1986). It is not within the scope of this chapter to discuss in detail the various CAIV programs now available. However, the following are examples of the more current interactive video speechreading programs: Auditory-Visual Laser Videodisc Interactive System (ALVIS), developed by Kopra et al., 1987; Computer-Assisted Speech Perception Evaluation and Training (CASPER), designed by Boothroyd and his co-workers (Boothroyd, 1987); Computer-Aided Speechreading Training Program (CAST) designed by Pichora-Fuller and Benguerel (1991); and Computerized Laser Videodisc Programs for Training Speechreading and Assertive Communication Behaviors, developed at the University of Iowa Hospitals by Tye-Murray and her associates (1988). Most of these CAIV programs include both analytic and synthetic-based activities for speechreading instruction, including a tracking component. There is little doubt that more computer-generated speechreading programs will be developed for use by the hearing impaired in the future. However, it also is clear that the traditional face to face format, involving both patient and clinician, will continue to be an important and viable format for audiologic rehabilitation as well.

■ MANUAL COMMUNICATION

Vision can be used by the hearing impaired for communication in another manner besides speechreading. Physical gestures and facial expressions have always been used by humans to express emotions and to share information. The transmission of thoughts in this manner undoubtedly preceded the verbal form of communication. As stated earlier in this chapter, manual communication is comprised of specific gestural codes. That is, a visual message is transmitted by the fingers, hands, arms, and bodily postures using specific signs or fingerspelling. In general, manual communication is used by a high percentage of the deaf to communicate with other individuals also having manual communication skills. The various forms of manual communication are used in isolation or in combination with speech.

Types of Manual Communication

Numerous forms of manual communication have evolved. The major types, along with spoken English, are briefly described and compared in Table 5.6 (Smith, 1984).

TABLE 5.6

Forms of Manual and Spoken Communication

AMERICAN SIGN LANGUAGE (ASL)	PIDGIN SIGN LANGUAGE (PSE)	SIGNED ENGLISH	LINGUISTICS OF VISUAL ENGLISH (LOVE)	SIGNING EXACT ENGLISH (SEE 2)	SEEING ESSENTIAL ENGLISH (SEE 1)	FINGER-SPELLING	CUED SPEECH	ENGLISH
Independent language; visual manual mode; own grammar; own syntax; signs are meaning based; has dialects, regionalisms, slang, puns; can be written; wide range of vocabulary covering minute differences in meaning; may borrow from other languages; is verbal, but also makes use of nonverbal elements.	A combination of elements from ASL and the sign systems, ranging from the more ASL-like (occasionally called Ameslish) to the more English-like (sometimes called CASE—Conceptually Accurate Signed English). Usually contains few if any sign markers (see Signed English); yet makes frequent use of fingerspelled English words. Used in conjunction with speech in interpreting and college teaching. Signs are meaning based.	Signed in accordance with English grammar, but signs are meaning based; specially invented sign markers for important affixes in English; invented by Bornstein; used widely in education.	Essentially the same as SEE 2, but has a method of writing each sign; used in education; invented by Wampler; usage is diminishing.	Signs are word based; special signs for all affixes in English; signed in strict accordance with English; invented by Zawolkow, Pfetzing and Gustason; widely used in education; very influential.	Signs are based on word roots (morphemes) (trans/port/a/tion); an extreme form of word-based signs; invented by Anthony; not popular in U.S., but still common in Iowa and Colorado schools for the deaf; signs for all affixes.	Manual representation of the written language; one hand shape for each letter of alphabet; used to borrow English words in ASL; when used with speech and speechreading, it is called the Rochester Method.	Employs 8 hand shapes in 4 positions on the face, and used in conjunction with lip movements to enable a deaf person to lipread more easily; based on sound with the syllable as the basic unit; devised by Orin Cornett at Gallaudet College.	Independent language; aural–oral mode; own grammar; own syntax; words are meaning based; contains dialects, regionalisms, slang, puns; can be written; wide range of vocabulary covering minute differences in meaning; may borrow from other languages; is verbal, but also makes use of nonverbal elements.

Artificial pedagogical systems, invented for educational purposes

Nonverbal communication: natural gestures, facial expression, body movements, body language, pantomime

Source: From W. H. Smith, personal communication, 1984.

Smith pointed out that the only two pure languages represented in this group are English and American Sign Language.

American Sign Language, also referred to as ASL or Ameslan, was the first form of manual communication established, independent of existing oral languages, by the deaf. Consequently, the original sign language was indeed a unique "natural" language. Approximately one-half million deaf and hearing individuals use this language (Baker and Cokely, 1980). Interestingly, many individuals learn ASL via their deaf peers and associates rather than from their parents. Padden (1980) reports that it is probably the only language that is not learned from parents. Although most deaf adults are proud that they communicate via ASL and are annoyed by teachers and others who are adverse to its use, the fact that they learned it from other children rather than from their parents influences their attitudes about sign language (Vernon and Andrews, 1990). The signs associated with ASL possess four identifying physical characteristics: hand configuration, movement, location, and orientation. In fact, Stokoe (1978) claims that there are 19 basic symbols for hand-shapes, 12 basic symbols for locations, and 24 basic symbols for movement. Although these parameters, referred to as *cheremes* by Stokoe et al. (1965), are different from spoken lexical items, they may be viewed as analogous to the distinctive features of speech. These features are illustrated in Figure 5.3. The prosodic features of ASL are provided by facial expressions, head tilts, body movement, and eye gazes (Vernon and Andrews, 1990).

Because ASL is a language, it consists of words. However, there is not a corresponding sign to represent each English word, just as there is no unique relationship between the words used in English, French, Portuguese, Chinese, or Japanese. All languages were developed using a common code for the exchange of information. Also, the structure of each language is as unique as is its vocabulary (code). Thus, "Ni qui guo zhong-guo mei-you?" probably looks and sounds peculiar and un-

> Cheremes are the most basic and visually distinct units of sign language.

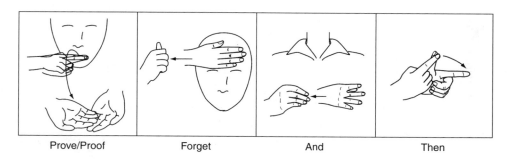

| Prove/Proof | Forget | And | Then |

FIGURE 5.3

Four signs used in ASL representing the features of handshape (DEZ), movement/signation (SIG), tabulation where sign is produced (TAB), and palmar direction of the hands.
Source: From L. Riekehof (1978). *The Joy of Signing.* Springfield, MO: Gospel Publishing House.

intelligible to those of us native to the United States, but the sentence is logical and meaningful to someone in Taiwan. Similarly, ASL is not a form of English, but rather a distinct language produced manually that requires just as unique a translation of English as does any foreign language.

Some of the over 6000 signs that are part of ASL can be decoded intuitively. These signs are classified as iconic, meaning that they are imageries of English words. The signs in Figure 5.4 will be familiar to most readers, even those who have never been exposed to manual communication, specifically ASL.

SIGNED ENGLISH SYSTEMS. There is evidence that only deaf adults are truly proficient at using ASL. When most hearing individuals attempt to communicate manually with the deaf using ASL, they often attempt to use the signs of ASL in a manner that more closely resembles English grammatically. This counterpart to ASL is commonly referred to as Pidgin Sign Language. In other words, Pidgin Sign Language involves combining ASL with English to some extent. If the signer makes considerable English-related modifications, then the result is Pidgin Signed English.

Other attempts have been made to seriously alter ASL so that it closely resembles English, and these are referred to as sign systems. Sign systems, which have been developed mainly by educators for use in educating the deaf, are contrived and have not evolved naturally, so they are not considered to be languages.

Signed English is a system in which the English words that appear in a message are signed in that same order. To indicate tense, person, plurality, and possession a sign marker is used as a suffix to the signed word. Seeing Essential English (SEE 1) was developed by David Anthony, a deaf individual, as a means of presenting English visually to the deaf as it is presented auditorily to normal hearing children. Anthony suggested that the word order of the message parallel the word order used in English. Signing Exact English (SEE II) is an outgrowth of SEE I. The purpose of this

Iconic signs closely represent the respective actions or things. They are easily presented and understood, sometimes even by those not fluent in signing.

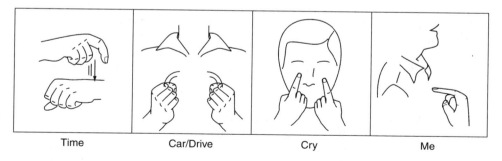

| Time | Car/Drive | Cry | Me |

FIGURE 5.4

Four iconic signs. The signs are visual images of the English words they represent.
Source: From L. Riekehof (1978). *The Joy of Signing.* Springfield, MO: Gospel Publishing House.

system is to maintain the syntactic structure of SEE I without making the system unintelligible for those using ASL. Linguistics of Visual English (LOVE) was established at approximately the same time as SEE II was initiated. Again, this was an attempt to refine another sign system aimed at approximating English. The vocabulary is more limited than that of SEE I and SEE II. It attempts to mirror spoken English by making signed movements that correspond to the number of syllables uttered in a spoken word. Yet LOVE is primarily a manual system identical to SEE II. The reader is urged to read the works of Scheetz (2001) and Vernon and Andrews (1990) for a historical and more detailed discussion of these systems.

FINGERSPELLING. Another method of communicating manually is to have senders spell the words with their fingers. That is, instead of using pencil and paper, speakers spell their message in the air by using various handshapes to represent the letters in the English alphabet. This mode of communication, fingerspelling, represents the 26 letters of the English alphabet by 25 handshapes and two hand movements (see Figure 5.5). Collectively these are also referred to as the manual alphabet. The letters *i* and *j* are produced by the same handshape, with the *j* being produced by moving the hand in a hook or *j*-like motion. The letter *z* is made by moving a unique handshape in the form of a *z*. Although fingerspelling is an exact and effective means of communication, it is the least efficient form of manual communication; each letter of each word must be produced, which makes it a relatively laborious means of communicating. Because no additional characters are included in the alphabet nor digits in the numeric system, a person can learn to transmit a message via fingerspelling in a relatively short time. However, because of the rapidity with which one learns to "spell" a message and because of the similarity in the production of *e*, *o*, *m*, and *n* and between the letters *a* and *s*, the reception of fingerspelling requires considerable practice and concentration. As mentioned in the discussion of speechreading, the similarity among letters and sounds becomes more confounding during discourse than in isolation. But, as in every other form of communication, predictability mitigates this problem. Today, fingerspelling is used to supplement all forms of manual communication by expressing proper names, technical terms, and events that cannot be conveyed by signs. An application of fingerspelling is the Rochester Method, in which the teachers and students simultaneously "spell" what they are expressing orally.

Cued speech also has applications for speech therapy.

CUED SPEECH. Some professionals have promoted the use of cued speech as an ancillary tool in speechreading instruction (Cornett, 1967, 1972). The intent of Cornett's (1967) cued speech system (some would prefer to classify it as a manual system) is to use hand cues to reduce the confusion produced by speechreading homophenous phonemes, making speechreading more accurate and effective. Cornett selected four hand positions and eight handshapes near the mouth to facilitate communication in the overall management of the hearing impaired. See Figure 5.6.

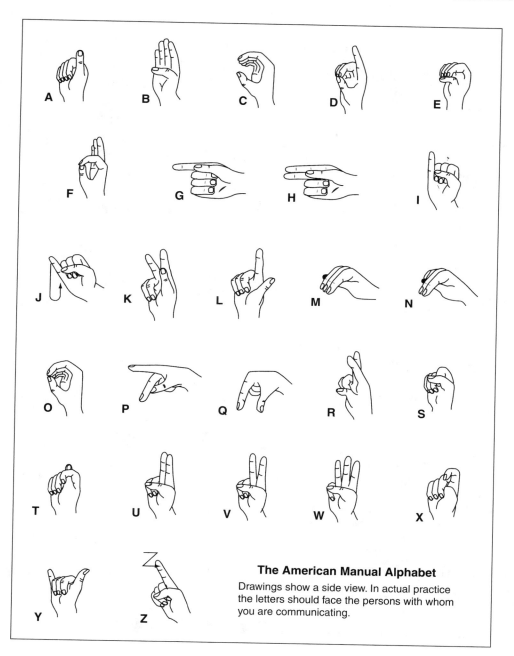

The American Manual Alphabet

Drawings show a side view. In actual practice the letters should face the persons with whom you are communicating.

FIGURE 5.5

American manual alphabet. The hand positions are shown as they appear to the person reading them.

Courtesy of Gallaudet College, Washington, D.C.

Chart I

Cues for English Vowels

	Group I (Base Position)		Group II (Larynx)		Group III (Chin)		Group IV (Mouth)	
Open	[a:]	(fäther) (gŏt)	[a]	(thăt)	[o:]	(fôr) (ought)		
Flattened-Relaxed	[ʌ] [ə]	(but) (the)	[i]	(is)	[e]	(gĕt)	[i:]	(feet) (meat)
Rounded	[ou]	(note) (boat)	[u]	(gŏod) (put)	[u:]	(blue) (food)	[ə]	(ûrn) (hẽr)

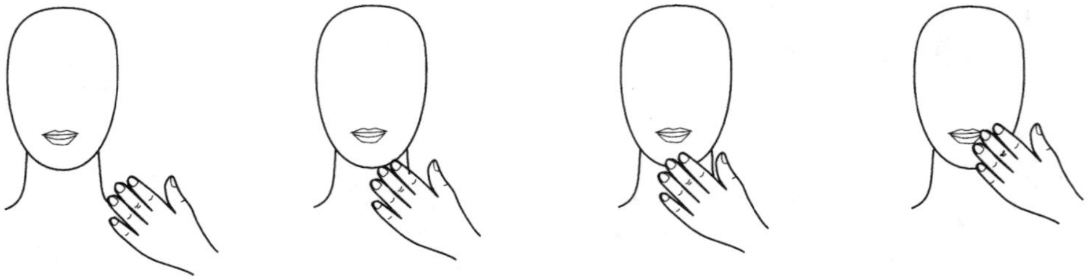

Chart II

Cues for English Consonants

T Group*	H Group	D Group	ng Group	L Group	K Group	N Group	G Group
t	h	d	(ng)	l	k	n	g
m	s	p	y (you)	sh	v	b	j
f	r	zh	ch	w	th (the)	hw**	th (thin)
					z		

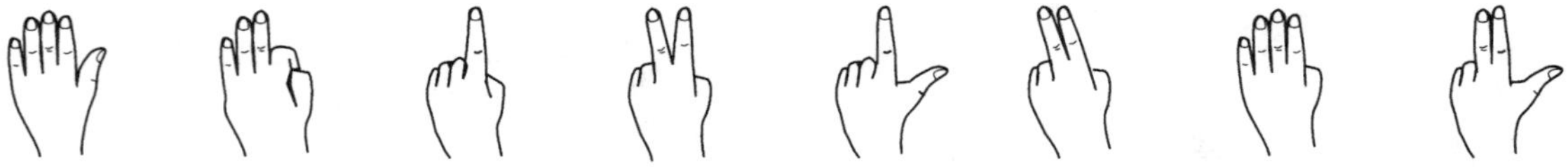

Note: The T group cue is also used with an isolated vowel—that is, an individual vowel not run with a final consonant from the preceding syllable.

FIGURE 5.6

Hand positions and handshapes used in cued speech.

Source: From R. Cornett (1967). Cued Speech. *American Annals of the Deaf, 112,* 3–13.

SUMMARY POINTS

- Speechreading and the use of manual communication are two important aspects of audiologic rehabilitation that involve the use of vision by those with hearing loss.
- Speechreading is a complex process that involves a large number of variables associated with the speechreader and other components of oral communication.

- Speechreading assessment can be done with a variety of formal and informal test protocols, using vision-only or combined vision–hearing conditions.
- Intensive training in speechreading is not frequently done. When carried out, both analytic and synthetic skill development activities are included.
- Shorter forms of audiologic rehabilitation are frequently used that encourage and assist those with hearing impairment to maximize the use of the speech-reading skills that they already have.
- Manual communication consists of sign language, sign systems, and finger spelling.
- American Sign Language, or ASL, is the language of the Deaf.
- Sign systems have been developed that modify ASL to make it more consistent with English. These systems are often used in educational programs.
- Fingerspelling, an adjunct to signing, uses the manual alphabet to spell out words in a message.

RECOMMENDED READING

Alpiner, J., & McCarthy, P. (Eds.). (2000). *Rehabilitative audiology: Children and adults* (3rd ed.). Philadelphia: Lippincott Williams and Wilkins.
Gagne, J. P., & Tye-Murray, N. (Eds.). (1994). Research in audiological rehabilitation: Current trends and future directions (Monograph). *Journal of the Academy of Rehabilitative Audiology, 27.*
Hipskind, N. (1978). Aural rehabilitation for adults. *Otolaryngologic Clinics of North America, 11,* 823–834.
Paul, P. (2001). *Language and deafness* (3rd ed.). San Diego, CA: Singular Publishing Group.
Scheetz, N. (2001). *Orientation to deafness* (2nd ed.). Boston: Allyn and Bacon.
Tye-Murray, N. (1998). *Foundations of aural rehabilitation.* San Diego, CA: Singular.
Valente, M., Hosford-Dunn, H., and Roeser, R. (2000). *Audiology: Treatment.* New York: Thieme.

REFERENCES

Albright, P., Hipskind, N., & Schuckers, G. (1973). A comparison of visibility and speechreading performance on English and Slurvian. *Journal of Communication Disorders, 6,* 44–52.
Alpiner, J. G. (1978). *Handbook of adult rehabilitative audiology.* Baltimore, MD: Williams & Wilkins.
Alpiner, J., & McCarthy, P. (Eds.). (2001). *Rehabilitative audiology: Children and adults* (3rd ed.). Baltimore, MD: Williams & Wilkins.
Baker, C., & Cokely, D. (1980). *American sign language: A teachers resource test on grammar and culture.* Silver Spring, MD: T. J. Publishers.
Berger, K. (1972a). *Speechreading: Principles and methods.* Baltimore, MD: National Educational Press.
Berger, K. (1972b). Visemes and homophenous words. *Teacher of the Deaf, 70,* 396–399.
Bevan, R. C. (1988). *Hearing-impaired children: A guide for parents and concerned professionals.* Springfield, IL: Charles C Thomas Publishers.

Binnie, C. A., Jackson, P., & Montgomery, A. (1976). Visual intelligibility of consonants: A lipreading screening test with implications for aural rehabilitation. *Journal of Speech and Hearing Disorders, 41,* 530–539.

Boothroyd, A. (1987). CASPER, computer-assisted speech perception evaluation and training. In *Proceedings of the 10th Annual Conference of the Rehabilitation Society of North America.* Washington, DC: Association for Advancement of Rehabilitation Technology.

Boothroyd, A. (1988). Linguistic factors in speechreading. In C. L. DeFilippo & D. G. Sims (eds.), New reflections on speechreading (Monograph). *Volta Review, 90* (5), 77–87.

Bruhn, M. E. (1929). *The Muelkr–Walle method of lip reading for the deaf.* Lynn, MS: Nicholas Press.

Bunger, A. M. (1944). *Speech reading—Jena method.* Danville, IL: The Interstate Co.

Campbell, C., Polomeno, R., Elder, J., Murray, I., & Altosaar, A. (1981). Importance of an eye examination in identifying the cause of congenital hearing impairments. *Journal of Speech and Hearing Disorders, 46,* 258–261.

CHABA, Working Group on Communication Aids for the Hearing-Impaired. (1991). Speech-perception aids for hearing impaired people: Current status and needed research. *Journal of the Acoustical Society of America, 90,* 637–685.

Clouser, R. A. (1976). The effects of vowel consonant ratio and sentence length on lipreading ability. *American Annals of the Deaf, 121,* 513–518.

Cornett, R. (1967). Cued speech. *American Annals of the Deaf, 112,* 3–13.

Cornett, R. O. (1972). *Cued speech parent training and follow-up program.* Washington, DC: Bureau of Education for the Handicapped, DHEW.

Cronin, B. (1979). The DAVID system: The development of an interactive video system at the National Institute for the Deaf. *American Annals of the Deaf, 124,* 615–618.

Daly, N., Bench, J., and Chappell, H. (1996). Gender differences in speechreadability. *Journal of the Academy of Rehabilitative Audiology, 29,* 27–40.

Dancer, J., Krain, M., Thompson, C., Davis, P., & Glenn, J. (1994). A cross-sectional investigation of speechreading in adults: Effects of age, gender, practice and education. *Volta Review, 96,* 31–40.

DeFilippo, C., & Scott, B. (1978). A method for training and evaluating the reception of ongoing speech. *Journal of the Acoustical Society of America, 63* (4), 1186–1192.

Dodd, B., & Campbell, R. (1987). *Hearing by eye: The psychology of lip-reading.* London: Erlbaum.

Erber, N. P. (1971). Effects of distance on the visual reception of speech. *Journal of Speech and Hearing Research, 14,* 848–857.

Erber, N. P. (1974). Effects of angle, distance and illumination on visual reception of speech by profoundly deaf children. *Journal of Speech and Hearing Research, 17,* 99–112.

Feehan, P., Samuelson, R., & Seymour, D. (1982). *CLUES: Speechreading for adults.* Austin, TX: Pro-Ed.

Fisher, C. G. (1968). Confusions among visually perceived consonants. *Journal of Speech and Hearing Research, 12,* 796–804.

French-St. George, M., & Stoker, R. (1988). Speechreading: An historical perspective. In C. L. DeFilippo & D. G. Sims (Eds.). New reflections on speechreading (Monograph). *Volta Review, 90* (5), 17–31.

Gaeth, I. H. (1948). *A study of phonemic regression in relation to hearing loss.* Unpublished doctoral dissertation, Northwestern University.

Garstecki, D. (1977). Identification of communication competence in the geriatric population. *Journal of the Academy of Rehabilitative Audiology, 10,* 36–45.

Garstecki, D., & O'Neill, J. J. (1980). Situational cues and strategy influence on speechreading. *Scandinavian Audiology, 9,* 1–5.

Gibson, E. J. (1969). *Principles of perceptual learning and development.* New York: Appleton-Century-Crofts.

Giolas, T., Butterfield, E. C., Weaver, S. J. (1974). Some motivational correlates of lipreading. *Journal of Speech and Hearing Research, 17,* 18–24.

Hardick, E. J., Oyer, H. J., Irion, P. E. (1970). Lipreading performance is related to measurements of vision. *Journal of Speech and Hearing Research, 13,* 92.

Haspiel, G. (1987). *Lipreading for children.* Washington, DC: Alexander Graham Bell Association for the Deaf.

Hefler, K. (1998). Auditory and auditory–visual recognition of clear and conversational speech by older adults. *Journal of the American Academy of Audiology, 9,* 234–242.

Hipskind, N. (1978). Aural rehabilitation for adults. *Otolaryngologic Clinics of North America, 11,* 823–834.

Hipskind, N. M., Nerbonne, G. P., & Gravel, J. S. (1973). The intelligibility of C.I.D. Auditory Test W-1 words as speechreading stimuli. *Journal of Communication Disorders, 6,* 1–10.

Jackson, P. L. (1988). The theoretical minimal unit for visual speech perception: Visemes and coarticulation. *Volta Review, 90,* 99–115.

Jackson, P. L., Montgomery, A. A., & Binnie, C. A. (1976). Perceptual dimensions underlying vowel lipreading performance. *Journal of Speech and Hearing Research, 19,* 796–812.

Jeffers, J., & Barley, M. (1971). *Speechreading.* Springfield, IL: Charles C Thomas.

Johnson, D., & Snell, K. B. (1986). Effects of distance visual acuity problems on the speechreading performance of hearing-impaired adults. *Journal of the Academy of Rehabilitative Audiology, 19,* 42–55.

Johnson, D., Caccamise, F., Rothblum, A., Hamilton, L., & Howard, M. (1981). Identification and follow-up of visual impairments in hearing-impaired populations. *American Annals of the Deaf, 126,* 321–360.

Kinzie, C. E., & Kinzie, R. (1931). *Lipreading for the deafened adult.* Chicago: John C. Winston.

Kopra, L., Kopra, M., Abrahamson, J., & Dunlop, R. (1986). Development of sentences graded in difficulty for lipreading practice. *Journal of the Academy of Rehabilitative Audiology, 19,* 71–86.

Kopra, L., Kopra, M., Abrahamson, J., & Dunlop, R. (1987). Lipreading drill and practice software for an auditory–visual videodisc interactive system (ALVIS). *Journal for Computer Users in Speech and Hearing, 3,* 58–68.

Kricos, P., & Lesner, S. (1982). Differences in visual intelligibility across talkers. *Volta Review, 84,* 219–225.

Lesner, S., Sandridge, S., & Kricos, P. (1987). Training influences on visual consonant and sentence recognition. *Ear and Hearing, 8,* 283–287.

Lewis, D. (1972). Lipreading skills of hearing impaired children in regular schools. *Volta Review, 74,* 303–311.

Lovering, L. (1969). *Lipreading performance as a function of visual acuity.* Unpublished doctoral dissertation, Michigan State University.

Mahshie, J. J. (1987). A primer on interactive video. *Journal for Computer Users in Speech and Hearing, 3,* 39–57.

Massaro, D. M. (1987). Speech perception by ear and eye: A paradigm for psychology inquiry. Hillsdale, NJ: Lawrence Erlbaum.

McCaffrey, H. (1995). Techniques and concepts in auditory training and speech-reading. Chapter 15 in R. Roeser & M. Downs (Eds.), *Auditory disorders in school children* (3rd ed.). New York: Thieme.

Miller, G. A., & Nicely, P. E. (1955). An analysis of the perceptual confusions among some English consonants. *Journal of the Acoustical Society of America, 27,* 338–352.

Montgomery, A. (1994). WATCH: A practical approach to brief auditory rehabilitation. *Hearing Journal, 10,* 10–55.

Montgomery, A., and Houston, T. (2000). The hearing-impaired adult: Management of communication deficits and tinnitus. In Alpiner, J., and McCarthy, P. (Eds.). *Rehabilitative audiology: Children and adults* (3rd ed.). Philadelphia: Lippincott Williams & Wilkins.

Montgomery, A. A., & Jackson, P. L. (1983). Physical characteristics of the lips underlying vowel lipreading performance. *Journal of the Acoustical Society of America, 73,* 2134–2144.

Montgomery, A. A., Walden, B. E., Schwartz, D. M., & Prosek, R. A. (1984). Training auditory–visual speech reception in adults with moderate sensorineural hearing loss. *Ear and Hearing, 5,* 30–36.

National Technical Institute for the Deaf. (1987). *NTID speechreading videotapes.* Washington, DC: Alexander Graham Bell Association for the Deaf.

New York League for the Hard of Hearing (1990). I see what you're saying. New York: Author.

New York League for the Hard of Hearing. (1991). *Assessment of adult speechreading ability.* New York: Author.

Nitchie, E. B. (1912). *Lip reading: Principles and practice.* New York: Frederick A. Stokes Co.

Nitchie, E. B. (1950). *New lessons in lip reading.* Philadelphia: J. B. Lippincott.

O'Neill, J. J. (1951). An exploratory investigation of lipreading ability among normal-hearing students. *Speech Monographs, 18,* 309–311.

O'Neill, J. J., & Oyer, H. J. (1981). *Visual communication for the hard of hearing* (2nd ed.). Englewood Cliffs, NJ: Prentice Hall.

Owens, E., & Blazek, B. (1985). Visemes observed by hearing-impaired and normal hearing adult viewers. *Journal of Speech and Hearing Research, 28,* 381–393.

Padden, C. (1980). The deaf community and the culture of deaf people. In C. Baker & R. Battison (Eds.), *Sign language and the deaf community: Essays in honor of William Stokoe.* Silver Spring, MD: National Association of the Deaf.

Pichora-Fuller, M. K., & Benguerel, A.-P. (1991). The design of CAST (computer-aided speechreading training). *Journal of Speech and Hearing Research, 34,* 202–212.

Pollack, D. (1964). Acoupedics. *Volta Review, 66,* 400.

Pollack, D. (1985). Educational audiology for the limited hearing infant and preschooler (2nd ed.). Springfield, IL: Charles C Thomas.

Romano, P., & Berlow, W. (1974). Vision requirements for lipreading. *American Annals of the Deaf, 119,* 393–396.

Ross, M. (1982). *Hard of hearing children in regular schools.* Englewood Cliffs, NJ: Prentice Hall.

Samar, V. J., & Sims, D. G. (1983). Visual evoked response correlates of speechreading performance in normal-hearing adults: A replication and factor analytic extension. *Journal of Speech and Hearing Research, 26,* 2–9.

Samar, V. J., & Sims, D. G. (1984). Visual evoked response components related to speechreading and spatial skills in hearing and hearing impaired adults. *Journal of Speech and Hearing Research, 27,* 23–26.

Sanders, D. A. (1993). *Aural rehabilitation* (3rd ed.). Englewood Cliffs, NJ: Prentice Hall.

Scheetz, N. A. (2001). Orientation to deafness (2nd ed.). Boston: Lenstok Press.

Shepard, D. C. (1982). Visual–neural correlate of speechreading ability in normal-hearing adults: Reliability. *Journal of Speech and Hearing Research, 25,* 521–527.

Shepard, D. C., DeLavergne, R. W., Fruek, F. X., & Clobridge, C. (1977). Visual–neural correlate of speechreading ability in normal-hearing adults. *Journal of Speech and Hearing Research, 20,* 752–765.

Smith, R. (1964). *An investigation of the relationships between lipreading ability and the intelligence of the mentally retarded.* Unpublished master's thesis, Michigan State University.

Stokoe, W. C. (Ed.). (1978). *Sign and culture, a reader for students of American sign language.* Silver Spring, MD: Lenstok Press.

Stokoe, W., Casterline, D., & Croneberg, C. (1965). *A dictionary of American sign language on linguistic principles.* Washington, DC: Gallaudet College Press.

Summerfield, Q. (1992). Lipreading and audio-visual perception. *Philosophical Transactions of the Royal Society of London,* January 29, 71–78. Royal Society of London.

Tye-Murray, N. (1993a). *Cochlear implants: Audiological foundations.* San Diego, CA: Singular Publishing Group.

Tye-Murray, N. (1993b). *Communication training for hearing-impaired children and teenagers: Speechreading, listening and using repair strategies.* Austin, TX: Pro-Ed.

Tye-Murray, N. (1997). *Communication training for hard-of-hearing adults and older teenagers: Speechreading, listening, and using repair strategies.* Austin, TX: Pro-Ed.

Tye-Murray, N., & Geers, A. (1997). The Children's Speechreading Enhancement Test (CHIVE). St. Louis, MO: Central Institute for the Deaf.

Tye-Murray, N., & Tyler, R. S. (1988). A critique of continuous discourse tracking as a test procedure. *Journal of Speech and Hearing Disorders, 53,* 226–231.

Tye-Murray, N., Tyler, R. S., Bong, B., & Nares, T. (1988). Computerized laser videodisc programs for training speechreading and assertive communication behaviors. *Journal of the Academy of Rehabilitative Audiology, 21,* 143–152.

Tyler, R., Preece, J., & Tye-Murray, N. (1986). *The Iowa phoneme and sentence tests.* Iowa City: University of Iowa Hospitals and Clinics.

Vernon, M., & Andrews, J. F. (1990). *The psychology of deafness: Understanding deaf and hard-of-hearing people.* New York: Longman.

Walden, B., Erdman, S., Montgomery, A., Schwartz, D., & Prosek, R. (1981). Some effects of training on speech perception by hearing-impaired adults. *Journal of Speech and Hearing Research, 24,* 207–216.

Walden, B., Prosek, R., Montgomery, A., Scharr, C., and Jones, C. (1977). Effects of training on the visual recognition of consonants. *Journal of Speech and Hearing Research, 20,* 130–145.

Wayner, D., & Abrahamson, J. (1996). *Learning to hear again.* Austin, TX: Hear Again.

Wedenberg, E. (1951). Auditory training of deaf and hard of hearing children. *Acta Otolaryngology* (Suppl. 94), *39,* 1–139.

Woodward, M. F., & Barber, C. G. (1960). Phoneme perception in lipreading. *Journal of Speech and Hearing Research, 3,* 212–222.

Yoshinaga-Itano, C. (1988). Speechreading instruction for children. In C. L. DeFilippo & D. G. Sims (Eds.). New reflections on speechreading (Monographs). *Volta Review, 90* (5), 241–254.

■ APPENDIXES

Appendix 5A: Utley—How Well Can You Read Lips?

This text, commonly referred to as the *Utley Test*, consists of three subtests: Sentences (Forms A and B), Words (Forms A and B), and Stories accompanied by questions that relate to each of the stories. Utley (1946) demonstrated that the Word and Story subtests are positively correlated with the Sentence portion of the test. Therefore, these are the stimuli most often used and associated with the *Utley Test*.

Utley evaluated her viewers' responses by giving one point for each word correctly identified in each sentence. A total of 125 words are contained in the 31 sentences on each form (Form A and B). Consequently, a respondent's score may range from 0 to 125 points. Utley suggested that homophenous words not be accepted when scoring the sentence subtest.

Utley administered the sentence subtest to 761 hearing-impaired children and adults, and the following descriptive statistics summarize her findings:

	FORM A	FORM B
Range	0–84	0–89
Mean	33.63	33.80
SD	16.36	17.53

PRACTICE SENTENCE

1. Good morning.
2. Thank you.
3. Hello.
4. How are you?
5. Goodbye.

UTLEY SENTENCE TEST—FORM A

1. All right.
2. Where have you been?
3. I have forgotten.
4. I have nothing.
5. That is right.
6. Look out.
7. How have you been?
8. I don't know if I can.
9. How tall are you?
10. It is awfully cold.
11. My folks are home.
12. How much was it?
13. Good night.
14. Where are you going?
15. Excuse me.
16. Did you have a good time?
17. What did you want?
18. How much do you weigh?
19. I cannot stand him.
20. She was home last week.
21. Keep your eye on the ball.
22. I cannot remember.
23. Of course.
24. I flew to Washington.
25. You look well.
26. The train runs every hour.
27. You had better go slow.
28. It says that in the book.
29. We got home at six o'clock.
30. We drove to the country.
31. How much rain fell?

From "A Test of Lipreading Ability" by J. Utley, 1946, *Journal of Speech and Hearing Disorders, 11*, pp. 109–116. Reprinted by permission.

Appendix 5B: The Denver Quick Test of Lipreading Ability

The *Denver Quick Test* is designed to measure adult ability to speechread 20 common everyday sentences. Sentences are presented "live" or taped by the tester and are scored on the basis of meaning recognition. No normative data are available to which individual scores may be compared; however, when the Quick Test was given without acoustic cues to 40 hearing-impaired adults, their scores were highly correlated (0.90) with their results on the *Utley Sentence Test* (Alpiner, 1982).

THE DENVER QUICK TEST OF LIPREADING ABILITY

1. Good morning
2. How old are you?
3. I live in (state of residence).
4. I only have one dollar.
5. There is somebody at the door.
6. Is that all?
7. Where are you going?
8. Let's have a coffee break.
9. Park your car in the lot.
10. What is your address?
11. May I help you?
12. I feel fine.
13. It is time for dinner.
14. Turn right at the corner.
15. Are you ready to order?
16. Is this charge or cash?
17. What time is it?
18. I have a headache.
19. How about going out tonight?
20. Please lend me 50 cents.

From "Evaluation of Communication Function" by J. Alpiner. In *Handbook of Adult Rehabilitative Audiology* (pp. 18–79) by J. Alpiner (Ed.), 1982. Baltimore: Williams & Wilkins. Reprinted by permission.

Appendix 5C: Craig Lipreading Inventory

The Craig Lipreading Inventory consists of two forms of 33 isolated words and 24 sentences. The vocabulary for these stimuli was selected from words used by children enrolled in kindergarten and first grade. A filmed version of the test is available. The test is usually presented "live," but may be videotaped by a clinician.

The viewer should be positioned 8 feet from the speaker. Each of the isolated words is preceded by a contextually meaningless carrier phrase, "show me." The respondent is provided with answer sheets that contain four choices for each stimulus. A single point is awarded for each of the words and sentences identified correctly. Consequently, maximum scores are 33 and 24 for the word test and sentence test, respectively.

Individual performances may be compared to the following mean scores obtained by Craig with deaf children:

	PRESCHOOL	NONPRESCHOOL
Words	62.5%–68%	68%–69%
Sentences	52.5%–62%	61.5%–63%

CRAIG LIPREADING INVENTORY

Word Recognition—Form A

1. white
2. corn
3. zoo
4. thumb
5. chair
6. jello
7. doll
8. pig
9. toy
10. finger
11. six
12. woman
13. fly
14. frog
15. grapes
16. goose
17. sled
18. star
19. sing
20. three
21. duck
22. spoon
23. ear
24. ice
25. goat
26. dog
27. cat
28. nut
29. milk
30. cake
31. eight
32. pencil
33. desk

SENTENCE RECOGNITION—FORM A

1. A coat is on a chair.
2. A sock and shoe are on the floor.
3. A boy is flying a kite.
4. A girl is jumping.
5. A boy stuck his thumb in the pie.
6. A cow and a pig are near the gate.
7. A man is throwing a ball to the dog.
8. A bird has white wings.
9. A light is over the door.
10. A horse is standing by a new car.
11. A boy is putting a nail in the sled.
12. A big fan is on a desk.
13. An owl is looking at the moon.
14. Three stars are in the sky.
15. A whistle and a spoon are on the table.
16. A frog is hopping away from a boat.
17. Bread, meat and grapes are in the dish.
18. The woman has long hair and a short dress.
19. The boys are swinging behind the school.
20. A cat is playing with a nut.
21. A man has his foot on a truck,
22. A woman is carrying a chair.
23. A woman is eating an apple.
24. A girl is cutting a feather.

Craig Lipreading Inventory

Word Recognition

Name: _____

Age: _____ Date: _____ School: _____

Ex.	fish	table	baby	ball
1.	kite	fire	white	light
2.	corn	fork	horse	purse
3.	two	zoo	spoon	shoe
4.	cup	jump	thumb	drum
5.	hair	bear	pear	chair

Word Recognition

Page 2

6.	yoyo	hello	jello	window
7.	doll	ten	nail	suit
8.	pig	pie	book	pear
9.	two	toe	tie	toy
10.	flower	finger	fire	feather
11.	six	sing	sit	kiss

Word Recognition

12.	table	apple	woman	rabbit
13.	fire	tie	fly	five
14.	four	frog	fork	flag
15.	grapes	airplane	tables	cups
16.	goose	tooth	shoe	school
17.	desk	sled	leg	nest

Word Recognition

18.	dog	sock	star	car
19.	wing	sing	ring	swing
20.	three	teeth	key	knee
21.	duck	rug	truck	gun
22.	moon	school	spoon	boot
23.	ear	hair	eye	egg

Word Recognition

24.	horse	house	ice	orange
25.	goat	gate	kite	girl
26.	dish	duck	desk	dog
27.	cat	cake	gun	coat
28.	nail	nut	nest	ten
29.	man	bat	milk	bird

Word Recognition   Page 6

30.	egg	cake	key	car
31.	eight	egg	cake	gate
32.	pencil	picture	mitten	pitcher
33.	wet	dress	nest	desk

CHAPTER 6

Language and Speech of the Deaf and Hard of Hearing

Deborah N. Seyfried Culbertson

Patricia B. Kricos

CONTENTS

■ INTRODUCTION

All of us possess personal attitudes toward language and modes of communication. These feelings form a basis for the way we choose to view the language abilities of persons with hearing loss. For example, a father of a child with profound hearing loss and a cochlear implant states, "I won't respond to my daughter unless she uses

Language is a broad term to describe a system of symbols used as a social tool for the exchange of information.

Morphology is the study of the minimal units of language that are meaningful, such as bug, -s for plural nouns or third-person verb tenses, -ing for present progressive, and -ed for past tense.

Phonology is the study of sound systems used in languages.

Pragmatics refers to the functional use of language.

Semantics is the study of word meanings and word relations.

Syntax is the aspect of language that governs the rules for how words are arranged in sentences.

spoken words." In contrast, a family with a young daughter with severe hearing impairment realizes that she is not responding well to amplified spoken language. Mom, Dad, and the two siblings go to the library, borrow all the sign language books, and start signing. An adolescent who is deaf begins a course of study at Gallaudet University and chooses not to use spoken language because it is not accepted by the Deaf community. All of these examples reflect "family" and personal attitudes toward language.

Professionals may respond to such family attitudes and choices toward language use in various ways. For many years, professionals established language programs based on their own principles and beliefs. With the passage of PL 99-457, however, our profession is moving in a new direction toward family-centered language programs (Roush & McWilliams, 1994). In family-centered programs, families are to be equal partners in language assessment, intervention, and decision making.

■ LANGUAGE AND COMMUNICATION

Factors Affecting Language Acquisition

To make an intelligent decision about language learning modes for children with hearing impairment, it is essential for parents and professionals to consider how hearing loss affects the acquisition of spoken language. The deteriorated speech signal resulting from hearing loss robs the child with hearing impairment of information regarding the form (phonology, syntax, morphology), content (semantics), and use (pragmatics) of language. Not surprisingly, language delay is a primary consequence of this information loss.

It must be stressed that, despite their language learning difficulties, children with hearing loss are not a homogeneous group when it comes to language acquisition. The three most obvious factors that might account for differences in language acquisition among children with hearing impairment are the degree of loss, age of onset, and whether other disabilities are present. Moeller, Coufal, and Hixson (1990), for example, noted a 30% incidence of educationally significant secondary disabilities in their population of children with hearing impairment.

Mayne and her coauthors (2000) reported that the significant predictors of early expressive language development in children who are deaf or hard of hearing included the child's age, the age of identification of the child's hearing loss (before or after 6 months), the child's cognitive status, and the presence or absence of one or more disabilities in addition to hearing loss.

In general, the greater the hearing loss, the greater the expected language delay. However, language abilities cannot be predicted solely on the basis of severity of hearing loss. Often, a range of language abilities can be observed in children with similar unaided audiograms. Surprisingly, some children with severe hearing impairment have age-appropriate language skills, while others have language difficulties that far exceed what would be expected for a given level of hearing loss. For the child with profound hearing impairment, the lack of sufficient speech information may preclude the acquisition of spoken language through audition. Even children who, at an early age, have mild fluctuating hearing losses secondary to otitis media may evidence significant delays in language development.

Encouraging reports regarding the substantial language gains made by children with cochlear implants have recently been reported. Svirsky and his coauthors (2000), for example, found that the mean rate of language acquisition in deaf children after implantation was similar to that of children with normal hearing and was considerably better than the development rate that would be expected from unimplanted children. Although there was a large amount of variability in the performance of the implanted children, the results of this study provide unambiguous evidence that many children will be given the opportunity to develop an oral linguistic system from the auditory input they receive from a cochlear implant. Positive results similar to these were also found by Tomblin and his coauthors (1999).

The following sections will discuss language characteristics for children with hearing impairment in two general age ranges: preschool (birth to age 5), and school age (age 5 through adolescence). Issues related to language assessment and management for all children are presented next. While speech is the oral means for expressing language, its separate presentation in latter sections is intended to simplify the discussion.

Language Characteristics of Preschool Children with Hearing Impairment

Carney and Moeller (1998) provide a thorough discussion of the impact of early onset hearing loss on language and literacy skills. The presence of hearing loss during the critical early periods of a child's development may deprive the child of unambiguous auditory and linguistic cues from the language models in his daily environment. The lack of opportunities to hear auditory language on a consistent basis may severely compromise the child's ability to develop the semantic, syntactic, morphologic, pragmatic, and phonologic aspects of language, which in turn greatly increases the likelihood of subsequent reading and academic difficulties. Although many children with hearing impairment, even of a severe degree, may have language skills commensurate with their age peers, most evidence significant delays in the various facets of language comprehension and production. There is a lack of consensus on the efficacy of various treatment approaches, communication modalities, and types of sensory aids for language and literacy competence in children who are hearing impaired. Some common language characteristics of children who are hearing impaired are shown in Table 6.1.

Importance of Parent–Child Interactions

Several authors have compared parent–child interactions of hearing parents with children who are normal hearing with those of hearing parents with children who are hearing impaired. These researchers have suggested that a child's hearing handicap can have a detrimental effect on parental communication styles. Goss (1970) was one of the first researchers to express concern regarding the verbal behavior of

TABLE 6.1

Some Common Characteristics of Language Usage by Children Who Are Hearing Impaired

Syntax

Shorter sentences (reduced mean length of utterances)
Simpler sentences (e.g., reduced use of complex syntactical constructions such as passive tense and relative clauses)
Overuse of certain sentence patterns (particularly subject–verb–object patterns)
Infrequent use of adverbs, auxiliaries, and conjunctions
Inappropriately constructed sentences (e.g., "The girl she want few some bread.")
Non-English word order
Incorrect usage of irregular verb tense

Semantics

Reduced expressive and receptive vocabulary
Limited understanding of metaphors, idioms, and other figurative language
Difficulty with multiple meanings of words (e.g., "row", "run")

Pragmatics

Restricted range of communicative intents (e.g., conversational devices, performatives, requests) in preschool children with hearing impairment
Lack of knowledge regarding conversational conventions, such as changing the topic or closing conversations
Limited knowledge and use of communication repair strategies

Family-centered intervention involves shared responsibility with the parents for the child's intervention, with the family retaining the ultimate decision making regarding intervention goals and services. A major goal of family-centered intervention is to strengthen family functioning, thus empowering the family to capitalize on its unique strengths when addressing the needs of the child with hearing impairment.

mothers with children who are hearing impaired. He observed that mothers of deaf children were less likely to use verbal praise, to ask for opinions and suggestions, and to use questions. He also noted that mothers of children who are hearing impaired were more likely to show disagreement, tension, and antagonism and to give more suggestions than were mothers of hearing children. These concerns have been expressed by other researchers (e.g., Kricos, 1982) and deserve careful consideration in view of the assertion by Mahoney and his coauthors (1998) that the responsiveness of parents is a critical determinant of the success of family-centered intervention programs. It is essential that the quality of interactions and the language learning environment that is provided by the parent be carefully evaluated.

Despite the concerns expressed by Goss (1970) and others, the professional must not assume that parental interactions will be aberrant. Lederberg and Everhart (1998) found that mothers of deaf and hearing children communicated with their children to the same extent, and that the mothers of the children with hearing impairment exhibited a number of functional adaptations to their child's hearing loss, such as using visual communication and tactile attention-getting strategies. However, these researchers found that the mothers primarily communicated via speech with their deaf babies and that the babies did not visually attend to much of their mothers' communication, thus receiving a less than ideal linguistic model.

Bilingual–Bicultural

There is considerable controversy in deaf education regarding the bilingual–bicultural approach to education of children with severe and profound hearing losses. This method is based on the premise that American Sign Language (ASL) is the native language of children with hearing losses and therefore should be the primary teaching language in school programs for children with hearing loss. Under this model, English is taught as a second language in written form, and the culture of Deaf individuals is emphasized in the curriculum. At this time, there is some evidence to support the efficacy of this approach, with several studies currently underway. Implementation of this model is another matter, however. For example, the majority of deaf children have hearing parents with no prior signing experience, and thus there should be concern about a lack of early exposure in ASL for these children.

Spencer (1993) studied the gestural–tactile and vocal–verbal communication behaviors of 36 mother–infant dyads. Mothers all had normal hearing while infants in half the dyads had hearing loss in the moderate to profound range. Unlike many children with hearing impairment, the children in this study were identified and provided with language programming and amplification prior to the age of 12 months. Interactive play sessions between mother-infant dyads were videorecorded when the children were 12 and 18 months of age.

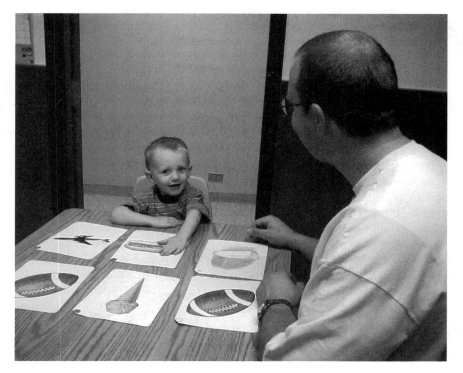

A young child works on communication skills in a therapy setting.

The two groups of infants did not differ significantly with respect to the overall number of intentional communication behaviors (i.e., combined vocal and gestural behaviors), the frequency of use of gestures, or the total number of communicative vocalizations. The groups did differ, however, with respect to the nature of their vocal and verbal productions. Children with normal hearing produced significantly greater numbers of canonical syllables (i.e., a consonant-like sound paired with a vowel), conventional vocalizations (imitations of animal sounds, vehicle noises, and nonrepresentational vocalizations like "uh-oh"), and single-element or multielement spoken or sign utterances. Correspondingly, Yoshinaga-Itano and Stredler-Brown (1992) also reported an overall low number of verbal communications (words and signs) for children with hearing impairment through the age of 18 months.

KNOWLEDGE OF SCHEMA IN PRESCHOOL CHILDREN. It has been suggested that early child language development is established through the use of daily routines in the child's life (Schirmer, 1994). The child, for example, experiences typical sequences of events and communication at dinner time, bath time, and bed time. Over time, the child stores and remembers a body of knowledge (called "schema") about these events and forms (Yoshinaga-Itano & Downey, 1986). Children with impaired hearing often have limited schemata for two main reasons. First, they have limited access to the language used by parents and siblings during daily routines. Children with hearing impairment who receive spoken language often will receive incomplete and distorted messages, while those receiving primarily signed or signed and spoken language will often receive incomplete and distorted messages because of the limited signing skills of family members. Second, children with hearing loss miss out on incidental learning opportunities. The child with normal hearing can overhear mom and dad talking about cleaning up the dinner dishes. The child with hearing loss may hear little of conversations unless they are directed toward him or her. In addition, parents using simultaneous communication may not sign communications if they are not directed toward their child. Thus, children with hearing impairment have reduced language input and the language they miss leads them to miss out on knowledge about their world.

SEMANTIC AND PRAGMATIC FUNCTIONS IN PRESCHOOL CHILDREN. Several investigators have reported that preschool children with hearing impairment exhibit a full range of pragmatic functions but limited semantic functions using nonverbal and verbal communication behaviors (Skarakis & Prutting, 1977).

Yoshinaga-Itano and Stredler-Brown (1992) provided data concerning the frequency of use of different nonverbal and verbal communicative intentions (e.g., comment on object–action, request object–action–information, answer, acknowledgment, and protest) for children with hearing impairment during parent-child play sessions. Data were provided for the following age ranges in months: 6–12, 13–18, 19–24, 25–30, and 31–36. All 82 children in this cross-sectional sample were hard of hearing (better ear pure-tone averages better than 70 dB HL, 44%) or deaf (better ear pure tone averages greater than 70 dB HL, 56%) and were enrolled in the Colorado Department of Health Home Intervention Program. Results showed that the overall number of nonverbal communicative intentions across categories increased with age. Children who were hard of hearing or deaf used a similar number of nonverbal communications. Verbal communication behaviors began to appear at 19 months of age, stabilized through 30 months, and then showed significant growth between 30 and 36 months. The children who were hard of hearing, however, showed significantly more verbal communications than the children who were deaf.

EARLY VOCABULARY IN PRESCHOOL CHILDREN. Few studies have investigated the early vocabulary of children with hearing loss. Normative data for the expressive vocabulary development of children who are deaf or hard of hearing were provided by Mayne et al. (2000). These investigators found that, on average, children whose cognitive quotients were 80 or greater and whose hearing losses had been identified by 6 months of age had a rate of vocabulary growth similar to children with normal hearing. Children whose hearing loss was identified after 6 months and/or whose cognitive status was compromised evidenced significant delays in their language acquisition rates.

The dramatic impact that early identification of hearing loss has on language acquisition was highlighted in what is sure to be considered a classic study by Yoshinaga-Itano and her co-authors (1998). The results of these authors' investigation of the language competence of early- and late-identified children with hearing loss clearly showed the advantages in language learning that are evident for children whose hearing loss is identified by 6 months of age. Figure 6.1 shows significantly better language competence in young children (1 to 3 years of age at the time of this study) whose losses were identified early. Figure 6.2 shows language acquisition as a function of both age of identification and cognitive status. What is particularly stunning in this figure is the fact that early-identified children with lower cognitive levels achieved essentially the same language levels as late-identified children with higher cognitive skills. These results should provide a strong impetus for the implementation of universal newborn hearing screening across the United States.

In 2000, eight more states passed legislation requiring hearing screening for all babies born in the state, bringing the total number of states that have adopted universal newborn hearing screening to 32.

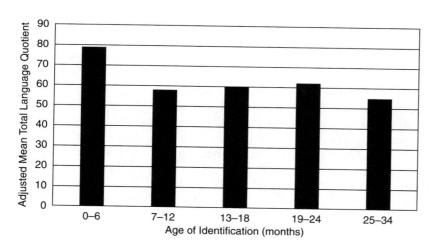

FIGURE 6.1

Adjusted mean total language quotients for groups based on age at identification of hearing loss.

Source: Reprinted with permission from *Pediatrics* 1998;102: 1161–1171.

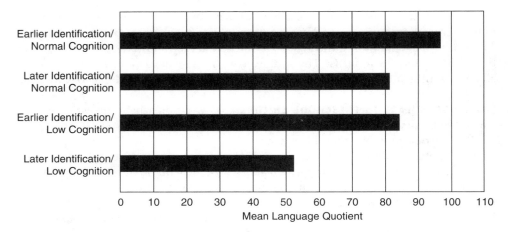

FIGURE 6.2

Mean total language quotient scores at 31 to 36 months by age at identification of hearing loss and cognition.

Source: Reprinted with permission from *Pediatrics* 1998;102: 1161–1171.

Language Characteristics of School-age Children with Hearing Impairment

The literature pertaining to the acquisition and use of language by school-age children who have hearing impairment is extensive and establishes a number of important concerns. Three major aspects of language have been evaluated in this population: (1) lexical–semantic skills, (2) syntactic–morphologic skills, and (3) pragmatic, or functional communication skills. Each of these will be briefly discussed.

LEXICAL–SEMANTIC SKILLS OF SCHOOL-AGE CHILDREN. The acquisition of the semantic component of language by children with hearing impairment may be mildly to profoundly delayed. Reduced vocabulary is common among individuals with hearing loss. Moeller, Osberger, and Eccarius (1986) and Osberger et al. (1986) administered a large battery of expressive- and receptive-language tests to children and young adults ranging in age from 4.5 to 20 years. Severe delays in the acquisition of lexical–semantic skills were observed across all age groups. On the average, the children's performance on the various measures of word knowledge was similar to that of a 6- to 8-year-old child with normal hearing. Marked difficulties with the semantic–lexical aspects of language have been documented by other investigators (Brenza, Kricos, & Lasky, 1981; Yoshinago-Itano, Snyder, & Mayberry, 1996).

SYNTACTIC–MORPHOLOGIC SKILLS OF SCHOOL-AGE CHILDREN. The difficulties in acquisition of English syntactic–morphologic skills by children who have hearing impairment have been extensively documented, and are even more pronounced than this population's difficulties with the semantic–lexical aspects of language. Descriptive studies of the syntactic abilities in this population have shown evidence of the following:

1. Restricted knowledge of word classes as evidenced by overuse of nouns and verbs and omission of function words.
2. Restricted knowledge of syntax as evidenced by overuse of the subject-verb-object sentence structure.
3. Syntactic delay with subsequent plateau in regard to syntactic abilities.
4. Deviant syntax in children with profound hearing impairment, e.g., misuse of morphological markers, omission of major sentence constituents, and asequential word order.

In their study of 145 children and young adults, ages 4.5 to 20 years, Moeller et al. (1986) found that few students evidenced language ages greater than 5 to 7 years in receptive syntax. Children who are hearing impaired have substantial difficulties with the more complex, subtle aspects of syntax (Yoshinago-Itano et al., 1996). Given the seeming inconsistencies in English syntax, it is not surprising that such difficulties are experienced by individuals with severe hearing impairment. Consider, for example, the following sentences: "I am going home."—"I am going to school."—"I am going to the store." It is no wonder that individuals with impaired hearing have difficulty sorting through the irregularities of the English language, ultimately generating sentences such as "I am going school" or "I am going to home."

PRAGMATIC SKILLS OF SCHOOL-AGE CHILDREN. The abilities of school-age children with impaired hearing to control the pragmatic aspects of language have, until fairly recently, received less attention from researchers. The limited research that has been conducted with older children, however, has delineated a number of concerns with the pragmatic aspects of language. Duchan (1988) reviews these studies, which show that many school-age children with hearing loss have difficulties with conversational turn-taking and topic initiations and maintenance. Studies of the pragmatic abilities of children who have been educated in a *total communication* program were reviewed by Johnson (1988). Although difficulties in turn-taking, topic identification, and communication repair were noted in these studies, there is at least some evidence that there is a steady progression of conversational skills in children with hearing impairment as they become older. Prinz and Prinz (1985) found that children's communication competence increased from ages 3 to 11 years (the ages of their subjects) as a result of their improved American Sign Language discourse strategies.

Total communication is a philosophy of communicating with children who are deaf using one or several modes of communication, including oral language, signed communication, written language, fingerspelling, gestures, facial expression, and Cued Speech, depending on the child's needs.

PLATEAU IN LANGUAGE ACQUISITION FOR SCHOOL-AGE CHILDREN. More disturbing than the delays in the development of language skills in children with hearing impairment is the apparent plateau in development of these skills, which has been documented in numerous studies (Boothe, Lasky, & Kricos, 1982). For example, Moeller, et al. (1986) found little growth in semantic and syntactic skills of children with severe hearing losses after 12 to 13 years.

Yoshinaga-Itano and Downey (1996) caution, however, that it would be erroneous to assume that *no* language growth occurs after age 12 years. Although a decrease

Metacognition refers to the child's knowledge and awareness of the thinking process and is tied closely to the child's use of higher symbolic language for reasoning and problem solving.

in skills for both metacognitive processing strategies and semantic language may occur for many children who are hearing impaired around 12 years of age, these authors point out that significant developmental increases will most likely occur in both semantic and syntactic skills after age 12.

PRELITERACY AND LITERACY ISSUES. Another issue in language development for the child with impaired hearing is the development of literacy (reading and writing) skills. Low reading and writing proficiency skills for children with hearing impairment have been related to limited oral language skills that serve as a base for literacy. Children with hearing loss also may not be exposed to the range and amount of prereading and reading activities as children with normal hearing (Limbrick, McNaughton, & Clay, 1992). Unfortunately, little attention has been directed toward establishing the precursors to reading and writing in this population.

An important precursor to reading ability is the development of phonological awareness. Phonological awareness is the ability to recognize that words consist of individual syllables, onsets and rimes, and phonemes and is related to the success with which children learn to read and spell. According to Miller (1997), prelingual deafness may inhibit phonemic awareness, although it does not preclude its formation. The ability to speechread does not provide enough phonological information to eliminate the need to access the acoustic parameters of speech. Although speechreading ability appears to be a good predictor of later phonological development, it is not adequate for complete development of phonological awareness (Dodd, McIntosh, & Woodhouse, 1998; Laybaert, 1998).

Onsets Sand rimes are the terms frequently used by reading specialists to denote the parts of words that children must learn to segment as they develop their phonological awareness skills. In words such as bat, cat, that, flat, rat, and mat, the onset of the word is the initial consonant or consonant blends, and the rimes are the rhyming word endings (-at).

Children with normal hearing learn about printed materials when they are very young. Infants and toddlers see and are shown letters and words on pictures, toys, and television, and in books. Parents read story books, traffic signs, and television ads. In contrast, children with hearing impairment may not have the same amount of exposure to these literacy experiences. This may be due to an unintentional overemphasis on spoken-language development in the early years with the expectation that reading and writing will be taught later in the elementary school setting. Literacy development and literacy facilitation activities are discussed by van Kleeck and Schuele (1987) and Schuele and van Kleeck (1987). Ewoldt (1985) has described a school-based literacy program for children with hearing impairment that included story telling, story creation, and free time for drawing and writing. Such activities may be crucial because reading is a critical skill for the child with hearing impairment. It provides for vocabulary expansion throughout life. Reading skills also allow the child who is deaf access to captioned television and the teletype device for the deaf (TDD).

Language Assessment

Measures used for assessing the language of children with hearing impairment can be categorized as follows: (1) communication checklists, (2) formal language tests, and (3) communication/language sample analyses. Many of the assessments most commonly used with young children with hearing impairment are those developed and standardized for use with children with normal hearing. Use of these assessments allows one to consider the language skills of children with hearing loss with reference to their normal-hearing peers. One could determine, for example, that Johnny, age 7, who has hearing impairment, has a vocabulary score typical of a 4.5-year-old child with normal hearing. Standard assessments typically indicate that spoken-language proficiency is usually delayed in children with impaired hearing. Assessments standardized on children with hearing impairment do exist. These assessments are likely to be most available to clinicians working in settings with a steady caseload of children with hearing impairment.

Because relatively few measures of language are specifically designed for children with hearing impairment, the clinician often needs to consider use of language-evaluation measures that were devised for and standardized with children with normal hearing. Language measures such as the Peabody Picture Vocabulary Test (PPVT; Dunn & Dunn, 1997), the Expressive One-Word Picture Vocabulary Test-Revised (EOWPVT-R; Gardner, 1990), and the Test of Language Development (TOLD; Newcomer & Hammill, 1977) can be administered to children with impaired hearing. However, caution in the administration, scoring, and interpretation of test results is warranted when these tests are administered to children who have impaired hearing. For example, one should not compute or use mental ages or IQ scores for the child with impaired hearing, because low scores usually reflect only the child's language delay. A few language assessment tests have been developed for and normed on children with hearing impairment (Table 6.2).

LIMITATIONS AND CAUTIONS IN USING FORMAL LANGUAGE MEASURES. Receptive language tests typically involve oral presentation of a word or sentence and require a picture-pointing response by the child. If a child with impaired hearing responds incorrectly, it is difficult to determine whether a language or a perceptual problem is responsible. Using printed stimulus items puts too much reliance on the child's reading abilities, making it difficult to ascertain whether a language or a reading problem is responsible for the child's errors. Even signing of the stimulus items is not without difficulties. The iconic nature of some signs may help the child to match the sign with the pictured response; thus, a true measure of the child's linguistic skills is not accomplished.

Formal measures may not provide a true measure of a child's linguistic skills in everyday conversations, in which the child has access to situational and linguistic cues to help decipher what is being said. The need to combine formal and informal strategies for language assessment of children with hearing impairment is delineated in an excellent article by Moeller (1988).

ESSENTIAL CONDITIONS FOR EVALUATING LANGUAGE ABILITIES. Several factors must be kept in mind when evaluating the language of a child with hearing impairment. First, sensory devices such as hearing aids or cochlear implants should be checked for proper function. Second, the test environment should be optimized by reducing noise and other environmental distractions. Third, when spoken language is used during testing, the clinician should make a conscious effort to allow the child full access to speechreading cues. This might necessitate allowing the child time to look down at a picture and then look back at the tester's face prior to presentation of the test item.

TABLE 6.2

Language Assessment Tests Designed for Children with Hearing Impairment

TEST	NORMED	SCREENING VERSION AVAILABLE	NUMBER OF SUBTESTS	NUMBER OF VERSIONS	FORMAT	MODE OF COMMUNICATION
Test of Syntactic Ability (TSA) (Quigley, Steinkamp, Power, & Jones, 1976)	Normal hearing and hearing impaired	Yes (2 different versions)	20	1	Paper and pencil	Written
Grammatical Analysis of Elicited Language (GAEL) (Moog & Geers, 1979; 1981; Moog, Kozak, & Geers, 1983)	Hearing impaired	No	0	3 (presentence, simple sentence, and complex sentence)	Props, modeled scripts, imitation	Oral, total communication
Teacher Assessment of Grammatical Structures (TAGS) (Moog & Kozak, 1983)	Normal hearing	No	0	3 (presentence, simple sentence, complex sentence)	Teacher rates child using sentences in daily classroom activities	Oral, signed English
Spontaneous Language Analysis Procedure (SLAP) (Kretschmer & Kretschmer, 1978)	Hearing impaired	No	6	1	Child in conversation	Any
Carolina Picture Vocabulary Test (Layton & Holmes, 1985)	Hearing impaired	No	0	1	Picture pointing	Total Communication
Rhode Island Test of Language Structure (Engen & Engen, 1983)	Normal hearing and hearing impaired	No	0	1	Picture pointing	Any
Scales of Early Communication Skills (Moog & Geers, 1975)	Hearing impaired	No	3	1	Demonstration and observation	Any
SKI-HI Language Development Scale (Tonelson & Watkins, 1979)	Hearing impaired	No	2	1	Parent observation	Any

An extremely important factor in language evaluation is that persons administering language tests be proficient users of the child's primary communication mode and language, whether that be spoken language only, spoken language + Cued Speech, spoken language + Signed English, or American Sign Language. Otherwise, test results will be invalid, reflecting misunderstanding of test instructions and desired responses rather than language ability. Luetke-Stahlman and Luckner (1991) have emphasized the concept of "first-language" assessment. That is, children with severe hearing impairment may not necessarily develop English as their first or native language. If their parents are manually communicating adults who are deaf, the child's first language may be American Sign Language (ASL). Even if their parents have normal hearing, which is true in the majority of cases, the children may not necessarily have acquired English skills, but rather, developed their own manner of communication including gesture, invented and formal sign language, and/or oral words (Luetke-Stahlman & Luckner, 1991).The assessment procedures that have been outlined in this chapter apply mainly to English language acquisition, and may not be appropriate for a child who has developed another form of communication. Ideally, either the examiner will have signing skills, including ASL and manually coded English, or someone with these skills will be available to assist in the language evaluation, when necessary.

Communication and Language Management for Preschool and School-age Children with Hearing Impairment

Carney and Moeller (1998) describe a number of treatment goals for language development of deaf children, including the following:

1. Enhanced parent–child communication in the chosen communication modality or language
2. Understanding of increasingly complex concepts and discourse
3. Acquisition of lexical and world knowledge
4. Development of verbal reasoning skills as a foundation for literacy attainment
5. Enhanced self-expression and acquisition of pragmatic, syntactic, and semantic language rules
6. Development of spoken, written, and/or signed narrative skills

Two traditional intervention formats have predominated in language intervention with children with hearing impairment: One emphasizes syntactic mastery and stresses the need for drill and practice, and the other emphasizes the need for a more natural or experiential approach to language learning. While language drills may be employed in the elementary and upper school years, they are of little meaning or interest to the young child with hearing impairment. In addition, heavy use of highly structured drills does not allow children time for social interaction and conversation.

Children with normal hearing have a wide range of conversational skills that children with hearing impairment may not have. Drilling on vocabulary labels or simple sentence forms does not allow a child with hearing loss to discover how to

Cued Speech involves the use of hand positions and shapes to resolve some of the ambiguities associated with trying to speechread words that look alike on the lips. Unlike fingerspelling, which is based on letters, the hand supplements associated with Cued Speech are based on sounds.

American Sign Language is frequently referred to as ASL. It is a form of manual communication used by culturally Deaf individuals in the United States and has a unique grammar that is not based on English.

Discourse refers to an extended verbal act, such as a conversation.

Contingent responding means that what caregivers say to (or do for) their young language learning children depends on the children's preceding utterances. For example, caregiver imitation of or response to the child's utterances can be reinforcing to the child, resulting in the child's repetition of the utterance or continued engagement in dialogue with the caregiver.

hold and maintain a conversation. Consequently, exposure to communication functions, forms, and structures in everyday contexts should be the primary goal of early communication development programs. As noted previously, children with hearing impairment may miss out on a great deal of incidental learning (e.g., others' conversations). Thus, an important part of language facilitation with the young child with impaired hearing is creating experiences that allow the child to discover and learn about a wide range of everyday events and reasons to communicate about them. Language facilitation strategies are applicable to all children with hearing impairment regardless of whether they are developing spoken and/or signed language.

It is important for parents, teachers, and clinicians to facilitate rather than directly teach language targets and forms. Rather than drill or dictate what the child says, adults can learn to facilitate the child's use of conversational skills. True conversation is characterized by contingent and relevant responses, shared topics, and a mutual frame of reference. For example, instead of requiring the child to label all the fruit in the fruit bowl, mom can show the child the bowl of fruit and follow the child's conversational lead.

Adults may need to learn to be responsive and contingent. Parents who talk, talk, talk may believe that they are teaching lots of language. In the meantime, where is the child's opportunity to talk or communicate? The parents can miss out on the child's special interest and focus, or on the child's attempt to enter the conversation. If the child does use words and/or gestures, then the adult needs to acknowledge the communication. For example, if the child reaches for the apple in the fruit bowl the parent could respond, "Oh, you want the red apple" rather than ignoring the child and continuing to instruct "Now, this is a red apple, and this a green pear, and this is a yellow banana."

Even with knowledgeable language modelers and an abundance of contextually rich communication exchanges, some structure and practice will be necessary for language to develop in children who are hearing impaired, especially those with more severe losses. However, syntactic and semantic principles must be presented under appropriate pragmatic conditions. Wilbur et al. (1989) attribute many of the difficulties children with impaired hearing have with linguistic structures to the practice of teaching them language using sets of unrelated sentences, with each sentence presented in isolation, devoid of any pragmatic or semantic context. A focus on isolated sentences may ultimately teach the child syntactic word order for certain syntactical devices, such as determiners, indefinite pronouns, and modals, but fails to teach the child under what pragmatic situation it would be appropriate and useful to employ the device.

The signing abilities of parents, instructors, and clinicians is critical to language development for children using a total communication approach. Moeller and Luetke-Stahlman (1990) studied parental use of simultaneous communication with their preschoolers who were deaf. All parents had sign language MLUs that were lower than their own child's MLU. Parents rarely signed or spoke syntactically or semantically complex utterances. And, unlike parents who were deaf, these parents with normal hearing rarely used fingerspelling to introduce new words. This writer remembers the comment of one father of a deaf child who said, "I don't need to know much sign language because my son only knows five signs." Clinicians and educators need to find ways to help parents gain, and understand the importance of, sign language proficiency. For example, videotape sign series are now available to help families learn sign language (e.g., *Sign with Me: A Family Sign Language Curriculum;* Moeller & Schick, 1993). Challenging as it may be, the instructor(s), parents, and siblings must be proficient in sign language in order for the child to develop language at a normal rate. If those communicating with the child are proficient in signing, every conversation can serve to aid language proficiency in the child with hearing impairment.

STRATEGIES FOR DEVELOPING CONVERSATIONAL SKILLS. Schirmer (1994) discusses several conversational approaches that facilitate language development. These approaches encourage the child's practice as a conversation partner learning how and when to initiate, take turns, and end conversations. The strategies employ real and role-played conversations. As such, they help the child become more communicatively proficient with all language aspects, not just syntax or morphology.

One technique discussed by Schirmer was *recasting*. Adults communicating with the child target syntactic–semantic structures for development. If and when the child uses incomplete or inappropriate forms during conversation, the adult recasts the utterance maintaining the child's meaning but providing the appropriate form. For example, if the child says, "Daddy eated cookie" the parent responds, "Yes, daddy ate the cookie." The parent does not require the child to correct his or her original utterance. This technique has been found to facilitate language development in children with hearing impairment.

Children with hearing impairment often have underdeveloped schema or limited knowledge concerning everyday events like what happens during a trip to the doctor's office (Yoshinaga-Itano & Downey, 1986). Schema can be developed by purposefully planning experiential learning events. For example, Dad could read a book about a trip to the doctor for a check-up, Dad and child could talk about visiting the doctor for a check-up, prepare for the trip to the doctor (e.g., take a bath and leave at the appointed time), visit the doctor and talk about the office and check-up, and later remember and tell Mom about the visit to the doctor's office.

When real-life schema building experiences cannot be arranged, adults can set up conversational scenarios or imaginary play scenes. The child and adult can pretend a "going-to-the-doctor scene" including what happens prior to and during the visit. The role-played scene still allows the child to learn about language and conversation in that setting.

Practical suggestions for teaching language use, content, and form are also provided by Luetke-Stahlman and Luckner (1991). They point out that much of the success in teaching the pragmatic aspects of language will depend on the teacher's and caretaker's ability to create an abundance of meaningful language opportunities for the child to communicate in routine situations. Several saboteur strategies are suggested to provide the child with opportunities to use language that has been mastered. One type of activity, for example, is to violate a routine event. At the dinner table, set the table by placing the plates and silverware on the chairs, or forget to put the child's favorite, mashed potatoes, on the table. These sabotaging activities provide

Sabotage activities provide motivation and opportunity for children to use and practice their emerging language skills. For example, a child may be presented with a desirable object that has been placed in a clear jar with a lid that is childproof. This increases the likelihood that the child will engage in communicative interaction with the caregiver, and the caregiver is provided with an opportunity to stimulate the child with the language needed to make a request for assistance, such as "open please."

Real-life activities are helpful in building language skills.

opportunities for the child to protest, request, comment, and tease, and ensure that the child has ample opportunity to use language in a meaningful context.

The same requirement to create real needs in the context of natural settings is stressed by Luetke-Stahlman and Luckner (1991) for the semantic and syntactic aspects of language. Suggestions for helping children expand their English vocabularies are provided. One technique is the use of semantic mapping, in which a new word, such as *satisfactory,* is explained in graphic form using words the child already knows, such as *excellent* and *terrible.* Communication games, such as barrier games, can provide opportunities for children to use their emerging syntactic skills in a fun, meaningful way.

PRELITERACY AND LITERACY ACTIVITIES. In addition to facilitating conversational skills, parents and clinicians will also want to provide early preliteracy and literacy activities for the young child with hearing impairment. Words on labels and traffic signs can be pointed out to the child, and story reading and retelling can be used to develop early awareness of reading and print. Children should also be allowed the opportunity to draw pictures, trace letters, and watch their stories be written down by their parents. Literacy activities for children with hearing impairment have been presented by Truax (1985) and Staton (1985).

BILINGUAL EDUCATION FOR CHILDREN WHO ARE DEAF. The history of education of children who are deaf has been marked by continual controversy regarding communication approach. For years, the argument was centered mainly on whether oral or manual communication was more appropriate for children with severe and profound hearing losses. In recent years, educators have increasingly embraced a bilingual–bicultural approach to communication with education of these children. Interest in the bilingual approach was sparked by Johnson, Liddell, and Erting (1990), who suggested that the academic curriculum would be more accessible to children who are deaf if it was presented in American Sign Language (ASL), which they felt should be the child's primary language. Under the model proposed by Johnson et al. (1990), ASL would be used for academic instruction and interpersonal communication in the classroom. English skills would be taught through written language, with explanations given using ASL. Johnson et al. (1990) argue that it is time to stop pathologizing deafness, and that acceptance of ASL as the primary language of children who are deaf will yield better academic success *and* ultimately greater English language competency than presenting instruction solely in English. An excellent discussion of rehabilitative issues in the bilingual education of children who are deaf is presented by Lieberth (1990). She poses a number of unanswered questions regarding the bilingual education model, including whether competency in English can be developed through writing, how parents with normal hearing will acquire competency in sign language, and how the relationship between children who are deaf and their parents with normal hearing will be affected by the child's bilingualism. Stewart (1993) emphasizes that bilingual–bicultural programs should not have exclusive use of ASL as the ultimate goal, but rather should provide for consistent and complete linguistic input in the target language as well. Thus, ASL and English-based signing could serve as complementary communication tools. Like Lieberth (1990), Stewart (1993) raises

Given the dismal picture of language skills of children who are hearing impaired that has been portrayed in this chapter, should the clinician assume that *all* children with hearing loss will show language learning difficulties and delays? Not at all! The children who are least likely to evidence significant language delays are those whose hearing loss is in the mild to moderate range who have above-average cognitive and linguistic processing skills and supportive learning environments (Gilbertson & Kamhi, 1995). And at the other end of the spectrum are children with hearing impairment who have additional learning disabilities that exacerbate their language learning difficulties. It is imperative that each child be evaluated without prior expectations of how children with hearing loss should or will perform in the language arena.

a number of questions regarding the current move in deaf education toward a bilingual education model. It is only through the gathering of data from controlled investigations that we will be able to answer these questions and to document the efficacy of a bilingual model of education for children who are deaf.

SPEECH CHARACTERISTICS, ASSESSMENT, ■ AND MANAGEMENT

Early management: speech–language–hearing intervention provided prior to 6 months of age.

Early identification: identification of hearing loss prior to six months of age.

Many parents, teachers, and clinicians advocate the development of oral communication skills to the greatest extent possible. The focus of this section reflects that attitude. However, this perspective is not meant to deny that other means of communication, such as sign language, are beneficial and essential. Indeed, not all children with hearing loss will be predominately oral communicators. The following discussion will address hearing as a foundation for speech sound development, early vocalizations of the child with hearing loss, speech intelligibility, speech characteristics of those with hearing loss, and considerations for speech assessment and management.

HEARING AS THE FOUNDATION FOR SPEECH SOUND DEVELOPMENT. Infants do not produce intelligible words until about 1 year of age. However, their early ability to recognize and differentiate speech sounds is a critical precursor to the production of those words (Sininger et al., 1999). In fact, a fetus hears speech at approximately 28 weeks gestation (Moore, Perazzo, and Braun, 1995), and by 6 months of age the child has learned to discriminate the sounds of his native language (Downs and Yoshinaga-Itano, 1999). Normal hearing allows for the development of speech perception. What are the effects of early auditory deprivation such as that produced by hearing loss? Studies of early auditory deprivation in animals show changes in the morphology and function of the central auditory system through which speech acoustic information is carried and processed.

Evidence suggests that babies are learning to listen to and differentiate the speech sounds of their own language during the first 6 months of life. Is this first 6 months a critical period for the development of spoken language? Downs and Yoshinaga-Itano (1999) reviewed the speech and language abilities of children with hearing loss identified prior to age 6 months and those identified later. Amazingly, children who were identified early and had no other complicating conditions typically had speech and language abilities *within the normal range* for their age. Downs and Yoshinaga-Itano proposed that identification and management of hearing loss by 6 months of age are the most effective strategy for developing normal speech and language. Yoshinaga-Itano (1997) found that many children whose hearing loss had been identified and managed prior to 6 months developed normal speech by age 5 years.

> Early and appropriate intervention is the most effective strategy for developing normal speech and language in children with hearing loss (Yoshinaga-Itano, 1997).

EARLY VOCALIZATIONS OF THE CHILD. In order to consider early vocalizations of the child with hearing loss, review of normal infant vocalizations is necessary. Normal-hearing babies develop vocalizations in an ordered sequence from birth to their first words (Stoel-Gammon & Otomo, 1986). They move through the following sequence of sound productions: crying and vegetative sounds (burps, coughs, sneezes), cooing and laughing, reduplicated babbling (same consonant–vowel syllable produced in a repetitive string, babababa), and variegated babbling (change in consonant–vowel syllable in a string, badabada) with sentence-like intonation (Oller, 1980). Between 11 and 14 months, children produce some speech sound combinations called *vocables* to consistently represent meaning (Owens, 1990). For example, the child may call her blanket "bee" on a consistent basis. Some time around the first birthday the child will begin producing her first words.

Infants with hearing loss vocalize also. Like normal-hearing babies they coo, squeal, growl, babble (Stoel-Gammon & Otomo, 1986); produce similar vowel positions and a greater proportion of velar–back consonants at 12 to 15 months (Smith, 1982); and show similar development of place of articulation of consonants and in the frequency of babbling. In contrast to infants with normal hearing, they produce fewer consonantlike sounds from 6 to 10 months of age (Stoel-Gammon & Otomo, 1986; Oller & Eilers, 1988). Oller and Eilers, for example, reported that whereas babies with normal hearing started canonical babbling (reduplicated babbling) between 6 and 10 months of age, babies with hearing loss showed onsets between 11 and 25 months and showed fewer instances of canonical babbling. Until the 1990s and the increased use of universal newborn hearing screening, relatively few children with hearing loss were identified within the first year of life, much less studied with respect to vocal behaviors. Research in this area should expand, given the widespread use of universal newborn hearing screening.

SPEECH INTELLIGIBILITY. Speech intelligibility refers to the proportion of speech that can be understood by a listener. Typically, speech intelligibility is evaluated by requiring a speaker to produce sentences that are recorded. The recording is then played to listeners who are asked to identify the words in the sentences, with percent of correct word identification indicating overall intelligibility. Two main factors affect intelligibility: the experience of the listener with deaf speech and the difficulty level of the vocabulary and sentence structure for the speaker. Listeners experienced with deaf speech yield higher intelligibility scores, and simpler vocabulary and sentences yield higher intelligibility scores (Monsen, 1975). Monsen, for example, reported that, although many studies indicated an average of 20% intelligibility for those with severe to profound hearing loss, his use of simpler sentence materials resulted in an average of 76.7% intelligibility. Also, the typical measure of speech intelligibility involves listener identification of words in unrelated sentences from a tape recording. This task does not allow face to face clues and context that can add substantially to real-world speech intelligibility.

Not only does intelligibility affect daily conversation, but it also affects perceptions of a speaker's cognitive competence and personality. Speakers who have good or moderately good speech intelligibility are perceived much more positively than speakers with poor intelligibility (Most et al., 1998). This is true for listeners who

Infant vocalizations: sounds such as crying, coughing, cooing, laughing, babbling, and vocables (word approximations) that precede spoken words.

Speech intelligibility: proportion of speech understood by a listener.

both have and have not had experience in listening to deaf speech. This may explain why some deaf speakers choose not to use speech, even though they may be capable of producing some intelligible words. Plant (1999), for example, reported on a deaf speaker who exhibited 80% to 90% intelligibility with contextual and face to face cues to listeners and yet who still chose not to use his speech in daily life.

Levitt et al. (1987) studied the speech and language of 120 children 10 to 14 years of age and found that speech intelligibility was directly related to the degree of hearing loss. However, there is considerably greater variability in speech intelligibility for children whose hearing losses are at or exceed 90 dB HL. Osberger et al. (1994) suggested dividing this population into the following categories based on their hearing thresholds at 500, 1000, and 2000 Hz:

1. Gold hearing aid users: pure tone thresholds of 90 to 100 dB HL with no thresholds greater than 105 dB HL at any of the three frequencies
2. Silver hearing aid users: pure tone thresholds of 101 to 110 at two of three frequencies
3. Bronze hearing aid users: pure tone thresholds greater than 110 dB HL at two of three frequencies

Mean speech intelligibility for children grouped in this way was (1) gold hearing aid users, 72%; (2) silver hearing aid users, 22%; and (3) bronze hearing aid users, 4%.

Although unaided hearing thresholds might allow for some prediction of speech intelligibility, aided audiometric thresholds and tests of speech perception abilities (Smith, 1975) should provide a better indicator of a given child's speech intelligibility. Plotting of the aided audiogram on a Familiar Sounds Audiogram (see Figure 6.3), for example, can allow one to predict what speech sounds might be available through audition to serve as a basis for speech development.

One highly controversial issue related to speech intelligibility is the effect of communication mode. Some argue that the early use of sign language diverts attention from spoken language, resulting in poor speech intelligibility. Others argue that competence in sign language might have little impact on speech intelligibility, whereas competency in a language might benefit reading and writing performance (Stuckless & Birch, 1997). Osberger et al. (1994) compared the speech intelligibility of children with cochlear implants using total communication and children with cochlear implants using oral communication. The children using oral communication had significantly better intelligibility. Potential causes of improved intelligibility for those using oral communication included (1) more intensive speech training, (2) teachers in total communication programs not having expertise in speech training, (3) higher expectations for oral communication set by parents and teachers, and

---

Does early sign language use inherently limit the development of intelligible speech? Or are children in total communication environments simply limited in their exposure to and use of speech?

FAMILIAR SOUNDS AUDIOGRAM

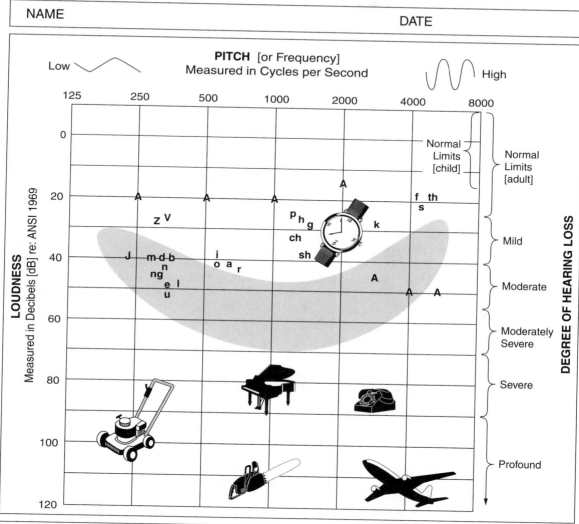

FIGURE 6.3

Aided thresholds (A) plotted on the Familiar Sounds Audiogram.

(4) peer use of speech. There is no evidence that the use of sign language itself detracts from speech intelligibility. However, it appears that some total communication programs give little attention to speech use and development and that this could easily explain why children in these programs have poorer speech intelligibility.

Speech Characteristics, Assessment, and Management for Individuals with Prelingual Hearing Loss

The following discussion will address the speech characteristics, assessment, and management concerns for two categories of individuals with prelingual hearing loss: those with hearing loss in the mild to moderately severe range (i.e., unaided pure tone thresholds ≤70 dB HL) and those with hearing loss in the severe to profound range (i.e., unaided pure tone thresholds >70 dB HL). A final section will address the speech of persons with acquired hearing loss (i.e., onset after 5 years of age).

Prior to this discussion, it is important to present two key tenets related to speech concerns for those with hearing loss. These tenets have been summarized by Robbins (1994). First, advancements in hearing aid technology and the availability of multichannel cochlear implants have allowed those with profound hearing loss greater access to speech acoustic cues than ever before. Despite these technological advances, the development of intelligible speech in children with prelingual profound hearing loss is still a challenge. Second, speech training must be fit into the realm of establishing overall communicative competence. Robbins suggested six guidelines for achieving this: (1) integrate auditory and speech goals, (2) follow a "dialogue" rather than "tutorial" format, (3) use bridging activities to promote real-world carryover, (4) practice communication sabotage, (5) use contrasts in perception and production, and (6) select speech goals that enhance communicative competence. One enjoyable and meaningful way to develop and practice speech sound listening discrimination and production with young children is to establish associations between familiar toys or actions and their sounds. Srinivasan (1996) provides a chart for clinicians and parents (see Table 6.3). The child can listen to family members "moo" when playing with the toy cow and be encouraged to "moo" also. (See Robbins, 1994, and Estabrooks, 1994, for sample speech activities.)

INDIVIDUALS WITH MILD TO MODERATELY SEVERE PRELINGUAL HEARING LOSS

SPEECH CHARACTERISTICS OF INDIVIDUALS WITH PRELINGUAL MILD TO MODERATELY SEVERE HEARING LOSS. Although published data are sparse, children with mild to moderately severe hearing loss generally have intelligible speech (Jensema et al., 1978; Elfenbein, Hardin-Jones, & Davis, 1994). The predominant speech errors of this population are related to the misarticulation of single consonants (Elfenbein et al., 1994) and consonant blends (Cozad, 1974).

Knowledge of speech acoustics and the typical sloping audiometric configuration would suggest that errors might be most common for speech sounds of low intensity, high frequency, and/or short duration. Complexity of formation, visibility, and developmental order of acquisition are also considerations in the speech errors of this population. Sounds most commonly in error are the affricates, fricatives,

TABLE 6.3
Listening Sounds List

SOUND	ASSOCIATED OBJECT	ASSOCIATED ACTION	ASSOCIATED PHRASE
ah	airplane (high pitch) truck (low pitch)		
oo	train (*woo woo*), owl (*hoot hoot*), ghost (*boo!*), cow (*moo*), dog (*woof woof*)		"Oops!"
ee	mouse (*ee ee ee*), bird (*cheep cheep*),	sweep down the slide ("Whee!")	
ai			"Hi!" "Bye bye!"
au	cat (*meow*),	down, around	"Ouch!"
o	rabbit (*hop hop*),	hop	hot, pop, "All gone!" knock (on the door)
oe		open, roll over	"Row, row the boat" "Roll (the ball)"
ay	horse (*neigh*)		"Hooray!"
a	duck (*quack*) sheep (*baaa*)		
u	up	run	"Uh oh!"
oi	pig (*oink*)		
m	ice cream (*Mmm!*)		"Mama," more, "Yumm! Yumm!"
n		knock	"No!"
w		walk, wind, wash, wipe	
b	bubbles, bus (*buh buh buh*)		"Bye! Bye!"
p	pop boat (*putt putt*)	pour, pat, pull/push	
t	clock (*tick tock*)	turn, tiptoe	
d	hammer (*duh duh duh*)		
k		cut	
g		go, drinking (*guh guh guh*)	
sh		Sleeping (*shh!*)	
s	snake (*sss*)		
f		off (take ___ *off*)	
l		lalling to a tune (*lah lah lah* . . .)	
z	bee (*zzzz*)		
h	witch (*hee hee hee*)	laughing ("Ha! Ha! Ha!")	"It's hot!"
y	yo yo		"Yuk", yes

Source: Srinivasan, 1996.

and blends (Elfenbein et al., 1994). Elfenbein, Hardin-Jones, and Davis found that the most common error types were substitutions (57%), followed by distortions (29%), and omissions (14%). The types of speech errors made by children with mild to moderately severe hearing loss resemble the errors made by younger children with normal hearing.

Phonologic assessments have been made of children with hearing loss to indicate rule-governed speech behaviors. Two sets of researchers have reported phonologic analyses of children with hearing loss in the mild to moderately severe range (Oller & Kelly, 1974; West & Weber, 1974). They found that these children were producing accurate vowels and were showing phonological processes used by younger children with normal hearing (e.g., voicing avoidance, fronting of consonants). Oller and Kelly proposed that children who are hard of hearing develop and use speech sounds in the same order as children with normal hearing.

SPEECH ASSESSMENT OF INDIVIDUALS WITH MILD TO MODERATELY SEVERE LOSS. The child with hearing loss in the mild to moderately severe range typically has speech errors comparable to normal-hearing children with articulation or phonological delays. Therefore, the practice of using standard articulation tests and phonologic analyses appears justified. One caution for the tester is to consider the vocabulary level of the stimulus words or items used and the need for replacing words or items not within the child's vocabulary. Formal assessments of vowel production, voice quality, and suprasegmental features may not be called for, given that these speech characteristics are less likely to be problematic for children with mild to moderately severe hearing losses. However, possible evaluation procedures are discussed in the assessment section for children with severe to profound hearing loss.

SPEECH MANAGEMENT OF INDIVIDUALS WITH MILD TO MODERATELY SEVERE LOSS. With early and appropriate amplification, many children with hearing loss in the mild to moderately severe range can be expected to have highly intelligible speech. However, children whose losses remain undetected and/or not amplified may be expected to manifest more extensive speech errors. Gordon-Brannan, Hodson, & Wynne (1992), for example, presented a case of a child in phonological treatment who showed significant gains only after his trough-shaped hearing loss was identified and he was fitted with hearing aids. In many cases, the clinician's major efforts will be directed toward articulation and/or phonological treatment. Standard articulation and/or phonological treatment techniques are generally appropriate with some special considerations and modifications to programming.

Several considerations should be kept in mind while undertaking such treatment. First, children with normal hearing who have articulation or phonologic disorders are capable of using auditory feedback cues. Children with hearing loss may need visual, tactile, and/or kinesthetic cues to compensate for their inability to hear certain speech sound distinctions.

Second, the clinician must be familiar with the child's aided hearing thresholds in order to identify which speech sounds are not likely to be within the child's residual hearing range. This information can be gained by plotting the child's aided hearing thresholds on the Familiar Sounds Audiogram (see Figure 5.1). For sounds not within the child's aided hearing range, nearly total reliance on other cues for speech sound production is likely.

Third, the clinician should be familiar with the impact of co-articulation, since speech sounds change when paired with different speech sounds. Consequently, training on isolated speech sound productions should be limited and instead should move quickly to the production of sounds in meaningful words and phrases. For children with hearing loss in the birth to 3-year age range, Cole (1992) advocates use of the following guidelines:

1. Selecting and sequencing the child's speech targets based on normal developmental information
2. Maximizing and ensuring optimal residual hearing
3. Having parents and clinicians target spoken language goals during normal everyday activities (p. 74)

INDIVIDUALS WITH PRELINGUAL HEARING LOSS IN THE SEVERE TO PROFOUND RANGE

SPEECH CHARACTERISTICS OF INDIVIDUALS WITH PRELINGUAL HEARING LOSS IN THE SEVERE TO PROFOUND RANGE. Studies have indicated that the average intelligibility of children with severe to profound hearing loss is approximately 20%, although individual ratings vary from 0% to 100% (Carney, 1986). These children may exhibit difficulties with consonant production, vowel and diphthong production, and voice quality (Hudgins & Numbers, 1942). For purposes of discussion, speech characteristics in this population will be discussed under the categories of respiration, resonance, phonation, and articulation and phonology. Because this categorization simplifies the discussion, we must remain aware that respiratory, resonatory, phonatory, and articulatory and phonologic behaviors are interactive and co-occur during ongoing speech. Smith (1982) cautions that the speech of children who are deaf actually represents "stacks of errors which are complex and interrelated" (p. 27). Children with severe to profound hearing loss also exhibit faulty suprasegmental features. The discussion of suprasegmental errors will be followed by assessment and management considerations.

RESPIRATION. Clinicians and investigators have observed that individuals with severe to profound hearing loss may speak only a few syllables on a single exhalation of air (Forner & Hixon, 1977). Hutchinson and Smith (1976), for example, noted high airflow rates (i.e., air wastage) during production of some consonant segments. Forner and Hixon (1977) studied abdomen and ribcage movement in 10 young adult males with severe to profound hearing losses. Unlike speakers with normal hearing, these subjects, who had poor speech intelligibility, initiated speech at low lung volumes, uttered only a few syllables at a time with air wastage during the pauses between segments, and continued to speak with lung volumes well below functional residual capacity. Cavallo et al., (1991) studied chest wall movements before vowel production in seven adult males. Ribcage and abdominal movements were recorded, and lung volume was estimated based on measures from a mercury strain gauge. Before vowel production, the speakers with hearing loss demonstrated expansion of the ribcage and contraction of the diaphragm comparable to that seen in speakers with normal hearing. However, speakers with hearing loss lost significantly more air during the short adjustment period immediately prior to vowel production. These investigators proposed that speakers with hearing loss delay the adduction of vocal folds prior to phonation that would normally limit loss of air. They further suggested that this might explain why some speakers with hearing loss initiate speech at or below functional residual capacity for the lungs.

Resonance: vibration of air in the throat, oral cavity, and/or nasal cavity; resonance problems include hypernasality and hyponasality.

RESONANCE. Both hyponasality and hypernasality have been observed in the speech of those with severe to profound hearing loss (Smith, 1975). The presence of resonance problems is interesting, given that acoustic information on nasality is found in the lower frequencies, where speakers with hearing loss may have more residual hearing (Borden, Harris, & Raphael, 1994). In these cases, individuals might be trained to make use of auditory cues to nasality, resulting in improved resonance.

Phonation: vocalizations produced with vocal fold vibration; problems with phonation include breathy voice quality with inadequate vocal fold adduction, abnormally high fundamental voice frequency, and excessive voice intensity with excessive vocal fold resistance.

PHONATION. Studies of respiration led investigators to link air wastage prior to and during the production of speech with insufficient vocal fold adduction, rather than to respiratory difficulties. Inadequate vocal fold adduction has been directly observed in speakers with hearing loss when producing vowels (Metz, Whitehead, & Whitehead, 1984). This incomplete closure can result in the overall perception of breathy voice quality and in the perception of voiceless sounds being substituted for voiced sounds (McGarr & Whitehead, 1992).

Control of fundamental frequency of the voice is also primarily a function of laryngeal events. When compared to normal-hearing peers, persons who are deaf may use higher average fundamental frequency, as observed by Angelocci, Kopp, and Holbrook (1964). However, some do retain normal average fundamental frequency, as observed by Monsen (1979). Another observation is that the range of fundamental frequencies produced across utterances is reduced in the speech of the deaf.

Speech intensity, another aspect of phonation, is also primarily a function of laryngeal activity. Unfortunately, data on voice intensity for speakers with hearing loss are limited. Reduced intensity, excessive intensity, and reduced intensity variations across utterances have all been observed in this population. Reduced intensity and lack of intensity variation have been related to pervasive breathiness and low lung volume during speech. Excessive intensity has been related to excessive glottal resistance.

ARTICULATION AND PHONOLOGY. Variability seems to be one of the hallmarks of speech production among those with severe to profound hearing loss. Despite the variability, some typical errors have been identified. First, patterns of consonant and vowel errors can be identified. Second, consonant misarticulation is much more common than vowel or diphthong misarticulation.

The following categorizations of vowel error patterns, offered originally by Hudgins and Numbers (1942), have been substantiated in more recent research:

1. Vowel neutralization (i.e., the tendency for all vowels to resemble the neutral schwa)
2. Diphthong and vowel confusions (e.g., /aI/ for /a/ or /a/ for /ai/)
3. Nasalization of vowels

The perception of vowel neutralization has been verified by acoustic and physiologic studies, including studies indicating centralized or static tongue position across vowels (Tye-Murray, 1991).

Children with hearing loss produce consonants less accurately than vowels on both spontaneous and imitative tasks (Geffner & Freeman, 1980). Hudgins and Numbers (1942) categorized the most common consonant error of children who are deaf in the following way:

1. Voicing errors (e.g., substitution of /b/ for /p/)
2. Omission and distortion of consonants (e.g., omission of velars and final consonants)
3. Omission of consonants in blends (e.g., /tap/ for /stap/)
4. Nasalization of consonants

Voicing errors may include voiced or voiceless confusions, devoicing of final consonants, and omission of final voiced consonants (Hutchinson et al., 1978).

Studies of tongue placement during consonant production have been conducted using a technique called *palatometry*. Palatometry involves the placement of a thin custom-fit pseudopalate over the child's hard palate and maxillary teeth. The pseudopalate has a set of 96 electrodes, which when contacted by the tongue, show as contact points on a display screen. Figures 6.4 and 6.5 (Dagenais, 1992), respectively, show the pseudopalate and the computer's visual display targets for a selected

Palatometry: a pseudopalate with 96 contact electrodes is fit like a dental retainer against the speaker's hard palate, and the speaker then views a computer display that shows the appropriate tongue to palate contacts while adjusting her tongue to match the target.

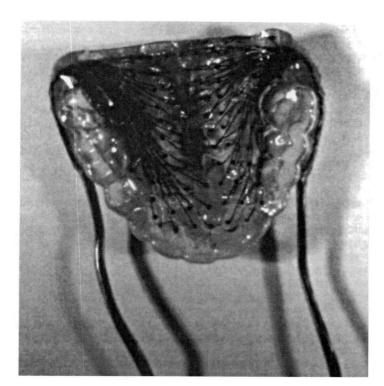

FIGURE 6.4

Palatometry pseudopalate showing the 96 contact electrodes.

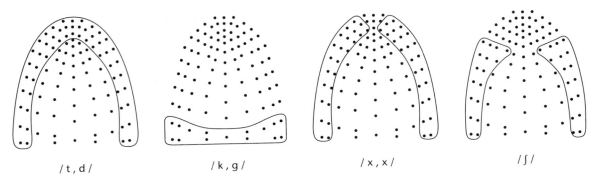

/ t , d /   / k , g /   / x , x /   / ʃ /

FIGURE 6.5

Contact patterns used for training consonants with palatometry.

set of consonants. Results of palatometry studies have indicated that children with profound hearing loss have idiosyncratic tongue to palate contacts as compared to speakers with normal hearing (Dagenais & Critz-Crosby, 1991).

In addition to individual phoneme errors, speech of persons who are deaf is sometimes characterized by reduced coarticulatory movements. The production of a speech sound in an utterance can be influenced by both preceding sounds and subsequent sounds. Reduced co-articulation in deaf speakers has been related to slower and less precise movement of the tongue (Okalidou and Harris, 1999).

Data suggest that cochlear implants allow for the greatest speech acoustic information for the development of speech sound production in children with profound hearing loss. Toby, Geers, and Brenner (1994) compared matched groups of hearing aid users, cochlear implant users, and tactile device users across a 3-year period and found significantly better speech sound production in children with cochlear implants. Children with cochlear implants showed significantly greater overall improvement in their production of intelligible vowels and consonants and were more accurate in producing some of the less visible place features (e.g., velars) and manner features (e.g., glides).

SUPRASEGMENTAL ASPECTS. Suprasegmental features include changes in duration, intensity, and fundamental frequency across syllables in an utterance. Suprasegmentals are important because they communicate an individual's emotional intent, the urgency of a message, and linguistic stress. Suprasegmental problems in deaf speakers can contribute substantially to poor intelligibility (Gold, 1980).

Individuals who are deaf speak at an overall rate 1.5 to 2 times slower than that of speakers with normal hearing (Tye-Murray, 1992). Slow speaking rate has been related to prolongation of individual phonemes and the presence of lengthy pauses within utterance. It is interesting to note that some investigators have reported improved intelligibility for slower speaking rates (Osberger & Levitt, 1979). Thus, overall slow speaking rate may, in part, serve as an appropriate compensatory adjustment.

Speakers with hearing loss have been found to use more and longer pauses in addition to within-phrase pauses during utterances. Speakers with normal hearing

Suprasegmental features: variations in intensity, fundamental frequency, and duration of syllables and pauses across an utterance; problems with suprasegmentals include overall slow speaking rate, within-phrase pauses, excessive fundamental frequency variation, and less than normal fundamental frequency variation.

tend to avoid within-phrase pauses. Although speakers who are deaf often exhibit abnormal pause behaviors, Osberger and Levitt (1979) found little associated effect on speech intelligibility.

Differences in intonation of deaf speakers have been consistently associated with reduced speech intelligibility (Formby & Monsen, 1982). Both excessive pitch variation and less than normal pitch variation have been observed. Atypical intonation has been associated with lower overall speech intelligibility (Formby & Monsen, 1982).

In summary, speakers who are deaf may have difficulty adjusting duration, intensity, and intonation within an utterance. These suprasegmental difficulties may result in faulty linguistic stress and reduce overall speech intelligibility.

Speech Assessment of Individuals with Severe or Profound Hearing Loss

Comprehensive speech evaluation of those with severe or profound hearing loss should include perceptual measures of intelligibility, articulation and phonology, suprasegmental features, and voice characteristics. The additional use of acoustic and/or physiologic measures is typically restricted to those who have access to the instrumentation. In this section, four general areas of evaluation will be considered.

MEASURES OF SPEECH INTELLIGIBILITY. Assessment and improvement of speech intelligibility would appear to be important goals for speakers with severe or profound hearing loss. Percent of intelligible word scores and intelligibility ratings are the most widely used measures, and difficulties arise with each.

As indicated previously, often speakers are required to produce sentences and listeners later identify the words that they hear, with percent of correct words

Adult deaf individuals may undertake speech therapy to improve intelligibility.

reflecting percent of speech intelligibility. However, the speech intelligibility score can vary widely depending on the following:

1. Complexity of vocabulary and sentences spoken
2. Presence or absence of contextual cues
3. Presence or absence of visual and lipreading cues
4. Listener experience with deaf speech

Thus, one score will typically represent the intelligibility only for that speaking–listening situation (Monsen, 1979).

Another type of assessment tool, the rating scale, has been presented by the National Technical Institute for the Deaf (NTID; Subtelny, 1977). This procedure requires a set of listeners who first are trained in the use of a 5-point rating scale. The scale ranges from 1 (speech cannot be understood) to 5 (speech is completely intelligible). Obviously, most clinicians would probably have only one listener—herself—to make these rating judgments.

Requiring deaf children to read sentences may underestimate intelligibility due to a child's difficulty in reading fluently. Assessment of intelligibility for picture description tasks or conversational samples, instead, can indicate how the child's knowledge of spoken language affects speech intelligibility. We can use these samples to calculate the number of totally intelligible utterances, number of totally unintelligible utterances, and number of intelligible and unintelligible words.

MEASURES OF ARTICULATION AND PHONOLOGY. Standard articulation tests have been used in the assessment of children with hearing loss (Abraham, Stoker, and Allen, 1988). Although these tests are not normed for children with hearing loss, they do indicate phonemes produced accurately, phonemes produced inaccurately, and the types of speech sound errors (substitution, distortion, omission).

Clinicians who have larger numbers of children with hearing loss may choose to obtain assessment tools specific to this population. Some evaluations, that is, phonetic evaluations, address whether the child is capable of producing a speech sound through imitation or in conversational speech. Ling (1976) developed the Phonetic Level Evaluation specifically for children with severe to profound hearing loss. On the Phonetic Level Evaluation, the child imitates nonsense syllables. Imitative target syllables include consonants and consonant blends in the initial and final positions of syllables and vowels and diphthongs. Toby, Geers, and Brenner (1994) reported on the use of the CID Phonetic Inventory, an evaluation tool that includes imitation of suprasegmentals, vowels and diphthongs, initial consonants, initial consonants with alternating vowels, final consonants, and final alternating consonants. Miccio et al. (1990) cautioned that deaf children may be able to imitate or spontaneously produce a large range of speech sounds and yet not use these sounds contrastively to produce words in ongoing speech.

A second type of evaluation, phonologic evaluation, indicates whether speech sounds are produced accurately and contrastively in conversation. Phonologic evaluation typically uses a speaking sample other than that produced through imitation of the clinician or through reading sentences. Ling (1976) suggested that in order to

Phonetic repertoire: a set of speech sounds that a child can produce regardless of whether they are used appropriately in everyday speech.

Phonologic system: speech sounds that are used in a rule-based way in everyday speech.

obtain a valid picture of phonologic skills a tape recording be made of the child in all five of the different types of discourse: conversation, description, narration, question, and explanation. The clinician would then analyze the tape-recorded sample to determine which speech sounds are and are not used accurately and consistently.

PERCEPTUAL ASSESSMENT OF SUPRASEGMENTALS AND VOICE CHARACTERISTICS. Speech and voice characteristics are most often assessed by clinicians who listen to and rate the characteristics of a spoken passage or spontaneous speech sample. Some clinicians, for example, may use Wilson's voice rating system (1977) in which judgments are made related to laryngeal valving, pitch, nasality, intensity variability, and pitch variability. In addition, Wilson urges clinicians to check for the presence of voice deviations such as diplophonia, audible inhalation, pitch breaks, and phrasing irregularities.

ACOUSTIC AND PHYSIOLOGIC DISPLAYS. Instrumentation providing displays of acoustic characteristics of speech are generally more likely to be available to clinicians than physiologic instrumentation. Commonly used equipment that displays acoustic features includes the Visi-Pitch (Kay Elemetrics, Inc.), which can indicate fundamental frequency and intensity, and the IBM SpeechViewer, which can indicate the mean frequency and standard deviation of frequency across an utterance, mean intensity and standard deviation of intensity across an utterance, and percentage of utterance voiced. Physiologic instrumentation can be used to assess respiratory function, nasality, and tongue to palate contacts. A spirometer can be used to assess speech initiatory lung volumes and other patterns of respiratory adjustment. A nasometer can be used to determine the presence of hyponasality or hypernasality. And a palatometer can be used to indicate whether an individual is making appropriate tongue to palate contacts.

Speech Management for Individuals with Severe or Profound Hearing Loss

Nearly all investigators who have studied speech production in persons who are deaf are struck by the extreme variability in error patterns among individuals. Such differences highlight the importance of individualizing speech management procedures. With the advent of universal newborn screening comes the opportunity to potentially prevent speech and language delay in children born with hearing loss. Yoshinaga-Itano & Apuzzo (1998a, 1998b) again remind us that children identified and provided appropriate amplification and family-centered intervention no later than 6 months of age typically develop speech and language in the normal range.

A critical concern with speech training is that it be as meaningful as possible. Speech is used to express meaning. Speech sounds that cannot be heard and developed through the use of optimal amplification or cochlear implant use may require the use of additional visual and/or tactile cues. However, training should not focus on lengthy motor drills of sounds in meaningless syllables. Speech sound training should move quickly to the use of meaningful words. In accordance with a whole-language philosophy, speech targets should appear in words that a child would learn about in natural contexts. A child, for example, would not simply learn the label "duck" when working on production of the /d/ and produce it each time the clinician showed a toy duck. The child would read about ducks, play with ducks, go see ducks at the duck pond, and talk about birds that are ducks and birds that are not ducks. In addition, the development of sounds in different phonetic contexts is also important to ensure the development of coarticulation.

Four major approaches may enhance speech training in persons with hearing loss: (1) early and consistent use of devices to provide optimal use of residual hearing, (2) anatomic and pictorial monitoring, (3) visual cues, and (4) use of complex feedback aids.

Most individuals with hearing loss possess some residual hearing, and its use should be maximized. This is the primary and best means for providing feedback for the development of speech. An important question to ask is whether the client's hearing aid, FM system, cochlear implant, or vibrotactile system provides her with as many speech sounds as possible. It would be ideal if clinicians could assume that clients are receiving the most speech sounds possible with the assistance of their sensory devices. But the fitting of devices, particularly in children, can be a tricky bit of educated guesswork. If the clinician questions the audibility of speech for a given client, consultation and possibly referral to the child's audiologist would be appropriate. Another related question is whether the client has the best device for allowing speech development? Tobey, Geers, and Brenner (1994) reported on three matched groups of children with profound hearing loss that received intensive speech training, but who were fit with either hearing aids, cochlear implants, or vibrotactile devices. All three groups showed improvement in imitative speech production and percent of intelligible words, but the children with cochlear implants showed the greatest gains. And yet it should be noted that children with cochlear implants still have difficulty in developing intelligible speech (Robbins, 1994).

Anatomic and pictorial monitoring has also been used to help establish speech sound production. Anatomic charts, sagittal sections of the head with a mobile tongue, and pictures of tongue shape may be useful in some cases. Some of these models are available commercially, but they can also be made without undue expense. The problem with these aids is that they provide a static picture, whereas the production of a speech sound is not static. It may be wise to use these types of models only in the initial stages of sound production and only as a last resort.

Another approach to improving speech production is visual stimulation by the clinician and/or visual monitoring with the use of a mirror. Some information concerning speech production is available visually. However, excessive attention to visual feedback may be hazardous. The visual characteristics of sounds dramatically change as a function of context. For example, /ʃ/ looks considerably different in the words "shoe" and "she."

Complex feedback aids or devices have also been used to assist in training speech production. Most devices provide for visual monitoring of acoustic features of speech, such as the VisiPitch and IBM SpeechViewer. The VisiPitch allows for display of fundamental frequency of the voice and intensity variation across an utterance. The IBM SpeechViewer allows for child-friendly displays, with loudness

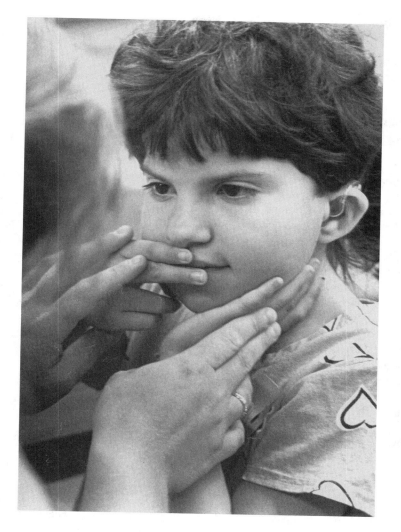

Providing feedback is an important element of speech therapy with the hearing impaired.

indicated by the changing size of a balloon, pitch indicated as changes on a thermometer, and vowel accuracy indicated by a monkey dropping a coconut from a tree. Vowel production and fundamental frequency treatment benefits have been documented with the use of the IBM SpeechViewer (Pratt, Heintzelmann, & Deming, 1993; Ryalls et al., 1995). However, there is no proof that the system is more effective than traditional therapy approaches or that it produces carryover to everyday speech. In addition, children appear to lose interest in the displays across multiple sessions. Consequently, these types of devices may be of greatest benefit as a supplementary treatment tool and in providing objective measures of treatment efficacy.

One type of feedback display shows tongue placement. The palatometer, described earlier, gives feedback on contact points of the tongue. Reports of palatometry training with children who are deaf have been promising, but the system is not widely available for use (Dagenais, 1992). Dagenais suggested that speech training might begin with the use of these systems to establish correct articulatory placement for sounds in nonsense syllables and single-syllable words and then move to more traditional approaches that emphasize words and phrases.

Speech Characteristics of Individuals with Postlingual Profound Hearing Loss

Descriptions of speech abilities in individuals with acquired hearing loss have been limited. Acquired deafness in those with well-developed speech appears to produce a gradual rather than immediate deterioration of speech. Hearing plays a role in the long-term monitoring and maintenance of speech coordination (Zimmerman & Rettaliata, 1981). A wide variation in speech production abilities has been observed in this population. Cowie and Douglas-Cowie (1983), for example, reported intelligibility scores ranging from 10% to above 90% in a sample of 13 adults. These investigators also reported that reduced intelligibility and voice quality or slurring resulted in negative reactions by the listeners judging the speech samples. The wide variation in speech production has been related primarily to age at onset of hearing loss, although degree of hearing loss and hearing aid history also have been considered secondary factors (Cowie, Douglas-Cowie, & Kerr, 1982). The following specific speech errors were observed in this population according to Kishon-Rabin et al. (1999): (1) decreased vowel space due to centralization of the first two formants, (2) inaccurate production of /s/ and /sh/, (3) similar voice onset time values for voiced and voiceless plosives, (4) substitution of /r/ with /w/, and (5) tendency to omit consonants in the final position of words. Kishon-Rabin et al. also reported that after receiving cochlear implants their postlingually deafened adults showed significant improvements in speech and voice quality over a 2-year period.

SUMMARY

Who should be responsible for speech and language intervention for individuals with hearing loss? The audiologist, speech–language pathologist, teacher of the hearing impaired, and family members will all have a role in the management of the child with hearing loss. All have complimentary and sometimes overlapping contributions toward language facilitation. The audiologist will have the greatest expertise in monitoring the child's hearing loss, establishing and ensuring that sensory devices are providing the maximum amount of speech acoustic cues, and communicating to others about the aspects of speech that may be inaudible to the child. The speech–language pathologist will have the strongest background and training in current language intervention techniques, including ways to establish more family-centered intervention. The teacher of the hearing impaired will offer means of tutorial and educational support and may be the most proficient of the professionals with respect to knowledge and use of sign language. The family is the constant in the child's life (Crais, 1991); as such, the family's needs and choices are critical to the success and carryover of language and speech intervention. The true challenge of family-centered intervention is working out the collaboration and consultation between the family and professionals involved in the management of the child with hearing loss.

SUMMARY POINTS

- The presence of hearing loss in children does not preclude language development, although it can have a serious impact on the child's overall language competence.
- The inability to hear auditory language on a consistent, unambiguous basis may severely compromise the child's ability to develop the semantic, syntactic, pragmatic, and phonologic aspects of language.
- Although there are several language measures specifically designed for children with hearing impairment, the clinician will probably need to supplement these measures with assessment tools that were designed and standardized with children who have normal hearing.
- For most children with severe hearing loss, a combination of language drill and experiential language stimulation will be necessary to enhance language development.
- Early identification and intervention are essential to optimize the child's chance of developing age-appropriate language skills.
- Because hearing is the foundation for speech development, hearing aid and/or cochlear implant use must be implemented as soon as possible to provide children with hearing loss access to speech acoustic information.
- The development of speech in children with congenital hearing loss can best be promoted when hearing loss identification, home intervention, and amplification are provided within the first 6 months of life.
- Infants with hearing loss do vocalize. However, studies suggest differences in their babbling behaviors when compared to normal-hearing babies.
- Children with mild to moderately severe hearing losses (up to 70 dB HL) typically have highly intelligible speech with predominately articulation and phonological errors.
- Children with severe and profound hearing losses (>70 dB HL) are much more variable with respect to speech intelligibility and speech errors. Intelligibility in this population ranges from 0% to 100%, with possible errors in vowel and diphthong production, consonant production, respiration for speech, resonance, phonation, and suprasegmental speech characteristics.

RECOMMENDED READING

Carney, A. E., & Moeller, M. P. (1998). Treatment efficacy: Hearing loss in children. *Journal of Speech Language and Hearing Research, 41,* S61–S84.

Estabrooks, W. (1994). *Auditory–verbal therapy for parents and professionals.* Washington, DC: Alexander Graham Bell Association for the Deaf.

Ling, D. (1989). *Foundations of spoken language for hearing-impaired children.* Washington, DC: Alexander Graham Bell Association for the Deaf.

Mayne, A. M., Yoshinaga-Itano, C., Sedey, A. L., & Carey, A. (2000). Expressive vocabulary development of infants and toddlers who are deaf or hard of hearing. *Volta Review, 100*(5) (monograph), 1–28.

Srinivasan, P. (1996). *Practical aural habilitation for speech–language pathologists and educators of hearing-impaired children.* Springfield, IL: Charles C Thomas.

Svirsky, M. A., Robbins, A. M., Kirk, K. I., Pisoni, D. B., & Miyamoto, R. T. (2000). Language development in profoundly deaf children with cochlear implants. *Psychological Science, 11,* 153–158.

Tomblin, J. B., Spencer, L., Flock, S., Tyler, R., & Gantz, B. (1999). A comparison of language achievement in children with cochlear implants and children using hearing aids. *Journal of Speech Language and Hearing Research, 42,* 497–511.

Yoshinaga-Itano, C., & Downey, D. M. (1996). Development of school-aged deaf, hard-of-hearing, and normally hearing students' written language. *Volta Review, 98,* 3–7.

RECOMMENDED WEB SITES

Cochlear implants:
http://www.hearusa.com

Alexander Graham Bell Association for the Deaf and Hard of Hearing:
http://www.agbell.org

Resource for families of children with hearing loss:
http://www.gohear.org

Free videos and library on oral deaf education:
http://www.oraldeafed.org

IBM SpeechViewer III with downloadable demonstration program:
http://www-3.ibm.com/able/snsspv3.html
http://www.listen-up.org/speech.htm

REFERENCES

Abraham, S., Stoker, R., & Allen (1988). Language assessment of hearing-impaired children and youth: Patterns of test use. *Language, Speech, and Hearing Services in the Schools, 19,* 160– 173.

Angelocci, A. A., Kopp, G. A., & Holbrook, A. (1964). The vowel formants of deaf and normal-hearing eleven-to-fourteen year old boys. *Journal of Speech and Hearing Disorders, 29,* 156–170.

Bankson, N. (1977). *Bankson Language Screening Test.* Baltimore, MD: University Park Press.

Boothe, L., Lasky, E., Kricos, P. (1982). Comparison of the language abilities of deaf children and young deaf adults. *Journal of Rehabilitation of the Deaf, 15,* 10–15.

Borden, G. J., Harris, K. S., & Raphael, L. J. (1994). *Speech science primer: Physiology, acoustics, and perception of speech* (3rd ed.), Baltimore, MD: Williams and Wilkins.

Brenza, B. A., Kricos, P. B., & Lasky, E. Z. (1981). Comprehension and production of basic semantic concepts by older hearing-impaired children. *Journal of Speech and Hearing Research, 24*, 414–419.

Caniglia, J., Cole, N. J., Howard, W., Krohn, E., & Rice, M. (1972). *Apple tree: A patterned program of linguistic expanse through reinforced experiences and evaluations.* Beaverton, OR: Dormac, Inc.

Carney, A. E. (1986). Understanding speech intelligibility in the hearing impaired. *Topics in Language Development, 6*(3), 47–59.

Carney, A. E., & Moeller, M. P. (1998). Treatment efficacy: Hearing loss in children. *Journal of Speech, Language, and Hearing Research, 41*, S61–S84.

Carrow, E. (1973). *Test of Auditory Comprehension of Language.* Austin, TX: Learning Concepts.

Cavallo, S. A., Baken, R. J., Metz, D. E., & Whitehead, R. L. (1991). Chest wall preparation for phonation in congenitally profoundly hearing-impaired persons. *Volta Review, 12*, 287–299.

Cole, E. B. (1992). Promoting emerging speech in birth to three year-old hearing-impaired children. *Volta Review, 94*, 63–77.

Cowie, R. I. D., & Douglas-Cowie, E. (1983). Speech production in profound post-lingual deafness. In M. E. Lutman & M. P. Haggard (Eds.), *Hearing science and hearing disorders.* New York: Academic Press.

Cowie, R. I. D., & Douglas-Cowie, E., & Kerr, A. G. (1982). A study of speech deterioration in post-lingually deafened adults. *Journal of Laryngology and Otology, 96*, 101–112.

Cozad, R. L. (1974). *The speech clinician and the hearing-impaired child.* Springfield, IL: Charles C Thomas.

Crais, E. R. (1991). Moving from "parent involvement" to family-centered services. *American Journal of Speech-Language Pathology, 9*, 5–8.

Dagenais, P. A. (1992). Speech training with glossometry and palatometry for profoundly hearing-impaired children. *Volta Review, 94*, 261–282.

Dagenais, P. A., & Critz-Crosby, P. (1991). Consonant lingual–palatal contacts produced by normal-hearing and hearing-impaired children. *Journal of Speech and Hearing Research, 34*, 1423–1435.

Dodd, B., McIntosh, B., & Woodhouse, L. (1998). Early lipreading ability and speech and language development of hearing-impaired pre-schoolers. In Campbell, R., Dodd, B., & Burnham, D. (Eds.), *Hearing by ear and eye II: Advances in the psychology of speechreading and auditory–visual speech* (pp. 283–301). United Kingdom: Psychology Press.

Downs, M. P., & Yoshinaga-Itano, C. (1999). The efficacy of early identification and intervention for children with hearing impairment. *Pediatric Clinics of North America, 46*(1), 79–87.

Duchan, J. F. (1988). Assessing communication of hearing-impaired children: Influences from pragmatics. In R. R. Kretschmer & L. W Kretschmer (Eds.), Communication assessment of hearing-impaired children: From conversation to classroom [Monograph]. *Journal of the Academy of Rehabilitative Audiology, 21*(Suppl.), 19–41.

Dunn, L., & Dunn, L. (1997). Peabody Picture Vocabulary Test–Revised (RPVT-3). Circle Pines, MN: American Guidance Service.

Elfenbein, J. L., Hardin-Jones, M. A., & Davis, J. M. (1994). Oral communication skills of children who are hard of hearing. *Journal of Speech and Hearing Research, 37*, 216–226.

Engen, E., & Engen, T. (1983). *Rhode Island Test of Language Structure*. Austin, TX: PRO-ED.

Formby, C., & Monsen, R. B. (1982). Long-term average speech spectra for normal and hearing-impaired adolescents. *Journal of the Acoustical Society of America, 71*, 196–202.

Forner, L. L., & Hixon, T. J. (1977). Respiratory kinematics in profoundly hearing-impaired speakers. *Journal of Speech and Hearing Research, 20*, 373–407.

Gardner, M. E. (1990). *Expressive One-Word Picture Vocabulary Test–Revised*. Novato, CA: Academic Therapy Publications.

Geffner, D. S., & Freeman, L. R. (1980). Assessment of language comprehension of six-year-old deaf children. *Journal of Communication Disorders, 13*, 455–470.

Gilbertson, M., & Kamhi, A. G. (1995). Novel word learning in children with hearing impairment. *Journal of Speech, Language, and Hearing Research, 38*, 630–642.

Gold, T. (1980). Speech production in hearing-impaired children. *Journal of Communication Disorders, 13*, 397–418.

Gordon-Brannan, M., Hodson, B., & Wynne, M. K. (1992). Remediating unintelligible utterances of a child with a mild hearing loss. *American Journal of Speech Language Pathology*, 28–37,

Goss, R. (1970). Language used by mothers of deaf children and mothers of hearing children. *American Annals of the Deaf, 115*, 93–96.

Hudgins, C. V., & Numbers, E. C. (1942). An investigation of the intelligibility of speech of the deaf. *Genetic Psychology Monographs, 25*, 289–392.

Hutchinson, J. M., & Smith, L. L. (1976). Aerodynamic functioning during consonant production by hearing-impaired adults. *Audiology and Hearing Education, 2*, 16–24.

Hutchinson, J. M., Smith, L. L., Kornhauser, R. L., Beasley, D. S., & Beasley, D. C. (1978). Aerodynamic functioning in consonant production in hearing-impaired children. *Audiology and Hearing Education, 4*, 23–31.

Jensema, C. J., Karchmer, M. A., & Trybus, R. J. (1978). *The rated speech intelligibility of hearing-impaired children: Basic relationships*. Washington, DC: Gallaudet College Office of Demographic Studies.

Johnson, H. A. (1988). A sociolinguistic assessment scheme for the total communication student. In R. R. Kretschmer & L. W. Kretschmer (Eds.), Communication assessment of hearing-impaired children: From conversation to classroom [Monograph]. *Journal of the Academy of Rehabilitative Audiology, 21*(Suppl.), 101–129.

Johnson, R. E., Liddell, S. K., & Erting, C. J. (1990). *Unlocking the curriculum: Principles for achieving access in deaf education*. Gallaudet Research Institute Working Paper 89-3. Washington, DC: Gallaudet University.

Kishon-Rabin, L, Taitelbaum, R., Tobin, Y., & Hildesheimer, M. (1999). The effect of partially restored hearing on speech production of postlingually deafened adults with multichannel cochlear implants. *Journal of the Acoustical Society of America, 106*(5), 2843–2857.

Kretschmer, R. R., & Kretschmer, L. W. (1978). *Language development and intervention with the hearing impaired*. Baltimore, MD: University Park Press.

Kricos, P. B. (1982). Response of mothers to the nonverbal communication of their hearing-impaired preschoolers. *Journal of the Academy of Rehabilitative Audiology, 15*, 51–69.

Kricos, P., & Aungst, H. (1984). Cognitive and communication development in hearing impaired preschool children. *Sign Language Studies, 43*, 121–140.

Laybaert, J. (1998). Phonological representation in deaf children: The importance of early linguistic experience. *Scandinavian Journal of Psychology, 39*, 169–173.

Layton, T. L., & Holmes, D. W. (1985). *Carolina Picture Vocabulary Test.* Austin, TX: PRO-ED.

Lederberg, A. R., & Everhart, V. S. (1998). Communication between deaf children and their hearing mothers: The role of language, gesture, and vocalizations. *Journal of Speech, Language, and Hearing Research, 41,* 887–899.

Lieberth, A. K. (1990). Rehabilitative issues in the bilingual education of deaf children. *Journal of the Academy of Rehabilitative Audiology, 23,* 53–61.

Limbrick, E. A., McNaughton, S., & Clay, M. M. (1992). Time engaged in reading: A critical factor in reading achievement. *American Annals of the Deaf, 137*(4), 309–314.

Ling, D. (1976). *Speech and the hearing-impaired child: Theory and practice.* Washington, DC: Alexander Graham Bell Association for the Deaf.

Ling, D. (1989). *Foundations of spoken language for hearing-impaired children.* Washington, DC: Alexander Graham Bell Association for the Deaf.

Luetke-Stahlman, B., & Luckner, J. (1991). *Effectively educating students with hearing impairments.* New York: Longman.

Mahoney, G., Boyce, G., Fewell, R. R., et al. (1998). The relationship of parent–child interaction to the effectiveness of early intervention services for at-risk children and children with disabilities. *Topics in Early Childhood Special Education, 18,* 5–17.

Markides, A. (1967). *The speech of deaf and partially-hearing children with special reference to factors affecting intelligibility.* Unpublished master's thesis, University of Manchester.

Mayne, A. M., Yoshinaga-Itano, C., Sedey, A. L., & Carey, A. (2000). Expressive vocabulary development of infants and toddlers who are deaf or hard of hearing. *Volta Review, 100*(5) (Monograph), 1–28.

McGarr, N. S., & Whitehead, R. (1992). Contemporary issues in phoneme production by hearing- impaired persons: Physiologic and acoustic aspects. *Volta Review, 94,* 33–45.

Metz, D., Whitehead, R., & Whitehead, B. (1984). Mechanics of vocal fold vibration and laryngeal articulatory gestures produced by hearing-impaired speakers. *Journal of Speech and Hearing Research, 27,* 62–69.

Miccio, A., Ingrisano, D., & Balkany, T. (1990). Emergence of phonological contrasts following cochlear implantation. Paper presented at the annual meeting of the American Speech–Language–Hearing Association.

Miller, P. (1997). The effect of communication mode on the development of phonemic awareness in prelingually deaf students. *Journal of Speech, Language, and Hearing Research, 40,* 1151–1163.

Moeller, M. P. (1988). Combining formal and informal strategies for language assessment of hearing-impaired children. Communication assessment of hearing-impaired children: From conversation to classroom. In R. R. Kretschmer & L. W. Kretschmer (Eds.), Communication assessment of hearing-impaired children: From conversation to classroom [Monograph]. Supplement, *Journal of the Academy of Rehabilitative Audiology, 21,* 73–101.

Moeller, M. P., & Luetke-Stahlman, B. (1990). Parents' use of signing exact English: A descriptive analysis. *Journal of Speech and Hearing Disorders, 55,* 327–338.

Moeller, M. P., & Schick, B. (1993). *Sign with me parent workbook.* Omaha, NE: Center for Hearing Loss in Children.

Moeller, M., Coufal, K., and Hixson (1990). The efficacy of speech-language intervention: Hearing impaired children. *Seminars in Speech-Language Pathology,* 11:227–241.

Moeller, M. P., Osberger, M. J., & Eccarius, M. (1986). Receptive language skills [Monograph 231]. *Language and learning skills of hearing-impaired students, Asha Monographs*, 41–54.

Monsen, R. B. (1979). Acoustic qualities of phonation in young hearing-impaired children. *Journal of Speech and Hearing Research, 22*, 270–288.

Moog, J. S., & Geers, A. E. (1975). *Scales of early communication skills for hearing impaired children.* St. Louis: Central Institute for the Deaf.

Moog, J. S., & Geers, A. E. (1979). *Grammatical analysis of elicited language—simple sentence level.* St. Louis, MO: Central Institute for the Deaf.

Moog, J. S., & Geers, A. E. (1983). *Grammatical analysis of elicited language–presentence level.* St. Louis, MO: Central Institute for the Deaf.

Moog, J. S., & Kozak, V. J. (1983). *Teacher assessment of grammatical structures.* St. Louis, MO: Central Institute for the Deaf.

Moore, J. K., Perazzo, L. M., & Braun, A. (1995). Time course of axonal myelination in the human brainstem auditory pathway. *Hearing Research, 87*, 21.

Most, T., Weisel, A., & Matezky, A. (1996). Speech intelligibility and the evaluation of personal qualities by experienced and inexperienced listeners. *Volta Review, 98*(4), 181–190.

Muter, V. (1997). Segmentation, not rhyming, predicts early progress in learning to read. *Journal of Experimental Child Psychology, 65*, 370–396.

Newcomer, P., & Hammill, D. (1977). *Test of Language Development.* Los Angeles: Western Psychological Services.

Okalidou, A., & Harris, K. S. (1999). A comparison of intergestural patterns in deaf and hearing adult speakers: Implications from an acoustic analysis of disyllables. *Journal of the Acoustical Society of America, 106*(1), 394–409.

Oller, D. K. (1980). The emergence of speech sounds in infancy. In G. Yeni-Komishan, J. Kavanaugh, & C. A. Ferguson (Eds.), *Child Phonology: Vol 1. Production* (pp. 93–112). New York: Grune and Stratton.

Oller, D., & Eilers, R. E. (1988). The role of audition in infant babbling. *Child Development, 59*, 441–449.

Oller, D., & Kelly, C. A. (1974). Phonological substitution processes of a hard-of-hearing child. *Journal of Speech and Hearing Disorders, 39*, 65–74.

Osberger, M. J., & Levitt, H. (1979). The effect of timing errors on the intelligibility of deaf children's speech. *Journal of the Acoustical Society of America, 66*, 1316–1324.

Osberger, M. J., Moeller, M. P., Eccarius, M., Robbins, A. M., & Johnson, D. (1986). Expressive language skills [Monograph 23]. In M. J. Osberger (Ed.), *Language and learning skills of hearing-impaired students* (pp. 54–65). Asha Monographs. Washington, DC: Asha.

Owens, R. E. (1990). Development of communication, language, and speech. In G. H. Shames & E. H. Wiig (Eds.), *Human communication disorders* (pp. 30–73). Columbus, OH: Merrill Publishing Co.

Plant, G. (1999). Speech training for young adults who are congenitally deaf: A case study. *Volta Review, 100*(1), 5–17.

Pratt, S. R., Heintzelmann, A. T., & Deming, S. E. (1993). The efficacy of using the IBM SpeechViewer Vowel Accuracy Module to treat young children with hearing impairment. *Journal of Speech and Hearing Research, 36*, 1063–1074.

Prinz, P. M., & Prinz, E. A. (1985). If only you could hear what I see: Discourse development in sign language. *Discourse Processes, 8*, 1–19.

Quigley, S. P., Monranelli, D. S., & Wilbur, R. B. (1976). Some aspects of the verb system in the language of deaf students. *Journal of Speech and Hearing Research, 19,* 536–550.

Quigley, S. P., Steinkamp, M., Poer, D., & Jones, B. (1978). The test of syntactic abilities. Beaverton, OR: Dormac.

Robinshaw, H. M. (1995). Early intervention for hearing impairment: Differences in the timing of communicative and linguistic development. *British Journal of Audiology, 29,* 315–334.

Roush, J., & McWilliam, R. A. (1994). Family-centered early intervention: historical, philosophical, and legislative issues. In J. Roush & N. D. Matkin, (Eds.), *Infants and toddlers with hearing loss: Family-centered assessment and intervention* (pp. 3–23). Baltimore, MD: York.

Ryalls, J. LeDorze, G., Boulanger, H., & Laroche, B. (1995). Speech therapy for lowering vocal fundamental frequency in two adolescents with hearing impairments: A comparison with and without the IBM SpeechViewer. *Volta Review, 97,* 243–250.

Schirmer, B. R. (1994). *Language and literacy development in children who are deaf.* New York: Maxwell Macmillan International.

Schuele, M. A., & van Kleeck, A. (1987). Precursors to literacy: Assessment and intervention. *Topics in Language Disorders, 7*(2), 32–44.

Sensenbaugh, R. (1996). Phonemic awareness: An important early step in learning to read. *Eric Digest,* D119–D120.

Seyfried, D. N., & Waldron, C. (1993). Pediatric aural rehabilitation: Combining the expertise of speech–language pathologists and audiologists. Short Course offered at Speech–Language–Hearing Association of Virginia, Reston, Virginia.

Sininger, Y. S., Doyle, K. J., & Moore, J. K. (1999). The case for early identification of hearing loss in children. *Pediatric Clinics of North America, 46*(1), 1–14.

Skarakis, E. A., & Prutting, C. A. (1977). Early communication: Semantic functions and communication intentions in the communication of the preschool child with impaired hearing. *American Annals of the Deaf, 122,* 392–394.

Smith, B. L. (1982). Some observations concerning pre-meaningful vocalization of hearing- impaired infants. *Journal of Speech and Hearing Disorders, 47,* 439–441.

Smith, C. R. (1975). Residual hearing and speech production in deaf children. *Journal of Speech and Hearing Research, 18,* 795–811.

Spencer, P. E. (1993). Communication behaviors of infants with hearing loss and their hearing mothers. *Journal of Speech and Hearing Research, 36,* 311–321.

Srinivasan, P. (1996). on disc. Practical aural rehabilitation for speech–language pathologists and educators of hearing-impaired children. Springfield, IL: Charles C Thomas.

Staton, J. (1985). Using dialogue journals for developing thinking, reading, and writing with hearing-impaired students. *Volta Review, 87*(5), 127–153.

Stewart, D. A. (1993). Bi-bi to MCE? *American Annals of the Deaf, 138,* 331–337.

Stoel-Gammon, C., & Otomo, K. (1986). Babbling development of hearing-impaired and normally hearing subjects. *Journal of Speech and Hearing Disorders, 51,* 33–41.

Stuckless, E. R., & Birch, J. W. (1997). The influence of early manual communication on the linguistic development of deaf children. *American Annals of the Deaf, 142*(3), 71–78.

Subtelny, J. D. (1977). Assessment of speech with implications for training. In. F. Bess (Ed.), *Childhood deafness: Causation, assessment, and management* (pp. 183–194). New York: Grune & Stratton.

Svirsky, M. A., Robbins, A. M., Kirk, K. I., Pisoni, D. B., & Miyamoto, R. T. (2000). Language development in profoundly deaf children with cochlear implants. *Psychological Science, 11,* 153–158.

Tomblin, J. B., Spencer, L., Flock, S., Tyler, R., & Gantz, B. (1999). A comparison of language achievement in children with cochlear implants and children using hearing aids. *Journal of Speech, Language, and Hearing Research, 42,* 497–511.

Tonelson, S., & Watkins, S. (1979). *SKI*HI language development scale.* Logan, UT: Hope, Inc.

Truax, R. (1985). Linking research to teaching to facilitate reading–writing–communication connections. *Volta Review, 87*(5), 155–169.

Tye-Murray N. (1991). The establishment of open articulatory postures by deaf and hearing talkers. *Journal of Speech and Hearing Research, 34,* 453–459.

Tye-Murray, N. (1992). Articulatory organizational strategies and the roles of auditory information. *Volta Review, 94,* 243–260.

van Kleeck, A., & Schuele, C. M. (1987). Precursors to literacy: Normal development. *Topics in Language Disorders, 7*(2), 13–31.

West, J. J., & Weber, J. L. (1974). A phonological analysis of the spontaneous language of a four-year-old hard-of-hearing child. *Journal of Speech and Heating Disorders, 38,* 25–35.

Wilbur, R., Goodhart, W., & Fuller, D. (1989). Comprehension of English modals by hearing-impaired students. *Volta Review, 91,* 5–18.

Wilson, F. B. (1977). *Voice disorders.* Austin, TX: Learning Concepts.

Yoshinaga-Itano, C., & Apuzzo, M. L. (1998a). Identification of hearing loss after age 18 months is not early enough. *American Annals of the Deaf, 143*(5), 380–387.

Yoshinaga-Itano, C., & Apuzzo, M. L. (1998b). The development of deaf and hard of hearing children identified early through the high-risk registry. *American Annals of the Deaf, 143*(5), 416–424.

Yoshinaga-Itano, C., & Downey, D. M. (1986). A hearing-impaired child's acquisition of schemata: Something's missing. *Topics in Language Disorders, 7*(1), 45–57.

Yoshinaga-Itano, C., & Downey, D. M. (1996). Development of school-aged deaf, hard-of-hearing, and normally hearing students' written language. *Volta Review, 98,* 3–7.

Yoshinaga-Itano, C., & Stredler-Brown, A. (1992). Learning to communicate: Babies with hearing impairments make their needs known. *Volta Review, 94,* 107–129.

Yoshinaga-Itano, C., Sedey, A. L., Coulter, D. K., & Mehl, A. L. (1998). Language of early- and later-identified children with hearing loss. *Pediatrics, 102,* 1161–1171.

Yoshinaga-Itano, C., Snyder, L. S., & Mayberry, R. (1996). How deaf and normally hearing students convey meaning within and between written sentences. *Volta Review, 98,* 9–38.

Zimmerman, G., & Rettaliata, P. (1981). Articulatory patterns of an adventitiously deaf speaker: Implications for the role of auditory information in speech production. *Journal of Speech and Hearing Research, 24,* 169–178.

Psychosocial Aspects of Hearing Impairment and Counseling Basics

Kris English

C O N T E N T S

■ INTRODUCTION

Adjusting to hearing impairment and accepting recommendations regarding audiologic rehabilitation can be a difficult process for many individuals, as well as for their families. This chapter will describe a range of psychological, social, and emotional difficulties frequently experienced by persons with hearing impairment across the life-span. In addition, a description of basic counseling concepts will be provided to demonstrate how professionals can help individuals with hearing loss to contend with the problems of living with hearing loss and identify and assume ownership of their individual solutions.

■ PSYCHOSOCIAL ASPECTS OF HEARING IMPAIRMENT

No hearing loss is exactly like another, but there are some ways to organize our understanding of this impairment. First to be recognized is the distinction between the terms *deaf* and *hard of hearing*. About 28 million individuals in the United States have some degree of hearing impairment, and more than 90% of these persons can be described as being *hard of hearing*: that is, having a mild, moderate, or severe hearing loss and some ability to understand speech with the use of hearing aids or other amplification. The remaining persons with hearing impairment have a bilateral profound hearing loss and would be described as being *deaf*, whereby, even with powerful hearing aids, speech generally is not perceived in auditory-only perceptual situations. Another important distinction is needed between the concepts of *being deaf* (having a bilateral profound hearing loss) and *being Deaf*. The latter phrase, with the capital D, refers to a cultural identification with the Deaf community; this distinction and the unique concerns of cultural Deafness will be reviewed in a later section.

deaf: profound degree of hearing loss, whereas *Deaf* connotes a pride in associating with a group who share the same culture (i.e., the Deaf community).

Initially, however, we will consider some general psychosocial and emotional implications of living with hearing loss, first among children and adolescents (that is, growing up with hearing impairment) and then among adults (acquiring hearing impairment).

Growing Up with Hearing Loss

The most significant consequence of growing up with a hearing loss is the difficulty in perceiving others' words, because this limitation has a direct effect on the ability to develop one's own words and subsequent language skills. Even a mild degree of hearing loss can adversely affect vocabulary development and the subtle intricacies of language use. When language development is delayed, there is a cascading effect on many aspects of a child's psychosocial development, including self-concept, emotional development, family concerns, and social competence.

Self-concept or self-image: how one sees oneself.

SELF-CONCEPT. Individuals are not born with their self-concepts intact; rather, *self-concept is learned* by absorbing the input, feedback, and reactions from those around us. Children typically internalize such reactions without question, and allow others' attitudes to define themselves to themselves. Children are likely to think these thoughts: "I see myself the way you tell me you see me. If you see me as loved or unlovable, capable or not capable, a delight or a trial—this is how I see myself."

It appears that children with hearing loss are at risk for developing a relatively poor self-concept, most likely from negative reactions regarding their communication difficulties and also from being perceived differently as hearing aid users. For example, Cappelli and colleagues (1995) collected information from 23 hard of hearing children, ages 6 to 12, as well as from 23 children with no hearing loss, matched by sex and classroom. From a "Self Perception Profile for Children," it was found that children with hearing impairment perceived themselves as less socially accepted than their non-hearing impaired peers. Another recent study (Bess, Dodd-

Murphy, & Parker, 1998) asked more than 1200 children with mild hearing loss to answer questions such as this: "During the past month, how often have you felt badly about yourself?" Overall, children with mild hearing loss exhibited significantly higher dysfunction in self-esteem than children without hearing loss (self-esteem or self-regard being an evaluative component of self-concept). The researchers concluded that "even mild losses can be associated with increased social and emotional dysfunction among school aged children" (p. 350).

Children who grow up with hearing loss not only receive negative feedback and reactions because of their communication difficulties, but also because of the cosmetic issue of looking different. Our society has yet to accept hearing aids as a neutral technical device; instead, there tends to be a negative association with hearing aid use, with biased assumptions of reduced abilities, attractiveness, and intelligence. Many studies have examined this phenomenon, often called the *hearing aid effect* (Blood, Blood, & Danhauser, 1977), by showing subjects a set of pictures of individuals, some wearing visible hearing aids and some not. All characteristics were identical except for the presence of hearing aids; yet when the instruments were visible, individuals were given lower scores in almost every category of intelligence, personality, attractiveness, and capability. It appears that the very presence of a hearing aid can cause overall negative reactions.

> Hearing aid effect: a psychological reaction to the presence of a hearing aid; the viewer has negative assumptions about the hearing aid user.

It is encouraging to note that preschool children seem less likely to hold these negative and preconceived notions (Riensche, Peterson, & Linden, 1990) and that teens may be becoming more accustomed to and accepting of hearing aids among their peers (Stein, Gill, & Gans, 2000). But, in general, if the appearance of a device on or in the ears creates a negative reaction among people who see it, their reaction is likely to be perceived by the hearing aid user, which can adversely effect the user's self-concept. We would do a disservice to children growing up with hearing loss to dismiss society's reactions to hearing aids as a non-issue or to downplay it as "only the other person's problem." Edwards (1991) reminds us that "it is the wearing of the device which 'amplifies' the difference between the child with hearing loss and his or her peers" (p. 7), and children deserve our honesty in acknowledging that this difference does exist. (To experience the hearing aid effect firsthand, college students [with normal hearing] are frequently assigned to wear a very visible pair of hearing aids for a full day around their community and record their subjective impressions of those around them as well as their own reactions.)

Since "the acquisition of language is essential for the development of self" (Garrison & Tesch, 1978, p. 463), it follows that a delay in language acquisition would adversely affect the development of self. This correlation in fact has been demonstrated in several studies, described in the next section.

EMOTIONAL DEVELOPMENT. An individual uses language to describe, interpret, and ultimately understand the abstract nature of his or her emotions. Because of concomitant language deficits, children growing up with hearing loss may have limited experience in self-expression and a subsequent delay in awareness and understanding of their own emotions, as well as the emotions of others. By virtue of having a hearing loss, they frequently miss overhearing adults and older children talk about and verbally manage their feelings about situations (see Figure 7.1).

FIGURE 7.1

Missing out on adult conversations about emotions.

Aunt Betty reminded me that this is the anniversary of her father's death. She is a little shaky, but she does feel better remembering all the good times while growing up. Still, that explains why she was so subdued the other day, I was pretty worried about that . . . .

Affective vocabulary: words and phrases that describe feelings or emotional reactions (e.g., discouraged, elated, bored, upset).

Researchers have shown that children with hearing loss are often less accurate in identifying others' emotional states than children without hearing loss and have a poorer understanding of affective words. Understanding affective vocabulary has been positively related to personal adjustment (Greenberg & Kusche, 1993), so these findings reinforce our understanding of the contributions of communication to self-understanding. (For further information about the importance of general emotional development, readers are referred to Goleman, 1995.)

FAMILY CONCERNS. More than 90% of children with hearing loss are born into families with normal-hearing parents. The vast majority of these parents have little or no experience with hearing loss, so the diagnosis of hearing loss is devastating news, a moment frozen in time that they never forget. Even if parents have suspected hearing loss for some time before the diagnosis, they still report experiencing sadness, as well as relief, for having their suspicions confirmed. From their reports, it appears that most parents experience emotional reactions consistent with the stages or phases of the "grief cycle" (Kubler-Ross, 1969). The grief cycle includes a progressive set of emotional reactions, starting with shock, because the information generally was not expected, and denial, because the information does not reconcile with one's dreams for the future. When the reality of the situation begins to sink in, parents in grief may find themselves feeling depressed or helpless for a time while they attempt to cope with the implications of the diagnosis. The final stage of this cycle is acceptance, but more than one parent has been heard to say that they feel the term *resignation* is more accurate. Other reactions include depression, sorrow, confusion, and vulnerability, and they have been known to resurface at unexpected times in the family's development. Luterman (1996) reminds us that it is inappropriate for a professional to expect families to be "over their grief by now"; families have the right to feel the way they feel, and professionals must refrain from passing judgment. It is important to keep in mind that we do not predictably "march through" stages of grief and ultimately recover to be the same person as before. Parents report moving back and forth within these emotional reactions during different stages of their child's development, and often they find themselves almost as grieved by a new event as when they first received the diagnosis of hearing loss.

Grief cycle: a pattern of reaction and adjustment to loss.

Over time, parents work their way past their own anticipated self-concept of being parents of a "perfect" child to the new reality of being parents of a child who has a hearing loss, and this process can be harder for some parents than for others. Kricos (2000) writes about professionals' perceptions of parents who are struggling with acceptance:

> Parents in the denial stage may appear to clinicians to be blocking efforts to initiate the intervention program. However, it should be remembered that this initial reaction to the diagnosis may provide a time for parents to search for inner strength and accumulate information. The goal for clinicians during this stage of grieving is to find ways of not merely tolerating parental denial but accepting it, while still offering, to the best of their abilities, the services the child needs. Unfortunately, parents who appear to be denying their child's hearing impairment are often perceived by clinicians as foolish and stubborn, when they should be perceived as loving parents who, for the time being, cannot accept the professional's diagnosis of such a severe disability in their child. (pp. 279–280)

Even as parents work through their emotional reactions, difficulties may persist, again because of communication. Several studies have described a tendency in mother–child interactions to be more rigid and more negative when the child has a hearing loss. Verbal exchanges are briefer and more directive and include less

Family counseling can assist in establishing successful parent-child attachment.

praise compared to mothers whose children have normal hearing (Pipp-Siegel & Biringen, 2000). Without intervention, these communication styles can have an impact on the quality of parent–child attachment.

Professionals may inadvertently contribute to parental confusion or stress by emphasizing issues that are not at the forefront of parents' concerns. For instance, upon first fitting hearing aids on a child, professionals are likely to intone these instructions: "Mrs. Tomas, you will want to make sure that Isabella wears these hearing aids every waking hour. That way, she will have the best conditions to develop speech and language." Although an accurate statement, this clinical approach may miss the mark for many parents; it might be more helpful to "speak their language" by "saying the same thing differently." For example,

> Mrs. Tomas, the more Isabella wears her hearing aids, the more she will learn from your voice how much you love her and cherish her; the more she will learn when you are teasing and when you are serious about obeying you; the more she will be part of family jokes and family lessons and family history . . .

At the time that all this is happening, Isabella will also have optimal conditions to develop speech and language, but it has been presented in a context that families can understand and use. In addition, the undue pressure of "pleasing the professional" has been removed; instead, the parent has been acknowledged as a competent adult who has a lot to manage and who will do her best for her child as her energy level allows.

SOCIAL COMPETENCE. As children grow up, their social world expands to include same-age peers. Here, too, difficulties have been observed among children with hearing loss: because of their delay in developing communication skills, children with hearing loss have fewer opportunities for peer interactions, making it difficult to learn "the social rules governing communication" (Antia & Kreimeyer, 1992, p. 135). Poor and limited communication results in poor social competence, which includes these skills (Greenberg & Kusche, 1993):

> Social competence: skills for successful and satisfying personal relationships.

- Capacity to think independently
- Capacity for self-direction and self-control
- Understanding the feelings, motivations, and needs of self and others
- Flexibility
- Ability to tolerate frustration
- Ability to rely on and be relied on by others
- Maintaining healthy relationships with others

It would appear that children with hearing loss are at risk in developing these social competencies. For instance, a group of parents of 40 children with hearing impairment completed a questionnaire that indicated overall that their children had more than typical problems interacting with others and establishing friendships (Davis et al., 1986). The children themselves were interviewed, and 50% ($N = 20$) expressed their own concerns about peers and social relationships. Most children stated that they would not mention wearing hearing aids because of "a fear of being teased and embarrassed, and many others reported spending most of their time alone" (p. 60). The researchers wondered if these social problems were typical among most preadolescents, so they conducted the same interview among 58 children without hearing loss. After factoring out the responses from two children who had just moved to a new school, only 12% (*N* = 7) of these children reported having difficulty with making friends or getting teased.

SPECIAL ISSUES IN ADOLESCENCE. Most of the information reviewed so far has focused on elementary school children. The teen years present new challenges and heighten the intensity of existing ones. Adolescence is a stage of life with important developmental tasks, including peer group affiliation, identity formation, occupational preparation, and adjustment to physiologic changes (Altman, 1996). During these turbulent times, self-consciousness increases, as well as uncertainty and mood swings. All teens, with or without hearing loss, may feel besieged with emotions that they find hard to articulate, and the presence of hearing loss can exacerbate teens' struggles for self-awareness and self-expression.

Peer relationships take paramount importance for teens, yet these relationships may be strained when hearing loss is involved. Mothers have reported that their teenage children seemed less emotionally bonded to their friends when hearing loss was a variable and also rated these friendships as higher in aggression (Henggeler, Watson, & Thelan, 1990). Being with other teens with hearing loss may be more important than expected, when we consider how peer relationships help teens to define themselves. Most of the 220 mainstreamed students in one study indicated that they preferred to spend most of their time with other students with hearing impairment, finding these relationships deeper and more satisfying (Stinson, Whitmore, & Kluwin, 1996).

The desire to conform to group expectations seems to peak in ninth grade (Kimmel & Weiner, 1995). For teens with hearing loss, this desire will probably include the desire to reject amplification for the sake of conformity. This desire may also represent a struggle to accept oneself as a person with a disability. The hearing aid effect is probably still in play, although there is some evidence that the magnitude of negative effect has lessened in the last 10 years (Stein et al., 2000). Overall, however, it is agreed that "during adolescence, being different is generally not valued" (Coyner, 1993, p. 19).

During these years, students need to develop appropriate social or interpersonal skills to advocate for their needs as they transition to college or work settings. This developmental task frequently is not supported, resulting in high school graduates who move on to higher education or work placements without learning how to describe and request the services that they need to succeed (English, 1997; Flexer, Wray, & Leavitt, 1990). Professionals who serve adolescents face the challenge of helping with the here and now issues of self-identity, as well as concerns of the imminent future, and the former may seem so paramount that the latter is overlooked.

SUMMARY. This section described a range of possible psychosocial and emotional difficulties that might occur as a result of growing up with a hearing loss. Self-concept can be affected because of communication limitations, as well as parental attachment, emotional development, and social competency. Interventions are available to help to reduce these effects, and they should be used when concerns arise (English, 2001). The following section will consider how similar psychosocial issues can affect persons who acquire hearing loss in their adult years.

Acquiring Hearing Loss

Although relatively few children are born with hearing loss, most individuals, if they live long enough, acquire some degree of hearing loss as part of the aging process. Frequently, adults also acquire hearing loss as a side effect of some medications or as a result of head injury or noise exposure. Adults are not immune to the psychological, emotional, and the previous social effects described with respect to children. Parallel categories will be considered here as they apply to adults: self-concept, psychoemotional reactions, and family and social concerns.

SELF-CONCEPT. It has long been noted that adults can be reluctant to admit to having a hearing loss and to take steps toward remediation. When people seek help from an audiologist, they have usually waited an average of 7 years from the time that they first noticed hearing problems. During these years, they may attempt to dismiss the problem as the fault of others (e.g., accusing people of mumbling) or using other avoidance techniques. Another indicator that adults have a difficult time adjusting to their self-concept of a person with hearing loss is the fact that only about 20% of the population who would benefit from the use of hearing aids actually obtain and use them. When asked, people in the remaining 80% indicate cosmetic concerns as second only to the cost of hearing aids (Kochkin, 1996).

To underscore the effect of hearing aids on self-concept, consider the following study: a group of older women with hearing loss were divided in half, but only the women in one group were fit with hearing aids (Doggett, Stein, & Gans, 1998). All subjects then interacted with unfamiliar same-age peers who later rated them on attractiveness, friendliness, confidence, and intelligence. The subjects who wore the

Helping the person to understand the underlying basis for a hearing disability facilitates adjustment to it.

hearing aids were rated as less confident, less friendly, and less intelligent than the subjects not wearing hearing aids. The remarkable point about this study is that the raters did not even notice the hearing aids and so were not responding to their appearance! The authors surmised that the subjects wearing hearing aids displayed less confidence, friendliness, and intelligence because they projected a negative self-image. Again, as with children, ignoring the hearing aid effect with adults is akin to ignoring the proverbial elephant standing in the middle of the living room. It would be naïve to assume that, because they are self-confident adults in most other aspects of their lives, they are invulnerable to this undeniable cosmetic concern.

PSYCHOEMOTIONAL REACTIONS. In addition to avoidance and worry about cosmetics, adults have reported a full range of other emotions and psychological reactions to hearing loss, including anger ("Why is this happening?"), anxiety and insecurity ("What will this mean about my future?"), stress (especially before the effects of the hearing loss are well understood, for instance, in understanding speech in restaurants), resentment, depression, and grief. The grief cycle was mentioned earlier with respect to parents and the diagnosis of hearing loss in children, but adults also experience a type of grief when their suspicions about deteriorating hearing have been confirmed. Its expression can be very subtle, as depicted in the following scenario:

Case Study

A 92-year-old man sought a hearing evaluation to address recent listening difficulties. Test results confirmed that he had a mild to moderate hearing loss, and hearing aids were recommended to help him to meet his listening goals. Upon hearing this, he lowered his head, sighed deeply, and said, "I've always thought of hearing aids as only for old people." His audiologist waited with him quietly, and in less than 1 minute he raised his head, shook himself slightly, and asked, "Well, what do we do first?" That moment was a very brief but real expression of grief: "I am vulnerable, mortal, getting farther and farther away from my youth."

When we are excluded from a conversation, it is human nature (because we are naturally egocentric) to suspect that the conversation is about us. Adults with hearing loss struggle regularly with *conversational exclusion,* which can lead to behaviors that would suggest paranoia. However, it is vital that we do not confuse these reactions with the paranoia associated with schizophrenia and other mental health problems; this kind of paranoia is actually a natural reaction to the situation. At the same time, such reactions should not be dismissed as unimportant: if persons with hearing loss feel actively ignored or talked about or excluded, they may not have associated these reactions with the existence of hearing loss and may experience an undefined sense of disquiet or confusion.

FAMILY CONCERNS. Family members take the brunt of the stress while a member is coming to accept the fact that his or her hearing is changing. They are blamed for not speaking clearly or for purposefully leaving the person with hearing loss out of the conversation. Because communication is difficult, families do tend to talk around the patient or, if asked to repeat something, to minimize the effort by responding, "Never mind, it wasn't really important." Significant others (particularly spouses) often assume the responsibility of "hearing" for the family member, by explaining what was missed, covering up for miscommunications, taking responsibility for all telephone contacts, or worrying about possible social embarrassment when a response is unrelated to the comment made. In half-jest, adults with hearing loss have been known to introduce their spouses this way: "Have you met my hearing aid?"

The person with hearing loss usually does not realize the burden that this spouse carries. When the patient and spouse take identical surveys to describe the effects of the hearing loss on their lives, the spouse usually reports greater problems before a hearing aid fitting and greater benefit after the hearing aid fitting than the patient does. These reports tell us a great deal about the stress of the hearing loss on the nonimpaired spouse or significant other.

Other family members may experience frustration and disappointment when communication by phone or in person is ineffective, and the person with the hearing loss may internalize these problems as a rejection of themselves rather than of the communication problems. A downward spiral can occur: "It's too hard to talk to Dad so I'll keep the details to a minimum." Dad resents the limitation and contributes even less to the communication efforts.

SOCIAL CONCERNS. When communication becomes gradually more difficult, our social world can constrict accordingly. The adult with hearing loss may opt out of favorite activities because the listening challenges are too stressful. When efforts are made to interact as if no hearing loss exists, misunderstandings typically occur (believing a comment was a joke when it was meant to be serious or completely misunderstanding a comment); this may result in embarrassment, possible blame directed to the communication partner, and eventually the use of avoidance techniques. Regular attendance to religious, family, and leisure activities becomes curtailed, often with excuses about losing interest, rather than recognizing the root of the problem. This social withdrawal has been shown to lead to depression. It is not uncommon to find adults not making the connection between the change in their life-styles and their gradual hearing loss.

Avoidance techniques: strategies used to postpone acknowledgment of a difficult situation.

SUMMARY. Acquiring hearing loss in adulthood is usually a gradual, insidious process and is usually recognized by family and friends before being recognized by the person whose hearing is becoming impaired. Before, during, and after confirmation of hearing loss, adults may experience many of the same psychosocial difficulties that children do.

About Being Deaf

So far we have considered the psychosocial and emotional effects of hearing loss in general. Several studies have noted that the more severe the hearing loss, the more severe the psychosocial and emotional problems can be (Warren & Hasenstab, 1986). These kinds of severe difficulties have been described by Meadow (1976, 1980), who reported how deaf children and adults have been characterized as compulsive, egocentric, and rigid. Deficits in empathy have been described (Bachara, Raphael, & Phelan, 1980), as well as higher than expected levels of anxiety (Harris, Van Zandt, & Rees, 1997) and a condition called "primitive personality" among deaf individuals (Vernon, 1996):

> This disorder involves a combination of extreme educational deprivation (usually functional illiteracy), miniscule social input and knowledge, including awareness of appropriate social behavior, immaturity, and a generally psychologically barren life. While not psychotic, individuals with primitive personalities are not able to cope with life in our complex modern society. When the communication handicap of deafness is not dealt with, educationally and psychologically, primitive personality is a frequent result. (p. 237)

Although few deaf people experience a genuinely "extreme deprivation," most do contend with limited language input that can result in a reduced repertoire of coping skills. Frustrations and worries that cannot be verbally expressed can escalate into impulse disorder behaviors or depression. It must be understood that psychological difficulties are not caused by the hearing loss per se, but rather by the communication problems that result from hearing loss. If these kinds of concerns present themselves, a referral to a qualified psychologist or other counselor is in order.

Impulse disorder: having difficulty controlling one's initial reactions or impulses; acting without considering consequences.

BEING DEAFENED. The previous paragraphs focused on issues of individuals who were born deaf. Persons who become deafened in their adult years (late-onset deafness) have a uniquely stressful situation, because they have no preestablished ties to the Deaf community, yet also face challenges in maintaining their ties to the hearing world. Communication may be limited to writing notes or speechreading, neither procedure being very conducive to spontaneous or lengthy conversation. A sense of isolation is likely to occur, as well as anger, frustration, denial, or depression (Zarrella, 1995).

Depression may result not only from the difficulties in communication, however. Speech communication occurs at a "symbolic" level of hearing, as defined by Ramsdell (1960). But there are other levels of hearing as well, including the *warning* or environmental level and the *primitive* level, which means hearing sounds so basic to our lives that we are not even aware of their occurrence. Virtually every action we make, every activity in our environment, produces a sound to which we react, often unconsciously. Persons who suddenly lose their hearing frequently report that the world has become "dead" to them. For example, to see a door shut forcefully and not hear the anticipated slam tend to make deafened people feel they are no longer interacting with the world around them. Even more distressing may be the absence of sound produced by the self, such as our own footsteps or voices. Ramsdell stressed that the depression of a deafened person occurs because he "is not aware of the loss he has suffered at the primitive level. . . . He is unaware that there is such a thing as this primitive level in the first place" (p. 464).

Fortunately, hearing aids and cochlear implants often provide much psychological relief to many deafened adults. Recovering some degree of sound perception, even if only at the primitive level, can result in reduced anxiety and depression.

"Deafness with a Capital D"

Deaf community: a group of individuals who share cultural similarities in language (ASL), mores, traditions, and values.

About 2 million people in the United States not only have a profound hearing loss and derive no benefit from hearing aids (i.e., being audiologically deaf), but they also identify themselves as members of the Deaf community (being culturally deaf). This cultural affiliation is described by Vernon and Andrews (1990):

> Membership in the deaf community involves identification with deaf people, shared experiences in school and work, and active participation in group activities with other deaf people. . . . Most notably, deaf community members share frustrating experiences trying to communicate in the hearing world. . . . [S]ome hearing individuals, such as educators, counselors, and spouses, can be "courtesy" members. However, only deaf persons can really know what deafness means. Neither social class nor sex nor religion are important attributes for membership; the most distinguishing criteria are communication skill and preference. (pp. 7–8)

Communication within the Deaf community is based on the use of American Sign Language (ASL), a manual language with its own syntax and rules of use (with roots in French and English) (see Chapter 5). Deaf theater and Deaf poetry thrive across the country, notably at Gallaudet University in Washington, DC, the only liberal arts university for the Deaf in the world. In addition to having its own language, like other cultures the Deaf community has its own traditions, mores, and values. The passing on of these values and traditions and even ASL is not accomplished through the more common vertical enculturation process from parent to child, because only about 10% of deaf children are born to deaf parents (a phrase usually shortened as "deaf of deaf"). Instead, the transference of culture has occurred horizontally, among peers in residential schools or in postsecondary settings like colleges or communities.

Enculturation process: shaping or raising children according to values defined by a culture.

Deaf persons tend to marry other Deaf persons and usually (but not always) would prefer to have children who also have profound hearing loss, like themselves (see the following Case Study). Connections to the Deaf community are usually life-long, and elderly deaf individuals typically maintain friendships established in their childhood (Becker, 1980).

Case Study

The topic for the day in Audiology 101 was the early identification of hearing loss. A young man named Tony sat in the front of the class to follow the sign language interpreter. He raised his hand and explained with both speech and sign language, "This topic is particularly important to me because my wife and I just had a baby last Saturday." The class applauded, and he continued, "Yes, because both she and I are deaf, they tested our baby's hearing. Unfortunately, he didn't pass the test." The class responded with silent nods of the head to show they were sorry. But he wasn't done—with a twinkle in his eye, he added, "Yes, he can hear." The collective jaw of the entire class dropped, and a few students laughed uncomfortably. Even though it was said teasingly, he wanted the class to understand that their preference would have been for a child who was deaf as they were, and the fact that the baby had normal hearing was a type of "failed test" to them.

The psychological, emotional, and social development of Deaf individuals will be influenced by all the same variables as those who are not culturally Deaf. Are they raised in families that accept them for who they are? Is communication easy to establish and sustain? Is the ability to express oneself and be understood and accepted part of one's experience? The topic of "being Deaf" is far too complex to cover in depth here; for more information about the psychology of deafness, the reader is referred to the Recommended Reading at the end of this chapter. Readings on the phenomenon of Deaf culture are also provided.

"KNOWING IS NOT ENOUGH": ■ COUNSELING BASICS

Having an understanding of the psychological, social, and emotional effects of living with hearing loss ("knowing" about its effects) satisfies one level of professional development. However, persons with hearing loss expect more from the professionals who serve them: they expect active support as they adjust to their situation and have consistently expressed disappointment that, in general, they do not receive it (Glass & Elliot, 1992). Clearly, then, "knowing" about these concerns is not enough. The next step in professional development is to advance from "knowing" to "know-how," as in knowing how to provide the personal adjustment support that our patients and their families need and expect. Extensive materials are available on developing this know-how, but this section will provide only highlights on counseling basics. Readers are strongly encouraged to seek formal coursework in counseling as it relates to their discipline, both in their training program and in informal training throughout their professional careers.

Important Distinctions

Before proceeding, we must be clear about the following terms. When we refer to counseling, we are not referring to psychotherapy or psychoanalysis, whereby mental health professionals (i.e., psychiatrists and psychologists) use their professional training to help clients to find ways to solve pervasive life problems. *Psychotherapy* helps patients to explore unconscious behavior patterns in order to alter ways of relating and functioning by examining and challenging personal history and by analyzing the meanings of one's responses (Cormier & Hackney, 1999; Crowe, 1997). Psychotherapy generally views the patient as being ill and searches for the cause of a person's problems, which might be rooted in family relationships or childhood trauma.

Counseling, in comparison, is designed to help people to develop "here-and-now strategies for coping with life, decision making, and current problems" (Shames, 2000, p. 6). Social workers, school counselors, ministers, and other spiritual leaders are professional counselors. Whereas psychotherapy attempts to affect major personality changes, counseling focuses on supporting personal adjustments to situations by helping a person to understand his or her feelings and engage in problem solving (see Figure 7.2).

Nonprofessional counseling may not be as familiar a concept, but it occurs routinely: a financial planner will counsel on tax problems, a teacher will counsel on test-taking strategies, an audiologist will counsel on hearing conservation, and so on (Kennedy & Charles, 1989). These examples involve content or *informational counseling,* which is one facet of nonprofessional counseling; but all professionals on occasion will work with clients or students facing emotional crises as well (e.g., the stress associated with financial risk or the despair and discouragement from failing an important exam). When the emotional crisis is related to the professional's specialty, *nonprofessional personal adjustment support* becomes a second facet of nonprofessional counseling.

Professional boundaries: notable distinctions between professions as they approach common areas of concern.

Professional boundaries must be respected, of course. Nonprofessional counselors must define relationships by boundaries that clarify the roles and functions of individuals in the relationship (Stone & Olswang, 1989). When a professional begins to feel uncomfortable with either the content or the intensity of the interaction, he or she can assume that a boundary is being approached, and it is probably an appropriate time to refer the patient or parent to a professional counselor.

What We May Think Counseling Is

Counseling is often narrowly perceived as *explaining:* a professional talks while a patient or parent listens to information about the audiogram, the anatomy of the ear, the benefits and limitations of hearing aids and cochlear implants, and the range of communication options. Undoubtedly, explaining is an essential aspect of service delivery, because patients, parents, and family members want and need information. Providing this information is called *content counseling* or *informational counseling* and is vital to audiologic rehabilitation.

The primary characteristic of content counseling is its tendency to become a one-way direction of communication (i.e., the professional talks and the patient or parent listens). If a patient or parent wants to talk about any of the psychosocial or emotional concerns discussed previously, how is he to interact with this one-way stream of information? It isn't possible; so when personal adjustment issues present

FIGURE 7.2

Important distinctions.

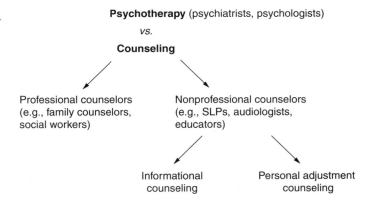

themselves, another direction in communication needs to be made available, a two-way conversation in which they can talk more and the counselors talk less. This two-way direction of interaction is a key component of personal adjustment counseling.

What Counselors Say Counseling Is

The counseling profession describes this kind of two-way conversation as a facilitative process, whereby the patient is given room, time, and permission to "tell his story." Stone, Patton, and Heen (1999) call this process "developing a learning conversation." In our context, we encourage the patient or parent to teach us what life with hearing loss is like for them and what their concerns are at that moment. This approach respects patients and parents as the experts of their lives and requires us to drop our assumptions that we somehow know how they feel.

The Counseling Process

The facilitative or counseling process (Figure 7.3) involves the following steps (adapted from Egan, 1998):

1. Help patients tell their story
2. Help patients clarify their problems
3. Help patients take responsibility for their listening problems (challenge themselves)
4. Help patients establish their goals
5. Develop an action plan
6. Implement the plan
7. Ongoing evaluation

Without care and reflection, audiological rehabilitation may rush through step 1, bypass steps 2 and 3, and pick up again at step 4; in other words, the professional may assume he or she already knows the patient's story and begin setting goals immediately (taking over the rehabilitation or adjustment process, rather than developing a partnership with the patient).

Long-term success in adjusting to hearing loss may ultimately depend on the effective management of the first three steps, because they usually involve an understanding of the psychosocial and emotional impact of living with a hearing loss.

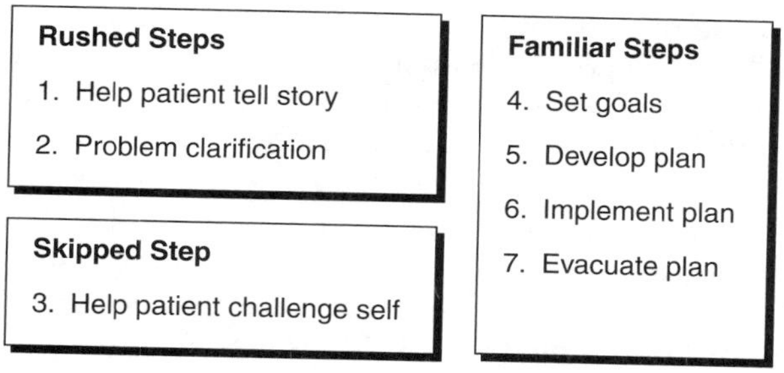

Rushed Steps

1. Help patient tell story
2. Problem clarification

Skipped Step

3. Help patient challenge self

Familiar Steps

4. Set goals
5. Develop plan
6. Implement plan
7. Evacuate plan

FIGURE 7.3

Counseling process as it might be applied to some audiologic rehabilitation situations.

This chapter will conclude with a discussion of how to incorporate these steps in audiological rehabilitation.

HELP PATIENTS (OR PARENTS) TELL THEIR STORY. Every patient and every parent has a unique perspective on living with a hearing loss. There is an inherent danger for professionals to assume that "we've heard it all before," and therefore we truly understand their struggles and frustrations and fears. This tendency is called *habituation*. While we surely have a general impression of these problems, we can never know what it is really like, exactly, for Ms. Juarez or Mr. Percy or 10-year-old Isaac. It is essential first that professionals conscientiously ask each patient, "What is it like for you?" And then listen carefully to each individualized response.

If a patient says, "No one understands how hard this is for me," it is not helpful to say that we do understand, because in fact we do not know how it is for this patient. A response such as "Most people with hearing loss experience these difficulties" does not help the patient feel personally understood, but only clumped into an impersonal category of "others." A response that focuses only on the patient, such as "You are having a tough time right now," gives the patient the message that she was heard and understood.

Self-assessments: paper and pencil questionnaires or surveys to help persons to describe their listening problems to themselves and others.

Using a self-assessment instrument can be very helpful in providing the opportunity for a patient to tell his story. While a patient takes the time to consider and describe his communication problems (part of step 2), he is also provided the opportunity to expand on the items that are of particular concern. Describing one's communication difficulties is an act of personal self-disclosure that may make a patient feel uncomfortable; however, the exercise of reading and talking about a standardized, neutral set of questions can take the pressure off, because both patient and professional are looking at the instrument, rather than at each other.

HELP PATIENTS CLARIFY THEIR PROBLEMS. Because the development of hearing loss in adults can occur slowly over several years, or because parents of children with hearing loss have a complicated life to juggle, or because children with hearing loss have limited experience in expressing their feelings and concerns, considerable time is needed to help individuals to describe and clarify their actual communication problems, as well as their emotional reactions to them and the psychosocial ramifications. Earlier, self-assessment instruments were mentioned as a strategy to help patients to tell their stories—and, as they tell their stories, not only are they being heard but they are getting clear in their minds what these problems are. Many instruments are available, and the reader is referred to Geier (1997) for a compilation of more than 30 of them. For example, the Abbreviated Profile of Hearing Aid Benefit (APHAB) (Cox & Alexander, 1995) poses 24 statements in the areas of ease of communication and communicating in adverse conditions (background noise, reverberation, etc.). An example of such a statement is "I have trouble hearing a conversation when I am with family at home." The patient describes his or her perception from "Always" to "Never" and receives the opportunity to recognize that such difficulties are a common aspect of living with a hearing loss. Many instruments open the door to a discussion about psychosocial reactions to hearing loss; for instance, the Self-Assessment of Communication (SAC) (Schow & Nerbonne,

1982) asks this question: "Does any problem or difficulty with your hearing upset you?" Responses range from "Almost always" to "Almost never," and it is up to the patient to decide whether he or she is comfortable with this kind of self-disclosure.

Self-assessments are not the only way to help patients to clarify their problems; conversation and carefully selected questions can also provide this opportunity. The point here is that patients need to understand their problems before they can develop solutions for them.

HELP PATIENTS TAKE RESPONSIBILITY FOR THEIR LISTENING PROBLEMS. Once patients clarify their communication and/or interpersonal problems, it might be assumed that they are ready to solve them. However, we have already learned that the psychosocial and emotional aspects of hearing loss can interfere with logical problem solving (using hearing aids to their best advantage, etc.). There is a real risk at this stage for the professional to take over and tell the patient or parent what to do: obtain and use hearing aids, learn sign language, or enroll in speechreading classes, for example. But like any other personal problem, the patient has to accept responsibility for the problem in order to commit herself to the solution. Far too often, patients agree to purchase hearing aids, but with no personal commitment or sincere intention to use them. It is probable that there are more hearing aids in drawers than on ears.

Another behavior that indicates that patients are not yet assuming the responsibilities of living with hearing loss is the common complaint that communication breakdowns occur because other people speak too softly, or they mumble, or children speak too quickly and with high voices. As long as the patient insists that everyone else should just speak more clearly, he is shirking his own role in successful communication. To help patients move past this stage of inaction, audiological

Good communication between marriage partners is vital in understanding the impact of hearing loss.

rehabilitation must take its cue from other helping professions and place responsibility for successful rehabilitation squarely on the patient. Once the problems have been clarified, we must ask, "And now, what are *your* listening goals? As you identify them, I will support you in attaining these goals."

This may be the point where the adult patient says, "I want to hear my grandchildren when they visit—but I won't wear hearing aids." He has identified two goals and (for the purpose of our discussion), unfortunately, they are incompatible. The ultimate decision is still his: he won't be able to hear his grandchildren without hearing aids, so what does he want to do about that? No amount of persuading will make a genuine difference; the patient has to find the internal resources to commit to his decision.

Not all adults struggle with the cosmetics of hearing aids, but, if they do, they can be encouraged to conduct a type of cost–benefit analysis: that is, compare the social costs of hearing aid use to the listening benefits that they seek. Which provides the outcome more valuable to them? If the listening benefits are perceived as greater, they might be more willing to tolerate the social costs of hearing aid appearances.

Another way to describe this thought process is called "substituting *but* for *and*;" that is, trade the word *but* for the word *and*. Initially, an adult may believe, "I want to hear my grandchildren better *but* I dislike how these hearing aids look." This way of thinking pits one condition against the other, and they mutually exclude each other. The adult could be asked to try thinking in these terms: "I want to hear my grandchildren better *and* I dislike how these hearing aids look." Including the possibility of both conditions coexisting at the same time gives the adult another way to look at the situation, one that could move her past a mental block to one that could help her to meet her goals (Kelly, 1992).

When to Refer

It is not uncommon for patients and parents to present with difficulties that cannot be accounted for by the hearing loss alone. Marital problems, family dissension, parenting dilemmas, financial or legal stress, fragile emotional and mental health, all these situations can be exacerbated by the presence of hearing loss; but treating the hearing loss will not resolve the fundamental problems. There is no easy answer to the question "When should I refer to a professional counselor?"; however, the answer is apparent when the professional sees a situation outside his expertise and scope of practice. It is strongly recommended that a referral system be established in advance so that, when the need to refer arises, a phone contact is immediately provided to the patient. This preparation will suggest to the patient that an outside referral is not rare and that the professional is aware of and is adhering to his or her professional boundaries.

Summary

The second half of this chapter takes the reader beyond an awareness of patients' psychosocial difficulties with hearing loss to an awareness of how the professional's interactions with patients can support (or hinder) their adjustment process. The basic concepts were these: listen carefully as the patient tells her story, help her to identify her listening problems, and help her to assume ownership for her problems so that she can commit to the solutions. If a professional finds herself wondering, "If this patient didn't want these hearing aids, why did she come for an evaluation in the first place?" the professional did not spend time in the beginning to hear the patient's story (i.e., her perception of her problems) and whether she was ready to take on the challenge of adjusting to hearing aid use. Following the counseling process through each step will lead to a deeper and more accurate understanding between patient and professional and facilitate the development of a therapeutic relationship with mutual goals.

SUMMARY POINTS

- Many persons with hearing loss experience a range of psychological, social, or emotional difficulties, although it is impossible to know exactly how a hearing loss affects a particular individual unless he or she specifically tells us.
- Because of resultant language delays, children with hearing loss may experience difficulties with self-expression and self-awareness, which can affect their ability to empathize with others and to achieve age-appropriate social skills.
- Adults who acquire hearing loss may also experience problems as they adjust to the consequences of the disability, including the acceptance of hearing aids.
- The Deaf culture does not see hearing loss as a disability, but rather a difference in abilities. Like other communities, its members share core values and traditions and also share the use of a common language (ASL).
- Counseling techniques are often used to help patients to accept and develop solutions for their listening problems.

RECOMMENDED READING

Audiologic Counseling

Clark, J. G., & Martin, F. (1995). *Effective counseling in audiology.* Englewood Cliffs, NJ: Allyn & Bacon.

Crowe, T. A. (Ed.). (1997). *Applications of counseling in speech–language pathology and audiology.* Baltimore, MD: Williams & Wilkins.

English, K. (2001). *Counseling children with hearing impairment and their families.* Boston: Allyn and Bacon.

Luterman, D. M. (1996). *Counseling persons with communication disorders and their children* (3rd ed.). Austin, TX: Pro-Ed.

Shames, G. H. (2000). *Counseling the communicatively disabled and their families: A manual for clinicians.* Boston: Allyn and Bacon.

Psychology of Deafness

Marschark, M. (1993). *Psychological development of deaf children.* New York: Oxford University Press.

McCay, V., & Andrews, J. (1990). *The psychology of deafness: Understanding deaf and hard of hearing people.* New York: Longman.

Paul, P. V., & Jackson, D. W. (1993). *Toward a psychology of deafness.* Boston: Allyn and Bacon.

Deaf Culture

Greenberg, J. (1970). *In this sign.* New York: Holt, Rinehart and Winston.

Holcomb, R. (1996). *Deaf culture our way.* San Diego, CA: Dawn Sign Press.

Padden, C., & Humphries, T. (1990). *Deaf in America: Voices from a culture.* Cambridge, MA: Harvard University Press

Preston, P. (1995). *Mother father deaf: Living between sound and silence.* Cambridge, MA: Harvard University Press.

RECOMMENDED WEB SITES

Association of Late Deafened Adults:
http://www.alda.org

Self-help for Hard of Hearing People:
http://www.shhh.org

"Beyond Hearing" listserv, Duke University:
http://www.saywhatclub.com/r-bh.htm

National Association of the Deaf:
http://www.nad.org

Gallaudet University:
http://www.gallaudet.edu

National Technical Institute for the Deaf:
http://www.ntid.edu

REFERENCES

Altman, E. (1996). Meeting the needs of adolescents with impaired hearing. In Martin, F., & Clark, J. G. (Eds.), *Hearing care for children* (pp. 197–210). Boston: Allyn and Bacon.

Antia, S., & Kreimeyer, K. (1992). Social competence intervention for young children with hearing impairments. In Odom, S., McConnell, S., & McEvoy, M. (Eds.), *Social competence of young children with disabilities: Issues and strategies for intervention* (pp. 135–164). Baltimore, MD: Paul H. Brookes Publishing Co.

Bachara, G., Raphael, J., & Phelan, W. (1980). Empathy development in deaf preadolescents. *American Annals of the Deaf, 125,* 38–41.

Becker, G. (1980). *Growing old in silence.* Berkeley: University of California Press.

Bess, F. H., Dodd-Murphy, J., & Parker, R. (1998). Children with minimal sensorineural hearing loss: Prevalence, educational performance, and functional status. *Ear and Hearing, 19*(5), 339–355.

Blood, G. W., Blood, M., & Danhauser, J. L. (1977). The hearing aid "effect." *Hearing Instruments, 20,* 12.

Cappelli, M., Daniels, T., Durleux-Smith, A., McGrath, P. J., & Neuss, D. (1995). Social development of children with hearing impairments who are integrated into general education classrooms. *Volta Review, 97,* 197–208.

Cormier, S., & Hackney, H. (1999). *Counseling strategies and interventions* (5th ed.). Boston: Allyn and Bacon.

Cox, R., & Alexander, O. (1995). The abbreviated profile of hearing aid benefit. *Ear and Hearing, 16,* 176–186.

Coyner, L. (1993). Academic success, self-concept, social acceptance, and perceived social acceptance for hearing, hard of hearing, and deaf students in a mainstream setting. *Journal of the American Deafness and Rehabilitation Association, 27*(2), 13–20.

Crowe, T. (1997). Approaches to counseling. In T. Crowe (Ed.), *Applications in counseling in speech–language pathology and audiology* (pp. 80–117). Baltimore, MD: Williams and Wilkins.

Davis, J., Elfenbein, J., Schum, R., & Bentler, R. (1986). Effects of mild and moderate hearing impairments on language, educational, and psychosocial behavior of children. *Journal of Speech and Hearing Disorders, 51,* 53–62.

Doggett, S., Stein, R., & Gans, D. (1998). Hearing aid effect in older females. *Journal of American Academy of Audiology, 9*(5), 361–366.

Edwards, C. (1991). The transition from auditory training to holistic auditory management. *Educational Audiology Monograph, 2,* 1–17.

Egan, G. (1998). *The skilled helper* (6th ed.). Pacific Grove, CA: Brooks/Cole.

English, K. (1997). *Self-advocacy for students who are deaf and hard of hearing.* Austin, TX: Pro-Ed.

English, K. (2001). *Counseling children with hearing impairment and their families.* Boston: Allyn and Bacon.

Flexer, C., Wray, D., & Leavitt, R. (1990). *How the student with hearing loss can succeed in college: A handbook for students, families, and professionals.* Washington, DC: Alexander Graham Bell Association for the Deaf.

Garrison, W. M., & Tesch, S. (1978). Self-concept and deafness: A review of research literature. *Volta Review, 80,* 457–466.

Geier, K. (1997). *Handbook of self-assessment and verification measures of communication performance.* Columbia, SC: Academy of Dispensing Audiologists.

Glass, L., & Elliot, H. (1992). The professional told me what it was but that was not enough. *Shhh, 13*(6), 26–28.

Goleman, D. (1995). *Emotional intelligence: Why it can matter more than IQ.* New York: Bantam Books.

Greenberg, M. T., & Kusche, C. A. (1993). *Promoting social and emotional development in deaf children: The PATHS project.* Seattle: University of Washington Press.

Harris, L. K., Van Zandt, C. E., & Rees, T. H. (1997). Counseling needs of students who are deaf and hard of hearing. *School Counselor, 44,* 271–279.

Henggeler, S. W., Watson, S. M., & Thelan, J. P. (1990). Peer relations of hearing-impaired adolescents. *Journal of Pediatric Psychology, 15*(6), 721–731.

Kelly, L. J. (1992). Rational–emotive therapy and aural rehabilitation. *Journal of the Academy of Rehabilitative Audiology, 25,* 43–50.

Kennedy, E., & Charles, S. (1989). *On becoming a counselor: A basic guide for non-professional counselors.* New York: Consortium.

Kimmel, D. C., & Weiner, I. B. (1995). *Adolescence: A developmental transition.* New York: Wiley & Sons.

Kochkin, S. (1996). Customer satisfaction and subjective benefit with high performance hearing aids. *Hearing Review, 3*(12), 16–26.

Kricos, P. B. (2000). Family counseling for children with hearing loss. In Alpiner, J., & McCarthy, P. A. (Eds.), *Rehabilitative audiology: Children and adults* (3rd ed.) (pp. 275–302). Philadelphia: Lippincot Williams & Wilkins.

Kubler-Ross, E. (1969). *On death and dying.* Macmillan Publishing Co.

Luterman, D. L. (1996). *Counseling persons with communication disorders and their families* (3rd ed.). Austin, TX: Pro-Ed.

Meadow, K. (1976). Personality and social development of deaf persons. *Journal of Rehabilitation of the Deaf, 9,* 3–16.

Meadow, K. (1980). *Deafness and child development.* Berkeley: University of California Press.

Pipp-Siegel, S., & Biringen, Z. (2000). Assessing the quality of relationships between parents and children: The Emotional Availability Scales. *Volta Review, 100*(5) (monograph), 237–249.

Ramsdell, P. (1960). The psychology of the hard of hearing and the deafened adult. In H. Davis, H., & Silverman, S. (Eds.), *Hearing and deafness* (pp. 459–473). New York: Holt, Rinehart and Winston.

Riensche, L., Peterson, K., & Linden, S. (1990). Young children's attitudes toward peer hearing aid wearers. *Hearing Journal, 43*(10), 19–20.

Schow, R., & Nerbonne, M. (1982). Communication screening profile: Use with elderly clients. *Ear and Hearing, 3,* 135–147.

Shames, G. H. (2000). *Counseling the communicatively disabled and their families: A manual for clinicians.* Boston: Allyn and Bacon.

Stein, R., Gill, K., & Gans, D. (2000). Adolescents' attitudes toward their peers with hearing impairment. *Journal of Educational Audiology, 8,* 1–6.

Stinson, M. S., Whitmore, K., & Kluwin, T. N. (1996). Self perceptions of social relationships in hearing-impaired adolescents. *Journal of Educational Psychology, 88*(1), 132–143.

Stone, D., Patton, B., & Heen, S. (1999). *Difficult conversations: How to discuss what matters most.* New York: Viking Press.

Stone, J. R., & Olswang, L. B. (1989). The hidden challenge in counseling. *Asha, 31,* 27–31.

Vernon, M. (1996). Psychosocial aspects of hearing impairment. In Schow, R., & Nerbonne, M., (Eds.), *Introduction to audiologic rehabilitation* (3rd ed.) (pp. 229–263). Boston: Allyn and Bacon.

Vernon, M., & Andrews, J. (1990). *The psychology of deafness: Understanding deaf and hard of hearing people.* New York: Longman.

Warren, C., & Hasenstab, S. (1986). Self-concept of severely to profoundly hearing impaired children. *Volta Review, 88,* 289–296.

Zarrella, S. (1995, November 20). Providing services for adults with late-onset hearing loss. *Advance for Speech–Language Pathologists and Audiologists, 11.*

Audiologic Rehabilitation Services in the School Setting

Kris English

CONTENTS

■ INTRODUCTION

Recent data have indicated that when a hearing loss is identified early and when amplification and early intervention are in place by 6 months of age a child is much more likely to acquire age-level language and learning milestones (Downs &

Yoshinaga-Itano, 1999). This kind of aggressive management is just the start of many years of audiologic rehabilitative services as a child progresses through the educational system. This chapter will examine school-based audiologic rehabilitative (AR) services by addressing three questions:

- *Why* are AR services required in school settings?
- *What* AR services are provided in schools?
- *Who* is responsible for AR services in the school environment?

WHY AR SERVICES ARE REQUIRED IN SCHOOL SETTINGS: THE EDUCATIONAL CONSEQUENCES ■ OF HEARING IMPAIRMENT

Hearing impairment is considered to be an educationally significant disability. Unless immersed at home and at school in a signing environment, children learn language through the auditory system. If the auditory input is distorted or inconsistent, the child can experience a variety of difficulties in language development, such as reduced vocabulary development, delayed syntax development, and inappropriate use of morphological markers and figurative speech (Davis et al., 1986; Ling, 1976). Table 8.1 provides a set of typical language milestones and how they can be delayed by a profound hearing loss. Chapter 6 provides more detailed information as well.

Because most academic success depends on a competent use of language, these deficits in a child's language development can have a direct effect on cognitive development (learning). Children with profound hearing impairment (HI) have often been found to have depressed math scores and reading levels that plateau at the fourth- or fifth-grade reading level (Boothroyd, 1982). One study measured the reading skills of 1250 students with HI in Iowa and noted a leveling off of reading skills at a fourth-grade reading level by the age of 16 (Davis et al., 1982). In a book entitled *Deaf Children in America*, Allen (1986) described even lower reading scores, less than third-grade levels, among 18-year-olds. In the 21st century, our futures depend on the ability to acquire and use a broad information base; thus, children with hearing impairment start out with a marked disadvantage. Audiologic rehabilitative services are needed now more than ever to help children to stay competitive in school and in the marketplace.

Degree of Loss: Terminology

deaf: having a bilateral profound hearing loss; Deaf: having a cultural identification with the Deaf community.

This chapter conforms to terminology found in federal law when describing hearing loss. The term *hearing impairment* is nonspecific in that it only indicates that some kind of hearing loss is present, but it does not describe the degree, or nature of the loss (conductive, sensorineural, mixed) or whether it is unilateral or bilateral. The term *hard of hearing* describes a child who has mild to severe loss in one or both ears. The term *deaf* is synonymous with severe to profound bilateral hearing loss (meaning that the child obtains very little benefit from amplification in understanding speech). (When the term *Deaf* appears with a capital D, it is meant to denote a cultural identification with the Deaf community, described more fully in Chapter 7.)

TABLE 8.1

Impact of Profound Hearing Loss on Language Development

AGE	CHILD WITH NORMAL HEARING	CHILD WITH PROFOUND HEARING LOSS
18 months	Vocabulary of 25 words	No words
2–3 years	Understands directions, uses short sentences, asks questions	Few words, yells and points to express desires
3–4 years	Makes long sentences	Some single words
4–5 years	Uses "why" and "how," past and future tense; 2000-word vocabulary	Has more single words
5–6 years	Grammar and syntax used correctly	Asks the names of things
6–7 years	Approximately 16,000 words	Asks questions
7–8 years	22,000 words	Uses mostly nouns, some verbs, pronouns, articles
9–10 years	Sentence length of approximately 12 words	Reading vocabulary at approximately 15% of normal
17 years	>80,000 words	Vocabulary <3rd grade

There is a strong relationship between the degree of hearing loss and the degree of educational impact: the more severe the loss, the more difficult learning can be. However, it would be a mistake to assume that a mild hearing loss would have little or no impact on learning; even a mild loss can put a child at risk for academic failure. A recent study of 1218 children with minimal hearing loss showed that 37% had failed a grade (Bess, Dodd-Murphy, & Parker, 1998). In addition, a statistically high number had poorer communication skills than children with no hearing loss and, as a group, they exhibited more problems in stress, social support, and self-esteem. These authors cited another study (Davis et al., 1986) that found that children with minimal hearing loss "could have as much or more difficulty on verbal, educational, and psychosocial tasks as a child with a mild or moderate loss" (p. 340). We are learning that any type of hearing loss presents the risk of academic failure and psychosocial difficulties, and no loss can be discounted as insignificant.

We cannot even assume that children with hearing impairment in only one ear, with normal hearing in the other ear (unilateral hearing loss), are not experiencing academic difficulties. It was once thought that one normal ear was sufficient; however, it has been found that children with unilateral hearing loss are 10 times more likely to fail a grade by age 10 compared to normal-hearing children (Bess, Klee, & Culbertson, 1986; English & Church, 1999). *The degree of hearing loss, by itself, cannot be used as a predictor of academic achievement or as a determiner of the level of support provided in a school.*

The exact prevalence rate depends on how hearing loss is defined; for instance, some states include in their census children with unilateral hearing loss or mild

Minimal hearing loss: lacking the ability to hear most pure tones softer than 20 dB.

conductive hearing loss while others do not. Some states consider hearing loss to be present when a child does not respond to a pure tone at 15, 20, or 25 dB HL. Depending on the screening methods and definitions of hearing loss, studies have described incidence rates ranging from 3% to 15% (Johnson, 2000). If a conservative estimated prevalence rate of 3–4% is used, this would mean that among the 46 million schoolchildren in the United States approximately 1–2 million children have some degree of hearing impairment.

Mandated by Law

Because hearing loss is an educationally significant disability, by federal law these children are entitled to a free appropriate public education (FAPE), which means access to "special education and related services which are provided at public supervision and direction, and without charge" (34 CFR § 300.4[a]). In other words, the services needed to support the education of a child with hearing loss are paid for by public funds, rather than by parents. The term *appropriate* is intentionally left undefined, with the understanding that each child's educational program will be based on individual requirements. Some of the related services include a range of audiologic rehabilitative services, to be discussed in a subsequent section.

IDEA: Individuals with Disabilities Education Act: guarantees educational rights to children with disabilities.

The law under discussion is called the *Individuals with Disabilities Education Act* (IDEA). It was first enacted in 1975 as the Education for All Handicapped Children Act (Public Law 94-142). Before PL 94-142 was passed, parents who had children with disabilities were frequently denied the right to enroll their children in the public school system. The passage of PL 94-142 was a milestone in ongoing efforts to protect the rights of all persons with disabilities. The actual law can be located in Volume 34 of the *Code of Federal Regulations* (CFR), found in all law school libraries and many general university and public libraries. The volume is divided into sections, designated with this § symbol. Readers are encouraged to refer to this original source as they develop a background in special education issues.

The mandate of a free appropriate public education was described earlier as a key component of this law. A second mandate, directly related to our discussion of audiologic rehabilitative services, can be found in 34 CFR § 300.303: "Each public agency shall insure that the hearing aids worn in school by children with hearing impairment, including deafness, are functioning properly." This requirement has often been the door-opener to audiologic rehabilitative services in school settings. If a parent asks, "How is your school meeting this requirement?" the school (the "public agency") must demonstrate that it has a program in place to monitor and check hearing aid and classroom amplification systems.

The U.S. Congress is required to reauthorize this law every few years, which allows for the opportunity to refine, update, and possibly expand on the original version. The first reauthorization occurred in 1986, when the Education of the Handicapped Amendments (PL 99-457) were passed. All educational services, including audiologic rehabilitation, were expanded to include children from birth to 5 years of age. This development formally brought audiologic rehabilitation into the area of early intervention services for infants and toddlers and their families.

The next reauthorization occurred in 1990. At this time, the law (PL 101-476) was renamed the Individuals with Disabilities Education Act (IDEA). This law used the term "disability" rather than handicap, and substituted the term "children with disabilities" for "handicapped children," codifying the use of *people-first* language. Persons with disabilities asked for this change, preferring to be considered persons first, who also happen to have a disability. Terms such "mentally retarded children" or "the hearing impaired" are now revised to say "children with mental retardation" or "individuals with hearing impairment."

People-first language: an identification of an individual before the mention of a disability.

Amendments to IDEA were passed in 1997, and the changes included requirements to make educational goals as functional as possible (i.e., related to classroom performance and classroom expectations). It also required programs to provide progress reports at least as often as parents are informed of the progress of children without disabilities and to include the general education teacher in meetings to ensure integration of special education goals into the general education curriculum. By law, the IDEA will continue to be reexamined every 4 or 5 years to ensure that children with hearing loss and other disabilities receive an appropriate education. A timeline of these legislative events can be found in Table 8.2.

Key Components of IDEA

Throughout these reauthorizations, three critical components have remained constant. The first was the guarantee of a free appropriate public education (FAPE), which was discussed previously. The other two components are these:

- That FAPE is to be provided in the least restrictive environment (LRE).
- That a child's educational program will be documented with the use of the Individual Education Program (IEP).

Least Restrictive Environment

The concept of LRE is often considered to be synonymous with mainstreaming, or educating children with disabilities in a local public school among children without

LRE continuum: a range of educational options, from regular education in one's neighborhood to a residential school.

TABLE 8.2	
Timeline of Special Education Legislative Acts	
YEAR	LAW
1975	PL 94-142: Education of All Handicapped Children Act
1986	PL 99-457: Education of Handicapped Act Amendments (including services to children from birth to age 5)
1990	PL 101-476: Individuals with Disabilities Education Act (IDEA)
1997	IDEA Amendments (IEPs must have functional goals, etc.)

disabilities. However, it is important to note that IDEA does not mandate mainstreaming per se, but simply the consideration of the least restrictive environment for the most appropriate education. Therefore, LRE is essentially open to interpretation and consequently remains imprecise.

EDUCATIONAL OPTIONS. To help schools make educational placement decisions, the Code of Federal Regulations states the following: "Each public agency shall insure that a continuum of alternative placements is available to meet the needs of children with disabilities for special education and related services" (34 CFR § 300.551[a]). Placement options include variations of the following settings:

- Full-time regular education classroom in the child's neighborhood school.
- Regular education with in-class support, such as instruction from a speech–language pathologist or teacher of children who are deaf or hard of hearing.
- Regular education, with pull-out sessions held in another classroom.
- Part-time regular education classroom; part-time special education in a resource room.
- Full-time special education in a separate or self-contained classroom held by a teacher of children with hearing loss, with a small number of other children with hearing loss, often in the child's general neighborhood.
- Full-time special education in a separate facility (often called a *center-based program*), not necessarily in the child's neighborhood.
- Residential school, with a large number of children with hearing loss and many teachers of children with hearing loss. Some children live on campus during the week; some attend as day students.

LRE: Least restrictive environment: where the child has most access to academic, social, and emotional support.

The LRE continuum is represented in Figure 8.1.

Case 1: Laurie

Laurie is five years old and has a severe bilateral hearing loss, identified before her first birthday. She has received a range of services from that time, wears two hearing aids all day, and is currently enrolled in a kindergarten program in her neighborhood and is also receiving therapy consistent with an auditory–verbal approach (i.e., a strong emphasis on developing listening skills) in a private clinic. Her language development is delayed but measurably improving, and her social skills are age appropriate. Her mother has been told by school officials that the first-grade placement should be at a specialized program, which would involve a bus ride of over an hour both ways. This placement would use sign language in its instruction, but Laurie's parents have been committed to an auditory–verbal approach for 4 years. They are therefore opposed to this placement recommendation because of the distance and because of the communication methods used. They will have to meet with the school administrators to make their case, and because they have learned their rights, they expect their understanding of the term "least restrictive environment" to carry the day.

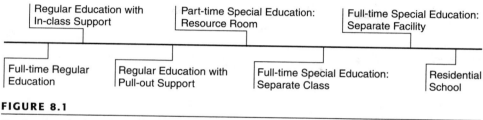

FIGURE 8.1

Continuum of educational placements.

In the first 15 years of special education, placement decisions considered the concept of mainstreaming as a move from special education to regular education. That is, children with hearing loss would most likely be placed in a special education environment, and as the child demonstrated grade-level competencies in math or in reading, he or she would gradually spend more time in a regular education classroom. In the last decade, there has been a reconsideration of this concept, and now the philosophy of *inclusion* is being applied, resulting in an initial placement of the child in a regular education program and the provision of supports or special services to help the child succeed in this placement. Only when it is clear that individualized or small-group instruction is necessary is the child taken from the class and provided help in resource room instruction or other educational placement.

Figure 8.2 gives the current distributions of students with hearing impairment across a variety of educational placements (U.S. Department of Education, 1998). It shows a growing trend toward placing children with hearing loss in regular

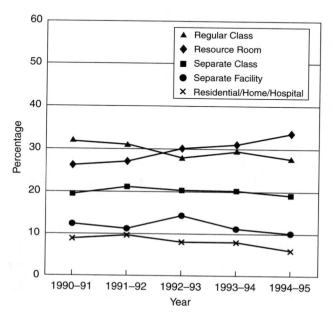

FIGURE 8.2

Percentage of students with hearing impairment ages 6 to 12 by type of educational environment: 1990–1991 to 1994–1995.

Source: U.S. Department of Education, Office of Special Education Programs, Data Analysis System (DANS).

education classrooms. Research supports the effectiveness of inclusive classroom placements, but the concept is not without its dissenters. Interpreters of this regulation repeatedly caution that it is not appropriate to generalize about LRE among children with hearing loss. *The determination of the LRE for each child must be made on an individual basis.*

LRE FOR A CHILD WITH HI. For a child with a hearing impairment, the preceding interpretation of least restrictive environment may not be appropriate. A child with a mild to moderately severe hearing loss may succeed in a regular education classroom if full support is provided to address the variety of language and listening needs that can impede learning. Because so much learning (social as well as academic) is language based, it is impossible to generalize about the appropriate environment for individuals who are hard of hearing.

The appropriate environment becomes a more complicated issue for the child who is deaf. The Commission on Education of the Deaf (1988) held that placement of a deaf child in a regular classroom, even with an interpreter, may be more restrictive than placement in a fully signing environment with deaf peers. Because of communication difficulties, a deaf child may experience unique academic, social, and

---

Case 2: Carlos

Carlos was identified as having a bilateral profound hearing loss at age 6 months. His family decided on total communication as his primary mode of communication and began to attend sign classes offered by the Early Intervention program. He attended a preschool that included many other deaf children and had developed several friendships there. By the time he was ready for kindergarten, most of his family were fairly fluent in sign, and Carlos was developing early reading skills.

Because his preacademic skills were near age level, it was decided that Carlos would attend his neighborhood school with a sign language interpreter. He was to be the only deaf child in the school, but he was friendly and gregarious, and it was assumed he would "fit right in." His new teacher spent the summer learning sign language to achieve as much direct communication as possible.

Everyone was surprised that it took Carlos several months to acquire the skills needed to use an interpreter effectively. Even more surprising was the difficulty his classmates had in adjusting to the presence of the interpreter. Although he tried to be inconspicuous, most of Carlos's classmates did not feel comfortable communicating with Carlos through the interpreter. Their initial attempts were to speak to Carlos directly and, when that failed, to mime their intentions. Eventually, the role of the interpreter was understood, but both he and the classroom teacher noted that communication between Carlos and his peers was restricted to the essentials: providing abbreviated directions, one or two word answers, and so on. The natural interaction that had occurred in the preschool environment was missing here. Because of the communication limitations, Carlos was effectively alone in a room full of people. When asked if he would like to go to a kindergarten with his signing deaf friends from preschool, he looked happier than he had all year. It became clear that, for Carlos, the regular education environment was more, not less, restrictive.

emotional complications in the regular classroom. If such is the case, the regular classroom is not the LRE for a deaf child: "Placing a deaf child in the regular classroom without the language needed to function as a participant seriously impedes, if not precludes, the child from receiving any worthwhile education in the class" (p. 33).

In response to these concerns, the U.S. Department of Education (DOE) issued "policy guidance" to states and school districts regarding the LRE for children with severe to profound hearing loss (*Federal Register*, October 30, 1992, *57*[211], pp. 49274–49276). Noting that "the communicative nature of the disability is inherently isolating" (p. 49274), the DOE advised that the LRE provisions of the IDEA may be incorrectly interpreted for children who are deaf. The following factors are of paramount importance when determining the LRE for a child who is deaf:

- Communication needs and the child's and family's preferred mode of communication
- Linguistic needs
- Severity of hearing impairment and potential for using residual hearing
- Academic level
- Social, emotional, and cultural needs of the child, including opportunities for peer interactions and communications

The DOE reminded educators that "The provision of FAPE is paramount, and the individual placement determination about LRE is to be considered within the context of FAPE" (p. 49275). In other words, no interpretation of LRE is meant to override the provision of an appropriate education.

The Individualized Education Program

The services to be provided to a child with a hearing loss are described in a document called an Individualized Education Program (IEP). It has been said that the IEP is not only a collection of forms, but also a *process:* that is, a group of interested persons (parents, teachers, school administrators, and related service providers such as audiologists, speech–language pathologists, school nurses, etc.), referred to as the Individualized Education Program Committee (IEPC), spend considerable time reviewing a child's current level of skills, and decide on reasonable goals for the upcoming year. The process involves a great deal of sharing, learning, and ultimately agreeing on how to implement the child's educational program. Parents can request a revisit of this process at any time to consider changes in the child or other variables.

IEP: Individualized Educational Program: a written report describing a child's current level of performance, annual goals, and procedures used to meet these goals.

As mentioned earlier, services are available to families as soon as a disability has been identified. From birth to age 3, services are tailored to the needs of the child within the context of the family (rather than the need of the child alone), so the document used to describe these services is called the Individualized Family Service Plan (IFSP).

The Communication Debate

Perhaps the most important consideration regarding educational placement is the communication method used. Unfortunately, this is a very complex matter, involving one of the oldest debates in education regarding the best way to teach a child with hearing impairment. This *communication debate* focuses on how to provide language instruction to children who are deaf. Students of audiologic rehabilitation will want to have a working knowledge of the issues; however, the choice of approach ultimately lies with parents, and professionals do not serve parents well by persuading them to adapt an approach that does not fit with their family. See Recommended Reading at the end of this chapter for more information on these topics.

The communication options include an oral–aural approach (i.e., using speech and hearing), a combination of signing with speech and hearing (total communication), a system called Cued Speech, and the use of sign only. Each approach is briefly described here.

ORAL–AURAL APPROACH. This method emphasizes speech communication (oral), optimal use of amplified residual hearing (aural), and the development of speechreading (formerly known as lipreading), while discouraging the use of sign language. This approach was espoused by Alexander Graham Bell (1847–1922), who, in addition to his other accomplishments, was a skilled speech teacher. Supporters of the oral–aural approach feel that "with spoken language, opportunities for higher education are less restricted, a more extensive range of careers is open, and there is greater employment security. Those who can talk also face fewer limitations in the personal and social aspects of their lives" (Ling, 1990, p. 9).

A relatively recent refinement of the oral–aural approach is the *auditory–verbal approach*. The primary difference between these approaches is that the auditory–verbal approach makes a concerted effort during aural rehabilitation therapy to remove visual cues, encouraging the child to develop the auditory system with directed listening practice. Speechreading is used as a secondary rather than primary teaching strategy. To stimulate auditory development, the therapist reduces or eliminates visual information by covering most of his or her face while presenting the speech stimuli (Estabrooks, 1994).

Approximately 30% of the schoolchildren with hearing loss in the United States are instructed in the oral–aural or auditory–verbal approaches.

TOTAL COMMUNICATION. To capitalize on the visual information provided by sign language, *total communication* (TC) was introduced in the 1960s. TC incorporates the use of many modalities at once: signing, speech, listening, and speechreading, as well as the contributions of nonverbal communication (body language and facial expressions). The nature of the signing depends on the background of the educator, who may use American Sign Language (ASL), or a sign system such as Signed Exact English (SEE), or a combination of ASL and SEE called Pigeon Sign, described in detail in Chapter 5. Briefly, ASL is recognized as a legitimate language with a rich lexicon and a fully developed linguistic structure. Its roots are in French Sign Language, and it has been in existence for over 200 years. Unlike most languages, ASL has the unique characteristic of being learned from deaf peers rather than from hearing family members (Hoffmeister, 1990). Because fewer than 10% of deaf children are born of deaf parents, ASL is typically learned from deaf friends and other adults, rather than from parents. In spite of this limited access to ASL, supporters feel that it should be the language of instruction for all children who are deaf.

Whereas ASL has evolved as a natural *sign language*, SEE is a *sign system* (i.e., a way to sign English words) created in the 1960s to address concerns regarding low reading and writing skills. SEE uses manual markers for linguistic concepts (e.g., plurality and tense) to correspond directly to the structures of the English language and follows the exact word order of English. SEE is just one of several artificial systems; readers of historical records will come across references to many versions. The use of these systems has diminished since the 1980s, for the most part being replaced with Pidgin Sign.

> Sign system: not a language, but a method of depicting an oral language like English with manual symbols.

Like other pidgin languages, Pidgin Sign combines elements of different languages, in this case a manual language (ASL) and a spoken language (English). Pidgin Sign is a "contact language . . . a result of something that occurs when two groups of people need or desire to communicate" (Luetke-Stahlman & Luckner, 1991, p. 10). In an exchange, a hearing person communicating with Pidgin Sign is likely to omit articles such as "the" or "a/an" or the "ing" endings of gerund verbs as in ASL. The word order, however, is usually identical to English, while in ASL the word order could be quite different (e.g., adjectives following rather than preceding nouns, as in "shoes brown").

Although the type of sign will vary from one classroom to another, total communication (TC) is the general practice found around the country; it is used in about 66% of classroom instruction for children with hearing loss.

CUED SPEECH. Another approach developed in the 1960s is called *cued speech*. Cued speech is not a language but a visual support system to facilitate speechreading. Hand shapes made close to the face represent phonemes, which helps the speechreader discriminate between similar phonemes. For example, the phonemes /k/ and /g/ require distinct handshapes (/k/ as if pointing to the throat with the index and middle fingers, while the /g/ points with all five fingers), thus providing the speechreader with a visual cue to the voiced or unvoiced component of the phonemes. Cued speech can be found in concentrated areas across the United States, but only in about 1% of classroom instruction (Kipila & Williams-Scott, 1990).

> Cued Speech: a set of handshapes to help with speechreading sounds that look virtually identical (compare "Friday" to "fried egg").

USING SIGN ONLY. In 1988, the Commission on the Education of the Deaf recommended yet another approach, called a *bilingual–bicultural* ("bi–bi") approach. This approach advocates teaching ASL as a deaf child's first language and that written English be taught as a second language. Speech production and listening skills are not emphasized. Its implementation requires teachers to be native or fluent users of ASL, and, as one might expect, not many teachers are so well qualified. Approximately 1% of students are immersed in the bi–bi approach (Coryell & Holcomb, 1997).

■ AR SERVICES PROVIDED IN SCHOOLS

This section will describe a range of school-based audiologic rehabilitative services (American Speech–Language–Hearing Association, 1993):

- Screening and assessment of hearing impairment
- Management of amplification

- Direct instruction and indirect consultation
- Hearing conservation
- Evaluation and modification of classroom acoustics
- Transition planning to postsecondary placements

Screening and Assessment

Screening for hearing loss is an essential audiologic rehabilitative service. Schools are usually required to screen all school-age children at select grades to determine the existence of unidentified hearing loss (e.g., in kindergarten and grades 1–3, and 12). Because more and more children are demonstrating mild hearing loss in the high frequencies (most likely due to high levels of noise exposure), these screening programs have become more valuable than ever in identifying hearing problems that may not be evident to parents, teachers, or the child.

In addition to screening, children with *known* hearing loss must have an annual hearing assessment to determine the stability of the loss and to reconsider the appropriateness of the child's hearing aids and other amplification systems. Assessment information should include conventional hearing test information, speech recognition and speechreading abilities in quiet and in noise, and functional performance with amplification.

Play audiometry provides useful information concerning hearing loss with preschoolers.

Management of Amplification

Managing amplification is a critical audiologic rehabilitative service. Amplification includes personal hearing aids, personal FM systems, cochlear implants, sound field amplification, and assistive devices. Without a systematic monitoring program, hearing aids and personal FM systems can be expected to have a 50% failure rate of operation (Lipscomb, Von Almen, & Blair, 1992; Robinson & Sterling, 1980). Educational audiologists have agreed that, given the high and unacceptable likelihood of malfunction, a monitoring program should be established, consisting of a daily visual inspection and listening check and at least one electroacoustic analysis every semester of each hearing aid and FM device (English, 1991). When such a program is rigorously applied, the malfunction rate can be as low as 1% (Langan & Blair, 2000). Given the importance of amplification to a child's academic success, a zero tolerance for malfunction rates should be established in each school.

Direct Instruction and Indirect Consultation

When children have hearing loss, they usually need direct instruction in developing their listening skills, speech production, and use of language. These supports may be provided within the classroom, one on one, or in small groups or children may leave the classroom to join a teacher, SLP, or audiologist in another (resource) room.

When a child is deaf, this type of direct instruction may not have as much relevance given the level of hearing loss and limits of amplification. Audiologists and SLPs may then pay particular attention to a child's communication strategies in a broader view. An educational audiologist at the Governor Baxter School for the Deaf in Maine described their Communication Strategies curriculum with these four categories (Snow, 2000):

PRAGMATICS

Kindergarten: Identify strangers versus friends versus family; express wants, needs, and preferences.

Grades 5 and 6: Support and justify actions and answers; understand and use hints; recognize sarcastic comments by wording and facial expressions.

LITERACY

Kindergarten: Recognize and practice writing phone numbers; use name signs for all classmates; recognize written names of classmates.

Grades 5 and 6: Read English and change to ASL; give basic directions in ASL.

LIFE SKILLS

Kindergarten: Order food successful, using picture-pointing menu; speechread one's name.

Grades 5 and 6: Carry on a conversation with a hearing peer via print.

DEAF CULTURE

Kindergarten: Identify self and familiar people as Deaf or hearing; introduce self using name sign.

Grades 5 and 6: Understand the purpose of interpreters; learn significance of Deaf theatre and poetry.

If a child's needs are not very involved or if personnel are not available for direct support, indirect consultation may take place among teachers and related service providers. An audiologist may train the teacher how to do a daily hearing aid check, because it is not possible for the audiologist to do it herself every day, or an SLP may provide an informal inservice on how to develop language skills within the curriculum, rather than work with the child directly.

Hearing Conservation

Because society is becoming increasingly noisy and because children are being exposed to ever-higher noise levels, the incidence of high-frequency noise-induced hearing loss in children is on the rise. Noise exposure comes from toys, snowmobiles, and other engines, but most often from music through headphones. The output from personal radio systems through headphones can exceed 115 dB. The hearing loss caused by this noise trauma is permanent and entirely preventable; therefore, school programs are required to develop educational training programs to teach all children about hearing health and hearing loss prevention. Health textbooks typically do not cover this topic, so it is usually left to the communication disorders specialist (audiologist, speech–language pathologist, teacher of children with hearing impairment) to develop age-appropriate lessons. Programs typically include a description of the auditory system, the effects of noise on this system, and a review of preventive measures. These programs have proved to be very effective (Bennett & English, 1999; Chermak, Curtis, & Seikel, 1996), but they are also time intensive and are often considered a luxury item on the menu of services delivered.

Hearing conservation: teaching children how to protect their hearing from high noise levels.

Evaluation and Modification of Classroom Acoustics

Classroom acoustics is the up-and-coming topic in audiologic rehabilitative services in schools. The reason why will be provided later, but first we need to consider the three variables that can affect the acoustic environment of a classroom: noise levels, reverberation, and distance between teacher and student. The *noise level* of the typical classroom can be very high, often louder than the teacher's voice. Children talk while working in small groups, feet shuffle on linoleum floors, heat and air conditioning systems turn on and off, computers hum, and so on. The higher the noise level, the harder it is for children with hearing impairment to hear oral instruction. In fact, when the noise level is just slightly higher than the teacher's voice, a child with hearing loss will understand very little of what she says. Unfortunately, most classrooms currently have background noise levels that exceed acceptable levels.

Even if a room is quiet, it can still have problems with *reverberation*. Reverberation is another word for *echo* and refers to the prolongation of sound as sound waves reflect off the hard surfaces in a room. Excessive reverberation occurs when floors have linoleum or tile instead of carpet or the walls and ceilings are covered with plaster instead of acoustic tile. Reverberation interferes with speech perception by overlapping with the energy of the direct signal of the teacher's voice. A child with hearing impairment cannot interpret this distorted speech quickly enough, so reverberation is as much a problem as high noise levels. *Reverberation time* (RT) is a value used to indicate the amount of time it takes for a sound to decay 60 dB from its initial onset. For optimal perception of speech, it has been recommended that the RT in a classroom not exceed 0.3 second; however, the RT for most classrooms typically ranges from 0.4 to 1.2 seconds (Crandall & Smaldino, 1994).

The third variable to consider with respect to classroom acoustics is the *distance* between teacher and student. Teachers move around the room most of the day, so the distance between teacher and student will vary from one minute to the next. The distance will affect the perceived sound level of the teacher's voice: the sound level for most conversational speech is approximately 60 dB SPL measured from 6 feet away, but this level drops as the distance between speaker and listener increases. When teachers stand a distance away, their voices may become too soft for most HI children to hear and understand, even with good hearing aids.

Hearing aids are limited not only by distance, but also by their nonselective amplification of all sounds in the classroom. Background noise sources such as overhead fans, buzzing fluorescent lights, and shuffling feet all contribute to the auditory input, and it can be very difficult to discriminate speech from this noise. An ideal solution to these listening challenges is the use of wireless personal FM (frequency modulated) amplification systems. These personal systems have two components. The first is the teacher's microphone and transmitter unit, which picks up and transmits the teacher's voice. The microphone may be attached to a lapel or worn on a neck loop or headset.

The second component of the system is the student's receiver and amplifier, a unit that picks up the FM signal carrying the teacher's voice, amplifies it, and delivers it to the student's ears. This receiver can be an attachment to a personal hearing aid or a small unit resembling a personal radio or cassette player (see Chapter 2).

With an FM system, the teacher's voice is transmitted by a frequency-modulated (FM) signal to the student's receiver, which works very much like a personal radio station. The teacher's mouth is approximately 6 to 8 inches away from the microphone and, because the teacher's voice is transmitted by FM signal rather than air waves, the student perceives this voice as if the teacher were always speaking 6 to 8 inches away from his or her hearing aid microphone (overcoming the limitation of distance). Reception stays consistent up to a distance of 200 feet. With an FM system, the problem of direction of the speaker is also eliminated. The clarity of the teacher's voice is not affected as she turns away from the listener (changing directions).

FM: a radio signal that carries the speaker's voice directly to a receiver.

In addition to overcoming the problems of distance and direction, FM systems also address the problem of hearing in noise. FM systems are designed to amplify and transmit the teacher's voice at intensity levels well above the environmental noise, creating a favorable signal-to-noise listening condition. Controls are available to receive input from the FM microphone only (e.g., to listen to a lecture when the teacher is the only one talking), hearing aid plus FM input together (to hear both teacher and classroom conversation), or hearing aid microphone only (to hear class discussion only when the teacher is working with other students).

The FM advantage: amplifying a speaker's voice above background noise, while not being affected by distance or direction.

These factors combine in what is called *the FM advantage* (Flexer, Wray, & Ireland, 1989, p. 14). The FM advantage consists of overriding the negative effects of noise by increasing the teacher's voice, as well as eliminating the adverse effects of distance and direction.

Another way of improving classroom acoustics is to amplify the entire classroom with the use of sound field amplification, usually recognized as a type of PA system. By amplifying the teacher's voice via loud speakers placed around the classroom, the problems with background noise and distance can be reduced. With a sound field system, the teacher wears a wireless microphone (an FM transmitter), and her voice is transmitted to an FM receiver and amplifier and one or more speakers placed around the room. She is free to move as before, but, regardless of her position, her voice will be amplified to all corners of the room. Sound field amplification has been found to enhance academic performance not only for children with hearing loss, but also for children whose first language is not English, who have language disorders, or who have mild mental retardation (Rosenberg et al., 1999).

Sound field amplification: amplifying an entire area (the sound field), such as a classroom or auditorium.

A new variation of the concept of amplifying the whole classroom is to amplify the small area around the student. Desktop speakers are being used with students who change rooms across the day; they take both the microphone and book-sized speaker with them as they move from math to science class, for example.

It is important to note that amplifying the sound field (the classroom area) does not completely overcome reverberation problems, so a classroom would still need to be evaluated to determine how to reduce the amount of hard surfaces. The usual first modifications are to carpet the floor and to install acoustic tile on the ceiling.

Why the current interest in classroom acoustics? Because the overall record of poor acoustic environments has attracted the interest of the federal government as an issue of access for persons with disabilities. Just as restaurants are required to provide menus in Braille and government offices must have restroom facilities that can accommodate wheelchairs, so, it is reasoned, the acoustics of a school should allow full *acoustic access* to oral instruction. Acoustic standards are being developed and can be followed on the Web site for the Federal Architecture and Transportation "Access" Board: www.edfacilities.org/ir/acoustics.html. The evaluation of classroom acoustics will be an increasing responsibility for persons providing audiologic rehabilitative services in the school setting and an exciting opportunity to positively affect the education of children with hearing loss.

Transition Planning to Postsecondary Placements

Ultimately, audiologic rehabilitative services are expected to support a child through to a successful high school graduation, but even here planning for the future is required. Once students graduate, the special education safety net is no longer in place for students with hearing loss. To prepare for the transition to placements after high school (college, vocational training, and work settings), students are required to meet with teachers and parents to develop an Individualized Transition Plan (ITP). If the student plans on attending a particular college, a representative of the college should attend this meeting; likewise, representatives from vocational training programs or work settings should provide input, as deemed necessary. The purpose of this transition planning is to ensure that the student has time to prepare for the requirements needed to enter college or vocational training or for job placement. The law reads "The IEP for each student, beginning no later than age 16 (and at an earlier age, if deemed appropriate), must include a statement of each public agency's and each participating agency's responsibilities, or linkages, or both, before the student leaves the school setting" (34 CFR § 300.45).

ITP: Individualized Transition Plan: a long-term plan to arrange for further education or job training after high school.

This transition planning is especially important when we consider college placements. Although students with hearing loss enter college programs at the same rate as students without hearing loss, their drop-out rate is much higher (71% compared to 47%) (Bullis & Egelston-Dodd, 1990; Welsh, 1993). It would appear that college career success depends as much on the ability to develop a social support system and to obtain and use support systems (interpreters, note takers, FM systems) as on the ability to earn good grades. Materials are available to help students to prepare for college, particularly in the area of being one's own advocate for supports and services (DuBow, Geer, & Strauss, 1992; English, 1997).

Deaf students may be particularly interested in attending colleges with an emphasis in Deaf culture, such as Gallaudet University (the only liberal arts college for the Deaf in the world) in Washington, DC, or the National Technical Institute for the Deaf (NTID) in Rochester, New York. On the west coast of the United States, the California State University at Northridge (CSUN) also has a large Deaf student enrollment. Transition to these environments requires planning as well, and students need a great deal of support during this process (English, 1993).

How Services Are Provided

Although these AR responsibilities are carefully described, they are not implemented as widely as one would expect. Earlier it was mentioned that 1–2 million schoolchildren are estimated to have some degree of hearing loss; however, according to annual data collected by the U.S. Department of Education, less than 10% of children with hearing loss receive the audiologic services to which they are entitled (U.S. Department of Education, 1997) (see Table 8.3). The reasons why children with hearing loss are underserved vary from one region to the next, but a common reason seems to be that parents are not fully aware of their rights to these services.

TABLE 8.3

Number of Children Ages 6 to 21 Served under IDEA, Part B, by Disability during the 1995–1996 School Year

STATE	MULTIPLE DISABILITIES	HEARING IMPAIRMENTS	ORTHOPEDIC IMPAIRMENTS	OTHER HEALTH IMPAIRMENTS	VISUAL IMPAIRMENTS
Alabama	1,322	976	537	1,476	408
Alaska	428	201	80	324	49
Arizona	1,341	1,249	748	677	469
Arkansas	823	579	152	2,349	183
California	5,333	8,643	10,253	11,710	3,453
Colorado	2,755	1,030	2,942	0	318
Connecticut	1,695	749	225	3,204	509
Delaware	0	181	496	0	114
District of Columbia	8	41	86	135	27
Florida	0	2,559	4,614	2,138	992
Georgia	0	1,286	805	3,936	512
Hawaii	228	309	148	385	69
Idaho	382	317	133	603	84
Illinois	0	2,982	2,592	2,630	1,109
Indiana	827	1,460	979	1,183	726
Iowa	516	849	1,078	8	203
Kansas	1,541	570	499	2,154	213
Kentucky	1,387	760	426	1,602	433
Louisiana	933	1,447	1,289	4,507	475
Maine	1,868	279	97	967	100
Maryland	4,594	1,233	518	3,038	370
Massachusetts	2,584	1,346	867	1,149	598
Michigan	2,344	2,712	8,000	0	830
Minnesota	0	1,685	1,380	3,525	377
Mississippi	392	571	1,216	0	214
Missouri	640	1,114	700	2,499	367
Montana	484	211	64	535	72
Nebraska	418	584	505	1,227	218
Nevada	391	325	215	459	98
New Hampshire	337	257	161	1,994	117
New Jersey	11,916	1,320	639	666	334
New Mexico	929	453	441	920	189

New York	16,166	4,938	2,622	10,952	1,460
North Carolina	1,440	1,966	982	6,283	589
North Dakota	0	99	125	249	52
Ohio	11,217	2,431	2,274	2,942	984
Oklahoma	1,457	710	373	753	294
Oregon	0	1,500	1,071	2,174	549
Pennsylvania	1,385	2,884	1,234	455	1,345
Puerto Rico	1,237	792	549	789	545
Rhode Island	199	190	149	834	70
South Carolina	402	992	763	1,163	388
South Dakota	493	156	112	203	55
Tennessee	1,827	1,295	1,163	7,260	937
Texas	3,313	5,450	5,004	21,523	2,081
Utah	1,406	767	185	631	347
Vermont	88	147	77	548	34
Virginia	3,751	1,239	772	4,148	500
Washington	3,237	2,387	1,050	13,778	339
West Virginia	0	377	219	754	199
Wisconsin	0	1,232	1,397	1,383	389
Wyoming	0	164	152	532	56
American Samoa	13	10	1	2	3
Guam	46	30	20	34	14
Northern Marianas	34	8	6	5	1
Palau	6	4	4	1	3
Virgin Islands	23	24	11	23	20
Bureau of Indian Affairs					
U.S. and Outlying Areas	94,156	68,070	63,200	133,419	25,484
50 States, D.C., P.R.	94,034	67,994	63,158	133,354	25,443

Source: U.S. Department of Education, 1997.

■ AR SERVICE PROVIDERS IN SCHOOL SETTINGS

School-based AR services are provided in a team approach, with the following professionals working as team members.

Teachers

Not too long ago, most children with hearing impairment were taught in small, self-contained classes run by teachers specially trained to teach them. This model still exists, but now, because of the movement toward inclusion (discussed earlier), many of these teachers may be assigned to several schools to provide support to children as they attend their neighborhood schools. Support may consist of direct instruction, individually or in small groups, or indirect consultation with the general classroom teacher. This collaboration is essential since most regular education teachers receive little training about hearing loss. Information on adapting curriculum, verifying hearing aid function, and the like, is shared, as well as reports on student progress.

Audiologists

School-based audiologists have developed a specialty called educational audiology, often considered to be audiology *plus,* that is, clinical audiology skills *plus* an understanding of the school culture, legal mandates, and the roles and responsibilities unique to the school setting (Berg et al., 1996; English, 1995). A primary limitation

One-on-one speech therapy focused on articulation.

to the provision of these services has been the relatively small number of audiologists hired to serve children in schools. The American Speech–Language–Hearing Association (ASHA) (1993) has conservatively estimated the need to be one audiologist for every 12,000 schoolchildren. This 1:12K ratio would necessitate hiring at least 4200 audiologists, but for over a decade only about 1000 educational audiologists have been employed by schools. Because of this hiring shortage, provision of services may be shared by any of the following professional colleagues.

Speech–Language Pathologists

Speech–language pathologists (SLPs) are the professionals most likely to provide speech and language therapy and auditory training. They may be the persons responsible for ensuring that a child's hearing aids are functioning, troubleshooting basic problems, and reporting any problems to the audiologist. SLPs usually provide support to the classroom teacher by describing how to provide visual cues, promote speechreading opportunities, control for acoustic problems, and so on. SLPs also often conduct hearing screening programs.

Related Support Personnel

Approximately 30% of children with hearing loss have additional disabilities, such as vision loss, autism, and mental retardation (Schildroth & Hotto, 1993). Therefore, associated AR services are also provided by the following, as well as others:

- School nurses, for medications and other health concerns, as well as hearing screening
- School psychologists, for assessment of verbal and nonverbal intellectual abilities
- Adaptive physical education teachers, for large motor and balance development
- Mobility and orientation specialists, for children with visual impairments

It is not at all unusual for these professionals to have a limited background in the area of hearing loss, which makes it all the more important to take a team approach in providing services.

■ SERVICES FOR CHILDREN WITH AUDITORY PROCESSING PROBLEMS

Up to this point, we have considered the audiologic rehabilitative services only for children with hearing impairment. However, in the last few years, increased attention is being paid to children who have normal hearing sensitivity, but deficits in their ability to understand what they hear. We can appreciate the depth of this problem when we realize that the vast majority of a school day requires a child to listen to her teacher's instruction, understand it, remember it, and respond to it. Imagine a classroom teacher giving the following instructions: "Class, I want you to take out your yellow math book and turn to page 197. Do only the even-numbered problems and then leave your paper on my desk. When you are done, you may do some silent reading until 10:40." A child with an auditory processing problem might be easily confused with this long set of instructions, or she might sufficiently understand until other children start making noise as they reach for their books, pencils, and paper. Such a child may look distracted or "off task" as she looks around trying to figure out what to do, and to a teacher her behaviors might appear hyperactive or immature.

Because auditory processing (listening) is an invisible behavior, it may be difficult for teachers to realize that it involves instantaneous complex cognitive activity, specifically, receiving, symbolizing, comprehending, interpreting, storing, and recalling auditory information or, put more simply, "what we do with what we hear" (Lasky & Katz, 1983, p. 5). The Task Force on Central Auditory Processing (1996) has defined five assessment areas and six related symptoms, including sound localization and auditory discrimination. As summarized in Chapter 9, current procedures typically measure only four:

- *Temporal aspects of hearing or pattern recognition:* the ability to rapidly and accurately sequence auditory information.
- *Monaural discrimination:* the ability to perceive degraded words or words in competion when signal and competition are present in one ear.
- *Understanding binaural acoustic information* such as a signal in one ear by ignoring competition in the other.
- *Understanding binaural (dichotic) information* that is heard in two ears at once.

When a child has problems with one or more of these listening challenges, he or she may have an *auditory processing disorder* (APD). Until recently, the term *central auditory processing disorder* (CAPD) has been used, but since "central" and "processing" are redundant words, it has been recommended that the term auditory processing disorders be used for clarity (Jerger & Musiek, 2000).

As mentioned, secondary behaviors that arise as a consequence of listening problems provide us with clues to the possible presence of APD. Adults are first alerted to listening difficulties when they observe the following in a child:

1. Responding inconsistently to auditory stimuli. For example, sometimes a child successfully follows a set of directions, yet other times becomes confused with the same task.
2. Demonstrating a relatively short attention span or becoming easily fatigued when confronted with long or complex listening activities.
3. Appearing overly distracted by both auditory and visual stimuli. Some children with APD feel compelled to respond immediately and fully to everything they hear, see, and touch and are unable to filter out relevant from irrelevant stimuli. Among auditory stimuli, the hum of a computer and the bubbling of a fish-tank in class may command as much attention as the teacher's voice, and the child is unable to ignore the background noises as irrelevant. These behaviors are also consistent with attention deficit hyperactivity disorder (ADHD), and a differential diagnosis can be difficult to achieve.
4. Frequently requesting that information be repeated: saying "huh?" more often than other children.

APD: Auditory processing disorder: a range of difficulties with auditory information, in spite of normal hearing acuity.

5. Having problems with short- and long-term memory skills, such as counting; reciting the alphabet or the days, weeks, and months of the year; or recalling a home address or phone number.

The overall impression of a child with APD is one who seems generally inattentive, "out of it," restless, forgetful, or impatient or acts socially inappropriately. Listening difficulties often surface in third grade, when classroom instruction becomes less directed. Such difficulties may even be apparent from the first days of formal schooling, because listening is the mode by which a prereader acquires information. However, it is also imperative to remember that the types of behaviors listed previously are seen in all children at some time, depending on general health and energy levels, personal worries or other distractions, a variety of other learning disabilities, or the presence of temporary hearing loss due to ear infections and allergies (Chermak & Musiek, 1997).

Because APD is difficult to diagnose and because there is no standard definition of the disorder, there is no specific count of the number of children who have auditory processing problems. Approximately 8 million to 12 million schoolchildren in the United States have learning disabilities, and many of them have APD. It appears that more boys have APD than girls, and many have allergies and a positive history of chronic ear infections (Keith, 1995). APD is typically considered a learning disorder and is often just one aspect of a more complex language–learning disorder. There are different kinds of processing problems, including the following:

■ Difficulties attending to speech with competing noise in the background (important when we consider the usual noise level in classrooms)
■ Difficulties hearing the differences in sounds and words (an essential skill for phonetic reading and spelling)

In addition to these kinds of problems, there is evidence that some children's auditory systems are not as efficient in the speed of transmission (slower neural activity) and that it may take longer than normal for signals to travel from the outer ear to the brain. If a delay like this is occurring, it could be said that a child cannot listen as fast as a teacher is talking (Bellis, 1996).

Providers of AR services in schools may be called on to make a diagnosis of APD and provide remediation as needed. Traditional auditory training techniques have been successfully applied to help children with normal hearing to develop listening skills: for example, learning to discriminate differences in long versus short tones or high versus low tones, as well as the sounds in words. Computer games (e.g., Earobics) have been designed to help a child to listen and discriminate between these kinds of sounds (see the end of the chapter for Web site information). If a child has difficulties ignoring background noise, many listening activities are presented while a tape of white noise or cafeteria noise is played as a method of desensitization. Activities are also provided to develop auditory memory, and to help a child "listen faster" by presenting stimuli with increasing speed. An innovative program called FastForward has been designed to help children to improve this last auditory skill: by logging onto the Internet, a child uses a computer to work through

> ### Case 3: Kim
>
> Kim is 7 years old and is in second grade. His classmates have been acquiring beginning reading skills for several months, but he did not understand the teacher's instruction about "letter sounds," and he was getting farther and farther behind. He was discouraged and struggling with his self-perception of "being stupid." He had been seeing a reading tutor for 2 months and was not making any progress. His motivation to learn was almost nonexistent.
>
> He was diagnosed as having an auditory processing problem, specifically with not being able to hear the subtle differences in sounds. Using several modalities (visual cues, kinesthetic cues, etc.), he was taught first to recognize and describe the differences between long and short tones on a keyboard and between low and high frequencies. He was taught to perceive the differences between similar consonants and vowels and consonant–vowel combinations.
>
> In the beginning, he was not eager to "work on listening." However, he enjoyed the one on one interaction and soon changed his attitude about learning. By the end of the 12-week session, he had learned how to translate these listening games to reading skills and was dismissed from the program.

a series of games that are individualized to his or her processing speed. Speech sounds are electronically altered and are made increasingly more challenging to perceive. Scores are entered to the FastForward's mainframe, and subsequent games are modified to increase or decrease the level of difficulty as needed. Readers are referred to the end of the chapter for Web site information.

In addition to direct therapy, environmental modifications have been suggested, such as minimizing the negative effects of noise by eliminating unnecessary noise sources (replacing buzzing fluorescent lightbulbs or placing carpet on the floor to absorb chair and feet noise) and increasing the "signal" of a teacher's voice by installing classroom amplification. Coping and problem-solving strategies are usually taught, such as learning how to make lists and use calendars, pretutoring key vocabulary and concepts, and using a "study buddy" (Masters, Stecker, & Katz, 1998).

Children with APD can usually improve their listening skills and become actively engaged in communication and learning. However, after experiencing repeated failure and fatigue from effort, children with APD can present motivational problems, creating a downward spiral of discouragement even when they try hard. Remediation must include opportunities to promote and reward a student's efforts to persist when faced with a difficult task.

SUMMARY POINTS

- Hearing loss has educational significance, and children with hearing loss are entitled to AR services to support their educational programs.

- AR services include testing, amplification management, modified instruction, and consideration of classroom acoustics.
- AR services are documented in a child's IEP and are intended to provide a free appropriate public education in the least restrictive environment.
- Children with normal hearing and auditory processing problems benefit from many of the same AR services.
- AR services in school settings are provided to children by a team of professionals: primarily teachers, audiologists, and speech–language pathologists.

RECOMMENDED READING

Cohen, L. (1995). *Train go sorry: Inside a Deaf world.* New York: Vintage Books.

Cohen provides a unique insider's perspective of Deaf culture. Although hearing, she grew up in a residential school for the deaf in New York as the daughter of a teacher there. She was generally accepted by the Deaf community, but at the same time was aware of a vast cultural divide.

Winefield, R. (1987). *Never the twain shall meet: Bell, Gallaudet, and the communications debate.* Washington, DC: Gallaudet University Press.

The author provides an objective review of the issues dividing the oral–aural and manual approaches by presenting a historical account of the beginning of the communications debate and its long-term ramifications with respect to Deaf culture and deaf identity.

Berg, F. (1993). *Acoustics and sound systems in schools.* San Diego, CA: Singular Publishing Group.

Commission on Education of the Deaf. (1988). *Toward equality: Education of the deaf.* Washington, DC: U.S. Government Printing Office.

English, K. (1995). *Educational audiology across the lifespan: Serving all learners with hearing loss.* Baltimore, MD: Paul H. Brooks.

Johnson, C. (2000). Management of hearing in the educational setting. In J. Alpiner & P. McCarthy (Eds.), *Rehabilitative audiology: Children and adults* (3rd ed.). Baltimore, MD: Lippincott Williams & Wilkins.

Roeser, R., & Downs, M. (Eds.). (1995). *Auditory disorders in children* (3rd ed.). New York: Thieme.

RECOMMENDED RESOURCES

Software

Earobics: a CD program designed to help children improve their listening skills. www.scicom.com

FastForward: an Internet-based auditory training program designed for children with auditory processing problems: www.scienticlearning.com

Johnson, C., Seaton, J., & Benson, P. (1997). *Educational audiology handbook.* San Diego, CA: Singular Group Publications.

This text gives an in-depth review of the roles and responsibilities of the audiologist in school settings, it also has a CD with more than 500 pages of forms to help to document services and provide a standardized method of service delivery.

Web Sites

Acoustics Standards Update:
www.edfacilities.org/ir/acoustics.html

Alexander Graham Bell Association:
www.agbell.org

Auditory Verbal International:
www.auditory-verbal.org

Educational Audiology Association:
www.eduaud.org

IDEA Amendments:
www.ed.gov/offices/OSERS/IDEA/the_law.html

National Association of the Deaf:
www.nad.org

National Cued Speech Association:
www.cuedspeech.org

REFERENCES

Allen, T. (1986). Patterns of academic achievement among hearing-impaired students: 1974 and 1983. In Schildroth, A. N., & Karchner, M. A. (Eds.), *Deaf children in America* (pp. 161–206). San Diego, CA: College Hill Press.

American Speech–Language–Hearing Association. (1993). Guidelines for audiology services in the schools. *Asha, 35*(Suppl. 10), 24–32.

Bellis, T. J. (1996). *Central auditory processing disorders in the educational setting: From science to practice.* San Diego, CA: Singular Group Publishing.

Bennett, J. A., & English, K. (1999). Teaching hearing conservation to school children: Comparing the outcomes and efficacy of two pedagogical approaches. *Journal of Educational Audiology, 7,* 29–33.

Berg, F., Blair, J., Viehweg, S., & Wilson-Vlotman, A. (1986). *Educational audiology for the hard of hearing child.* Orlando, FL: Grune & Stratton.

Bess, F. H., Dodd-Murphy, J., & Parker, R. A. (1998). Children with minimal sensorineural hearing loss: Prevalence, educational performance, and functional status. *Ear and Hearing, 19*(5), 339–354.

Bess, F., Klee, T., & Culbertson, J. L. (1986). Identification, assessment, and management of children with unilateral sensorineural hearing loss. *Seminars in Hearing, 7*(1), 43–50.

Boothroyd, A. (1982). *Hearing impairments in young children.* Englewood Cliffs, NJ: Prentice Hall.

Bullis, M., & Egelston-Dodd, J. (1990). Priorities in the school-to-community transition of adolescents who are deaf. *Career Development for Exceptional Individuals, 13*(10), 71–82.

Chermak, G., & Musiek, F. (1997). *Central auditory processing disorders: New perspectives.* San Diego, CA: Singular Group Publishing.

Chermak, G., Curtis, L., & Seikel, J. (1996). The effectiveness of an interactive hearing conservation program for elementary school children. *Language, Speech, and Hearing Services in Schools, 27*(1), 29.

Commission on Education of the Deaf. (1988). *Toward equality: Education of the deaf.* Washington, DC: U.S. Government Printing Office.

Coryell, J., & Holcomb, T. K. (1997). The use of sign language and sign systems in facilitating the language acquisition and communication of deaf students. *Language, Speech, and Hearing Services in Schools, 28,* 384–394.

Crandall, C., & Smaldino, J. (1994). An update on classroom acoustics for children with hearing impairment. *Volta Review, 96,* 291–306.

Davis, J., Elfenbein, J., Schum, R., & Bentler, R. (1986). Effects of mild and moderate hearing impairments on language, educational, and psychosocial behavior of children. *Journal of Speech and Hearing Disorders, 51,* 53–62.

Davis, J., Shepard, N., Stelmachowicz, P., & Gorga, M. (1982). Characteristics of hearing impaired children in the public schools: Part I. Psychoeducational data *Journal of Speech and Hearing Disorders, 46,* 130–137.

Downs, M., & Yoshinaga-Itano, C. (1999). The efficacy of early identification and intervention for children with hearing impairment. *Pediatric Clinics of North America, 46*(1), 79–87.

DuBow, S., Geer, S, & Strauss, K. (1992). *Legal rights: The guide for deaf and hard of hearing people* (4th ed.). Washington, DC: Gallaudet University Press.

English, K. (1991). Best practices in educational audiology. *Language, Speech, and Hearing Services in Schools, 22,* 283–286.

English, K. (1993). Students with hearing impairment in higher education: A follow-up study. *Educational Audiology Monograph, 3,* 27–31.

English, K. (1995). *Educational audiology across the lifespan: Serving all learners with hearing impairment.* Baltimore, MD: Paul H. Brookes.

English, K. (1997). *Self-advocacy skills for students who are deaf and hard of hearing.* Austin, TX: Pro-Ed.

English, K., & Church, G. (1999). Unilateral hearing loss in children: An update for the 1990s. *Language, Speech, and Hearing Services in Schools, 30,* 26–31.

Estabrooks, W. (Ed.) (1994). *Auditory–verbal therapy.* Washington, DC: Alexander Graham Bell Association for the Deaf.

Flexer, C., Wray, D., & Ireland, J. (1989). Preferential seating is NOT enough: Issues in classroom management of hearing impaired students. *Language, Speech, and Hearing in Schools, 20,* 11–21.

Hoffmeister, R. (1990). ASL and its implications for education. In Bornstein, H. (Ed.), *Manual communication: Implications for education* (pp. 108–127). Washington, DC: Gallaudet University Press.

Individuals with Disabilities Education Act. (IDEA), PL 101-476. (October 30, 1990). Title 20, U.S.C. 1400 et seq: *US Statutes at Large, 104,* 1103–1151.

Jerger, J., & Musiek, F. (2000). Report of the Consensus Conference on the diagnosis of auditory processing disorders in school-aged children. *Journal of the American Academy of Audiology, 11*(9), 467–474.

Johnson, C. D. (2000). Management of hearing in the educational setting. In Alpiner, J., & McCarthy, P. (Eds.), *Rehabilitative audiology: Children and adults* (3rd ed.). Baltimore, MD: Lippincott Williams & Wilkins.

Keith, R. (1995). Tests of central auditory processing. In Roeser, R., & Downs, M. (Eds.), *Auditory disorders in children* (3rd ed.)(pp. 101–116). New York: Thieme.

Kipila, E., & Williams-Scott, B. (1990). Cued speech. In Bornstein, H. (Ed.), *Manual for communication: Implications for education* (pp. 151–185). Washington, DC: Gallaudet University Press.

Langan, L., & Blair, J. C. (2000). "Can you hear me?" A longitudinal study of hearing aid monitoring in the classroom. *Journal of Educational Audiology, 8,* 24–26.

Lasky, E. Z., & Katz, J. (1983). *Central auditory processing disorders: Problems of speech, language, and learning.* Baltimore, MD: University Park Press.

Ling, D. (1976). *Speech and the hearing impaired child.* Washington, DC: Alexander Graham Bell Association for the Deaf.

Ling, D. (1990). Advances underlying spoken language development: A century of building on Bell. *Volta Review, 92*(4), 8–20.

Lipscomb, M., Von Almen, P., & Blair, J. C. (1992). Students as active participants in hearing aid maintenance. *Language, Speech, and Hearing Services in Schools, 23*(3), 208–213.

Luetke-Stahlman, P., & Luckner, J. (1991). *Effectively educating students with hearing impairments.* New York: Longman.

Masters, M. G., Stecker, N. A., & Katz, J. (1998). *Central auditory processing disorders: Mostly management.* Boston: Allyn and Bacon.

Robinson, D. O., & Sterling, G. R. (1980). Hearing aids and children in school: A follow-up study. *Volta Review, 82,* 229–235.

Rosenberg, G., Blake-Rahter, T., Heavner, J., Allen, L., Redmond, B., Phillips, J., & Stigers, K. (1999). Improving classroom acoustics (ICA): A three-year FM sound field classroom amplification study. *Journal of Educational Audiology, 7,* 8–28.

Schildroth, S., & Hotto, S. (1993). Annual survey of hearing impaired children and youth: 1991–92 school year. *American Annals of the Deaf, 138,* 163–171.

Snow, L. (2000). Educational audiology at a bilingual school for the Deaf: An identity crisis? *Educational Audiology Review, 17*(1), 4–5.

Task Force on Central Auditory Processing-ASHA. (1996). Central auditory processing: Current status of research and implications for clinical practice. *American Journal of Audiology, 5*(2), 41–54.

U.S. Department of Education. (1997). *Nineteenth annual report to Congress on the implementation of the Individuals with Disabilities Education Act.* Washington, DC: U.S. Government Printing Office.

U.S. Department of Education. (1998). *Elementary and secondary educational statistics: School year 1997–98.* Washington, DC: U.S. Department of Education National Center for Educational Statistics.

Welsh, W. (1993). Factors influencing career mobility of deaf individuals. *Volta Review, 95,* 329–339.

Comprehensive Approaches to Audiologic Rehabilitation

Audiologic Rehabilitation for Children: Assessment and Management

Mary Pat Moeller
Ronald L. Schow
Dorothy Johnson

CONTENTS

■ INTRODUCTION

This chapter will provide a comprehensive discussion of audiologic rehabilitation for children as provided at two major levels: (1) parent–infant/preschool and (2) the school years. Before specific components that constitute the rehabilitation process are addressed, however, the reader will get a brief overview of prevalence and service delivery statistics, applicable definitions and terms, a general profile of the client, typical rehabilitation settings at various age levels, and the identification and assessment process.

■ PREVALENCE OF LOSS AND LEVEL OF SERVICE

Of all audiologic rehabilitation efforts, those focusing on the child are probably the most frequently applied. While numbers vary depending on the criteria used, it is commonly reported that there are approximately 50,000 youngsters who are deaf in the United States' educational system (about 1 in every 1000 children) and that well over 90% of them receive special services. There are 20 to 40 in every 1000 children (2% to 4%) who can be considered to be permanently hard of hearing in both ears at levels poorer than 20 dB HL in the speech range, and there is a much poorer rate of service for the hard of hearing as compared to the deaf. This estimate would suggest that 1 million to 2 million school-age youngsters in the United States are seriously hard of hearing; but when we include minimal hearing loss with levels poorer than 15 dB HL (bilateral or unilateral) and high-frequency losses, we add another 3 million children. Conductive or temporary losses add at least another 1.5 million. Inclusion of the younger population (0 to 5 years) could put the total at close to 10 million children with hearing loss (Bess, Dodd-Murphy, & Parker, 1998; Niskar et al., 1998).

Recent study of minimally hard of hearing children in Tennessee shows that they experience excessive grade repetition (Bess et al., 1998). When hearing loss in the Iowa public schools was studied extensively, the rate of mild to moderate sensorineural and mixed losses was relatively constant in school children from grades K to 12. Conductive, temporary losses decreased as the children got older, but high-frequency, noise-induced types of losses increased (Shepherd et al., 1981). The level of services (the percentage of youngsters receiving rehabilitation help) reported in Iowa for youngsters having sensorineural and mixed losses varies by the degree of loss. Specifically, there was only a 27% level of service for the mildest losses, but up to a 92% level for the worst losses. Although Iowa was then considered to have exemplary services (70 school audiologists, 500 speech–language pathologists, 100 teachers of the hearing impaired) for its school-age children with hearing impairment, the state was found to be serving only 46% of all such youngsters with some kind of special placement or itinerant service. Also, slightly less than 50% of the overall sensorineural–mixed group was amplified. These data indicate a clear need to address, in a more comprehensive fashion, the needs of children with hearing impairments of all types and degrees.

■ TERMS AND DEFINITIONS

As noted in Chapter 1, a rigid distinction between habilitation and rehabilitation is not being made in this book. Although some prefer to use the word *habilitation* when dealing with children having prelingual hearing impairments, we use the term *audiologic rehabilitation* because of its generic usage in the profession.

Audiologic rehabilitation for the child may be viewed best as an advocacy, in which the rehabilitation professional works with the parents and the child to identify needs in relation to the hearing loss and subsequently arranges to help meet those needs. Needs resulting from hearing loss are detailed in the chapters on amplification (Chapters 2 and 3), auditory and visual skill development (Chapters 4 and

5), speech–language communication (Chapter 6), psychosocial (Chapter 7), and educational issues (Chapter 8), all of which are contained in the first section of this book. Audiologic rehabilitation (AR) includes both assessment and management (see discussion in Chapter 1). While all these AR needs are important, they should be approached differently for various children, depending, among other variables, upon the degree and time of onset of the hearing loss and the age of the child. Consequently, in order to be meaningful, a discussion of audiologic rehabilitation should be seen in the context of a profile of possible clients. The following section specifically focuses on severity and type of hearing loss, age of child, and other disabilities.

■ PROFILE OF THE CLIENT

Hearing Loss

Deafness categories for children include *congenital* (present at birth), *prelingual* (onset before 3 to 5 years), and *postlingual* (onset at or after age 5). Youngsters with congenital deafness should generally be served through early-intervention programs, which include parent–infant and preschool programs. As soon as the loss is identified (preferably by 6 months of age or before) the parent–infant or individual family service plan (IFSP) should start. Preschool programming typically begins when the child is about 3 years of age and may run concurrently with parent–infant programming. Ideally, children continue with such programs until AR services are provided in connection with school placement. Youngsters with prelingual deafness, with onset after birth, will generally receive similar treatment. Children with postlingual deafness, however, will most likely be served only in the schools.

A variety of children who are hard of hearing also participate in audiologic rehabilitation. Youngsters with milder losses are sometimes identified early and receive AR through early intervention. Other youngsters with slight or mild losses are not identified and/or do not receive assistance until after they start school. Indeed, some losses are progressive and reach significant dimensions only as the child gets older. One type of slight to mild loss involves middle-ear infections, which result in conductive hearing problems. Frequently, such losses are of a transient nature, but in other cases they persist over a long period and require rehabilitation assistance. These conductive problems can have an educational impact on children even if the loss is only on the order of 15 dB HL.

Since many more children are hard of hearing than are deaf, most AR work should be performed with children who are hard of hearing (although audiologic rehabilitation should not be neglected with either group). Involvement with children who are deaf may be more intensive because of the greater problems caused by the severity of the hearing loss. The child with more pronounced hearing loss tends to experience more language, speech, and educational difficulties, and more remedial efforts will, therefore, be necessary (see Table 1.2). In this chapter we describe the various types of rehabilitative efforts, without precisely distinguishing between service models for children who are deaf and those for children who are hard of hearing. Although this approach involves some loss of specificity, it is necessary in order to avoid excessive duplication. There is, naturally, much in common

Congenital refers to hearing loss present at birth. Prelingual refers to the onset of hearing loss prior to the acquisition of spoken language. Postlingual refers to the onset of hearing loss after spoken language has been acquired.

The individual family service plan (IFSP) is required by special education law to guide birth to age 3 services. It is developed in collaboration with the family to identify family and child strengths and needs and to outline objectives for the early intervention program.

in AR services regardless of the degree of hearing loss or the mode of communication used. Thus, the reader must selectively apply AR techniques consistent with the individual child's needs.

Age

If the assumption is made that children become adults somewhere between 18 and 21 years of age, graduation from high school provides a natural line of demarcation between childhood and adulthood. In that case, we may separate the years from birth to 18 into two basic divisions: those before school years (0 to 5) and the school years themselves (5 to 18). In addition, we may make a number of other subdivisions, including the years of infancy and toddlerhood (0 to 3), the preschool years (3 to 5), and the kindergarten, grade school, junior high, and high school years (5 to 18).

In this chapter, we use the two-way division (0 to 5 and school years), since children who are deaf or hard of hearing generally undergo a major adjustment of rehabilitation services when they enter regular school programming. Before that, audiologic rehabilitation includes parent–infant and preschool programs. When kindergarten begins, the school personnel will generally take over rehabilitation responsibilities from the early-intervention–preschool professional. These age ranges are general; consequently, some children progress through intervention programs more quickly than others. Services are not time locked, but sequential, depending on the child's progress.

Other Disabling Conditions

Multidisciplinary approach involves a team of specialists from a variety of disciplines in the child's care.

Youngsters with hearing impairment often have other disabling conditions such as visual impairments, motor disabilities, or mental retardation. The percentage is on the order of 26% to 30%, based on data from national surveys of young children with hearing impairment (SKI-HI Institute, 1994; see also Chapter 8). Improvements in medical science have resulted in the survival of more children with multiple disabilities. This underscores the need for a multidisciplinary approach to rehabilitation in which important professionals coordinate all services to ensure integrated treatment of the child. (See Chapter 11, Case 1, for an example in working with such a youngster.)

■ REHABILITATION SETTINGS AND PROVIDERS

AR settings and providers are determined to a great extent by the child's age, the severity of the hearing loss, and the presence of other handicapping conditions. Typically, services start as family-centered programs in the home coordinated by a parent advisor, and progress through preschool programs up through the formal school years. Throughout the rehabilitation process, the services of many professional disciplines are called upon in addition to continued strong parental involvement. Figure 9.1 contains an overview of the AR process as it relates to the roles of clinical audiologists, educators, and medical personnel.

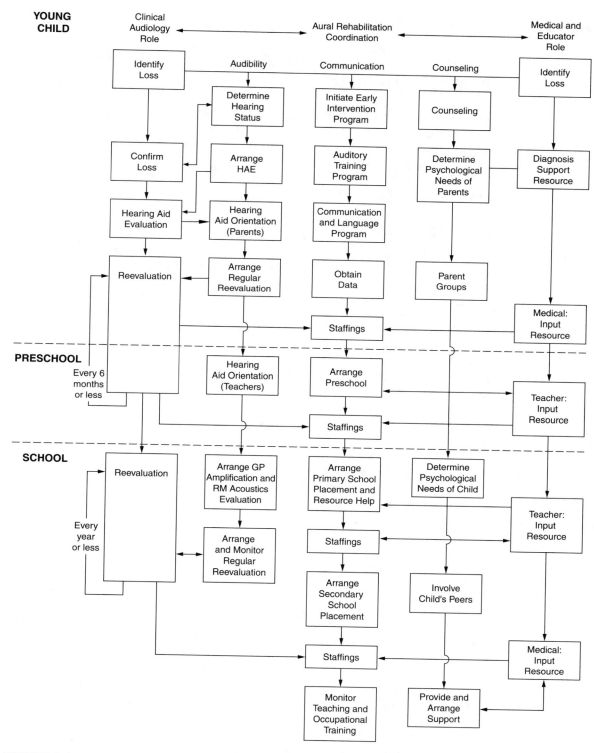

FIGURE 9.1

Overview of the AR process.

IDENTIFICATION AND ASSESSMENT PROCEDURES
■ WITH CHILDREN

Early identification of children with hearing impairment or who are at risk for hearing impairment is critical for successful rehabilitation. Also, proper diagnosis requires precise and appropriate screening and assessment instruments, administered, scored, and interpreted by skilled professionals. The following sections will present prevailing trends in these areas as well as implications for amplification and the overall AR process.

Early Identification

As indicated previously, audiologic rehabilitation personnel are frequently involved in early identification of hearing loss. Naturally, early audiologic rehabilitation efforts cannot be initiated until the presence of hearing loss is known. The status of these identification efforts is in a stage of rapid development and refinement, and methods are constantly being updated (White, Maxon, & Behrens, 1992). Recent technological advances allow for identification of hearing loss soon after birth through the use of two objective tests of hearing, otoacoustic emissions (OAE) and auditory brainstem response (ABR). The National Institutes of Health (NIH-NIDCD) (1993), the Joint Committee on Infant Hearing (2000), and the American Academy of Pediatrics (1999) have endorsed the practice of universal screening of hearing in newborns, and a majority of states across the nation have enacted legislation and initiated screening programs. Current newborn hearing screening procedures have been found to be more effective than previously used high-risk screening programs (Norton et al., 2000). These initiatives allow for proactive management by identifying the majority of hearing losses early in life.

> Two objective tests of hearing used in early identification programs are otoacoustic emissions (OAE) and auditory brainstem response (ABR).

Current newborn screening protocols may miss some infants with sensorineural hearing loss, including those with onset of hearing loss after the newborn period or those with auditory neuropathy (Norton et al., 2000). Therefore, professionals and parents should be aware of risk factors and warning signs for hearing loss. Risk factors include (1) family history, (2) in utero infections such as rubella or cytomegalovirus, (3) anomalies of head or face, (4) low birthweight, (5) hyperbilirubinemia requiring transfusion, (6) ototoxic medications, (7) meningitis, (8) low Apgar scores, (9) mechanical ventilation of five days or longer signifying severe asphyxia, and (10) findings associated with a syndrome. Once children with a high risk are identified, diagnostic screening is used to determine whether or not a hearing loss actually exists. When it is established that a loss exists, early intervention efforts can begin.

With ABR and OAE it is possible to determine if the baby's responses are consistent with those seen in youngsters with normal hearing. When responses are not normal, the child is rescheduled for full audiological diagnostic testing. This retest should occur preferably by three months of age. The advantage of this early hospital screening is that no other occasion or place prompts such universal participation until the child enters school, when it is too late to be looking for congenital hearing loss.

Beyond these early screening efforts, some hearing losses in very young children are identified by physicians. Usually such identification is based upon the report of alert parents who notice that their child does not respond appropriately to sound or fails to develop speech and language at the expected time. When organized screening or high-risk programs are not available, attentive physicians and parents are the major sources for hearing-loss identification. The dimensions of the loss can subsequently be established through testing in an audiology clinic.

School Screening

Most children with severe hearing losses and some with milder losses are identified before they enter school. A number of children, however are not identified until they reach school age. Nearly all schools in the United States conduct a pure tone hearing screening program beginning with kindergarten children or first-graders. Although the specifics of these programs vary, a good model has been recommended by the American Speech–Language–Hearing Association (ASHA, 1997). Most children identified in school hearing-conservation programs demonstrate conductive hearing loss. The rehabilitation efforts, therefore, involve coordination with parents, medical practitioners, and teachers. Some children with previously unidentified sensorineural losses may also be identified in these school programs. In such cases, medical referral is indicated to clarify the medical aspects of the loss, followed by audiologic rehabilitation assistance provided by educational audiologists or other personnel.

Medical and Audiologic Assessment

Before audiologic rehabilitation is initiated, the child should undergo a medical examination as well as a basic hearing assessment. Complete, definitive results are not always available on very young children. When the child is old enough, results from such assessments should include information on both ears, giving: (1) otoscopic findings, (2) degree and configuration of loss, (3) type of loss and cause, (4) speech (clarity of hearing) recognition ability, (5) most comfortable level (MCL), (6) threshold of discomfort (TD), and (7) hearing aid performance and audibility measures. Functional skills in the areas of academic achievement, language, and amplification systems should also be evaluated (Roush & Matkin, 1994).

Sometimes there is a tendency to omit certain aspects of testing, as, for example, speech recognition on youngsters with severe to profound losses, and sometimes there is a failure to consider hearing-aid insertion gain measures at all frequencies and at varying input levels.

Medical clearance becomes necessary when decisions about amplification are made. After initial hearing-aid fitting, regular assessments should take place even for children with sensorineural losses, since temporary conductive loss may occur and complicate the hearing situation, especially in young children. Audiologic data

School screening is important to identify children when they reach school age.

should be obtained on a regular basis so that, if necessary, amplification or other dimensions of the rehabilitation program can be changed. In the early and preschool years, children should be seen for audiologic assessment at least every six months. After that they should be clinically tested at least once a year.

ASPECTS OF AUDIOLOGIC REHABILITATION: EARLY INTERVENTION FOR PARENT–INFANT ■ AND PRESCHOOL

Rehabilitation Assessment

With children, the extensive rehabilitative assessments that generally precede management (see model in Chapter 1) are integrated with management more than with adult clients. Thus, we outline here an ongoing assessment approach to the audiologic rehabilitation of the young hearing-impaired child, beginning at the confirmation of the loss and continuing through the child's school years. Throughout the audiologic rehabilitation process, the dimensions and implications of the child's disability require constant diagnostic scrutiny. As suggested in the AR model (Chapter 1), the rehabilitation assessment includes (1) consideration of communication status, (2) overall participation variables, including psychosocial and educational issues, (3) related personal factors, and (4) environmental conditions.

Management

ENVIRONMENTAL COORDINATION AND PARTICIPATION

FAMILY-CENTERED PRACTICES: AN ASSESSMENT AND INTERVENTION FRAMEWORK. In recent years there has been an increasing appreciation for the central role family relationships play in a child's development (Bailey, 1987). Many professionals contend that the young child cannot be effectively evaluated or instructed apart from the ecological system of the family. There is recognition that developmental influences are bidirectional: the infant's responses affect the family and the family's responses affect the infant. Recognition of the importance of these relationships on the child's development has led to interventions that focus on the child within the family system.

These concepts are not necessarily new to the field of audiologic rehabilitation. It has long been recognized in early-intervention programs for children with hearing impairment that parents are in the best position to provide models of language and auditory stimulation for their child throughout daily routines. In the 1970s, several home demonstration programs were established to guide parents of infants who are deaf in the early stimulation of language. These programs recognized the importance of capitalizing on optimal periods for language acquisition, and the value of taking advantage of the natural parent–child interactions of daily living to develop language and auditory skills. Model demonstration home programs were established in Nashville at the Bill Wilkerson Hearing and Speech Center, at the Central Institute for the Deaf in St. Louis, and at the Lexington School for the Deaf in New York. Another highly successful parent–infant program, the SKI-HI Model (Watkins & Clark, 1993), began in Utah in 1972. This program focused on the training of parent advisors who could provide home-based services to families of young deaf and hard of hearing children. Through its preparation of trainers model, the SKI-HI program developed a network of parent educators that has spanned 45 states and numerous rural communities. The John Tracy Clinic provided outreach guidance to parents through its correspondence courses. During this era, David Luterman developed an early intervention program that focused primarily on the support needs of the family. Another unique program that evolved in the early 1970s was the Infant Hearing Resource in Portland, Oregon, which has played a major role in personnel preparation (both preservice and inservice) for parent infant intervention.

These forerunner programs continue to excel today. They have been joined by additional model programs. A text entitled *Infants and Toddlers with Hearing Loss: Family Centered Assessment and Intervention* (Roush & Matkin, 1994) describes these various model programs. A commonality of the majority of the models described in this text is their evolution over the years from an emphasis on child-centered practices to an emphasis on family-centered practices.

In the 1970s and 1980s, it was not uncommon for parent–infant programs to focus *primarily* on the needs of the child. Certainly, parent support was given in many ways, but the priority goals of early intervention dealt with child needs.

Family-centered practice includes a focus on family-identified needs, efforts to form partnerships with parents to address child needs, and empowerment of families as the primary decision makers for their child. Child-centered practice refers to an intervention that provides direct service for the child, with limited direct involvement of the parent in intervention.

With the passage of PL 99-457 (now included in PL 101-476), emphasis on early-intervention programs for all children with special needs has shifted toward family-centered care. Two primary features characterize family-centered programs: (1) an emphasis on *family support* as a primary intervention goal and (2) the expectation that families may select their level of involvement in decision making, program planning, and services. Winton and Bailey (1994) describe family-centered programs as being willing "to develop a collaborative relationship with each family and to provide services in accordance with family values and priorities" (p. 24). Programs that are family centered recognize the central role that relationships play in development. Professionals respect the expertise and perspectives of families, and seek to establish balanced partnerships with parents. They employ naturalistic strategies and build relationships that lead to identification of family strengths and priorities (Moeller & Condon, 1994).

Natural environments are promoted in federal early intervention laws. The term is used to promote the provision of services in the home or in community settings that families routinely access.

Consistent with the concept of family-centered practice, federal legislation (Part C of IDEA) also requires the provision of early intervention services in *natural environments*. Although this term has been interpreted in a variety of ways, the intention is that infants and their families should receive services in the home or in routinely accessed community settings, rather than in clinics or center-based programs. The purpose of early intervention is to support and assist families in providing learning opportunities for their infant within the activities, routines, and events of everyday life. Parent advisors are encouraged to integrate their coaching within typical routines and settings that comprise daily events for the family. It is believed that infants will have more opportunities to develop requisite skills if parents and other caregivers have been involved in the planning and have learned to incorporate strategies into daily routines using items that are part of their own households.

Family-centered practices and the concept of parent–professional partnerships are valuable tools to implement in response to universal newborn hearing screening programs. As a result of early screening efforts, infants are identified more than 2 years earlier than they were previously. This requires that the content of early intervention shift to focus on the parent–infant relationship in ways that support parent–

infant attachment, bonding, and social reciprocity in communication. The professional works together with the family to promote a nurturing and responsive social and communicative environment. Some professionals prefer the term *early development,* rather than *intervention,* to characterize this work. The concept of *development* captures the joint goals of nurturing infant growth through parent–infant interaction and of supporting the growth of parenting skills. Professionals need to cultivate the skills of being sensitive and responsive to family identified needs in order to implement such programs.

> Parent–professional partnerships involve family members collaborating with professionals to identify needs and implement strategies to encourage infant development.

EFFECTIVENESS OF EARLY INTERVENTION: FAMILY AND CHILD OUTCOMES. The primary goal of early detection and hearing intervention programs, then, is to maximize sensitive periods for language development in infancy by promoting a responsive social and communicative environment. Studies suggest that several important benefits accrue when families are systematically involved in intervention.

Research has shown that interventions can influence families in the following positive ways:

1. *Reduce familial stress.* Stress can alter the emotional availability of parents and affect the caregiver style, resulting in less than optimum interactions (Brofenbrenner, 1974). Early intervention programs have been shown to reduce the anxiety and stress parents experience following diagnosis of a child's hearing impairment (Meadow-Orlans, 1995; Hadadian & Merbler, 1995; Greenberg, 1983).

2. *Support parental self-confidence.* Parent–professional partnerships, a cornerstone of family-centered practice, are designed to empower parents and build their self-confidence for parenting the child. Social support given in early intervention has significant positive effects on mothers' interaction with children who are deaf (Meadow-Orlans & Steinberg, 1993). These factors are associated with improved long-term outcomes for the child (Schlesinger & Acree, 1989). However, Calderon, Bargones, and Sidman (1998) found that parents who had late access to intervention did not demonstrate high levels of confidence or independent understanding of ways to enhance the child's communication. This finding further supports the need for early family support programs.

3. *Promote or support responsive communicative interactions.* Calderon (2000) demonstrated the positive impact on a child's language, reading, and social skills when mothers developed effective skills for communicating with the child. Some hearing parents of deaf children are able to make intuitive adjustments to their parenting style to enhance communicative interactions with the child (Lederberg & Prezbindowski, 2000). For others, this aspect of the program has primary importance.

Most professionals are strongly committed to the notion that early intervention is effective and essential for infants with hearing loss. However, objective documentation of the effectiveness of early intervention has been limited (see Calderon and Greenberg, 1997, for a comprehensive review of past research). Bess and Paradise (1994) raised concern for the lack of empirical evidence to support early intervention during debates about the advisability of universal newborn hearing screening. Their article prompted a resurgence of interest in examining intervention outcomes in relation to ages of identification.

Several recent studies demonstrate that early intervention is effective in preventing or reducing the consequences of hearing loss on child language and literacy development. Some selected primary findings are the following:

1. Children who are identified prior to 6 months of age consistently outperform later-identified children on measures of language, administered through 3 years of age (Yoshinaga-Itano et al., 1998). Moeller (2000) found that age of enrollment in intervention was a significant predictor of vocabulary and verbal reasoning skills at 5 years of age. Children enrolled in services early (in this case, below 11 months of age) had better vocabulary and verbal reasoning skills at age 5 than their later identified counterparts.

2. In the Yoshinaga-Itano et al. (1998) study, the early identification advantage was observed regardless of a number of background variables, such as communication mode, degree of hearing loss, or socioeconomic status.

3. Children enrolled in services prior to 6 months of age, on average, showed near normal rates of language development through age 3 years, whereas later identified children showed delayed development (Yoshinaga-Itano et al., 1998).

4. Family involvement was found to be a significant contributor to child outcomes. It was concluded that children will benefit most from early identification that is paired with comprehensive interventions that actively involve families (Moeller, 2000).

5. Age of entry in intervention predicts better short- and long-term language performance, and better language performance is associated with better early reading skills and more positive social–emotional adjustment (Calderon & Naidu, 2000).

6. When mothers become actively involved as strong communication partners with their children, their children demonstrate better language development, early reading skills, and social–emotional development (Calderon, 2000).

The implications of these collective findings are clear. Environmental influences can have a significant impact on the child's development. Alleviation of stress in the family system will contribute to positive interactions and to a healthy language environment. Rehabilitative efforts that facilitate a nurturing interaction style between parent and child are likely to have long-term positive consequences for the child. Child-centered programs that fail to address the needs of the family system are likely to be of limited success.

SHIFTING ROLES IN THE AUDIOLOGIC REHABILITATION PROGRAM. As early-intervention programs work to implement PL 99-457, many are finding the need for program modification and reconceptualization of professional roles. Bernstein and Morrison (1992) surveyed 134 programs for children with hearing impairment and identified a lack of readiness in most programs to provide the comprehensive services required by the law.* Brinker, Frazier, and Baxter (1992) stressed the need for programs to examine

---

*Survey studies indicate that many programs lack substantial family participation and tend to implement child-centered approaches (Roush, Harrison, and Palsha, 1991).

how family-centered care can best be approached with disadvantaged families. Winton and Bailey (1994) noted the lack of professional training for working with infants and families as a barrier to overcome in implementing family centered practices.

One of the most dramatic role shifts occurring in audiologic rehabilitation as a result of family centered practice goals is that decision-making authority is to rest with family members. Professionals are challenged to help parents gain the skills and knowledge to be effective advocates and decision makers for their child. Previously, professionals made many of the decisions regarding the habilitative management of the child. Now professionals are being challenged to work as partners with families in assessment, management, and decision making. So, for example, in the parent advisor–family partnership, the parent advisor relies on family members to direct the thrust of the services. The young child's needs are expressed as part of the family's concerns. Family members know the child's likes, dislikes, time schedules, favorite toys and activities, food preferences, and many other matters that the parent advisor can't be expected to know. One mother stated, "The advisor I worked with was wise enough to know that no one knows my child better than I do. She respected my suggestions and opinions as much as I respected hers" (Glover et al., 1994, p. 323). Being understanding of the family's cultural values and practices enhances the partnership. As the parent advisor–family partnership develops and as respect and trust mature, the parent advisor has the opportunity to help family members explore their feelings, clarify their concerns and desires for the child, and see and appreciate the child's unique skills and strengths. Other examples of collaborative decision making with parents are contained in Chapter 11 (see Case 2).

A second major shift in service delivery influences the roles of the AR clinician. In order to meet comprehensive family and child needs, professionals must employ transdisciplinary teamwork. No one discipline has all the knowledge and expertise to adequately address the comprehensive nature of most cases. The AR clinician in

> Professionals need to shift their traditional roles and ensure that families are placed in the role of primary decision makers for the child.
>
> Transdisciplinary teamwork refers to a process in which team members collaborate and are interdependent. Rather than each member separately working with the child and sharing viewpoints, team members work together and integrate their perspectives.

Parent Perspectives on Early Intervention Teams as Told in SKI-HI Parent Interviews and Team Surveys, 1995–1998

A good team is "a lifesaver if it works right. Team members have training in areas that I need their help in, but I know my child best. . . . I think a team can be a lifeline when you are feeling so helpless for a little while and frightened."

"There needs to be more correlation in services . . . each service provider tends to come in and do their own thing. I could use more help in coordination as it is difficult for a parent to coordinate all of the services."

Asked if parents feel listened to or heard, one parent said, "No! Team members need to ask us as parents what our goals are for our child."

"Usually team members ask me as the parent which would be best for my child and family if there is a difference of opinion. We then proceed in the direction that I think is best."

Source: Working Together on Early Intervention Teams (B. Glover, 1999, pp. 13–14, 42, 48, 60). Used with permission.

> ### Perspectives of Professionals on Early Intervention Teams as Told in SKI-HI Professional Interviews and Team Surveys, 1995–1998
>
> "It is a new concept for some people. But, I think once people participate on a team they will realize how it works to benefit families. On our team we write a group report of the assessment instead of everybody writing a separate report. We gather the information that everybody has, then we take turns writing the report. . . . This makes it a lot easier and less fragmented for family members."
>
> "It was very difficult at first because team members were holding their own ground and not wanting to share information with other team members. It is not like that now. . . ."
>
> "I think that the families I work with are not as overwhelmed as they used to be. Before, there were lots of different service providers coming in at different times to work on different things with their child. Now we are coordinating our goals, and we look at service for the child in a holistic approach with the service coordinator directing the activities that are carried out with the child and family."
>
> *Source: Working Together on Early Intervention Teams* (B. Glover, 1999, pp. 17, 18, 70). Used with permission.

a parent-advisor role has a particularly critical role on the team. Because the parent advisor has frequent contact with the family in their home (e.g., one to two times per week), this professional is often in a good position to gain a full understanding of the family's strengths and priorities, and to work with the parent to implement strategies to achieve these priorities. The parent advisor may also serve in a role of case coordination with the assistance of a Services Coordinator.

The parent advisor–AR clinician can and should draw upon the resources of a community-based team of professionals, depending on the needs that present themselves. Parent advisors need to cultivate the skills for collaborative consultation and teamwork in order to effectively serve families. Idol, Paolucci-Whitcomb, and Nevin (1986) state, "Collaborative consultation is an interactive process that enables teams of people with diverse expertise to generate creative solutions to mutually defined problems. The outcome is enhanced and altered from the original solutions that any team member would produce independently" (p. 9).

> Collaborative consultation comes about when team members contribute diverse expertise to creatively solve intervention problems.

IMPLICATIONS OF FAMILY-CENTERED INTERVENTION FOR ASSESSMENT PRACTICES. Extensive and ongoing assessment of a child's needs is fundamental to pediatric audiologic rehabilitation (see model in Chapter 1). Assessment is critical for determining priority intervention needs, determining outcomes, and ascertaining the most efficacious approaches. Assessment practices have been expanded in some of the following ways as a result of early intervention mandates:

1. *Ongoing assessment by a transdisciplinary team leads to the development of an Individualized Family Service Plan (IFSP).* This document, created in collaboration

with family members, serves as a road map to the intervention. The **IFSP** process requires that the AR team (a) describe the infant's present levels of achievement across major developmental domains, (b) determine family strengths and list family-identified needs, and (c) identify the major outcomes expected for the infant and family. In many states, services coordinators assist team members in clarifying and addressing family needs.

2. *Professionals should observe and understand family interactions and needs before giving advice or instruction.* Following diagnosis, parents may lack confidence in their skills for parenting a child with hearing loss. Yet, in most cases, parents have discovered effective and nurturing ways to interact with their babies. When professionals sensitively observe and identify such strengths, they lead the parent to recognize, "Oh, I *do* have skills to meet the challenges ahead." Rather than expert advice giver, the AR clinician acts as a good listener and observer and, later, as a coach.

3. *Assessment needs to address the infant, primary caregivers and their interaction* (Sparks, 1989). Useful infant evaluation tools include (a) naturalistic contexts, (b) a focus on strengths in the parent–infant interaction, and (c) methods for recruiting input and observations from the family.

4. *Clinicians must respect the decision-making authority of the family.* Families with newly identified infants with hearing loss are met with many decisions related to their child's management (e.g., various hearing aid options, sensory device options, and communication options). The process of making important decisions should be one of collaborative problem solving between the family and clinicians (Moeller, Coufal, and Hixson, 1990). Parents need access to the full range of information, objective guidance, and opportunities to observe strategies that appear to be successful with their infant. With this information base, families can make their own informed decisions.

The Boys Town National Research Hospital has implemented a program called the Diagnostic Early Intervention Project (DEIP), which is dedicated to helping parents learn and objectively discover what approaches work best for the child and family before deciding on modes or placements (Moeller & Condon, 1994). Figure 9.2 shows a schematic model of the stages in the DEIP process. Within this process, there is an openness between the clinician and family to explore options on a continuum and determine objectively which option will best meet the presenting needs. The team and parents collect objective data on family concerns, audiological variables (learning rate in auditory training, amplification success), communication variables (rate of phonological learning, rate of language development), learning variables (play and cognition, learning styles), and medical–genetic issues (presence of additional disabilities) to aid in decision making. Each child and family is unique, with an individualized profile of strengths and needs. Thus, the team avoids a "one size fits all" approach, and rather explores various approaches to determine the "best fit" that will lead to communicative success.

The SKI-HI program also has an excellent home-based program to enable families to make appropriate communication methodology choices. A series of discussions is available for the parent advisor and family to use as they explore different

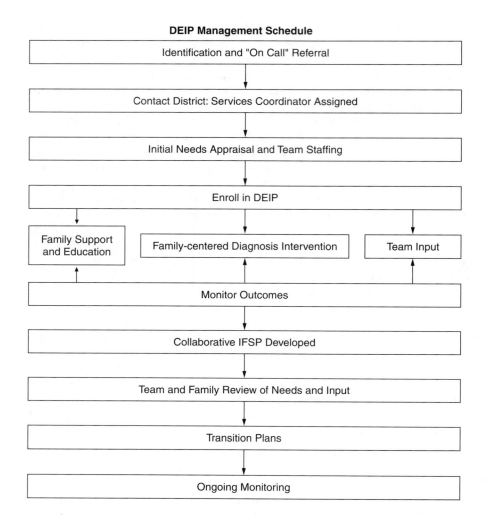

FIGURE 9.2

Diagnostic early intervention project model.
Source: Moeller and Condon (1994).

communication methodology options. The discussions include information about the various methodologies as well as suggested activities and supplemental readings. Parent advisors and family members together observe, document, explore, and discuss a variety of child and family factors that are important to consider as they make methodology choices. After a communication methodology decision has been reached, SKI-HI programming resources are available in all communication methodology areas (including Bilingualism) that will promote the child's and family's communication interaction in that methodology.

TEAM STAFFINGS. The specific intervention priorities for a particular family are determined as part of the IFSP process. The clinician and parent will regularly monitor the infant's progress by collecting data in such areas as hearing-aid usage and adjustment, auditory development, vocabulary growth, receptive and expressive language accomplishments, and phonological development. With such information as a basis, team staffings can be held every three to six months to discuss progress monitoring and adjust strategies as needed. At the staffings, perspectives can be shared from other disciplines, such as psychology, pediatrics, audiology, education, as well as other professions involved with the family. The goals of the staffings are to tailor programs to meet the needs of individual children and families.

IMPLICATIONS OF FAMILY-CENTERED CARE FOR INTERVENTION. Family-centered parent–infant programs, then, focus on family members as the primary interventionists. The audiologic rehabilitation specialist provides guidance and coaching to the family in several key content areas: (1) fitting and adjustment of amplification and assistive devices; (2) auditory learning (use of residual hearing); and (3) techniques for optimizing communicative development (speech, language, signing, cognitive, and preliteracy skills). Another vital content area for the program is helping the family meet their support needs and providing activities that promote psychosocial well-being. Once the child is of preschool age (around three years old), services typically shift to center-based models where the child attends a preschool. These services are commonly provided in a self-contained program for children who are deaf or hard of hearing, in a reverse-integrated preschool deaf program, in a special-needs multi-categorical classroom, or in a regular preschool program with support services from an AR specialist. Wherever the service delivery or whatever the model, family-centered practices continue to be vital. Families learn at the parent–infant level to be knowledgeable advocates for their children. They become intricately involved in influencing the child's success. It would be a mistake to "graduate" the child into a center-based program and minimize the contributions family members can make. Instead, programs should continue to address family needs, family support, and family guidance into the preschool years. In the next sections we describe approaches in each of the key content areas at the parent–infant and preschool levels.

AUDIBILITY, AMPLIFICATION, AND ASSISTIVE DEVICE ISSUES

HEARING-AID FITTING. Once preliminary medical and audiologic findings are available on the child, the selection of amplification, when appropriate, becomes an early goal in the rehabilitative program. Many experts agree that hearing aids are extremely important tools in early-intervention programs in helping children develop their residual hearing and their speech and language abilities. Unfortunately, as previously noted, many youngsters with hearing impairment do not typically use amplification. Consequently, the efforts of the audiologic rehabilitationist may need to be directed toward achieving that goal. The hearing aid fitting will be performed by an audiologist who may also be providing other rehabilitative services (see Figure 9.1). If the AR therapist does not perform the fitting, he or she will want to review its adequacy. In recent years, the focus in fitting children has been to move away from procedures based on threshold to those focusing more on how the amplified speech range fits into the child's usable hearing range. The Desired Sensation Level (DSL) method is an example of this latter approach and is reviewed in Chapter 2. Although hearing aid fitting is a first priority, other assistive amplification devices should also be considered, such as classroom FM equipment for the older child.

TYPE AND ARRANGEMENT OF AID. The type of aid and the arrangement (monaural, binaural, or other special fitting, such as a direct input feature or integrated FM capability) need careful attention and review in the AR process. Behind the ear (BTE) aids are used by most children from infancy through the teenage years (Bentler, 1993). Some children, especially teenagers, use in the ear or canal aids. While requiring special adjustment, these are feasible for use by certain individuals. (See a discussion of various hearing aid issues in Chapter 2, which covers hearing aid fitting procedures.) From a rehabilitative standpoint, binaural fittings are nearly always the rule, since children with hearing impairment require every educational advantage possible. Unfortunately, the minority of hearing impaired children with bilateral losses are using binaural aids. Various reports place this minority at somewhere between 20% and 40% (Bentler, 1993). Even after a careful analysis to eliminate the children with bilateral losses who were not candidates for a second aid, Matkin (1984) found that only 38% of the children who could use two aids were doing so. In some settings, the use of aids by children is excellent, as in one local school district where 22 of the 23 children are properly fitted. But all settings do not have such excellent services.

If children are found to have little usable residual hearing or serious progressive loss, cochlear implants may be considered (see Chapter 3). Promising results with children who have been implanted are leading to an increased use of these implants, which have now been used on well over 3000 children between the ages of 2 and 17 years since the FDA approved such use beginning in June 1990. Implant device surgery is very expensive, and when children are implanted, extensive audiologic rehabilitation follow-up is needed.

HEARING-AID FEATURES

1. *Earmold fit and gain setting of aid.* With very young or fast-growing children, the earmold will need to be changed frequently to ensure a well-fitting mold and to provide adequate gain without feedback even though feedback is less of a problem now with the new technology. Turning the gain down will help eliminate the feedback, but it is an unacceptable long-term solution. The therapist should not rely entirely on the clinical audiologist or the dispenser for this assessment, but should personally monitor the earmold condition on each rehabilitation visit. In some situations, the audiologic rehabilitationist is trained to make ear impressions. This can be a valuable asset to the program, especially considering the frequency of mold changes in an adequate program (see Table 9.1).

2. *Real-ear measures.* Precise information on aided results can be obtained with real-ear measures, which provide accurate and complete information (see Chapter 2). They make it possible to evaluate benefit from the aid thoroughly without requiring more than passive cooperation from the the child.

Desired sensation level (DSL) is a computer-based method of determining a child's usable hearing with amplification.

In addition to hearing aids, assistive listening devices like FM systems for use in noisy environments (e.g., classrooms) should be considered.

TABLE 9.1

Average Months per Set of Earmolds for Children Whose Molds Were Replaced at the First Evidence of Feedback Difficulty[a]

	Average Months per Mold	
DEGREE OF LOSS (dB)	<2½-YEAR-OLD CHILD (N = 25)	2½- TO 5-YEAR OLD CHILD (N = 27)
Mild (30–55)	3.0	5.2
Moderate (56–75)	2.7	4.1
Severe (76–90)	2.5	5.6
Profound (91–110)	2.0	4.6

Reprinted by permission: SKI-HI data.

[a]Also included are average loss and gain values for children in total project (N = 52) with properly fitting molds. Mean loss pure tone average (PTA), 75 dB; mean aided loss, 44 dB; mean gain, 31 dB.

3. *Electroacoustic assessment of aid.* An electroacoustic check of the hearing aid should provide information on the frequency response, the gain, the SSPL, and the distortion of the instrument (see Chapter 2 for a description of this process). These data can help uncover inadequacies in the amplification that can otherwise be devastating to the child's progress in the rehabilitation program. Electroacoustic checks are particularly helpful in the case of distortions, which are not found in the real-ear tests, and when biologic listening checks do not reveal a distortion problem.

4. *Five-sound test of aid.* In connection with hearing-aid adjustment, it may be helpful for the AR therapist to use the five-or-six-sound test described by Ling (1989). According to Ling, the sounds /u/, /a/, /i/, /ʃ/, /s/ and sometimes /m/ can be used to determine the effectiveness of an aid. With the infant, visually reinforced audiometry can be used to determine if the child can hear these sounds. Older children can simply indicate they hear the sounds by imitating or giving a detection response.

HEARING-AID ORIENTATION. It is helpful for parents, teachers, school personnel, and other involved professionals to be knowledgeable about the auditory mechanism and hearing so that they can help monitor hearing aid use. This information can be provided in home visits, in clinic counseling sessions, in parent groups, and through inservice training in the school setting. (See suggestions in Chapter 10).

The benefit of hearing-aid use may not be readily obvious to parents or teachers, especially in cases where auditory communication is minimal. The purposes of hearing-aid use may include some or all of the following: verbal communication, signal or warning function, and environmental awareness. Parents must recognize why their child is wearing an aid, since with younger children, parents have the major responsibility for maintaining the aid and ensuring that it is used regularly. If parents understand hearing aids, they will be encouraged to help their child form good habits of use.

The hearing aids will be more acceptable to the child when they function properly, but the procedures for obtaining hearing-aid accessories, repairs, or loaners will vary with local conditions. The AR provider should be aware of these conditions in order to be an effective resource person.

REMEDIATION OF COMMUNICATION ACTIVITY

AUDITORY LEARNING: PARENT–INFANT AND PRESCHOOL LEVELS. There are many natural opportunities in the home setting for exposing the child to sound. Once the child is fitted with appropriate amplification, the parents and clinician work to provide meaningful and frequent auditory experiences to encourage the child to rely on his or her residual hearing. For many children, systematic introduction to sounds during the early years will have a positive impact on language learning. Effective stimulation of residual hearing is critical to the development of spoken communication. Early auditory learning training should consist of observing and promoting the child's listening experiences in many meaningful daily activities. As Marlowe (1984) recommended, the clinician should "stress listening to people sounds rather than environmental sounds unless the latter are incorporated in meaningful experiences" (p. 6).

> Auditory learning activities for infants should focus on observing and promoting natural listening opportunities throughout natural daily routines.

A variety of materials have been developed that describe auditory skill development. Erber (1982) developed a particularly useful model that distinguishes between levels of detection, discrimination, identification, and comprehension (a complete discussion of Erber's model is contained in Chapter 4). Table 9.2 contains a related description of a sequence of listening skills and techniques parents can use to develop these skills. Parents need not see these as discrete, sequential stages; however, it is helpful for them to be aware of a general hierarchy and that some skills will develop later than others. Detailed suggestions for how to help an infant or a preschool child develop auditory skills can also be found in Watkins and Clark (1993) and Ling and Ling (1978).

Teachers and clinicians in the preschool setting can also take advantage of natural opportunities to encourage the children to rely on their residual hearing. It is common for clinicians in preschool settings to integrate auditory challenges throughout curriculum lessons. Rather than specifying a "listening lesson" or "listening time," clinicians integrate auditory learning as a process that pervades all activities. This can be challenging in a total communication program, where the focus is on visual learning. Clinicians in TC settings need to make a conscious effort to provide realistic auditory challenges to the child that support other communicative goals. Erber's (1982) concept of adaptive auditory skill development is very useful at the preschool level. This concept implies that a clinician constantly is monitoring a child's level of success with a particular auditory contrast or task, and adjusting the task as necessary to bring about successive approximation to the goal.

> Adaptive auditory skill development refers to the continual monitoring of a child's responses and adjustment of the level of difficulty of the task to bring about success or further challenge.

An innovative auditory development curriculum for the preschool and school-age level was developed by an interdisciplinary team at the University of Miami and the Dade County Public Schools Model Program. This unique program (entitled the Miami CHATS curriculum) is a comprehensive curriculum, that integrates goals for

TABLE 9.2		
Auditory Skill Development Sequence		
AUDITORY SKILLS	**CHILD'S BEHAVIOR**	**STIMULATION SKILLS**
1. Attending and Detection	Child attends to environmental sounds and voices. Child attends to distinct speech sounds.	Use auditory clues, show child sources of sound. Focus on highly communicative sounds (e.g. food preparation; bath noises; hearing name called).
2. Recognizing	Child recognizes objects and events from their sounds.	Point out sounds and reinforce child's recognition of sources. Allow sound to be child's first source of information. Contrive opportunities for child to respond to meaningful sounds and associate them with sources.
3. Locating	Child locates sound sources in space.	Create localization opportunities and reinforce all child attempts to localize. Recognize that localization gives clues to the sound's source and meaning. Involve child in social games like "hide and seek" to develop localization.
4. Distances and levels	Child locates sound sources at increased distances and above and below.	Create opportunities for child to hear sounds above, below, and at distances; reinforce child's responses. Use distance listening games to help child tune "selective attention" to sound.
5. Environmental discrimination, identification, and comprehension	Child discriminates, identifies, and comprehends environmental sounds.	Repeatedly stimulate the child with meaningful environmental sounds and reinforce child's discrimination, identification, and comprehension of sounds. Tie these sounds to natural communication routines.
6. Vocal discrimination, identification, and comprehension	Child discriminates, identifies, and comprehends gross vocal sounds, words, and phrases.	Provide natural opportunities for child to discriminate, identify, and comprehend onomatopoeic sounds, words, and phrases. Present contrasting verbal signals within playful social routines.
7. Speech discrimination, identification, and comprehension	Child discriminates, identifies, and comprehends fine speech sounds: vowels, then consonants.	Provide stimulation of vowel, then consonant sounds in meaningful words and situations. Create opportunities for child to demonstrate discrimination, identification, and comprehension of these words.

cochlear implant, hearing aid, or tactile aid users. The goals of the curriculum are to provide professionals with a systematic guide to the integration of sensory aids to facilitate the ability of the child with hearing impairment to produce and comprehend oral communication (Vergara and Miskiel, 1994).

It is important for AR clinicians to fit auditory-skill development within a conceptual model of speech and language learning. For many children with hearing loss, the auditory channel is viable for language learning, given appropriate amplification and stimulation. Boothroyd (1982) and Ling (1976) stress the primacy of the auditory channel for speech and language learning. Throughout the course of development, the AR clinician should closely integrate listening goals with those of speech and language learning. For example, a preschool child learning to discriminate temporal patterns should also be working on production of the appropriate number of syllables in simple word approximations. The child learning to detect sounds should have opportunities to answer in a socially appropriate manner when his or her name is called. A child with residual hearing benefits from auditory-based correction when a speech error is made. Ling (1976) stresses the importance of helping the child establish an auditory feedback loop. That is, auditory skills need to develop to the point where the child can self-monitor his speech productions through audition. These goals are realistic for many children with appropriate amplification. Language, audition, and phonological acquisition are intricately related processes, that should be addressed in an integrated fashion. Rather than "auditory training" the notion is "auditory learning" or "auditory communication." For some children, progress toward auditory goals will be slow, due to limitations of residual hearing. Alternative sensory communication devices may be considered by the team in these cases.

Documentation of learning rates in audition is useful in selecting intervention approaches and in ascertaining the need for additional sensory aids. Dillon and his colleagues described a Goal Attainment Scaling Procedure used with adults to ascertain the efficacy of various devices or approaches (Dillon et al., 1991). Moeller (1993) adapted this approach for use with infants and preschoolers. The scaling approach allows the AR clinician to systematically track the child's progress across different goals and situations. Table 9.3 illustrates an example of this procedural adaptation. It is also relevant for the AR clinician to carefully monitor changes in a child's phonological development. Substantive changes in vocal and phonological behaviors are often indicators of auditory learning. Oller (1983) cites the onset of true babbling as a critical benchmark, typically observed from 7 to 10 months of age in normally developing infants. Often, the babbling stage is delayed in children who are deaf.

COMMUNICATION AND LANGUAGE STIMULATION: PARENT-INFANT. At the same time that auditory-skill development is being initiated in the home, the clinician helps parents build upon their communication strategies with the child. Effective interaction between parent and child is fundamental to the process of language acquisition. The communicative interaction between the child and family members is a primary focus of parent-infant rehabilitation.

When parents and professionals team together in a partnership, intervention can proceed in a fashion of joint discovery (Moeller & Condon, 1994). During home

TABLE 9.3

Examples of Goal Attainment Scaling with Infant Auditory Goals from IFSP

AUDITORY GOALS FROM IFSP

A. Child will respond meaningfully to common environmental sounds.
B. Child will be spontaneously alert when name is called.
C. Child will respond with appropriate action to simple, functional commands.
D. Child will respond to functional phrases in distracting environments.
E. Child will wear hearing aids full waking hours.

SPECIFIC GOAL ACCOMPLISHMENT

Goal	A	B	C	D	E	Comments 3/93
Always						A-microwave, door knock, bath water garage opener, dog
Most of the Time	✓				✓	B-Needs to be in listening set
Half of the Time			✓			C-Come here, no no, stop, yeah!!!
Occasionally		✓		✓		E-hearing aid use is problem at day care
Never						

Taking the *primary listening situations* from the IFSP goals, rate the child's current responses in the targeted listening environments (See attached example).

CHILD RESPONDS TO:

	Sounds at Home		Calling Name		Functional Phrases		Functional Phrases		Wears Hearing Aids	
	Alert	I.D.	Close	Distant	1 to 1	Group	Day Care	Church	Home	Sitter
Always										
Most of the Time										
Half of the Time										
Occasionally										
Never										
Not Applicable										

Proposed by Moeller, Boys Town National Research Hospital (1993).

×- -×- -× = 3/93   •——•——• = 9/93

intervention sessions, family members engage the infant in stimulating routines, and the parent and clinician actively monitor the child's responses and adjust techniques as necessary. Family members also receive guidance, information, and support during home visits. The SKI-HI home visit program (see Figure 9.3) is an excellent example of a model that includes a comprehensive management approach.

When the home is the primary intervention setting, the parent advisor and parent use the natural environment and daily events as the milieu for teaching. As much as possible, parents, siblings, and other significant persons in the child's life are encouraged to be "in the driver's seat" in the intervention sessions. Instead of bringing an adult-directed lesson plan with demonstration activities, the parent advisor and parent take advantage of natural interaction situations to practice the provision of nurturing input for the child. For example, a parent advisor might take advantage of the siblings' affinity for a "ring around the rosy" game to emphasize the skill of sound detection for the deaf toddler. A toddler's feeding time can become an ideal time for reinforcing prelinguistic communicative signals and strengthening turn taking. Bedtime storybook sharing is one of many natural opportunities to contribute to the infant's or toddler's literacy development (Watkins, 1999). Reinforcing toddler games and toys available in the home can also be introduced to encourage language and thinking, but they should not be the primary focus. Parents are supported when language and auditory intervention schemes can fit into the

> Language and auditory development techniques need to be incorporated into natural parenting routines.

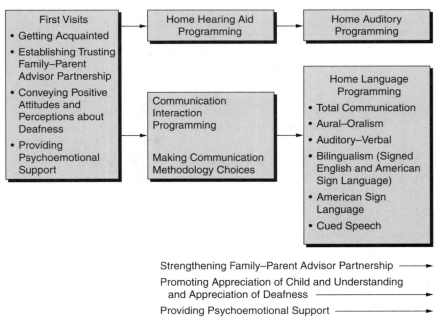

FIGURE 9.3

SKI-HI home visit programming.

rhythm and habits of their daily lives. Parents may need help to discover that it is their "all-day-long" routine interactions with the child that build language skills (Simmons-Martin & Rossi, 1990), not structured "sit-down" therapy activities. Language and auditory intervention strategies need to fit within the context of natural positive parenting.

A primary focus of the intervention program is promoting nurturing and effective interactions between the parents and the infant. Although mothers of children who are deaf have been described as being overly controlling in interactions with their children, there are many examples in clinical practice of parents who interact in highly facilitative ways with their infants who are deaf and hard of hearing. Perhaps family-centered practices will result in different characterizations of maternal and paternal styles. Some parents will need direct guidance to develop facilitative styles with their infants. However, the parent advisor should not assume this to be the case. There may be many strengths that can be built upon in the parent–child interaction.

During home intervention sessions, the parents and parent advisor work together to implement nondirective language stimulation approaches. Some primary techniques include:

1. Ensuring that family members recognize the infant or toddler's prelinguistic communication signals (e.g., gestures, vocalizations, eye gaze, cries, points, etc.).
2. Helping parents interpret communication signals as conversational "turns" and then provide semantically appropriate responses, such as comments or expansions. For example, if the child reaches for the bottle and vocalizes, does the parent recognize that this was a complex signal? How does the parent respond? Optimally, the parent will interpret the child's intention and put the child's idea into words (e.g., "Oh, you want more milk. Here's your bottle.").
3. Facilitating the establishment of conversational turn-taking between primary interactants and the child. Are family members following the child's interest and conversational lead? How does the child respond when family members follow his lead? What activities promote extended turn taking?
4. Helping parents consider the need to contrive developmentally appropriate opportunities for the child to respond to auditory stimuli in the environment. When the child responds to meaningful sounds, how does the family react? Do they comment on the child's observation and give the sound a name? Do they take the child to the sound and reinforce that it is the source of the sound?
5. Guiding the parents in taking advantage of everyday occurrences to expose the child to relevant language concepts. What language concepts occur naturally and are of interest to the child? What is the child curious about? Primary language targets become evident from observing typical interactions and also from following the child's interest lead.
6. Guiding family members to provide the words for what a child is trying to express. This involves helping family members to be accurate interpreters of the child's message and then providing the verbal model for that message.
7. Helping family members develop positive ways to secure and maintain the child's visual attention. Joint attention on objects is positively correlated with

vocabulary acquisition in young children. Some evidence suggests that hearing mothers may not always use the most facilitative strategies for securing joint attention on objects. Deaf mothers of children who are deaf have been observed to implement effective strategies in this regard. Further study of approaches by parents who are deaf would provide useful input for working with parents with normal hearing.

8. Helping family members use parallel talk strategies that describe what the child is doing, seeing or thinking while experiencing an event.

9. Guiding parents in strategies for encouraging cognitive and sensorimotor play skills within communicative routines. Parents should learn to encourage the early pretend skills of the toddler, mapping language onto these accomplishments.

A comprehensive summary of methods for establishing effective parent/child communication is included in Table 9.4.

Several resources are useful in helping family members implement an indirect language stimulation approach. One was developed at the Hanen Early Language Resource Centre in Toronto for children with speech and language delay. The program provides inservice training to professionals and distributes a parent guidebook entitled, *It Takes Two to Talk* (Manolson, 1985). This program can be very useful to clinicians in encouraging developmentally appropriate interactions with infants. Curricular materials for guiding parents and professional training are also available from the Infant Hearing Resource (Parent/Infant Communication, Schuyler & Sowers, 1998) and from Project SKI-HI (Watkins & Clark, 1993). Also, Infant Hearing Resource recently published a guidebook with videotapes called "For Families." This material is especially useful and practical for guiding early listening and communication.

For those children who begin to use signs, families are in need of access to sign classes and materials. Two videocassette family sign programs for families of young children are currently available. One was produced by the SKI-HI Institute and is available from Home Oriented Program Essentials, 1856 North 1200 East, Logan, Utah, 84341. A more recent program has been developed at Boys Town National Research Hospital. This video program entitled, *Sign with Me: A Family Sign Program* (SWM) focuses on the sign communication needs of parents of children who are deaf, ages birth through three years. SWM is available from Boys Town Press, 13603 Flanagan Blvd., Boys Town, Nebraska, 68010 402-498-651. It includes focus on signing skills, parenting principles and language stimulation strategies. It is being produced in both American Sign Language and Manually Coded English versions. Parents receive supplemental workbooks with the videotapes that provide additional guidance in parenting principles and language stimulation techniques. This program specifically targets helping parents develop a signing style that is consistent with a visual equivalent of motherese. The tapes also include comprehension tests, using a variety of sign models, including children.

Families involved in signing programs often desire and benefit from opportunities to learn about deaf culture. Furthermore, many parents are seeking resources and support for learning American Sign Language (ASL). The SKI-HI Institute has developed and tested Deaf Mentor Programming, which enables family members

"Motherese" or "parentese" are terms used to describe the baby talk that parents use when they talk to a young infant. Adults make a number of modifications to their speech (e.g., shorter, simpler ideas with higher pitch and varied intonation), which are believed to support infants' language development.

TABLE 9.4	
Some Methods for Parents to Establish Effective Communication with Their Child Who Is Deaf or Hard of Hearing	

Identify the child's early use of signals and respond interactively	Understand the importance of early communication and how babies learn to communicate Identify child's early communication Respond to child's early communication Use interactive turn-taking Respond appropriately to child's cry Encourage smiling and laughing in early interactions Give child choices Utilize daily routines for communication
Optimize daily communication in the home	Minimize distracting noises Get close to child and on child's level Establish eye contact and direct conversation to child Provide a safe, stimulating communication environment Communicate frequently with child each day
Optimize parent communication with child in early interactions	Understand how parents communicate to babies and young children Increase the "back and forth" exchanges in turn-taking Encourage vocalization in communicative interactions Use touch and gestures in communicative interactions Use facial expressions and intonation in communicative interactions Interact with child about meaningful here-and-now experiences; make an experience book

Source: The SKI-HI Model: A Resource Manual for Family-centered Home-based Programming for Infants, Toddlers, and Pre-School Children with Hearing Impairments (S. Watkins and T. Clark, 1993, p. 262). Used with permission.

to learn American Sign Language and to learn about deaf culture. The program utilizes the services of adults who are deaf as mentors and models of the language and culture of the deaf. These Deaf Mentors make regular visits to the home, interact with the child using ASL, show family members how to use ASL, and help the family understand and appreciate deafness and deaf culture. Meanwhile, the family continues to receive visits from a parent advisor who focuses on helping the parents promote English acquisition in the young child who is deaf. In this way, the family and child use both English and ASL and participate comfortably in both the hearing and deaf worlds. A variety of Deaf Mentor materials are currently being developed at the SKI-HI Institute, including guides for teaching families ASL, information on deaf culture, and Deaf Mentor Program operation guides. An array of data has been obtained on the children and families receiving Deaf Mentor Programming. These data were compared with data on children who were not receiving bilingual–bicultural programming. Children receiving this early bilingual–bicultural (bi–bi) Deaf Mentor programming made greater language gains during treatment time, had considerably larger vocabularies, and scored higher on measures of communication, language, and English syntax than the matched children who did not receive this

Shared Reading Project

An innovative and practical program developed by David Schleper (1996) at Gallaudet University has supported hearing parents who want to incorporate ASL and/or visual principles into their communication with young children. The Shared Reading Project (SRP) is designed to support deaf children's literacy development through the provision of fluent models of storytelling. Deaf individuals are trained to go into family homes and coach the parents in visual methods for sharing books with their young children. This innovative program has been implemented through support from Gallaudet in several states across the United States. A most innovative application has been developed in the state of Washington through the efforts of Nancy Hatfield and Howie Seago. In this application, the SRP is brought to families throughout the state through videoconferencing technology. Information on this approach may be found at www.srvop.org.

programming (Watkins, Pittman, & Walden, 1998). Data on program operation, service satisfaction from persons involved in the program, and cost effectiveness also were obtained (Watkins, Pittman, & Walden, 1996).

Hatfield and Humes (1994) also describe a parent–infant program that has incorporated a bilingual–bicultural model, and Busch and Halpin (1994) describe an approach to incorporating deaf culture into the early-intervention program. Many professionals and deaf persons stress the importance of considering the natural ways that American Sign Language, a visual-spatial language, is organized and the potential advantages this language organization may have for the young learner who is deaf.

These approaches are useful because parents with normal hearing need considerable support to develop good communication with their children who are deaf through the visual mode.

According to Moeller, Schick, and Williams (1994) good communication should include the following:

1. Developing a lexicon that allows parents to sign simple, conversational phrases to the young child.
2. Developing fluency and prosody in their signing, following principles of visual motherese, used by parents and children, both of whom are deaf.
3. Developing parents' ability to understand a range of signers, including children.
4. Developing parents' ability to sign at a level more complex and diverse than the child's, and participate in contingent, nondirective interactions with the child.
5. Learning to tell stories in an animated, fluent fashion.
6. Maintaining the child's visual attention.

SPEECH STIMULATION: PARENT–INFANT AND PRESCHOOL. We believe that children in parent–infant programs should not receive formal speech training, which typically involves drill and correction. Instead, we believe parents and professionals should be aware of the general sequence in which speech sounds emerge and then provide extensive modeling of speech at a level that encourages children to move to the next stage of development. An excellent source on speech development for children who are

[Margin notes:]

Fluency of sign refers to the smoothness, accuracy, and flow of movement from one sign to the next. Prosody relates to the ways a signer segments thought units and stresses certain ideas in the message.

Contingent responses are those that relate to the child's idea or follow the child's communicative lead. Nondirective interactions are those that refrain from controlling the interaction through commands and questions. Instead, the parent follows the child's lead.

Preschool Language Stimulation Strategies

1. *Children should be regarded as active learners, not passive recipients of information.* Clinicians need to recognize that children bring to tasks past experiences, knowledge, and assumptions that contribute to learning. By exploiting children's background knowledge during lessons, clinicians help children to construct new knowledge in a mentally active manner. This can happen through provision of choices, teacher-guided questioning, and opportunities to solve problems (see Moeller & Carney, 1993, for further discussion).

2. *Children who are deaf or hard of hearing typically benefit from a systematic approach to vocabulary development.* Typically, developing children access word meanings and experiential knowledge through overhearing the conversations of others. Children with hearing loss may have less access to this path for developing word and world knowledge. Therefore, vocabulary development approaches that seek to expand world knowledge and build connections between new and established words are useful with this population. Yoshinaga-Itano and Downey (1986) describe such an approach.

3. *Developmentally appropriate practices should be at the foundation of any program serving preschoolers.* Guidelines from the National Association for the Education of Young Children are included in Table 9.5 (Bredekamp, 1987).

4. *Question asking should be a priority goal with children who are deaf and hard of hearing.* For all children, language serves as a powerful tool for accessing information and making discoveries about the world. One of the most frequent verbalizations of a 4-year-old is "Why?" Children who are deaf or hard of hearing are equally curious. If children with hearing loss are encountering difficulty forming questions, they benefit from supportive contexts, modeling, and multiple opportunities to participate in question asking. Activities and routines that purposely provoke curiosity are ideal.

5. *Question understanding is also a priority so that children benefit from classroom discourse routines that guide thinking.* In quality preschool programs, many teachers use collaborative learning methods within learning centers. During explorative activities, teachers use questions to elicit observations and guide children's thinking and discovery. A useful classroom discourse model for developing children's ability to respond to questions of increasing abstraction was developed by Blank, Rose, and Berlin (1978). Emphasis on answering increasingly abstract questions helps to develop children's verbal reasoning skills.

6. Quality preschool programs recognize that language (whether oral, signed, or written) is a tool for conveying meanings and for communicating purposefully. Language "lessons," then, need to be integrated in pragmatically appropriate contexts that have communicative value.

7. *Thematic or literature-based units can be a useful way to present concepts and vocabulary in an organized manner with relevant topical links.* Themes should be developmentally appropriate, interesting, and relevant to the child's communicative needs.

8. *Opportunities for exploration through play should be provided regularly.* Children learn thinking, language, and social skills through playful exploration. Adults can guide children's learning during play by using thought provoking questions, by pointing out or instigating problems in need of solution, and by helping the child to make and express choices. Children benefit from a play process that includes (a) opportunities to learn to verbally plan prior to playing, (b) support from adult play partners in the form of descriptive comments,

Children are not passive learners. They actively construct meaning by testing out ideas, manipulating materials, asking questions, and making discoveries.

> problem-solving opportunities, and questions, and (c) a period devoted to verbally recall-
> ing what happened during play (Hohmann, Banet, & Weikart, 1979).
>
> **9.** Children benefit in many ways from exposure to quality children's literature. Story-
> telling should be a daily curricular component. Exposure to stories helps children expand
> upon event knowledge (scripts), develop a notion of story grammar, and prepare for future
> literacy tasks. There are many indications in the literature that children who are read to with
> regularity at home become the most literate. Parents should be actively involved in the
> storytelling program. The *Sign with Me* curriculum described above includes storytelling
> demonstration tapes called "Read with Me" for signing parents (Snow, 1983).
>
> **10.** Children at the preschool level benefit from exposure to early literacy opportuni-
> ties. These include reading books and being read to, demonstrating knowledge about
> books (e.g., book handling, reading pictures, recognizing environmental print), beginning to
> recognize simple print forms, being exposed to functional uses of print, and having oppor-
> tunities to explore with written symbols.

deaf or hard of hearing is *Speech and the Hearing Impaired Child* (Ling, 1976). Another useful source, by Cole (1992), is *Listening and Talking: A Guide to Promoting
Spoken Language in Young Hearing-impaired Children.*

Oller (1983) has identified stages in normally developing infants' vocal development, that are useful to consider. From birth to two months, infants are in a *phonation stage,* where they produce comfort sounds that may be precursors to vowel

---

TABLE 9.5

Guidelines for Developmentally Appropriate Practices

1. The clinician or teacher prepares the learning environment and plans activities to promote discoveries and exploration.
2. Content and strategies presented are age appropriate.
3. Curriculum techniques are adjusted to respond to children's learning style, personality, or cultural background.
4. Child-initiated, but adult-supported play is primary vehicle of encouraging developmental growth in all domains.
5. Developmental and learning domains are integrated within the curriculum (e.g. motor, social, language, cognitive, emotional).
6. Learning materials are concrete, real, and relevant to the experiences of young children.
7. Learning materials are presented at various developmental levels to interest and challenge children. They are non-sexist and reflect cultural diversity.
8. Play materials allow for sensorimotor, symbolic, and constructive play.
9. Adults are responsive and comforting. They encourage independence and treat children with respect and dignity.
10. Adults use discipline techniques that guide children to learn self-control, redirect children to use more acceptable behaviors to resolve conflict, and remind children of rules.

Source: Adapted from Bredekamp, 1987.

production. At this stage, syllables with consonants or vowels are rare. Infants enter a *cooing stage* during the 2- to 3-month period. They produce comfort sounds often articulated in the back of the oral cavity. These are not well formed, mature syllabic productions. Next is the expansion stage (4 to 6 months). Infants at this stage produce various new sound types, like squeals, growls, yells, whispers, and a variety of isolated vowel sounds with occasional vowel tract closure, making simple consonant vowel syllables, and forming "marginal" babbling. Mature syllables are not yet evident, though. The next stage is considered to be a developmental landmark, and is called the *canonical stage* (7 to 10 months). At this point, infants produce well-formed, reduplicated syllables like /mamama/ or /dadada/. This is considered to be a critical stage, as these syllables function as phonetic building blocks of words. Nonreduplicated canonical utterances (e.g., /bi/, /ada/, /imi/) are also heard frequently at this stage. The period of 11 to 12 months brings about the variegated babbling stage. Here, infants systematically produce utterances with differing consonantal or vocalic elements. Useful clinical systems for transcribing and studying infant vocalizations have been described by Stoel-Gammon and Cooper (1984).

In most cases, infants who are deaf or hard of hearing spontaneously produce some vocalizations. Parents should encourage the child to develop an abundance of vocalizations by being responsive to the child's vocal attempts (Ling, 1989). Parents can respond by smiling, moving closer to the child, interpreting the vocal attempt communicatively, and imitating the child (Cole, 1992).

Parents can also encourage the child's initial vocalizations by providing animated models of vocalizing during active play with the child.

> Marginal babbling develops in the period from 4 to 6 months and occurs when the baby produces simple consonant–vowel (cv) syllables. Canonical babble includes strings of repetitive syllables (e.g., /bababab/) and emerges between 7 and 10 months of age.

As the child is being gently bounced on the parent's knee, the parent can say /up-up-up/. Vocalizations like /a-boo; a-boo/ would be appropriate during a peek-a-boo game. Parents should be encouraged to respond warmly to reinforce any early accidental vocalizations. At the expansion and canonical babbling stages, parents can reinforce the child's vocal exploration by imitating and modeling interesting auditory patterns. The parent can say, "You said up-up-up! Let's ride horsey up-up-up the hill." For the older infant, new sounds can be imitated and then repeated in syllable chains and then used in simple words ("/ha-ha-ha/— yes, that is HOT!").

Parents should encourage the infant's development of early suprasegmental aspects of speech. Breath control can be developed through playful duration games, where the child is encouraged to vocalize long or short sounds (e.g., vocalizing /u:/ while the sand pours out of a container).

Intensity and pitch control can be developed in play where the child is encouraged to make soft and loud (e.g., whisper while the baby doll sleeps; make a loud voice to wake her up) and high and low sounds. Speech rhythms can be learned by encouraging the child to participate in play activities in which speech tempos are produced slowly and quickly (e.g., during a horsey-back ride, the movement and the sound can be contrasted from slow to fast repetitions).

At the preschool level, children often benefit from a goal-oriented approach to speech development. This process begins with a comprehensive analysis of the child's speech-production skills to determine appropriate intervention targets. This might include a phonologically-based assessment (e.g., Test of Phonology; Bankson & Bernthal, 1990), an articulation test, or a procedure specifically designed for deaf and hard of hearing students (Ling, 1976). The decision about which type of assessment to use depends on the diagnostic questions of the clinician and the skill level and residual hearing of the child. For some children who are hard of hearing, for example, a developmental phonological process approach can be very useful. Whatever tools are chosen, the clinician should be well informed about the typical characteristics of speech in children with hearing loss.

> A comprehensive appraisal of speech should include assessment of (1) functional auditory skills; (2) phonetic level skills; (3) phonological skills; (4) suprasegmental and vocal behaviors; (5) stimulability for sound production or emergence of skills; and (6) speech intelligibility.

Often an oral mechanism assessment is valuable. In our opinion, the speech assessment should not rely solely on imitative productions, but should examine spontaneous productions and extent of carryover, as well.

When working on speech, AR clinicians should encourage the child to rely as much as possible on residual hearing.

A thorough discussion of the many speech training approaches is beyond the scope of this chapter. Speech development should always be viewed within the broader context of communication, with emphasis on speech generalization and carryover. See Chapter 6 of this book for a discussion of various speech management approaches.

A task has complex cognitive and linguistic demands when it challenges the child to think abstractly and to respond by understanding or using complex language forms.

Too often, speech training materials are presented at a basic level. They require labeling of pictures or creating simple ideas from pictured stimuli. Children may have difficulty with carryover of speech skills when tasks are abstract and demand a lot of their mental attention. Training materials that incorporate increasingly complex cognitive–linguistic demands will help children to generalize. At the same time, the child is working on materials useful for language and cognitive development. When the child is ready, approaches that integrate several levels of goals are both useful and expedient.

COUNSELING AND PSYCHOSOCIAL ASPECTS. During the early years of the child's life, the psychosocial aspects of the hearing deficit are, for a great part, related to the parents as the primary caregivers and teachers. Parenthood is a great challenge for all fathers and mothers. The added responsibility of having a child with hearing impairment enhances this challenge in various degrees and ways.

Needs of Parents. Psychosocial support is vital for the parents of infants with hearing impairment. Mindel and Vernon (1987) wrote that "unless parents' emotional needs are attended to, the programs for young hearing handicapped children have limited benefit" (p. 23).

Concepts Common to Recommended Speech Training Approaches for Children with Hearing Impairment

1. The speech training program should exploit the use of residual hearing to the fullest extent possible. Auditory and speech development should be closely integrated in this process.

2. Adult expectations can have a significant impact on a child's development of speech. In the classroom and at home, children benefit from regular encouragement to rely on speech to the best of their abilities. This should not be implemented to the degree that it interferes with communication. However, adults need to recognize the value of regular, brief practice opportunities in natural contexts (Ling, 1976) and the value of high expectations.

3. Many programs find that collaborative consultation models work well for integrating speech into the classroom. The speech–language clinician or AR clinician works closely with the preschool classroom teacher to determine how speech intervention targets can be incorporated naturally in classroom activities. Consultants can assist the teacher in maintaining appropriate and challenging expectations for speech and auditory skill development in the classroom. Although individual speech intervention is often valuable, there may be problems with generalization and carryover if speech is not emphasized in natural routines and contexts. A collaborative team approach can be very effective in accomplishing the goal of generalization of speech skills.

4. For some children with limited or no residual hearing, speech acquisition can be difficult and tedious. It is essential that the AR clinician provide intervention goals that are achievable and functional, and that they be presented in fun, motivating lessons that are supportive of the child.

5. Speech development should always be viewed within the broader context of communication. Speech generalization and carryover are critical steps in intervention. Carotta, Carney, and Dettman (1990) discussed a systematic plan for carryover of speech targets that involved the gradual inclusion of the target in increasingly abstract and cognitively demanding contexts. Using the preschool discourse model described earlier (Blank et al., 1978), they proposed a series of activities that took the child through a progression from cognitively simple to cognitively challenging language contexts. For example, if the child was working on a vowel like /au/, the sound would be included in phonologically based activities in the following manner:

   a. Matching perception (simplest level of abstraction)
     Name objects seen in a bag (cow, mouse, towel)
   b. Selective analysis of perception
     Name something that is . . . (attentive to one or two categorical characteristics).
     Example: Name an animal (cow, mouse)
     Example: Name something little and brown (mouse)
   c. Reordering perception
     Identify similarities: How are a cow and a mouse the same?
   d. Reasoning about perception
     Forming a solution from another person's perspective
     The man saw a nail sticking out of the house. What should he do? (pound the nail; sit down and pout)

During the child's early years, the parent advisor is often the key person in enabling families to understand hearing loss and deal creatively and positively with the child. Because over 90% of children who are deaf or hard of hearing have parents with normal hearing, these parents typically have had little or no experience with deafness. Although family members may not know much about deafness, they have hopes and dreams for their child, and they have many concerns and questions. Often family members are confused and surprised by the variety of emotions they experience by having a family member who is deaf or hard of hearing. The competent parent advisor is able to listen to family members sensitively and with more care, interact with them, and provide needed support, information, and skills.

One of the most valuable contributions the parent advisor can make to the family is to gently and gradually help the family understand and appreciate deafness. Rather than perceiving deafness as a "pathology," a "problem," or "something to be feared," parent advisors can help families to see deafness as a unique human experience that may include linguistic and cultural aspects. Perhaps the very best way for families to understand and appreciate deafness is to interact with deaf persons themselves. The Deaf Mentor Program at the SKI-HI Institute provides the opportunity for families to interact regularly with adults who are deaf (Deaf Mentors).

Of course, the process of understanding and appreciating deafness and the situation of having a child who is deaf is gradual. For most parents with normal hearing the initial reaction to the diagnosis of deafness includes shock, denial, and confusion. Parents have wished for and expected a "normal" child. Now their dreams are shattered, and they feel devastated and helpless. The shock has numbed them into a state of immobility. They may be unable to assimilate what information is given them. Sometimes, after learning the diagnosis for the first time, parents are utterly and literally lost, unable even to locate their cars in the parking lot.

After the initial shock, denial, and confusion stage, some parents experience anger, depression, and guilt: "Why me?" Luterman (1987) noted:

> Anger comes from a violation of expectations. Parents have many expectations about their unborn children, not the least of which is that they will be normal. When they find that the child does not hear normally and cannot be cured, they feel cheated and wonder why they were singled out. (p. 42)

Anger also results from loss of control of personal freedom. Parents may experience a kind of aesthetic disavowal of the child with hearing impairment as they envision the restrictions the child may impose on their plans for the future. Anger also results from not knowing how to help the child. In addition to anger, parents often experience strong guilt feelings, manifested by overindulging the child who has hearing impairment, or placing excessive demands on him. If these findings of guilt and despair are not resolved, parents begin an unending search for a "magic cure" by a doctor who will deny the difficulty or the location of the "best" school.

This period of anger, depression, and guilt can be followed by a time of withdrawal, solitude, and introspection. As parents learn about deafness and interact with persons who are deaf, they come to see that these people reside, work, produce, and lead normal lives in society. Arrival at this stage does not preclude con-

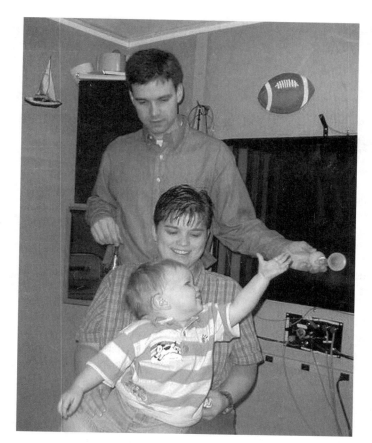

When parents have to accept that their child has a hearing loss, it can be helpful if they watch the hearing tests and observe first-hand the sounds their children can hear and cannot hear.

tinued problems and adjustments. On the contrary, as new crises surface, as new programs, new medical problems arise, parents may go through additional emotional adjustments.

Gradually, most parents come to see that their child has a future and they begin to accept the disability. Acceptance of the disability leads the parents back to the feelings they were experiencing toward their child before the diagnosis of deafness. The duration of each stage depends upon the parents. Some stages may pass in a matter of minutes, others may last for months or years, and, as indicated, the parents may reexperience some of the stages later in their lives. Generally, however, parents go through the stages just described. (See Chapter 7 for additional detail. There, this period is divided into four stages: shock, denial, depression, and acceptance.)

SUPPORT FOR PARENTS. It is the responsibility of the parent advisor first and foremost to convey positive attitudes and perceptions about deafness to family members. Deaf adults (mentors) are invaluable in enabling families to understand and appreciate deafness. For parents experiencing the stages of grief described above, the parent advisor will want to sensitively help the parents deal with these stages. The parent advisor will not want to hurry parents through the stages or encourage avoidance of them; rather, parents should be skillfully, but gently, helped to progress from one stage to the next. The following discussion offers some suggestions as to how this may be accomplished. (See also case examples, Chapter 11.)

During the first stage, which is characterized by confusion and denial, the parent advisor–audiologic rehabilitationist establishes contact with the family. This is done immediately after the diagnosis of a hearing loss. The professional's role is to offer emotional support and realistic hope. The parent advisor explains programs that will involve all family members and how these programs will help the child who is deaf or hard of hearing.

During the next stage, anger and depression, the parent advisor may erroneously try to counteract the parents' emotions by helping them feel less depressed. At this period, the parent advisor needs to exhibit genuine understanding and good listening skills rather than attempt to talk the parents out of their feelings (Moses, 1985).

The effective parent advisor contributes greatly to the third stage, that of quietude and introspection. It is during this time that parents usually open up and ask questions about the future of their child, educational considerations, and society's perception of them and of their youngster. Perhaps the most important contribution the parent advisor can make during this stage is to plan with the parents constructive activities for family members that help the child's listening, communicative, and language abilities. When the parents see the child responding, growing, and learning, acceptance occurs. They realize they have a child who can be taught and loved just like any other child.

CONSULTATION BETWEEN PSYCHOLOGIST AND AR THERAPIST. Some parents do not move easily through the stages just outlined. On the way they may have problems: unrealistic expectations for the child, overprotection, rejection, or confusion over conflicting information about educational methods. They may have problems with general childrearing practices, such as discipline and sibling rivalry. The parent advisor may need special help from psychologists or social workers in dealing with these problems. Sessions can be set up between the parent advisor and the psychologist or social worker for this purpose. The psychologist or social worker can offer suggestions that can in turn be tried by the parent advisor in the home or discussed with the family as appropriate. For parents who want psychological counseling, the AR therapist should act as facilitator and ensure such therapy is arranged.

NEEDS OF AND SUPPORT FOR THE CHILD. Successful resolution of parental anxieties, warm acceptance of the child who is deaf, and establishment of communication with the child promote normal psychosocial development. However, the child may also present social, emotional, or psychological problems. Consequently, the therapist must have a knowledge of what to expect from the child with hearing impairment in these developmental areas.

Development scales established by Vincent et al. (1986) and others enable professionals to know what behaviors a child should exhibit at a particular age (see re-

> ## Support Group Meetings
>
> Another invaluable way of giving psychosocial support to parents is to arrange parent group meetings. "There is probably no greater gift that a professional can give to families than to provide them with a support group. Groups are marvelous vehicles for learning and emotional support" (Luterman, 1987, p. 113). Support group meetings are part of many early-intervention programs. Often eight or nine meetings are held, once a week, with a psychologist or social worker in charge. The first part of each meeting often consists of a presentation by a professional. Such topics as Language Development, Communication Methods, Development of Self-concept, and Making the Home Environment Responsive can be discussed. The last part of each meeting is devoted to group interaction. Luterman (1987) described the benefits of support group interactions: (1) They enable members to recognize the universality of their feelings; members come to appreciate that others in the group have similar feelings; (2) they give participants the opportunity to help one another; and (3) they become a powerful vehicle for imparting information.
>
> Parents are great sources of help and comfort to other parents. In attending support group meetings we have been constantly impressed with the amount of help and moral support parents give each other. Inclusion of adults who are deaf in support groups is highly recommended. Such adults can describe their experiences of being deaf and answer questions about deafness that professionals with normal hearing simply cannot do.

source website). The audiologic rehabilitationist observes the child's behaviors and determines what age levels they typify. In addition to developmental scales, the therapist should arrange for appropriate developmental and psychosocial assessments for the child. These tests should be administered by competent psychologists who are familiar with hearing-impaired children. According to Davis (1990), this may be difficult since "most psychologists receive little or no training in testing or working with hearing-impaired children" (p. 36).

If the child is lagging in a specific area, the audiologic rehabilitationist can seek help from other professionals such as child development specialists, psychologists, social workers, occupational and physical therapists, pediatricians, and nurses.

ASPECTS OF AUDIOLOGIC REHABILITATION:
■ SCHOOL YEARS

Rehabilitation Assessment: IEP Meeting

Public law stipulates that primary and secondary school placements must be based on assessments of the child, which are reviewed in an individualized educational program (IEP) meeting (see Chapter 8). The IEP meetings serve to develop, review, or revise educational program goals for the student. The AR therapist is responsible for completing an appropriate assessment prior to the IEP meeting. The AR therapist working with the school-age student may be an educational audiologist,

An individual educational plan (IEP) is a document developed for each student receiving special education services in the schools. Required by law, this document includes specific objectives and progress indicators.

an educator of the hearing impaired, a speech–language clinician, or some other professional charged with the responsibility of coordinating components of the child's educational support services. Assessment of the school-age child includes the four general areas described in the AR model presented in Chapter 1:

1. Communication status, including audiologic and amplification issues, receptive and expressive language, and social communication skills.
2. Overall participation variables of academic achievement, psychosocial adaptation, and prevocational and vocational skills.
3. Related personal factors.
4. Environmental factors.

In many cases, multi-disciplinary input is valuable in gaining a comprehensive understanding of student needs. Assessment guidelines are available in Moeller (1988) and Alpiner and McCarthy (2000). Consistent with the goal of ecologically valid assessment practices, it is useful to include a classroom observation and/or teacher questionnaires regarding the student's performance in that setting. As the section on communication rehabilitation stresses, classroom communication behaviors are unique and complex. Many standardized tests do not reflect the kinds of language skills that are required in the classroom setting. Therefore, observations in that setting and teacher impressions offer invaluable insights for the IEP The SIFTER (Screening Instrument for Targeting Educational Risk; see resource website) is an example of an efficient tool for recruiting teachers' impressions of the student's performance in relation to her peers. A member of the assessment team or a representative of the team who is familiar with the results of the assessment (often the audiologic rehabilitationist) must attend the IEP meeting along with the teacher, parents and child, as appropriate. Based on the educational recommendations from the child's IEP, the AR therapist proceeds to arrange for or provide the needed services. Excellent guidelines for comprehensive service provision have been published by the National Association for State Directors of Special Education. You can obtain these guidelines, developed by the deaf initiatives project, by writing: Deaf Guidelines Document, c/o National Association of State Directors of Special Education, 1800 Diagonal Road, Suite 320, Alexandria, Virginia 22314.

Management

ENVIRONMENTAL COORDINATION AND PARTICIPATION. As a part of the overall coordination, the therapist is responsible for maximizing the child's learning environment (classroom), assisting in securing ancillary services, promoting development of social skills, and arranging for special college preparation or occupational training. If the primary educational programming is delivered by someone other than the AR therapist (e.g., the teacher), the therapist needs to assume a supporting role and assist the teacher in these areas.

CHILD LEARNING ENVIRONMENT (CLASSROOM MANAGEMENT). School placement alternatives are necessary so that the best educational setting can be selected. For the older child, additional placement options are available beyond those listed for the preschool child.

> ## Placement Options
>
> The range of options includes (1) integration into public schools with ancillary services like speech therapy; (2) day school or day classes for the hearing impaired; (3) resource rooms where the child with hearing impairment learns communication skills and is integrated into regular classrooms for less language-oriented subjects, such as math and physical education; (4) residential school placement; and (5) team-taught combined classes of normal and hearing-impaired youngsters. (See Chapter 8 on school placement alternatives for a discussion of these options.)

The audiologic rehabilitationist is responsible for informing the child's teachers of the conditions that will optimize learning; that is, seating, lighting, visual aids, and reduction of classroom noises. Helpful guides for teachers who have children with hearing impairment in their classrooms have been written (see also Appendix). In addition, the therapist should ensure that an appropriate student–teacher ratio is maintained.

The AR therapist should also promote home and school coordination. Cooperation can be facilitated by regular conferences between parents and teachers, periodic visits to the home by the teacher, notes, newsletters, and special student work sent home to the parents, telephone conversations, and allowing parents to participate in classroom activities.

ANCILLARY SERVICES. The therapist may also need to help set up ancillary services required for the hearing-impaired child. Services like otologic assessments and treatment; occupational or physical therapy; medical exams and treatment; social services; and neurologic, ophthalmologic, and psychological services are important components of the welfare of a child with hearing impairment. Finally, secondary students with hearing impairment in public school programs may require the services of notetakers or interpreters.

DEVELOPMENT OF SOCIAL SKILLS. In a study of 40 mainstreamed students with hearing impairment, Davis et al. (1986) found a high incidence of social problems, including peer acceptance difficulties. Over 50% of the students with hearing impairment expressed concerns with peer relations, in contrast to 16% of similar concerns expressed by hearing students. The authors stressed the need for increased attention by school programs to the development of positive self-esteem and social interactions in students with hearing impairment. The AR clinician should monitor the social adjustment of the student with hearing impairment and make appropriate referrals as needed. The school counselor or other mental health professional can be supportive in addressing the social integration of the student. Refinement of social language skills can also be supportive of this goal area.

AUDIBILITY, AMPLIFICATION, AND ASSISTIVE DEVICE ISSUES. If children obtain their hearing aids during the early intervention period and go through the adjustment and orientation steps described earlier in this chapter, they have a good start on dealing with amplification concerns. However, this area requires a continued focus, since new amplification needs or problems may arise when children enter school. Regular hearing aid reassessment at 6-month to 1-year intervals and daily monitoring of the aid by school personnel should occur. Unfortunately, such regular monitoring is often neglected. Therefore, audiologic rehabilitation personnel need to be vigilant in this area (see Chapter 8). The major deficit for these children is their impaired hearing. Therefore, the most obvious management is to restore as much of that hearing through amplification devices and excellent acoustic listening conditions as possible. In this manner, we may remove the need for some therapy that would otherwise be required.

Daily hearing aid monitoring is an essential, but often neglected, practice.

HEARING AIDS. Some children with hearing impairment are not identified until they reach school, and some of them receive their first amplification attention at this time. As indicated in the section on early intervention, when children with hearing losses are identified, they should also be evaluated medically and audiologically. After specific assessment information has been obtained, the way is cleared for carefully evaluating the place of amplification in the overall management program. Children with mild or more serious losses in the speech frequencies should proceed with a hearing-aid assessment, and additional audiologic rehabilitation can assist them in hearing-aid orientation aspects, as described previously.

Children with slight losses, high-frequency losses, or chronic conductive losses present a more difficult problem in terms of amplification. A careful assessment of such children's language and speech status and a report on their ability to function in the classroom will help determine whether they can function successfully without amplification. Preferential seating can provide some help, but this is, at best, an imperfect and perhaps only temporary solution. Some have recommended fitting hearing aids on children with chronic conductive losses and have shown

Successful hearing aid fitting is based on gathering accurate audiologic information, which can be a challenging activity with young children.

that it is a feasible alternative (Northern & Downs, 1991). Another possible solution is temporary use of FM amplification devices until the hearing problems are resolved. Such units may also be used for children with slight sensorineural losses. However, when a hearing aid can be fitted comfortably, it is generally better to fit children with sensorineural losses with aid(s) while they are younger. As they get older, they tend to become more concerned about the unfortunate social stigma associated with amplification devices. In contrast, children who use amplification from an early age know how much it can help them and are less likely to part company with it as they get older. Nevertheless, getting children to use their hearing aid(s) on a regular basis may be one of the greatest challenges faced by the AR therapist.

Teachers and parents and, later, the child himself can provide information on how regularly the hearing aid is used. The therapist should seek out this information and try to modify behavior when necessary. Young children will often respond to methods like public charting of their daily hearing aid use. The child can be made responsible for the charting. Older children should understand the purpose for amplification. When they are old enough, therefore, they need to receive the same instruction and information about their hearing loss as their parents were given previously. (See Amplification/Assistive Devices under Early Intervention in this chapter.)

Full-time use of an aid is preferable, in part because the child is less likely to forget or lose the instrument. With older children, however, it is sometimes unrealistic. In the case of mild loss, the aid may provide little, if any, benefit in many play or recreational circumstances. The teenager, therefore, may elect not to use the aid during these times. The audiologic rehabilitationist may help the young person identify the situations where the aid should be used.

As the child gets older, she can begin to assume the responsibility for the care and management of the hearing aid. At that point, the AR therapist should teach the child about hearing aid function, repair, and use (see Chapter 2). Maintenance of children's hearing aids is often neglected, as shown in a series of studies starting with Gaeth and Lounsbury (1966). These writers found that approximately half the hearing aids in their study were not in working order and parents were generally ill informed about the rudiments of aid care. Unfortunately, that situation has not improved appreciably as reflected in subsequent studies, nearly all of which have shown 50% poor function among children's aids (Blair et al., 1981). Furthermore, school programs have been similarly negligent about maintaining children's aids, even though some projects have demonstrated that children's aids may be substantially improved by regular maintenance.

Older children can be taught to take full responsibility for the care and maintenance of their amplification devices, including recognizing times when devices are not functioning properly.

In cases where the child's management skills are deficient due to age or length of experience with the aid, help and instruction should be provided (see Hoverstein, 1981, and Chapter 8 for suggestions).

ASSISTIVE LISTENING DEVICES AND CLASSROOM ACOUSTICS. Other aspects of amplification that become important in the school years include use of classroom amplification systems and the concern for quiet classroom environments. While no knowledgeable person would dispute the importance of quiet conditions for persons with hearing impairment, there has been some controversy about whether school-age youngsters should use educational (FM) auditory systems instead of personal hearing aids.

Personal hearing aids have improved appreciably over the past years so they now provide good fidelity, cosmetic appeal, and often built-in FM systems (see Chapter 2). In addition, they allow good student to student communication and self-monitoring by the child, and in small groups they provide satisfactory amplification for teacher to student communication purposes.

Chapter 2 contains a description of the different types of classroom amplification equipment in use. *FM radio-frequency* systems, used almost exclusively now, allow teacher and students more freedom and flexibility than other systems. Personal systems are used in the majority of cases but increasingly more classrooms are being outfitted with sound field systems wherein between two and four loudspeakers allow all students in the classroom to benefit from an improved auditory signal (Flexer, 1993). These sound field systems have the advantage that they provide improved listening to students with hearing impairment without any stigma, which may be associated with using special equipment that they alone must wear. Personal FM systems may also be used with hearing aids by direct audio hookup and by induction loop transmission. The older forms of classroom amplification, the *standard* or *hard-wire* systems and *induction loop amplification* (ILA) systems, are still used for some special applications. One other device is the *infrared system,* which utilizes light rays for transmission. The infrared system is usable in classes, auditoriums, and public buildings and for personal use and TV watching by some persons with hearing impairment.

> FM radio-frequency amplification systems are commonly used in classroom settings to control the effects of background noise and distance on understanding of the spoken message.

The audiologic rehabilitationist must be knowledgeable about the various types of equipment and must be able to instruct others in daily operation and monitoring. Occasionally, AR professionals will also be asked to recommend the best arrangement for a particular setting. More frequently, they will simply be responsible for regularly evaluating, or getting someone else to evaluate, the function of existing systems. Several sources (Ross, 1987; Bentler, 2000; Johnson et al., 2000) contain thorough discussions of factors that should be considered when evaluating amplification equipment. Suffice it to say that attention should be given to (1) electroacoustic considerations, (2) auditory self-monitoring capability of the units, (3) child-to-child communication potential, (4) signal to noise ratios, (5) binaural reception, and (6) simplicity and stability of operation.

OTHER ASSISTIVE DEVICES. It is important that the youngster with hearing impairment be introduced to other available accessory devices that can be useful in a variety of situations. Such devices include amplifiers for telephone, television, and radio; decoders for television; signal devices for doorbells and alarm clocks; and so forth. These devices are described in Chapter 2. In addition, therapy materials are available to help in familiarization (Castle, 1984).

SOUND TREATMENT. Well-functioning group amplifying systems will be more effective if used in an acoustically treated environment. In this regard, youngsters with hearing impairment with sensorineural losses will have more serious difficulties than the child with normal hearing when noise is present. When all sounds are amplified, it is important to avoid excessive reverberation in the amplified environment. Reverberation occurs when reflected sound is present and added to the original sound. In an unbounded space (anechoic chamber) there is no reverberation. A sound occurs, moves through space, and is absorbed. However, in the usual listening environment like a classroom, sound hits various hard surfaces as it fans out in all directions, and it is reflected back. Consequently, not only the original unreflected sound, but a variety of reflected versions of the sound are present at once. This results in less distinct signals since signals are "smeared" in the time domain.

Reverberation time (RT) is a measure of how long it takes before a sound is reduced by 60 dB once it is turned off. In an anechoic chamber, RT is near 0 seconds. In a typical classroom it is around 1.2 seconds. However, in a sound-treated classroom, one with carpets, acoustical tile, and solid-core doors, the RT can be on the order of 0.4 second. Finitzo-Heiber and Tillman (1978) showed the effect of RT and environmental signal to noise (S/N) ratio. The S/N ratio is a measure of how loud the desired signal (such as a teacher's voice) might be, compared to other random classroom noise. A +12-dB S/N ratio is considered acceptable for children with hearing impairment while +6 S/N and 0 S/N ratios are more typical of ordinary classrooms. As seen in Table 9.6, the speech identification of both children with normal hearing and children with hearing impairment is adversely affected when S/N ratios are poorer and RTs are increased. The performance of the child who is hard of hearing is more adversely affected by poor conditions than it is for children with normal hearing.

In the ordinary classroom, noise levels tend to be about 60 dBA, but in an open classroom they rise to 70 dBA. Gyms and cafeterias have noise levels of 70 to 90

> Reverberation time is a measure of how long it takes for a sound to be reduced by 60 dB once it is turned off. Signal to noise (S/N) ratio measures the level of the teacher's voice in relation to background noise. Both of these characteristics of a room can influence word recognition.

TABLE 9.6

Mean Word Recognition Scores of Normal Hearing and Hearing Impaired Children under a High-fidelity (Loudspeaker) and through an Ear-level Hearing Aid Condition for Various Combinations of Reverberation and S/N Ratios

| | | MEAN WORD RECOGNITION SCORE (%) | | |
| | | NORMAL GROUP (PTA = 0 TO 10 dB) | HEARING IMPAIRED GROUP (PTA = 35 TO 55 dB) | |
Reverberation Time (RT) (sec)	S/N Ratio (dB)	Loudspeaker	Loudspeaker	Hearing Aid
0.4	+12	83	69	60
	+6	71	55	52
	0	48	29	28
1.2	+12	69	50	41
	+6	54	40	27
	0	30	15	11

Source: Adapted from "Room Acoustics' Effects on Monosyllabic Word Discrimination Ability for Normal and Hearing Impaired Children" by T. Finitzo-Heiber and T. Tillman, 1978, *Journal of Speech and Hearing Research, 21*, pp. 440–458.

Barriers

Two commonplace barriers to successful education of deaf and hard of hearing students in regular education settings are the following:

   1. Classroom educators and administrators often underestimate the impact of the child's language problems on academic performance. Because the child who is hard of hearing, for example, may speak well on the surface and carry on conversations effectively, the teacher assumes that the child's language is "intact." Teachers may focus on whether or not the child can "hear" the instruction rather than whether or not the child can effectively process and understand the language of instruction. Blair, Peterson, and Viehweg (1985) documented significant lags in achievement of students with mild hearing impairment by the fourth grade when compared to their grade-mates with normal hearing. Teachers need to become aware of common language weaknesses that will interfere with academic development unless addressed.

   2. Too often, support services are provided in a fragmented fashion.

---

dBA, with high amounts of reverberation. A carpeted classroom with five students and a teacher generates about 40 to 45 dBA of random noise. According to Finitzo-Heiber (1988), since voices at close range average 60 to 65 dBA, the S/N ratio in sound-treated classrooms may be +20 dB if the listener is close to the teacher. If the listener is farther away from the teacher, the signal will get weaker and the S/N ratio will be poorer. In view of poor performance by youngsters who are hard of hearing in noisy conditions (see Table 9.6), it is recommended that class noise levels be 45 dBA for gym and arts and crafts classes, but 30 to 35 dBA in the classrooms where these students spend most of their time. It has also been suggested that noise levels of about 50 dBA may be more feasible. This would allow minimally acceptable S/N ratios of +15 to 20 dB. Reverberation times are easier to reduce than noise levels. Thus, carpeting, acoustical tile, and even commercially available foam sheets may be placed in classrooms to help absorb noise. A feasible goal may be to reduce the RT to 0.3 to 0.4 second. In addition, provisions should be made to keep the child with hearing impairment close to the speaker (teacher). This can be accomplished through use of group amplification (FM) equipment, since the location of the microphone is, in effect, the position at which listening occurs. Extensive rationale and methods for providing sound treatment are available elsewhere (Berg, 1993).

   To summarize, the audiologic rehabilitationist plays a crucial role in providing and encouraging both routine and extensive checks of individual and group amplifying systems and in obtaining adequate sound treatment in the educational setting.

COMMUNICATION AND LANGUAGE STIMULATION: SCHOOL-AGE LEVEL. The goal is for all facets of the child's program to be closely integrated, with the focus of the AR program being on building language skills to support academic success. To accomplish this goal, the AR clinician must be in regular communication with the child's educational team and be aware of the communicative demands of the classroom and the academic curriculum.

School-age students are placed in a variety of educational settings. Yet many students who are deaf and hard of hearing spend some time in inclusive educational environments, where the language demands can be complex. Several premises guide quality practices when serving these students.

1. *Intervention goals should be based on a comprehensive evaluation of a student's individual strengths and areas of need in communication and language.* In designing a comprehensive evaluation for an individual school-age student, the AR clinician should consider the language demands of the classroom and curriculum. Questions similar to the following can be helpful in designing a classroom-relevant evaluation process.

- Does the student understand paragraph-length or story-length conversation?
- Can the student recall facts from information presented by the teacher?
- Does the student understand abstract questions related to the curriculum?
- Is the student able to recall past events in well-organized narratives?
- Does the student take the listener's perspective into account when sharing information?
- Is the student able to use complex language functions efficiently (e.g., persuading someone, making comparisons and contrasts, summarizing ideas, justifying an answer, using cause–effect reasoning)?
- Does the student recognize when she or he does not understand? If so, what strategies are used to seek clarification?
- Does the student have strong vocabulary skills, supported by an extensive world knowledge? How does the student go about learning new words?
- Can the student shift the manner of conversation for different partners (e.g., peer versus person in authority)?
- Is the student able to use complex grammatical forms (e.g., embedded, subordinate clauses)?

Although this is not an exhaustive list, it illustrates the process of probing the kinds of language skills that are typically challenged in school environments. Formal tests need to be supplemented with informal procedures and language sampling in order to examine some of these issues.

2. *Intervention should focus on skills that will support the student's functioning in the classroom* (Wallach & Miller, 1988). The following example illustrates this point. For a student who relies on residual hearing, AR often focuses on auditory skill training. Clinicians sometimes present isolated auditory discrimination activities. It is unclear how such training might generalize to the classroom setting. The AR clinician can support classroom functioning by focusing on skills that lead toward *successful classroom listening behaviors.* Examples include

1. listening for the main idea in a paragraph,
2. drawing a conclusion from several details,
3. making comments relevant to the remarks of other students in a discussion, and
4. recognizing when a critical piece of information has been missed and appropriately seeking clarification.

It can be helpful to observe the student in the classroom and/or request input from the teacher on the student's listening habits.

3. *School-age students often need opportunities to expand their world knowledge and link new vocabulary words to existing knowledge.* Delays and gaps in vocabulary and word knowledge are common in students with hearing loss. Vocabulary delays can interfere with reading comprehension and with understanding of academic discussions. It is not sufficient to teach new words in isolation (e.g., sending home a list of unrelated spelling words to be practiced and memorized). Rather, students need support in building networks of associated meanings. As an example, suppose that you heard the word *barracuda* in a conversation. Immediately, you would consider options for what the word might mean (e.g., a fish, a type of car, a song, an aggressive person). Then you hear your friend say, "Oh, I forgot my barracudas this morning." Right away, you revise your hypothesis. In essence, you do a "best of fit analysis." You draw on your knowledge of grammar to help you. The words "*my* barracuda*s*" tip you off that it cannot be any of the word meanings mentioned before and that it is likely a personal item that can be carried. If you knew that your friend was a swimmer and then the friend added, "I prefer my barracudas because they don't leave rings around my eyes," you would conclude that she was talking about goggles. Vocabulary training needs to help students to use their fund of word knowledge and experience to figure out what words mean and to store new words in relation to associated meanings. Some excellent strategies for implementing such an approach are discussed by Yoshinaga-Itano and Downey (1986).

4. *Many students will benefit from opportunities to work on self-expression at the narrative level.* During a school day, students are asked to express themselves in various modes (e.g., giving an explanation, justifying a response, or writing a theme). If a need is identified in this area, the AR clinician can provide practice and support at the narrative level of conversation. Emphasis on the organization of face to face narratives may positively influence written language as well. Some narrative functions that are common in school include explaining, describing, debating, negotiating, comparing and contrasting, justifying, summarizing, predicting, and using cause–effect reasoning. AR clinicians can devise activities that address these literate language functions. For example, a student might be encouraged to take an opinion poll related to a recent political event. Functional speech intelligibility can be reinforced while the student asks others for their opinions. He can then be asked to draw summary statements and explain them to a peer. Finally, he could be encouraged to write an article for the school paper about his discoveries.

> Narratives involve the telling of stories in various forms. One commonly used narrative form is a personal narrative through which a student shares a past event with another.

5. *As the school years progress, demands for verbal reasoning increase. Therefore, students may benefit from interventions designed to encourage verbal reasoning skills.* AR clinicians can take advantage of any daily problem to support the student's expansion of problem-solving skills. It is useful to guide the student in analyzing the nature of the problem (e.g., I left my assignment at home and I will get an F if I fail to turn it in) and alternative solutions (e.g., brainstorming ways to get the assignment finished in time). The student can then be guided in evaluating the various alternatives and needed resources, leading to the selection of the best alternative. The student should evaluate both the outcomes and ways to prevent this problem in the future. These strategies can help the student learn useful problem-solving processes that can be implemented when faced with peer conflicts, social pressures, or other everyday problems. It is also useful to discuss the feelings that result from problems and their consequences. Students may have a limited fund of affective vocabulary. Gaining a better understanding of affective words and their relation to problem situations can increase students' awareness of themselves and of the perspectives of others.

6. *Some school-age students will profit from emphasis on study skills and other classroom survival skills.* If at all possible, the AR clinician should observe a student in the classroom or interview the teacher about the student's responsiveness in the classroom. Input from these sources is useful in the identification of priority needs. For example, one student had significant difficulty identifying key points for notetaking. He tried to write down all the points from a class lecture. This resulted in a lack of organization and many missing elements in his notes. The IEP team decided to provide a notetaker to ease the processing demands on the student. The AR clinician used the notetaker's transcripts to illustrate some key points about organizing notes and studying from notes. The student learned about what to attend to in the lecture from this process. Through observation and discussions with the teacher, a priority need was effectively addressed.

This list is not meant to be inclusive. Rather, it illustrates examples of priority areas for many students who are of school age. It emphasizes the importance of selecting goals that will support the student to function as well as possible in the learning and social environments at school. This can only come about when the AR clinician works closely with the educational team to identify skills that need to be addressed so that the student can communicate more effectively in the classroom. Sensitivity to the language learning demands of a student's school program will lead to the selection of relevant interventions.

COUNSELING AND PSYCHOSOCIAL ASPECTS (SPECIAL CASE)

ADJUSTMENTS FOR MILD LOSSES AND AUDITORY PROCESSING PROBLEMS.

Children with mild hearing problems (i.e., mild sensorineural loss, conductive loss) and those with central auditory processing disorders (CAPD or APD) may require communication rehabilitation along with children who demonstrate more pronounced losses. Although the language-related problems may be minimized in the case of milder losses, they are apt to be present and require attention. A careful multidisciplinary assessment of the child's difficulties should be conducted consisting of reports from teachers, parents, the child, and others in addition to observation and diagnostic testing.

Most authorities agree that CAPD involves one of the following:

1. Delay in development
2. Disordered development
3. A specific central lesion

Such difficulties may be part of a general perceptual problem involving vision and hearing or a general intellectual problem, or CAPD may occur in isolation. CAPD

Auditory processing disorder (APD) involves either a delay in development, a disorder in development, or a specific central lesion. APD often accompanies attention deficits, specific learning disabilities, and/or speech–language delays.

often occurs in conjunction with attention deficit hyperactivity disorder (ADHD) and/or learning disorder (LD) and/or speech–language (SL) deficits.

When intelligence and peripheral hearing are within normal limits and the child seems to be showing deficits mainly in hearing tasks, then CAPD, rather than a more general problem, may be the cause, and this is possible with or without these other conditions (ADHD, LD, SL). In these cases, a rehabilitation evaluation focused on CAPD is indicated. ASHA (1996) has indicated that possibly five or six different related symptoms or assessment areas may be evaluated in CAPD, but usually current batteries only assess a more limited number of these. Musiek and Chermak (1994) have recommended that four of the ASHA areas be assessed: 1) monaural tasks in background competition, 2) auditory pattern recognition, and tasks involving 3) binaural separation and 4) integration. A Multiple Auditory Processing Assessment (MAPA battery) that follows this recommendation has been found to separately measure these four tasks and is now available through Auditec of St. Louis, Missouri (Domitz & Schow, 2000; Schow, et al., 2000).

The advantage of these developments in assessment is that audiology is emerging from the imprecision of an earlier era in CAPD. Now that ASHA has defined the areas of concern in APD and assessments are being developed to measure these areas, remediation strategies can be focused specifically on any or all of the four deficit areas and then can be measured again posttherapy to determine improvement. For example, the recent use of FastForward, a commercial product used more and more in schools, (see resource website), may remediate problems in auditory pattern recognition. As data using this and other remediation methods are gathered to test this assumption, more will be learned about ways to help children. Although specific remediation may be indicated at times, the child with CAPD can also be helped with strategies that improve the signal (through improvement of the signal to noise ratio), and they may be helped by being taught improved cognitive strategies for learning and remembering. Chermak and Musiek (1992) offered a series of helpful suggestions (see Table 9.7) that address such improved signal and cognitive strategies. These recommendations may be useful to the child regardless of the particular problems. In the future, it appears that audiologic rehabilitation specialists working with school-age children will be equipped with improved methods for evaluating and remediating CAPD.

SUMMARY

This chapter has provided an introduction to the process of audiologic rehabilitation at two distinct levels: the early intervention level and school-age service levels. Although services in these settings are provided by a variety of personnel and in various communication modes, one professional—the parent advisor or the AR therapist—often assumes the important roles of coordinating service provision and serving as an advocate for children and families. This chapter has emphasized the critical importance of family-centered practice and the role of the family throughout the child's educational program. After appropriate assessment and selection of intervention priorities, including a communication system, audiologic rehabilitation services throughout the child's life focus on four major areas: (1) environmental

TABLE 9.7

Management of Central Auditory Processing Disorders

FUNCTIONAL DEFICIT	STRATEGIES	TECHNIQUES
Distractibility and inattention	Increase signal to noise ratio	ALD/FM system; acoustic modifications preferential seating
Poor memory	Metalanguage	Chunking, verbal chaining, mnemonics, rehearsal, paraphrasing, summarizing
	Right hemisphere activation	Imagery, drawing
	External aids	Notebooks, calendars
Restricted vocabulary	Improve closure	Contextual derivation of word meaning
Cognitive inflex: predominantly analytic or predominantly conceptual	Diversify cognitive style	Top-down (deductive) and bottom-up (inductive) processing, inferential reasoning, questioning, critical thinking
Poor listening comprehension	Induce formal schema to aid organization, integration, and prediction	Recognize and explain connectives (additives; causal; adversative; temporal) and patterns of parallelism and correlative pairs (not only/but also; neither/nor)
	Maximize visual and auditory summation	Substitutions for notetaking
Reading, spelling, and listening problems	Enhance multisensory integration	Phonemic analysis and segmentation
Maladaptive behaviors (passive, hyperactive, impulsive)	Assertiveness and cognitive behavior modification	Self-control, self-monitoring, self-evaluation, self-instruction, problem solving
Poor motivation	Attribution retraining: internal locus of control	Failure confrontation, attribution to factors under control

Source: Chermak and Musiek, 1992.

coordination and integration of services; (2) audibility, amplification and assistive device issues; (3) communication activity rehabilitation with a model of language and literacy attainment; and (4) counseling and psychosocial support for the child and family. At the school-age level, the importance of integrated service delivery that considers the unique communicative demands of the classroom setting has been emphasized. Rehabilitation presents challenges to parents, children, and therapists. Nevertheless, if proper attention is given to all of these aspects, prospects for effective management may be very good. If the problems of the child with hearing impairment are underestimated or neglected, the student may experience long-term negative consequences on language, literacy, and social skill attainment. Aggressive and early management of children who are deaf or hard of hearing through audiologic rehabilitation is therefore very important.

- Rehabilitative management of children who are deaf and hard of hearing begins with comprehensive, transdisciplinary evaluation. During intervention, ongoing assessment is necessary to document outcomes, make appropriate adjustments to therapy routines, and identify additional intervention priorities.

- Universal newborn hearing screening procedures allow for identification of hearing loss in the neonatal period, much earlier than in the past. To gain maximal benefit, early identification needs to be paired with early intervention programs that seek to involve and support families.

- Most early intervention programs seek to offer family-centered practices. In this approach, families are empowered in their roles as decision makers for the child, professionals seek to form balanced partnerships with parents, and family-identified needs are addressed through collaborative teamwork.

- Families in early intervention programs benefit from full access to information on options to guide decision making. Stress is reduced when informal and formal support systems (e.g., support group meetings) are made available. Parent advisors use coaching methods to support families in providing a nurturing language environment for infants with hearing loss.

- Appropriate management of personal amplification and FM systems is a primary step in facilitating a child's use of residual hearing. Children benefit from regular monitoring of amplification, encouragement to wear devices their full waking hours, and opportunities to listen throughout daily routines. Auditory learning can be fostered during natural interactions.

- Preschool-age children benefit from language intervention techniques that stimulate thinking, problem solving, and active learning. Children should be encouraged to master question–answer routines, because this aspect of language supports them in making discoveries about the world.

- Because children who are deaf and hard of hearing have fewer opportunities to "overhear," they may experience gaps and delays in vocabulary and world knowledge. Both preschool- and school-aged children profit from approaches that help them to build networks of word meanings. They need to learn to tie new information to familiar concepts.

- Speech development programs for children with hearing loss should be structured to maximize the child's reliance on residual hearing. When children strengthen their reliance on listening skills, they often learn to self-monitor, which contributes to the generalization of speech training.

- The AR specialist should be involved as a team member in providing input to the child's IFSP (birth to 3 years) or IEP (3 years on). In the school-age years, AR specialists need to communicate regularly with the educational team so that goals will relate to the student's classroom communicative needs.

- Family members should be involved in the child's AR program throughout the course of the child's education. Furthermore, children with any degree of hearing loss may be candidates for some level of AR service. Team approaches benefit all children, but especially those with multiple disabilities.

RECOMMENDED READING

Alpiner, J. G., & McCarthy, P. A. (2000). *Rehabilitative audiology: Children and adults.* (3rd ed.) Baltimore, MD: Williams & Wilkins.

American Speech–Language–Hearing Association. (1993). Guidelines for audiology services in the schools. *Asha, 35* (suppl. 10), pp. 24–32.

Cole, E. B. (1992). *Listening and talking: A guide to promoting spoken language in young hearing impaired children.* Washington, DC: Alexander Graham Bell Association for the Deaf.

DeCondie-Johnson, C., Benson, P. V., and Seaton, J. B. (1997). *Educational audiology handbook.* San Diego: Singular.

Roeser, R., & Downs, M. (Eds.). (1995). *Auditory disorders in children* (3rd ed.). New York: Thieme.

Roush, J., & Matkin, N. D. (1994). *Infants and toddlers with hearing loss.* Baltimore, MD: York Press.

Watkins, S., and Clark, T. C. (1993). *SKI*HI resource manual. Family-centered, home-based programming for infants, toddlers, and preschool-aged children with hearing impairment.* Logan, UT: HOPE, Inc.

RECOMMENDED WEB SITES

www.sivop.org

www.clerccenter.gallaudet.edu

www.boystownhospital.org

www.skihi.org

www.babyhearing.org

REFERENCES

Alpiner, J. G., & McCarthy, P. A. (2000). *Rehabilitative audiology: Children and adults.* (3rd ed.) Baltimore, MD: Williams & Wilkins.

American Academy of Pediatrics. (1999). Newborn and infant hearing loss: Detection and Intervention. Task Foce on Newborn and Infant Hearing. *Pediatrics, 103,* 527–530.

ASHA. (1996). American Speech-Language-Hearing Association. Central auditory processing: Current status of research and implications for clinical practice. *American Journal of Audiology, 5*(2), 41–54.

ASHA. (1997). American Speech–Language–Hearing Association. Committee on Audiometric Evaluation. *Guidelines for audiologic screening,* 1–60. Rockville, MD.

Bailey, D. J. (1987). Collaborative goal setting with families: Resolving differences in values and priorities for service. *Topics in Early Childhood Education, 7*(2), 59–71.

Bankson, N. W., & Bernthal, J. E. (1990). *Bankson–Bernthal test of phonology.* San Antonio, TX: Special Press.

Bentler, R. A. (1993). Amplification for the hearing-impaired child. In Alpiner, J. G., and McCarthy, P. A., (Eds.), *Rehabilitative audiology: Children and adults.* Baltimore, MD: Williams and Wilkins.

Berg, F. S. (1993). *Acoustics and sound systems in schools.* San Diego, CA: Singular.

Bernstein, M., & Morrison, M. (1992). Are We Ready for PL99-457? *AAD, 137*(1), 7–13.

Bess, F. H., & Paradise, J. L. (1994). Universal screening for infant hearing impairment: not simple, not risk-free, not necessarily beneficial, and not presently justified. *Pediatrics, 93,* 330–334.

Bess, F. H., Dodd-Murphy, J., & Parker, R. A. (1998). Children with minimal sensorineural hearing loss: prevalence, educational performance, and functional status. *Ear Hear, 19*(5), 339–54.

Blair, J., Petersen, M., & Viehweg, S., (1985). The effects of mild sensorineural hearing loss on academic performance of young school-age children. *Volta Review, 87*(2), 87–93.

Blair, J., Wright, K., & Pollard, G. (1981). Parental understanding of their children's hearing aids. *Volta Review, 83,* 375–382.

Blank, M., Rose, S., & Berlin, L. (1978). *The language of learning: The preschool years* (pp. 8–21). New York: Grune & Stratton.

Boothroyd, A. (1982). *Hearing impairments in young children.* Englewood Cliffs, NJ: Prentice Hall.

Bredekamp, S. (1987). *Developmentally appropriate practice in early childhood programs serving children from birth through age 8* (expanded ed.). Washington, DC: National Association for the Education of Young Children.

Brinker, R., Frazier, W., & Baxter, A. (1992). Maintaining involvement of inner city families in EI programs through a program of incentives: Looking beyond family systems to social systems. *OSERS News in Print. Winter, 4*(1), 9–19.

Bronfenbrenner, U. (1974). *Is early intervention effective? A report on longitudinal evaluations of preschool programs* (vol. II). (Department of Health, Education and Welfare, Office of Human Development, Office of Child Development, Children's Bureau, Department of Health, Education, and Welfare Publication No. OHD-76-30020). Washington, DC: U.S. Government Printing Office.

Busch, C., & Halpin, K. (1994). Incorporating deaf culture into early intervention. In B. Schick & M. P. Moeller (Eds.), *Proceedings of the Seventh Annual Conference on Issues in Language and Deafness.* Omaha, NE: Boys Town National Research Hospital, 117–125.

Calderon, R. (2000). Parental involvement in deaf children's education programs as a predictor of child's language, early reading, and social–emotional development. *Journal of Deaf Studies and Deaf Education, 5*(2), 140–155.

Calderon, R., Bargones, J., & Sidman, S. (1998). Characteristics of hearing families and their young deaf and hard of hearing children: Early intervention follow–up. *American Annals of the Deaf, 143*(4), 347–362.

Calderon, R., & Greenberg, M. T. (1997). The effectiveness of early intervention for deaf children and children with hearing loss. In Guralnick, M. J. (Ed.), *The effectiveness of early invention* (pp. 455–483). Baltimore, MD: Paul H. Brookes.

Calderon, R., & Nadiu, S. (2000). Further support for the benefits of early identification and intervention for children with hearing loss. *Volta Review, 100*(5), 53–84.

Carotta, C., Carney, A. E., & Dettman, D. (1990). Assessment and analysis of speech production in hearing-impaired children. *Asha, 32,* 59(A).

Castle, D. (1984). *Telephone training for hearing-impaired persons: Amplified telephones, TDD's, codes.* Washington, DC: Alexander Graham Bell Association for the Deaf.

Chermak, G. D., & Musiek, F. E. (1992). Managing central auditory processing disorders in children and youth. *American Journal of Audiology, 61–65.*

Cole, E. B. (1992). *Listening and talking: A guide to promoting spoken language in young hearing impaired children.* Washington, DC: Alexander Graham Bell Association for the Deaf.

Davis, J. (1990). Personnel and service. In Davis, J. (Ed.), *Our forgotten children: Hard of hearing pupils in the school* (2nd. ed.). Washington, DC: Self Help for the Hard of Hearing.

Davis, J., Effenbein, J., Schum, R., & Bentler, R. (1986). Effects of mild and moderate hearing impairments on language, educational, and psychosocial behavior of children. *Journal of Speech and Hearing Research, 51*(1), 53–63.

Dillon, H., Koritschoner, E., Battaglia, J., Lovegrove, R., Ginis, J., Mavrias, G., Carnie, L., Ray, P., Forsythe, L., Towers, E., Goulias, H., & Macaskill, F. (1991). Rehabilitation effectiveness I: Assessing the needs of clients entering a national hearing rehabilitation program. *Australian Journal of Audiology, 13,* 55–65.

Domitz, D., & Schow, R. L. (2000). Central auditory processes and test measures: ASHA revisited. *American Journal of Audiology, 9,* 63–68.

Erber, N. P. (1982). *Auditory training.* Washington, DC: Alexander Graham Bell Association for the Deaf.

Finitzo-Heiber, T. (1988). Classroom acoustics. In Roeser, R., & Downs, M. (Eds.), *Auditory disorders in school children* (pp. 221–233). New York: Thieme-Stratton.

Finitzo-Heiber, T., & Tillman, T. (1978). Room acoustics' effects on monosyllabic word discrimination ability for normal and hearing impaired children. *Journal of Speech and Hearing Research, 21,* 440–458.

Flexer, C. (1993). Management of hearing in an educational setting. In Alpiner, J. G., and McCarthy, P. A. (Eds.), *Rehabilitative audiology: Children and adults* (2nd ed., pp. 176–210). Baltimore, MD: Williams and Wilkins.

Gaeth, J., & Lounsbury, E. (1966). Hearing aids and children in elementary schools. *Journal of Speech and Hearing Disorders, 31,* 283–289.

Glover, B. (1999). *Working together on early intervention teams.* Logan, Utah: SKI-HI Institute.

Glover, B., Watkins, S., Pittman, P., Johnson, D., & Barringer, D. G. (1994). SKI-HI home intervention for families with infants, toddlers, and preschool children who are deaf or hard of hearing. *Infant–Toddler Intervention: The Transdisciplinary Journal, 4*(4), 319–332.

Harrison, M., & Roush, J. (1996). Age of suspicion, identification and intervention for infants and young children with hearing loss: A national study. *Ear and Hearing, 17,* 55–62.

Hatfield, N., & Humes, K. (1992). Developing a bilingual-bicultural parent-infant program: Challenges, compromises and controversies. In B. Schick & M. P. Moeller (Eds.), *Proceedings of the Seventh Annual Conference on Issues in Language and Deafness.* Omaha, NE: Boys Town National Research Hospital.

Hohmann, M., Banet, B., & Weikart, D. (1979). *Young children in action.* Ypsilanti, MI: High/Scope Press.

Hoverstein, G. (1981). A public school audiology program: Amplification maintenance, auditory management, and inservice education. In Bess, F., et al. (Eds.), *Amplification in education.* Washington, DC: Alexander Graham Bell Association for the Deaf.

Idol, L., Paolucci-Whitcomb, P., & Nevin, A. (1986). *Collaborative consultation.* Rockville, MD: Aspen.

Lederberg, A., & Prezbindowski, A. (2000). Impact of child deafness on mother–toddler interaction: Strengths and weaknesses. In Spencer, P., Erting, C., & Marschark, M. (Eds.), *The deaf child in the family and school* (pp. 73–92). Mahwah, NJ: Lawrence Erlbaum.

Ling, D. (1976). *Speech and the hearing impaired child: Theory and practice.* Washington, DC: Alexander Graham Bell Association for the Deaf.

Ling, D. (1989). *Foundations of spoken language in hearing impaired children.* Washington, DC: Alexander Graham Bell Association for the Deaf.

Ling, D., & Ling, A. (1978). *Audiologic habilitation: The foundations of verbal learning in hearing-impaired children.* Washington, DC: Alexander Graham Bell Association for the Deaf.

Luterman, D. (1987). *Deafness in the family.* San Diego, CA: College-Hill Press.

Manolson, A., (1985). *It takes two to talk* (2nd ed.). Toronto: Hanen Early Language Resource Centre.

Marlowe, J. A. (1984). The auditory approach to communication development for the infant with hearing loss. In Perkins, W. (Ed.), *Current therapy of communication disorders: Hearing disorders* (pp. 3–9). New York: Thieme-Stratton.

Matkin, N. D. (1984). Wearable amplification: A litany of persisting problems. In Jerger, J. (Ed.), *Pediatric audiology: Current trends* (pp. 125–145). San Diego, CA: College-Hill Press.

Meadow-Orlans, K. P. (1995). Sources of stress from mothers and fathers of deaf and hard of hearing children. *American Annals of the Deaf, 140,* 352–357.

Meadow-Orlans, K. P., & Steinberg, A. G. (1993). Effects of infant hearing loss and maternal support on mother–infant interaction at 18 months. *Journal of Applied Developmental Psychology, 14,* 407–426.

Mindel, E. D., & Vernon, M. (1987). *They grow in silence: The deaf child and his family* (2nd ed.). Silver Spring, MD: National Association of the Deaf.

Moeller, M. P. (1988). Language assessment strategies [Monograph Supplement]. *Journal of the Academy of Rehabilitative Audiology, 21,* 73–99.

Moeller, M. P. (September, 1993). Auditory learning: Efficacy and validation issues. Paper presented at the 1993 Conference on Developments in Pediatric Audiology: Assessment and Amplification. Omaha, NE: Boys Town National Research Hospital.

Moeller, M. P. (2000). Early intervention and language outcomes in children who are deaf and hard of hearing. *Pediatrics, 106*(3) 43, 1–9.

Moeller, M. P., & Carney, A. E. (1993). Assessment and intervention with preschool hearing-impaired children. In Alpiner, J., & McCarthy, P. (Eds.), *Rehabilitative audiology: Children and adults* (2nd ed.) (pp. 106–136). Baltimore, MD: Williams & Wilkins.

Moeller, M. P., & Condon, M.-C. (1994). D.E.I.P.: A collaborative problem-solving approach to early intervention. In Roush, J., & Matkin, N. D. (Eds.), *Infants and toddlers with hearing loss* (pp. 163–194). Baltimore, MD: York Press.

Moeller, M. P., Coufal, K., & Hixson, P. (1990). The efficacy of speech–language intervention: Hearing impaired children. *Seminars in Speech and Language, 11*(4), 227–241.

Moeller, M. P., Schick, B., & Williams, K. T. (1994). Sign with me: A family sign program. In Schick, B., & Moeller, M. P., (Eds.), *Proceedings of the seventh annual conference on issues in language and deafness.* Omaha, NE: Boys Town National Research Hospital.

Moses, K. L. (1985). Infant deafness and parental grief: Psychosocial early intervention. In Powell, F., et al. (Eds.), *Education of the hearing impaired child* (pp. 85–102). San Diego, CA: College-Hill Press.

Musiek, F. E., & Chermak, G. D. (1994). Three commonly asked questions about central auditory processing disorders: Assessment. *American Journal of Audiology, 3,* 23–27.

National Institute on Deafness and other Communication Disorders. (1993, March 1–3). *National Institutes of Health Consensus Statement: Early identification of hearing impairment in infants and young children.* Bethesda, MD: Author. http://odp.od.nih.gov/consensus/cons/092/092 intro.htm

Niskar, A. S., Kieszak, S. M., Holmes, A., Esteban, E., Rubin, C., & Brody, D. (1998). Prevalence of hearing loss among children 6 to 19 years of age: the Third National Health and Nutrition Examination Survey. *Journal of the American Medical Association, 8,* 279(14), 1071–1075.

Northern, J., & Downs, M. (1991). *Hearing in children* (4th ed.). Baltimore, MD: Williams & Wilkins.

Norton, S. J., Gorga, M. P., Widen, J. E., Folsom, R. C., Sininger, Y., Cone-Wesson, B., Vohr, B., & Fletcher, K. A. (2000). Identification of neonatal hearing impairment: Summary and recommendations. *Ear and Hearing, 21*(5), 529–535.

Oller, D. K. (1983). Infant babbling as a manifestation of the capacity for speech. In Gerber, S. E., & Mencher, G. T., (Eds.), *The development of auditory behavior* (pp. 221–236). New York: Grune & Stratton.

Oller, D. K., & Eilers, R. E. (1988). The role of audition in infant babbling. *Child Development, 59,* 441–449.

Pugh, G. (1994). *Deaf and hard of hearing students: Educational service guidelines.* NASDSE, Alexandria, VA.

Ross, M. (1987). Classroom amplification. In Hodgson, W., & Skinner, P. (Eds.), *Hearing aid assessment and use in audiologic habilitation* (3rd ed., pp. 231–265). Baltimore, MD: Williams & Wilkins.

Ross, M., & Tomassetti, C. (1987). Hearing aid selection for preverbal hearing impaired children. In Pollack, M. C. (Ed.), *Amplification for the hearing impaired* (3rd ed., pp. 213–253). New York: Grune & Stratton.

Ross, M., Brackett, D., & Maxon, A. (1991). *Assessment and management of mainstreamed hearing-impaired children: Principles and practices.* Austin, TX: Pro-Ed.

Roush, J., & Matkin, N. D. (1994). *Infants and toddlers with hearing loss.* Baltimore, MD: York Press.

Roush, J., Harrison, M., & Palsha, S. (1991). Family-centered early intervention: The perceptions of professionals. *America Annals of the Deaf, 136*(4), 360–366.

Schuyler, V., & Sowers, N. (1998). *Parent infant habilitation: A comprehensive approach to working with hearing-impaired infants and toddlers and their families.* Portland: HIR Publications.

Shepherd, N., Davis, J., Gorga, M., & Stehnachowicz, P. (1981). Characteristics of hearing impaired children in the public schools: Part I. Demographic data. *Journal of Speech and Hearing Disorders, 46,* 123–129.

Simmons-Martin, A. A., & Rossi, K. G. (1990). *Parents and teachers: Partners in language development.* Washington, DC: Alexander Graham Bell Association for the Deaf.

Sinclair, J. S., & Freeman, B. A. (1981). The status of classroom amplification in American education. In Bess, F. et al. (Eds.), *Amplification in education.* Washington, DC: Alexander Graham Bell Association for the Deaf.

SKI-HI Institute. (1994). *SKI-HI 1992–1993 national data report.* Logan UT: Utah State University, SKI-HI Institute.

Snow, C. E. (1983). Literacy and language: Relationships during the preschool years. *Harvard Educational Review, 53*(2), 165–189.

Sparks, S. M. (1989). Assessment and intervention with at-risk infants and toddlers: Guidelines for the speech–language pathologist. *Topics in Language Disorders, 10*(1), 43–56.

Vergara, K. C. & Miskiel, L. (1994). *CHATS: The Miami cochlear implant, auditory and tactile skills curriculum.* Intelligent Hearing Systems. Miami, FL.

Vincent, L., Davis, J., Brown, P., Broome, K., Funkhouser, K., Miller, J., & Gruenewald, L. (1986). *Parent inventory of child development in nonschool environment.* Madison: University of Wisconsin, Department of Rehabilitation Psychology and Special Education.

Wallach, G., & Miller, L. (1988). *Language intervention and academic success.* Boston: College-Hill Press.

Watkins, S. (1999). *The gift of early literacy for young children who are deaf or hard of hearing and their families.* Logan, Utah: SKI-HI Institute.

Watkins, S., & Clark, T. C. (1993). *SKI*HI resource manual: Family-centered, home-based programming for infants, toddlers, and preschool-aged children with hearing impairment.* Logan, UT: HOPE, Inc.

Watkins, S., Pittman, P., & Walden, B. (1996). Bilingual-bicultural enhancement for infants, toddlers, and preschoolers who are deaf through deaf mentors in family-centered early home-based programming (The Deaf Mentor Project), Final Report to U.S. Department of Education, Office of Special Education Programs. Logan, UT: SKI-HI Institute.

Watkins, S., Pittman, P., & Walden, B. (1998). The deaf mentor experimental project for young children who are deaf and their families. *American Annals of the Deaf, (29).*

White, K. R., Maxon, A. B., & Behrens, T. R. (1992) Neonatal hearing screening using evoked otoacoustic emissions: The Rhode Island Hearing Assessment Project. In Bess, F. H., & Hall, J. W. (Eds.). *Screening children for auditory function.* (pp. 207–214). Nashville, TN: Bill Wilkerson Center Press.

Winton, P. J., & Bailey, D. B., Jr. (1994). Becoming family centered strategies for self-examination. In Roush, J., & Matkin, N. D. (Eds.), *Infants and toddlers with hearing loss* (pp. 23–42). Baltimore, MD: York Press.

Yoshinaga-Itano, C., & Downey, D. (1986). A hearing-impaired child's acquisition of schemata: Something's missing. *Topics in Language Disorders, 7*(1), 45–57.

Yoshinaga-Itano, C., Sedey, A. L., Coutler, B. A., & Mehl, A. L. (1998). Language of early and later-identified children with hearing loss. *Pediatrics, 102*(5), 1168–1171.

APPENDIX

GENERAL SUGGESTIONS FOR THE CHILD WITH HEARING IMPAIRMENT IN THE REGULAR CLASSROOM

1. The child with hearing impairment should be encouraged to watch the teacher whenever he is talking to the class.

2. The teacher should use natural gestures when they complement, not substitute for speech.

3. Whenever reports are given or during class meetings, have children stand in the front of the class so the child who is hard of hearing can see lips.

4. During class discussions, let the child who is hard of hearing turn around and face the class so he can see the lips of the reciter.

5. To help the child follow instructions accurately, assignments should be written on the board so she can copy them in a notebook.

6. Like other children with sensory defects, the child with impaired hearing needs individual attention. The teacher must be alert to every opportunity to provide individual help to fill gaps stemming from the child's hearing defect.

7. Ask the child with hearing impairment if he understands after an extensive explanation of arithmetic problems or class discussion. Write key words of an idea or lesson on the chalkboard or slip of paper.

8. Enlist class cooperation in understanding the problem of the child with hearing impairment. Designate a student to be her helper in assignments, someone who notes that she is on the right page and doing the right exercise. However, do not let the child with hearing impairment become too dependent on her "helper."

9. The child with impaired hearing should be seated no further than five to eight feet from the teacher. He should be allowed to shift his seat in order to follow the change in routine. This position will enable him to see the teacher's face and to hear her voice more easily.

10. If the child's hearing impairment involves only one ear or if the impairment is greater in one ear than the other, seat the child in the front with the poorer ear toward the noisy classroom and the better ear turned to the teacher or primary signal. When both ears have the same loss, center placement is recommended.

11. Seat the child with hearing impairment away from the heating/cooling systems, hallways, playground noise, etc.

12. If a choice of teachers is possible, the child with a hearing loss should be placed with the teacher who enunciates clearly. Distinct articulation is more helpful than a raised voice.

13. The child with hearing impairment should be carefully watched to be sure she is not withdrawing from the group or that she is not suffering a personality change as a result of her hearing impairment. Make her feel like "one of the gang."

14. Be natural with the child who is hard of hearing. He will appreciate it if he knows you are considerate of his disability.

15. In the lower grades, watch particularly that the student with hearing impairment does her part and is not favored or babied.

16. Use visual aids in your presentation of lessons. Visual aids provide the hearing impaired with the association necessary for learning new things.

17. Encourage the child with hearing impairment to accept his disability and inspire him to make the most of it. Maintain his confidence in you so be will report any difficulty.

18. Parents should know the truth about their child's achievement. If marking is lenient because of the disability, the parents should know that the child is not necessarily equaling the achievement of a child with normal hearing.

19. Students with hearing impairment need special encouragement when they pass from elementary to junior high school and later into senior high. The pace is swifter. There is much more discussion. Pupils report to five or more teachers instead of one.

20. As the youngster with hearing impairment approaches the age of 16, be especially watchful. She may want to give up. Explain that she needs much preparation to enjoy a life of success and happiness.

HOW TO HELP A CHILD WITH HEARING IMPAIRMENT USE SPEECHREADING SKILLS MORE EFFECTIVELY

1. Don't stand with your back to the window while talking (shadow and glare make it difficult to see your lips).
2. Stand still and in a place with a normal amount of light on your face while speaking.
3. Keep your hand and books down from your face while speaking.
4. Don't talk while writing on the chalkboard.
5. Be sure you have the child's attention before you give assignments or announcements.
6. Speak naturally. Do not exaggerate or overemphasize. It is to be expected that it will be more difficult to hold the attention of the child who is hard of hearing. Never forget that the hearing impaired get fatigued sooner than other children because they not only have to use their eyes on all written and printed work, but also have to watch the lips.
7. Particular care must be used in dictating spelling. Use the words in sentences to show which of two similar words is meant (i.e., "Meet me after school" and "Give the dog some meat"). Thirteen words look like "meat" when spoken, such as been, bead, and beet. The word "king" shows little or no lip movement. Context of the sentence gives the child the clue to the right word. Have the child who is hard of hearing say the words to himself before a mirror as he studies his spelling lesson.
8. If the child who is hard of hearing misunderstands, restate the question in a different way. Chances are you are using words with visual images that are difficult to speechread. Be patient and never skip her. Be sure that things are understood before you move ahead.

Audiologic Rehabilitation for Adults and Elderly Adults: Assessment and Management

Kathy Pichora-Fuller
Ronald L. Schow

C O N T E N T S

■ INTRODUCTION

The provision of services for adults with hearing impairment has always been challenging, but with an ever expanding elderly population and with new technology increasingly available, this challenge is larger than ever. The great majority of adults with hearing disability acquire hearing loss due to illness, accident, noise exposure, and aging, but most lose their hearing through the aging process. Senior adults continue to live longer and be more active. However, a major ingredient for maintaining and enhancing quality of life is to maintain communication skills. Most individuals experiencing hearing loss will retain some residual hearing, but what they lose will erode their ability to hear others effectively, and *communication activity* will be lost, usually in a gradual process. Hearing loss will therefore gradually reduce their *participation* in many rewarding activities of life. Both *personal* and *environmental factors* will interact to complicate this process.

■ PROFILE OF THE ADULT CLIENT

Hearing Loss over the Life-span

Inevitably the loss of hearing leads to misunderstandings and stress for the individual and for family and close associates. Usually, this leads to an awareness that hearing loss is present, but this is often difficult for adults to accept. It may be some time before family, friends, or the stress associated with hearing loss will convince the individual to have his or her hearing screened or tested, leading to a firm identification of the loss. The prevalence data for hearing loss illustrate that this is most likely to occur in the later years.

   The prevalence of hearing loss increases with advancing age as reflected by Table 10.1 and Figure 10.1. These numbers suggest that hearing problems increase gradually throughout life, because there are substantial numbers of younger adults

TABLE 10.1

Prevalence Rates of Hearing Impairment, per 100 Persons, in the Civilian, Noninstitutionalized Population of the United States

AGE GROUP IN YEARS	NUMBER	PREVALENCE RATE (%)
3–17	968,000	1.8
8–24	650,000	2.6
25–34	1,659,000	3.4
35–44	2,380,000	6.3
45–54	2,634,000	10.3
55–64	3,275,000	15.4
65–74	4,267,000	23.4
75+	4,462,000	37.7
All	20,295,000	8.6

Rates are based on 1990–1991 interview data from the National Center for Health Statistics (Ries, 1994).

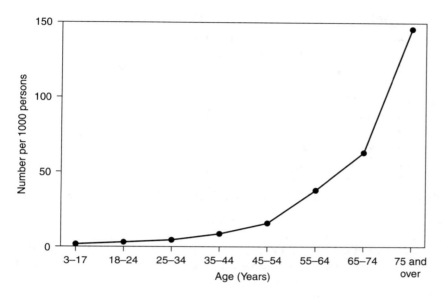

FIGURE 10.1

Average annual age-specific number of persons three years of age and over who cannot hear and understand normal speech per 1000 persons: United States, 1990–1991.
Source: Ries, 1994.

who have hearing loss due to various causes besides age. Table 10.1 gives an estimate of impairment or hearing loss based on interview data; Figure 10.1 shows disability or communication activity data based on hearing and understanding speech. So the numbers are slightly different, but in both cases we see that hearing problems increase even for younger adults but dramatically as we get into the retirement years. We will deal with the elderly somewhat separately, because the majority of those who have hearing problems and the great bulk of those who need hearing rehabilitation are elderly. As a group, the elderly are similar in many ways, but they also present a different, somewhat more complicated profile.

Hearing losses increase dramatically as we grow older.

■ PROFILE OF THE ELDERLY CLIENT

A younger person readapts to a new situation more readily than an older individual who is more limited in options. As the support system continues to decrease with age, the frequency and severity of significant life-style changes, described by Ronch and Van Zanten (1992) and summarized next, continue to increase. Although most aging persons undergo a certain degree of change in every area listed, their capacity to adapt to these changes is highly individualized and personal, depending on genetic inheritance, life experiences, traditional ways of dealing with life, and past and present environmental factors.

PERSONAL AND ENVIRONMENTAL FACTORS

1. *Physical condition:* loss of youth; changes in physiological and biological aspects of the body cause poor health and its emotional consequences.
2. *Emotional and sexual life:* loss of significant others through death, separation, and reduction in sexual activity due to societal expectations, health, personal preference, or death of partner.

3. *Members of the family of origin:* parents, brothers, and sisters become ill or die.
4. *Marital relationship:* strain due to death or illness of spouse, estrangement due to empty nest syndrome, pressures due to retirement.
5. *Peer group:* friends die or become separated by geographical relocation for health, family, or retirement reasons.
6. *Occupation:* many older people retire.
7. *Recreation:* becomes scarce due to physical limitation or unavailability of opportunities.
8. *Economics:* income is reduced by retirement, limited income is tapped by inflation or medical costs not covered by insurance.

Physical and Mental Health and the Aging Process

Some people appear youthful well into their 80s, whereas others manifest old-age behaviors by their early 40s.

The increasing number of life-style changes results in a more heterogeneous population than that of any other age group. It is therefore impossible to assess accurately the effect of aging based solely on a person's chronological age. Not all individuals of the same age experience aging in the same way. Some people appear youthful well into their 80s, while others manifest old age behaviors by their early 40s.

Most elderly persons are in relatively good health, but, as reported by the U.S. Bureau of the Census (1990), approximately 9% of adults 65 to 69 years old need assistance with their everyday activities, and this increases to 45% for those 85 and over. Only a small proportion of the aging population has physical disabilities so severe as to interfere with successful rehabilitative treatment.

To some degree, the senior adult is required to adjust to a certain amount of physical disability and reduced activity level. As each new physical problem becomes apparent and is reinforced by the inevitable continuance of deterioration, the consequences of age can, significantly affect an individual's attitude toward self-fulfillment. This is why it is difficult to discuss the physical and mental factors contributing to the aging process as separate entities. The interaction between the two is symbiotic, with changes in one almost certainly influencing the other. As senior adults confront life-style changes, not all can readily adapt. Concomitant declines in sensory and motor skills and increased risk of illness and injury create a loss of independence and personal control. Senility, long regarded as the inevitable consequence of growing older, is no longer attributed entirely to biochemical changes associated with aging, nor is it considered entirely unalterable. Behaviors otherwise described as senile (e.g., inattentiveness, inappropriate responding) may in reality result from hearing loss. In fact, studies have shown that hearing loss has an adverse effect on quality of life and on emotional, behavioral, and social well-being. Bess et al. (1989) found a systematic relationship between hearing loss and function–psychosocial status in 153 elderly subjects, and determined that hearing loss accounted for a significant amount of the variation when they controlled for demographic variables like age, number of illnesses, and medication amounts.

Hearing Loss

PRESBYCUSIS. When the aging process, the most common cause of hearing impairment, produces such a loss, it is called presbycusis. In its most common form, presbycusis is a gradual process initially affecting hearing sensitivity for the higher frequencies of a pure tone audiogram. As the deficit progresses, the ability to understand speech, especially in the presence of background noise, becomes increasingly impaired.

PHONEMIC REGRESSION. In some older individuals, presbycusis is characterized by a more severe word recognition problem than would be expected on the basis of the pure tone threshold configuration. This phenomenon, referred to as phonemic regression (Gaeth, 1948), causes perceptual confusions and distortions of the phonetic elements of speech and may not be overcome by amplification alone. Increasing the intensity of speech is not always helpful, because phonemic regression is generally attributed to a central auditory processing disorder (CAPD or APD). Gaeth concluded that there is a central auditory origin for phonemic regression when he found little relationship between this condition and age, duration of loss, educational or socio-economic background, intelligence, or reaction time scores. More recently, Jerger et al. (1990) found that when CAPD could be identified with various tests these subjects would perceive a greater hearing problem than those without CAPD.

Economic Status and Retirement

Adjustments to radical life-style changes are made easier when economic factors are not a concern. A higher income allows great mobility to seek better health care and to continue supportive social contacts. The affluent, socially active older person is more inclined to compensate for the detrimental effects of age by purchasing necessary medications, eyeglasses, dentures, or hearing aids. Low-income persons, on the other hand, have fewer options. Women are particularly vulnerable to economic stresses, especially if they have not been in the work force. Because husbands were often the wage earners, widows often have no or limited savings.

Retirement is perhaps the primary factor for change in the senior adult's economic status. Loss of employment not only may alter financial security, but may also reduce social interaction and erode self-esteem.

Although most older individuals are not considered poor, many live on fixed incomes and have their prime financial asset tied up in the equity of their home. The financial benefit of selling the house is frequently offset by the emotional stress produced by the subsequent loss of neighborhood, territorial familiarity, security, and environmental surroundings.

The economic status of senior citizens who live in long-term extended care facilities is usually lower than that of their counterparts who reside in privately owned homes.

Living Environments

Older adults may live independently, with family members, or in some type of health care facility. Most live in their own residence, while only 15% live with a relative other than their spouse or a nonrelative. Many elderly adults are confined to their homes due to financial and health considerations and are often cared for by their spouses or children. Just over 50% of the aging population live with a spouse.

Just over 50% of the elderly live with a spouse.

The number living alone rapidly increases with advancing age until 47% are doing so when they are 85 years or over (Taeuber, 1992).

The older individual is likely to require professional health care beyond the capabilities of the family environment. For some, this may necessitate only limited assisted care, but health care facilities most often associated with the aging population are nursing homes that provide long-term care. About 52% of women versus 33% of men will use a nursing home before they die. In addition, 70% of women who die at 90 have lived in a nursing home. Those in nursing homes represent an older segment of the geriatric population with generally more advanced physical and mental deterioration. Furthermore, they are more socially isolated, with about half having no nearby relatives. Families frequently use nursing homes for those near death, and most admissions are short term (three-quarters are for less than a year) (Taeuber, 1992).

For nursing home residents and the hospitalized elderly, hearing loss is very common. Schow and Nerbonne (1980) evaluated 202 nursing home residents from five facilities and found that 82% of their sample demonstrated pure tone threshold averages (PTAs) of 26 dB HL or greater, with 48% exhibiting PTAs of at least 40 dB HL.

Palliative nursing care occurs in the final stages of a person's life.

Palliative care occurs when saving a life drops in priority and patients are being nursed through the final stages of life. In our experience, nurses doing such care may make audiology referrals because they want to communicate with people at this stage, even though this may have been less important when the nurses earlier were preoccupied with other forms of care. We should not assume that it is unimportant to do audiologic rehabiltation with very ill people who have little time to live.

■ MODEL FOR REHABILITATION

In Chapter 1 and in Schow (2001) a model and flow chart were presented to provide an overall framework for audiologic rehabilitation. The flow chart is shown in Figure 10.2 to provide a frame of reference as we describe rehabilitation for adults. As noted there, this work is divided into rehabilitative assessment and the treatment itself. The core concerns within assessment and management derive from the anchor points provided by the WHO concepts of activity and participation, as explained in Chapter 1. Included also are personal and environmental factors. There are four fundamental areas within assessment and four within management. These are summarized with the acronyms CORE and CARE, suggesting the core assessment issues and the rehabilitative care needed to treat the patient.

Assessment

The traditional case history is actually a form of self-report, but more formal self-report procedures are also available.

The CORE areas of assessment include Communication impairment and activity limitations, Overall participation variables, Related personal factors, and Environmental factors. In most cases, communication findings may be drawn chiefly from diagnostic audiometry and self-report. Within the area of overall participation variables, the audiologist and client should consider social, emotional, educational, and vocational issues, among others. Related personal factors include such things as client attitude and other disabilities or personal conditions that may confound the

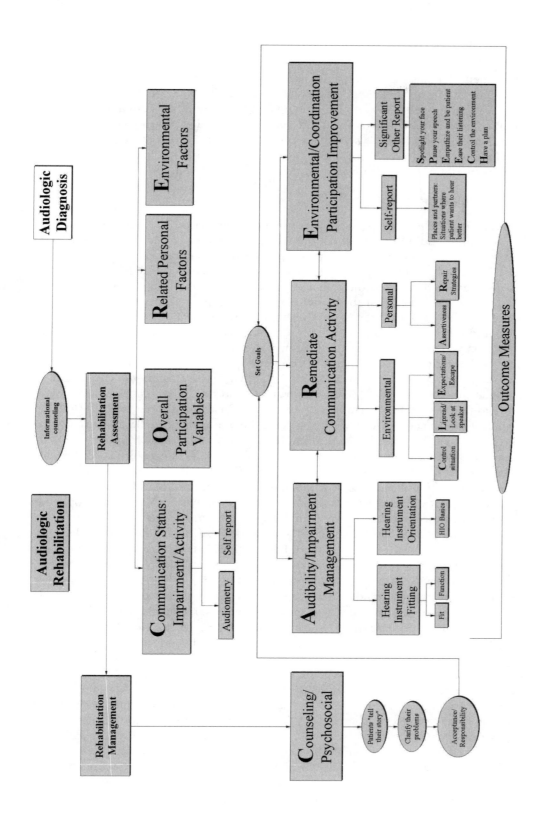

FIGURE 10.2

Model for audiologic rehabilitation.

treatment. Finally, the issue of environmental factors encourages consideration of the general context in which the person lives and must communicate. Through this assessment process the audiologist is invited to consider the fundamental issues that bear on rehabilitation. This need not be an extended process, because a good case history and a focused self-report often help us to address these issues. Nevertheless, we need to see these four matters as comprising a rehabilitation battery, and none of these important elements should be neglected.

Treatment

On the treatment side we see the four aspects summarized by the acronym CARE. Counseling, Audibility–amplification, Remediation for communication activities, and Environmental coordination and participation improvement are the focus here. Counseling should include information dispensed to the client based on our assessment findings, and through an interactive process it should allow the client to help set goals for what they would like to accomplish in treatment. Treatment goals will fall into three areas: audibility, activity, and participation.

Audibility treatment usually involves amplification. In many current cases this is the only focus of treatment. But through the current model we propose not only a more precise understanding of the elements within audibility management, but a broader focus to treatment that includes activity and participation issues as proposed by the WHO model. Hearing instrument and audibility treatment involve the fit and function of the instrument, plus hearing instrument orientation (HIO). *Fit* has to do with such matters as the style of the aid or the specific assistive device preferred by the client, plus issues like obtaining a suitable mold impression. *Function* has reference to matters such as whether audibility is accomplished through digital or other aids. These matters of *fit and function* have been thoroughly discussed in Chapter 2. *Hearing instrument orientation (HIO)* should cover some fundamental topics. The typical dispensing audiologist may use a handout to cover the basics when they perform this part of the audibility management.

Communication activity issues should be addressed by all those fitting hearing aids and others involved in hearing rehabilitation. One approach in this area involves asking the client to consider at least five important communication concepts. These include (1) control the situation, (2) lipread, (3) realistic expectations or escape, (4) assertiveness, and (5) repair strategies. As noted in the model, these matters involve both personal and environmental factors. A small handout also can be used to help to reinforce these concepts, which would be explained by the audiologist and reinforced throughout the entire dispensing process. More advanced communication work may be used to follow up and provide more intensive help.

The final area of treatment involves *environmental and participation* issues. We recommend, for most audiologists dispensing hearing aids, that this concern can be most easily addressed through the use of self-report. When clients select a few areas of major concern wherein they have serious communication difficulties, as they do within appropriate self-report approaches, these generally translate into goals whereby the clients would like to improve their communication activities and their participation possibilities. If the dispensing audiologist helps the client to select at least one unique area of concern, then outcome measures can be used to measure improvement. When self-report questionnaires contain standard situations in which most persons with hearing difficulties experience problems, standardized data are available that allow comparison with the client being treated. By use of the self-report it is thus possible to derive important outcome measures with prefitting and postfitting scores that address a variety of participation areas. We like self-report tools that also include measures of use and satisfaction, in addition to the benefit measures that are situation specific.

We believe that this AR model will be helpful for those doing the most common form of rehabilitative audiology, that is, hearing instrument fitting and follow-up for adults. It is broader, however, than the narrow rehabilitation concerns surrounding amplification. The model is based on the WHO (2000) concept of disability and provides a relatively simple protocol for audiologic rehabilitation with the hope that more precision and unanimity might be obtained in this work. By laying out a recommended protocol for those involved in dispensing and by providing supportive materials to facilitate the adoption of this approach, as we do in this chapter and elsewhere we hope to move toward the acceptance of a more standardized procedure in rehabilitation (Schow, 2001).

Montgomery (1994) recommended a simple protocol based on the acronym WATCH, which he hoped would inspire more audiologists to standardize their approach to rehabilitation at the time of hearing aid fitting. Others (Goldstein and Stephens, 1981; Stephens, 1996a; Gagné and Jennings, 2000, for example) have also proposed models to help us to better understand the rehabilitation process, but none of these previous efforts has incorporated the WHO model. With this broader focus and grounding within WHO, we are hopeful that the acronyms from this model will simplify the concepts and help the student to somewhat standardize rehabilitative work.

■ REHABILITATION SETTINGS

Rehabilitative care for hearing is delivered in a variety of settings. These include university speech and hearing clinics, community hearing centers, hospitals, otologic clinics, senior citizen centers, vocational rehabilitation offices, audiology private practices, and hearing aid sales offices.

University Programs

Early adult audiologic rehabilitation centers were provided in university training programs that served World War II veterans with hearing loss. The focus was directed toward improvement of the adult's communication skills through the use of appropriate amplification and communication training, with counseling and education of adults with hearing impairment and their families and significant others.

This early approach continues to influence present-day programs. At the Idaho State University Hearing Clinic, for example, faculty and students provide a comprehensive program of hearing care (see Schow, 2001 and Brockett & Schow, 2001). After diagnostic audiology, rehabilitation assessment, and counseling, consideration is given to solving audibility deficits through the use of personal amplification systems used alone or in conjunction with assistive listening devices. After the devices are fit, the client is given hearing instrument orientation through a process

TABLE 10.2

Handout of Suggestions for Hearing Instrument Orientation (HIO)

HIO BASICS

Hearing expectations. Even the most advanced hearing aid technology will not give you normal hearing. Also, remember that even people with normal hearing do not understand everything all the time. Some situations will be difficult. Properly fitted hearing aids will allow you to hear soft sounds better while keeping loud sounds appropriately loud. You may find, however, that sounds such as water running, crackling newspaper, wind blowing, crying babies, or dishes in a restaurant will sound different. This difference may be annoying, but with continued use and adjustment to the hearing aids it should become acceptable.

Instrument operation. Be sure that you understand the controls on your hearing aid. What controls are on your aid: volume control, T-coil switch, memory button, directional microphone switch, others? Review each control and be sure that you can adjust it. Ask for help if you need to go over the controls again. Practice and patience will help while you are learning. Experiment to find the best way to use the telephone, but remember not to hold it too close to your hearing aid and that tilting it slightly to the side can prevent feedback. Assistive devices for telephone use are available if you continue to have difficulty.

Occlusion effect. The occlusion effect is an echo that you may hear that can make your voice sound more hollow. If you notice this bothering you, bring it to the attention of your hearing care professional.

Batteries. These come in different sizes. Write your correct size and number here _____. Batteries usually last 1 to 2 weeks depending on how much you wear your hearing aids. Be sure you know how to obtain replacements. The battery has to be inserted with the shiny side facing up. If you cannot change your battery, be sure to ask for help. Keep batteries away from children because they are dangerous if swallowed or placed inside the nose or ear.

Acoustic feedback. Feedback is the squealing sound that your hearing aids sometimes make. It happens when the amplified sound gets into the microphone. If you hear it when you hold the hearing aid in your hand, you know that your hearing aid is turned on. If you hear it when the hearing aid is in your ear, you know that the earmold is not snug or the volume is too high. If you cannot wear your hearing aids at the best loudness level without feedback, ask your hearing care professional for help.

System troubleshooting. If your hearing aid is not working, first check the battery. Then check if there is wax in the microphone or receiver opening. Remove the wax using the simple tools that come with your hearing aids. If you still have problems, ask your hearing care professional for help.

Insertion and removal. It is very important to learn how to insert and remove your hearing aids properly because, if you find it difficult or uncomfortable to do this you won't want to use the aid. Practice regularly to improve and maintain your skill. Ask if you need more help.

Cleaning and maintenance. Wax or other debris can block the opening on the microphone or receiver. Learn how to use tissues, brushes, and wax loops to keep your hearing aids clean. Clean your hearing aids every day and not just when there is a problem.

Service. Knowing where and how to get service on the hearing aid is important. Read your warranty to be sure you understand it. Take advantage of the regular follow-up appointments that the hearing care professional will schedule for you. The usual life of hearing aids is 4 to 5 years if they are well cared for, but one day you will need new hearing aids even if your hearing stays the same.

TABLE 10.3

Handout of Communication Suggestions to Help the Person with Hearing Loss

CLEAR

Control your communication situations. Maximize what you are trying to listen to and minimize anything that gets in the way of what you are trying to hear. Position yourself so that you can see the talker well and hear him most clearly and with the least interference from others. Turn on some lights or move your conversation to an area that is better lit. Move conversations away from noisy areas. If the talker is too far away or the interference from others is too bothersome, you can mic that person with an assistive device. In short, whenever you can be sure to control the lighting or your position in the room and favor your better ear if you have one.

Look at and/or lipread the talker to ease the strain of listening. Watch the person so you can read body language, facial expressions, and lip movements to clarify information that is hard to hear. Remember that much of the information that is hard to hear is easy to see. Lipreading is easier if you face the person directly, but you can also get useful information from the side. In general, the closer the better, but 5 to 10 feet away is ideal.

Expectations need to be realistic. When the situation is just too difficult, you can use communication escape strategies to help you to reduce frustration. If you are realistic about how well you can hear, you may decide that some situations are unreasonably difficult. Anticipate the fact that you will likely have difficulty, and plan options for dealing with a breakdown in communication. For example, if a restaurant is a difficult listening situation, rather than staying at home, agree to have another person in your party explain the specials to you or do the ordering. This is called an anticipatory strategy.

Assertiveness can help others understand your hearing difficulties. Let others in your conversation know that you have difficulty hearing and encourage them to get your attention before talking and to look at you when they speak. Let them know that short, uncomplicated sentences are easier to understand than longer, complicated ones. Being timid will not serve you well; you must speak up and be assertive in order to move the conversation away from a noisy area or ask the talker to slow down or talk louder. Be pleasantly assertive and let your needs be known. Most people will want to be helpful in these circumstances.

Repair strategies for communication breakdown can help you *and* the talker. If you miss important information and you don't understand enough of what is being said, repeat back what you *did* hear and ask them to clarify what you missed. You can ask others to speak more loudly or slowly or distinctly. You can ask them to spell a word or even write it down. Counting on your fingers may help with numbers. Develop different ways to repair a conversation, and do it in an interesting way or with a sense of humor if possible. Saying "I'm going to listen the best I can now, so please say that once more" as you face and watch the person is a more pleasant way to ask for repetition than simply saying "What?" You can also reduce the need for repairs by being the one who begins a conversation or by being sure you know what the topic is before you enter into a conversation.

---

called HIO BASICS, and the client is given a handout (Table 10.2) to facilitate this process. Communication activities are routinely treated through the use of a program called CLEAR, and this has a handout also (Table 10.3). Self-report information is used to assess aspects of participation that the client is concerned about and chooses to address. (We use the Glasgow Hearing Aid Benefit Profile for this purpose). In addition, we provide a handout called SPEECH (Table 10.4) for family members

TABLE 10.4

Handout of Communication Suggestions to Help the Person to Communicate with Someone Who Has a Hearing Loss

SPEECH

Spotlight your face and keep it visible. Keep your hands away from your mouth so that the hearing impaired person can get all the visual cues possible. Be sure to face the speaker when you are talking and be at a good distance. Avoid gum, cigarettes, and other distractions when possible. And be sure not to talk from another room and expect to be heard.

Pause slightly between the content portions of sentences. Slow, exaggerated speech is as difficult to understand as fast speech. However, speech at a moderate pace with slight pauses between phrases and sentences can allow the hearing impaired person to process the information in chunks.

Empathize and be patient with the hearing impaired person. Try plugging both ears and listen for a short while to something soft that you want to hear in an environment that is distracting and noisy. This may help you to appreciate the challenge of being hard of hearing, and it should help you to be patient if the responses seem slow. Rephrase if necessary to clarify a point and remember, empathy, patience, empathy!!!

Ease their listening. Get the listener's attention before you speak and make sure that you are being helpful in the way you speak. Ask how you can facilitate communication. The listener may want you to speak more loudly or more softly, more slowly or faster, or announce the subject of discussion, or signal when the topic of conversation shifts. Be compliant and helpful, and encourage the listener to give you feedback so you can make it as easy as possible for him or her.

Control the circumstances and the listening conditions in the environment. Maximize communication by getting closer to the person. If you can be 5 to 10 feet away, that is ideal. Also, move away from background noise and maintain good lighting. Avoid dark restaurants and windows behind you that blind someone watching you.

Have a plan. When anticipating difficult listening situations, set strategies for communication in advance and implement them as necessary. This might mean that at a restaurant you carry on the communication with a server instead of having your hard of hearing family member or friend do so.

and friends to teach them some basic concepts about communication. In this manner, rehabilitation addresses these broad concerns in working to solve impairment problems through improved audibility, communication activity is targeted with common useful remedies, and participation issues are chosen by the client that, when solved, will improve their quality of life. Usually, the approach is individual. Occasionally, clients choose to attend four 2-hour group sessions. Significant others, usually spouses, may be included in audiologic rehabilitation.

Community Centers and Agencies

Community medical centers and hearing societies, such as those in New York City and a few other large cities, provide rehabilitation settings and classes where participants are usually highly motivated and well directed toward management of their problems. Vocational rehabilitation offices provide adults whose hearing is impaired with access to networks of assessment and management services that are often important for optimizing their potential for gainful employment and for helping them function as contributing members of a community.

Military

Various audiologic rehabilitation programs are available for current and former military personnel in military and Veterans Administration Medical Centers. Programs range from one-time, 1-hour hearing instrument orientation sessions after hearing aid fitting to comprehensive programs meeting over an intense 3-day period. Generally, the sessions are individual, but some group sessions may be conducted, such as at Water Reed Army Medical Center in Washington, D.C. Rehabilitation covered may include counseling, self-assessment inventories, orientation, communication, and assertiveness training.

Consumer Groups

An important hearing rehabilitation source may be found in such groups as the Self-Help for Hard of Hearing People, Inc. (SHHH) (see the resource Website). SHHH has existed since 1979 and has a nationwide network of support groups for all persons who are hard of hearing. SHHH can be described as a self-help, social, outreach, and advocacy group. SHHH publishes a periodical and sponsors an annual convention. Local chapters hold monthly social activities and informative meetings. Consumer groups provide a vehicle by which adults with hearing impairment can improve their ability to self-manage their problems. They promote installation of group amplification systems in theaters, churches, lecture halls, and other public meeting places. But the involvement of informed hearing specialists is important if these groups are to do the most good.

Hospitals, Medical Offices, Private Practice Audiologists, and Hearing Instrument Specialists

It is estimated that well over 90% of all hearing rehabilitation services are offered by audiologists or other dispensers in private practice or by those affiliated with hospital or medical groups. These services generally do not extend beyond the fitting of a hearing aid, orientation to its use, and counseling regarding management of hearing problems. The concern about these services provided in such settings is that they are so limited and do not extend much beyond the fitting of a hearing aid. For most adults with hearing impairment, this service appears to satisfy their rehabilitative needs. But in many cases the hearing aid does not resolve their major communication difficulties. Nor do such limited services begin to meet the needs of those few clients who have very complex rehabilitation issues. Audiologists comprise about half of those dispensing hearing aids, while the remainder are hearing instrument specialists in sales offices (Skafte, 2000). Hearing instrument specialists also tend to provide only limited help with hearing aids and associated devices and assist in initial adjustment to hearing aid use. Few of such specialists are trained to provide extensive rehabilitative services.

■ REHABILITATION ASSESSMENT

Audiometry and self-report are typically used to measure hearing impairment and communication activity limitations. Although we have extensive audiometric methods for measuring hearing impairment, monographs edited by Schow and Smedley (1990) and Newman and Jacobsen (1993) focused attention on the use of self-report techniques to measure not only impairment, but also its primary and secondary consequences. The need to combine audiometric measures with self-report assessment for determining hearing impairment and its consequences is a priority for clinicians and researchers involved in hearing loss management. Fortunately, audiologists in the United States are giving greater attention to these self-report instruments. Schow et al. (1993) reported that self-assessment use by ASHA audiologists had increased from 18% in 1980 to 37% by 1990. In 2000, use of self report increased to 58% (Millington, 2001).

Assessment of the consequences of hearing loss is important in the audiologic rehabilitation process for several reasons. First, there is a need to obtain information that will help us to understand the hearing loss and communication consequences of hearing impairment. Second, an assessment of the psychological consequences of the hearing loss is needed. Emotional and psychological problems may be more detrimental to the well-being of the individual in a way that goes beyond the organics of the loss and the effect on communication. Client input is helpful in dealing with this aspect of audiologic rehabilitation. Self-report procedures can be used both pre- and posttherapy, thereby allowing a measure of improvement in communication function and emotional, social, and vocational well-being. It is expected that efforts in both audiometric and self-report assessment will continue to expand and improve in order to provide more adequate information about hearing loss and its consequences.

Audiologic Testing

The audiometric assessment assists in two areas: (1) diagnosis and (2) rehabilitation. The basic diagnostic test battery consists of pure tone air and bone conduction audiometry, speech threshold tests, word recognition tests, immittance, and measures of uncomfortable level (UCL). The basic audiometric battery results indicate whether a hearing loss exists, the degree and type of loss, and if the loss is likely to be remedied medically or surgically or compensated for through amplification. A variety of test procedures may be added to the standard assessment battery to differentiate cochlear from retrocochlear problems, determine vestibular function, assess middle ear function, and measure central auditory processing ability.

The standard diagnostic battery, followed by hearing aid fitting and hearing instrument orientation (HIO), will generally address the most basic audiologic rehabilitation needs. However, there is a need to go further and develop relevant goals and activities for improving communication skills and address participation aspects of the loss. We should extend the assessment to include identification of those circumstances under which clients experience their greatest communication difficulties and tailor treatment to improve their functioning as they select places where or persons who they want to hear better.

Assessment by Self-report

As explained in Chapter 1, the overall effect of hearing loss is called disability by the World Health Organization (WHO, 2000). One part of disability can be measured audiometrically as hearing loss (called impairment by the WHO), and another part, communication activity limitation, can be measured by self-report. A loss of hearing is measured easily in terms of decibels on an audiometric grid or percent correct on a word recognition test, thereby yielding numerical indicators of the amount of hearing impairment. Unfortunately, these numbers are not indicators of the day to day consequences that may be manifested by hearing impairment. We know from experience, for example, that two individuals with the same numerical hearing loss may encounter entirely different problems as a result.

CASE HISTORY. A case history interview is actually a form of self report and is one way of obtaining information on the day to day activity limitations resulting from a hearing deficit. The history, along with the audiogram, provides the clinician with an initial impression of the client.

OTHER FORMS OF SELF-REPORT. Within the past 30 years, significant efforts have been made to assess hearing consequences beyond the traditional case history. Alternative approaches used for assessment are discussed in the section that follows, and their role in audiologic rehabilitation is explained. Most of these instruments involve self-report by questionnaire. Such questionnaires have been used in an abbreviated form for screening purposes to select rehabilitation candidates, in longer versions to explore a small number of consequences resulting from the hearing problem, or in very comprehensive instruments that explore multiple (up to 22) dimensions of the hearing loss.

Schow and Gatehouse (1990) summarized a variety of fundamental concerns related to self-report, including the need to consider different hearing domains (e.g., impairment, disability) in test design and use, a detailed listing of about 20 instruments used in self-report of hearing, specific applications for which self-report may be used, and a variety of psychometric issues that need careful attention. More recently, Noble (1998) has further underscored the importance of self-report in a thorough update on these methods. Self-report instruments are easy and inexpensive to use. They can be used for a wide variety of purposes and with different populations and are noninvasive and nonthreatening. These factors account for their wide popularity for hearing and other concerns. By assessing the psychosocial and other consequences of hearing loss using self-report, AR clinicians can much more adequately address audiologic rehabilitation. They can measure not only communication difficulties that may require amplification, but also other concerns such as tinnitus and dizziness. These instruments can also promote systematic follow-up to identify effective or ineffective management. This includes outcome measures to determine whether hearing aids are adequate and/or if other rehabilitation efforts have been successful.

In a survey of ASHA audiologists (see Table 10.5), the self-reports most used in the USA were identified. Details about these procedures may be found in the resource web site and also in other sources (Alpiner & Schow, 2000).

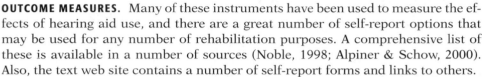

OUTCOME MEASURES. Many of these instruments have been used to measure the effects of hearing aid use, and there are a great number of self-report options that may be used for any number of rehabilitation purposes. A comprehensive list of these is available in a number of sources (Noble, 1998; Alpiner & Schow, 2000). Also, the text web site contains a number of self-report forms and links to others.

In our judgment, two approaches to self-report lend themselves nicely for use by those fitting hearing aids. Because the great majority of rehabilitation is being done in such dispenser settings, we are including a description of these two approaches and copies of them to facilitate their use (see Tables 10.6 and 10.7). These two approaches are called the Glasgow Hearing Aid Benefit Profile (GHABP) and the Client Oriented Scale of Improvement (COSI) (Gatehouse, 1999; Dillon, James, & Ginis, 1997).

Both of these self-report procedures lend themselves to a tailored use by the client and can be adapted nicely for any individual or unique purpose. This is one of their best features, which has made them very sensitive and useful as outcome measures. The more comprehensive tool is the GHABP and so we will describe it first. This extremely practical tool for hearing aid fitting is contained on both sides of a single sheet of paper. On one side it features questions on four standard situations (listening to TV, speaking one on one, speaking in a small group, and speaking with someone under noisy conditions). For each of these situations the client is asked questions that measure activity limitation (disability) and participation restriction (handicap), and both of these are with reference to the unaided condition.

TABLE 10.5

Use of Various Adult Self-assessment Questionnaires (Millington, 2000)

	2000 $N = 218$[a]	
QUESTIONNAIRES	N	%
APHAB	58	27
COSI	53	24
HHIE	36	17
HHS	21	10
SAC/SOAC	9	4
GHABP	6	3
Other	26[b]	12

[a]Of responding clinically active ASHA audiologists, these 127 (58%) were the only ones who reported use of such adult questionaires.

[b]Four of these were a unique, informal, or in-house forms.

TABLE 10.6

Glasgow Hearing Aid Benefit Profile

Date of Assessment ....

Date of Review ....

Hospital Number ....
Name ....
Address ....
....

Does this situation happen in your life? 0 _____ No 1 _____ Yes		**LISTENING TO THE TELEVISION WITH OTHER FAMILY OR FRIENDS** **WHEN THE VOLUME IS ADJUSTED TO SUIT OTHER PEOPLE**			
How much difficulty do you have in this situation?	How much does any difficulty in this situation worry, annoy or upset you?	In this situation, what proportion of the time do you wear your hearing aid?	In this situation, how much does your hearing aid help you?	In this situation, with your hearing aid, how much difficulty do you now have?	For this situation, how satisfied are you with your hearing aid?
0__N/A 1__No difficulty 2__Only slight difficulty 3__Moderate difficulty 4__Great difficulty 5__Cannot manage at all	0__N/A 1__Not at all 2__Only a little 3__A moderate amount 4__Quite a lot 5__Very much indeed	0__N/A 1__Never/Not at all 2__About ¼ of the time 3__About ½ of the time 4__About ¾ of the time 5__All the time	0__N/A 1__Hearing aid no use at all 2__Hearing aid is some help 3__Hearing aid is quite helpful 4__Hearing aid is a great help 5__Hearing is perfect with aid	0__N/A 1__No difficulty 2__Only slight difficulty 3__Moderate difficulty 4__Great difficulty 5__Cannot manage at all	0__N/A 1__Not satisfied at all 2__A little satisfied 3__Reasonably satisfied 4__Very satisfied 5__Delighted with aid
Does this situation happen in your life? 0 _____ No 1 _____ Yes		**HAVING A CONVERSATION WITH ONE OTHER PERSON WHEN** **THERE IS NO BACKGROUND NOISE**			
How much difficulty do you have in this situation?	How much does any difficulty in this situation worry, annoy or upset you?	In this situation, what proportion of the time do you wear your hearing aid?	In this situation, how much does your hearing aid help you?	In this situation, with your hearing aid, how much difficulty do you now have?	For this situation, how satisfied are you with your hearing aid?
0__N/A 1__No difficulty 2__Only slight difficulty 3__Moderate difficulty 4__Great difficulty 5__Cannot manage at all	0__N/A 1__Not at all 2__Only a little 3__A moderate amount 4__Quite a lot 5__Very much indeed	0__N/A 1__Never/Not at all 2__About ¼ of the time 3__About ½ of the time 4__About ¾ of the time 5__All the time	0__N/A 1__Hearing aid no use at all 2__Hearing aid is some help 3__Hearing aid is quite helpful 4__Hearing aid is a great help 5__Hearing is perfect with aid	0__N/A 1__No difficulty 2__Only slight difficulty 3__Moderate difficulty 4__Great difficulty 5__Cannot manage at all	0__N/A 1__Not satisfied at all 2__A little satisfied 3__Reasonably satisfied 4__Very satisfied 5__Delighted with aid
Does this situation happen in your life? 0 _____ No 1 _____ Yes		**CARRYING ON A CONVERSATION IN A BUSY STREET OR SHOP**			
How much difficulty do you have in this situation?	How much does any difficulty in this situation worry, annoy or upset you?	In this situation, what proportion of the time do you wear your hearing aid?	In this situation, how much does your hearing aid help you?	In this situation, with your hearing aid, how much difficulty do you now have?	For this situation, how satisfied are you with your hearing aid?
0__N/A 1__No difficulty 2__Only slight difficulty 3__Moderate difficulty 4__Great difficulty 5__Cannot manage at all	0__N/A 1__Not at all 2__Only a little 3__A moderate amount 4__Quite a lot 5__Very much indeed	0__N/A 1__Never/Not at all 2__About ¼ of the time 3__About ½ of the time 4__About ¾ of the time 5__All the time	0__N/A 1__Hearing aid no use at all 2__Hearing aid is some help 3__Hearing aid is quite helpful 4__Hearing aid is a great help 5__Hearing is perfect with aid	0__N/A 1__No difficulty 2__Only slight difficulty 3__Moderate difficulty 4__Great difficulty 5__Cannot manage at all	0__N/A 1__Not satisfied at all 2__A little satisfied 3__Reasonably satisfied 4__Very satisfied 5__Delighted with aid
Does this situation happen in your life? 0 _____ No 1 _____ Yes		**HAVING A CONVERSATION WITH SEVERAL PEOPLE IN A GROUP**			
How much difficulty do you have in this situation?	How much does any difficulty in this situation worry, annoy or upset you?	In this situation, what proportion of the time do you wear your hearing aid?	In this situation, how much does your hearing aid help you?	In this situation, with your hearing aid, how much difficulty do you now have?	For this situation, how satisfied are you with your hearing aid?
0__N/A 1__No difficulty 2__Only slight difficulty 3__Moderate difficulty 4__Great difficulty 5__Cannot manage at all	0__N/A 1__Not at all 2__Only a little 3__A moderate amount 4__Quite a lot 5__Very much indeed	0__N/A 1__Never/Not at all 2__About ¼ of the time 3__About ½ of the time 4__About ¾ of the time 5__All the time	0__N/A 1__Hearing aid no use at all 2__Hearing aid is some help 3__Hearing aid is quite helpful 4__Hearing aid is a great help 5__Hearing is perfect with aid	0__N/A 1__No difficulty 2__Only slight difficulty 3__Moderate difficulty 4__Great difficulty 5__Cannot manage at all	0__N/A 1__Not satisfied at all 2__A little satisfied 3__Reasonably satisfied 4__Very satisfied 5__Delighted with aid

(continued)

TABLE 10.6

Continued

We have dealt with some of the situations that in our experience can lead to difficulty with hearing. What we would now like you to do is to nominate up to four new situations in which it is important for you as an individual to be able to hear as well as possible.

How much difficulty do you have in this situation?	How much does any difficulty in this situation worry, annoy or upset you?	In this situation, what proportion of the time do you wear your hearing aid?	In this situation, how much does your hearing aid help you?	In this situation, with your hearing aid, how much difficulty do you now have?	For this situation, how satisfied are you with your hearing aid?
0__N/A 1__No difficulty 2__Only slight difficulty 3__Moderate difficulty 4__Great difficulty 5__Cannot manage at all	0__N/A 1__Not at all 2__Only a little 3__A moderate amount 4__Quite a lot 5__Very much indeed	0__N/A 1__Never/Not at all 2__About ¼ of the time 3__About ½ of the time 4__About ¾ of the time 5__All the time	0__N/A 1__Hearing aid no use at all 2__Hearing aid is some help 3__Hearing aid is quite helpful 4__Hearing aid is a great help 5__Hearing is perfect with aid	0__N/A 1__No difficulty 2__Only slight difficulty 3__Moderate difficulty 4__Great difficulty 5__Cannot manage at all	0__N/A 1__Not satisfied at all 2__A little satisfied 3__Reasonably satisfied 4__Very satisfied 5__Delighted with aid
How much difficulty do you have in this situation?	How much does any difficulty in this situation worry, annoy or upset you?	In this situation, what proportion of the time do you wear your hearing aid?	In this situation, how much does your hearing aid help you?	In this situation, with your hearing aid, how much difficulty do you now have?	For this situation, how satisfied are you with your hearing aid?
0__N/A 1__No difficulty 2__Only slight difficulty 3__Moderate difficulty 4__Great difficulty 5__Cannot manage at all	0__N/A 1__Not at all 2__Only a little 3__A moderate amount 4__Quite a lot 5__Very much indeed	0__N/A 1__Never/Not at all 2__About ¼ of the time 3__About ½ of the time 4__About ¾ of the time 5__All the time	0__N/A 1__Hearing aid no use at all 2__Hearing aid is some help 3__Hearing aid is quite helpful 4__Hearing aid is a great help 5__Hearing is perfect with aid	0__N/A 1__No difficulty 2__Only slight difficulty 3__Moderate difficulty 4__Great difficulty 5__Cannot manage at all	0__N/A 1__Not satisfied at all 2__A little satisfied 3__Reasonably satisfied 4__Very satisfied 5__Delighted with aid
How much difficulty do you have in this situation?	How much does any difficulty in this situation worry, annoy or upset you?	In this situation, what proportion of the time do you wear your hearing aid?	In this situation, how much does your hearing aid help you?	In this situation, with your hearing aid, how much difficulty do you now have?	For this situation, how satisfied are you with your hearing aid?
0__N/A 1__No difficulty 2__Only slight difficulty 3__Moderate difficulty 4__Great difficulty 5__Cannot manage at all	0__N/A 1__Not at all 2__Only a little 3__A moderate amount 4__Quite a lot 5__Very much indeed	0__N/A 1__Never/Not at all 2__About ¼ of the time 3__About ½ of the time 4__About ¾ of the time 5__All the time	0__N/A 1__Hearing aid no use at all 2__Hearing aid is some help 3__Hearing aid is quite helpful 4__Hearing aid is a great help 5__Hearing is perfect with aid	0__N/A 1__No difficulty 2__Only slight difficulty 3__Moderate difficulty 4__Great difficulty 5__Cannot manage at all	0__N/A 1__Not satisfied at all 2__A little satisfied 3__Reasonably satisfied 4__Very satisfied 5__Delighted with aid
How much difficulty do you have in this situation?	How much does any difficulty in this situation worry, annoy or upset you?	In this situation, what proportion of the time do you wear your hearing aid?	In this situation, how much does your hearing aid help you?	In this situation, with your hearing aid, how much difficulty do you now have?	For this situation, how satisfied are you with your hearing aid?
0__N/A 1__No difficulty 2__Only slight difficulty 3__Moderate difficulty 4__Great difficulty 5__Cannot manage at all	0__N/A 1__Not at all 2__Only a little 3__A moderate amount 4__Quite a lot 5__Very much indeed	0__N/A 1__Never/Not at all 2__About ¼ of the time 3__About ½ of the time 4__About ¾ of the time 5__All the time	0__N/A 1__Hearing aid no use at all 2__Hearing aid is some help 3__Hearing aid is quite helpful 4__Hearing aid is a great help 5__Hearing is perfect with aid	0__N/A 1__No difficulty 2__Only slight difficulty 3__Moderate difficulty 4__Great difficulty 5__Cannot manage at all	0__N/A 1__Not satisfied at all 2__A little satisfied 3__Reasonably satisfied 4__Very satisfied 5__Delighted with aid

TABLE 10.7

Client Oriented Scale of Improvement

Name: _____ Category: New _____   <u>Degree of Change</u>   <u>Final Ability</u>
                                                                                    (with hearing aid)
Audiologist: _____   Return _____

Date: 1. Needs Established _____   Person can hear

     2. Outcome Assessed _____   10% 25% 50% 75% 95%

<u>SPECIFIC NEEDS</u>

Indicate Order of Significance

		Worse	No Difference	Slightly Better	Better	Much Better	CATEGORY	Hardly Ever	Occasionally	Half the Time	Most of Time	Almost Always
☐	....											
☐	....											
☐	....											
☐	....											
☐	....											

NATIONAL ACOUSTIC LABORATORIES

Categories
1. Conversation with 1 or 2 in quiet
2. Conversation with 1 or 2 in noise
3. Conversation with group in quiet
4. Conversation with group in noise
5. Television or Radio @ normal volume
6. Familiar speaker on phone
7. Unfamiliar speaker on phone
8. Hearing phone ring from another room

9. Hear front door bell or knock
10. Hear traffic
11. Increased social contact
12. Feel embarrassed or stupid
13. Feeling left out
14. Feeling upset or angry
15. Church or meeting
16. Other

Once a hearing aid is fitted, then use time, benefit, residual disability, derived benefit, and satisfaction are measured with reference to these same situations. On the other side of the paper, similar questions are asked based on up to four situations supplied by the client that involve hearing problems. Therefore, up to eight situations can be used in deriving scores in the seven areas of disability, handicap, use, benefit, residual disability, derived benefit, and satisfaction. Any of the four standard items that are not experienced by the person in everyday life are eliminated from the scoring. Percentage scores are derived in all seven areas. We think this comprehensive measurement is important and helpful in checking outcomes in hearing aid fitting. Gatehouse has a Web site (see end of chapter) showing that such measures are useful in comparing benefit and satisfaction from different hearing aids, such as behind the ear and in the ear. He also has a method for scoring differences in these areas between an old and a new hearing aid that can be used with a client. This is called the Glasgow Hearing Aid Difference Profile.

The COSI method is also very useful as an outcome measure and is designed to meet individual needs. It encourages the client to pick up to five situations in which help with hearing is required, where they want to hear better. After the hearing aid is fit, the client is asked to rate on a 5-point scale how much improvement or change the hearing aid has provided and how well they now hear in the various situations with the hearing aid in place. It is a very simple and straightforward scale, but it has been shown to be as valid as much longer scales. It does not, however, have the advantage of using a set of standard situations like the GHABP does.

CORE Assessment Overview

Audiologic testing and self-report are the fundamental tools for assessment, but a continuing need exists for assessment protocols that present a broader, meaningful profile of the adult with hearing impairment. Loss of hearing sensitivity is only one aspect of a complex set of interacting variables, both personal and environmental, that cumulatively interact and affect the hearing problem. Therefore, the assessment process should focus widely, and all four assessment aspects in the model used throughout this book need to be considered.

1. *Communication status* assessment should include both impairment and activity limitations. Once audiologic testing and self-report are completed, there should be reasonably thorough information in these areas.

2. *Overall participation variables* include concerns about social, psychological, educational, and vocational issues. Self-report procedures like the GHABP provide useful information about the social and emotional–psychic dimension of the loss, because they ask how worried or upset the client has become over four standard situations, as well as the unique listening situations that the client has chosen to focus on. It also addresses vocational and educational issues if the clients have been concerned enough to list these as specific situations on the second part of the GHABP. In general, an open-ended procedure as in the GHABP is valuable for teasing out participation concerns, but a follow-up interview may help uncover other areas of concern, and an effort should be made to touch on any aspect of a person's life that may have special relevance.

3. *Related personal factors* that interact with hearing loss include, among others, health status, activity level, and manual dexterity. Attitude and motivation also are key issues, but for older persons changes in health status have perhaps the most significant effect on an individual's ability to participate actively in remediation. Difficulties with motor coordination, vision, memory, or general health may prohibit an aging person from initiating or sustaining interest in the intervention process. The senior citizen may not be enthusiastic about involvement in audiologic rehabilitation when other disabilities, unrelated to the hearing loss, are life threatening and cause greater concern. These disabilities are generally more severe among residents in extended health care facilities, but can be managed. In a report on 62 nursing home residents who wore amplification, Smith and Fay (1977) concluded that almost 30% required daily assistance from staff due to severe health limitations.

4. *Environmental factors* include not only where a person lives and the social circumstances in which they choose to participate, but they also include all aspects of the environment that may facilitate or impede adjustment to and improvement from the effects of the loss. This includes the community and support systems. Environmental factors can often be modified, but first we have to know and understand how they contribute to the problem.

■ REHABILITATION MANAGEMENT

Following assessment, various forms of audiologic rehabilitation can be undertaken. A common set of management principles applies to most cases, and a large number of adults have similar auditory abilities and quality of life issues. Nevertheless, the specific form of rehabilitation will vary between individuals and over time because of the personal and dynamic nature of adjustment to hearing loss in adulthood. In the management process, the rehabilitative audiologist works together with the individual with hearing loss and his or her communication partners to find a combination of solutions that will enable listening goals to be attained and maintained in a wide range of life circumstances. The audiologic management process coherently integrates specific forms of rehabilitation consistent with CARE (Figure 10.2):

1. *Counseling,* which focuses on identifying, understanding, and shaping the attitudes and goals that influence help seeking, decision making, and action taking, with an emphasis on the factors that predispose, enable, and reinforce individuals in their adjustment to hearing difficulties and associated stresses. The audiologist gives the client information based on the results of the assessment and, through an interactive process with the client, goals are set to address needs at three levels: audibility, activity, and participation.

2. *Audibility and instrumental interventions,* in which hearing aids, cochlear implants, and/or a variety of assistive listening devices (ALDs) are discussed, selected, and fitted, with provision of appropriate pre- and posttrial education to ensure the effective use of these technologies. This level of intervention addresses amplification issues in terms of the fit and function of devices and orientation to them.

3. *Remediation for communication activities,* which focuses on changing behaviors that will contribute to enhancing the communication performance of listeners with their communication partners in hearing-demanding activities and environments, including when and how to use devices and other strategies.

4. *Environmental coordination and participation improvement,* with an emphasis on the social and physical supports (in the health care system, the community, and in occupational, educational, and/or family contexts) required to ensure that rehabilitation achieves the individual's goals for participation in everyday life, especially in the priority situations that are targeted in the client-specific goals for rehabilitation.

Issues and Imperatives in Audiologic Management of Adults

Before turning to a more specific consideration of the four aspects of audiologic management, it is worthwhile to consider issues and imperatives that continue to be important for practice and research in rehabilitative audiology. Many important questions remain.

Issues	**Imperatives**
Why don't more hard of hearing adults seek and benefit from audiologic rehabilitation?	Audiologists must tailor rehabilitation to the changing needs of individuals over the adult life-span, because adjustment to hearing loss is a dynamic process.
What role do the nonaudiometric characteristics of the individual play in adjustment to hearing loss?	Audiologists must cultivate their role in facilitating adjustment to hearing loss in terms of how the adult preserves communicative competence and constructs an identity as a hard of hearing person, because there are powerful links between hearing, communicative competence, and identity.
How could more effective solutions be achieved in the everyday lives of hard of hearing adults by combining various forms of rehabilitation?	Audiologists must extend interventions to the individual's communication partners and physical environment, because the social and physical context have a profound impact on the individual's experience of hearing loss.

WHY DON'T MORE ADULTS SEEK AND BENEFIT FROM AUDIOLOGIC REHABILITATION AND HOW MIGHT REHABILITATION BE IMPROVED BY CONSIDERING THE DYNAMIC PROCESS OF ADJUSTING TO HEARING LOSS? Some individuals who lived with hearing loss as children or teenagers continue to experience hearing loss as adults. Some adults become late-deafened. Some experience sudden hearing loss. Some undergo medical or surgical treatments ranging from middle ear reconstruction, to removal of acoustic neuroma, to cochlear implantation. For many, exposure to hazardous levels of recreational or occupational noise over extended periods of time results in permanent sensorineural hearing loss. Hearing conservation programs to prevent hearing loss and identify early signs of hearing loss may be considered as an early type of hearing care along a continuum of care for adults who, sooner or later, will need various forms of audiologic rehabilitation. Nevertheless, the vast majority of adults experience very gradual age-related declines in hearing. Willott (1991) defines *presbycusis* as referring to "the decline in hearing associated with various types of auditory system dysfunction (peripheral and/or central) that accompany aging and cannot be accounted for by extraordinary ototraumatic, genetic, or pathological conditions. The term *presbycusis* implies deficits not only in absolute thresholds but in auditory perception, as well."

By age 75, almost half of the general adult population and the vast majority of those living in residential care facilities have a clinically significant degree of threshold hearing loss. But many listeners first notice problems in hearing in everyday life much earlier. Difficulties often begin in the fourth decade, especially in challenging listening conditions, such as when there is background noise or reverberation, even though there may be no real problems in quiet surroundings (CHABA, 1988). Importantly, once hearing difficulties are noticed, it is common for adults to delay help seeking for hearing problems by years and sometimes even decades. Although numerous studies have documented this delay in help seeking, the reasons for it remain a topic of research.

An older adult with a good audiogram may notice problems hearing in noisy everyday situations, even though he or she has no problem hearing in quiet situations.

Much of the research on rehabilitative audiology for adults has considered hard of hearing adults who are already receiving audiologic services, either adults obtaining their first hearing aid or long-time hearing aid users. Over the last decade, a handful of studies has compared adults who have not consulted audiologists about hearing problems to those who have (Brink et al., 1996; O'Mahoney et al, 1996; Swan & Gatehouse, 1990). There have also been a small number of studies that examined help seeking and the specific rehabilitative needs associated with the particular life circumstances of subpopulations of hard of hearing people, for example, university students and faculty (McCormick et al, 1994), industrial workers (Getty & Hétu, 1991; Hétu & Getty, 1991), residents of nursing homes (Pichora-Fuller & Robertson, 1994), individuals holding strong religious beliefs (Conran & Binzer, 2000), and even inmates in penitentiaries (Dahl, 1994). There has also been increased awareness that women and men adjust differently to hearing loss (Garstecki & Erler, 1995; Hallberg et al., 1996). Regrettably, research has seldom examined how and why the rehabilitative needs of hard of hearing individuals in different circumstances evolve over time.

The pressing need to consider adjustment to hearing loss as a dynamic process has fueled new research. Rather than dismissing adults in the early stages of hearing loss as poorly motivated or "not yet ready for a hearing aid" innovative audiologists around the world are discovering how to use health education or promotion approaches to prepare adults for the eventuality of instrumental and behavioral forms of rehabilitation (Carson & Pichora-Fuller, 1997; Garstecki & Erler, 1997; Stephens, 1996b; Worrall et al., 1998). Recent research on help seeking and adjustment to hearing loss should help rehabilitative audiologists to develop new management approaches for adults living with hearing loss whose abilities, needs, and aspirations change over time and with life circumstances (Noble, 1998; Worrall & Hickson, in press).

HOW DO NONAUDIOMETRIC CHARACTERISTICS OF THE INDIVIDUAL PLAY A ROLE IN AD-JUSTMENT TO HEARING LOSS AND HOW MIGHT REHABILITATION BE IMPROVED BY FACIL-ITATING THE PRESERVATION OF COMMUNICATIVE COMPETENCE AND THE CONSTRUCTION OF AN IDENTITY AS A HARD OF HEARING PERSON? Over the last decade, much has been learned about age-related changes in auditory abilities, but clinical tests have not yet been developed to measure many of the important changes in temporal and central auditory processing that are thought to contribute to the particular difficulties that middle-aged and older adults have understanding spoken language, especially in noise. At the same time as auditory processing abilities are gradually deteriorating, many other changes also occur over the adult life-span. Over the last decade, much has been learned about age-related changes in perception and in emotional, social, cognitive, and linguistic performance (Craik & Salthouse, 2000). Nonauditory changes no doubt have a bearing on adjustment to hearing loss in adulthood, as well as on communication competence in general. In trying to understand how adults experience hearing loss, it helps to consider life-span changes that they experience, especially changes that alter real or perceived communicative competence.

As age-related auditory and nonauditory changes slowly but surely make it more and more difficult for older adults to continue as competent communicators, their self-image and social relations are challenged (Hummert & Nussbaum, 2000). In adjusting to hearing loss, adults are adjusting to changes in how they define themselves and relate to others. Like delay in seeking help for hearing problems, failure to benefit from rehabilitation also seems to hinge on the process of adjustment. All too often, difficulty accepting and adjusting to hearing loss seems to undermine readiness for and benefit from rehabilitation; yet the primary goal of rehabilitation has seldom been explicitly formulated in terms of helping the hard of hearing adult to adjust to hearing loss or the related experiences of handicap in everyday life (Stephens et al., 1998).

Traditionally, audiologic rehabilitation has been primarily concerned with fitting hearing aids in an attempt to restore lost auditory abilities. It was expected that diminished communicative competence would, in turn, also be restored once amplification was provided. Traditionally, hearing aids have been the cornerstone of audiologic rehabilitation, and most adults who seek and receive rehabilitation services usually do so in connection with obtaining a hearing aid. However, despite miniaturization and advances in hearing aid technology over the years, it is still the case that only about one-fifth of adults who might benefit from a hearing aid own one (Kochkin, 1996, 1999, 2000). Furthermore, greater than half who are fitted with aids abandon or greatly limit their use a short time thereafter, and only a small number who continue to use hearing aids succeed in overcoming all their hearing problems (Holmes, 1995). There has been a long-standing assumption that, if only the amplified signal could be sufficiently improved, more people would seek help sooner, and hearing instruments would be successfully adopted by currently dissatisfied users, as well as by the vast untapped market that might benefit from amplification but have never tried it. Nevertheless, the technological imperfections of hearing aids do not seem to adequately explain why this form of rehabilitation meets with such resistance and lack of success. It now seems obvious that other factors need to be considered (Kricos, 2000).

The importance of social, psychological, and environmental issues in adjustment to hearing loss has received increasing attention in the last decade (Borg, 1998; Ross, 1997). On the one hand, unmanaged hearing loss may have an adverse effect on the physical, cognitive, emotional, behavioral, and social function of aging adults; on the other hand, the participation of adults with hearing loss may not be restricted so long as rehabilitation, including optimization of social and physical supports, enables them to fulfill their personal and social goals in everyday life. Whereas the causal direction of the link between hearing loss and personal or social adjustment may be open to debate, the eventual establishment of the link between them for most aging adults is evident. The nature of these links needs to be better understood and incorporated into rehabilitative approaches (Pichora-Fuller & Carson, 2000).

Sadly, even for those who have entered into the rehabilitative process, the simple reality is that most persons who are deaf or hard of hearing, who undergo assessment for their hearing problems, are not evaluated as thoroughly as we recommend. Furthermore, many adults receive only a semblance of the idealized treatment that we summarize in this chapter. For most adults, hearing aids, and sometimes ALDs, along with pre- and postpurchase counseling and orientation tailored to the life circumstances of the individual, will be the key components of audiologic rehabilitation. But hearing aid dispensing on its own, with no goal other than making a sale, will be woefully inadequate. Unfortunately, such narrow, sale-focused, hearing aid counseling and orientation are often provided in a terribly abbreviated fashion (see the survey of rehabilitation procedures on the website provided with this text). Therefore, rehabilitation-oriented audiologists have proposed methods of counseling and orientation that will be simple and readily used by more practitioners (Gagné, 2000). In most cases, counseling and orientation need not be complicated nor go on interminably. Client centered efforts that focus on real needs and problem solving will allow us to achieve effective rehabilitation as soon as the problems are solved. These efforts will also take into consideration the life context of the person, including many nonauditory age-related changes in abilities, needs, and aspirations. The main challenge facing rehabilitative audiologists today is to find management approaches based on a deeper understanding of the adult with hearing loss and how different forms of rehabilitation can be combined to achieve solutions tailored to meet their specific abilities, needs, and aspirations in a timely and effective fashion (Dillon & So, 2000; Stephens et al., 2000).

HOW DOES SOCIAL AND PHYSICAL CONTEXT INFLUENCE THE EVERYDAY EXPERIENCE OF HEARING LOSS AND HOW MIGHT REHABILITATION ACHIEVE MORE EFFECTIVE SOLUTIONS BY COMBINING DIFFERENT FORMS OF REHABILITATION, INCLUDING INTERVENTIONS EXTENDING BEYOND HARD OF HEARING INDIVIDUALS TO INCLUDE THEIR COMMUNICATION PARTNERS AND PHYSICAL ENVIRONMENTS AS CRUCIAL SOURCES OF SUPPORT? Audiologists usually work in offices and clinics where they assess the rehabilitative needs of people in highly artificial conditions. Most clinical tests are conducted in a sound attenuating booth using standardized materials presented under earphones or over one or two loudspeakers. Many of the most challenging social and physical dimensions that confront listeners in everyday life are difficult

Two clients being familiarized with ALDs.

if not impossible to assess directly in typical clinical settings. For example, even though the concerns of family members often motivate first visits to the audiologist, the problems plaguing the communicative interactions between the person with hearing loss and family members are infrequently appraised, either indirectly or directly (Hétu et al., 1993). In response to this gap, over the last decade, rehabilitative methods have been developed to assess more naturalistic conversational behavior and to provide conversational therapy for both persons with hearing loss and their communication partners (Erber, 1988, 1996; Erber et al., 1999; Tye-Murray, 1997). To give another example, many challenges posed by the physical dimensions of everyday listening environments are not tapped by typical clinical procedures. In the real world, multiple sound sources surround the listener, and these sources are altered by room acoustics. The listener must attend to wanted sounds and concentrate on a goal while ignoring extraneous sounds and distractions posed by competing tasks (e.g., a mother trying to have a conversation with her husband while a child is demanding help). In response to these gaps, approaches have been developed for evaluation and intervention concerning hearing tactics (Andersson et al., 1994; Stephens et al., 1999) and/or modification and design of improved acoustical environments. The incorporation of such approaches into the management of hearing loss expands the tool kit of the audiologist to include more than instruments such as hearing aids, cochlear implants, and ALDs.

Most rehabilitation programs combine several important components. These components are consistent with the CARE management model used in this text (see Chapter 1 and Figure 10.2). First, the audiologist counsels the hard of hearing adult about hearing loss, explores its significance in the particular life circumstances of the individual, and determines the needs and goals of the person and significant others. This step is crucial insofar as it culminates in the statement of prioritized objectives for rehabilitation. Treatment goals fall into three main areas to be improved: audibility, activity, and participation. Depending on the objectives that have been set, a customized combination of interventions can be initiated and continued contingent on ongoing reevaluation. To improve audibility, the client will likely be familiarized with instruments, usually hearing aids and/or ALDs. Activity-specific communication skills may be improved through training in visual attentiveness, use of repair strategies or communication tactics, conversational management, and enhancement of goal-directed decision making and assertiveness. Participation may be improved by involving key communication partners, such as family members, other professionals, or caregivers, in therapy and/or by modifying the physical environment, including the use of ALDs in public places.

Outcome measures that look at use, benefit, and satisfaction with interventions can be used to help to document the effectiveness of programs (Cox et al., 2000), while goal-specific outcome measures can be helpful in determining the progress of individuals (Gagné, McDuff, & Getty, 1999). The Glasgow and COSI can be used to evaluate hearing aid delivery programs and/or individuals fit with devices. Indeed, as will be noted later, outcome measures have been used to demonstrate how programs can dramatically improve our efforts at rehabilitating hearing aid users (Brooks, 1989). Novel outcome measures have also been developed and used to demonstrate the value of ALDs (Lewsen & Cashman, 1997; Pichora-Fuller & Robertson, 1997), communication therapies (Erber, 1988, 1996; Robertson et al., 1997), and interventions involving modification of the social and physical environment (Pichora-Fuller & Carson, 2000). Further development of outcome measures is still needed, especially as the rehabilitative tool kit expands and objectives shift from an emphasis on impairment and audibility to a greater emphasis on participation in everyday life (Wilkerson, 2000; Worrall & Hickson, in press). Given the increasingly wide range of choices of outcome measures, audiologists need to know which suit their particular purposes in planning individual treatments or group programs (Beck, 2000; Stephens et al., 2000), and in evaluating the results of rehabilitation (Bentler & Kramer, 2000; Gatehouse, 2000). Such evidence is extremely important, because it is important for audiologists to continue to improve service delivery. There are many disbelievers among those who need our services, and favorable outcome findings are increasingly needed for documentation to those who pay for services.

Counseling and Psychosocial Considerations

The varying degrees of adjustment to hearing loss within the adult population reflect the heterogeneity of the group. Life-styles, hearing-related demands, and experiences of hearing loss vary widely. In counseling, the rehabilitative audiologist needs to begin by listening to the client so that the person's attitudes toward hearing loss and his or her goals in seeking help for hearing loss can be identified and understood. Not surprisingly, the way in which the client experiences hearing loss and expresses issues and concerns about these experiences is unlikely to be cast in scientific terms such as decibels and hertz or hair cell counts. By listening to the client, the audiologist begins to build a bridge between the client's lived experience of hearing loss and their own professional understanding of the results of the formal audiologic and self-report assessment. Building the bridge between these kinds of knowledge sets the stage for the important relationship that must develop between the client and clinician if rehabilitation is to succeed (Clark, 1996). Counseling can then turn to reflection on these attitudes and goals, as well as to a consideration of possible courses of rehabilitative action. Decision making may be guided by discussing factors specific to the life circumstances of the client that have or will predispose or impede taking rehabilitative action (e.g., the positive or negative reaction of a husband to his wife's new hearing aid), factors that will enable taking a rehabilitative step (e.g., providing a college student with written information about FM systems to give to the professors who will be asked to wear a transmitter in class), and factors that will reinforce the continuation of the rehabilitative action (e.g., joining a hard of hearing peer support group). It should be abundantly clear that, although two clients may have the same audiogram and hearing aid, the personal and environmental factors that influence their decision making and action taking may be very different. It is also important to note that the role of the audiologist is itself one of the factors to be considered (e.g., a routine schedule of follow-up appointments may be critical to the client's success).

> The client will succeed in taking and maintaining rehabilitative action if the factors that predispose, enable, and reinforce change are optimized.

Communication is never perfect; even people with normal hearing experience miscommunication and vary in their communication behaviors and styles (Coupland et al., 1991). Differences between communicators will influence how hearing loss affects communication. Compounding the effects of hearing loss on communication, individual differences and age-related changes in emotional, social, cognitive, perceptual, and linguistic status are likely to influence the process of adjustment and readiness for audiologic rehabilitation. Two main functions of communication are *exchange of information* and *social interaction*. Both functions contribute to communication, but their relative importance varies depending on the communicators and their roles in a situation (Pichora-Fuller et al., 1998). As people age, emotional aspects of social interaction, especially with close friends and family, tend to become increasingly important, but acquiring new knowledge or information tends to become relatively less important (Isaacowitz et al., 2000). Even mild hearing loss can interfere with information exchange (e.g., when a college student listens to the details of instructions in the classroom, phonemes must be perceived with a high degree of accuracy and new vocabulary must be learned); in contrast, social interaction may remain well preserved in the early stages of hearing loss (e.g., when an elderly spouse judges a partner's emotions, prosodic or visual cues may be adequate) (Villaume et al., 1994). In setting rehabilitative goals, it is important to understand the kind of communicator that the person has been in the past and to determine his or her current and anticipated priorities for communication in the context of specific relationships and roles.

One adult may be a well-educated professional who has always been socially active and a leader in the community. Such a person may be an exceptionally skilled communicator who is motivated to listen carefully and to draw from nonverbal cues during difficult information-intense communicative situations (e.g., public meetings). Although participation in such situations may be restricted by a mild hearing loss, the person may be well prepared and motivated to embark on rehabilitation to resolve communication problems. Another adult with the same hearing loss may not have been so socially outgoing or adept at adjusting to new situations and may be concerned primarily about being able to communicate with close family members, especially a spouse, in the confines of the familiar surroundings of their home. The same hearing loss may pose less of a threat to participation for this individual, partly because the spouse is able and willing to manage communication breakdowns and partly because unfamiliar and challenging communication situations are avoided; however, the individual may be far less able to overcome communicative obstacles when it becomes necessary to do so (e.g., when admitted to hospital). It is noteworthy that gender differences in adult adjustment to hearing loss have only fairly recently been recognized as important, and evidence continues to mount showing that hearing loss may take a greater toll on women than men, partly because of the centrality of communication in the roles of wife and mother and partly because women receive less social support from others in adjusting to hearing loss (Hallberg et al., 1996; Hétu et al., 1993). There is still much more to learn about the functional significance of hearing and hearing loss to everyday communication.

> The hard of hearing adult may hear well enough to participate appropriately in many communication situations, yet struggle in other communication situations.

Even the ageist stereotypes held by family members and professional caregivers can influence an individual's success in adjusting to hearing loss, because such stereotypes can have a profound effect on actual behavior over the long term (Ryan et al., 1986). In challenging situations, verbal messages are likely to be misinterpreted and inappropriate responses may result. Family and friends may be confused by the inconsistency in the person's apparent communicative ability, and they may attribute the person's moments of seeming inattentiveness and lack of appropriate social interaction to a number of causes, ranging from indifference to senility, any of which may lead to less and less social interaction between the aging individual and various communication partners. When deprived of social interaction, due to either a hearing loss and/or the stereotyped attitudes of those around them, older persons become frustrated and may increasingly avoid situations in which difficulties are encountered (i.e., family gatherings, church, movies, and other social activities that they enjoyed previously). Such a loss in close interpersonal communication can lead to decreased stimulation, resulting in depression and self-depreciation. The stereotyped expectations become a self-fulfilled prophecy in what has been called the "communication predicament of aging" (Figure 10.3).

Ultimately, many older persons with hearing impairment exhibit what has been described clinically as the "geriapathy syndrome" (Maurer, 1976):

> The individual feels disengaged from group interaction and apathy ensues, the product of the fatigue which sets in from the relentless effort of straining to hear. Frustration, kindled by begging too many pardons, gives way to subterfuges that disguise misunderstandings. The head nods in agreement with a conversation only vaguely interpreted. The voice registers approval of words often void of meaning. The ear strives for some redundancy that will make the message clearer. Finally, acquiescing to fatigue and frustration, thoughts stray from the conversation to mental imageries that are unburdened by the defective hearing mechanism.

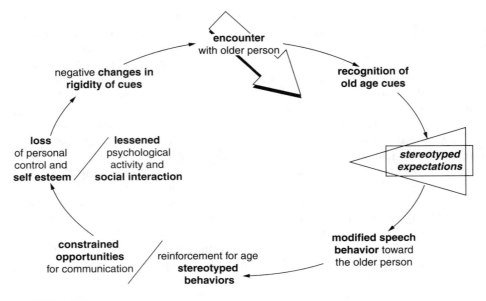

FIGURE 10.3

Communication predicament of aging.

Source: From Ryan et al., 1986. Copyright 1986. Reprinted with permission of Elsevier Science.

> The pattern described by clinicians as geriapathy has also been expressed by older adults themselves, as demonstrated in the following comment written by an older woman at a meeting of the Canadian Hard of Hearing Association: "When you are hard of hearing you struggle to hear; when you struggle to hear you get tired; when you get tired you get frustrated; when you get frustrated you get bored; when you get bored you quit.—I didn't quit today."

The comments made to audiologists by adults who are hard of hearing provide rich insights into how they experience communication situations in everyday life. The following sample of quotes illuminates various obstacles to communication and how the causes and consequences of hearing problems may be manifested. These words also suggest areas to be addressed in rehabilitation. In counseling, the audiologist must be alert to such comments because of their value in guiding rehabilitation planning. Furthermore, as a communication expert, the audiologist is uniquely positioned to provide a positive communication experience for the client, thereby demonstrating that solutions to the problems that they describe can be achieved. It is especially important that the audiologist rise above ageist sterotypes when interacting with other adults.

Hearing Loss

These comments provide insights into some of the ways that hearing loss affects people:

Mary: I can appreciate young children being considered inattentive or disruptive in school from this lack of hearing and assimilation and not comprehending why because they don't know that they can't hear. It's not that I don't understand but rather that it is so tiring to listen.

Tom: Jokes aren't funny if you have to ask for a repetition.

Patricia: It's hard to be intimate with my partner when whispers can't be heard and the lights have to be on for lipreading.

Henry: There's no privacy in this home for the aged—no one would hear a knock on the door so people just barge into rooms to find a resident; conversations are never quiet.

These comments suggest helpful tactics that could be addressed in conversational therapy:

Marjorie: By completely sounding each word, the speaker goes more slowly and it gives me time to translate the sounds to meaning. Most TV or radio speakers are too fast, and while I am trying to make sense of the first statement, they are away on to the third or fourth sentence, so I soon have to drop out and so lose interest. Asking for repetition seems to be a way of giving the brain cells time to put sounds into meaning.

Mike: In a group, when someone new begins talking, by the time I figure out who it is, I have lost the thread of the conversation. When I know the topic, I have no problem, but when the topic changes I get lost.

To deal with obstacles to communication and the stresses associated with hearing loss, the effortfulness of listening, and frequent miscommunications, adults adopt coping behaviors. Rehabilitation planning requires that the audiologist appreciate how persons experience stress and how they cope with it. Lazarus and Folkman (1984) proposed a model of stress and coping that can be readily applied to the situations of adults who are hard of hearing. In their model, the person and the environment are considered to be in a dynamic, bidirectional relationship. Stress entails the constant appraisal of this relationship. When the relationship is perceived to pose a threat, challenge, or harm to the person, then it becomes stressful and a coping response is required. Problem-focused coping responses are directed at the cause of stress (e.g., gathering information or solving problems). Emotion-focused coping responses are directed at regulating stress (e.g., avoiding problems). Distress continues until coping is successful in restoring balance in the relationship between the person and the environment.

Studies of adults who are hard of hearing have found that coping behaviors fall into two general categories: (1) controlling the social scene and (2) avoiding the social scene (Hallberg & Carlsson, 1991). Controlling is similar to problem-focused coping. The person actively manages communication situations assertively by

Coping responses can be problem focused or emotion focused.

altering the social and physical environment and taking responsibility for the outcomes of these actions. Coping behaviors include giving verbal and/or nonverbal instructions to communication partners, using technology, and/or adjusting seating or lighting in a room. Although these coping behaviors seem laudable, they may create feelings of helplessness and negative feelings when attempts to control the situation fail and it begins to seem that it is not possible to maintain control. Repeated experiences of helplessness may ultimately result in abandonment of attempts to control the situation.

Avoiding is similar to emotion-focused coping. The person who is hard of hearing minimizes hearing loss by joking about it or making positive comparisons between the self and others. The person may avoid challenging communication situations and choose not to use conspicuous hearing technologies. Rather than disclose the hearing problem or the need for accommodation, strategies such as lipreading, positioning oneself near a talker, pretending to understand, or remaining silent may be used to camouflage hearing problems (Jaworski & Stephens, 1998). Avoiding behaviors seem maladaptive, but they may be essential during some phases of adjustment when the person's self-esteem is vulnerable or the person has too little energy to solve problems. It is intriguing to consider that such avoidance may be a key factor in the limited use of hearing aids by those with hearing loss. However, prolonged avoiding may result in social isolation or redefinition of the self as less competent.

The relationship between *personal factors* and *environmental factors* and the ensuing stress lead to coping responses.

Everyone encountering stress engages in a mixture of coping behaviors, and it is important to reexamine these adjustment methods as they relate to hearing impairment in adulthood. What works for one person may not work for another, and what works for a given person at one time may not work at another time, with success necessarily depending on the nature of the person, the environment, and the person–

Trade-Offs

An example of the trade-offs between controlling and avoiding are demonstrated in the following example. A middle-aged man, attending a peer support group for the hard of hearing, proudly explained to the group how he and his wife had decided to manage the "going to a restaurant for dinner scene." The couple were united in their conviction that the most important part of going out for dinner was for them to enjoy each other's company. By comparison, the man was clear in his mind that he had no interest in social interaction with the restaurant staff. Furthermore, the man did not feel that his masculinity was threatened in any way if his wife did the talking with the restaurant staff, and his wife did not have any hesitation about taking on the responsibility for the required information exchange with these strangers. Both members of the couple were prepared to use an audio input extension microphone to increase the privacy and reduce the stress of their conversation throughout the dinner. After clearly defining what was important, or not, to them in the situation, they agreed on solutions that accomplished their goals, without jeopardizing their roles and relationships. On the one hand, the scenario demonstrates control insofar as action was taken to address important needs (enjoying each other's company); on the other hand, avoiding was a reasonable choice to minimize stress associated with unimportant aspects of the situation (who communicated with the staff). Deciding what is important and what is not is crucial to goal setting and sets the stage for developing an action plan for coping.

environment relationship at a given time. There is no universally correct form of coping and no stock recipe for managing hearing loss.

Coping styles learned in childhood continue to be utilized throughout one's lifetime to deal with the normal stresses of living, but the ways in which aging adults cope with communicative challenges are also influenced and modified by their interactions with others who may or may not support particular coping behaviors. Given the strong influence of family and caregivers on communicative behavior in older adults, it is helpful to the audiologist to consider how the adjustment of the client may be predisposed or reinforced not only by the client's own behaviors, but also by the behaviors of significant others. In the model of learned dependency, two main patterns of interactions between older people and their social partners in everyday activities in private dwellings and in residential care facilities were described as the *dependence–support script* and the *independence–ignore script* (Baltes & Wahl, 1996). These scripts highlight how older adults maintain and develop dependent and independent behaviors. In the dependence–support script, the dominant pattern was one in which older people engaging in dependent behaviors were immediately attended to and given positive reinforcement. For example, when a man who is hard of hearing waits for his wife to answer the phone, she reinforces his avoidance of the phone by answering it herself and, in the ensuing phone conversation with a mutual friend, she makes decisions for her husband without passing the phone to him or even consulting with him. After many such events, he begins to doubt his ability to manage conversations on the phone to the extent that he doesn't answer it at all, even when he is alone, thereby eventually losing independence. The less common independence–ignore script was one in which older people engaging in independent behaviors were ignored or discouraged. For example, if a woman tried to put on her own hearing aid (an independent act), her husband might say "I told you I would help you with that; you never get it in right" (a dependence–supportive act). Sadly, in the study, constructively engaged or proactive social behaviors (e.g., talking to another person) were reinforced only 25% of the time, and more frequently such independent behaviors were discouraged. Ultimately, the older person surrenders independence and complies with the expectations of dependence.

On a positive note, the communication enhancement model in Figure 10.4 suggests how to counteract the communication predicament of aging (Ryan et al., 1995). Accordingly, the audiologist should encourage family and caregivers to use independence-supporting behaviors. A daughter can make comments like "It is so great to get your input on this decision" when the hearing aid is worn or a conversational repair strategy is used, thereby encouraging her mother to take an active role in family discussions. A nurse can use a personal amplifier to ease a resident's communication effort. Successful communication experiences will predispose, enable, and/or reinforce the behavior changes targeted as goals for the client.

In summary, in counseling the audiologist and client explore the complex backdrop against which the rehabilitation plan will be enacted, including the client's attitudes, activity and participation goals, coping and communication styles, coexisting health issues, the influence of family and caregivers, and the personal and environmental factors that have and will support or impede adjustment to hearing loss. Counseling culminates in setting objectives. Objectives should be

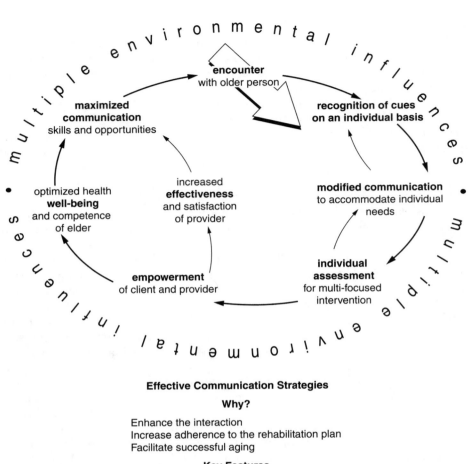

Effective Communication Strategies

Why?

Enhance the interaction
Increase adherence to the rehabilitation plan
Facilitate successful aging

Key Features

Be 'inspiring' *vs* 'dispiriting'
Convey high expectations
Facilitate communication skills of older client
Seek feedback about how communicating
Affirm personhood by listening
Recognize individual life goals and strategies
Assess collaboratively
Assess and build on strengths
Negotiate treatment plan

FIGURE 10.4

Communication enhancement model.

Source: From Ryan et al., 1995.

clearly stated and specify *who* will do *what, how much,* by *when.* Objectives can target behavioral or environmental changes to be adopted by the person who is hard of hearing or by significant others. Examples of a priority rating of objectives developed from an analysis of complaints for a particular client are provided in Table 10.8

TABLE 10.8

Complaints, Objectives, and Recommended Action Steps in Priority Order for an Example Case

INITIAL COMPLAINT	OBJECTIVES FOR END OF THE THIRD WEEK OF THE TRIAL PERIOD	ACTION
A. Audibility objectives addressed by practicing volume control skills with hearing aid		
1. Turning TV up too loud (daughter's complaint)	Mrs. Carter will find her comfortable TV listening level 100% of the time when watching the news by adjusting her hearing aid after the daughter has preset the level.	Practice adjusting TV and hearing aid volume with Mrs. Carter and daughter in a quiet room.
2. Inability to hear whispers, soft sounds	Mrs. Carter will detect car turn indicator sound 100% of the time when driving in her neighborhood (to be confirmed by daughter on a trip at the end of the 3 weeks).	Explain and practice how to adjust hearing aid volume depending on the level of the target signal and degree of background noise.
B. Activity objectives addressed by conversational therapy with client and partner		
3. Daughter tired of repeating conversation	Mrs. Carter's daughter will reduce needed repetitions in a 10-minute sample of daily conversation by 50% from the amount needed on samples taken on 3 days pretrial.	Instruct daughter to turn off background sounds (e.g., radio, TV), make eye contact before talking, state and confirm topic changes, and slow speech rate during conversation.
4. Difficulty understanding conversation with friends in the dining room	Mrs. Carter will understand the gist of 90% of conversations with her friend Mrs. Brown during lunch in the dining room at their facility (to be self-assessed by Mrs. Carter).	Explain benefits of visual attention to the talker and how to select a seat away from noise sources and discuss when two preferred repair strategies could help.
C. Participation objectives addressed by use of ALD (FM system)		
5. Confusion at church services	Mrs. Carter will demonstrate to her daughter that she understood 100% of the announcements made at the Sunday service of the third week.	Explain and try new hearing aid with existing FM system at her church.
6. Frustration on Senior Adult Center bus outings	Mrs Carter will increase her understanding of messages from the driver by 75% as demonstrated to the recreation staff who accompany the seniors on outings.	FM System and its use with the hearing aid to be explained to the bus driver and the recreation staff and to be used on the bus.

(explained in more detail later). Over time, evaluation of whether goals have been achieved will become an important topic of discussion between the audiologist and the client and significant others as they go on to make new decisions and set new rehabilitative goals to meet new or changing needs.

Amplification and Instrumental Interventions to Achieve Audibility

Amplification is the most common form of rehabilitation. First, the audiologist must determine if the client is ready for a hearing aid or ALD. A decision to go ahead with instrumental rehabilitation will depend on the nature and degree of the client's hearing loss, the nature of the client's activity and participation needs, and the client's willingness to trade the potential benefits against the burdens of using an instrument. Having decided to go ahead with instrumental rehabilitation, the next steps for the audiologist are to fit an appropriate device, ensure that it functions as expected, and counsel and orient the client to its use and care.

IS THE CLIENT READY FOR AN INSTRUMENT? Sensorineural hearing loss is not medically treatable at the present time, but the alternative choice, wearable amplification, is not highly regarded among adults of any age. Hearing loss is stigmatizing (Hétu, 1996). By putting on a hearing aid for the first time, the hard of hearing person discloses to the world that he or she has a hearing loss and is not "normal". Hearing aids are considered to be ugly, unkind associations are made between deafness and dumbness, and uncharitable jokes about deafness and aging are prevalent. In addition to the social costs, wearing a hearing aid also has other costs: the initial high financial costs of hearing aids, ongoing costs for batteries and maintenance, continued lack of knowledge and confusion about the service delivery system, and transportation costs and time needed for visits to clinics and hearing aid offices. These costs are not readily offset by the acoustic benefits of amplification. Furthermore, even the acoustical benefits may fall short, because even the latest digital hearing aids continue to be of limited benefit in adverse noisy or reverberant acoustical environments. In a recent survey of members of the hard of hearing association in the United Kingdom, the first priority was to improve hearing aids (endorsed by 100%), and the second priority (endorsed by 95%) was to educate the general public about hearing loss (Stephens, 1996b). It is essential for further progress that there be a combination of improved and appropriately fit technology, along with reduction of stigma by changing societal attitudes toward hearing, hearing loss, and increasing hearing accessibility.

A client may not be ready to purchase a hearing aid for a number of reasons. Results of a questionnaire interview survey conducted over 20 years ago among a random sample of 153 elderly individuals who had not purchased hearing aids pointed to a number of obstacles. Responding to the question "What prevents older persons with hearing difficulties from getting help?", 47% of the respondents cited the high cost of aids as the prime reason, 15% indicated lack of knowledge concerning where to go for assistance and what services were available, 11% attributed lack of transportation as the main problem, and 7% cited pride and vanity as the primary reasons for not seeking help. The remaining 20% described a variety of other problems, including fear of doctors and hearing aid dealers, lack of awareness of a hearing difficulty, projected determination to get by without assistance despite the handicap, and unfavorable reports about hearing aids from relatives and friends (Lundberg, 1979). Despite advances in technology, studies over the intervening decades have found similar results (Holmes, 1995).

Reasons for seeking help are also varied. Studies have repeatedly found that help seeking for hearing loss depends more on perceived disability (activity limitation) and handicap (participation restriction) than on measured impairment (audibility reduction), with those who feel themselves to be more handicapped seeking help sooner (Brink et al., 1996; Gilhome Herbst, Meredith, & Stephens, 1991; Swan & Gatehouse, 1990). Older persons who accept hearing loss as a "normal part of aging," tend to report less handicap, and tolerate greater hearing impairment than younger persons before seeking audiologic assistance for their problems (Brink et al., 1996; Garstecki & Erler, 1996; Lutman, 1991). While social pressure, especially from family members, who themselves may experience handicap, is a major incentive for help seeking for hearing loss, lack of referral from primary care physicians is a major disincentive (Humphrey et al., 1981; Lichtenstein et al., 1988). Of course, it is possible that hearing impairment has less effect on many older adults because of their particular life circumstances, including their greater social expertise and less demanding communication goals. In keeping with the communication enhancement model, the audiologist will need to explore the participation goals of each person as an individual in his or her own person–environment relationships. Readiness for a hearing aid or ALD must be appraised within this context.

Acknowledging the need for amplification represents considerably more than simply admitting to a sensory deficit within this age group. It is inevitably linked to recognition of the reality of aging, an acknowledgment that another bodily system is failing and that control in life situations is at risk. As one woman emphatically stated during a hearing aid counseling session, "Well, I suppose this thing will go along with my dentures, glasses, and support brace. It's getting so it takes me half the morning to make myself *whole!*" Nonetheless, most older persons can benefit from appropriately fitted hearing aids and/or ALDs if the predisposing, enabling, and reinforcing conditions are optimized.

FIT AND FUNCTION OF THE INSTRUMENT. Although amplification is worn by individuals of all ages, most people who wear aids are beyond the sixth decade of life (Holmes, 1995). This trend has been obvious for many years and it is only likely to increase as the population ages. Over the last two decades, hearing aids have become increasingly miniaturized, and at the same time there have been advances such as greater sophistication in hearing aid selection and fitting techniques, programmable technology, better consumer protection through FDA regulations, and increased professional awareness of the need for adequate rehabilitative follow-up. Nevertheless, hearing aid users still express serious concerns, which can be instructive in helping avoid certain pitfalls. Smedley and Schow (1990) summarized a large number of these complaints based on their survey of 490 elderly users. Most complaints fell into four categories: (1) the negative effects of background noise (28%), (2) fitting, comfort, and mechanical problems (25%), (3) concerns that the aid provides too little benefit (18%), and (4) feelings that the cost of aids, batteries, and repairs is excessive (17%).

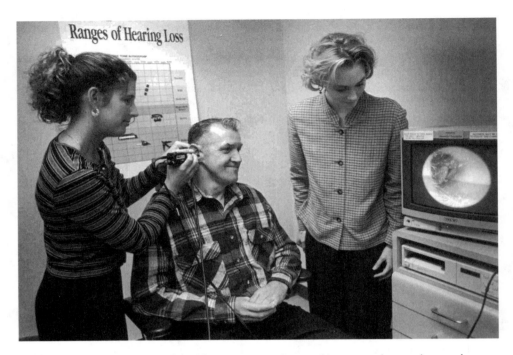

Inspection of the outer ear with a video-otoscope prior to taking an ear impression can be helpful in hearing aid fitting.

Some solutions will come from further improvements in digital signal processing and other technological advances. Other solutions will come from improvements in and wider use of ALDs. A seemingly endless number of products and devices are now available for assisting adults in a variety of situations. The hearing aid may be looked on as a general purpose device, while ALDs serve a variety of special listening needs, such as telephone listening, TV listening, or listening in large meeting rooms where the listener is some distance from the talker. A number of other listening and speaking devices are available, ranging from simple hardwire amplification systems for use in automobiles to infrared and FM systems for use in nursing homes, churches, and auditoriums (see Chapter 2 for a complete listing of devices; see also Lubinski & Higginbotham, 1997). Some ALDs are used instead of conventional hearing aids, while others are used in conjunction with them. ALDs may be preferred over hearing aids by younger adults in the early stages of hearing loss who have very specific needs (e.g., hearing on the telephone or in a classroom). They may also be the device of choice for very old adults whose co-occurring cognitive, vision, or dexterity problems increase the difficulty of using conventional hearing aids.

For biologically older adults, it may be necessary to modify the conventional assessment techniques used to determine the fit and function of instruments as described in Chapter 2. First, the length and number of appointments may need to be modified. Susceptibility to fatigue, lengthened reaction time, and a lower frustration threshold may mandate shorter sessions and the need for return visits to complete the evaluation. Although this recourse is often not desirable because of transportation problems, it may be necessary in view of other factors, including variability in performance scores (some of which may be associated with time of day or other health issues), necessity for additional assessment, and, perhaps most crucial, the need for concurrent counseling.

Second, different tests may need to be selected. Conventional word lists, sound field procedures, real-ear measurements, and programmable adjustments may need to be altered or expanded to capture pertinent auditory processing abilities, even though at the same time it may be necessary to abbreviate testing due to the older patient's diminishing alertness and susceptibility to fatigue. Depending on the environments in which the person will be using the hearing aid or ALD, tests for sentence comprehension in cafeteria noise or with competing speech (intelligible background conversation) may provide a more valid estimation than monosyllabic word lists in quiet surroundings. Matthies et al., (1983) found that the age-related decrement in speech intelligibility in noise tended to disappear over a 90-day period as their subjects gained experience wearing amplification in noise, although others have reported that older hearing aid users do not show the same benefits from *acclimatization* as do younger adults (Cox et al., 1996), presumably because of central processing problems that are not remedied by amplification (Chmiel & Jerger, 1996). Care should be taken to assess benefit from a hearing aid after a period of acclimatization following 6 to 12 weeks of exposure to amplification. Prior to that time, overall improvements are subject to additional change and thus are suspect.

The degree of acclimatization of the individual to amplification will not be known without repeated testing over time.

Third, hearing aid selection may be highly influenced by nonauditory considerations. The number of hearing aid choices may be restricted by the individual's lack of management skills or by firmly entrenched attitudes as to what type of instrument will or will not be tolerated. Fourth, additional types of appointments may need to be planned. The biologically aging segment of the population often requires more extensive follow-up, including counseling, supervised orientation, hearing aid earmold modifications, and consultation with caregivers, communication partners, and/or other health care professionals.

The question of whether aging persons should wear one hearing aid or binaural amplification is an individual one, depending on the degree of central processing deficit in binaural hearing (Grose, 1996) and, to a great extent, on prosthesis management and financial capabilities, which should be weighed against perceived gains in social receptive skills. An added variable is the attitudinal difference between wearing one instrument as opposed to two. Thus, it is not uncommon to hear an elderly person comment, "I don't need two of these, do I? I'm not deaf!" Apparently, if one hearing aid represents a milestone in adjustment to sensorineural aging, two become a millstone! Nevertheless, life satisfaction is greater for those who can adjust to appropriately fitted binaural amplification, and this is likely to increase as newer technologies implement more sophisticated binaural signal processing schemes that may offset some kinds of central auditory processing deficits. Birk-Nielsen (1974) noted in comparing monaural versus binaural amplification that two aids reduced the amount of social hearing handicap among older persons. This two-ear advantage includes better speech perception in noise, reduced localized autophony (voice resonance), improved spatial balance and localization, and improved sound quality. Among those who have physical, financial, or cosmetic limitations or whose quiescent life-styles fail to support the need for two instruments, the choice of which ear to fit becomes an issue. Considerations that enter into this decision among older adults include (1) earedness for social communication gain in quiet and in noise, (2) severity of arthritic or other physical involvement in the arms and hands as related to prosthesis manipulation, (3) handedness, (4) accustomed ear for telephone use, and (5) life-style factors affecting sidedness, such as driving a car or location of bed in a convalescent home.

On the one hand, newer signal processing hearing aids with built-in automatic controls have provided relief for some whose dexterity problems would make manipulations such as adjusting the volume control difficult. On the other hand, some advanced hearing aid features may be inappropriate for the frail elderly with co-occurring cognitive, vision, and dexterity problems. In particular, the success of hearing aids depends to a great extent on the individual's ability to handle and maintain the prosthesis. Some hearing aid companies have developed special features to accommodate the physical limitations of older persons by offering oversize or touch-type volume controls, foolproof battery compartments, attachments to reduce risk of loss, and fingernail slots or removal handles for easier removal of in the ear hearing aids. A few hearing aid manufacturers have grown concerned about the special needs of elderly persons in nursing homes and convalescent hospitals, persons whose dexterity and visual, tactile, neuromuscular, and memory difficulties contraindicate conventional forms of amplification. Therefore, Frye Electronics, for example, designed an inexpensive rechargeable body-type amplifier that features a large, red volume control and accommodates a variety of hearing loss candidates. The visibility of a body aid may benefit nursing home residents with poor management skills and visual limitations. Similarly, when earmold insertion becomes prohibitively challenging, headset-style ALDs are often preferred because they are easier to put on, but also because they can be removed without assistance, thereby supporting independence. A set of helpful tips concerning hearing aid and earmold choices for the specific challenges posed by frail elderly clients with co-occurring cognitive, vision, and dexterity problems is listed in Tables 10.9, 10.10, and 10.11 (Fairholm, 2001).

Older adults with physical and cognitive limitations require special accommodations, and it is often even more important to include caregivers in the rehabilitation plan for such individuals. Furthermore, those with central auditory processing problems often are not good candidates for hearing aids because increased audibility of the amplified signal does not overcome their need for better signal to noise conditions. Such central auditory processing deficits, usually involving declines in temporal and binaural processing, may not be apparent from the results of a conventional hearing test, but may be revealed during a comprehensive audiologic assessment. Nonetheless, Kricos et al., (1987) endorsed the need to counsel patients with central auditory processing deficits (CAPD) about the benefits and limitations of amplification. Hearing aids may not produce significantly improved speech recognition scores, but may allow centrally impaired persons to maintain what these investigators describe as "more natural auditory contact with the world" (p. 341). Furthermore, Stach (1990) has shown that ALDs may provide some help for these CAPD cases because they are designed specifically to overcome adverse signal to

TABLE 10.9

Tips for Challenges Presented by Clients with Cognitive, Vision, or Dexterity Problems

Challenge	**Client fiddles and pulls off hearing aid**
Suggestion	Low-profile in the ear aid with screw set volume control and removal notches
Rationale	May defy removal because fitting offers less to grab on to
	Fewer controls can be inadvertently changed
Limitations	Clients with very severe losses need the greater gain of a BTE
	Clients who still gets the aid off may dismantle, swallow, or discard it
Challenge	**Client will not tolerate or constantly loses hearing aids**
Suggestion	Box and headphone-style personal amplifier used under supervision when caregivers converse with client (possibly wireless)
Rationale	Light headset is often accepted better than an aid inserted into the ear
	Personal amplifiers are less expensive and more robust than hearing aids
	Caregiver holds the device, speaking into the microphone, and giving a good signal to noise ratio
Limitations	Communication opportunities restricted to times when caregivers are available
	Some caregivers will not bother to use the device
	Caregivers need to check, troubleshoot, and change batteries for the device
Challenge	**Client loses everything**
Suggestion 1	Line attachment from aid to back of collar
Rationale	By attaching the aid to clothing it will not be lost if the client takes it out
	Caregivers can see from a distance if the aid is in place or out of the ear
Limitations	Some clients will fiddle with line
	Some clients change or take off clothes such as sweaters during the day
	Some clients refuse a line attachment due to cosmetic concerns
Suggestion 2	Brightly colored hearing aid shells
Rationale	Aid is more visible to caregivers in or out of the ear
	Different colors (for example, red for right and blue for left) help staff to identify which aid is for which ear
Limitations	Cosmetic concerns
Suggestion 3	Label aid with client's name (emboss custom shells, engrave or taped on BTE)
	Note serial numbers, especially for aids that cannot easily be labeled
Rationale	If a lost aid is found, it can be traced back to its owner
Limitations	Aids may not be found (e.g., aids may be thrown into the garbage or flushed down the toilet)
Suggestion 4	Insure the hearing aid through household or specific hearing aid policies
Rationale	Insurance will pay for replacement aid
Limitations	Premiums may increase after a claim or insurance may be discontinued after an aid is lost once
Challenge	**Client with vision or dexterity problems (loss of finger mobility or sensation) wants to be independent**
Suggestion 1	Full shell in the ear aid with built-up volume control or screw-set volume control and adaptive compression providing automatic gain control
	Removal handle
	Size 13 batteries

(continued)

TABLE 10.9	
Continued	

Rationale	This hearing aid style is easiest to insert and remove
	Volume control either does not have to be manipulated or it is built up for easier manipulation
	The removal handle allows easier removal of aid from ear, even for a client unable to insert the aid
	Size 13 batteries are easier for client or caregiver to manipulate
Limitations	Some client dexterity does not allow manipulation of aids even with these modifications
	Some caregiver assistance may be required, and if the client will not accept assistance, the client may not be able to use a hearing aid
Suggestion 2	Under the chin "stethoscope" style of personal amplifier
Rationale	Even clients with hands severely crippled by arthritis can place these devices on their ears, and the on-volume wheel is large, easy to feel, and easy to see
Limitations	Rechargeable battery pills may be hard for clients to manipulate
	Device may move around and be knocked, causing microphone noise
	Microphone needs to be placed facing away from, not toward, the body
	Food spillage may damage the device
Challenge	**Client with vision or dexterity problems and insufficient gain without feedback, even with a power BTE**
Suggestion	Personal amplifier fit with custom molds and power buttons
Rationale	Personal amplifiers are less expensive than body aids, have fewer controls to manipulate, and may be rechargeable
Limitations	Frequency and output of personal amplifier need to be a good match to hearing loss and loudness tolerance
Challenge	**Hearing aid user unable to manipulate a telecoil switch who wants to use the phone**
Suggestion 1	For monaural hearing aid users, use amplified phone on the other ear
Rationale	Avoids feedback problems, microphone noise, and the need to remove the hearing aid when using the phone
Limitations	Clients with usable hearing in only one ear will not be able to use this option
Suggestion 2	Amplified telephone held away from the hearing aid microphone
Rationale	Avoids feedback when the hearing aid is used on the "microphone" setting
Limitations	Hearing aid may still feed back
	Advantage of cutting out background noise when using the telecoil is lost
Suggestion 3	Place a foam pad on the telephone ear piece
Rationale	Cushions ear and reduces feedback when hearing aid is on microphone setting
Limitations	Foam pad may interfere with placement of phone when hanging up
	Feedback from hearing aid may persist
Challenge	**Client with memory problems or confusion trying to manage hearing loss alone or with help from caregivers**
Suggestion	Keep the hearing aid as simple as possible
	ITE style with screw-set volume control if possible

TABLE 10.9

Continued

	If BTE style is needed for gain, cover the volume wheel and MTO switch (use commercial volume cover, tape, or plastic cling wrap tightly wrapped around volume wheel and MTO switch)
	Use battery door as on (open)–off (closed)
Rationale	Reduce possibility of confusion, resulting in ineffective use of hearing aid
Limitations	Battery will sometimes fall out when the battery door is opened
	Client has to take hearing aid out of ear if turned off
	Client may not accept lack of volume control

TABLE 10.10

Considerations in Selection of Advanced Hearing Aid Features for the Frail Elderly

HEARING AID FEATURE	WHY IT MIGHT BE A PROBLEM FOR THE FRAIL ELDERLY
Multiple programs	Trouble pressing buttons to change between programs
	Trouble remembering when or why to use different programs
Directional microphone	Lack of sound from behind is confusing
	May startle and fall when approached from behind
	Those in wheelchairs need to hear caregivers as they push the wheelchair from behind
	Difficulty switching between omnidirectional and directional microphones.
Remote controls	May be confusing
	May be easily lost

TABLE 10.11

Earmold Considerations for the Frail Elderly

CONCERN	PRECAUTIONS
Skin is delicate and breaks down easily	Alleviate earmold pressure points
	Earmold should not be excessively tight
	Cut tubing long enough for BTE aids
Ear canal cartilage is very flexible	Use soft earmold impression material to avoid distention during impression making
	Take open-mouth impressions because ear canal may be very mobile during chewing or talking
	Take impressions with dentures if they are usually worn, but not if they are seldom worn

noise conditions. When the rehabilitation program incorporates appropriate supports, it has been shown that even those living in residential care are able to benefit from ALDs (Lewsen & Cashman, 1997; Pichora-Fuller & Robertson, 1997). Certainly, the recommendation for amplification should not be ignored or contraindicated because of central impairments without a quantitative assessment of potential benefits during a reasonable trial period with different devices. A consideration of contextual factors will guide decision making.

Assessing benefits in the real-world context may be easier for frail clients and may provide crucial information about the nature of the social and physical environment and the supports that are available to the person. This information will guide the choice of technology best suited to the participation needs of the individual. Greater opportunity for communication will provide motivation for using a hearing aid (Lubinski, 1984). Peer support may inspire a new hearing aid user to try and continue use of a hearing aid (Carson, 1997; Dahl, 1997). If caregivers or volunteers are willing to assist with the hearing aid and their involvement becomes part of the rehabilitation plan, a hearing aid may be an option for a person with cognitive impairment who would not be able to manage the device independently (Hoek et al., 1997). If a participation priority of the person is attending group activities (e.g., bingo in the cafeteria), an FM system may provide a vital improvement in signal to noise ratio that would not be achieved with a personal hearing aid. If telephone conversations with family in another city are a participation priority, a telephone amplifier may be sufficient, cheaper, and easier to manage than a hearing aid with a T-switch. The hearing aid evaluation process among the elderly may encompass the entire 30- to 60-day trial period offered by the dispenser, often taxing the patience of those whose primary interest is sale closure. However, the clinical audiologist must remain steadfast in terms of ethical responsibilities toward even the slowest clients and must remain open to alternative or complementary solutions.

Several methods are available for measuring the perceived benefit of amplification and, indeed, self-report has been shown to be useful in dealing with acclimatization issues (see Chapter 2). Smedley and Schow (1992) used benefit, use, and satisfaction measures, including Self-assessment of Communication/Significant Other Assessment of Communication and a simple 7-point scale, and showed how these may help provide feedback from users of new devices, such as the newer programmable hearing aids. Brooks (1989) used a relatively simple self-report tool of 39 items, the Hearing Assessment Questionnaire (along with measurements of hearing aid use time) to evaluate 758 newly fitted patients seen over 1 year. The data produced in this extremely valuable study clearly demonstrate the importance of extensive counseling and hearing aid orientation (see Figure 10.5). Brook's work carefully controlled for age and hearing loss of the clients, and it may be noted that hearing aid use time for those who are extensively counseled improved dramatically (in some cases by a factor of 2). Diligent follow-up is perhaps even more important for the frail elderly because their needs and abilities may change unexpectedly. When appropriate supports are in place for this special population, regular use and benefit from amplification can be maintained by experienced hearing aid wearers, even though first time use of a hearing aid would be unlikely to succeed (Hoek et al., 1997; Parving & Phillip, 1991; Pichora-Fuller & Robertson, 1997). Use or benefit or satisfaction may be useful measures for those who are still participating in

(a) Distribution of 758 subjects fitted with NHS BTE hearing aids according to age and hearing loss, and whether (EC) or not (NEC) extra counseling was provided.

		Age (Years)							
		≤60		61–70		71–80		≥81	
		EC	NEC	EC	NEC	EC	NEC	EC	NEC
Hearing Loss (dB)	≤41	39	68	53	60	43	57	7	11
	41–50	19	16	23	30	34	49	28	32
	51–60	9	8	7	11	19	25	27	22
	61–70	2	4	2	6	7	11	10	19

(b) Average daily use time for patients having NHS aids supplied without extra counseling, as a function of degree of hearing loss and age when fitted.

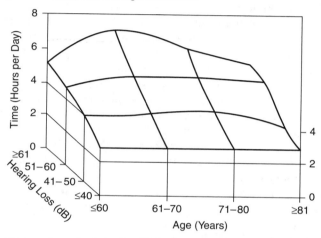

(c) Average daily time use for patients having NHS aids supplies with extra counseling, as a function of degree of hearing loss and age when fitted.

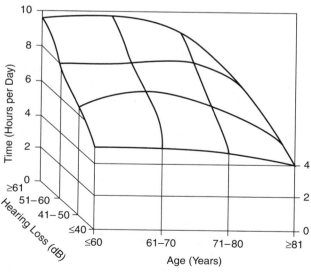

FIGURE 10.5

Data from Brooks (1989) based on United Kingdom National Health Service (NHS) provision of hearing aids.

379

activities, and for those who have stopped participating in activities and have already become more socially isolated, increases in the number of activities in which the individual participates may provide a telling outcome measure (Pichora-Fuller & Robertson, 1994). For those with a significant degree of cognitive impairment, questionnaires are too difficult, but benefit from amplification has been demonstrated by other kinds of outcome measures, such as staff observations of reductions in behavioral problems (Palmer et al., 1999). Clearly, counseling and ongoing support and follow-up are necessary to success in many cases.

COUNSELING AND ORIENTATION TO INSTRUMENTS. Initial experiences with the hearing aid or ALD, especially in the first 2 weeks, are critical. The audiologist should be ready for any problem that might occur among the client, the instrument, and the environment. Counseling, either face to face or by telephone, is a continuing commitment that is based on the adjustment needs of the individuals and their partners. As pointed out earlier, the reasons for rejection of devices are infinite, ranging from simple management difficulties to complex attitude adjustment problems. The clinician must allow these reasons to surface early in the trial period before rejection becomes ingrained. An important concept to be aware of during counseling is that rejection often works in tandem with other age-related deficits that undermine appropriate use of the device. For example, rejection and reduced short-term memory may combine to become counterproductive, as summed up in the statement of an 89-year-old woman who, during a moment of exasperation, announced, "I can never remember which way the battery goes in, and I hear better without this thing, anyway!" Needless to say, she had the battery inserted backward. Other problems may be less obvious.

Even if the person wearing the hearing aid does not notice much benefit from amplification, it is possible that his or her communication partner does notice improvement in terms of not finding talking so stressful: "Harry doesn't think my voice is any easier to hear, but now I don't have to shout at him so it really makes my life a lot easier!" The primary complaints of the client, family members, and friends during the preintervention phase should be readdressed during the trial period. Information from an example case illustrates the utility of this approach. The preintervention counseling session included the list of complaints and associated objectives to be reviewed at follow-up as shown in Table 10.8.

Consequently, audiologic surveillance in the first 2 weeks was aimed not only at use of the hearing aid, but also at taking appropriate measures to reduce or eliminate each complaint. Two additional strategies for addressing the complaints were an introduction to conversational therapy for the client and her daughter and familiarization with the use of an FM system in challenging acoustical conditions. The conversational therapy targeted the frustration of the daughter during conversation with her mother, and it also targeted communication with a close friend in the dining hall at the residence of the client. An FM system was already available in the client's church, and its use in conjunction with the hearing aid was practiced with both client and daughter. Furthermore, the use of an FM system would enable listening to the bus driver on outings, and the driver and recreational staff were involved in implementing this solution. Considered separately from the environment, the hearing aid would have been doomed to failure given the person's usual seating choices, the high level of reverberation in the church, and the high level of noise on the bus. Similarly, the overloud TV volume control was corrected by allowing the daughter to adjust the loudness to a "comfortable" level while the client was seated in her customary chair with her aids turned to half-gain. This listening level was subsequently marked on the TV volume control with an easily visible fingernail polish. Had this solution failed to meet the objectives, the next step would have been to consider using a television device providing FM transmission of the signal directly to the hearing aid wearer. Setting clear and measurable objectives helped to clarify that the rehabilitation plan was on track during the follow-up appointment during the trial period.

INDIVIDUAL ORIENTATION. The majority of hearing aid and ALD users receive help within an individual rather than a group orientation structure (Schow et al., 1993; Millington, 2001). Although group sessions have certain advantages that will be discussed later, many are not able to meet regularly in the group environment. Individual sessions permit rehabilitation to focus more on accomplishing the specific goals of the individual. Whenever possible, it is important to have significant other persons in attendance during therapy sessions or even to conduct sessions on site in locations where the target activities take place (e.g., at the chapel or in the dining hall of a care facility), one reason being to facilitate carryover to the person's everyday participation in real-world environments.

Frequently, individual device orientation focuses on developing competence in using the device. A prerequisite to achieving audibility is for clients and/or their caregivers to become skilled at handling, operating, and caring for the hearing aid or ALD. These skills are difficult for older adults to acquire, but even middle-aged adults may need more help than is routinely provided, as suggested by a study of working-aged adults in which it was found that one in four new hearing aid owners had problems operating their aid at their 1-month postfitting follow-up appointment (Alberti et al., 1984). Common problems for users of all ages are improper placement of the aid, insertion of the mold, operation of the controls, and battery insertion. All clients should be given instruction in these important skills, as well as being given written information that they can continue to refer to over time. An example handout for clients is **HIO BASICS** (see Table 10.2). Handouts may need to be translated into foreign languages or produced in large print for those with vision problems. For those requiring more intensive instruction, step-by-step training in these skills can be highly successful (Maurer, 1979). In such training, the skill to be acquired (e.g., inserting the earmold) is broken down into discrete steps that are repeated until each is mastered. At each step, encouraging comments are provided by the audiologist as successes are achieved. It is also crucial for the client to learn how to judge if he or she has been successful or not, often on the basis of tactile and visual cues regarding how the earmold looks and "feels in the ear" when it is properly seated, how it "feels to the fingers" when it is properly seated, and how it "feels to the fingers" when it is grasped properly. Such programs may be completed in a single session or over multiple sessions. Skills should always be reevaluated at follow-up to ensure that they have been maintained and to further refine them.

> The necessary skills in operating and caring for hearing aids and assistive devices should be checked to be sure that no further training is needed.

Group AR activities can help clients learn about hearing aids.

ORIENTATION IN GROUPS. Some persons may fit into a group training structure rather than, or in addition to, individual sessions. This will not be feasible for everyone, however, because all do not have attitudes or cultural beliefs that favor group interaction with strangers; they may prefer meeting times that do not coincide with the group meeting time; or they may simply prefer or need the individual attention created by a one on one situation. But when group sessions are feasible, they can be very helpful. Aging individuals may be understimulated. As noted earlier, their nucleus of peers is smaller than in previous years, and the opportunity to participate in a group experience is often welcomed. An important aspect of a small group is the opportunity to share information. In addition to the benefits to those receiving information, sharing information is often a positive experience for the information giver. In such meetings, the audiologist takes the position of group leader and facilitates discussions by (1) bringing out those persons who are reluctant to share their experiences, (2) inhibiting those few who might dominate the group, (3) permitting the discussion topics to surface from the group rather than from the clinician, (4) acting as a resource person when expertise is needed, and, most importantly, (5) acting as a good listener. Achieving homogeneous grouping (i.e., bringing together persons who have similar perceived communication problems, as revealed in self-assessment profiles), when feasible, may be desirable. It may also be advantageous to mix more expert experienced hearing aid users with beginners so that peer teaching and modeling can be incorporated into group sessions.

Like individual orientation sessions, group sessions also tend to focus mostly on the use of hearing aids, with lesser amounts of attention on communication strategies, auditory training, ALDs, and speechreading (Schow et al., 1993). In ad-

hearing aid orientation listed in Chapter 2 and in the HIO BA-
neeting is one that (1) is primarily success rather than prob-
ides an element of entertainment, (3) focuses on no more than
ves, (4) incorporates sharing of ideas in a counseling medium,
h a clear understanding of how each member can take charge
:quired learning through carryover activities. The clinician
)hesiveness by asking members to contact each other by tele-
)ns; for example, the objective of a homework assignment
on called to guess who the "mystery caller" is and report on
next group meeting. Additional help in planning group meet-
he resource website.

. The significant other person should understand the pros-
n components, and the conditions under which it should be
information regarding basic troubleshooting, warranty, and
e proficient at inserting and removing the instrument. It is
written description of this information and resources for obtaining further information on particular topics. Resource information always includes the audiologist's phone number, as well as information such as the following:
the location and telephone number of a local drug store providing low-cost batteries, suppliers of special alerting, wake-up, or other communication devices; information on captioned films for television; lists of local facilities with hearing
accessibility options (e.g., loops or FM systems); a schedule for planned hearing aid
checks; notices of audiologic rehabilitation meetings, and call-back for annual audiologic assessment. Furthermore, in addition to learning new information and
communication skills so that they can help the person with the hearing loss; significant others themselves must adjust to living with a person with hearing loss;
they may benefit as much as the client from group discussions with peers in which
information and common experiences may be shared (see Table 10.4).

ADVOCACY IN RESTRICTIVE ENVIRONMENTS. Just as it is important to set objectives that
address the goals of individuals, at the institutional level, the best method for securing the participation of the administration and staff of convalescent hospitals,
nursing homes, high-rise facilities for the aging, and senior adult centers is to find
out what needs they perceive can be addressed by the audiologic rehabilitation program. Unfortunately, they may perceive the hearing problems of their clientele to
rank low in priority when compared to the sleeping, eating, cleaning, entertainment, and other health needs within the facility. Most staff lack knowledge of hearing loss and hearing aids, and they may not perceive hearing help to fall within their
job description. Sometimes it is difficult to gain entry into a restrictive environment
on the basis of one client who has a hearing impairment and needs carryover assistance. A workable strategy for overcoming staff resistance is to seek out the staff
member who is most likely to appreciate the communication and listening needs of
the person (e.g., the activities director) and explain that you are working with the
client and his or her family. Sometimes housekeeping or nutrition staff spend more
time communicating with residents than do nurses. Offer to provide services that will

help all staff involved in the case to work more easily with the client. Another possibility is to offer a more general information session on hearing and aging as an inservice activity aimed at helping the staff to understand and manage all clientele with hearing difficulties. A stimulating, solution-oriented inservice presentation nearly always produces advocates among residents, family, volunteers, and staff members, individuals who later may become allies in the rehabilitation plan. Once allies are made, interest is maintained through a recognized need for further education as well as an open communication line to the audiologist's office. Leaving a designated staff member with this public service gesture and a copy of your professional credentials removes much of the suspicion frequently associated with the doorstep intervention tactics of some commercial vendors.

Elsewhere we have reported on a variety of experiences in providing hearing services for nursing homes (Hoek et al., 1997; Pichora-Fuller & Robertson, 1997; Schow, 1992). In a number of such homes where hearing was tested we found that only about 10% of potential hearing aid candidates were using amplification, whereas another 20% responded that they had hearing aids but were not using them. Importantly, rehabilitation has been shown to be valuable in maintaining the use of devices by those in residential care. Therefore, the need for rehabilitation is apparent and residents will be at a disadvantage if it is not provided. A multistep program is proposed as an effective plan for ensuring that hearing services are available in these facilities (see Table 10.12).

Face to face interactions between the rehabilitative audiologist and those in residential facilities will be crucial, but in some situations other media, ranging from posters and videotapes to the Internet, may augment face to face interactions. Hurvitz and colleagues (1987) demonstrated an effective self-paced computer AR program designed to provide communication training to a nursing home population. Their software program covers content related to (1) mechanism of the ear, (2) audiograms, (3) management of the hearing problem, (4) speechreading, (5) hearing aids, and (6) communication skills training. Short informational paragraphs are presented followed by multiple-choice questions in a user-friendly format. Patients trained with this program showed more knowledge gains than in a conventional group classroom approach. Health information on the Internet has growing appeal to many adults who want to find or review information on health topics at a time and place of their own choosing. In the future, Internet connection will no doubt be used to facilitate more immediate communication between the audiologist and staff, family, or residents at different locations that are geographically distributed.

Remediation for Communication Activities

Traditionally, communication rehabilitation has focused on auditory–visual communication training, with an emphasis on speechreading and auditory training. Typically, it was provided when counseling and instrumental interventions proved insufficient. In light of the growing understanding of the lengthy but important process of adjusting to hearing loss, many rehabilitative audiologists today offer communication rehabilitation to a broader segment of the population and in more varied forms that target more specific activity goals. All clients should be familiarized

TABLE 10.12

Multistep Program for Those in Residential Care

1. Screening of hearing, as required by federal law, with pure tones, visual inspection (including determination of need for removal of cerumen), and self- and staff members' assessment of hearing (e.g., Nursing Home Hearing Handicap Index).
2. Cerumen management as indicated, followed by thorough diagnostic testing for those who fail screening, along with charting and informing staff of results and arranging for referrals as needed.
3. Consultation with communication partners if appropriate to identify objectives of staff, family, or significant others.
4. Identification of objectives for rehabilitation for individuals and subgroups of residents who share particular interests or activities (e.g., attending services in chapel, going on bus outings).
5. Selection of candidates for devices, trials with hearing aids or ALDs in context, and thorough orientation for those who are reestablishing use or becoming new users of devices.
6. Inservices to staff, including instruction on the auditory mechanism, explanation of the causes and effects of hearing loss in the elderly, discussion of the role of the audiologist and facility staff in hearing health care, development of skills in using and caring for amplification devices, and guidance on how to encourage independent communication behaviors and an environment that facilitates positive interpersonal relationships among residents and staff.
7. Recommend changes to routines and physical environment that will enable best use of amplification and assistive technology.
8. Implement method for ongoing monitoring of and help for all amplification users and key communication partners, including family, staff, peers, and volunteers.

with the principles of communication rehabilitation in discussion with the audiologist, and written materials should be provided for the client to refer to later or share with significant others. An example of such a handout is CLEAR (see Table 10.3). In addition to introducing these general principles to clients, their specific activity goals can also be addressed by individual or group communication remediation tailored to their needs.

As in the past, audiovisual communication rehabilitation may be provided to those whose needs have not been met adequately by amplification. The analytic approaches to speechreading and auditory training have been encompassed into a more holistic conversation-based approach to communication rehabilitation, and this form of rehabilitation has targeted people who are hard of hearing and their communication partners (Erber, 1988, 1996; Tye-Murray, 1997). In addition to communication remediation for those using amplification, communication training is now being provided to assist individuals in the process of adjusting to hearing loss who may not yet be ready to try a hearing aid. Exciting new programs use a health promotion approach in programs for older adults with no known clinically significant hearing loss so that they will be better prepared for taking-action when they do begin to experience hearing problems (Worrall et al., 1998).

> **"Bridge" Therapy**
>
> Individual speechreading instruction was deemed appropriate for a 62-year-old woman who had suffered loss of hearing in one ear due to Ménière's disease. Socially active in the community and reluctant to disclose her impairment to others, the woman preferred the privacy of individual therapy. She was an avid bridge player and participation in her bridge club was of utmost importance to her. To address her single goal of retaining excellent ability to participate in bridge games, individual therapy activities were chosen that satisfied the same five ingredients described earlier for a good group meeting. One such therapy activity consisted of "playing" bridge through a two-way mirror with only visual cues for statements, such as "I bid three spades," "I pass," and so forth. The woman improved her ability to speechread the language of her favorite game. This proved fortuitous, since the signs of Ménière's syndrome (roaring tinnitus, vertigo, and nausea) signaled the eventual loss of hearing in her good ear. As her hearing loss deteriorated further, additional goals were formulated and therapy activities undertaken.

The traditional synthetic approaches to auditory and lipreading training have also been recast in communication remediation insofar as contextual cues and world knowledge are used to compensate for the acoustic speech cues that are misperceived or not heard. Peripheral and central auditory processing problems, including loss of hearing sensitivity, slowing of neural processing of messages, and increased difficulty understanding in noise, interact with deficits in working memory storage during communication (Schneider & Pichora-Fuller, 2000). A peripheral high-frequency hearing loss alters coding of the speech signal, thereby affecting comprehension of the content of the message and even influencing the ongoing response to the message: "Mr. Jacobson was helping his grandson paint the family shed. 'Gramps,' the younger person said, 'let's quit for awhile and go get some thinner.' The older man stared in amazement at his grandson, 'Go get some dinner? Son, we just had lunch!' "

Increasing inability to ignore background conversations and noises while attending to primary messages further interferes with the encoding and storage of conversational content to such an extent that some elderly individuals cope by avoiding these situations. Furthermore, the message-delivery speed of the nightly television newscaster simultaneously stresses auditory temporal processing as well as cognitive/linguistic processing such that older listeners experience more misperceptions of sounds and greater difficulty comprehending because they simply cannot "keep up." Vision loss is also extremely common in older adults and stresses on perceptual and cognitive processing may also undermine their ability to read (Schneider & Pichora-Fuller, 2000; Wingfield & Stine-Morrow, 2000). As a result, intellectual currency with events in the world may slip, affecting both the acquisition of new general knowledge and the recall of the specific content of conversations with others. The comprehension of content, therefore, becomes jeopardized by misperceptions of sound and misunderstanding, as well as lapses in recent memory, with possible consequences being the older person's loss of trust in reality or even denial or disbelief in it.

Mrs. Andrew's chief complaint about her new hearing aid was lack of battery life.

"Are you opening the battery case at night when you're not using the instrument?" the audiologist inquired.

"Heavens no. You didn't tell me to do that!"

"Yes, she did, mother," the daughter chimed in. "Don't you remember? It's even stated in that booklet in your purse."

"Well, this is the first time I've *heard* about it," the older woman retorted.

The critical implication of hearing loss for an aging individual is that it affects the lenses through which the client views reality. Thus, when the speech signal and content of messages are altered, the older person comes to distrust what others say as well as her own interpretation of communicative events. Restoring control and trust in communication may become an objective for communication rehabilitation that is accomplished in conversational therapy.

When communication needs become apparent in a wider range of everyday life situations, and when reduced communicative competence comes to have far-reaching effects on the person's well-being, a broader approach to communication training becomes essential. Conversation-based communication training has been promoted over the last decade or more by Erber (1988, 1996) and is explained in Chapters 4 and 5. Just as in face to face communication, conversation-based therapy necessarily engages the person in auditory and visual perception of speech. However, the therapy stresses how the person can take advantage of and manipulate many of the redundant sources of information that are available in the communicative interaction, including many aspects of the person–environment relationship. Whereas some sources of information come from the external world (e.g., seeing the waitress approach a table in a restaurant), others come from internally stored knowledge of the world (e.g., knowledge that restaurant script for ordering food often begins by the waitress asking the customers if they are ready to order). During therapy, clients learn how they can optimize the usefulness of available information, especially by using conversational strategies. For example, miscommunication resulting from misperceived speech sounds can be overcome if conversational strategies are used to establish the topic. In the earlier example, the confusion arising from the *thinner–dinner* misperception would have been repaired more gracefully if the grandfather had been more cautious and asked "What do you want to get?" before jumping to a conclusion that he actually recognized to be inconsistent with the situation. For audiologic rehabilitation to be successful for the older person, positive change must be brought about in the entire social–communicative milieu.

Conversation-based therapy cultivates the communication skills pertaining to the four elements in any communication situation: listener, talker, message, and environment. The client develops skills in each area: (1) listening (and watching) to comprehend; (2) coaching talkers to produce more easily understood speech and language (e.g., by suggesting helpful accommodations, such as "Could you keep your hand away from your face and speak slower?"); (3) using linguistic and world knowledge to interpret the meaning of the message; and (4) altering the acoustical and lighting properties of the situation to improve the signal and reduce interference from extraneous sources. The communication partner also develops corresponding skills pertaining to each of the skill areas. Both the client and the communication partner develop methods that are effective for them in their relationship with each other. These methods may be different for spouses who have lived together for 50 years than for a college student and his new professor or for a 90-year-old with dementia and the nurse providing her with palliative care in a hospice. The audiologist–counselor, acting in the multiple roles of diagnostician, hearing aid specialist, audiologic rehabilitation specialist, and gerontologist, becomes an integral part of the client's milieu.

It is worth noting that hearing loss in one communication partner may coexist with hearing loss in the other partner. It is also common for one or both partners to have another communication disorder. Spouses may develop vocal pathology as a result of chronically raising their voice to be heard by their hard of hearing partners. Spouses may have trouble hearing the poorly intelligible or soft voices of partners with Parkinson's. Most individuals who have had total laryngectomy surgery are within the senior adult age group and have hearing difficulties. Furthermore, since esophageal speech generally has reduced intensity and less well defined vowel formants, persons with laryngectomies are less intelligible to peers, who are also likely to be aging and hard of hearing. Withdrawal from social situations may result from the combination of hearing and speaking difficulties and may affect the relationship between spouses and friends. Communicative rehabilitation often entails using visual cues to improve speech perception; however, this may not be an option for the many older adults with vision loss. In one home for the aged, the audiologist was surprised when a woman who was blind asked to join the lipreading class until the woman explained that she wanted to learn how to talk more clearly so that her roommate who was hard of hearing would be able to lipread her better. It may become necessary to address the other communication issues of the client or even the communication issues of the spouse in order to achieve a solution in communication rehabilitation.

The counselor–audiologist is positioned between the aging client and reality, because the counselor's own communication skills and knowledge are called into play to assist the older person in restructuring the client's life-style to ameliorate or compensate for the hearing impairment to achieve participation. The audiologist may even play the role of the client when the communication partner is receiving conversational training or the role of the communication partner when the client is being trained. The ability to re-create these roles is enhanced by the use of Erber's HELOS (hearing loss simulator), which can be used to introduce the effects of hearing impairment into the signal heard by a person with normal hearing (Erber, 1988); but the therapy can also be done without HELOS. Importantly, such role playing enables the audiologist to model more effective communication strategies, and it also promotes empathy, mutual respect and consideration, and sharing of experiences with and between the client and their communication partner(s).

During communication rehabilitation, as in all stages of audiologic rehabilitation, the empathy achieved through listening will have great effect on the outcome of the rehabilitation program. Slower in adapting to change and more fixed in their

---

Allowing Client to Register Complaints

Client: My voice is so difficult with these aids on. [Shakes head.] I don't think I can get used to them.

Audiologist: Uh-huh.

Client: Do I sound like this to others? My voice sounds so gravelly.

Audiologist: Hmm.

Client: I wonder if I've been talking too loud to people . . . before I got these, I mean. [Eyes brighten.] Well, I certainly keep my voice down now.

Audiologist: Uh-huh.

Client: I can hear a whisper now . . . in a quiet room. But . . . Oh, the racket when I'm doing dishes! I took them off and put them on the window sill.

Audiologist: Uh-huh.

Client: I could hear the clerk in the checkout line yesterday. Heard everything he said. . . .

Audiologist: Hmm.

Client: I suppose it's a matter of . . . getting used to them. [Nods head.] They help . . . they really do.

---

attitudes than younger persons with hearing impairment, elderly patients demand more professional time for their feelings to surface. In some instances, the audiologist can bring about positive changes by simply *permitting the client to register complaints,* thereby achieving a more favorable outlook in decision making. Listening helps the audiologist to appreciate the delicate balance between the client's enjoyment of hearing and the perceived nuisances of the new device. Listening also helps the audiologist learn from the ingenuity of clients who find their own novel solutions to problems. The many personal preferences, attitudes, and beliefs of clients will guide the setting of objectives and the selection of an action plan for rehabilitation that can be reevaluated over time.

Environmental Coordination and Participation Improvement

As demonstrated so far in this chapter, a well-coordinated rehabilitation program for adults requires an organized body of knowledge about the clientele. This includes clinical sensitivity toward persons in general who are at various life-span stages, a thorough understanding of the individual in question, and prioritization of this information into a meaningful rehabilitative plan. Directive, informational counseling that includes "laundry lists" of questions, often constructed on the basis of stereotypes, is not well advised. Although such an approach may be useful for some purposes, the salience of the information sampled in this noninteractive, narrow

Client Profile

Areas of intake information that provide context for the overall coordination of the program:

- Hearing status, including history, duration, and potential site(s) of lesion, as well as self-assessment of the hearing problems and assessments by significant other persons.
  - What problems are the most important to this person and his or her partners?
  - What are the past, present, and desired activities of this person?
- Previous help seeking and medical or prosthetic intervention.
  - What factors contributed to the success or failure of previous rehabilitative action?
- Associated health issues, such as arthritis, neuromuscular limitations, visual problems, tinnitus, and memory difficulties.
  - To what extent do physical, mental, social, or economic conditions make this individual dependent on others?
- Personal and environmental factors that will predispose, enable, and reinforce decision making and action taking.
  - What kinds of social or environmental supports would be needed by the individual in his or her activities?
  - What costs and benefits might influence rehabilitative choices?

manner may be lost in the undertow of real needs and feelings that surface when the clinician simply listens to the client. In too many instances, failure or rejection of hearing amplification or other treatment during the intervention process is due either to lack of clinical sensitivity toward the individual client's needs, feelings, and goals or to insensitivity toward the subpopulation of adults to which the individual belongs. Adults are heterogeneous and their particular needs must be determined by the audiologist. The elderly segment of the world population of persons with hearing impairment has a wealth of life experiences that may influence their course of rehabilitation both positively and negatively. There is also variability among younger adults, including young adults completing their education and vocational training, adults raising young families, adults caring for aging parents, working adults in stressful senior positions, and adults with unusual health or occupational challenges. For older and younger adults alike, their need for audiologic services may range from minimal to extreme. Each case must be appreciated in a dynamic context.

The pervading question is whether the rehabilitation program will make a significant, positive impact on the life satisfaction of this person. A well-developed client profile, based on both formal assessment measures and informal information gathering during counseling, substantially increases the probability of successful audiologic rehabilitation. Thus, the profile permits an educated focus on current aspects of the person's life-style. It addresses client needs, rather than those of the clinic or the practitioner. It delineates whether the individual is a candidate for intervention, the particular plan that should be tailored to meet the person's needs, the hypothetical objectives and terminal goals that might be accomplished, significant other persons who should be involved, environmental modifications that will be needed to achieve a solution for the person, and where, when, and under whose auspices the program should be carried out. The individual's adjustment to hearing loss and preparedness for taking rehabilitative action is foremost in the rehabilitative agenda, but rehabilitation may well fall short of meeting the individual's goals if the importance of social and physical environmental supports is overlooked.

Most of the complaints of adults about their hearing difficulties, for example, are about participation in a specific situation or role: "I can't hear in church," "I can't understand the lecturer when my classmates are talking," "I don't watch the news on television, because the announcer talks too fast," "I feel like I'm letting my teenage son down because I can't have conversation with him without making him repeat all the time." Knowledge about such concerns provides for a practical, operational baseline from which positive rehabilitative changes can be measured. Newer self-assessment measures such as the Glasgow and COSI are useful for identifying the needs of the individual and documenting changes with respect to these needs. More informal information gathering during counseling, however, is still necessary if the audiologist is to fully appreciate how personal, social, and physical environmental factors should best be tackled to achieve a successful rehabilitative solution.

The key to whether significant other persons should be included in the plan and subsequent coordination of the rehabilitation program is the extent of their present and potential contribution toward the elderly individual's life satisfaction and the achievement of their top priority goals. Observing interactions between the client and others may reveal the kind of support that they will provide and whether they will be allies during intervention. Perhaps one of the paramount questions that the clinician should ask on an intuitive level is whether significant others' support is based on a valid concern for the individual or whether it is irregular or counterproductive, or independence or dependence supporting. Relatives, friends, and staff members in the geriatric environment can constitute important links in the rehabilitative chain and can be helped by review of a handout like the one shown in Table 10.4. Others who may act in concert with the audiologist to facilitate adjustive behaviors include members of the professional community who have knowledge about the client and his or her family support system, culture, and life-style. Relevant parties may include members of the clergy, physicians, welfare workers, and administrators or leaders of organizations and clubs in which the client holds membership.

The physical environment may also be crucial to the client's ability to participate fully. Environmental supports can be optimized by selecting favorable environments or modifying unfavorable environments. The client may need to investigate which restaurants are quiet and well lit and learn how to pick the best table and seat. Where choices are not possible, modifications may be required. Noise and reverberation may need to be reduced by interior decorating (e.g., carpeting, upholstery, drapes) or architectural changes to increase sound absorption by room surfaces. Electromagnetic interference can also interfere with participation by people who are hard of hearing. For example, when a department head in a large company moved into her new office, she was horrified to discover that she was unable to use her T-switch for the telephone or with ALDs in the conference room. To the embarrassment of the architect, the acoustical consultant who was hired to assess the problem determined that the problem was caused by the high level of electromagnetic interference produced in a machine room located directly below the new offices. A large insulating panel was installed by the employer to eliminate the problem. The nature of the client's problem and the method for solving it eluded the audiologist, whose clinical measures showed that there was no change in the client's hearing and that her devices were working properly. The cooperation of the employer and the expertise of the architect and acoustical consultant were vital to achieving the environmental piece of the solution. Greater involvement of professionals and policy makers responsible for the built environment will likely be seen as audiologic rehabilitation catches up with other rehabilitative fields in which accessibility adaptations (e.g., ramps for wheelchairs) have long been accepted as societal obligations, especially in workplaces or public educational, health, and law facilities.

Further Illustration of CORE and CARE

The approach recommended in this chapter suggests that the rehabilitation of hearing loss should be based on the strategy suggested by CORE and CARE (See Figure 10.2). We further note that most of the rehabilitation done by audiologists is done in connection with hearing aid fitting. We know that in a certain number of special cases, such as with a cochlear implant client, that rehabilitation may be much more involved, but these special cases will be the exception. We therefore want to provide a clear emphasis on hearing aid fitting, and before concluding this chapter we would like to describe a client recently seen in our clinic to illustrate how this rehabilitation procedure plays out in real life in the case of a hearing aid client. This individual, John, was a male, age 54, who had been experiencing hearing problems for the past few years, which finally prompted him to have his hearing tested with the idea he might need hearing aids. In the C (communication) assessment phase, we tested hearing by audiometry and self-report. The audiogram revealed equal results in both ears, and so the better ear thresholds were 1K = 35, 2K = 50, 4K = 60 (Figure 10.6). The loss was sensorineural and, based on better ear thresholds and the system used in our clinic for sorting hearing loss into exclusive groups, we placed the loss into our category F1 (see Chapter 1 and the resource web site).

We also had John complete a Glasgow (GHABP) scale. At an initial interview and before any decision was made about hearing aids, the Glasgow allowed us to measure the initial disability or communication activity limitation. This score is based on four standard listening situations and up to four situations supplied by the client that are of concern. John provided two areas of hearing concern beyond the four standard ones, and his Glasgow results for the relevant six items are shown in Figure 10.7. The percentage disability score (*activity limitation*) obtained on the Glasgow for John was 60%. Scoring procedures and practice in scoring for the Glasgow can be accessed on the web site that goes with this text.

In terms of O (overall) participation, we considered vocational, social, and emotional issues. John said his work as a janitor was not affected by his hearing, but his major concerns were in social activities and some emotional problems related to these social activities. Again the Glasgow was helpful in measuring this handicap or *participation restriction*, because it measured how much his hearing

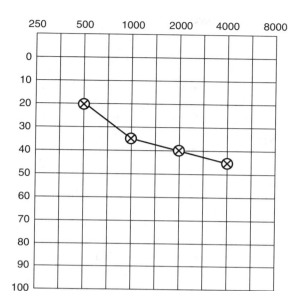

FIGURE 10.6

John, age 54, initial audiogram.

Ear/Test	PTA	SRT	%	Level
Right	32	35	88	60
Left	32	30	84	60

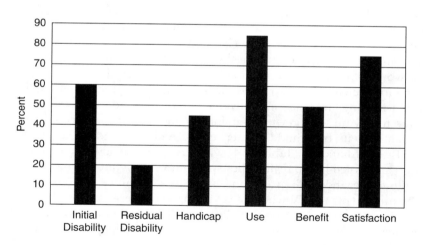

FIGURE 10.7

Glasgow (GHABP) findings for John. Pre hearing aid results are initial disability and handicap. Post fitting results are residual disability, use, benefit and satisfaction.

problems cause him to be worried, annoyed, or upset in the six situations. This score was 45%.

We have gathered and published scores on over 800 clients sorted into exclusive hearing categories, and when we compared John's two scores (60% and 45%) with others who have hearing losses in the same category as his, we found that he was within one standard deviation of the mean for all clients with such a hearing loss (see data in Chapter 1 and on the resource web site). However, his scores were located toward the upper end of that midrange, showing that he has more than average *activity limitation* and *participation restrictions*. We also explored R (related personal) and E (environmental) factors that had a bearing on John's hearing loss. We found his attitude about improving his hearing was excellent (a type I) and that he is an extrovert who would like to get out more if his hearing were better. In terms of environmental issues, his wife also would like him to socialize more and encouraged him to obtain hearing aids. She filled out a Glasgow also, modified for use by a significant other person. Thus we considered all four of the CORE issues.

As John told us his story during the C (counseling) phase of the treatment, goals were determined based on input from him. These goals were set in the areas of A (audibility) and R (remediation of communication activities) and in terms of E (environmental or participation goals). By counseling and setting goals in these three areas, we recommend a reasonably standardized procedure in rehabilitation (CARE) much as we do in diagnostic audiology. (Schow, 2001). After John decided to obtain hearing aids, the necessary decisions were made about fit and function of the aid, and ear impressions were made. When he came back to pick up his hearing aids, we used the HIO BASICS handout (Table 10.2) in a 45-minute session for hearing instrument orientation. A week later in a second 45-minute follow-up session, the remediation of communication issues was addressed with the CLEAR handout (see Table 10.3). This provided John with some help in fundamental areas of concern surrounding communication. Had John been interested in getting more help in these areas we would have recommended our four sessions of group therapy, which are provided twice each semester, but John did not elect to enroll for these sessions, which are provided free with all of our hearing aid fittings.

John did elect to focus his efforts in the next two 45-minute follow-up sessions on the two environmental participation issues that he had identified as a major concern on his Glasgow. John was concerned that he could not hear his grandchildren when they come for their weekly visit. Also, he was concerned about hearing TV when his wife is watching and he cannot turn the volume as loud as he would like it. We spent a full follow-up session with John talking about ways that he could improve communication with his granddaughter, age 10, and his grandson, age 8. We went over the SPEECH handout (Table 10.4) with his wife to help her communications with him and urged her to review these communication improvement suggestions with the two grandchildren. He and his wife determined to control the environment by turning off the TV when he is visiting with these children, and by getting them to sit closer and watching their lips, he felt he could improve his success in communication. Also, in another follow-up session we helped him to obtain a listening device for his TV that was successful for use when his wife watched TV with him. We sent a Glasgow scale to John 6 months after he first came to our clinic and found that he now had only 20% residual disability, which is a reduction of 40% from the first assessment. He was using the aids at an 85% level and receiving good reported benefit (50%) and was satisfied at a 75% level of satisfaction.

Certainly, all rehabilitation outcomes will not be this straightforward and successful. But new goals may be set based on outcome measures when the initial plans do not yield good success. When the entire CORE–CARE package is used with clients, we believe that good outcomes can occur on a consistent basis.

SUMMARY

The audiologic rehabilitation specialist has a unique opportunity to provide services to the adult population over a large life-span range, although the majority will be retired adults. The complexity of changes occurring in advanced age, together with the difficulties encountered due to auditory deficits, requires that the audiologist become resourceful and willing to modify established techniques and protocols. The audiologist can contribute to a positive future for aging persons who are hard of hearing—a future that is of higher quality, more productive, and/or less isolated. Better communication skills may help to lessen the stress caused by other disabilities, as well as facilitate ongoing social interaction between older adults and their environments.

The need for specialized training in adult life-span changes and gerontology among graduate students specializing in speech and hearing sciences becomes increasingly apparent as longevity increases and the population ages (Kricos & Lesner, 1995). The last decade has seen a substantial growth in our knowledge of aging in general and auditory aging in particular. Following on these advances in research, it is now time for a greater commitment to training in gerontology among graduate programs in the United States so that audiologists can take on a leadership role in the care of aging persons who are hard of hearing. Addressing the problems of adults who are hard of hearing is a professional challenge that we must all face together.

SUMMARY POINTS

- The great majority of adults with hearing disability acquire hearing loss due to illness, accident, noise exposure, and aging, but most lose their hearing through the aging process.
- Hearing loss leads to misunderstandings and stress for the individual, family, and friends.
- A number of personal and environmental factors may complicate the situation for elderly persons with hearing loss.
- Presbycusis is the name for age-related hearing loss.
- Phonemic regression is a common presbycusic problem wherein there is a more severe word recognition problem than would be expected on the basis of hearing thresholds.
- It is not uncommon for over 80% of a nursing home population to have hearing loss.
- The CORE and CARE model of rehabilitation employed throughout this text provides the framework for rehabilitation assessment and management.
- Rehabilitation settings include university speech and hearing clinics, military facilities, community centers, medical clinics, and private practice offices of dispensers.
- Assessment begins with audiometry and self-report and progresses to concerns about participation, personal, and environmental factors.
- Two self-report measures, the COSI and the GHABP, are used in assessment and are also extremely valuable later as outcome measures.

- Rehabilitative goals must be set by considering the current audibility, activity, and participation needs of the individual.
- The personal and social and physical environmental factors supporting or impeding decision making and action taking must be considered when goals are set.
- Goals should clearly state and specify *who* will do *WHAT, HOW MUCH*, and by *WHEN.*
- Goals must be reevaluated and reset as needed at the time of follow-up, a crucial step in the rehabilitative cycle.
- Rehabilitation involves change on the part of the individual who is deaf or hard of hearing, but may also involve his or her communication partners or necessitate changes in the physical environment.
- More people will seek and benefit from rehabilitation as technology improves, but it will also be crucial for stigmas to be reduced by social change.
- Even individuals who do not use amplification might benefit from other forms of rehabilitation.
- Adjustment to hearing loss is a dynamic process that we do not yet fully understand.

RECOMMENDED READING

Craik, F. I. M., & Salthouse, T. A. (Eds.). (2000). *The handbook of aging and cognition* (2nd Ed.). Mahwah, NJ: Lawrence Erlbaum.

Erber, N. P. (1996). *Communication therapy for adults with sensory loss* (2nd Ed.). Melbourne, Australia: Clavis Publishing.

Hummert, M. L., & Nussbaum, J. (Eds.). (2000). *Aging, communication, and health: Linking research and practice for successful aging.* Mahwah, NJ: Lawrence Erlbaum.

Kricos, P. B., & Lesner, S. A. (Eds.). (1995). *Hearing care for the older adult: Audiologic rehabilitation.* Boston: Butterworth-Heinemann.

Lubinski, R., & Higginbotham, J. (Eds.). (1997). *Communication technologies for the elderly: Vision, hearing, and speech.* San Diego, CA: Singular Group Publishing.

Noble, W. (1998). *Self-assessment of hearing and related functions.* London: Whurr.

Tye-Murray, N. (1997). *Communication training for older teenagers and adults: Listening, speechreading & using conversation strategies.* Austin, TX: PRO-ED.

Willott, J. F. (1991). *Aging and the auditory system: Anatomy, physiology, and psychophysics.* San Diego, CA: Singular Group Publishing.

Worrall, L., & Hickson, L. (in press). *Communication disability in aging: Prevention and intervention.* San Diego, CA: Singular Group Publishing.

RECOMMENDED WEB SITES

This Web site has about 70 different AR links broken down into "devices" "communication" and "other."
http://www.pitt.edu/~commsci/aural.htm

Perry Hanavan's site which defines AR and includes about 30 links.
http://www.augie.edu/perry/ear/ardefine.htm

By far the most comprehensive AR site available. It is very stable and has been there for years with regular updating. It has over 100 sites that are AR related. http://ctl.augie.edu/perry/ar/ar.htm

Gatehouse web site for GHABP
http://www.ihr.gla.ac.uk/ghapb

REFERENCES

Alberti, P. W., et al. (1984). Aural rehabilitation in a teaching hospital: Evaluation and results, *Annals of Otology, Rhinology and Laryngology, 93*(6), 589–594.

Alpiner, J. G., & Schow, R. L. (2000). Rehabilitative evaluation of hearing-impaired adults. In Alpiner, J., & McCarthy, P. (Eds.), *Rehabilitative audilology: Children and adults* (3rd ed.). Baltimore, MD: Williams & Williams.

Andersson, G., et al. (1994). Behavioural counselling for subjects with acquired hearing loss: A new approach to hearing tactics. *Scandinavian Audiology, 23,* 249–256.

Baltes, M. M., & Wahl, H-W. (1996). Patterns of communication in old age: The dependence-support and independence-ignore script. *Health Communication, 8* (3), 217–231.

Beck, L. (2000). The role of outcomes data in health-care resource allocation. *Ear and Hearing, 21*(4), Supp., 89S–96S.

Bentler, R. A., & Kramer, S. (2000). Guidelines for choosing a self-report outcome measure. *Ear and Hearing, 21*(4), Supp., 37S–49S.

Bess, F., et al. (1989). Hearing impairment as a determinant of function in the elderly. *Journal of the American Geriatric Society, 37,* 123–128.

Birk-Nielsen, H. (1974). Effect of monaural versus binaural hearing and treatment. *Scandinavian Audiology, 3,* 183–187.

Borg, E. (1998). Audiology in an ecological perspective—development of a conceptual framework. *Scandinavian Audiology, 27,* Supp. 49, 132–139.

Brink, R. H. S van den, et al. (1996). Attitude and help-seeking for hearing impairment. *British Journal of Audiology, 30,* 313–324.

Brockett, J., & Schow, R. L. (2001). Web site profiles common hearing loss patterns. *Hearing Journal, 54*(8) in press.

Brooks, D. (1989). The effect of attitude on benefit obtained from hearing aids. *British Journal of Audiology, 23,* 3–11.

Carson, A. J. (1997). Evaluation of the "To Hear Again" program. *Journal of Speech–Language Pathology and Audiology, 21,* 160–166.

Carson, A. J., & Pichora-Fuller, M. K. (1997). Health promotion and audiology: The community–clinic link. *Journal of the Academy of Rehabilitative Audiology, 30,* 1–23.

CHABA: Committee on Hearing, Bioacoustics, and Biomechanics. (1988). Speech understanding and aging. *Journal of the Acoustical Association of America, 83,* 859–895.

Chmiel, R., & Jerger, J. (1996). Hearing aid use, central auditory disorder, and hearing handicap in elderly persons. *Journal of the American Academy of Audiology, 7,* 190–202.

Clark, P. G. (1996). Communication between provider and patient: Values, biography, and empowerment in clinical practice. *Aging and Society, 16,* 747–774.

Conran, T., & Binzer, S. (2000, July). Personal beliefs in adaptation to hearing loss. Paper presented at the XXVII International Congress of Psychology, Stockholm, Sweden.

Coupland, N., Wiemann, J. M., & Giles, H. (1991). Talk as "Problem" and communication as "Miscommunication": An integrative analysis. In Coupland, N., Giles, H., & Wiemann, J. M. (Eds.), *"Miscommunication" and problematic talk* (pp. 1–17). Newbury Park, CA: Sage.

Cox, R., et al., (1996). Benefit acclimatization in elderly hearing aid users. *Journal of the American Academy of Audiology, 7*, 428–441.

Cox, R., et al., (2000). Optimal outcome measures, research priorities, and international cooperation. *Ear and Hearing, 21*(4) Supp., 106S–115S.

Dahl, M. (1994). Hard-of-hearing inmates in penitentiaries. *Journal of Speech–Language Pathology and Audiology, 18*, 271–277.

Dahl, M. (1997). To Hear Again: A volunteer program in hearing health care for hard-of-hearing seniors. *Journal of Speech–Language Pathology and Audiology, 21*, 153–159.

Dillon, H., & So, M. (2000). Incentives and obstacles to the routine use of outcome measures by clinicians. *Ear and Hearing, 21*(4) Supp., 2S–6S.

Dillon, H., James, A., and Ginis, J. (1997). Client oriented scale of improvement (COSI) and its relationship to several other measures of benefit and satisfaction provided by hearing aids. *Journal of American Academy of Audiology, 8*, 27–43.

Erber, N. P. (1988). *Communication therapy for hearing-impaired adults.* Victoria, Australia: Clavis.

Erber, N. P., et al., (1999). Caregiver communication training program. *Speech Pathology Australia,* June, 12–14.

Fairholm, D. (2001). Vancouver/Richmond Health Board Community Audiology Centre Outreach to Hard of Hearing Seniors Program, personal communication.

Gaeth, J. (1948). *A study of phonemic regression associated with hearing loss.* Unpublished doctoral dissertation, Northwestern University.

Gagné, J.-P. (2000). What is treatment evaluation research? What is its relationship to the goals of audiologic rehabilitation? Who are the stakeholders of this type of research? *Ear and Hearing, 21*(4) Supp., 60S–73S.

Gagné, J.-P., & Jennings, M. B. (2000). Audiological rehabilitation intervention services for adults with acquired hearing impairment. In Valente, M., Hosford-Dunn, H. & Roesor, R. Audiology treatment. New York: Theme.

Gagné J.-P., McDuff, S., & Getty, L. (1999). Some limitations of evaluative investigations based solely on normed outcome measures. *Journal of the American Academy of Audiology, 10*, 46–62.

Garstecki, D. C., & Erler, S. F. (1995). Older women and hearing. *American Journal of Audiology, 4*, 41–46.

Garstecki, D. C., & Erler, S. F. (1996). Older adult performance on the communication profile for the hearing impaired. *Journal of Speech and Hearing Research, 39*, 28–42.

Garstecki, D., & Erler, S. (1997). Counseling older adult hearing instrument candidates. *High Performance Hearing Solutions, 1*, 14–18.

Gatehouse, S. (1999). Glasgow hearing aid benefit profile: Derivation and validation of a client-centered outcome measure for hearing-aid services. *Journal of American Academy of Audiology, 10*, 80–103.

Gatehouse, S. (2000). The impact of measurement goals on the design specification for outcome measures. *Ear and Hearing, 21*(4) Supp., 100S–105S.

Getty, L., & Hétu, R. (1991). Development of a rehabilitation program for people affected with occupational hearing loss. II. Results from group intervention with 48 workers and their spouses. *Audiology, 30,* 317–329.

Gilhome Herbst, K. R., Meredith, R., & Stephens, S. D. G. (1991). Implications of hearing impairment for elderly people in London and in Wales. *Acta Otolaryngologica,* Supp. 476, 209–214.

Goldstein, D. P., & Stephens, S. D. G. (1981). Audiological rehabilitation: Management model I. *Audiology, 20,* 432–452

Grose, J. H. (1996). Binaural performance and aging. *Journal of the American Academy of Audiology, 7,* 168–174.

Hallberg, L., & Carlsson, S. (1991). A qualitative study of strategies for managing a hearing impairment. *British Journal of Audiology, 25,* 201–211.

Hallberg, L., R.-M., & Jansson, G. (1996). Women with noise-induced hearing loss: An invisible group? *British Journal of Audiology, 30,* 340–345.

Hétu, R. (1996). The stigma attached to hearing impairment. *Scandinavian Audiology, 25,* Supp. 43, 12–24.

Hétu, R., & Getty, L. (1991). The development of a rehabilitation program for people affected by occupational hearing loss I: A new paradigm. *Audiology, 30,* 305–316.

Hétu, R., Jones, L., & Getty, L. (1993). The impact of acquired hearing impairment on intimate relationships: Implications for rehabilitation. *Audiology, 32,* 363–381.

Hoek, D., et al. (1997). Community outreach to hard-of-hearing seniors. *Journal of Speech–Language Pathology and Audiology, 21,* 199–208.

Holmes, A. (1995). Hearing aids and the older adult. In Kricos, P. B., & Lesner, S. A. (Eds.), *Hearing care for the older adult: Audiologic rehabilitation* (pp. 59–74). Boston: Butterworth-Heinemann.

Humphrey, C., Gilhome Herbst, K., & Faurqi, S. (1981). Some characteristics of the hearing-impaired elderly who do not present themselves for rehabilitation. *British Journal of Audiology, 15,* 25–30.

Hurvitz, J., et al., (November, 1987). Comparison of two aural rehabilitation methods in a nursing home. Paper presented at the ASHA National Convention, New Orleans.

Isaacowitz, D. M., Charles, S. T., & Carstensen, L. L. (2000). Emotion and cognition. In Craik, F. I. M., & Salthouse, T. A. (Eds.). *The handbook of aging and cognition* (2nd ed.; pp. 593–632). Mahwah, NJ: Lawrence Erlbaum.

Jaworski, A., & Stephens, D. (1998). Self-reports on silence as a face-saving strategy by people with hearing impairment. *International Journal of Applied Linguistics, 8,* 61–80.

Jerger, J., Oliver, T., & Pirozzolo, F. (1990). Speech understanding in the elderly. *Journal of the American Academy of Audiology, 1,* 17–81.

Kochkin, S. (1999). "Baby boomers" spur growth in potential market, but penetration rate declines. *Hearing Journal, 52(1),* 33–48.

Kochkin, S. (1996). Marke Trak IV: 10-year trends in the hearing aid market—has anything changed? *Hearing Journal, 49(1),* 23–34.

Kochkin, S. (2000). Marke Trak V: "Why my hearing aids are in the drawer": The consumers' perspective. *Hearing Journal, 53(2),* 34–42.

Kricos, P. B. (2000). The influence of non-audiological variables on audiological rehabilitation outcomes. *Ear and Hearing, 21*(4) Supp., 7S–14S.

Kricos, P., et al. (1987). Perceived benefits from amplification as a function of central auditory status in the elderly. *Ear and Hearing, 8,* 337–342.

Lazarus, R. S., & Folkman, S. (1984). *Stress, appraisal and coping.* New York: Springer.

Lewsen, B. J., & Cashman, M. (1997). Hearing aids and assistive listening devices in long-term care. *Journal of Speech–Language Pathology and Audiology, 21,* 3, 149–152.

Lichtenstein, M. J., Bess, F. H., & Logan, S. A. (1988). Validation of screening tools for identifying hearing-impaired elderly in primary care. *Journal of the American Medical Association, 259* (19), 2875–2878.

Lubinski, R. (1984). The environmental role in communication skills and opportunities of older people. In Wilder, C., & Weinstein, B. (Eds.), *Aging and communication: Problems in management* (pp. 47–57). New York: Haworth.

Lundberg, R. (1979). *Research survey.* Unpublished manuscript, Portland State University.

Lutman, M. E. (1991). Hearing disability in the elderly. *Acta Otolaryngologica,* Supp. 476, 239–248.

Matthies, M., Bilger, R., & Roezchowski, C. (1983). SPIN as a predictor of hearing aid use. *Asha, 25*(10), 61.

Maurer, J. E. (1976). Auditory impairment and aging. In Jacobs, B. (Ed.), *Working with the impaired elderly* (pp. 72). Washington, DC: National Council on the Aging.

Maurer, J. E. (1979). Aural rehabilitation for the aging. In Bradford, L. J. & Hardy, W. G. (Eds.), *Hearing and hearing impairment* (pp. 319–338). New York: Grune & Stratton.

McCormick, M., et al. (1994). Hearing accessibility in a university setting: Reflections on the audiologic therapeutic process. *Journal of Speech–Language Pathology and Audiology, 18,* 260–266.

Millington, D. (2001) Audiologic rehabiltation practices of ASHA audiologists: Survey 2000. Unpublished masters thesis, Idaho State University.

Montgomery, A. A. (1994). WATCH: A practical approach to brief auditory rehabilitation. *Hearing Journal, 47*(10), 10, 53–55.

Newman, C. W., & Jacobsen G. P. (1993). Self-assessment of hearing. *Seminars in Hearing, 14*(4), 299–384.

Noble, W. (1998). *Self-assessment of hearing and related functions.* London: Whurr.

O'Mahoney, C. F. O., Stephens, S. D. G., & Cadge, B. A. (1996). Who prompts patients to consult about hearing loss? *British Journal of Audiology, 30,* 153–158.

Palmer, C. V., et al., (1999). Reduction in caregiver-identified problem behaviors in patients with Alzheimer disease post-hearing-aid fitting. *Journal of Speech and Hearing Research, 42,* 312–328.

Parving, A., & Phillip, B. (1991). Use and benefit of hearing aids in the tenth decade— and beyond. *Audiology, 30,* 61–69.

Pichora-Fuller, M. K., & Carson, A. J. (2000). Hearing health and the listening experiences of older communicators. In Hummert, M. L., & Nussbaum, J. (Eds.), *Aging, communication, and health: Linking research and practice for successful aging* (pp. 43–74). Mahwah, NJ: Lawrence Erlbaum.

Pichora-Fuller, M. K., & Robertson, L. F. (1994). Hard of hearing residents in a home for the aged. *Journal of Speech–Language Pathology and Audiology, 18,* 278–288.

Pichora-Fuller, M. K., & Robertson, L. (1997). Planning and evaluation of a hearing rehabilitation program in a home-for-the-aged: Use of hearing aids and assistive listening devices. *Journal of Speech–Language Pathology and Audiology, 21,* 174–186.

Pichora-Fuller, M. K., Johnson, C., & Roodenburg, K. (1998). The discrepancy between hearing impairment and handicap in the elderly: Balancing transaction and interaction in conversation, *Journal of Applied Communication Research, 25,* 99–119.

Robertson, L., et al. (1997). The effect of an aural rehabilitation program on responses to scenarios depicting communication breakdown. *Journal of Speech–Language Pathology and Audiology, 21,* 187–198.

Ronch, J. L. Van Zanten. (1992). Who are these aging persons? In Hull, R. (Ed.), *Rehabilitative audiology* (pp. 185–213). New York: Grune & Stratton.

Ross, M. (1997). A retrospective look at the future of aural rehabilitation. *Journal of the Academy of Rehabilitative Audiology, 30,* 11–28.

Ryan, E. B., et al. (1986). Psycholinguistic and social psychological components of communication by and with the elderly. *Language and Communication, 6,* 1–24.

Ryan, E. B., et al. (1995). Changing the way we talk with elders: Promoting health using the Communication Enhancement Model. *International Journal of Aging and Human Development, 41,* 89–107.

Schneider, B., & Pichora-Fuller, M. K. (2000). Implications of perceptual deterioration for cognitive aging research. In Craik, F. I. M., & Salthouse, T. A. (Eds.), *The handbook of aging and cognition* (2nd Ed., pp. 155–219). Mahwah, NJ: Lawrence Erlbaum.

Schow, R. L. (1992). Hearing assessment and treatment in nursing homes. *Hearing Instruments, 43*(7), 7–11.

Schow, R. L. (2001) A standardized AR battery for dispensers. *Hearing Journal, 54*(8) 10–20.

Schow, R. L., & Gatehouse, S. (1990). Fundamental issues to self-assessment of hearing. *Ear and Hearing, 11*(5, Suppl.), 6–16.

Schow, R. L., & Nerbonne, M. A. (1980). Hearing levels among Elderly nursing home residents. *Journal of Speech and Hearing Disorders, 45*(I), 124–132.

Schow, R. L., & Smedley, T. C. (1990). Self-assessment of hearing. *Ear and Hearing, 11*(5, Suppl./Special Issue).

Schow, R. L., et al. (1993). Aural rehabilitation by ASHA audiologists; 1980–1990. *American Journal of Audiology, 2*(3), 28–37.

Skafte, M. D. (2000). The 1999 hearing instrument market—the dispensers' perspective. *Hearing Review, 7*(6),8–40.

Smedley, T. C., & Schow, R. L. (1990). Frustrations with hearing aid use: Candid observations from the elderly. *Hearing Journal, 43*(6), 21–27.

Smedley, T. C., & Schow, R. L. (1992). Satisfaction/disability rating for programmable vs. conventional aids. *Hearing Instruments 43*(11), 34–35.

Smith, C. R., & Fay, T. H. (1977). A program of auditory rehabilitation for aged persons in a chronic disease hospital. *Asha, 19,* 417–422.

Stach, B. (1990). Hearing aid amplification and central processing disorder. In Sandlin, R. E. (Ed.), *Handbook of hearing aid amplification,* Vol. 2 (pp. 87–111). Boston: College-Hill Press.

Stephens, S. D. G. (1996a). Hearing rehabilitation in a psychosocial framework. *Scandinavian Audiology, 25,* Supp. 43, 57–66.

Stephens, S. D. G. (1996b). Evaluating the problems of the hearing impaired. *Audiology, 19,* 105–220.

Stephens, S. D. G., Jones, G., & Gianopoulos, I. (2000). The use of outcome measures to formulate intervention strategies. *Ear and Hearing, 21*(4) Supp., 15S–23S.

Stephens, S. D. G., et al. (1998). Use of patent-specific estimates in patient evaluation and rehabilitation. *Scandinavian Audiology, 27,* Supp. 49, 61–68.

Stephens, S. D. G., et al. (1999). An analysis of the communication tactics used by hearing-impaired adults. *British Journal of Audiology, 33,* 17–27.

Swan, I. R. C., & Gatehouse, S. (1990). Factors influencing consultation for management of hearing disability. *British Journal of Audiology, 24,* 155–160.

Taeuber, C. (1992). *Sixty-five plus in America*. Washington, DC: U.S. Department of Commerce, Economics and Statistics Administration. Bureau of the Census.

U.S. Bureau of the Census. (1990). *The need for personal assistance with everyday activities: Recipients and caregivers, current population reports*, Series P-70, No. 19, Table B. Washington, DC: U.S. Government Printing Office

Villaume, W. A., Brown, M. H., & Darling, R. (1994). Presbycusis, communication, and older adults. In Hummert, M. L., Wiemann, J. M., & Nussbaum, J. F. (Eds.), *Interpersonal communication in older adulthood: Interdisciplinary theory and research* (pp. 83–106). Thousand Oaks, CA: Sage.

Wilkerson, D. (2000). Current issues in rehabilitation outcome measurement: Implications for audiological rehabilitation. *Ear and Hearing, 21*(4) Supp., 80S–88S.

Wingfield, A., & Stine-Morrow, E. A. L. (2000). Language and speech. In Craik, F. I. M., & Salthouse, T. A. (Eds.), *The handbook of aging and cognition* (2nd Ed., pp. 359–416). Mahwah, NJ: Lawrence Erlbaum.

World Health Organization (WHO). (2000). *International classification of functioning, disability, and health.* (pp. 25–43), Geneva, Switzerland: World Health Organization

Worrall, L., et al. (1998). An evaluation of the *Keep on Talking* program for maintaining communication skills into old age. *Educational Gerontology, 24,* 129–140.

Implementing Audiologic Rehabilitation: Case Studies

Case Studies: Children

Mary Pat Moeller

C O N T E N T S

■ INTRODUCTION

Each child with hearing loss presents with a unique constellation of abilities and needs. An individualized approach to diagnostics and case management is essential.

Children with hearing loss represent a heterogeneous group, with highly individual characteristics and needs. Differences in degree of hearing loss, family constellation and resources, medical history, language abilities, school support, and styles of learning contribute to each child's unique profile. The five case examples that follow describe individualized approaches to case management, with process-oriented strategies for problem solution. In each of the cases that follow, two concepts are central to the intervention: (1) clinicians must ascertain intervention priorities through differential diagnosis and careful determination of a child and family's primary needs; and (2) individualized management requires a process of clinical decision making and objective monitoring of the efficacy of intervention (see Chapter 9).

The process of pediatric audiologic rehabilitation is complex and challenging. Parents and clinicians face numerous management decisions early in the course of audiologic rehabilitation. Should the child's rehabilitation focus on auditory–oral development or is a visually oriented approach needed? If a visual approach is needed, should it be oriented toward American Sign Language or Manually Coded English? What type of amplification will best meet this child's needs? Should sensory communication aids be considered? Will the child's needs be met in an inclusive educational setting, or will a specialized setting better serve this child? Answers to these and other management questions are rarely simple and rarely without controversy. Parents face many of these questions at a time when they are trying to cope with the diagnosis of hearing loss. They deserve objective guidance that is based on thoughtful examination of the child's needs and abilities in light of the options available.

Parents should have access to information about all communication options and guidance based on thoughtful evaluation of the child and the family's needs.

AR service delivery for children is further complicated by the increasing incidence of children with hearing loss who have significant secondary disabilities. These children require sophisticated assessment and management through a team approach. Federal mandates require that early intervention be provided in a family-centered manner (Roush & Matkin, 1994). This has brought about a reconceptualization of the professional's role in the decision making and management process. The goal of empowering family members in the management of the child's needs also requires a diverse and individualized approach, given the wide range of family systems represented in the clinician's caseload. Each of these factors dictates the need for objective, individually tailored approaches and flexible, innovative service delivery models.

The case studies that follow represent five unique concerns that influenced the course of rehabilitative management:

1. Family-centered intervention for a child with multiple disabilities.
2. Clinical decision making: a student's decision to receive a cochlear implant.
3. Issues affecting educational placement decisions.
4. Late identification in a child who was hard of hearing: auditory–linguistic considerations.
5. Diagnostic therapy: a tool for solving complex intervention problems.

In each of the following cases, multidisciplinary service delivery was necessary and advantageous. No one discipline has all the skills and expertise to address the complex nature of the problems that often present themselves. The audiologic rehabilitation specialist needs to cultivate the skills of working as a team member, joining in collaborative consultation with allied professionals and parents. Multidisciplinary perspectives contribute to a holistic understanding of the child's and family's needs.

Although the cases described are based on real persons, names and other biographical facts have been changed to maintain patient confidentiality.

CASE 1   JOEY: FAMILY-CENTERED
■ INTERVENTION: MULTIPLE DISABILITIES

AR specialists working at the parent/infant level are meeting new professional challenges, including the opportunity to work with very young infants in the context of the family system (see Chapter 8). It has been estimated that 33% to 38% of infants with hearing loss have complex developmental needs resulting from secondary disabilities (Schildroth & Hotto, 1993; Moeller et al., 1990). This case illustrates the importance of transdisciplinary approaches to case management. Overall coordination among various professionals and families is essential in meeting the needs of deaf infants with additional disabilities (Moeller et al., 1990).

It has been estimated that between 33% and 38% of children with hearing loss have educationally significant secondary disabilities.

Background Information

Joey's profound bilateral sensorineural hearing loss was diagnosed through auditory brainstem response testing when he was 10 months of age. Subsequent behavioral testing demonstrated no response to speech or tonal stimuli at the limits of the equipment. Birth history records revealed that an emergency C-section was done at 36 weeks gestation due to fetal distress. Joey required oxygen and remained in the neonatal intensive care unit (NICU) for 5 days following birth. Neonatal complications included hyperbilirubinemia and cardiac and respiratory difficulties. Joey was on a heart monitor for the first seven months of his life. Joey also has a medical history of dizziness and balance problems, poor coordination, and hypotonia.

Joey was delayed in achieving developmental milestones. He sat unsupported at 10 months and walked at 18 months. At 4 years of age, Joey is not yet toilet trained. The parents began signing to Joey immediately after diagnosis of the hearing loss, and he produced his first sign at 13 months of age. The mother reported that Joey was producing signed phrases up until about 16 to 18 months. At that time, he discontinued use of many of the signs he knew and did not combine signs. Regression in both social and language behaviors was noted by the family.

Significant regression in language behaviors in toddlers may be association with autism.

Previous Rehabilitation

Joey had been served since infancy by a homebound early-intervention program. At two years of age, he was placed in a self-contained toddler and preschool program, where he was served by an educator of the deaf, a speech–language pathologist, and an occupational and physical therapist (OT/PT). Although Joey was

ABR and OAE testing are valuable in identifying hearing loss in a young child like Joey.

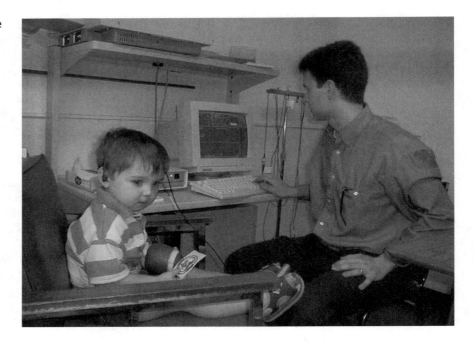

Fleeting visual attention, reduced functionality of communication, and self-stimulatory behaviors are not typical of a child who has hearing loss alone.

learning to cooperate with the routine of his preschool classroom, he demonstrated little evidence of learning from the group setting. He rarely initiated interactions or conversations with others. Although he knew over 100 signs, he rarely used them for functional communication. His attention to communication from others was fleeting. He demonstrated stereotypical and self-stimulatory behaviors. At 3½ years of age, Joey's family relocated and he was placed in a self-contained public school program for deaf students with support services in speech–language pathology and OT/PT, similar to those of his previous program. Joey's social, behavioral, and attentional difficulties continued in the new school environment. Joey's educational team and parents requested consultation from an AR team due to concerns for his inattention, slow language learning, and atypical behaviors.

A comprehensive, multidisciplinary assessment was initiated in response to the expressed concerns. The communication portion of the evaluation was conducted by a team of AR specialists, who relied on valid instruments relevant to the child's environment and informal observations to analyze Joey's needs. The assessment began with parent interviews. The mother expressed a primary concern that her son may have autism. The mother had read extensively on the subject and was an excellent reporter of her son's unique constellation of behaviors. She indicated that he had extreme fixations with lights and electronic equipment with switches. If left to his own devices, Joey would spend an entire day running and staring at lights or turning a VCR off and on. Although the parents had purchased numerous developmentally appropriate toys, these items did not hold Joey's attention. The mother indicated that Joey did not seem to know how to play with toys.

Joey's mother aptly described her son as socially isolated, preferring to be "in his own world." The family had learned to sign fluently to their son, but few rewards for this effort were forthcoming. Joey's communication remained extremely delayed in comparison to that of his deaf peers at school. The parents faithfully implemented full-time hearing-aid use, which they reported resulted in exacerbation of negative behaviors and self-stimulatory vocalizations. During the initial parent interview, Joey was allowed to play in an attractive playroom with numerous developmentally appropriate toys. Joey spent the entire period fixating on the lights in the room and did not become involved with toys or individuals present.

Formal, structured language testing is often inappropriate with a youngster who has fragile social interactions. The AR specialist found it necessary to identify ecologically valid assessment tools that would provide insights on Joey's communicative skills in a variety of environments. The Communication and Symbolic Behaviors Scales (CSBS) (Wetherby & Prizant, 1993) was an ideal selection in that it makes use of observational contexts that place few demands on the young child. Symbolic play skills and communicative means can be explored with this tool during semistructured play activities. In addition, the MacArthur Communicative Development Inventory (Dale & Thal, 1993), which is a parent report scale, gave the clinician valuable information on Joey's sign vocabulary used in the home. Results indicated that Joey used signs and gestures to communicate a small range of language functions (behavioral regulation, rejecting, and answering). His receptive sign vocabulary of 192 words was roughly equivalent to a 21-month developmental level. He presented as a curious and highly independent youngster. Rather than requesting help with a mechanical toy, for example, he would persist in trying to discover how to operate it.

Joey's warm and supportive home environment was a strength. The family had already learned through discovery various strategies to structure Joey's behavior and attention. They described the need to "Joey-proof" their home. In fact, the parents had become experts in helping their son succeed through environmental structuring. Many family strengths that could be incorporated in the individual family services plan (IFSP) were noted. The family was able to identify many primary needs. Foremost among them was the need for a definitive diagnosis so that appropriate management strategies and expectations could be implemented with Joey. In essence, the parents were "doing all the right things," yet watched as their child remained very delayed and became more difficult to manage. The parents expressed the need for a team to integrate perspectives and to understand their child in the holistic context of the family.

Joey was severely delayed in his symbolic skills, including play. His symbolic play skills at age four were commensurate with a 19- 22-month level. His constructional play skills were well in advance of his symbolic play skills. He exhibited difficulty integrating various sensorial inputs. For example, if Joey's hands were involved in sensory exploration activities, he was not able to attend to any other input. Activities in his classroom frequently seemed to cause a "sensory overload" for Joey. When this occurred, he would "tune into" lights or the feel of his shirt and "tune out" the language input around him.

Typically developing deaf children usually perform well on tests of symbolic play. Children with autism often have relative strengths in constructional play with deficits in symbolic play.

Environmental Coordination/Participation

Team members from various disciplines made multiple observations of Joey in an effort to make a differential diagnosis and understand his needs. Transdisciplinary team discussion centered on the constellation of major findings of (1) serious delays in symbolic language use (in spite of positive opportunities for language acquisition in the home), (2) history of regression in language and social behaviors, (3) limited social interaction, (4) significant delays in symbolic play with strengths in constructional play, (5) tendencies for obsessions with lights and mechanical objects, and (6) self-stimulatory behaviors. Based on these findings, it was the team consensus that Joey was exhibiting the characteristics of childhood autism in addition to profound deafness. This diagnosis had important implications for Joey's intervention program. The team psychologist was able to offer many insights into the impact of the two disabilities on behavior, learning, and daily living. He assisted the family in implementing a consistent behavior management program at home.

Communication Rehabilitation Adjustment

Joey's program, which was designed to meet the needs of young children who are deaf, required adaptation in view of Joey's complex needs. AR team members had the opportunity to observe Joey in his school placement and to problem solve with the school-based intervention team. Observations, and the adaptations and recommended strategies included:

An integrated team approach is required to effectively meet the complex needs of a child with multiple disabilities.

1. Joey presented with developmental needs across several domains (e.g., cognition, symbolic play, language, fine and gross motor, and social and sensory integration). This complex set of needs was difficult to address in a traditional deaf education classroom. It was determined that his needs would be better served in a special education preschool classroom, with teamwork between a teacher specializing in children with autism and a teacher of the deaf. The special educator had signing skills and was able to provide Joey with a range of developmental activities in a highly structured and predictable classroom routine. Services were also provided by occupational and physical therapists.

2. Joey's special education team worked together to incorporate highly functional learning activities with regular opportunities to communicate through sign. Emphasis was placed on individualized lessons and increasing one on one time.

3. Assistance from a behavioral specialist was implemented at home and at school. Emphasis was placed on reducing time spent with fixations and reducing aggressive behaviors.

4. Joey's parents were motivated to implement full-time hearing aid use, and they had accomplished this goal early in the rehabilitation program. However, behavior problems and inappropriate vocalizing escalated greatly when he wore amplification. The team and the parents agreed to remove amplification until other behaviors were brought under control. Amplification would be tried again in the future in the context of the overall behavior program. Although a medical team had suggested a cochlear implant, the parents recognized that there were many contradictions to the recommendation.

5. A priority for Joey's program was to strengthen the social foundation for language learning. He required indirect playful approaches, where he was motivated to remain in interaction with others and engage in turn-taking. Strategies from Greenspan's (1990) *Floor Time* program were useful in addressing this goal. This program focuses on goals such as engagement, two-way communication, establishing shared meanings, and developing emotional thinking. Through this program, adults learn a variety of strategies for following the child's lead and building communication circles through such behaviors as a slow and calm approach, gentle looks, supportive postures, and nonintrusive ways of supporting the child's themes and communicative attempts.

> Engagement refers to the ability of an infant to share an experience with a parent or caregiver, such as looking at objects together and smiling or laughing in response to an interaction with the object.

6. As Joey's parents found, structuring the environment was instrumental in helping him succeed. He needed boundaries in wide-open spaces. He learned better in rooms without access to switches. He responded well when his limits were clearly defined and he could be actively engaged in lessons.

Psychosocial and Counseling Aspects

It was critical for the educational and AR teams to consider family needs. In talking with the parents, it was clear that living with Joey 24 hours a day brought many challenges. Sleep disruption was common; going out in public was nearly impossible; controlling driven obsessions was a full-time job. Joey's parents did everything they could to help him. Even so, their rewards came very slowly and in unpredictable ways. It helped for the team to make recommendations that gave consideration to the impact on home life. The parents needed the team to address behavioral issues in a comprehensive and ongoing manner. They also needed a chance to talk to other parents of children like Joey. The family appreciated practical direction to allow them to cope with today and to be hopeful about tomorrow. Respite care opportunities and support from the extended family gave the parents needed breaks.

> Emotional thinking relates to a child's growing ability to understand what they themselves and others are feeling or wanting and how that affects their behavior.

CASE 2   MIKE: DECISION MAKING BY A ■ STUDENT RELATED TO COCHLEAR IMPLANTS

In some cases, successful rehabilitation dependents on the willingness of the family, the client, and the AR specialist to explore different options. When students are older, as in this case, they need to have access to the full range of information in order to take an active role in decision making. This case study illustrates the process a pre-teenager went through in making his decision to receive a cochlear implant and in adjusting to the device. The case illustrates how the AR program was modified as a result of implantation.

> Older students need to take an active role in decision making. In support of this process, they need access to the full range of available information.

Background Information

Mike was diagnosed with a severe to profound, bilateral sensorineural hearing loss when he was 15 months of age. Pregnancy and birth history were unremarkable and the etiology of hearing loss was unknown. Mike had a history of recurrent otitis media, for which he received medical treatment. He achieved developmental milestones as expected for age, with the exception of speech and language skills.

Mike's family lived in a small Midwestern community that provided limited early intervention services locally at the time. The parents enrolled him in the local parent–infant program and sought additional consultative guidance from agencies experienced with deaf infants. This provided them contact with other parents and support for decision making. The parents elected to implement a total communication approach with a strong emphasis on learning spoken communication. They focused on the integration of listening into daily routines and supported Mike in making rapid adjustment to full-time binaural hearing aid use. As Mike grew older, the parents exposed him to a rich variety of opportunities, including auditory experiences, such as instrumental music lessons.

Mike demonstrated a strong learning rate throughout the preschool years. He was a curious and eager learner. By 5 years of age, he demonstrated sign and oral language skills that were age appropriate. He relied on sign for information reception, but expressed himself primarily through oral means. His speech production skills were progressing, but conversational intelligibility was reduced. The prosodic characteristics of his speech were significantly affected by his hearing loss. He was successful in auditory recognition tasks with closed set materials, but had poor open set discrimination skills. Mike was enrolled in an individualized aural rehabilitation program that focused on (1) improving auditory identification and comprehension of linguistic messages, (2) reducing tendency to elongate and distort vowels, (3) reducing hypernasal resonance, (4) strengthening self-monitoring for the production of fricatives and affricates (often produced as stops), and (5) improving speech intelligibility in conversation. Throughout elementary school, this student was placed in regular classrooms with support services from an educational interpreter, a teacher of the deaf, and a speech–language pathologist. He utilized FM amplification in the classroom setting. Mike's socialization with hearing peers was affected by reduced speech intelligibility.

Aural Rehabilitation Plan: Preimplant

As the school years progressed, Mike became an avid reader and a strong student. His curiosity was evident each time he visited the audiologist and discussed ways that hearing aid circuitry might be improved. It was not surprising to the team, then, when he began to explore the topic of cochlear implants on the Internet at age 10½. Mike spent many months researching the topic. He was reluctant to undergo surgery, but considered the possibility that the device would provide him with better functional auditory skills than his conventional hearing aids. He asked to communicate with other students near his age who had received implants. He was interested in questioning students with both positive and limited outcomes from the device. He con-

---

Margin notes:

Prosodic characteristics of speech include such features as duration, pitch control, stress and intonation.

Hypernasal speech results when vocal sounds resonate through the nasal rather than the oral cavity. This is a common error in speech in students with limited residual hearing.

During his decision-making process, Mike questioned other students who had both positive and negative experiences with cochlear implants. This helped him to develop balanced expectations.

tacted several students by email and interviewed them. He discussed his impressions with his parents and then requested a cochlear implant orientation. The results of baseline and candidacy evaluations indicated that Mike had good closed set auditory identification abilities, but very limited open set word identification abilities (score of 4% on the PB-K test). Once it was determined that he was a candidate, Mike was scheduled to meet with a counselor, who discussed his expectations, reservations, and questions related to the device. He was judged to have a realistic view of what the implant would provide and was minimally concerned about appearance issues.

Mike underwent surgical implantation in the right ear just after his twelfth birthday. Following hookup and programming of the speech processor, Mike began his adjustment to the device. His AR program was modified to support this process.

Aural Rehabilitation Plan: Postimplant

In the first few months following implantation, Mike expressed some frustration in his attempts to understand the signal he was receiving. However, he was extremely motivated to resolve these issues and refused to switch back to his hearing aid. He wore his implant device full waking hours and devoted time to practicing listening lessons during daily routines. His parents reported a sense of disappointment. They noted that even though they had been cautioned against optimism they had hoped for their son to respond well immediately.

> Mike and his parents were disappointed with the outcome from the device immediately post hookup. It is not unusual for a student with this history to require a lengthy adjustment period.

However, as Mike worked at listening, he began to report significant progress in his recognition of what he was hearing. He noted that many previously unheard environmental sounds were now audible to him and that he had begun to recognize them when he heard them. He began to realize that the implant was providing access to a much wider range of sounds than he experienced with hearing aids.

It was critical to shift the emphasis of Mike's therapy program in light of this increased audibility and his access to a wider range of speech sounds, including fricatives. The therapist began with auditory closure (fill in the blank) activities to take advantage of his strong knowledge base, which helped him to predict the meaning of the unknown word presented through audition alone. As his confidence and closure skills strengthened, larger units of information were presented through audition alone. If Mike struggled, speechreading cues were added; however, with time this was less necessary. Listening skills were embedded in all aspects of the intervention program. Because of Mike's age, he was asked to be responsible for identifying what he wanted to work on in therapy. Some of these areas and strategies that were relevant to his overall goals were the following:

> Discourse tracking refers to a method by which students listen to utterances related to a topic and repeat verbatim the messages that they hear.

1. Mike was eager to strengthen his oral conversational understanding beyond the single utterance level. Discourse tracking activities were implemented with high-interest materials (e.g., tips for improving a tennis backhand; humorous materials like how to cheat at golf).

2. Mike wanted support to increase his social skills. Auditory-based role play activities were included to practice ways to (a) initiate and sustain innocuous, friendly topics of interest to peers, (b) respond appropriately to remarks of others,

(c) detect sarcasm in the voice (e.g., for humor recognition), and (d) tell good jokes with appropriate benign reactions.

3. Mike progressed to the point where he did not need interpreter support for face to face peer communication. However, group conversations and noisy contexts were challenging. Emphasis was placed on ways to manage such discourse situations, repair strategies, and listen in noise.

4. Mike did not believe that he was capable of conversing on the telephone. Utilitarian activities, like calling the golf course to get a tee time or ordering pizza, were practiced on a set of phones. Mike discovered that he was able to understand these predictable conversations fairly well, but being understood by the other party was a challenge. He learned ways to shape his intended message to heighten his intelligibility. He began to contact familiar peers to set up social activities.

> Mike needed to learn strategies for managing noisy settings and for maximizing his speech intelligibility over the telephone.

5. Mike wanted support to continue to refine his speech production skills. Focus was placed on auditory self-monitoring for production of fricatives, affricates, and ending sounds. He made more rapid progress than in the past due to increased audibility of these phonemes. In addition, emphasis was placed on more natural prosody, also enhanced by increased audibility. Opportunities for self-expression at the conversational level were incorporated in all the activities described above. Emphasis was placed on conveying meaning accurately and on self-evaluation.

6. Because open set word recognition was challenging, the clinician incorporated analytic training, using minimally paired contrasts that were increasingly challenging.

Intervention Outcomes

Two years following implantation, Mike continues to make progress in his auditory, speechreading, and spoken language skills. His scores on closed set auditory tests ranged from 90% to 100% at 24 months postimplantation. Figure 11.1 illustrates

FIGURE 11.1

Changes in open set auditory skills over time following implantation.

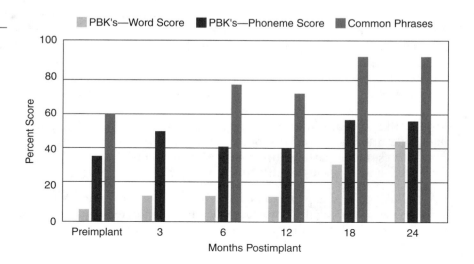

PBK's—Word Score ■ PBK's—Phoneme Score ■ Common Phrases

his scores over time on open set auditory recognition tasks. His best performance was in response to holistic messages, such as the Common Phrases tests, where he scored at 100% in getting the meaning and 90% in understanding of specific words. His prepost scores show steady improvement in the PB-K phoneme score, with slow but steady growth in the PB-K word discrimination scores.

Mike's oral conversational proficiency has been markedly strengthened by his use of the cochlear implant. His open set word discrimination scores tell little about the ease with which he is now able to participate in face to face conversation. Mike reports that his opportunities to socialize with peers have markedly increased in the past year. He is now able to participate in extended oral discourse through listening and speechreading. Spontaneous use of frication in his speech is observed over 75% of the time. Mike feels highly satisfied with his decision to receive a cochlear implant and recognizes many ways in which the device has supported his socialization and extended his communication opportunities.

As face to face conversation became more fluent, Mike's social opportunities greatly increased. This had an impact on his satisfaction with the device.

Summary

Mike was an active participant in steering the course of his audiologic rehabilitation program as he entered the teenage years. His case illustrates the importance of clear delineation of goals that are relevant to the client and persistence in working toward them. Mike and his family were initially disillusioned about his response to the cochlear implant. Mike needed support to leave his comfort zone to rely on new auditory capabilities provided by the implant. Over time, the family discovered that his efforts to adjust yielded many benefits. The ease of social communication was the most clear benefit, which greatly facilitated peer interaction and socialization in his school environment.

CASE 3   AMBER: ISSUES AFFECTING
■ EDUCATIONAL PLACEMENT

Audiologic rehabilitative management frequently includes provision of input to a child's IEP team related to educational placement. This case illustrates the importance of considering audiological, language, academic, and social factors in such decisions.

Background Information

Amber was referred for a multidisciplinary evaluation by the AR team when she was 6 years, 7 months of age. She was born in Korea and spent the first year of her life with a Korean foster family. Birth records indicated a normal, full-term delivery. An American family adopted Amber when she was 14 months of age. Amber walked at 14 months, was toilet trained at 4 to 5 years of age, and had few words at 3 years of age.

At 30 months of age, a bilateral, sensorineural hearing loss was identified. Audiological records indicated that the loss was progressive in nature, as shown in the serial audiogram in Figure 11.2. At the time of her first MDT evaluation, Amber's

A serial audiogram is used when progression is suspected. It logs the thresholds over time for ease of comparison.

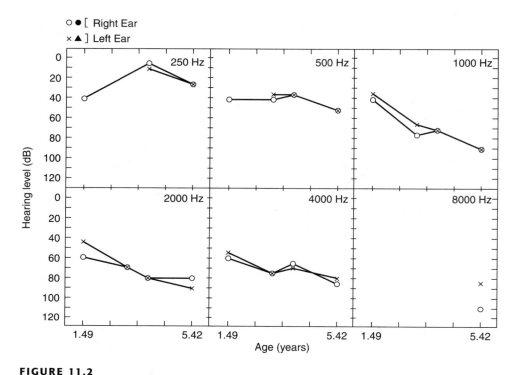

FIGURE 11.2

Case 3: Amber's serial audiogram.

hearing loss was borderline normal sloping to profound bilaterally (see Figure 11.3a). She received hearing aids at 3 years of age and was reported to have progressed well orally once she received amplification. Amber wore glasses for correction of visual acuity problems. She had a history of otitis media and tube insertion. Amber's parents requested a team evaluation during her first grade year to gain input on their daughter's progress and to determine if she was ready to access a regular classroom full time. At the point of evaluation, Amber was attending a self-contained classroom for hard of hearing children in the mornings and a regular first grade in the afternoons. The only concern raised by the school was Amber's tendency to "shut down" and avoid responding following some adult requests at school.

Assessment Findings

A profile can be a useful way to integrate results across disciplines in order to get a "total child" view.

The profile in Figure 11.3b summarizes the results of multidisciplinary findings in the areas of psychology, language, and communication. Filled circles represent the first evaluation; the ×s represent a 1-year follow-up evaluation. In the first evaluation Amber's language and academic skills were very delayed in comparison to the hearing peers with whom she was competing in class. Considering that she had limited language at age 3, however, the results were suggestive of a strong learning rate.

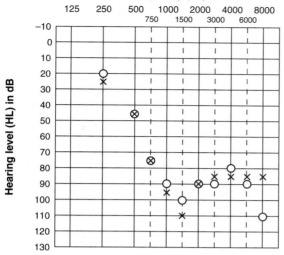

Frequency (Hz)

Key to Audiogram

Ear	R	L
AC (THD-49)	O	×
AC (ER-3A)	●	▲
BC (masked)	[	]
NR	↙	↘

Test Reliability:
fair – good
Method:
CPA

	⌐	— Unmasked BC
	▨	— Sound Field Warble Tones
SAT	— Speech Awareness
		Threshold
SRT	— Speech Reception
		Threshold
SL	— Sensation Level
SF	— Sound Field
BC	— Bone Conduction
ETF	— Eustachian Tube Function
→	— Single Responses

Effective Masking Level to Nontest Ear

Immittance Battery		Right	Left
Tymp	Normal		
	Abnormal		
Reflexes	Present		
	Absent		
	Elevated		
ETF	Vol (cc)	7.0	7.0
	Release (daPa)	266	—

	Ear	SRT	SAT	Level / %	Level / %	Level / %	Speech Materials
CD	R	45		105M / 28	100M / 64		PBK
	L	50		85M / 44	90M / 56		
Tape	SF/BC						

(M = masked)

Comments/Special Test
New hearing aids this fall
Phonak
Picofone PPSC2
P4 LCO V2

Audiologic Impression:

Borderline normal sloping to profound bilateral symmetrical (at most frequencies) loss w/tm perfs and previous progression

Recommendations:

1. Monitor hearing 3 mos
2. Aided testing w/aided threshold or probe mis tests and with aided word recognition
3. Monitor hearing aid function

Audiological Retest

3 mos
locally

FIGURE 11.3A

Case 3: Amber's initial audiogram.

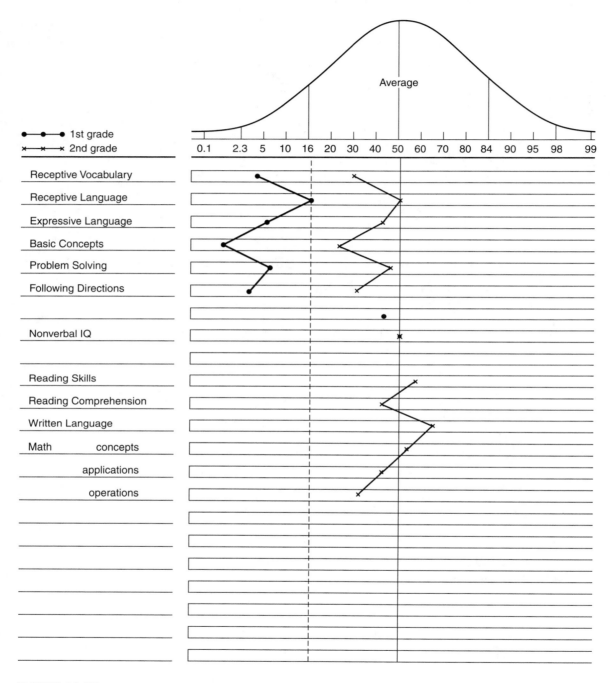

FIGURE 11.3B

Amber's profile of multidisciplinary findings.

Although there were errors in speech typical of a child with limited high-frequency audibility, her speech was developing well and was intelligible to unfamiliar listeners. She demonstrated receptive language abilities in the low average range for her age. Amber was imaginative in art and symbolic play. She had an engaging sense of humor and highly supportive home and school environments.

The primary concern identified during the evaluation was Amber's difficulties in self-expression. Extensive language sample analysis revealed expressive language formulation difficulties that were affecting her social skills in the mainstream environment. Amber's personal narratives were disorganized and reduced in complexity. For example, she attempted to explain to the examiner why she did not like witches in the following narrative. "I don't like witches. That . . . I have . . . my grandma have that one (pointing to a picture of a witch). It clap (demonstrates with her hands). And I have one. It's down in the basement . . . in my freezer (she means it is stored beside the freezer). Her clap (gestures). I don't like him. He say heehee-hee." Grammatical errors appeared to be related to audibility. Formulation difficulties were observed in her tendency to produce false starts, her reliance on nonspecific references, semantic errors, and reliance on gestures to help carry the message. These expressive language challenges were affecting her participation in class and her socialization with peers. When she was unsure how to express her idea, she would "shut down" as the school had observed. Her mother described several examples at school when Amber cried in order to solve a verbal problem instead of expressing herself. For example, another student inadvertently picked up Amber's materials and got in line. Amber responded by saying "Hey" and grabbing at the books. When the books were not returned to her, she began to cry.

Language formulation difficulties refer to problems that a child encounters in organization of ideas for self-expression.

False starts are instances when a speaker begins a phrase, but stops and revises it. Use of *nonspecific references* means the tendency to use indefinite words, like *it, that, thing,* instead of the specific name for items.

Recommendations for Management

Based on academic performance in the classroom, the parents were eager to fully mainstream their daughter for her second grade year. It was important to keep two points in mind when counseling the parents on this issue. First, the language demands of the first grade curriculum are fairly well controlled. Performance on first grade tasks may not be predictive of Amber's performance in the next few grades, in which demands for verbal reasoning and processing with less context support escalate. Second, Amber has a history of a strong learning rate. She was responsive to language stimulation techniques tried in diagnostic teaching. She appeared to have a good prognosis for improvement and would benefit from some additional language support, particularly in the area of expressive language formulation and social language use.

Amber had a team of highly skilled professionals at her school. After reviewing the findings with the parents and the school team, it was determined that continuing the half-day of self-contained placement and half-day of regular classroom placement was advisable. The teaching team selected the following priorities for her support program: (1) strengthen expressive language formulation through daily opportunities to narrate with support from the team; particular emphasis to be placed on school language functions (e.g., problem solving, reasoning, describing, explaining, sharing personal stories), (2) building vocabulary and using specific references, (3) reducing semantic errors, particularly those based in limited audibility (e.g., pronouns and prepositions), (4) strengthening emotive vocabulary, and (5) role playing to practice verbal social interactions with peers.

Follow-up Assessment

The parent and school team requested a follow-up assessment 1 year later as a way of monitoring their progress toward the established goals and reconsidering the parental goal of increasing mainstreaming opportunities. Audiological testing revealed that Amber's hearing thresholds had remained stable over the past year and that she was receiving good benefit from her amplification and FM systems. Language and academic retesting demonstrated significant progress in all areas of language and literacy. As illustrated by the ×s on the profile in Figure 11.3, Amber's language and academic scores were falling within the average range for her age and grade placement. Although Amber was still working through some formulation struggles at times, her personal narratives were better organized and contained few errors. She was able to express her ideas fluently much of the time. The school reported that Amber was getting along better with her peers and solving problems using verbal means. As a result of the positive findings, the parents and educators made a decision to mainstream Amber in the third grade with support services. This case illustrates that social–emotional and communication factors needed to be considered in the decision-making process. Academic test results, especially in the earliest grades, can be misleading in determining readiness for mainstreaming. Amber benefited greatly from an additional year of support, which resulted in stronger linguistic and social preparation for full integration.

> Communication and social findings should be considered along with academic performance when making decisions about mainstreaming and support needs.

CASE 4   GREG: LATE IDENTIFICATION
■ OF A HARD OF HEARING CHILD

Children who are hard of hearing can be difficult to identify, because they respond inconsistently to sounds around them. This inconsistency confuses parents and physicians, and may delay referral for hearing testing until evidence of speech and language delays prompts referral. Once the hearing loss is identified and amplification is fitted, the child may need to embark on the process of relearning auditory behaviors. This case illustrates the importance of audibility in the formation of language rules by a child who is hard of hearing. In this case, the child needed to learn new ways of gaining meaning from messages around him. His auditory training program needed to focus on helping him develop productive listening and comprehension behaviors.

Background Information

Greg's parents first began to express concerns about his hearing to their pediatrician when he was 2 years old. He was demonstrating inconsistent responses to sound and delayed speech and language development at that time. Results of audiologic testing at a community hospital suggested borderline normal hearing sensitivity in response to speech and narrowband stimuli. One and one-half years later, the parents continued to express concern for Greg's hearing, and testing revealed at least a mild to moderate sensorineural hearing loss in the better ear. However, the audiologist reported questionable test reliability, and Greg was referred for Auditory Brainstem Response testing. Results suggested the probability of a moderate to severe sensorineural hearing loss in at least the higher frequencies, with the right ear more involved than the left. Greg was then referred to a pediatric audiologic team. A severe rising to mild hearing loss in the right ear was confirmed through behavioral testing. Left ear testing revealed responses in the mild hearing loss range, rising to within normal limits at 1 khz, steeply sloping to the severe hearing loss range at 2 khz, and then rising to the mild hearing loss range in the higher frequencies. Given the unusual configuration of Greg's hearing loss (see Figure 11.4a), it was not surprising that he passed a screening evaluation that used speech and narrow bands of noise in sound field. Unfortunately, the referral for more definitive testing was delayed by the findings of the screening assessment. Medical–genetic evaluation revealed a family history of hearing loss, but etiology could not be confirmed.

Hearing aid fitting was complex, given the unusual audiometric configuration in the left ear. However, a binaural fitting was selected, with capability for direct audio input for FM amplification. Greg was immediately referred to an AR program for the purposes of evaluating his individual communication needs and determining considerations for educational placement.

Communication Activity Assessment

Greg demonstrated an unusual communication profile at 4 years of age. On standardized tests of language, his receptive language skills approximated a 2½-year level and his expressive language skills were equivalent to a 3-year level. On many tests, his expressive performance was stronger than comprehension. Analysis of conversational interactions was useful in understanding the complexity of his receptive and expressive language problems. It was evident from the outset that Greg was having serious difficulty understanding those around him. Table 11.1 contains a segment from an interactive language sample, where Greg was conversing with an audiologic rehabilitation clinician.

> Greg's comprehension difficulties were evident in the finding that expressive language was stronger than receptive.

A number of interesting patterns were reflected in Greg's spontaneous speech. Although most of his words were intelligible to the listener, it was difficult to understand Greg due to numerous semantic and grammatical errors in his spontaneous productions. It was suspected that Greg's unusual audiometric configuration had contributed to his formulation of unusual language rules. Spectral information he was receiving may have provided inconsistent cues about grammatical or semantic categories. For example, he frequently marked nouns with /s/, even when a morpheme was not required. He rarely inflected verbs. He was aware that words were marked with morphemes like /s/, but had no consistent basis for application of this rule. Lack of audibility of portions of the speech spectrum may have also led to semantic confusions. Greg confused gender (*girl* vs. *boy; man* vs. *lady*), used nouns as verbs, used pronoun forms randomly (with confusion of *I, you, be, she,* and *we*),

> Semantic errors refer to errors in the meaning of message. For example, referring to a *girl* as a *boy* is an error of meaning.

Frequency (Hz)

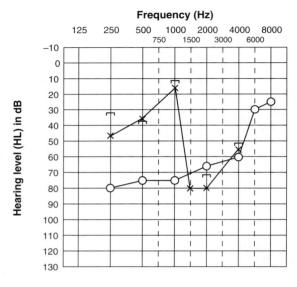

Key to Audiogram

Ear	Air	Bone
AC (THD-49)	○	×
AC (ER-3A)	●	▲
BC (masked)	[	]
NR	↙	↘

⌐	— Unmasked BC
▨	— Sound Field Warble Tones
SAT	— Speech Awareness Threshold
SRT	— Speech Reception Threshold
SL	— Sensation Level
SF	— Sound Field
BC	— Bone Conduction
ETF	— Eustachian Tube Function
+	— Single Responses

Test Reliability: Good

Method: CPA

Immittance Battery		Right	Left
Tymp	Normal	X	X
	Abnormal		
Reflexes	Present		
	Absent	X	X
	Elevated		
ETF	Vol (cc)		
	Release (daPa)		

Effective Masking Level to Non-Test Ear

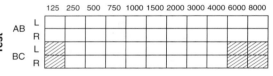

Ear	SRT	SAT	Level / %	Level / %	Level / %	Speech Materials
MLV R		25	105M			NU-Chips
CD L		10	105M			
Tape SF/BC						

(M = masked)

Comments/Special Test

Discrim scores 6/15-R, 5/15-L

Result of discrim testing may have been effected by vocab and attention

Audiologic Impression:

Recommendations:

FIGURE 11.4A

Case 4: Greg's initial audiogram.

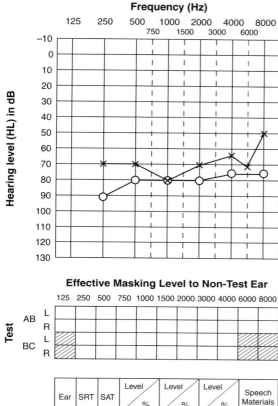

Frequency (Hz)

Key to Audiogram

Ear	Air	Bone
AC (THD-49)	○	×
AC (ER-3A)	●	▲
BC (masked)	[	]
NR	↙	↘

⌐ — Unmasked BC
▨ — Sound Field Warble Tones
SAT — Speech Awareness
          Threshold
SRT — Speech Reception
          Threshold
SL — Sensation Level
SF — Sound Field
BC — Bone Conduction
ETF — Eustachian Tube Function
+ — Single Responses

Test Reliability:
   Good
Method:
   Conv

	Immittance Battery	Right	Left
Tymp	Normal		
	Abnormal		
Reflexes	Present		
	Absent		
	Elevated		
ETF	Vol (cc)		
	Release (daPa)		

Effective Masking Level to Non-Test Ear

Ear	SRT	SAT	Level / %	Level / %	Level / %	Speech Materials
MLV R	85					
CD L	75					
Tape SF/BC						

(M = masked)

Comments/Special Test

R aid in for repair

Current em's working ok

Current use of fm at school via DAI to phonak aid

Audiologic Impression:

Recommendations:

FIGURE 11.4B

Case 4: Greg's recent audiogram (following progression).

TABLE 11.1	
Conversational Exchange between Greg and the Clinician	
E	Hi, Greg. How are you today?
C	Fours.
E	Oh, you are four years old. Well, how are you feeling?
C	Fine.
E	Greg, where's your mom?
C	My moms Greg go to the schools. The mom talk it the boats.
E	Oh. Hmmmm, you and mom came to school. Wow, I see you got a star!
C	I got stars my mom say no go outsides. Mom say do suns no go outside. Mom the all raining go put the backs the watch all raining.

C = child; *E* = examiner.

and had significant difficulty providing the appropriate semantic content in response to questions. Collectively, these errors appeared to be language "differences," rather than simple delays.

To understand better the nature of Greg's language problems, the AR clinician constructed probes to examine Greg's language processing strategies. For example, she observed his responses to various questions across contexts and tasks. Greg was having such difficulty understanding others that he had developed an overreliance on nonlinguistic comprehension strategies. Chapman (1978) described young children's normal developmental use of comprehension strategies in the face of complex linguistic input. Moeller (1988) has observed that students with hearing impairment may use such comprehension "short cuts" when their comprehension is taxed well into their school years. Greg demonstrated extreme reliance on these behaviors, due to pervasive comprehension difficulties. Greg used the following strategies in his attempts to make sense of input around him:

Nonlinguistic comprehension strategies refer to a child's use of cues other than the spoken message to figure out the meaning of a phrase. For example, the child might use context cues to understand what was said.

1. Attended to key words in the message to the exclusion of other information.
2. Predicted message intention based on situational context cues.
3. Nodded his head as if he understood.
4. Selected a key, recognizable word and made comments related to that topic (without respect for the current topic of conversation).
5. Controlled the conversational topic to avoid comprehension demands.
6. Said everything known about the topic in hopes that the answer was included in the content somewhere (global response strategy).

Greg was not able to answer any types of questions with consistency. Tracking of his responses revealed correct responses in fewer than 25% of the instances. In response to commands, he failed to recognize the need for action, and would instead imitate the command or nod his head. Greg's reliance on nonlinguistic strategies is evident in the discourse example provided in Table 11.2.

In this example, Greg showed his overdependence on context for determining what questions mean. He also demonstrated his tendency to use a global response strategy, and his assumption that "if she asks me the question again, my first re-

TABLE 11.2

Greg's Replies to Questions about Simple Objects

E	(*holding a boy doll*) Who is this?
C	Boy.
E	(*puts boy in helicopter*) Who is this?
C	Boy the helicopter.
E	(*holds up a mom doll*) Who is this?
C	Mom boy the helicopter.

C = child; *E* = examiner.

sponse must have been wrong." The clinician observed similar behaviors from Greg in his preschool class setting. He had a "panicked" expression on his face much of the time. Greg did not appear to expect to understand. Rather, he expected to have to guess. In the classroom, he frequently produced long, confused narratives. His teacher, in an effort to be supportive, would abandon her communication agenda and follow Greg's topic to any degree possible. This was problematic, however, in that Greg needed to learn to understand and respond with semantic accuracy to classroom discourse.

Management

REMEDIATION OF COMMUNICATION ACTIVITY: AUDITORY AND LINGUISTIC TRAINING. Once amplification was fitted, Greg was enrolled in a multi-faceted audiologic rehabilitation program. Individual auditory language therapy focused on development of productive comprehension strategies and reduction of semantic confusion through attention to appropriate auditory linguistic cues. A parent program was included, with focus on teaching the family natural ways to support Greg's comprehension. Greg had a tendency to imitate each message he heard, which interfered with processing and responding. The parents and therapist agreed to reduce emphasis on imitation and expression until success in comprehension could be increased. Further, the AR specialist provided collaborative consultation to Greg's classroom teacher. The school district provided Greg a diagnostic placement in a Language Intervention Preschool. His teacher was a speech–language pathologist. The teacher and AR specialist developed a scheme for helping Greg repair comprehension breakdowns and for helping him respond accurately in the classroom. Table 11.3 illustrates the type of teaching interaction that was implemented to scaffold or support Greg's emerging comprehension.

These classroom adaptations were successful in helping Greg begin to focus on the content of what he was hearing. As his auditory–linguistic behaviors strengthened, he began to revise language and discourse rules. His auditory language program focused specifically on helping him discriminate among linguistic elements that marked important semantic or syntactic distinctions. For example, he worked with the AR clinician in learning to distinguish pronoun forms (e.g., *I* vs. *you*), various morphological structures, and the meaning of various question forms. All

Because imitation interfered with processing, clinicians needed to reduce the emphasis on requests for speech imitation. Focus was placed on listening and comprehending.

TABLE 11.3

Classroom Interaction Designed to Support Greg's Emerging Discourse Skills

E	Good morning, Greg. Where's your mommy?
C	Mom Greg go go the school. My moms say Greg no go the school the rain. . . .
E	Just a minute, Greg. *Listen* to the question (*focusing prompt*).
E	Where *is* mom? (*highlighting prompt*) At home? In the car? Here at school? (*multiple choice prompt*).
C	Mom right there. At school! (*points to his mother in the hall—on her way in to be room mother today*).
E	Good, Greg! You answered my question! I asked, "where's mom?" You told me . . . right there! There she is!

C = child; *E* = examiner.

Source: Moeller, Osberger, and Eccarius, 1986.

intervention was incorporated in communicatively based activities to ensure the development of pragmatically appropriate conversational skills.

The AR clinician and teacher worked collaboratively to gradually shape in Greg productive listening and comprehension strategies. This was an essential step in helping Greg revise his expressive language behaviors. He needed to develop the confidence that he could understand and that his responses needed to be related to the conversational topic. Adjustment of Greg's approach to comprehension was necessary to prepare him for learning in a classroom environment.

Intervention Outcomes

Greg was responsive to the auditory–linguistic training program and to the supportive techniques used in the classroom to strengthen language processing. Greg continued to receive a team approach to his rehabilitation and education into his early elementary years. Although the ultimate objective was to enable him to profit from education in a regular classroom, the initial approach was conservative with emphasis on specialty services to help him develop the language foundation necessary for academic success. In this case, the conservative approach was especially fortuitous because Greg experienced progression in his sensorineural hearing loss during his early elementary years. The audiograms in Figure 11.4a and b illustrate the progression in thresholds that occurred, with the initial audiogram on the left and the final audiogram on the right. Hearing thresholds finally stabilized at a severe hearing loss level, with a bilaterally symmetrical configuration. Fortunately, optimal hearing aid fittings have been achieved (see Figure 11.5). Real-ear measures indicate that much of the speech spectrum is audible to Greg with properly fitted personal and FM amplification.

A language assessment was completed when Greg was 10 years of age. All language test scores fell solidly within the average range for his age in comparison to hearing peers. Previous comprehension and discourse problems were no longer present. In the context of a storytelling task, Greg produced complex utterances like,

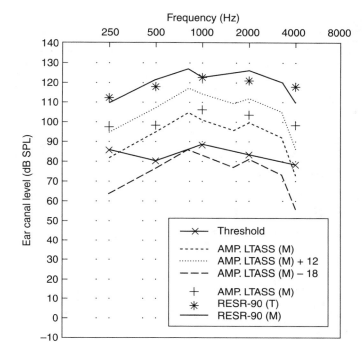

FIGURE 11.5

Results of real-ear measures illustrating audibility in relation to the long-term average speech spectrum.

"The boy says that the frog should stay on the land while the rest of them sail off on a raft." Greg's expressive language was semantically and grammatically appropriate for his age. Provision of support services will continue to be important for Greg, in spite of his strong language performance. When asked if he was having any problems in school, Greg reported, "Well, it is hard sometimes because you have to be quiet to hear the teacher, but the hearing kids keep talking. Then I always have to watch what everybody's doing, and then I'll know what I'm supposed to be doing."

Summary

This case has illustrated the critical importance that audibility plays in a child's language rule formation. It also underscores the importance of teamwork to address concerns in all the child's significant learning environments. With aggressive and continuous AR support, a child who is hard of hearing has an opportunity to overcome early delays. Appropriate management of amplification and auditory learning opportunities play a key role in this process.

CASE 5   STEVE: DIAGNOSTIC THERAPY: A TOOL
■ FOR SOLVING COMPLEX INTERVENTION PROBLEMS

One of the more challenging aspects of audiologic rehabilitation is the goal of determining the most efficacious intervention approach for solving a particular problem. This requires accurate and thorough differential diagnosis of a child's problems, and design of management strategies to address the child's needs in the most effective manner. The selection of intervention priorities following thorough problem analysis is like a craft, requiring skill, theoretical preparation, and insight. It is useful for the clinician to ask (1) If I select this goal, what difference will it make in the child's overall communicative functioning? (2) Will emphasis on this goal lead to generalization or impact on other communicative behaviors? (3) Is there any way to effect systemwide change with this approach?

This case illustrates the process of differential diagnosis and discovery-oriented therapy. It is often impossible to separate assessment from management. In fact, intervention is typically guided by the constant analysis of outcomes and clinical decision making. The case is used to illustrate this clinical decision making process.

> It is important for the clinician to consider the impact that a goal might have on generalization of language behaviors and enhancement of communicative function.

Background Information: Assessment of Hearing Loss and Amplification

Steve's hearing loss was identified when he was 11 months of age. Audiologic results throughout his early years indicated a profound, bilateral sensorineural hearing loss, with no response to speech or tonal stimuli at the limits of the audiometric equipment. At 11 months of age he was enrolled in a comprehensive, family-centered early intervention program (Moeller & Condon, 1994). Steve demonstrated little response to conventional amplification and was subsequently fitted with a Tactaid II+ vibrotactile device.

> A vibrotactile unit connects sound into vibratory sensation presented to the skin. This input provides basic cues for sound perception.

Previous Rehabilitation

During early intervention, Steve's clinician documented numerous developmental concerns. Steve demonstrated hypotonia, tactile defensiveness, motor overflow, and difficulties with visual attention. His family members participated fully in the program, and became fluent and competent signers. In spite of a nurturing language environment at home, Steve was slow to develop expressive language, and was delayed in social and play skills. Steve was referred for both neurological and OT/PT assessments, due to developmental concerns. Steve passed a gross screening assessment completed by a school-based OT/PT who felt that services were unnecessary. Neurological assessment revealed physical evidence of brain damage. Psychological assessment revealed that Steve had at least average nonverbal intelligence.

> *Hypotonia* is a term used to describe a child with low muscle tone. This condition can affect the strength, precision, and control of movements. *Tactile defensiveness* refers to a tendency to react negatively to touch or tactile sensations.

Differential Diagnosis and Assessment: Communication Problems and Signing Strategies

Steve was enrolled in a self-contained preschool program for deaf children at age 3, upon completion of the early intervention program. Family members continued to participate in parent and sibling sign classes, and to demonstrate follow-through at home. In spite of aggressive efforts, Steve continued to lag behind his peers, especially in his social use of language. Steve's teachers began to make systematic observations and modifications of his curriculum in an effort to bring about better results. Steve's teacher referred him for a formal diagnostic intervention program upon discovery of motor difficulties that appeared to be affecting his sign productions. She theorized that motor problems may have been constraining his efforts at self expression. An AR specialist began to work collaboratively with the classroom teacher in attempts to understand the problem better. The teacher provided the clinician with long lists of signs that were produced incorrectly by this child, rendering many of his spontaneous language attempts unintelligible.

The audiologic rehabilitationist observed Steve in the classroom and closely examined the lists of "mispronounced signs." She began to formulate diagnostic questions on the basis of language and phonological theories and careful observations of the child's production schemes. The first question asked was "Is there regularity to Steve's sign production errors?" Theories of phonology in spoken language suggest that children do not make random errors in production. Rather, they follow systematic rules, which have been described as developmental phonological processes (Edwards & Shriberg, 1983; Hodson, 1980). The clinician conjectured that Steve's sign production errors may also have been rule governed. If immature phonological processes were guiding his productions, this finding would impact management strategies.

The first step taken was to closely examine Steve's handshape productions on videotape. Only six primary handshapes were produced correctly, representing a restricted phonological repertoire for a 4-year-old. In fact, five of the six handshapes he could produce (*1, A, L, O,* and *B*) are among those observed in the earliest developmental productions of young deaf children acquiring native signs (Battison, 1978). Steve also used the *F* handshape in substitution for several other handshapes in common signs. The clinician constructed probes to determine whether or not Steve followed consistent rules in handshape substitutions or changes. For example, the clinician gathered sets of objects that had signs representing the spectrum of handshapes needed for basic lexical use in young deaf children. She recorded Steve's responses to these stimulus items and then analyzed the results for patterns.

Motoric Limitations in Signing

All of Steve's errors clustered into four production simplification patterns or "rules." These rules were described by the clinician as follows:

1. For all signs requiring two or more fingers to be isolated and spread, Steve would substitute an *F.* Thus, on signs like *AIRPLANE, PUMPKIN, WATER,* or *THREE,* all of which have distinctive handshapes, Steve produced *F.* His counting, for example was characterized as "1, F, F, 4, 4" instead of "1, 2, 3, 4, 5." This simplification rule was having a serious effect on sign intelligibility.
2. For signs that required flexion of the hand with two fingers extended together, Steve simplified to the *B* handshape. Thus, signs with handshapes using *N, U,* or *R* became *B.*
3. When signs required distal finger flexion or extension (e.g., *Y* in *PLAY, T* in *POTTY;* or *S* in *SHOE*), Steve produced the *A* handshape.
4. Signs that required a relaxed *C* production were produced in a highly flexed and spread position, in a clawlike manner.

The clinician observed some additional patterns that were of concern and led her to ask for a second opinion from occupational therapy. Steve demonstrated reversal of the sign path in some instances. He would watch his teacher sign *WITCH* (where the dominant hand comes from the nose downward to meet the nondominant hand) and he would sign it backward (with his dominant hand coming up to the nose from the non-dominant hand). On a sign like *BEAR*, which requires that the hands cross midline, he failed to cross his hands, and would instead place claw-hands separately on either side of his chest. He demonstrated associated reactions, which can be indicative of immature neurological development. That is, if one hand was producing a movement pattern (e.g., signing *GIRL*), his other hand would be at his side mimicking the action of the dominant hand. Finally, Steve appeared to have poor control of his nondominant hand, making it especially difficult for him to produce signs that required two different handshapes (e.g., *HELP*, *PUMPKIN*).

Related Personal Factors

When a child has trouble holding the trunk in a stable position, it makes it even more challenging to control the fine movements of the hands.

Associated reactions refer to extra motor movements that the child produces due to limited motor control. For example, if Steve was signing "cute" with his right hand, his left hand would move in the same manner as the right, even though this is a one-handed sign.

Following careful examination of the information to date, the clinician posed the next diagnostic question: "Are underlying motor problems influencing these simplification rules and production difficulties?" The clinician referred Steve to an occupational therapist (OT), who began serving in a consultative role with the AR team. The OT had experience with deaf children, and was sensitive to the motor production demands of signing. The OT identified the following problems:

1. Presence of Steve's asymmetric tonic neck reflex (ATNR) at age four years, reflecting an immature central nervous system. Typically, the ATNR disappears in the first few months of life in a normally developing infant.
2. Difficulties with proprioceptive perception (e.g., knowing what position the hand is in when not looking at it) and motor planning.
3. Reduced proximal trunk stability, making skilled distal movements of the hand difficult.
4. Overflow of movement from one side of the body to another, causing associated reactions and making it hard to isolate movement on one part of the body or move one limb differently from the other.
5. Tendency to avoid crossing the midline of the body.

Management: Sign Communication Rehabilitation

The clinician made the decision to address the motor production of signs as a primary intervention target because:

1. These problems were affecting conversational initiations and communicative success. Although the child was attempting to initiate social conversation with others, his signs were often misinterpreted or misunderstood, leading to frustration and social isolation.
2. The errors appeared to have a consistent rule base, which might allow for a process-oriented intervention that could result in system-wide change. That is,

if his phonological rules could be changed, several errors could be modified at the same time.

An individualized intervention was designed to address the motor sign production problems and needs. Given the constellation of motor problems, the clinician first employed successive approximation strategies. Her goal was to implement motor changes from the easiest change to those that would require more complex motor patterns. She took her lead in developing an intervention hierarchy from tracking the child's daily progress. The therapy program implemented a phonological process approach. Rather than address each error singly, the clinician worked on clusters of phonemes to try to bring about changes in the phonological rule structure (e.g., worked on all handshapes that required flexion of the hand and two or more fingers extended and spread).

Many developmental activities were implemented to give Steve natural opportunities to explore new motor patterns. For example, play with finger puppets on several fingers helped him learned to isolate fingers while flexing the fist. Matching the clinician's handshapes in plaster of paris or in fingerpaint gave him increased proprioceptive cues about new productive forms. Playful interaction games gave him large numbers of trials with target forms (e.g., play with various vehicles and with number games gave him opportunities to practice the 3 handshape, which he later used productively as a number or as a classifier for *VEHICLE-MOVING*). Breakdown–buildup strategies were useful in helping him understand complex patterns. When a sign required him to reverse the path, the clinician would break the task down for him by positioning herself beside him, allowing him to mirror the path. He was led through successive activities until he could successfully reverse the path. Similarly, signs that required midline crossing were produced in steps. He was asked to copy the clinician holding claw-hands side by side on the table for the sign *SPIDER*. Then he copied the action of crossing, and next copied the action of moving them forward. Later in intervention, he was expected to integrate the three motor patterns involved in this action. Minimal contrasts also helped Steve modify his signing behaviors. An activity was set up where letter cards of *F* were contrasted with small bags of three stickers. When Steve wanted the three stickers, but produced *F*, he received the letter card. He was motivated to win the stickers and quickly adjusted his handshape to communicate his desire clearly.

> Breakdown–buildup strategies are useful when a child has trouble analyzing the parts that are in a whole movement. The clinician might slow the sign or produce its parts and then build it back up to a whole. This can aid student processing.

The teacher, the parents and the OT were involved directly in the therapy program to ensure generalization of concepts to all intervention contexts. Through teamwork, all communication partners had the information they needed to adjust their expectations for Steve's phonological productions in sign.

Outcome Measures

Sessions were held three times weekly for a period of 4 months. Therapy data logs and post testing on untrained stimuli revealed the following results:

1. All target handshapes were produced accurately in spontaneous conversational contexts.
2. Changes in handshapes were maintained 6 months after diagnostic therapy was terminated.

3. Steve improved significantly in sign intelligibility and frequency of initiation of signed messages.
4. Bilateral coordination of signs was labored and continued to require intervention. A consultative approach to intervention in the classroom was employed to resolve remaining concerns.

Summary

The results of this case underscore the importance of professional collaboration in solving complex problems. The case further illustrates the value in implementing a diagnostic teaching approach where theory informs practice, and strategies and questions are continually modified to bring about positive results.

REFERENCES AND RECOMMENDED READING

Battison, R. (1978). *Lexical borrowing in American Sign Language.* Silver Spring, MD: Linstok Press.

Chapman, R. (1978). Comprehension strategies in children. In Kavanagh, J. & Strange, P. (Eds.), *Language and speech in the laboratory, school and clinic.* Cambridge, MA: MIT Press.

Dale, P., & Thal, D. (1993). MacArthur Communicative Development Inventory (Infant and Toddler Scales used). Center for Research in Language, UCSD, San Diego, CA.

Edwards, M. L., & Shriberg, L. D. (1983). *Phonology: Applications in communicative disorders.* San Diego, CA: College-Hill Press.

Greenspan, S. (1990). *Floor Time.* New York, NY: Scholastic, Inc.

Hodson, B. W. (1980). *The assessment of phonological processes.* Danville, IL: Interstate Printers and Publishers.

Moeller, M. P. (1988). Combining formal and informal strategies for language assessment of hearing-impaired children [monograph]. In Kretschmer, R. R., Jr., & Kretschmer, L. W. (Eds.), *Journal of the Academy of Rehabilitative Audiology, 21* (Suppl.), 73–101.

Moeller, M. P., & Condon, M. C. (1994). D.E.I.P: A collaborative problem-solving approach to early intervention. In Roush, J. & Matkin, N. D. (Eds.), *Infants and toddlers with hearing loss* (pp. 163–194). Baltimore, MD: York Press, Inc.

Moeller, M. P., Coufal, K., & Hixson, P. (1990). The efficacy of speech–language intervention: Hearing impaired children. *Seminars in Speech and Language, 11*(4), 227–241.

Moeller, M. P., Osberger, M. J., & Eccarius, M. (1986). Cognitively based strategies for use with hearing-impaired students with comprehension deficits. *TLD, 6*(4), 37–50. Aspen Publishers, Inc.

Roush, J., & Matkin, N. D. (1994). *Infants and toddlers with Hearing loss.* Baltimore, MD: York Press.

Schildroth, A. M., & Hotto, S. A. (1993). Annual survey of hearing impaired children and youth: 1991–92 school year. *American Annals of the Deaf, 138*(2), 163–171.

Schuyler, V. & Sowers, J. (1998). *Parent–infant communication* (4th Ed.). Portland, OR: Hearing and Speech Institute. Infant Hearing Resources.

Schuyler, V., Sowers, J., & Broyles, N. (1998). *For families.* Portland, OR: Hearing and Speech Institute. Infant Hearing Resources.

Wetherby, A., & Prizant, B. (1993). *Communication and symbolic behavior scales.* Chicago: Special Press.

R E C O M M E N D E D   W E B   S I T E

Schleper, D. R. (1996). W. W. Fifteen Principles of Reading to Deaf Children: The Shared Reading Project. Laurent Clerc National Deaf Education Center, Gallaudet University, Washington, DC.
http://clercccenter.gallaudet.edu

CHAPTER 12

Case Studies: Adults and Elderly Adults

Michael A. Nerbonne
Jeff E. Brockett
Dan F. Konkle
Alice E. Holmes

C O N T E N T S

■ INTRODUCTION

The five adult and elderly cases of audiologic rehabilitation described in this chapter involve a wide range of clients with hearing impairment, in terms of both age and communication-related difficulties. While special adjustments must be considered with some elderly patients, such as those found in nursing homes, in general, both adult and elderly persons will most often demonstrate the same kinds of communication problems and, therefore, be candidates for similar rehabilitation strategies. Thus, we have grouped these younger and older cases together and presented them in the same chapter. Although references are made to group therapy (as in Case 1) the major emphasis with each case is on addressing the specific, unique problems which each of these individuals is experiencing. Some of these problems relate as much to psychosocial influences as to auditory effects. Such influences need to be acknowledged in AR approaches.

Although a major goal for each case was to reduce communication-related difficulties, the specific audiologic strategies varied for each client depending on individual needs and motivation. The sampling of cases presented here ranges from involvement in hearing aid selection and orientation and counseling to traditional and more recently developed forms of individual and group communication rehabilitation. In addition, the pre- and post-implantation AR process for a challenging cochlear implant recipient is presented.

In the course of performing audiologic rehabilitation, the audiologist may encounter the wide range of cases described here. We hope that these cases will give some insights into the challenges and possibilities of this work. In general, the model followed here is the one detailed in the introductory chapter of this text (see Figure 1.2), which was inspired by the recently revised WHO (2000) classification scheme associated with rehabilitation. The model involves both assessment and remediation phases as part of the total audiologic rehabilitation process.

A variety of pre- and post-AR tests were used in an attempt to objectify the status of the clients during the assessment and management phases of therapy. Self-assessment tools are receiving increased emphasis in AR and several different communication assessment instruments have been used here, including both screening and diagnostic tools. Also, real-ear (probe tube microphone) measures are used with some cases, demonstrating the utility of this tool in the rehabilitation process. No single test battery is recommended; nor is it implied that one is best for all purposes. Instead, clinicians must select the tests that will be useful for determining the exact needs of the client, assisting in specific therapy strategies, and providing relevant outcome measures to assess the results of management. In addition to the tests and procedures used in this chapter, the reader may refer to numerous other chapters throughout the book for other relevant test and resource materials which may be useful in AR.

Even though all cases included here are based directly on real persons, minor adjustments have been made in the names used and the material presented in order to maintain the anonymity of the clients.

■ CASE 1   DR. M.: PROGRESSIVE HEARING LOSS

Case History

Dr. M. was a 69-year-old man who had retired 4 years earlier after a 40-year career as a college professor. He reported experiencing frequent difficulties in hearing, particularly at church, social functions, and plays that he and his spouse attended at the university's theater. Dr. M. had noted being aware of hearing difficulties for some time, including the last couple of years of his teaching career. The onset of his impairment was reportedly gradual and seemed to affect both ears equally.

Audiologic Rehabilitation Assessment

Figure 12.1 contains the audiometric results obtained with Dr. M. In general, he was found to possess a mild to moderate sensorineural hearing loss bilaterally. The results of speech audiometry were consistent with the pure tone findings and indicated that Dr. M. was experiencing significant difficulty in speech perception, especially if speech stimuli were presented at a typical conversation level (50 dB HL).

The Self-Assessment of Communication (SAC) and Significant Other Assessment of Communication (SOAC) (Schow & Nerbonne, 1982) screening inventories were administered to Dr. M. and his spouse to gather further information concerning the degree of perceived hearing handicap resulting from Dr. M.'s hearing loss. Using both of these measures provides valuable information about how hearing impaired persons view their hearing problems, as well as potentially valuable insights from the person who is communicating with the individual on a regular basis. Scores of 50% and 60% (raw scores: 30, 34) on SAC and SOAC tests presented a consistent pattern which, when evaluated according to research (see Table 12.1), provided further evidence that Dr. M. was experiencing considerable hearing-related difficulties (Schow et al., 1989).

Interestingly, some people with hearing impairment that is similar to Dr. M's will report much different (less or more) hearing disability. This important dimension obviously is quite individualized.

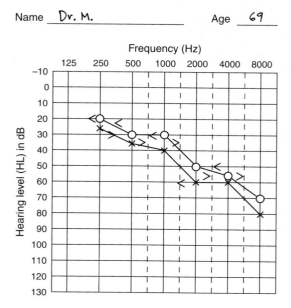

Audiological Record

Name Dr. M.   Age 69

Frequency (Hz)

	PTA	SRT	SAT	HL / PB
R	37	40		80 / 82
L	45	50		90 / 78
SF		35		50 / 52
Aided (Quiet)		20		50 / 80
Aided (Noise)				

Ear	Air	Bone
Right	O	<
Left	×	>
Aided	A	

NR — No Response
DNT — Did Not Test
CNT — Could Not Test
SAT — Speech Awareness Threshold

FIGURE 12.1

Audiometric results for Dr. M., Case 1.

TABLE 12.1		
Categories and Associated Scores for Classifying Primary and Secondary Effects of Hearing Loss (Hearing Disability or Handicap) When Using the SAC and SOAC		
CATEGORY	RAW SCORES	PERCENTAGE SCORES
No disability or handicap	10–18	0–20
Slight hearing disability or handicap	19–26	21–40
Mild to moderate hearing disability or handicap	27–38	41–70
Severe hearing disability or handicap	39–50	71–100

Source: Adapted from "Hearing Handicap Scores and Categories for Subjects with Normal and Impaired Hearing Sensitivity" by R. Schow and C. Tannahill, 1977, *Journal of the American Audiological Society, 3*, pp. 134-139. Also from *Communication Handicap Score Interpretation for Various Populations and Degrees of Hearing Impairment* by M. J. Sturmak, 1987, master's thesis, Idaho State University, and Schow et al., 1989.

On the basis of these test results and the patient's comments, a hearing-aid evaluation was recommended and scheduled.

Management

HEARING AID EVALUATION AND ADJUSTMENT. Prior to any testing associated with hearing aids, Dr. M. was advised about the option of utilizing behind the ear or in the ear style of hearing aids. Like most individuals facing this choice, Dr. M. expressed a clear preference for the in the ear style. Dr. M. was also advised that, because of the severity of his hearing loss and other factors such as improved localization abilities, binaural hearing aids would be advisable.

Care must be taken to get accurate and complete ear impressions. No matter how state of the art the circuitry of a hearing aid may be, if it doesn't fit well and feel comfortable the patient probably will not use it.

The hearing aid evaluation consisted of a series of probe-tube microphone real-ear measures with each ear, as well as soundfield speech audiometry. Data from the audiogram and real-ear measures were applied to an existing prescription approach (Libby, 1986) to determine the desired gain, frequency response and SSPL-90 values for the hearing aids to be fit in the right and left ears. This resulted in two ITE hearing aids being recommended with moderate gain and high-frequency emphasis. Venting of each unit was also deemed appropriate. Earmold impressions were taken and an appointment was scheduled for Dr. M. to be fit with his new aids once they were received from the manufacturer.

Dr. M. was fitted with his hearing aids at the next session and real-ear measures were taken to confirm the appropriateness of the insertion gain and OSPL-90 values for each unit. Soundfield speech audiometry was also used to evaluate further the degree of improvement provided by the binaural system. As seen in Figure 12.1, Dr. M.'s speech reception thresholds and speech recognition score improved significantly with the in the ear hearing aids. His comments concerning the aids were favorable and no further adjustments were made with either hearing aid. Following a thorough orientation to the operation and care of his new aids, Dr. M. was advised to return for subsequent follow-up appointments.

Dr. M.'s experience with his new hearing aids was, for the most part, positive. While still noting some problems hearing in group situations and at the theater, he definitely felt that the hearing aids were assisting him. Further discussion with Dr. M. regarding his hearing difficulties at the theater revealed that he had not yet tried the facility's infrared listening system. Encouraging him to do so, the audiologist explained the manner in which the system functions, as well as how Dr. M. could use the infrared receiver either with his hearing aids or as a stand-alone unit. Subsequent contact with Dr. M. revealed that he found the assistive listening device to be remarkably helpful.

While Dr. M. had adjusted well to his hearing aids and received substantial improvement as a result of their use, he did note some persistent communication difficulties. Because of this and his motivation for improvement, Dr. M. agreed to enroll in a short-term group audiologic rehabilitation program for adults.

COMMUNICATION TRAINING. Dr. M. was one of eight hearing impaired adults who participated in the weekly group sessions. Although the activities and areas of emphasis varied somewhat as a result of the interests and needs of each group of participants, the main components of the program generally followed those outlined by Giolas (1982). The individuals participating with Dr. M. were new hearing aid users with mild-to-moderate hearing losses. Consequently, emphasis was placed on the effective use of hearing aids, care and maintenance of the systems, and the way hearing aids can be supplemented by one or more types of assistive listening devices. Attention was also given to developing more effective listening skills and capitalizing on the visual information available in most communication situations. Interaction among the group participants was encouraged, and valuable information on a variety of topics was shared at each session.

Following the final session, Dr. M. stated that the sessions had been helpful to him. In addition to the practical information provided, such as where to buy batteries for his hearing aids and the use of hearing aids with the telephone, Dr. M. felt that a number of the communication strategies covered had been of benefit to him. The net result was that he felt much more confident when communicating with others.

Successful audiologic rehabilitation done with groups of adults will involve both structured content and informal information sharing among the participants. They can learn as much from each other as from the group facilitator.

Summary

It was clear from the start that Dr. M. had accepted his hearing problem and was motivated to seek out whatever assistance was available to him. His positive and cooperative behaviors, which would be categorized by Goldstein and Stephens (1981) as an example of a Type I attitude (see Chapter 10), facilitated the audiologic rehabilitation process and positively affected Dr. M.'s overall communication abilities. Motivation should be recognized as a key ingredient in successful audiologic rehabilitation with any individual with hearing impairment.

CASE 2   MR. B: HEARING LOSS, DEPRESSION,
■ AND SUCCESSFUL HEARING AID USE

Mr. B is a 70-year-old male who was brought in by his neighbor. Mr. B's wife of nearly 50 years passed away 1 year prior to this visit. His neighbor was concerned that Mr. B. was becoming depressed and a shut-in because of his difficulty in hearing. Mr. B reported having hearing problems for a very long time and that he had tried at least three different sets of hearing aids over the last 20 years. His newest set was approximately 7 years old and was not working. Even when these instruments were new, they reportedly "did him no good." When asked what he didn't like about his current hearing aids (when they were working), he said that "everything was too noisy and loud" and that he "was constantly fiddling with the hearing aids to try and hear better."

Informational Counseling

Following a complete evaluation, the test findings were explained to Mr. B in such a way that he could understand why he had so many communication difficulties. The audiologic rehabilitation process was described to him, but he seemed somewhat reluctant to proceed.

Rehabilitation Assessment

COMMUNICATION STATUS: IMPAIRMENT ACTIVITY LIMITATIONS

AUDIOMETRY AND COMMUNICATION ASSESSMENT. The results of a complete audiologic evaluation (see Figure 12.2) showed a moderate, symmetrical sensorineural hearing loss with a gradually sloping configuration. This is an F2 category (see website). His word recognition scores at a comfortable presentation level were 76% correct in the left ear and 84% correct in the right ear, using the CID W-22 word lists.

Mr. B's dynamic range was mapped at 500 and 4000 Hz. Results showed a dynamic range of 40 dB at 500 Hz and a significantly reduced dynamic range of 20 dB at 4000 Hz.

Mr. B's perception of his communication difficulty was assessed using the Self-assessment of Communication (SAC) (Schow and Nerbonne, 1982). A raw score of 22 indicated only a mild degree of perceived difficulty. His neighbor was given the Significant Other Assessment of Communication to get an estimate of how others perceived Mr. B's communication difficulty. A raw score of 30 was computed, indicating a higher perception of communication difficulty.

The Glasgow Hearing Aid Benefit Profile was used to provide additional information about Mr. B's perceived disability and handicap. Scoring the unaided portion resulted in a initial disability of 72% and a initial handicap of 59%.

Persons routinely engaging in only a limited amount of communication on a day to day basis sometimes tend not to report as much hearing disability as another person might who does more communicating.

OVERALL PARTICIPATION VARIABLES. Based on his report, Mr. B had little demand on his hearing. He lived alone and did not participate in any social activities. His family was distant and did not keep in touch with him very much. He avoided using

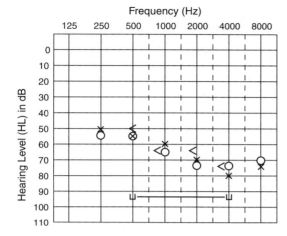

FIGURE 12.2

Audiogram for Mr. B., plus loudness discomfort levels at 500 and 4000 Hz.

	PTA	SRT	WRS	Level
R	65	60	84%	80
L	62	60	76%	80

the phone unless absolutely necessary. His neighbor thought that if Mr. B could hear better he would start to become more active and enjoy life more.

RELATED PERSONAL FACTORS. Mr. B. seemed very quiet and, although he did not resist being at the evaluation, he did not appear motivated to do anything about his hearing loss. His neighbor mentioned the word "depressed" several times in describing Mr. B's behavior.

ENVIRONMENTAL FACTORS. Because Mr. B lived alone, his communication environment was very restricted. In other words, aside from his neighbor and an occasional trip to the grocery store, he had little communication demand. When he was at home he watched TV and was able to turn the TV up loud enough to hear.

Rehabilitation Management

COUNSELING AND PSYCHOSOCIAL ISSUES. Mr. B did not have any problem believing and admitting that he had a hearing problem. It was difficult, however, for him to identify what bothered him the most about his hearing difficulty. Because he could manage his communication environment at home by avoiding the telephone and turning up the TV, his perception of "difficulty" was somewhat distorted.

After some discussion, Mr. B was asked if there were any situations that he would participate more in if he could hear better. He reported that he would like to hear on the telephone so that he could visit with his family and he wanted to hear well in a "group" situation.

It was clear that Mr. B had some reservations about proceeding, probably due to a combination of three unsuccessful hearing aid fittings in the past and low communication demands. However, getting him to hear better on the telephone and in group environments seemed like appropriate goals.

AUDIBILITY AND IMPAIRMENT MANAGEMENT

AMPLIFICATION (MODIFYING AUDIBILITY). New technology in amplification was discussed, particularly the ability of hearing aids to address how he needs to hear different levels of sound. When it was explained that hearing aids could be adjusted so that he could receive more gain for soft sounds, less gain for average sounds, and even less for loud sounds, he seemed very interested in pursuing a trial period. He was comfortable with the full-shell ITE style and, because his dynamic range across frequencies was different, two-channel, programmable instruments were considered in the design. Because the circuitry could manage the gain for different input levels, the hearing aids were ordered without a user-operated volume control.

When the hearing aids arrived, Mr. B.'s threshold and supra threshold information was entered and the Desired Sensation Level (DSL) I/O fitting formula (Seewald, 1992) was followed to preset the initial program for the hearing aids. Predicted insertion gain response curves matched the target gain curves for soft, average, and loud inputs reasonably well.

When Mr. B. arrived for his hearing aid fitting and orientation, he seemed excited and anxious to hear the new sound. The hearing aids were placed in his ears and the actual fit of the hearing aids was inspected. The aids slipped in easily and seemed stable once in place. Mr. B said that the hearing aids felt comfortable. The program was activated and he had an immediate positive reaction.

An informal, functional assessment was performed using a CD containing different types of speech and environmental sounds presented in a sound field. Using this method, gain levels for soft (<45 dB), average (45 to 65 dB), and strong (>65 dB) inputs were programmed in the hearing aid. The compression ratio in the channel assigned to the high frequencies, where Mr. B had a narrower dynamic range, was adjusted further to reduce loud sound amplification. Mr. B reported that soft sounds seemed "distant" but he could still identify the sound. Average sounds were reported to be comfortable, and higher-level inputs seemed loud but were not uncomfortable.

Newer hearing aids with multiple channels allow for greater flexibility in meeting the specific needs that a given individual may have.

As an objective measure, probe microphone measurements using modified DSL targets were used to evaluate insertion gain. Results showed good approximation of target in the low and mid frequencies, but the insertion response for soft, high-frequency sounds did not meet target gain values in the 3000–4000-Hz range. Gain in the channel assigned to the higher frequencies was increased to better address soft, high-frequency sounds; however, Mr. B then reported that speech was too "lispy." The hearing aids were returned to the previous setting.

Finally, a formal functional assessment was performed under unaided and aided listening conditions using CID W-22 word lists presented in a sound field at 50 dB HL. Mr. B was unable to correctly identify any of the words in the unaided condition, but scored 88% in the aided condition.

HEARING AID ORIENTATION. Even though Mr. B was an experienced user, basic hearing instrument orientation, HIO-BASICS, was discussed in detail. These topics included the following:

Hearing expectations: realistic ones

Instrument operation: on/off, telecoil, telephone use

Occlusion effect: user's voice with hearing aids in place

Batteries: tabs, how long they will last, removal, replacement, dangers

Acoustic feedback: what causes it, when is it OK; not OK?

System troubleshooting: what to do when there are problems

Insertion and removal: identifying left, right, insertion, and removal

Cleaning and maintenance: wax and debris cleaning, hair spray, excessive heat, etc.

Service, warranty, repairs, follow-up process, etc.

Mr. B was encouraged to maintain a journal of his experiences, both good and bad, so that appropriate adjustments to his hearing aids could be made.

Mr. B returned for his 2-week follow-up, and it was apparent from his attitude that his experience had been favorable. Mr. B reported that he was so pleased about how he was hearing that the night following his fitting he decided to go to a fiftieth wedding anniversary gathering. As expected, it was "too much, too soon" and he had to remove the hearing aids before the end of the evening.

Mr. B's journal included positive comments about how much "clearer" the TV sounded and that one on one conversations were much easier for him to hear. On the negative side, he felt that in situations where there was "a lot going on" (background noise) he could actually hear better with the hearing aids removed. He also commented that using the telephone was difficult because it sounded too soft. A combination of reducing gain and increasing the compression kneepoint for both channels was used to address his concerns about background noise. However, when he tried the telephone in our clinic, the volume still seemed too soft. Gain for the telephone coil circuit was increased and he reported that it was much better. He was scheduled for a 1-month follow-up appointment.

His 1-month follow-up visit was very positive. Competing noise situations were much better and he also reported doing much better on the telephone.

Mr. B's overall speech perception was improved dramatically when listening to speech presented at a routine conversation level.

REMEDIATE COMMUNICATION ACTIVITY. At each of his follow-up visits, Mr. B was given additional information about how to maximize his communication ability. The information included the following items from our CLEAR handout:

Control communication situations by avoiding noisy areas, poorly lit areas, and the like.

Look at speaker: visual cues from speakers are important and help make up for lost information.

Escape and expectations: be realistic about situations where it will be easy or difficult to hear. Plan strategies for dealing with unfavorable listening situations.

Assertiveness: let others know that you have difficulty hearing and encourage them to gain your attention before speaking and to look at you when they are talking.

Repair strategies: if a breakdown occurs in communication, repeat back to the speaker what you *did* hear and then ask them to clarify what you *did not* hear.

ENVIRONMENT AND COORDINATION: PARTICIPATION IMPROVEMENT. On Mr. B's 3-month follow-up, his neighbor (who initially referred him to our clinic) accompanied him. Both were extremely appreciative of what the hearing aids had done to improve his quality of life. Mr. B reported that he is attending more group functions (group communication goal), has kept in better touch with his family through the telephone (telephone goal), and is less intimidated by difficult communication situations. His neighbor reported that Mr. B. seemed much more outgoing and positive about himself and had been praising the effects of his new instruments to others.

Scoring of the aided portion of the Glasgow profile resulted in scores that supported Mr. B and his neighbor's comments. In the Hearing Aid Use category he scored an 80%, indicating a high level of hearing aid use. In the Hearing Aid Benefit category he scored 39%, indicating only a moderate amount of perceived benefit. For the Residual Disability category he scored 52%, indicating a reduced perception of disability (unaided initial disability was 72%). Finally, in the Satisfaction category his mean score was 91%, indicating a very high level of satisfaction with his hearing aids.

Summary

This is a classic case because it contains two very common issues in audiologic rehabilitation. The first issue relates to the amplification (modifying audibility) component of audiologic rehabilitation. Mr. B had a dynamic range problem, and his previous three sets of hearing aids did not manage differing input levels appropriately. He would turn the hearing aids up to hear soft sounds and then loud sounds would be too loud. When he was exposed to loud sounds, he would have to turn the hearing aids down. After a few weeks of use, he would just set the hearing aids to where loud sounds were comfortable and the result was inadequate gain for soft and average inputs. Current multichannel technology has the ability to address differences in dynamic range associated with hearing loss more effectively. Mr. B's new hearing aids were programmed to help to manage his problems related to loudness. This capability contributed much toward enabling Mr. B to be a successful hearing aid user this time around.

The second issue is that hearing loss often results in communication problems that can be perceived as depressionlike symptoms and can ultimately affect one's emotional well-being. Providing amplification can go a long way to relieving some of these problems, but effective rehabilitation should also address other appropriate aspects of communication. For example, effective use of communication strate-

Successful audiologic rehabilitation often can have a positive impact on an individual that goes beyond simply facilitating communication.

gies, establishing patient-based goals, the inclusion of the communication partner in rehabilitative efforts, and consideration of environmental situations all help to increase communication competence.

Synergy is a process in which the whole is greater than the sum of the parts. As with Mr. B, a definite synergy often occurs when the audiologic rehabilitation process for adults is managed multidimensionally and includes more than just targeting amplification.

■ CASE 3   DR. F.: MÉNIÈRE'S DISEASE

Case History

Dr. F. is a 58-year-old male university professor with a 24-year history of Ménière's disease. Ménière's was initially suspected when Dr. F. suffered two severe attacks of vertigo accompanied by nausea and a roaring tinnitus. Although Dr. F. characterized each attack as sudden, he admitted to a sensation of aural fullness that preceded both attacks. Following the second attack, medical and neurological assessments, coordinated by an otorhinolaryngologist, resulted in the diagnosis of Ménière's disease. Audiological findings at the time of diagnosis were negative for hearing impairment, and Dr. F. reported that he was counseled to manage the Ménière's symptoms by adherence to a dietary regimen designed to stabilize body fluid–blood levels and thus avoid or minimize secondary fluctuations in inner ear fluids.

Dr. F. felt that the dietary regimen was successful, because for the next 15 years he was relatively symptom free and only reported an occasional sensation of aural fullness. Periodic audiological monitoring during this 15-year period revealed a slight 10- to 15-dB decrease in hearing sensitivity for the left ear for the lower frequencies (i.e., 250 to 1000 Hz), but hearing thresholds remained within normal limits. No changes in sensitivity were noted for the right ear.

At age 49 years, Dr. F. suffered another severe Ménière's attack that lasted for several hours. An audiological assessment conducted 2 days later indicated a moderate sensorineural type of hearing loss in the left ear and a slight sensorineural type of loss for the right ear. The audiometric configuration for both ears was characterized by poorer hearing sensitivity for the lower compared to the higher frequencies. Speech audiometric results were consistent with pure tone findings for each ear. Audiological monitoring conducted over the next several months revealed a slight improvement in hearing sensitivity bilaterally. Dr. F. consistently denied communication problems and did not feel amplification would be beneficial.

Four years later, when Dr. F. was 53 years old, he suffered a series of three relatively mild Ménière's attacks during a 2-week period. The audiometric findings obtained 2 weeks after this series of attacks are presented in Figure 12.3. As can be seen, compared to the previously summarized audiometric findings, hearing sensitivity for the left ear had decreased to a moderately severe sensorineural loss characterized by a flat audiometric configuration. Pure tone thresholds for the right ear revealed a mild sensorineural hearing loss, with the lower frequencies most involved. Speech reception thresholds were compatible with pure tone findings

Ménière's disease is a disorder of the inner ear characterized by periodic episodes of vertigo (i.e., dizziness); fluctuating, progressive, low-frequency hearing loss; tinnitus (i.e., ringing in the ears); and a sensation of "fullness" or pressure in the ear. Onset typically is sudden and the symptoms can be very severe.

Name	Test Date	Birthdate	Audiometer	Clinician
Dr. F.				

Frequency in (Hz)

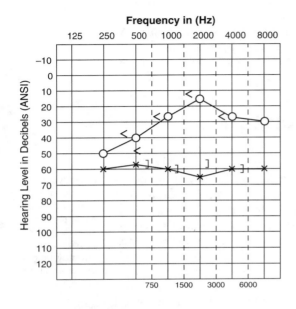

Immittance Results

Probe Hz
226 678   Tympanometry   Canal Volume

Right _____

Left _____

Acoustic Reflex (HL)

Stimulus Ear	Contralateral					Decay
	500Hz	1000Hz	2000Hz	4000Hz		
Right						
Left						
	Ipsilateral					
Right						
Left						

Effective Masking Level to Non-Test Ear

AB						
BC						

L R   L R   L R   L R   L R   L R

Ear	SRT	SDT	MCL	UCL	PTA	% Speech Recognition %					
						HL	SL	HL	SL	HL	SL
Right	30				27	92%					
Masking											
Left	60				60	46%					
Masking											
Sound Field											
Aided											
Masking											

Speech Audiometry   Recorded _____   Material Used: _____
     Live Voice _____   Type of Noise: _____

Modality	Ear		
	Left	Unspecified	Right
Air Conduction-Earphones Unmasked Masked	✗ □		○ △
Bone Conduction-Mastoid Unmasked Masked	>]	∧	< [
Soundfiled Aided		S A	
No Response	↘		↙

SRT   Speech Recognition Threshold   MCL   Most Comfortable Level   NR   No Response   CNT   Could Not Test
SDT   Speech Detection Threshold   UCL   Uncomfortable Level   DNT   Did Not Test   HL   Hearing Level

FIGURE 12.3

Pure tone air- and bone-conduction thresholds and speech audiometric findings for Dr. F.

for each ear, and his ability to understand speech (maximum word recognition score) was poor for the left ear (46%), but excellent for the right ear (92%). At this time, Dr. F. acknowledged he was having some difficulties understanding speech in noisy backgrounds. He noted that these problems were especially troublesome when he was required to listen to students during classroom discussions. Based on these observations, Dr. F. agreed to explore the use of amplification.

Audiologic Rehabilitation Assessment and Management

Dr. F.'s acknowledgment of communication difficulty represented an initial step in the rehabilitation sequence. Although it is sometimes convenient to view audiologic rehabilitation as a process comprised of a series of individually discrete events, in reality the assessment and management phases of rehabilitation typically overlap and often are characterized as an interrelated sequence of ongoing experiences. Such was the case of Dr. F., whose initial attempts to use amplification were not successful, and, as a consequence, he exited the rehabilitative process. Two years later, however, as Dr. F.'s communication difficulties increased, he again sought help for his hearing loss. The following sections provide a discussion of Dr. F.'s rehabilitative experiences that start with his initial efforts to seek help for his communication problems and culminate with his acceptance of amplification.

INITIAL EXPERIENCES WITH AMPLIFICATION. Following the series of three mild Ménière's attacks described previously (see Figure 12.3), Dr. F. made an appointment for a hearing aid evaluation at his university's audiology clinic. This was the same clinic that performed his audiological assessments following the Ménière's attacks. During his initial appointment, Dr. F. was informed about the advantages and disadvantages associated with hearing aid style and was advised that in the ear models probably would provide superior localization and enhanced amplification compared to behind the ear units. Also, Dr. F. was encouraged to wear two hearing aids in order to maximize potential binaural advantages. Furthermore, binaural amplification was stressed by counseling Dr. F. about auditory deprivation and the potential deleterious influence on his hearing if he only used one hearing aid. Based on this information, Dr. F. elected to pursue binaural hearing aids. Electroacoustic parameters for the hearing aids were selected based on the revised National Acoustic Laboratories (NAL–R) procedures (Bryne & Dillon, 1986), earmold impressions were obtained for each ear, and two linear in the ear hearing aids with appropriate circuitry to meet the NAL–R prescribed electroacoustic output parameters were ordered.

> A linear hearing aid maintains a constant gain while input intensities vary until maximum output is reached.

Upon receipt of the hearing aids, real-ear insertion gain measures were generated on Dr. F. to verify that the output of each hearing aid approximated that recommended by the NAL–R procedures. Dr. F. was counseled about the correct use and care of his new hearing aids and instructed to return to the audiology clinic if he experienced any problems. During this counseling session, it was stressed that Dr. F. was to try the hearing aids on a 30-day trial basis and that he could return the hearing aids at any time during this trial period for a complete refund if he did not feel that the aids were providing benefit.

Taking an ear impression for a new hearing aid.

Feedback is a term used to describe when a hearing aid squeals because the amplified sound from the aid leaks out of the user's ear canal, reaches the aid's microphone, and is then reamplified.

Over the next 3 weeks, Dr. F. returned to the clinic four times with complaints about his hearing aids. On his first return visit, Dr. F. expressed concern that when he turned the volume control of the left hearing aid to a comfortable listening level the unit squealed. This problem, known as feedback, was controlled by lowering the amount of high-frequency gain. Dr. F. returned 2 days later, complaining that things still sounded too loud and that he could not understand conversation. In fact, he felt that his ability to understand speech was worse when he wore the hearing aids than when he was not using amplification. Real-ear measures were again obtained and they revealed that both hearing aids were providing the prescribed amplification. An adjustment was made to the right hearing aid to increase slightly the amount of low-frequency gain. Dr. F. was informed that, because he was a new hearing aid user, it would take some time for him to adjust to all the "new sounds" he was now hearing, but that the adjustment would be faster the more he wore his hearing aids. Dr. F. returned 8 days later and reported that, despite wearing his hearing aids all the time, he continued to have difficulty understanding speech. He also noted that the right hearing aid continuously sounded noisy, especially when he listened in a quiet background. In an attempt to satisfy Dr. F., the high-frequency gain for the right hearing was adjusted to a lower output and Dr. F. reported that the aid did not sound as noisy. Dr. F. was again encouraged to wear the hearing aids as much as possible.

Ten days later Dr. F. returned to the clinic and announced that he was not satisfied and wanted to return the aids and get his money back. Dr. F. was concerned that he was being overpowered by the hearing aids. He did not feel that they helped during lectures, and, in fact, reported that he could hear better when teaching if he didn't use the hearing aids. He did state that the hearing aids made sounds louder and that he was more aware of environmental noises, but did not feel this "minor" advantage was worth the expense to buy the aids. Dr. F.'s money was refunded and he was informed to return to the clinic if he should change his mind about pursuing amplification.

SUBSEQUENT EXPERIENCES WITH AMPLIFICATION. For the next 2 years, Dr. F. managed his vocational, professional, and social obligations with difficulty. He tended to avoid social functions associated with high levels of background noise (e.g., parties, dinner engagements) unless they were related to professional responsibilities. Also, several of Dr. F.'s students and colleagues reported anecdotally that he frequently ignored their queries and comments. Dr. F. became particularly concerned when student evaluations of his classroom performance contained statements about his being inattentive and indifferent to questions. During this period of time, Dr. F. was becoming more aware of his communication problems and wondered if his hearing was getting worse. Thus, 2 years after returning the original hearing aids, he made an appointment at another audiology center to get his hearing rechecked and to explore again the possibility of using amplification.

Audiometric findings from that audiologic assessment were similar to those illustrated in Figure 12.3 and suggested that Dr. F.'s hearing sensitivity had remained stable during this 2-year interval. Dr. F. reviewed his communication problems with the audiologist and emphasized that he was worried particularly about his teaching performance. This was of special concern because his previous attempts to use hearing aids within the classroom environment failed to provide noticeable benefit. Dr. F. was advised by the audiologist that, instead of pursing linear-type amplification as with his previous hearing aids, he might want to try more advanced technology that used digital signal processing (DSP). DSP hearing aids are generally considered to be more flexible than linear models because their electroacoustic output can be programmed by a computer. Similar to his first hearing aid experience 2 years ago, it was recommended that Dr. F. should obtain two hearing aids.

Unlike his initial experience, however, Dr. F. was provided detailed counseling about his hearing loss. This counseling stressed that the differences in hearing sensitivity between his ears and the upward sloping audiometric configuration of his right ear made his hearing loss very difficult to fit with hearing aids. He was informed that he could expect some benefit from amplification, but that he should not expect the hearing aids to overcome completely his communication problems.

Dr. F. elected to try binaural DSP amplification. The selection of electroacoustic parameters for the DSP instruments was based on the desired sensation level [i/o] approach advocated by Seewald and colleagues (Seewald, 2000). These electroacoustic parameters were programmed into the hearing aids by a computer interface and were subsequently modified several times based on Dr. F.'s observations derived from various real-life listening situations. In addition, Dr. F. was encouraged to use his amplification systems in various configurations (i.e., monaural right ear, monaural left ear, unaided, binaural) and to keep a written log of his perceptions. In general, Dr. F. reported that, while the amplification units did not restore his hearing to normal, he felt that they provided substantial improvement compared to the previous linear units. More importantly, Dr. F. claimed that his hearing was better in most listening conditions when he wore the aids as compared to not using any amplification. Dr. F. noted that the hearing aids failed to provide improvement in conditions such as listening outdoors when the wind was blowing or listening in a background of noise characterized by a group of multitalkers.

Of most significance, however, Dr. F. observed that the hearing aids allowed him to be aware that his students were asking question during class, although he admitted that he did not always understand their questions. In this regard, Dr. F. was encouraged to become more of a self-advocate and to solicit student cooperation to enhance classroom communication processes. At the time of this writing, Dr. F. continues to be a satisfied hearing aid user.

Summary

This challenging case illustrates the point that rehabilitative management is a multifaceted process. Success depends on giving careful consideration to all facets of the process and, most importantly, to include the patient as an integral part of the program.

Although it is not completely clear why Dr. F. initially rejected amplification, it may be useful to speculate about several factors. First, it is possible that Dr. F.'s initial experience with hearing aids failed, in part, because he had an unrealistic expectation about the amount of benefit he would derive from amplification. If this were the case, Dr. F. may have entered into the rehabilitative process with the expectation that hearing aids would allow him to hear his students normally and that he would no longer have to worry about missing important information during class. Hence, Dr. F. would have been severely disappointed once he realized that the initial hearing aids did not provide the degree of benefit that he had expected. Indeed, unrealistic expectations about the amount of benefit to be derived from amplification are one of the primary reasons why individuals purchase hearing aids, but then elect not to use them. Recall that it was not until 2 years later during the second hearing aid evaluation that Dr. F. was counseled about the potential difficulties he might experience with amplification because of his particular hearing loss. This counseling may have sensitized Dr. F. to the fact that hearing aids would not cure all his problems and, in turn, assisted his acceptance of less than ideal hearing.

A second area that may have influenced Dr. F.'s use of amplification is the type of technology. His second set of hearing aids were DSP units that, in addition to being more flexible, were capable of processing incoming acoustic information into three bands (e.g., a low-, mid-, and high-frequency channel). Because the electroacoustic parameters of each band could be manipulated somewhat independently from the other bands, it is possible that the advanced technology resulted in a more appropriate fit between the DSP units and the unique characteristics of Dr. F.'s hearing loss compared to the initial linear units.

A third consideration is overall management of Dr. F.'s complaints during the initial evaluation. Dr. F.'s primary concern was that he could not understand his students during class. Rather than telling Dr. F. that he had to wear the hearing aids more in order to receive maximum benefit, an alternative strategy during the initial assessment would have been to have Dr. F. compare listening over a 2- or 3-day period, first without hearing aids, then with both hearing aids, and finally with only one hearing aid. This experience would have provided Dr. F. with an opportunity to compare directly the performance of various amplification arrays (i.e., monaural–binaural) to listening without hearing aids. Most important, however, this strategy would have made Dr. F. an active rather than passive participant in the rehabilitative process.

■ CASE 4   MRS. O.: COCHLEAR IMPLANT USER

Case History

Mrs. O. was a 55-year-old former school bus driver who had a progressive sensorineural hearing loss for approximately 25 years. She reported that her hearing loss was gradual in onset, with unknown etiology. She wore binaural behind the ear (BTE) programmable hearing aids, which she stated helped her to perceive pauses in speech and some intonation cues. Mrs. O. had tried using a transpositional hearing aid, but with little to no success. Mrs. O. indicated that her hearing loss severely affected interactions in her job setting. She changed job positions to become an aid on a school bus for disabled children, instead of being the driver. Her speech was very intelligible and her vision and overall health were good. Mrs. O. was seen initially for an evaluation for cochlear implant (CI) candidacy and speechreading therapy. According to the otologist on the CI team, Mrs. O. was a medically suitable candidate for CI surgery.

Transpositional hearing aids process sound much differently from conventional hearing aids and are mostly used in cases with profound sensorineural hearing loss. Basically, they shift or transpose energy found in the higher frequencies of sounds down to the lower frequencies, where they are more likely to be heard.

Diagnostic Information

Audiometric evaluation revealed a bilateral sensorineural hearing loss (Figure 12.4). Pure tone thresholds indicated a moderate loss at 250 Hz, rapidly dropping to a profound loss bilaterally. Mrs. O. was unable to respond to pure tone stimuli at the limits of the audiometer above 1500 Hz. Speech detection thresholds were obtained at 60 and 55 dB HL in the right and left ears, respectively. Her unaided word recognition scores were 0% in both ears, using the NU-6 word recognition test presented at her most comfortable loudness level in an auditory-only test condition.

Aided thresholds were obtained at 35 dB HL at 500 Hz and 55 dB HL from 750 through 3000 Hz. Further aided evaluation was completed with Mrs. O. using selected closed set subsets of the Minimal Auditory Capabilities Batteries (MAC) (Owens et al., 1981) at a 55-dB HL presentation level. She scored 48% on the

Name __Mrs. O.__   Date _____   Audiometer __GSI 16__

Tested By _____   DOB _____   Med Rec # _____   Reliability Excellent _____

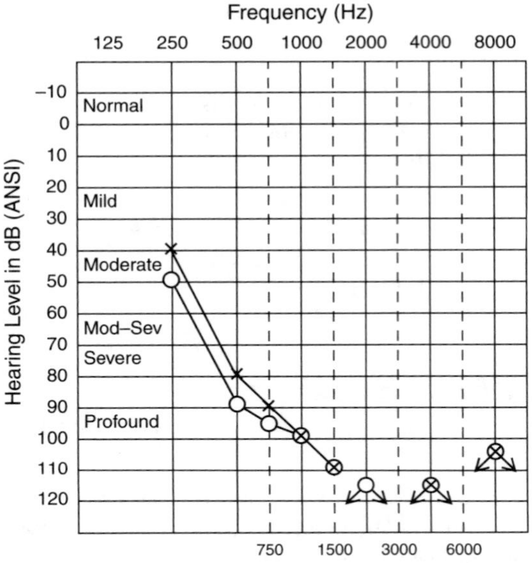

Speech Audiometry

	SRT/SAT		Discrimination		
	dBHL	MASK	%	MASK	Discrimination Level dBHL
Right	60		0		80
Left	55		0		80

Inserts Phones ___✓___   Head Phones _____

Audiogram Legend

	Left	Right
Air: Unmasked	O	×
Masked	△	□
Bone: Unmasked	∧	
Masked	[	]
No Response	□	□
Sound Filed:		
Aided	S	
Unaided	A	
Cochlear Implant	CI	

Comments:

FIGURE 12.4

Audiometric results for Mrs. O., Case 4.

Number of Syllables, and 55% on the Four Choice Spondee Subtests. The CID Everyday Sentence test was used to determine her open set speech perception abilities with and without speechreading. In the aided condition without speechreading, Mrs. O. repeated 4% of key words at a 55-dB HL presentation level. When visual cues were added, Mrs. O. scored 83%. Paper and pencil questionnaires were given to Mrs. W. and her husband to determine their expectations for a CI. Both Mr. and Mrs. O. indicated that they hoped the implant would enable Mrs. O. to use the telephone and to improve her communication abilities so that she could return to driving the school bus. Mrs. O. expected the implant to enable her to "hide" her hearing loss and that after surgery most people would not suspect that she had a hearing impairment.

Pre-CI Management

COUNSELING AND PSYCHOSOCIAL CONSIDERATIONS. Mrs. O. appeared to be a good candidate for a CI, based on the results of the pure tone and speech perception tests. However, it was apparent that she had unrealistic expectations. Extensive counseling was given to both Mr. and Mrs. O. on the limitations and benefits of the implant. They were told that the CI was designed as an aid to speechreading, not a replacement for visual cues. The CI would not give her normal hearing, and she would need to inform her communication partners that she had a hearing loss. It was explained that the majority of patients with CIs need visual cues to communicate and that telephone communication would continue to be a problem with an implant. Mrs. O. was put in contact with two current CI users who answered many of her questions.

> Experienced CI users can provide very valuable and relevant information to those considering an implant for themselves.

COMMUNICATION REMEDIATION. It was recommended that Mrs. O. receive communication therapy prior to surgery. She attended five sessions that focused on communication repair and anticipatory strategies. Discussions on ways to modify the environment and the use of nonverbal cues were also included. During these sessions, continued counseling was completed on the benefits and limitations of the implant.

CI SURGERY. Following the completion of this therapy and after CI expectations were reevaluated, recommendations for surgery were given. Mr. and Mrs. O. demonstrated a better understanding of the benefits and long-range therapy goals for CI use. Mrs. O. was successfully implanted with a multichannel CI. The entire electrode was inserted surgically with no complications.

Post-CI Management

AUDIBILITY AND AMPLIFICATION. Five weeks after surgery, Mrs. O. returned for electrical stimulation of her CI and follow-up therapy. Initially, Mrs. O. was seen on 2 consecutive days to program the CI processor and then for 10 more visits spread out over a 3-month interval for therapy and fine-tuning of her speech processor. Threshold and maximum comfort levels were obtained for each of her active electrodes. Four speech processing programs or MAPs, using both SPEAK and ACE processing strategies, were made and saved into her body-worn speech processor. Mrs. O. was instructed on how to change programs, and recommendations for different programs in different listening situations were made. During the fourth session, Mrs. O. was also fit with an ear-level speech processor that she could use as an alternative to the body-worn speech processor. Continued monitoring of her threshold and comfort levels and subsequent map modifications were made throughout her therapy sessions.

> Ear-level processors are becoming increasingly more popular among CI users.

AUDIOVISUAL TRAINING FOR COMMUNICATION. Therapy sessions consisted of training Mrs. O. in a hierarchy of auditory skills, including sound detection, word and sentence length discrimination and identification, pattern discrimination and identification in phrases and sentences, and identification of overlearned speech (common expressions). Drill work using consonant and vowel stimuli in auditory-only and auditory–visual modes was also used in each session. Her auditory-only vowel and consonant recognition improved from a pre-CI score of 8% to a post-CI score of 58%. Through speech tracking (DeFilippo & Scott, 1978), Mrs. O. practiced using the CI along with visual cues in understanding running speech. The use of communication strategies was stressed and practiced during the tracking exercises. Her auditory–visual tracking rates increased from a pre-CI score of 28 words per minute (wpm) to a post-CI score of 78 wpm. After 1 month of therapy, telephone use was introduced, using codes and overlearned speech. Mrs. O. found that she could communicate with her husband and two other familiar individuals on the phone, but had some difficulties in conversations with strangers. After 3 months of use she reported that she was beginning to use the telephone more frequently with family and friends.

COUNSELING AND COORDINATION. Throughout the therapy sessions, Mrs. O. kept an ongoing diary of her experiences with the CI. She listed wearing times, environmental sounds heard, and communication situations. From her diary and discussions in therapy, it was apparent that Mrs. O. was initially very disappointed with the CI. Even though she had tempered her expectations of the CI, she had still maintained hope that she would function as a person with normal hearing. The diary served as a focal point of behavioral counseling. Specific problems were discussed, pointing out both the benefits and limitations of the CI, along with possible strategies that she might use in each situation. For example, she reported frustration with conversing in noisy places such as on the school bus, in her car, and in restaurants. It was recommended that she use her external microphone in such situations to minimize the background noise. In addition, separate MAPs with reduced low-frequency information were put into her speech processor so that she could use these in noisy backgrounds. During this adjustment period, Mrs. O. also received a great deal of support from another cochlear implant user in her home town.

Interestingly, Mrs. O. felt that she could get just as much information from her hearing aid in the unaided ear as she could with the cochlear implant. She stated that she was primarily using speechreading to communicate. One month into the implant use, we recommended that she try using just the hearing aid for a couple of days. She returned the next week and reported that she had gone without the implant for 1 day and realized how much it was helping. At that point she stopped using the hearing aid in the unimplanted ear completely. Mrs. O. did not realize how much benefit she was getting from the implant until we performed speech recognition testing with and without her speech processor. After this, her attitude toward the CI and therapy greatly improved, as reflected in both her diary and discussions. From her diary, her use of the CI went from 8 hours a day to the time she got up in the morning until the time she went to bed at night.

At her 3-month evaluation, Mrs. O scored 94% on the CID Everyday Sentence test and 38% on the NU-6 word recognition test in the auditory-only condition at 50 dB HL with her implant. When visual cues were added, she was easily able to score 100% on the sentence materials.

On the job, Mrs. O. found the implant to be of great help, particularly in her abilities to hear environmental sounds that are important for safety. Eighteen months after her initial hookup, Mrs. O's supervisor recommended that she be re-

> The overall effectiveness of a CI for the recipient increases with time as he or she learns how to use the new, expanded information now available.

turned to her former position as a bus driver. She now drives a school bus for disabled children. The aid on her bus assists when she experiences difficulty with the bus intercom system. She continues with yearly appointments to monitor her progress with the implant. Both she and husband report continuing improvements in her communication abilities. Mrs. O. reported that she is now "at ease when speaking to both friends and strangers."

Summary

Cochlear implants offer an excellent opportunity for postlingually deafened adults to receive beneficial auditory information. Much variation in benefits can be seen across CI patients, from those who have good open set understanding even on the telephone to those who receive minimal auditory cues. Mrs. O. is representative of an average postlingually hearing impaired CI patient. She was able to speechread with greater ease, could identify many more environmental sounds, and had telephone skills using the CI when talking with familiar individuals. However, she still relies heavily on speechreading to communicate in many situations.

Mrs. O.'s case also illustrates the importance of a full program of pre- and post-AR therapy and counseling with CI candidates and their families. Often, patients expect the CI to be a "bionic ear." Even after their expectations are tempered prior to surgery, like Mrs. O., they may be disappointed that the CI cannot provide "normal" hearing. Audiovisual training and communication strategy therapy help the patients to learn to use the CI and deal with communication breakdowns. With appropriate training, the CI can improve the quality of life for an individual with profound hearing impairment.

CASE 5   MRS. E.: NURSING HOME ■ HEARING-AID USER

Case History

Mrs. E. was a 75-year-old resident of a local nursing home. She had been living in the facility for over 2 years and was quite alert mentally and able to move about the facility without any special assistance. Mrs. E. was using a hearing aid at the time she was first seen by an audiologist. It was later determined that she had been a longtime hearing aid user, having had four other instruments over a period of many years. Her present hearing aid was 5 years old and, according to Mrs. E., did not seem to be working as well as it once had.

Diagnostic Information

Initial efforts with Mrs. E. involved air conduction pure tone testing and tympanometry in a quiet room within the nursing home. As seen in Figure 12.5, the client had a moderate hearing loss, which was bilaterally symmetrical. Type A tympanograms were traced bilaterally, suggesting the presence of a sensorineural disorder in each ear.

It is possible (and sometimes necessary) to gather basic, relevant audiometric information outside the traditional audiologic test booth if certain measures are taken to ensure the validity of the results obtained.

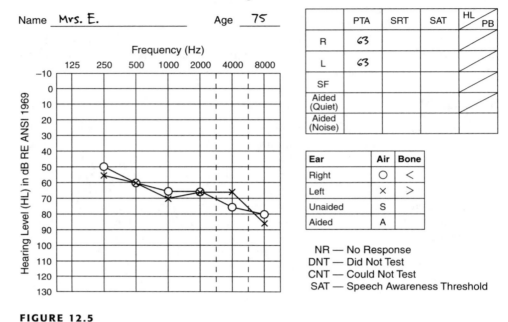

FIGURE 12.5

Audiometric results for Mrs. E., Case 5.

Audiologic Rehabilitation

The repair and reconditioning of a hearing aid can be viable alternatives if the instrument is not too old and is still appropriate for the user's hearing loss.

Mrs. E. was concerned about the condition of her hearing aid, complaining that it did not seem to help her as much as it had in the past. She also appeared to be experiencing an excessive amount of acoustic feedback and reported having difficulty getting the earmold into her ear properly.

The hearing aid was analyzed electroacoustically by the audiologist and was found to have a reduced gain and an abnormal amount of distortion. In discussing the feasibility of purchasing a new hearing aid, it became clear that Mrs. E. was not financially able to consider such a purchase. She was, therefore, advised to have her hearing aid serviced and reconditioned by the manufacturer. She was agreeable to this recommendation, and arrangements were made for this to occur.

In the course of working with Mrs. E. it became apparent that she needed a new earmold. In discussing this, Mrs. E. recalled that her current mold had also been used with her previous hearing aid. The mold was very discolored and did not appear to fit Mrs. E.'s ear canal and pinna adequately. The audiologist took an ear impression, which was sent to a laboratory for production of a new earmold.

In approximately two weeks, both the earmold and the hearing aid were returned. Mrs. E. was then fit with the reconditioned aid and her initial reaction was quite positive. She was instructed to use the aid as much as possible in the following days. A subsequent electroacoustic analysis of the instrument revealed an increase in gain and a significant improvement in the amount of distortion. Real-ear measures, taken at the nursing home with portable equipment, revealed satisfactory gain.

When she was seen again, Mrs. E. was still pleased with the help she was receiving from her hearing aid, but she indicated that she was still having difficulty inserting the earmold. Watching her attempt to do this herself made it apparent that Mrs. E. was not able to manipulate her hands sufficiently to allow her to insert the earmold without great effort. It was also apparent that she was not using an efficient method when inserting the mold. To assist her, Mrs. E. was given some basic instructions on how to best insert and remove the earmold. She was encouraged to practice the procedure and was visited by the audiologist several times during the next 2 weeks to review the procedure and to answer any questions she might have. During these visits it became apparent that Mrs. E.'s facility in placement of the earmold had improved.

Along with the work done with Mrs. E. to improve the way she inserted her earmold, several of the nursing home staff members working with Mrs. E. were also provided with information on how to put the earmold in properly. This allowed them to assist Mrs. E. in doing so each day. Both Mrs. E. and the staff also received helpful information on how to clean her earmold and basic instruction on the operation and use of her hearing aid.

More frequent monitoring of the status of some patients is important to facilitate success with audiologic rehabilitation.

Summary

Attempts to help Mrs. E. were successful. This is not always the case when working in a rehabilitative capacity with nursing home residents (Schow, 1982). Mrs. E.'s case illustrates one of the ways in which an audiologist can make a valuable contribution to a number of residents in a given nursing home. It is important first to identify those individuals within the facility for whom audiologic rehabilitation may be beneficial. Once this is done, the audiologist will generally work with each person individually, identifying those areas of AR that should be worked on. Individual needs must be considered, and the audiologist must be willing to devote the time necessary to accomplish the desired ends.

SUMMARY POINTS

- Hearing impairment can produce a variety of difficulties for an individual, and effective audiologic rehabilitation must address these particular needs.
- Information gathering, including discussions with the patient, the use of self-report scales, hearing tests, auditory–visual skills assessment, and other relevant sources of information, is an important component of audiologic rehabilitation.
- Successful intervention depends to a large extent on the degree of motivation possessed by the individual with hearing impairment.
- Today's hearing aids are complex instruments. Proper selection and fitting of these devices require extensive expertise and instrumentation in order to maximize their potential.

■ The intervention process can be threatened if the person with hearing impairment has unrealistic hopes and expectations related to a component of audiologic rehabilitation (e.g., a cochlear implant) that are impossible to fulfill. Clinicians need to monitor this continuously with their patients, especially in the early stages of intervention.

■ Comprehensive and effective hearing aid fitting, particularly for first-time users, should include an extensive orientation to hearing aid use and exposure to factors that facilitate communication.

REFERENCES

Byrne, D., & Dillon, H. (1986). The National Acoustics Laboratories' (NAL) new procedure for selecting the gain & frequency response of a hearing aid. *Ear and Hearing, 7*, 257–265.

DeFilippo, C., & Scott, B. (1978). A method for training and evaluating the reception of ongoing speech. *Journal of the Acoustical Society of America, 63*, 1186–1192.

Gatehouse, S. (1999). Glasgow hearing aid benefit profile: Derivation and validation of a client-centered outcome measure for hearing aid services. *Journal of the American Academy, of Audiology, 10*, 80–103.

Giolas, T. (1982). *Hearing handicapped adults.* Englewood Cliffs, NJ: Prentice Hall.

Goldstein, D., & Stephens, S. (1981). Audiological rehabilitation: Management model I. *Audiology, 20*, 432–452.

Libby, E. (1986). The 1/3–2/3 insertion gain hearing aid selection guide. *Hearing Instruments, 37*, 27–28.

Owens, E., et al. (1981). The minimal auditory capabilities (MAC) battery. *Hearing Journal, 34*(9), 32–34.

Schow, R. L. (1982). Success of hearing aid fitting in nursing home residents. *Ear and Hearing, 3*(3),173–177.

Schow, R. L., & Nerbonne, M. (1982). Communication screening profile: Use with elderly clients. *Ear and Hearing, 3*(3), 133–147.

Schow, R. L., et al. (1989). Self assessment of hearing in rehabilitative audiology: Developments in the U.S.A. *British Journal of Audiology, 23*, 13–24.

Seewald, R. (1992). The desired sensation level method for fitting children. *Hearing Journal, 45*, 36–46.

Seewald, R. (2000). An update of DSL [i/o]. *Hearing Journal, 53*(4), 10–16.

WHO (2000). World Health Organization. *International classification of functioning and disability.* ICI DH-2. Geneva, Switzerland: WHO.

■ AUTHOR INDEX

■ SUBJECT INDEX